W9-AWG-582

PRINCIPLES OF
# DATABASE AND KNOWLEDGE – BASE SYSTEMS
## SYSTEMS
VOLUME I

# PRINCIPLES OF COMPUTER SCIENCE SERIES

ISSN 0888-2096

## Series Editors
**Alfred V. Aho,** Bell Telephone Laboratories, Murray Hill, New Jersey
**Jeffrey D. Ullman,** Stanford University, Stanford, California

1. *Algorithms for Graphics and Image Processing**
   **Theo Pavlidis**
2. *Algorithmic Studies in Mass Storage Systems**
   **C. K. Wong**
3. *Theory of Relational Databases**
   **Jeffrey D. Ullman**
4. *Computational Aspects of VLSI**
   **Jeffrey D. Ullman**
5. *Advanced C: Food for the Educated Palate**
   **Narain Gehani**
6. *C: An Advanced Introduction**
   **Narain Gehani**
7. *C for Personal Computers: IBM PC, AT&T PC 6300, and Compatibles**
   **Narain Gahani**
8. *Principles of Computer Design**
   **Leonard R. Marino**
9. *The Theory of Database Concurrency Control**
   **Christos Papadimitriou**
10. *Computer Organization**
    **Michael Andrews**
11. *Elements of Artificial Intelligence Using LISP*
    **Steven Tanimoto**
12. *Trends in Theoretical Computer Science*
    **Egon Börger, Editor**
13. *An Introduction to Solid Modeling*
    **Martti Mäntylä**
14. *Principles of Database and Knowledge Base Systems, Volume I*
    **Jeffrey D. Ullman**

*These previously-published books are in the *Principles of Computer Science Series* but they are not numbered within the volume itself. All future volumes in the *Principles of Computer Science Series* will be numbered.

## OTHER BOOKS OF INTEREST

*Jewels of Formal Language Theory*
**Arto Salomaa**

*Principles of Database Systems*
**Jeffrey D. Ullman**

*Fuzzy Sets, Natural Language Computations, and Risk Analysis*
**Kurt J. Schmucker**

*LISP: An Interactive Approach*
**Stuart C. Shapiro**

# PRINCIPLES OF
# DATABASE AND KNOWLEDGE - BASE SYSTEMS
# VOLUME I

Jeffrey D. Ullman
*STANFORD UNIVERSITY*

COMPUTER SCIENCE PRESS

Copyright© 1988 Computer Science Press, Inc.

Printed in the United States of America.

All rights reserved. No part of this book may be reproduced in any form including photostat, microfilm, and xerography, and not in information storage and retrieval systems, without permission in writing from the publisher, except by a reviewer who may quote brief passages in a review or as provided in the Copyright Act of 1976.

*Computer Science Press*
*1803 Research Boulevard*
*Rockville, Maryland 20850*


**Library of Congress Cataloging-in-Publication Data**

Ullman, Jeffrey D., 1942-
    Principles of database and knowledgebase systems.

    (Principles of computer science series, ISSN 0888-2096 ; 14-    )
    Bibliography: p.
    Includes index.
    1. Data base management. 2. Expert systems (Computer science) I. Title.
II. Series. Principles of computer science series; 14, etc.
QA76.9.D3U443   1988                    005.74                    87-38197
ISBN 0-7167-8158-1


2 3 4 5 6 7 8 9   RRD   6 5 4 3 2 1 0 8 9 8

# PREFACE

This book is the first of a two-volume set that is intended as a replacement for my earlier book *Principles of Database Systems* (Ullman [1982] in the references). Since the latter book was written, it became clear that what I thought of as "database systems" formed but one (important) point in a spectrum of systems that share a capability to manage large amounts of data efficiently, but differ in the expressiveness of the languages used to access that data. It has become fashionable to refer to the statements of these more expressive languages as "knowledge," a term I abhor but find myself incapable of avoiding. Thus, in the new book I tried to integrate "classical" database concepts with the technolgy that is just now being developed to support applications where "knowledge" is required along with "data."

The first volume is devoted primarily to classical database systems. However, knowledge, as represented by logical rules, is covered extensively in Chapter 3. From that chapter, only the material on relational calculus, a "classical" database topic, is used extensively in this volume. We shall return to the topic of logic as a user interface language in the second volume, where it is one of the major themes. We also find in the first volume a discussion of "object-oriented" database systems, which, along with "knowledge-base systems," is an important modern development.

Chapter 1 introduces the terminology for database, object-base, and knowledge-base systems; it attempts to explain the relationships among these systems, and how they fit into an unfolding development of progresssively more powerful systems. Chapters 2 and 3 introduce us to data models as used in these three classes of systems; "data models" are the mathematical abstractions we use to represent the real world by data and knowledge. In Chapter 4 we meet several important query languages that are based on the relational data model, and in Chapter 5 we meet languages that are based on one of several "object-oriented" models.

Chapter 6 covers physical organization of data and the tricks that are used to answer, efficiently, queries posed in the languages of Chapters 4 and 5. Then, in Chapter 7 we discuss some of the theory for relational database systems, especially how one represents data in that model in ways that avoid redundancy and other problems. Chapter 8 covers security and integrity aspects of database systems, and in Chapter 9 we discuss concurrency control, the techniques that make it possible for many processes to operate on one database

v

simultaneously, without producing paradoxical results. Finally, in Chapter 10 we consider techniques for dealing with distributed database systems.

It is expected that the second volume will cover query optimization techniques, both for "classical" database systems (chiefly relational systems) and for the new class of "knowledge-base" systems that are presently under development, and which will rely heavily on the optimization of queries expressed in logical terms. We shall also find a discussion of some of these experimental systems. Finally, Volume II will cover "universal relation" systems, a body of techniques developed to make sense of queries that are expressed in natural language, or in a language sufficiently informal that the querier does not have to know about the structure of the database.

### Mapping the Old Book to the New

Readers familiar with Ullman [1982] will find most of that material in this volume. Only the chapters on optimization and on universal relations are deferred to Volume II, and a few sections of the old book have been excised. The material in the old Chapter 1 has been divided between the new Chapters 1 and 2. Sections 1.1 and 1.2 remain in Chapter 1, while Sections 1.3 and 1.4 form the core of Chapter 2 (data models) in the new book. Chapter 2 of the old (physical organization) now appears in Chapter 6, along with material on physical organization that formerly appeared in Sections 3.2, 4.2, and 5.1. Some of the material in the old Section 2.8 (partial-match queries) has been excised.

The remainders of Chapters 3 and 4 (network and hierarchical languages) appear in the new Chapter 5 (object-oriented langauges), along with new material on OPAL, which is a true, modern object-oriented language for database systems. The old Chapter 5, on the relational model, has been dispersed. Section 5.1, on physical structures, moves to Chapter 6, Section 5.2, on relational algebra, moves to Chapter 2 (data models), while Section 5.3, on relational calculus, moves to Chapter 3 (logic and knowledge). The old Chapter 6 (relational languages) becomes the new Chapter 4. The discussion of the language SQUARE has been omitted, but the language SQL is covered much more extensively, including an example of how SQL can be interfaced with a host language, C in particular.

Only Chapter 7 (relational theory) remains where it was and remains relatively unchanged. A discussion of the Tsou-Fischer algorithm for constructing Boyce-Codd normal form schemes is included, as well as a pragmatic discussion of the virtues and dangers of decomposition or "normalization." Chapters 8 (query optimization) and 9 (universal relation systems) are deferred to the second volume. Chapter 10 (security and integrity) becomes Chapter 8. The discussion on statistical databases is excised, but more examples, drawn from SQL and OPAL, are included. Chapter 11 (concurrency) becomes Chapter 9, and is expanded in several ways. Chapter 12 (distributed systems) is divided in two. The first half, on query optimization for distributed systems, is moved to Volume II, while the second half forms the core of the new Chapter 10; the latter includes not only distributed locking, but also covers other issues such as distributed agreement ("distributed commit").

## Exercises

Each chapter, except the first, includes an extensive set of exercises, both to test the basic concepts of the chapter and in many cases to extend these ideas. The most difficult exercises are marked with a double star, while exercises of intermediate difficulty have a single star.

## Acknowledgements

The following people made comments useful in the preparation of this volume: David Beech, Bernhard Convent, Jim Cutler, Wiebren de Jonge, Michael Fine, William Harvey, Anil Hirani, Arthur Keller, Michael Kifer, Hans Kraamer, Vladimir Lifschitz, Alberto Mendelzon, Jaime Montemayor, Inderpal Mumick, Mike Nasdos, Jeff Naughton, Meral Ozsoyoglu, Domenico Sacca, Shuky Sagiv, Yatin Saraiya, Bruce Schuchardt, Mary Shaw, Avi Silberschatz, Leon Sterling, Rodney Topor, Allen Van Gelder, Moshe Vardi, and Elizabeth Wolf.

Alberto Mendelzon, Jeff Naughton, and Shuky Sagiv also served as the publisher's referees. My son Peter Ullman developed some of the TEX macros used in the preparation of this manuscript. The writing of this book was facilitated by computing equipment contributed to Stanford University by ATT Foundation and by IBM Corp.

Corrections to the first printing were provided by: Francisco Carrasco, Chen-Lieh Huang, Elie Kanaan, Dorothee Koch, Byung-Suk Lee, Mike Migliore, Inderpal Mumick, Geoff Phipps, and Yumi Tsugi.

## Old Debts

The two editions of Ullman [1982] acknowleged many people who contributed to that book, and many of these suggestions influenced the present book. I thank in this regard: Al Aho, Brenda Baker, Dan Blosser, Martin Brooks, Peter deJong, Ron Fagin, Mary Feay, Shel Finkelstein, Vassos Hadzilacos, Kevin Karplus, Zvi Kedem, Arthur Keller, Hank Korth, Keith Lantz, Dave Maier, Dan Newman, Mohammed Olumi, Shuky Sagiv, Charles Shub, Joe Skudlarek, and Joseph Spinden.

Gerree Pecht, at Princeton, typed the first edition of the old book; vestiges of her original troff can be found in the TEX source of this volume. Luis Trabb-Pardo assisted me in translation of Ullman [1982] from troff to TEX.

J. D. U.
Stanford CA

# TABLE OF CONTENTS

# CHAPTER 1

Databases,
Object Bases,
and
Knowledge Bases

A database management system (DBMS) is an important type of programming system, used today on the biggest and the smallest computers. As for other major forms of system software, such as compilers and operating systems, a well-understood set of principles for database management systems has developed over the years, and these concepts are useful both for understanding how to use these systems effectively and for designing and implementing DBMS's. In this book we shall study the key ideas that make database management systems possible. The first three sections of this chapter introduce the basic terminology and viewpoints needed for the understanding of database systems.

In Section 1.4, we discuss some of the newer applications for which the classical form of database management system does not appear to be adequate. Then, we discuss two classes of enhanced DBMS's that are of rising importance. In Section 1.5 we mention "object-base" systems and discuss how they solve the problems posed by the new applications. Section 1.6 introduces us to "knowledge systems," which are generally systems implementing logic, in one or another form, as a programming language. A "knowledge-base management system" (KBMS) is then a programming system that has the capabilities of both a DBMS and a knowledge system. In essence, the highly touted "Fifth Generation" project's goal is to implement a KBMS and the hardware on which it can run efficiently. The relationships among these different kinds of systems are summarized in Section 1.7.

The reader may find some of the material in this chapter difficult to follow at first. All important concepts found in Chapter 1 will be covered in greater detail in later chapters, so it is appropriate to skim the material found here at a first reading.

## 1.1 THE CAPABILITIES OF A DBMS

There are two qualities that distinguish database management systems from other sorts of programming systems.

1.   The ability to manage persistent data, and
2.   The ability to access large amounts of data efficiently.

Point (1) merely states that there is a *database* which exists permanently; the contents of this database is the data that a DBMS accesses and manages. Point (2) distinguishes a DBMS from a file system, which also manages persistent data, but does not generally help provide fast access to arbitrary portions of the data. A DBMS's capabilities are needed most when the amount of data is very large, because for small amounts of data, simple access techniques, such as linear scans of the data, are usually adequate. We shall discuss this aspect of a DBMS briefly in the present section; in Chapter 6 the issue of access efficiency is studied in detail.

While we regard the above two properties of a DBMS as fundamental, there are a number of other capabilities that are almost universally found in commercial DBMS's. These are:

a)   Support for at least one *data model*, or mathematical abstraction through which the user can view the data.
b)   Support for certain high-level languages that allow the user to define the structure of data, access data, and manipulate data.
c)   *Transaction management*, the capability to provide correct, concurrent access to the database by many users at once.
d)   *Access control*, the ability to limit access to data by unauthorized users, and the ability to check the validity of data.
e)   *Resiliency*, the ability to recover from system failures without losing data.

### Data Models

Each DBMS provides at least one abstract model of data that allows the user to see information not as raw bits, but in more understandable terms. In fact, it is usually possible to see data at several levels of abstraction, as discussed in Section 1.2. At a relatively low level, a DBMS commonly allows us to visualize data as composed of files.

**Example 1.1:** A corporation would normally keep a file concerning its employees, and the record for an employee might have fields for his first name, last name, employee ID number, salary, home address, and probably dozens of other pieces of information. For our simple example, let us suppose we keep in the record only the employee's name and the manager of the employee. The record structure would look like:

```
record
    name:  char[30];
    manager:  char[30];
end
```

The file itself is a sequence of records, one for each employee of the company.
☐

In many of the data models we shall discuss, a file of records is abstracted
to what is often called a *relation*, which might be described by

EMPLOYEES(NAME, MANAGER)

Here, EMPLOYEES is the name of the relation, corresponding to the file mentioned in Example 1.1. NAME and MANAGER are field names; fields are often called *attributes*, when relations are being talked about.

While we shall, in this informal introductory chapter, sometimes use "file" and "relation" as synonyms, the reader should be alert to the fact that they are different concepts and are used quite differently when we get to the details of database systems. A relation is an abstraction of a file, where the data type of fields is generally of little concern, and where order among records is not specified. Records in a relation are called *tuples*. Thus, a file is a list of records, but a relation is a set of tuples.

## Efficient File Access

The ability to store a file is not remarkable; the file system associated with any operating system does that. The capability of a DBMS is seen when we access the data of a file. For example, suppose we wish to find the manager of employee "Clark Kent." If the company has thousands of employees, it is very expensive to search the entire file to find the one with NAME = "Clark Kent". A DBMS helps us to set up "index files," or "indices," that allow us to access the record for "Clark Kent" in essentially one stroke, no matter how large the file is. Likewise, insertion of new records or deletion of old ones can be accomplished in time that is small and essentially constant, independent of the file's length. An example of an appropriate index structure that may be familiar to the reader is a hash table with NAME as the key. This and other index structures are discussed in Chapter 6.

Another thing a DBMS helps us do is *navigate* among files, that is, to combine values in two or more files to obtain the information we want. The next example illustrates navigation.

**Example 1.2:** Suppose we stored in an employee's record the department for which he works, but not his manager. In another file, called DEPARTMENTS, we have records that associate a department's name with its manager. In the style of relations, we have:

EMPLOYEES(NAME, DEPT)
DEPARTMENTS(DEPT, MANAGER)

Now, if we want to find Clark Kent's manager, we need to navigate from EMPLOYEES to DEPARTMENTS, using the equality of the DEPT field in both files. That is, we first find the record in the EMPLOYEES file that has NAME = "Clark Kent", and from that record we get the DEPT value, which we all know is "News". Then, we look into the DEPARTMENTS file for the record having DEPT = "News", and there we find MANAGER = "Perry White". If we set up the right indices, we can perform each of these accesses in some small, constant amount of time, independent of the lengths of the files. □

## Query Languages

To make access to files easier, a DBMS provides a *query language*, or *data manipulation language*, to express operations on files. Query languages differ in the level of detail they require of the user, with systems based on the relational data model generally requiring less detail than languages based on other models.

**Example 1.3:** The query discussed in Example 1.2, "find the manager of Clark Kent," could be written in the language SQL, which is based on the relational model of data, as shown in Figure 1.1. The language SQL will be taught beginning in Section 4.6. For the moment, let us note that line (1) tells the DBMS to print the manager as an answer, line (2) says to look at the EMPLOYEES and DEPARTMENTS relations, (3) says the employee's name is "Clark Kent," and the last line says that the manager is connected to the employee by being associated (in the DEPARTMENTS relation) with the same department that the employee is associated with (in the EMPLOYEES relation).

```
(1)  SELECT MANAGER
(2)  FROM EMPLOYEES, DEPARTMENTS
(3)  WHERE EMPLOYEES.NAME = 'Clark Kent'
(4)      AND EMPLOYEES.DEPT = DEPARTMENTS.DEPT;
```

**Figure 1.1** Example SQL query.

In Figure 1.2 we see the same query written in the simplified version of the network-model query language DML that we discuss in Chapter 5. For a rough description of what these DML statements mean, lines (1) and (2) together tell the DBMS to find the record for Clark Kent in the EMPLOYEES file. Line (3) uses an implied "set" structure EMP-DEPT that connects employees to their departments, to find the department that "owns" the employee ("set" and "owns" are technical terms of DML's data model), i.e., the department to which the employee belongs. Line (4) exploits the assumption that there is another set structure DEPT-MGR, relating departments to their managers. On line (5) we find and print the first manager listed for Clark Kent's department, and technically, we would have to search for additional managers for the same department, steps which we omit in Figure 1.2. Note that the print operation on line (5) is not part of the query language, but part of the surrounding "host language," which is an ordinary programming language.

The reader should notice that navigation among files is made far more explicit in DML than in SQL, so extra effort is required of the DML programmer. The difference is not just the extra line of code in Figure 1.2 compared with Figure 1.1; rather it is that Figure 1.2 states how we are to get from one record to the next, while Figure 1.1 says only how the answer relates to the data. This "declarativeness" of SQL and other languages based on the relational model is an important reason why systems based on that model are becoming progressively more popular. We shall have more to say about declarativeness in Section 1.4. □

```
(1)  EMPLOYEES.NAME := "Clark Kent"
(2)  FIND EMPLOYEES RECORD BY CALC-KEY
(3)  FIND OWNER OF CURRENT EMP-DEPT SET
(4)  FIND FIRST MANAGER RECORD IN CURRENT DEPT-MGR SET
(5)  print MANAGER.NAME
```

**Figure 1.2**  Example query written in DML.

**Transaction Management**

Another important capability of a DBMS is the ability to manage simultaneously large numbers of *transactions*, which are procedures operating on the database. Some databases are so large that they can only be useful if they are operated upon simultaneously by many computers; often these computers are dispersed around the country or the world. The database systems used by banks, accessed almost instantaneously by hundreds or thousands of automated teller machines, as well as by an equal or greater number of employees in the bank branches, is typical of this sort of database. An airline reservation system is another good example.

Sometimes, two accesses do not interfere with each other. For example, any number of transactions can be reading your bank balance at the same time, without any inconsistency. But if you are in the bank depositing your salary check at the exact instant your spouse is extracting money from an automatic teller, the result of the two transactions occurring simultaneously and without coordination is unpredictable. Thus, transactions that modify a data item must "lock out" other transactions trying to read or write that item at the same time. A DBMS must therefore provide some form of *concurrency control* to prevent uncoordinated access to the same data item by more than one transaction. Options and techniques for concurrency control are discussed in Chapter 9.

Even more complex problems occur when the database is distributed over many different computer systems, perhaps with duplication of data to allow both faster local access and to protect against the destruction of data if one computer crashes. Some of the techniques useful for distributed operation are covered in Chapter 10.

## Security of Data

A DBMS must not only protect against loss of data when crashes occur, as we just mentioned, but it must prevent unauthorized access. For example, only users with a certain clearance should have access to the salary field of an employee file, and the DBMS must be able to associate with the various users their privileges to see files, fields within files, or other subsets of the data in the database. Thus, a DBMS must maintain a table telling for each user known to it, what access privileges the user has for each object. For example, one user may be allowed to read a file, but not to insert or delete data; another may not be allowed to see the file at all, while a third may be allowed to read or modify the file at will.

To provide an adequately rich set of constructs, so that users may see parts of files without seeing the whole thing, a DBMS often provides a *view* facility, that lets us create imaginary objects defined in a precise way from real objects, e.g., files or (equivalently) relations.

**Example 1.4:** Suppose we have an EMPLOYEES file with the following fields:

EMPLOYEES(NAME, DEPT, SALARY, ADDRESS)

and we wish most people to have access to the fields other than SALARY, but not to the SALARY field. In the language SQL, we could define a view SAFE-EMPS by:

```
CREATE VIEW SAFE-EMPS BY
SELECT NAME, DEPT, ADDRESS
FROM EMPLOYEES;
```

That is, view SAFE-EMPS consists of the NAME, DEPT, and ADDRESS fields of EMPLOYEES, but not the SALARY field. SAFE-EMPS may be thought of as a relation described by

SAFE-EMPS(NAME, DEPT, ADDRESS)

The view SAFE-EMPS does not exist physically as a file, but it can be queried as if it did. For example, we could ask for Clark Kent's department by saying in SQL:

```
SELECT DEPT
FROM SAFE-EMPS
WHERE NAME = 'Clark Kent';
```

Normal users are allowed to access the view SAFE-EMPS, but not the relation EMPLOYEES. Users with the privilege of knowing salaries are given access to read the EMPLOYEES relation, while a subset of these are given the privilege of modifying the EMPLOYEES relation, i.e., they can change people's salaries. □

Security aspects of a DBMS are discussed in Chapter 8, along with the related question of *integrity*, the techniques whereby invalid data may be detected and avoided.

## 1.2 BASIC DATABASE SYSTEM TERMINOLOGY

In this section we shall catalog several different ways in which database systems can be viewed, and we shall develop some of the terminology that we use throughout the book. We shall begin by discussing three levels of abstraction used in describing databases. We shall also consider the scheme/instance dichotomy, that is, the distinction between the structure of a thing and the value that the thing currently has. In the next section we discuss the different kinds of languages used in a database system and the different roles they play.

### Levels of Abstraction in a DBMS

Between the computer, dealing with bits, and the ultimate user dealing with concepts such as employees, bank accounts, or airline seats, there will be many levels of abstraction. A fairly standard viewpoint regarding levels of abstraction is shown in Figure 1.3. In the world of database systems, we generally have no reason to concern ourselves with the bit or byte level, so we begin our study roughly at the level of files, i.e., at the "physical" level.

### The Physical Database Level

A collection of files and the indices or other storage structures used to access them efficiently is termed a *physical database*. The physical database resides permanently on secondary storage devices, such as disks, and many different physical databases can be managed by the same database management system software. Chapter 6 covers the principal data structures used in physical database systems.

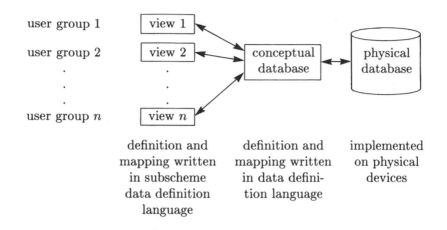

**Figure 1.3** Levels of abstraction in a database system.

## The Conceptual Database Level

The *conceptual database* is an abstraction of the real world as it pertains to the users of the database. A DBMS provides a *data definition language*, or DDL, to describe the conceptual scheme and the implementation of the conceptual scheme by the physical scheme. The DDL lets us describe the conceptual database in terms of a "data model." For example, we mentioned the relational model in Section 1.1. In that model, data is seen as tables, whose columns are headed by attributes and whose rows are "tuples," which are similar to records.

Another example of a suitable data model is a directed graph, where nodes represent files or relations, and the arcs from node to node represent associations between two such files. The *network model*, which underlies the program of Figure 1.2, is a directed-graph model. That program dealt with nodes (files) for employees, for departments, and for managers, and with arcs between them: EMP-DEPT between EMPLOYEES and DEPARTMENTS, and DEPT-MGR between DEPARTMENTS and MANAGERS.[1] Chapter 2 discusses data models in general, with the relational model described in Sections 2.3 and 2.4 and the network model described in Section 2.5. Logic as a data model is introduced in Chapter 3.

The conceptual database is intended to be a unified whole, including all the data used by a single organization. The advent of database management systems allowed an enterprise to bring all its files of information together and to see them in one consistent way—the way described by the conceptual database.

---

[1] The DEPARTMENTS node was never mentioned explicitly, being referred to only as "owner of current EMP-DEPT set" in line (3) of Figure 1.2.

This bringing together of files was not a trivial task. Information of the same type would typically be kept in different places, and the formats used for the same kind of information would frequently be different.

**Example 1.5:** Different divisions of a company might each keep information about employees and the departments to which they were assigned. But one division might store employee names as a whole, while another had three fields, for first, middle, and last names. The translation of one format into the other might not be difficult, but it had to be done before a unified conceptual database could be built.

Perhaps more difficult to reconcile are differences in the structure of data. One division might have a record for each employee and store the employee's department in a field of that record. A second division might list departments in a file and follow each department record by a list of records, one for each employee of that department. The difference is that a department suddenly devoid of employees disappears in the first division's database, but remains in the second. If there were such an empty department in each division, the query "list all the departments" would give different answers according to the structures of the two divisions. To build a conceptual scheme, some agreement about a unified structure must be reached; the process of doing so is called *database integration.* $\Box$

## The View Level

A *view* or *subscheme* is a portion of the conceptual database or an abstraction of part of the conceptual database. Most database management systems provide a facility for declaring views, called a *subscheme data definition language* and a facility for expressing queries and operations on the views, which would be called a *subscheme data manipulation language.* In a sense, the construction of views is the inverse of the process of database integration; for each collection of data that contributed to the conceptual database, we may construct a view containing just that data. Views are also important for enforcing security in a database system, allowing subsets of the data to be seen only by those users with a need or privilege to see it; Example 1.4 illustrated this use of views.

As an example of the general utility of views, an airline provides a computerized reservation service, including a collection of programs that deal with flights and passengers. These programs, and the people who use them, do not need to know about personnel files, lost luggage, or the assignment of pilots to flights, information which might also be kept in the database of the airline. The dispatcher may need to know about flights, aircraft, and aspects of the personnel files (e.g., which pilots are qualified to fly a 747), but does not need to know about employee salaries or the passengers booked on a flight. Thus, there may be one view of the database for the reservations department and another, very different one for the dispatcher's office.

Often a view is just a small conceptual database, and it is at the same level of abstraction as the conceptual database. However, there are senses in which a view can be "more abstract" than a conceptual database, as the data dealt with by a view may be constructible from the conceptual database but not actually present in that database.

For a canonical example, the personnel department may have a view that includes each employee's age. However, it is unlikely that ages would be found in the conceptual database, as ages would have to be changed each day for some of the employees. More likely, the conceptual database would store the employee's date of birth. When a user program, which believed it was dealing with a view that held age information, requested from the database a value for an employee's age, the DBMS would translate this request into "current date minus date of birth," which makes sense to the conceptual database, and the calculation would be performed on the corresponding data taken from the physical database.

**Example 1.6:** Let us emphasize the difference between physical, conceptual, and view levels of abstraction by an analogy from the programming languages world. In particular, we shall talk about arrays. On the conceptual level, we might describe an array by a declaration such as

$$\textbf{integer array } A[1..n; 1..m] \tag{1.1}$$

while on the physical level we might see the array $A$ as stored in a block of consecutive storage locations, by the rule:

$$A[i, j] \text{ is in location } a_0 + 4\big(m(i - 1) + j - 1\big) \tag{1.2}$$

A view of the array $A$ might be formed by declaring a function $f(i)$ to be the sum from $j = 1$ to $m$ of $A[i, j]$. In this view, we not only see $A$ in a related but different form, as a function rather than an array, but we have obscured some of the information, since we can only see the sums of rows, rather than the rows themselves. □

### Schemes and Instances

In addition to the gradations in levels of abstraction implied by Figure 1.3, there is another, orthogonal dimension to our perception of databases. When the database is designed, we are interested in plans for the database; when it is used, we are concerned with the actual data present in the database. Note that the data in a database changes frequently, while the plans remain the same over long periods of time (although not necessarily forever).

The current contents of a database we term an *instance of the database*. The terms *extension of the database* and *database state* also appear in the literature, although we shall avoid them here. However, the term *extensional database* will be used when speaking of knowledge-base systems in Chapter 3 to describe something quite close to the "current database."

Plans for a database tell us of the types of entities that the database deals with, the relationships among these types of entities, and the ways in which the entities and relationships at one level of abstraction are expressed at the next lower (more concrete) level. The term *scheme* is used to refer to plans, so we talk of a *conceptual scheme* as the plan for the conceptual database, and we call the physical database plan a *physical scheme*. The plan for a view is often referred to simply as a *subscheme*. The term *intention* is sometimes used for "scheme," although we shall not use it when talking of database systems.

**Example 1.7:** We can continue with the array analogy of Example 1.6. The description of arrays and functions given in that example was really schema information.

1. The physical scheme is the statement (1.2), that the array $A$ is stored beginning at location $a_0$, and that $A[i, j]$ appears in word

$$a_0 + 4\bigl(m(i - 1) + j - 1\bigr)$$

2. The conceptual scheme is the declaration (1.1); $A$ is an integer array with $n$ rows and $m$ columns.

3. The subscheme is the definition of the function $f$, that is,

$$f(i) = \sum_{j=1}^{m} A[i, j]$$

As an example of an instance of this conceptual scheme, we could let

$$n = m = 3$$

and let $A$ be the "magic square" matrix:

$$
\begin{array}{ccc}
8 & 1 & 6 \\
3 & 5 & 7 \\
4 & 9 & 2
\end{array}
$$

Then, the physical instance would be the nine words starting at location $a_0$, containing, in order, 8, 1, 6, 3, 5, 7, 4, 9, 2. Finally, the view instance would be the function $f(1) = f(2) = f(3) = 15$. $\square$

## Data Independence

The chain of abstractions of Figure 1.3, from view to conceptual to physical database, provides two levels of "data independence." Most obviously, in a well-designed database system the physical scheme can be changed without altering the conceptual scheme or requiring a redefinition of subschemes. This independence is referred to as *physical data independence*. It implies that modifications to the physical database organization may affect the efficiency of application programs, but it will never be required that we rewrite those programs just because the implementation of the conceptual scheme by the physical scheme has changed. As an illustration, references to the array $A$ mentioned in Examples 1.6 and 1.7 should work correctly whether the physical implementation of arrays is row-major (row-by-row, as in those examples) or column-major (column-by-column). The value of physical data independence is that it allows "tuning" of the physical database for efficiency while permitting application programs to run as if no change had occurred.

The relationship between views and the conceptual database also provides a type of independence called *logical data independence*. As the database is used, it may become necessary to modify the conceptual scheme, for example, by adding information about different types of entities or extra information about existing entities. Many modifications to the conceptual scheme can be made without affecting existing subschemes, and other modifications to the conceptual scheme can be made if we redefine the mapping from the subscheme to the conceptual scheme. Again, no change to the application programs is necessary. The only kind of change in the conceptual scheme that could not be reflected in a redefinition of a subscheme in terms of the conceptual scheme is the deletion of information that corresponds to information present in the subscheme. Such changes would naturally require rewriting or discarding some application programs.

## 1.3 DATABASE LANGUAGES

In ordinary programming languages the declarations and executable statements are all part of one language. In the database world, however, it is common to separate the two functions of declaration and computation into two different languages. The motivation is that, while in an ordinary program data exists only while the program is running, in a database system, the data persists and may be declared once and for all. Thus, a separate definition facility often makes sense. We shall also see that work is divided between specialized database languages and an ordinary, or "host," language. The reason why database systems commonly make this partition is discussed in Section 1.4.

### Data Definition Languages

As we have mentioned, the conceptual scheme is specified in a language, provided as part of a DBMS, called the data definition language. This language is not a procedural language, but rather a notation for describing the types of entities, and relationships among types of entities, in terms of a particular data model.

**Example 1.8:** We might define a relation describing the flights run by an airline with the data definition:

```
CREATE TABLE FLIGHTS(NUMBER:INT, DATE:CHAR(6),
    SEATS:INT, FROM:CHAR(3), TO:CHAR(3));
CREATE INDEX FOR FLIGHTS ON NUMBER;
```

This code is an example of the data definition language of SQL. The first two lines describe the relation, its attributes, and their physical implementation as integers and character strings of fixed length. The third line states that an index on the flight number is to be created as part of the physical scheme, presumably to make the lookup of information about flights, given their number, more efficient than if we had to search the entire file of flights. For example, the DDL compiler might choose a hash table whose key was the integer in the NUMBER field, and it might store FLIGHTS records in buckets according to the hashed value of the flight number. If there were enough buckets so that very few records are placed in any given bucket on the average, then finding a flight record given its number would be very fast. □

The data definition language is used when the database is designed, and it is used when that design is modified. It is not used for obtaining or modifying the data itself. The data definition language has statements that describe, in somewhat abstract terms such as those of Example 1.8, what the physical layout of the database should be. Detailed design of the physical database is done by DBMS routines that "compile" statements in the data definition language.

The description of subschemes and their correspondence to the conceptual scheme requires a *subscheme data definition language,* which is often quite similar to the data definition language itself. Sometimes, the subscheme language uses a data model different from that of the data definition language; there could, in fact, be several different subscheme languages, each using a different data model.

## Data Manipulation Languages

Operations on the database require a specialized language, called a data manipulation language (DML)[2] or query language, in which to express commands such as:

1. Retrieve from the database the number of seats available on flight 999 on July 24.
2. Decrement by 4 the number of seats available on flight 123 on August 31.
3. Find all flights from ORD (O'Hare airport in Chicago) to JFK (Kennedy airport in New York) on August 20.

---

[2] Do not confuse the general notion of "a DML" with the particular language DML (more properly "the CODASYL DML") that we introduced by example in Figure 1.2.

4. Enter (add to the database) flight 456, with 100 seats, from ORD to JFK on August 21.

Items (1) and (3) illustrate the querying of the database, and they would be implemented by programs like those of Figures 1.1 and 1.2. Item (2) is an example of an *update* statement, and it would be implemented by a program such as the following lines of SQL.

```
UPDATE FLIGHTS
SET SEATS = SEATS - 4
WHERE NUMBER = 123 AND DATE = 'AUG 31';
```

Item (4) illustrates insertion of a record into the database, and it would be expressed by a program (in SQL) like:

```
INSERT INTO FLIGHTS
    VALUES(456, 'AUG 21', 100, 'ORD', 'JFK');
```

The term "query language" is frequently used as a synonym for "data manipulation language." Strictly speaking, only some of the statements of a DML are "queries"; these are the statements, like (1) and (3) above, that extract data from the database without modifying anything in the database. Other statements, like (2) and (4), do modify the database, and thus are not queries, although they can be expressed in a "query language."

## Host Languages

Often, manipulation of the database is done by an *application program*, written in advance to perform a certain task. It is usually necessary for an application program to do more than manipulate the database; it must perform a variety of ordinary computational tasks. For example, a program used by an airline to book reservations does not only need to retrieve from the database the current number of available seats on the flight and to update that number. It needs to make a decision: are there enough seats available? It might well print the ticket, and it might engage in a dialog with the user, such as asking for the passenger's "frequent flier" number.

Thus, programs to manipulate the database are commonly written in a *host language*, which is a conventional programming language such as C or even COBOL. The host language is used for decisions, for displaying questions, and for reading answers; in fact, it is used for everything but the actual querying and modification of the database.

The commands of the data manipulation language are invoked by the host-language program in one of two ways, depending on the characteristics of the DBMS.

1. The commands of the data manipulation language are invoked by host-language calls on procedures provided by the DBMS.

| Program in ordinary<br>programming language | Program in extended<br>programming language |
|---|---|
| `CALL GET(B)` | `##GET(B)` |
| `A := B+1` | `A := B+1` |
| `CALL STORE(A)` | `##STORE(A)` |

**Figure 1.4**  Two styles of host language.

2.  The commands are statements in a language that is an extension of the host language. Possibly there is a preprocessor that handles the data manipulation statements, or a compiler may handle both host and data manipulation language statements. The commands of the data manipulation language will thereby be converted into calls to procedures provided by the DBMS, so the distinction between approaches (1) and (2) is not a great one.

The two forms of program are illustrated in Figure 1.4. In the second column, the double #'s are meant to suggest a way to mark those statements that are to be preprocessed.

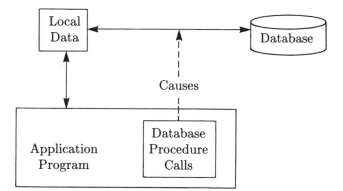

**Figure 1.5**  The data seen by an application program.

Figure 1.5 suggests how the application program interacts with the database. There is *local data* belonging to the application program; this data is manipulated by the program in the ordinary way. Embedded within the application program are procedure calls that access the database. A query asking for data causes the answer to be copied from the database to variables in the local data area; if there is more than one answer to be retrieved (e.g., "find all flights from ORD to JFK"), then these solutions are retrieved one at a time, when a "fetch" procedure is called by the application program. When inserting or modifying data, values are copied from the local data variables to the database, again in response to calls to the proper procedures. For example, the request to decrement by 4 the number of seats on a certain flight could be performed by:

1. Copying the number of seats remaining on that flight into the local data area,

2. Testing if that number was at least 4, and if so,

3. Storing the decremented value into the database, as the new number of seats for that flight.

### Database System Architecture

In Figure 1.6 we see a diagram of how the various components and languages of a database management system interact. On the right, we show the design, or database scheme, fed to the DDL compiler, which produces an internal description of the database. The modification of the database scheme is very infrequent, compared to the rate at which queries and other data manipulations are performed. In a large, multiuser database, this modification is normally the responsibility of a *database administrator*, a person or persons with responsibility for the entire system, including its scheme, subschemes (views), and authorization to access parts of the database.

We also see in Figure 1.6 the query-language processor, which is given data manipulation programs from two sources. One source is user queries or other data manipulations, entered directly at a terminal. Figure 1.1 is an example of what such a query would look like if SQL were the data manipulation language. The second source is application programs, where database queries and manipulations are embedded in a host language and preprocessed to be run later, perhaps many times. The portions of an application program written in a host language are handled by the host language compiler, not shown in Figure 1.6. The portions of the application program that are data manipulation language statements are handled by the query language processor, which is responsible for optimization of these statements. We shall discuss optimization in Chapter 11 (Volume II), but let us emphasize here that DML statements, especially queries, which extract data from the database, are often transformed significantly by the query processor, so that they can be executed much more efficiently than if they had been executed as written. We show the query processor accessing the database description tables that were created by the DDL program to ascertain some facts that are useful for optimization of queries, such as the existence or nonexistence of certain indices.

Below the query processor we see a *database manager*, whose role is to take commands at the conceptual level and translate them into commands at the physical level, i.e., the level of files. The database manager maintains and

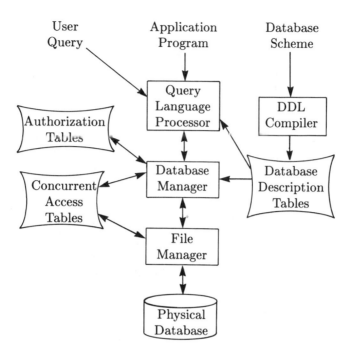

**Figure 1.6** Diagram of a database system.

accesses tables of authorization information and concurrency control information. Authorization tables allow the database manager to check that the user
has permission to execute the intended query or modification of the database.
Modification of the authorization table is done by the database manager, in
response to properly authorized user commands.

If concurrent access to the database by different queries and database manipulations is supported, the database manager maintains the necessary information in a specialized table. There are several forms the concurrency control
table can take. For example, any operation modifying a relation may be granted
a "lock" on that relation until the modification is complete, thus preventing simultaneous, conflicting modifications. The currently held locks are stored in
what we referred to as the "concurrent access tables" in Figure 1.6.

The database manager translates the commands given it into operations on
files, which are handled by the *file manager*. This system may be the general-
purpose file system provided by the underlying operating system, or it may be
a specialized system modified to support the DBMS. For example, a special-
purpose DBMS file manager may attempt to put parts of a file that are likely
to be accessed as a unit on one cylinder of a disk. Doing so minimizes "seek

time," since we can read the entire unit after moving the disk head once.

As another example of a possible specialization of the file manager, we indicated in Figure 1.6 that the file manager may use the concurrent access tables. One reason it might be desirable to do so is that we can allow more processes to access the database concurrently if we lock objects that are smaller than whole files or relations. For example, if we locked individual blocks of which a large file was composed, different processes could access and modify records of that file simultaneously, as long as they were on different blocks.

## 1.4 MODERN DATABASE SYSTEM APPLICATIONS

The classical form of database system, which we surveyed in the first three sections, was designed to handle an important but limited class of applications. These applications are suggested by the examples we have so far pursued: files of employees or corporate data in general, airline reservations, and financial records. The common characteristic of such applications is that they have large amounts of data, but the operations to be performed on the data are simple. In such database systems, insertion, deletion, and retrieval of specified records predominates, and the navigation among a small number of relations or files, as illustrated in Example 1.3, is one of the more complex things the system is expected to do.

This view of intended applications leads to the distinction between the DML and the host language, as was outlined in the previous section. Only the DML has the built-in capability to access the database efficiently, but the expressive power of the DML is very limited. For example, we saw in Section 1.1 how to ask for Clark Kent's manager, and with a bit more effort we could ask for Clark Kent's manager's manager's manager, for example. However, in essentially no DBMS commercially available in the late 1980's, could one ask in one query for the transitive closure of the "manages" relationship, i.e., the set of all individuals who are managers of Clark Kent at some level of the managerial hierarchy.[3]

The host language, being a general-purpose language, lets us compute management chains or anything else we wish. However, it does not provide any assistance with the task that must be performed repeatedly to find the managers of an individual at all levels; that task is to answer quickly a question of the form "who is $X$'s manager?"

The DML/host language dichotomy is generally considered an advantage, rather than a deficiency in database systems. For example, it is the limited power of the DML that lets us optimize queries well, transforming the algorithms that they express in sometimes surprising, but correct, ways. The same

---

[3] Some commercial DBMS's have a built-in facility for computing simple recursions, like managerial hierarchies, but they cannot handle any more complex recursion.

queries, written in a general purpose language, could not be optimized in such radical ways by known techniques. However, there are some new applications of database systems that do not follow the older paradigms, and in these applications, the integration of the data manipulation and host languages becomes important.

Typical applications in this class include VLSI design databases, CAD (computer-aided design) databases, databases of graphic data, and software engineering databases, i.e., databases that manage multiple versions of large programs. These applications are characterized by the need for fast retrieval and modification of data, as were the earliest DBMS applications, but they are also characterized by a need to do considerably more powerful operations on data than was required by the earlier applications. The following example is a simplification of, but in the spirit of, many applications in this class.

**Example 1.9:** Suppose we wish to use a database system to store visual images composed of cells and to construct images from recursively defined cells. For simplicity, we shall assume that images are black-and-white. A cell is composed of a collection of bits (*pixels*), each of which is either white (set) or black (reset). A cell also can contain copies of other cells, whose origins are translated to a specified point in the coordinate system of the containing cell.

For example, Figure 1.7 shows a cell, Cell1, containing two copies of Cell2; the latter is a picture of a man. The origin of Cell2, which we shall assume is the lower left corner, is translated for each copy, relative to the origin of Cell1. Thus, we might suppose that the figure on the left has its origin at $(x, y)$ coordinate $(100, 150)$ of Cell1's coordinate system, while the figure on the right might have its origin at $(500, 50)$. In addition, Cell1 contains a copy of another cell, not shown, with a picture of a tree. Finally, Cell1 has the pixels of the horizon line set directly, not as part of any subcell.

Cell2 and the cell for the tree may be defined recursively as well. For example, Cell2 may consist of copies of cells for the arms, leg, body, and face; the cell for the face may consist of copies of cells for eyes, mouth, and so on. The database stores only the immediate constituents of each cell. Thus, to find the status of all pixels in Cell1, we must query the database for all the pixels set directly in that cell, then query the database to find the points set in each of the constituent cells of Cell1. Those queries cause queries about the constituents of the constituents, and so on. □

As mentioned earlier, recursions are not generally handled by single queries to a conventional database system. Thus, we are forced to use the host language to store the image as we construct it. The DML is used to query the database repeatedly for the constituents of cells at progressively lower levels.

Storing the image is not hard for a typical $1000 \times 1000$ black-and-white graphic image; a bitmap representation of the drawing easily fits in main mem-

Cell1

**Figure 1.7**  Cells in a drawing database.

ory. However, VLSI images can be 100 times as large, and multicolored as well. A page of text, such as the one you are reading, can have more data still, when printed on a high-quality printer. When an image has that much data, the host language program can no longer store a bitmap in main memory. For efficiency, it must store the image on secondary storage and use a carefully designed algorithm for exploring the contents of cells, to avoid moving large numbers of pages between main and secondary storage. This is exactly the sort of task that a data manipulation language does well, but when written in the host language, the programmer has to implement everything from scratch. Thus, for graphics databases and many similar applications, the DML/host language separation causes us great difficulty.

**Integration of the DML and Host Language**

There are two common approaches to the problem of combining the fast access capability of the DML with the general-purpose capability of the host language.

1.  The "object-oriented" approach is to use a language with the capability of defining abstract data types, or classes. The system allows the user to embed data structures for fast access in those of his classes that need it. Thus, the class "cell" for Example 1.9, might be given indices that let us find quickly the constituents of a given cell, and the cells of which a given cell is a constituent.

2.  The "logical" approach uses a language that looks and behaves something like logical (if $\cdots$ then) rules. Some predicates are considered part of the conceptual scheme and are given appropriate index structures, while others are used to define views, as if they were part of a subscheme. Others may

be used as if they were part of a single application program.

We shall discuss the object-oriented approach further in the next section. Chapter 5 includes a discussion of OPAL, a data manipulation language that follows the principles outlined in (1). Section 1.6 introduces the logical approach, which is discussed in more detail in Chapter 3. The discussion of systems built along these lines is deferred to the second volume.

### Declarative Languages

There is a fundamental difference between the object-oriented and logical approaches to design of an integrated DML/host language; the latter is inherently declarative and the former is not. Recall, a *declarative language* is a language in which one can express what one wants, without explaining exactly how the desired result is to be computed. A language that is not declarative is *procedural*. "Declarative" and "procedural" are relative terms, but it is generally accepted that "ordinary" languages, like Pascal, C, Lisp, and the like, are procedural, with the term "declarative" used for languages that require less specificity regarding the required sequence of steps than do languages in this class. For instance, we noticed in Example 1.3 that the SQL program of Figure 1.1 is more declarative than the Codasyl DML program of Figure 1.2. Intuitively, the reason is that the DML program tells us in detail how to navigate from employees to departments to managers, while the SQL query merely states the relationship of the desired output to the data.

The declarativeness of the query language has a significant influence on the architecture of the entire database system. The following points summarize the observed differences between systems with declarative and procedural languages, although we should emphasize that these assertions are generalizations that could be contradicted by further advances in database technology.

1.  Users prefer declarative languages, all other factors being equal.
2.  Declarative languages are harder to implement than procedural languages, because declarative languages require extensive optimization by the system if an efficient implementation of declaratively-expressed wishes is to be found.
3.  It appears that true object-orientedness and declarativeness are incompatible.

The interactions among these factors is explored further in Section 1.7.

### 1.5 OBJECT-BASE SYSTEMS

The terms "object base" and "object-oriented database management system" (OO-DBMS) are used to describe a class of programming systems with the capability of a DBMS, as outlined in Section 1.1, and with a combined DML/host language having the following features.

1. *Complex objects*, that is, the ability to define data types with a nested structure. We shall discuss in Section 2.7 a data model in which data types are built by record formation and set formation, which are the most common ways nested structures are created. For example, a tuple is built from primitive types (integers, etc.) by record formation, and a relation is built from tuples by set formation; i.e., a relation is a set of tuples with a particular record format. We could also create a record one of whose components was of type "set of tuples," or even more complex structures.

2. *Encapsulation*, that is, the ability to define procedures applying only to objects of a particular type and the ability to require that all access to those objects is via application of one of these procedures. For example, we might define "stack" as a type and define the operations PUSH and POP to apply only to stacks (PUSH takes a parameter—the element to be pushed).

3. *Object identity*, by which we mean the ability of the system to distinguish two objects that "look" the same, in the sense that all their components of primitive type are the same. The primitive types are generally character strings, numbers, and perhaps a few other types that have naturally associated, printable values. We shall have more to say about object identity below.

A system that supports encapsulation and complex objects is said to support *abstract data types* (ADT's) or *classes*. That is, a class or ADT is a definition of a structure together with the definitions of the operations by which objects of that class can be manipulated.

## Object Identity

To see the distinction between systems that support object identity and those that do not, consider Example 1.2, where we discussed a file or relation

    EMPLOYEES(NAME, DEPT)

consisting of employee-department pairs. We may ask what happens if the News department has two employees named Clark Kent. If we think of the database as a file, we simply place two records in the file; each has first field "Clark Kent" and second field "News". The notion of a file is compatible with object identity, because the position of a record distinguishes it from any other record, regardless of its printable values.

However, when we view the data as a relation, we cannot store two tuples, each of which has the value

    ("Clark Kent", "News")

The reason is that formally, a relation is a set. A tuple cannot be a member of a set more than once. That is, there is no notion of "position" of a tuple within a relation the way records have a position within a file.

A system that supports object identity will sometimes be referred to as "object-oriented," even though that term generally implies support for abstract data types as well. Systems that do not support object identity will be termed *value-oriented* or *record-oriented*. All systems based on the relational model of data are value-oriented, as are systems based on logic. However, most of the earliest database systems were object-oriented in the limited sense of supporting object identity. For example, network-model systems are object-oriented in this sense.

One might naturally suppose that object-orientation is preferable to value-orientation, since the former implies one has an "address" or l-value for objects, from which one can obtain the object itself, that is, its r-value.[4] Going the other way, finding the l-value of an object given its r-value, is not generally possible. However, one can often fake object identity in a value-oriented system by use of a "surrogate," which is a field that serves as a serial number for objects. For example, employees usually are given unique ID numbers to distinguish them in the database. That is how two Clark Kent's in the News department would, in fact, be distinguished in a relational system.

In favor of value-orientation, it appears that object-identity preservation does not mesh well with declarativeness. Furthermore, encapsulation, which is another characteristic of object-oriented systems, appears antithetical to declarativeness, as well. We shall not try to argue here that these relationships must hold, but we observe in Section 1.7 how history supports these contentions.

## 1.6 KNOWLEDGE-BASE SYSTEMS

"Knowledge" is a tricky notion to define formally, and it has been made trickier by the fact that today, "knowledge" sells well. It appears that attributing "knowledge" to your software product, or saying that it uses "artificial intelligence" makes the product more attractive, even though the performance and functionality may be no better than that of a similar product not claimed to possess these qualities.

When examined, it appears that the term "knowledge" is used chiefly as an attribute of programming systems that support some form of declarative language. Further, it appears that declarative languages are universally some form of logic. For example, the SQL program of Figure 1.1 may appear to have nothing at all to do with logic, yet we shall see in Chapter 4 that SQL is really a syntactic sugaring of a form of logic called "relational calculus," which is introduced in Chapter 3.

---

[4] The l-value/r-value distinction refers to the difference in meaning between a variable occurring on the left and right of an assignment. In a statement like $A := B$, the value of variable $B$, that is, its r-value, is required, while for $A$, we require its location, or l-value, to perform the assignment.

We shall therefore sidestep the philosophical question of what "knowledge" is and use the term to refer to systems with declarative, logic-based languages. We shall distinguish between a *knowledge system* and a *knowledge-base management system* (KBMS). A KBMS is a system that

1. Provides what a DBMS provides (support for efficient access, transaction management, etc.), and
2. Provides a single, declarative language to serve the roles played by both the data manipulation language and the host language in a DBMS.

A knowledge system, on the other hand, is a system that supports only (2); i.e., it is a programming system with a declarative language.

In the late 1980's, there are no commercial KBMS's in the sense just given, although several systems in the design phase are mentioned in the bibliographic notes, and some of those will be described in Volume II. However, there are a variety of knowledge systems, at least if one accepts that declarativeness is a relative term and regards logic-based or rule-based systems as sufficiently declarative to qualify. These systems are variously known as "expert system shells," "production system languages," "logic programming languages," and by several other names. Knowledge systems will not be addressed in this book, although we shall focus on Prolog, probably the best-known knowledge system, to provide the notation for logic as knowledge that we use throughout the book.

The reader who is familiar with Prolog is aware that this language can be viewed as purely procedural, since it has a well-defined order in which the Prolog interpreter performs actions designed to answer queries posed logically. However, it is also possible, in many cases, to think of Prolog programs as if they were purely declarative, and database system applications provide many of the best examples. In this book, we shall take the "pure" or declarative viewpoint regarding what logical rules mean, even though they are expressed in the syntax of Prolog.

## Logical Rules

We shall give a brief introduction to the Prolog notation for logical rules here, deferring a more formal treatment for Section 3.1. To begin, Prolog statements are composed of "atomic formulas," which consist of a predicate symbol applied, as if it were a procedure name, to arguments. These arguments may be composed of constants (called atoms), variables, and function symbols; the latter are applied to arguments just as we would call a function in an ordinary programming language. Predicate symbols should be thought of as producing true or false as a result; i.e., they are Boolean-valued functions. Function symbols, on the other hand, may be thought of as producing values of any type one wishes.

Following Prolog conventions, predicate symbols, function symbols, and constants begin with a lower-case letter, with the exception that constants are also permitted to be integers. Variables must begin with a capital letter. Logical statements, often called *rules*, will usually be written in the form of *Horn clauses*, which are statements of the form: "if $A_1$ and $A_2$ and $\cdots A_n$ are true, then $B$ is true." The Prolog syntax for such a statement is:[5]

$B$ :- $A_1$ & $A_2$ & $\cdots$ & $A_n$.

The symbol :- can generally be read "if." Note the terminal period, which serves as an endmarker for the rule. If $n = 0$, then the rule asserts $B$ unconditionally, and we write it

$B$.

**Example 1.10:** The following two rules can be interpreted as an inductive definition of addition, if we attribute the proper meanings to the predicate symbol *sum* and the function symbol $s$. That is, $sum(X, Y, Z)$ is true exactly when $Z$ is the sum of $X$ and $Y$, while $s(X)$ is the successor of $X$, that is, the integer which is one more than $X$. Then the rules:

```
sum(X,0,X).
sum(X,s(Y),s(Z)) :- sum(X,Y,Z).
```

say that $X + 0 = X$, and that if $X + Y = Z$, then $X + (Y + 1) = (Z + 1)$. □

**Example 1.11:** We are more often interested in logical rules expressing information about the data in a database. We should appreciate the similarity between the logical notion of a predicate with its arguments and a relation name with its attributes. That is, we can think of a predicate as true for its arguments if and only if those arguments form a tuple of the corresponding relation. For instance, we can define a view SAFE-EMPS as we did in Example 1.4, by the logical rule:

```
safe-emps(N,D,A) :- employees(N,D,S,A).
```

In order to interpret the above rule, we must remember that EMPLOYEES has four fields, the NAME, DEPT, SALARY, and ADDRESS. The rule says that for all employee names $N$, departments $D$, and addresses $A$, $(N, D, A)$ is a fact of the *safe-emps* predicate if there exists a salary $S$, such that $(N, D, S, A)$ is a fact of the *employees* predicate. Note that in general, a variable like $S$, appearing on the right side of the :- symbol but not on the left, is treated as *existentially quantified*; informally, when reading the rule we say "there exists some $S$" after saying the "if" that corresponds to the :- symbol.

For another example of how information about data can be expressed in logical terms, let us suppose that we have our earlier EMPLOYEES relation, whose only attributes are NAME and DEPT, and let us also use the DEPART-

---

[5] Most Prolog versions use a comma where we use the ampersand.

MENTS relation, with attributes DEPT and MANAGER, as we did in Example 1.2. Then we could define the predicate $manages(E, M)$, with the intuitive meaning that manager $M$ manages employee $E$, by:

$$\text{manages(E,M)} \text{ :- employees(E,D) \& departments(D,M).} \qquad (1.3)$$

That is, $(E, M)$ is a *manages* fact if there exists a department $D$ such that $(E, D)$ is an *employees* fact and $(D, M)$ is a *departments* fact. In essence, we have used the above logical rule to create view, *manages*, which looks like a relation with attributes *name* and *manager*. The queries shown in Figures 1.1 and 1.2, to find Clark Kent's manager, could be expressed in terms of this view quite simply:

$$\text{manages('Clark Kent', X)} \qquad (1.4)$$

The value or values of $X$ that make (1.4) true are found by an algorithm essentially the same as the one that would answer Figure 1.1 or 1.2, but the logical rule (1.3) plays an important part in allowing the system to interpret what the query means. In a loose sense, we might suppose that (1.3) represents "knowledge" about the *manages* relationship. $\Box$

### Expressiveness of Logic

We mentioned in Section 1.4 that SQL and similar data manipulation languages do not have enough power to compute transitive closures, such as managerial hierarchies.[6] Logical rules using function symbols have all the power of a Turing machine; i.e., they can express any computation that can be written in conventional programming languages. Even logical rules without function symbols (a language we shall call "datalog" in Chapter 3) have power to express computations beyond that of conventional DML's, as the next example will suggest.

**Example 1.12:** Suppose we have a relation (or predicate) $manages(E, M)$, intended to be true exactly when employee $E$ reports directly to manager $M$. We may wish to define another predicate $boss(E, B)$, intending it to be true whenever $B$ is $E$'s manager, or his manager's manager, or his manager's manager's manager, and so on; i.e., *boss* is the transitive closure of *manages*. The predicate *boss* can be expressed in Horn clauses as

(1)  `boss(E,M) :- manages(E,M).`
(2)  `boss(E,M) :- boss(E,N) & manages(N,M).`

The above is a typical example of how logical rules can be used recursively, that is, used to define a predicate like *boss* in terms of itself. To argue that a

---

[6] Formally, the *transitive closure* of a binary relation $r$ is the smallest relation $s$ that includes $r$ and is *transitive*, i.e., $s(X, Y)$ and $s(Y, Z)$ imply $s(X, Z)$.

collection of logical rules defines something in particular, we need to formalize the meaning of rules, and we shall do so in Chapter 3. For the moment, the following intuitive argument should give the reader the flavor of the semantics of logical rules.

To begin, we must show that whenever the rules (1) and (2) tell us $boss(e, b)$ is true, then $b$ really is what we intuitively regard as a boss of $e$. That is, we must show there is a *management chain* from $e$ to $b$, i.e., a sequence of two or more individuals $c_1, \ldots, c_n$, where $e = c_1$, $b = c_n$, and $manages(c_i, c_{i+1})$ is true for all $i$, $1 \leq i < n$. If we discover $boss(e, b)$ by rule (1), it must be that $manages(e, b)$ is true, so surely $b$ is a boss of $e$; that is, there is a management chain with $n = 2$. Otherwise, we must discover $boss(e, b)$ by rule (2). Then there is some individual $c$ such that we already discovered $boss(e, c)$ (and therefore, $c$ is in the management chain above $e$), and also $manages(c, b)$ is a fact. Then $b$ is likewise in the management chain above $e$, so our inference of $boss(e, b)$ is correct.

Conversely, we must show that whenever $b$ is in the management chain above $e$, we can infer $boss(e, b)$. The proof is by induction on the length of the management chain $e = c_1, \ldots, c_n = b$. For the basis, which is $n = 2$, if $b$ is the immediate manager of $e$, then we can make the inference by rule (1). For the induction, if there is a chain of length more than one from $e$ to $b$, say

$$e = c_1, \ldots, c_n = b$$

then by the inductive hypothesis, we can infer $boss(e, c_{n-1})$, and we also are given $manages(c_{n-1}, b)$. Thus, we may use rule (2) to infer $boss(e, b)$. $\square$

**Example 1.13:** The following rules solve the problem posed in Section 1.4, of expanding the recursive definition of cells. We shall suppose the database stores a predicate $set(I, X, Y)$, meaning that the pixel with coordinates $(X, Y)$ is set (has value 1) in the cell named $I$. Also stored is the predicate $contains(I, J, X, Y)$, meaning that cell $I$ contains a copy of cell $J$, with the origin of the copy at position $(X, Y)$ of cell $I$. Then we can define the predicate $on(I, X, Y)$ to mean that point $(X, Y)$ is set in cell $I$, either directly or through one of $I$'s constituent cells.

```
on(I,X,Y) :- set(I,X,Y).
on(I,X,Y) :- contains(I,J,U,V) & on(J,W,Z) &
             X = U+W & Y = V+Z.
```

The first rule says a point is on if it is directly set. The second says that $(X, Y)$ is set in $I$ if there exists a cell $J$ such that a copy of $J$ appears in $I$ with origin translated to point $(U, V)$, the point $(W, Z)$ is on in $J$, and the translation from the origin of $I$ to point $(U, V)$, and from there to the relative point $(W, Z)$ takes us to $(X, Y)$ of the coordinate system of cell $I$. $\square$

## 1.7 HISTORY AND PERSPECTIVE

Figure 1.8 shows the development of database systems from their origin in the early 1960's, through the present. It incorporates the decade of the 1990's, which, we predict, will be the decade in which true knowledge-base management systems first become available. We also summarize three important characteristics of these systems:

1.  Whether they are object-oriented or value-oriented.
2.  Whether they support declarative query languages.
3.  Whether they separate the DML from the host language or integrate the two.

It was our contention in Section 1.4 that (1) and (2) are linked; only value-oriented systems can support declarative languages. So far, at least, the relationship has held.

| Decade | Systems | Orientation | Declarative? | DML/host |
|--------|---------|-------------|--------------|----------|
| 1960's | Network, hierarchical model as in Sects. 2.5, 2.6, 5.1–5.5 | Object | No | Separate |
| 1970's | Relational, as in Sects. 2.3, 2.4, Ch. 4 | Value | Yes | Separate |
| 1980's | OO-DBMS's, as in Sects. 2.7, 5.6, 5.7 | Object | No | Integrated |
| 1990's | KBMS's | Value | Yes | Integrated |

**Figure 1.8** Past and future history of database systems.

The earliest true DBMS's appeared in the 1960's, and they were based on either the network or the hierarchical data models, which we discuss in Sections 2.5, and 2.6. Languages based on these models appear in Chapter 5. These systems provided efficient access to massive amounts of data, but they neither integrated the DML and host languages, nor did they provide query languages that were significantly declarative. They were object-oriented in the sense that they supported object identity, although they did not support abstract data types.

The 1970's saw the advent of relational systems, following Codd's seminal paper (Codd [1970]). A decade of development was needed, with much of the research devoted to the techniques of query optimization needed to execute the declarative languages that are an essential part of the relational idea. As we mentioned, relational systems are declarative and value-oriented, but they do not easily allow us to integrate the DML and host languages.

We see the 1980's as the decade of object-oriented DBMS's in the true sense of the term; i.e., they support both object identity and abstract data types. These are the first systems to provide well-integrated data manipulation and host languages. However, in one sense, they represent a retrograde step: they are not declarative, the way relational systems are.

Our prediction is that in the 1990's, true KBMS's will supplant the OO-DBMS's just as the relational systems have to a large extent supplanted the earlier DBMS's. These systems will provide both declarativeness and integration of the DML/host language. We predict that they will be inherently value-oriented and logic-based. It also appears that there is much to be learned about query optimization before it is possible to implement commercial KBMS's. Much of Volume II is devoted to this technology of optimization.

## BIBLIOGRAPHIC NOTES

Most of the topics introduced in this chapter will be taken up again in later chapters, and we defer the references in those areas until they are studied more deeply. Here, we mention a few odd topics and give some references regarding knowledge-base systems that would otherwise not appear until the second volume.

### Three-Level Architecture

The three levels of abstraction—physical, conceptual, and view—appear in the "DBTG report" (CODASYL [1971]). They are also a feature of the "ANSI/SPARC report" (ANSI [1975]), where they are called internal, conceptual, and external, respectively. Tsichritzis and Klug [1978] is an informal introduction to a revised version of that report.

### Database Integration

We mentioned in Section 1.1 that the process of "database integration" is needed when files from several sources are combined to form a single database. El Masri and Wiederhold [1979] and Litwin [1984] give notations to assist in the process.

## DML/Host Language Dichotomy

Stonebraker and Rowe [1977] discuss the classical architecture of a DBMS that interfaces a data manipulation language to a host language, as was discussed in Section 1.3.

## Object-Oriented Systems

Baroody and DeWitt [1981] is an early discussion of object-oriented concepts in the context of database systems. Khoshafian and Copeland [1986] discusses object identity in database systems. Maier, Stein, Otis, and Purdy [1986] discusses the GEMSTONE OO-DBMS and Fishman et al. [1986] covers the IRIS OO-DBMS.

Maier [1986] is an attempt to integrate a logic-based language into an object-oriented setting. The relationship between object- and value-oriented database systems is explored in Wiederhold [1986] and Ullman [1987].

A problem with object-oriented systems that we have not discussed is what happens when one allows types that are subtypes of several incompatible types. Strategies for resolving the resulting conflicts (e.g., what does the procedure *insert* mean if two supertypes define that operation in different ways?) are discussed and unified by Minsky and Rozenshtein [1987].

## Knowledge-Base Systems

For a discussion of knowledge systems in artificial intelligence the reader may consult Tanimoto [1987] or Genesereth and Nilsson [1987], e.g. Frost [1986] is a text attempting to integrate database and knowledge-base concepts.

Brodie and Mylopoulos [1986] surveys recent work on the development of knowledge-base management systems. The design and development of certain systems in this class are described in Dayal and Smith [1986] (PROBE), Morris, Ullman, and Van Gelder [1986] and Morris et al. [1987] (NAIL!), Stonebraker and Rowe [1986a, b] (POSTGRES), and Tsur and Zaniolo [1986] (LDL).

## Prolog-Based Systems

Kowalski [1974] is a fundamental paper on Prolog, and Clocksin and Mellish [1981] is a popular tutorial on the language. We also recommend Maier and Warren [1988] for a discussion of the language and its implementation.

Some efforts to develop KBMS's have concentrated on interfacing a Prolog interpreter with a database management system. The original paper along these lines is Warren [1981].

Other works include Jarke, Clifford, and Vassiliou [1984], Bocca [1986], Moffat and Gray [1986], Walker [1986], and Sciore and Warren [1986]. The logic/data interface is also discussed by Kunifuji and Yokuta [1982] and Kellogg, O'Hare, and Travis [1986].

## General Sources

The bibliography by Kambayashi [1981] is getting out-of-date but is an extensive compendium of work in database systems prior to its publication. Date [1986], Korth and Silberschatz [1986], and Wiederhold [1983] contain large, general bibliographies; the latter also catalogs commercial database systems. Bernstein, Hadzilacos, and Goodman [1987] has extensive references on concurrency control and distributed systems. Wiederhold [1987] provides a large bibliography on file structures and physical design.

# CHAPTER 2

# Data Models
# for
# Database Systems

We now consider the principal models used in database systems. Section 2.2 introduces the entity-relationship model, which is used primarily as a database design tool. The relational model is discussed in Sections 2.3 and 2.4; the network model in Section 2.5, and the hierarchical model, which is based on collections of tree structures, in Section 2.6. In Section 2.7 we introduce the "object model," which is a synthesis of several models based on complex objects.

Chapter 3 is devoted to one particular data model, based on logic. This "datalog" data model plays an important role in most knowledge systems and KBMS's, and aspects of that model are also central to the relational model for database systems. We shall also meet, in Chapters 4 and 5, certain query languages based on the models we discuss here.

## 2.1 DATA MODELS

A *data model* is a mathematical formalism with two parts:

1. A notation for describing data, and
2. A set of operations used to manipulate that data.

Chapter 1 made brief mention of two important models. One is the relational model, where the notation for describing data is a set of names, called attributes, for the columns of tables. Another is the network model, which uses directed graphs to describe data. For neither of these models did we discuss the operations used to manipulate data, although examples were given in Figures 1.1 and 1.2.

## Distinctions Among Data Models

One might naturally ask whether there is one "best" data model for database systems. The multiplicity of models in use suggests not. Below, we list some of the differences among models that influence where and when they are best used.

1. *Purpose.* Most data models are intended to serve as the notation for data in a database and as a notation underlying the data manipulation language. The entity-relationship model, on the other hand, is intended as a notation for conceptual scheme design, prior to an implementation in the model of whatever DBMS is used. This model is therefore missing a notion of operations on data (although some have been proposed), and one could even argue that it should not be classified as a data model at all.

2. *Object- or Value-Orientedness.* Recall our discussion in Section 1.7. We believe that value-oriented models, in effect the relational and logical models, allow declarativeness, with a profound effect on the kind of languages those models support. Nondeclarative models require less optimization, so systems based on these models are often available years before similar systems with value-oriented models. The network, hierarchical, and object models each provide object identity, and therefore can be called "object-oriented." The entity-relationship model likewise may be seen as requiring object identity.

3. *Dealing with Redundancy.* All models have some way of helping the user to avoid storing the same fact more than once. Not only does such redundancy waste space, but it may cause the data to become inconsistent, because a fact gets changed one place but not another. Object-oriented models are generally better at dealing with redundancy, because one can create a single copy of an object and refer to it by pointers from many different places. A major theme in Chapter 7 is how one copes with redundancy in the relational model, through careful database scheme design.

4. *Dealing with Many-Many Relationships.* Often a database system needs to store a "many-many" relationship, in which each of one group of elements is related to "many" of another group (i.e., to zero, one, or more of that group) and vice versa. A canonical example is the relationship between courses and students, where a typical student takes several courses, and the typical course is taken by several students. The problem is that designing a storage structure so that one can answer efficiently queries of the form "what courses is a given student taking" and "what students are taking a given course" is not trivial. Each model we shall discuss has a way of coping with this potential efficiency problem. For example, the relational model throws the problem onto the physical design level, as we discuss in Section 6.11, and the network model outlaws many-many relationships, requiring that we factor them in a way we discuss in Section 2.5.

## 2.2 THE ENTITY-RELATIONSHIP MODEL

The purpose of the entity-relationship model is to allow the description of the conceptual scheme of an enterprise to be written down without the attention to efficiency or physical database design that is expected in most other models. It is normally assumed that the "entity-relationship diagram" thus constructed will be turned later into a conceptual scheme in one of the other models, e.g., the relational model, upon which real database systems are built. The transformation from entity-relationship diagram to, say, a network is fairly straightforward using constructions we shall give in this chapter, but obtaining the conceptual scheme that offers the most efficiency can be quite difficult and requires an understanding of design issues in the target model.

### Entities

The term "entity" defies a formal definition, much as the terms "point" and "line" in geometry are defined only implicitly by axioms that give their properties. Suffice it to say an *entity* is a thing that exists and is distinguishable; that is, we can tell one entity from another. For example, each person is an entity, and each automobile is an entity. We could regard each ant as an entity if we had a way to distinguish one from another (say paint little numbers on their backs).

The notion of distinguishability of entities is very close to object identity, which we discussed in Section 1.5. For this reason, the entity-relationship model is generally regarded as an object-oriented model.

### Entity Sets

A group consisting of all "similar" entities forms an *entity set*. Examples of entity sets are

1. All persons.
2. All red-haired persons.
3. All automobiles.

Notice from examples (1) and (2), persons and red-haired persons, that the term "similar entities" is not precisely defined, and one can establish an infinite number of different properties by which to define an entity set. One of the key steps in selecting a scheme for the real world, as it pertains to a particular database, is choosing the entity sets. As we shall see below, it is necessary to characterize all members of an entity set by a collection of characteristics called "attributes." Thus, "similarity" at least requires that a set of characteristics common to all members of the entity set can be found.

The notion of "entity set" is a scheme-level notion, in the terminology of Section 1.2. The corresponding instance-level notion is the current subset of all members of a given entity set that are present in the database.

**Example 2.1:** The California Department of Motor Vehicles may design its database scheme to have an entity set AUTOMOBILES. In the current instance of that entity set are all the automobiles presently registered in California, not all automobiles in the world or all the automobiles that could ever exist. □

## Attributes and Keys

Entity sets have properties, called *attributes*, which associate with each entity in the set a value from a *domain* of values for that attribute. Usually, the domain for an attribute will be a set of integers, real numbers, or character strings, but we do not rule out other types of values. For example, the entity set of persons may be declared to have attributes such as name (a character string), height (a real number), and so on.

The selection of relevant attributes for entity sets is another critical step in the design of a conceptual database scheme. An attribute or set of attributes whose values uniquely identify each entity in an entity set is called a *key* for that entity set. In principle, each entity set has a key, since we hypothesized that each entity is distinguishable from all others. But if we do not choose, for an entity set, a collection of attributes that includes a key, then we shall not be able to distinguish one entity in the set from another. Often an arbitrary serial number is supplied as an attribute to serve as a key.

**Example 2.2:** An entity set that included only U.S. nationals could use the single attribute "Social Security number" as a key. However, suppose we wished to identify uniquely members of an entity set including citizens of many countries. We could not be sure that two countries do not use the same identification numbers, so an appropriate key would be the pair of attributes ID_NO and COUNTRY. □

## Isa Hierarchies

We say $A$ **isa** $B$, read "$A$ is a $B$," if entity set $B$ is a generalization of entity set $A$, or equivalently, $A$ is a special kind of $B$. The primary purpose of declaring **isa** relationships between entity sets $A$ and $B$ is so $A$ can inherit the attributes of $B$, but also have some additional attributes that don't make sense for those members of $B$ that are not also members of $A$. Technically, each entity $a$ in set $A$ is related to exactly one entity $b$ in set $B$, such that $a$ and $b$ are really the same entity. No $b$ in $B$ can be so related to two different members of $A$, but some members of $B$ can be related to no member of $A$. The key attributes for entity set $A$ are actually attributes of entity set $B$, and the values of those attributes for an entity $a$ in $A$ are taken from the corresponding $b$ in $B$.

**Example 2.3:** A corporation might well have an entity set EMPLOYEES, with attributes such as ID_NO, NAME, and SALARY. If the corporation were a baseball team, certain of the employees, the players, would have other important attributes, like BATTING_AVG or HOME_RUNS, that the other employees would not have. The most sensible way to design this scheme is to have another entity set PLAYERS, with the relationship PLAYERS **isa** EMPLOYEES. Attributes like NAME, belonging to EMPLOYEES, are inherited by PLAYERS, but only PLAYERS have attributes like BATTING_AVG. □

## Relationships

A *relationship* among entity sets is an ordered list of entity sets. A particular entity set may appear more than once on the list. This list of entity sets is the scheme-level notion of a relationship. If there is a relationship $\mathcal{R}$ among entity sets $E_1, E_2, \ldots, E_k$, then the current instance of $\mathcal{R}$ is a set of $k$-tuples. We call such a set a *relationship set*. Each $k$-tuple $(e_1, e_2, \ldots, e_k)$ in relationship set $\mathcal{R}$ implies that entities $e_1, e_2, \ldots, e_k$, where $e_1$ is in set $E_1$, $e_2$ is in set $E_2$, and so on, stand in relationship $\mathcal{R}$ to each other as a group. The most common case, by far, is where $k = 2$, but lists of three or more entity sets are sometimes related.

**Example 2.4:** Suppose we have an entity set PERSONS and we have a relationship MOTHER_OF, whose list of entity sets is PERSONS, PERSONS. The relationship set for relationship MOTHER_OF consists of all and only those pairs $(p_1, p_2)$ such that person $p_2$ is the mother of person $p_1$.

An alternative way of representing this information is to postulate the existence of entity set MOTHERS and relationship MOTHERS **isa** PERSONS. This arrangement would be more appropriate if the database stored values for attributes of mothers that it did not store for persons in general. Then the relationship MOTHER_OF would be the list of entity sets

PERSONS, MOTHERS

To get information about a person's mother as a person, we would compose (in the sense of ordinary set-theoretic relations) the relationships MOTHER_OF and **isa**. □

## Borrowed Key Attributes

We mentioned in connection with **isa** relationships that if $A$ **isa** $B$, then the key for $A$ would naturally be the key attributes of $B$, and those attributes would not appear as attributes of entity set $A$. Thus, in Example 2.3, the key for entity set PLAYERS would most naturally be the attribute ID_NO of EMPLOYEES. Then a player would be uniquely identified by the ID_NO of the employee that is him.

There are times when we want the key for one entity set $A$ to be attributes of another entity set $B$ to which $A$ is connected by a relationship $\mathcal{R}$ other than

**isa.** It is only necessary that $\mathcal{R}$ provide, for each entity $a$ in $A$, a unique $b$ in $B$ to which $a$ is related. For instance, we assumed in Example 2.2 that individuals had attribute COUNTRY that, with ID_NO, formed a key for individuals. It is just as likely that the database design would include countries as another entity set, and there would be a relationship CITIZEN_OF relating individuals to countries. Then the key for individuals would be their ID_NO and the name of the country to which they were related by CITIZEN_OF.

Note that when "borrowing" key attributes, it is essential that the relationship to be followed leads to a unique entity in the target entity set. That must be the case when following an **isa** relationship, but it need not be the case in general; e.g., can individuals be citizens of two countries? Shortly, we shall investigate the matter of functionality of relationships, which tells us when an entity of one entity set is related, via a particular relationship, to a unique member of another entity set.

### Entity-Relationship Diagrams

It is useful to summarize the information in a design using *entity-relationship diagrams*, where:

1. Rectangles represent entity sets.
2. Circles represent attributes. They are linked to their entity sets by (undirected) edges. Sometimes, attributes that are part of the key for their entity set will be underlined. As a special case regarding attributes, we sometimes identify an entity set having only one attribute with the attribute itself, calling the entity set by the name of the attribute. In that case, the entity set appears as a circle attached to whatever relationships the entity set is involved in, rather than as a rectangle.
3. Diamonds represent relationships. They are linked to their constituent entity sets by edges, which can be undirected edges or directed edges (arcs); the use of arcs is discussed later when we consider functionality of relationships. The order of entity sets in the list for the relationship can be indicated by numbering edges, although the order is irrelevant unless the same entity set appears more than once on a list.

**Example 2.5:** Figure 2.1(a) shows a simple entity-relationship diagram, with three entity sets, EMPS, DEPTS, and MANAGERS. The first two are related by relationship ASSIGNED_TO and the second and third are related by MANAGES. For the present, we should ignore the arrows on some of the edges connecting the relationship diamonds to the entity-set rectangles. We show three attributes, NAME, PHONE, and SALARY, for EMPS; NAME is taken to be the key.[1] Departments have attributes NAME (of the department) and

---

[1] While we shall often imagine that "names" of entities can serve as keys for their entity

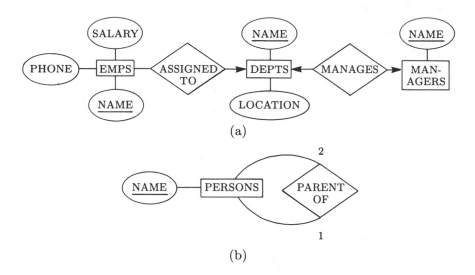

**Figure 2.1** Examples of entity-relationship diagrams.

LOCATION, while MANAGERS has only the attribute NAME.[2]

In Figure 2.1(b) we see an entity set PERSONS and we see a relationship PARENT_OF between PERSONS and PERSONS. We also notice two edges from PARENT_OF to PERSONS; the first represents the child and the second the parent. That is, the current value of the PARENT_OF relationship set is the set of pairs $(p_1, p_2)$ such that $p_2$ is known to be a parent of $p_1$. □

## Functionality of Relationships

To model the real world adequately, it is often necessary to classify relationships according to how many entities from one entity set can be associated with how many entities of another entity set. The simplest and rarest form of relationship on two sets is *one-to-one*, meaning that for each entity in either set there is at most one associated member of the other set. For example, the relationship MANAGES between DEPTS and MANAGERS, in Figure 2.1(a), might be declared a one-to-one relationship. If so, then in the database we never can find more than one manager for a department, nor can one person manage two or more departments. It is possible that some department has no manager at the

---

sets, it is very likely that two entities with the same name can exist. Surely there could be two employees with the same name. In practice, many entity sets, such as EMPS, would be given artificial keys, such as an employee ID number. However, we shall frequently pretend that "names" are unique to simplify the set of necessary attributes.

[2] An alternative formulation of this structure would give MANAGERS no attributes and have an **isa** relationship from MANAGERS to EMPLOYEES. We see this treatment of employees and managers in Example 2.6.

moment, or even that someone listed in the database as a manager currently has no department to manage.

Note that the one-to-oneness of this relationship is an assumption about the real world that the database designer could choose to make or not to make. It is just as possible to assume that the same person could head two departments, or even that a department could have two managers. However, if one head for one department is the rule in this organization, then it may be possible to take advantage of the fact that MANAGES is one-to-one, when designing the physical database.

## Many-One Relationships

In a *many-one* relationship, one entity in set $E_2$ is associated with zero or more entities in set $E_1$, but each entity in $E_1$ is associated with at most one entity in $E_2$. This relationship is said to be many-one *from $E_1$ to $E_2$*. That is, the relationship is a (partial) function from $E_1$ to $E_2$. For example, the relationship between EMPS and DEPTS in Figure 2.1(a) may well be many-one from EMPS to DEPTS, meaning that every employee is assigned to at most one department. It is possible that some employees, such as the company president, are assigned to no department.

The concept of a many-one relationship generalizes to relationships among more than two entity sets. If there is a relationship $\mathcal{R}$ among entity sets $E_1, E_2, \ldots, E_k$, and given entities for all sets but $E_i$, there is at most one related entity of set $E_i$, then we say $\mathcal{R}$ is many-one from $E_1, \ldots, E_{i-1}, E_{i+1}, \ldots, E_k$ to $E_i$.

## Many-Many Relationships

We also encounter *many-many* relationships, where there are no restrictions on the sets of $k$-tuples of entities that may appear in a relationship set. For example, the relationship PARENT_OF in Figure 2.1 is many-many, because we expect to find two parents for each child, and a given individual may have any number of children. The relationship of enrollment between courses and students, mentioned in Section 2.1, is another example of a many-many relationship, because typically, many students take each course and many courses are taken by each student.

While many-many relationships appear frequently in practice, we have to be careful how these relationships are expressed in the conceptual scheme of the actual database.[3] Many data models do not allow direct expression of many-many relationships, instead requiring that they be decomposed into several

---

[3] Recall that the entity-relationship design is not the conceptual scheme, but rather a sketch of one, and we need to translate from entities and relationships into the data model of the DBMS that is used.

many-one relationships by techniques we shall cover later in this chapter. As we indicated in the previous section, the reason is that no efficient data structures are available in these models for implementing many-many relationships. The relational model permits direct expression of many-many relationships, but the problem of efficient implementation is merely pushed down to the physical level.

### Indicating Functionality in Entity-Relationship Diagrams

In entity-relationship diagrams we use arcs, that is, edges with a direction indicated by an arrow, to indicate when a relationship is many-one or one-one. In the simplest case, a many-one relationship $\mathcal{R}$ from $A$ to $B$, we place an arc from the diamond for $\mathcal{R}$ to the rectangle for $B$. As an example, we may suppose that employees are assigned to at most one department, which explains the arrow from ASSIGNED_TO to DEPTS in Figure 2.1(a). More generally, if $\mathcal{R}$ involves three or more entity sets and is many-one to some entity set $A$, we draw an arc to $A$ and undirected edges to the other sets. More complicated mappings that are many-one to two or more entity sets will not be represented by an edge convention.

If $\mathcal{R}$ is one-one between $A$ and $B$, we draw arrows from $\mathcal{R}$ to both $A$ and $B$. For example, we may suppose that managers may manage only one department, and departments may have only one manager. That justifies the arcs from MANAGES to both DEPTS and MANAGERS in Figure 2.1(a). As an exception, if $A$ **isa** $B$, we draw an arc only to $B$.

**Example 2.6:** Let us introduce the example of a database that will reappear at many points throughout the book. In the town of Yuppie Valley, a small supermarket, the Yuppie Valley Culinary Boutique (YVCB) has purchased a microcomputer and is about to design a database system that will hold the information the store needs to conduct its business. After due consideration, the database administrator for the system, Sally Hacker, a Sophomore at Calvin Klein Senior High School in Yuppie Valley, who works in the store every Thursday afternoon, developed the entity-relationship diagram shown in Figure 2.2. We shall consider the reasoning that lies behind this diagram in the following paragraphs.

One important aspect of the YVCB business is dealing with suppliers. Thus, Sally decided that the database should have an entity set SUPPLIERS. In our example, we'll use only two attributes, SNAME, the key, and SADDR.[4] In practice, there would probably be several more attributes stored about suppliers, e.g., their phone number.

---

[4] Several entity sets will have an attribute that could logically be called "NAME." There is nothing preventing us from giving them all an attribute NAME, but we shall distinguish the different kinds of names by using attributes SNAME (supplier name), CNAME (customer name), and so on.

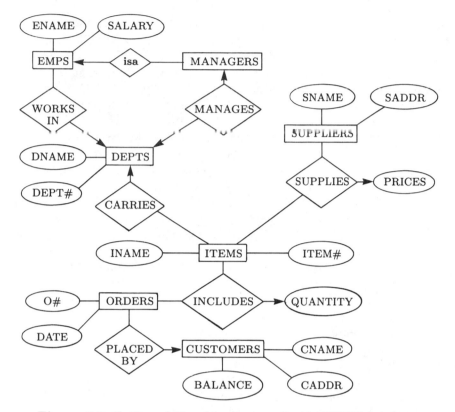

**Figure 2.2** Entity-relationship diagram for the YVCB database.

One important fact about suppliers that cannot be stored conveniently as an attribute is the set of items that each supplies. Thus, Sally specified an entity set ITEMS, with two attributes, INAME and ITEM#, either of which can serve as the key. To connect items and suppliers there is a many-many relationship SUPPLIES, with the intent that each item is related to all the suppliers that can supply the item, and each supplier is related to the items it can supply. However, a third entity set, which we call PRICES, is involved in the relationship. Each supplier sets a price for each item it can supply, so we prefer to see the SUPPLIES relationship as a ternary one among ITEMS, SUPPLI-ERS, and PRICES, with the intent that if the relationship set for SUPPLIES contains the triple $(i, s, p)$, then supplier $s$ is willing to sell item $i$ at price $p$.

If we look at Figure 2.2 we see a circle around entity set PRICES, rather than the customary rectangle. The reason is that PRICES presumably has only one attribute, the price itself. Thus, our exception to the way entity sets are represented applies, and we draw PRICES as if it were an attribute of the relationship SUPPLIES. That arrangement makes some sense if we view SUP-PLIES as representing item–supplier pairs, and the price as telling something about that pair.

Notice also that SUPPLIES has an arc to PRICES, reminding us that this relationship is many-one from ITEMS and SUPPLIERS to PRICES, i.e., given a supplier and an item, there is a unique price at which the supplier will sell the item. Also observe that we cannot normally break SUPPLIES into two or three binary relationships. For example, if we had one relationship between SUPPLIERS and ITEMS and another between SUPPLIERS and PRICES, then a supplier would be compelled to sell all items it sold at the same price; that is, we could not figure out which price goes with which item.

The YVCB is organized into departments, each of which has a manager and some employees. The attributes of entity set DEPTS are DNAME and DEPT#. Each department is responsible for selling some of the items, and store policy requires that each item be sold by only one department. Thus, there is a many-one relationship CARRIES from ITEMS to DEPTS.

The employees are represented by entity set EMPS, and there is a many-one relationship WORKS_IN from EMPS to DEPTS, reflecting the policy that employees are never assigned to two or more departments. The managers of departments are represented by another entity set MANAGERS. There is a one-to-one relationship MANAGES between MANAGERS and DEPTS; the one-to-one-ness reflects the assumption that in the YVCB there will never be more than one manager for a department, nor more than one department managed by one individual. Finally, since managers are employees, we have an **isa** relationship from MANAGERS to EMPS. To access the salary or name of a manager, we follow the **isa** relationship to the employee entity that the manager is, and find that information in the attributes SALARY and ENAME of EMPS.

Now, let us consider the bottom part of Figure 2.2. There we see another important entity set of the enterprise, the customers. The attributes of the entity set CUSTOMERS are CNAME, CADDR, and BALANCE. The first is the key, the customer's name. The second is the customer's address, and the third is the balance on the customer's charge account.

Customers place orders for food items, which are delivered by the YVCB. An order consists of a list of items and quantities placed by one customer. At-tributes of the entity set ORDERS are O# (Order number) and DATE, but the actual content of the order is represented by a relationship INCLUDES among ORDERS, ITEMS, and QUANTITY. The latter is a trivial entity set whose entities are the integers. Since a quantity has only its value as an attribute, we show it as a circle attached to the relationship INCLUDES. That relationship is many-one from ITEMS and ORDERS to QUANTITY, since each order can have only one quantity of any given item. Finally, the many-one relationship PLACED_BY from ORDERS to CUSTOMERS tells who placed each order. □

## 2.3 THE RELATIONAL DATA MODEL

The relational model, although not the data model used in the first database management systems, has grown slowly in importance since its exposition by E. Codd in 1970, to the point where it is generally the model of choice for the implementation of new databases. Perhaps the most important reason for the model's popularity is the way it supports powerful, yet simple and declarative languages with which operations on data are expressed. We may trace these capabilities to the fact that, unlike competing models, the relational model is value-oriented. That fact, in turn, leads to our ability to define operations on relations whose results are themselves relations. These operations can be combined and cascaded easily, using an algebraic notation called "relational algebra," which we introduce in the next section.

In comparison, we shall see in Chapter 5 that languages based on the object-oriented models do not have operations that can be composed easily. The reason is twofold.

1. Whatever the data model, relations are a useful way to express answers. Since relations do not support object identity, the result of an operation cannot itself be of the same type as the database in an object-oriented model. Thus, operations in such models cannot apply to the result of other operations.

2. Models that support abstract data types present another obstacle. The result of a useful operation is often of a new type. Such a type needs to have operations defined for it, so it cannot become immediately the operand of another operation.

### The Set-Theoretic Notion of a Relation

The mathematical concept underlying the relational model is the set-theoretic *relation*, which is a subset of the Cartesian product of a list of domains. Formally, a *domain* is simply a set of values, not unlike a data type. For example, the set of integers is a domain. So are the set of character strings, the set of character strings of length 20, the real numbers, and the set $\{0, 1\}$, for additional examples. The *Cartesian product* (or just *product*) of domains $D_1, D_2, \ldots, D_k$, written $D_1 \times D_2 \times \cdots \times D_k$, is the set of all $k$-tuples $(v_1, v_2, \ldots, v_k)$ such that $v_1$ is in $D_1$, $v_2$ is in $D_2$, and so on. For example, if we have $k = 2$, $D_1 = \{0, 1\}$, and $D_2 = \{a, b, c\}$, then $D_1 \times D_2$ is $\{(0, a), (0, b), (0, c), (1, a), (1, b), (1, c)\}$.

A *relation* is any subset of the Cartesian product of one or more domains. As far as databases are concerned, it is generally pointless to discuss infinite relations, so we shall assume that a relation is finite unless we state otherwise. For example, $\{(0, a), (0, c), (1, b)\}$ is a relation, a subset of the product $D_1 \times D_2$ mentioned above. The empty set is another example of a relation.

The members of a relation are called *tuples*. Each relation that is a subset of some product $D_1 \times D_2 \times \cdots \times D_k$ of $k$ domains is said to have *arity* $k$; another term for arity is *degree*. A tuple $(v_1, v_2, \ldots, v_k)$ has $k$ *components*; the $i$th component is $v_i$. A tuple with $k$ components is sometimes called a *$k$-tuple*. Often we use the shorthand $v_1 v_2 \cdots v_k$ to denote the tuple $(v_1, v_2, \ldots, v_k)$.

It helps to view a relation as a table, where each row is a tuple and each column corresponds to one component. The columns are often given names, called *attributes*. The set of attribute names for a relation is called the *relation scheme*. If we name a relation REL, and its relation scheme has attributes $A_1, A_2, \ldots, A_k$, we often write the relation scheme as $\text{REL}(A_1, A_2, \ldots, A_k)$.

**Example 2.7:** In Figure 2.3 we see a relation whose attributes are CITY, STATE, and POP. The arity of the relation is three. For example,

(Miami, Oklahoma, 13880)

is a tuple. The relation scheme for this relation is {CITY, STATE, POP}; if the relation were named CITYINFO, we might write the relation scheme as CITYINFO(CITY, STATE, POP). □

| CITY | STATE | POP |
|------|-------|-----|
| San Diego | Texas | 4490 |
| Miami | Oklahoma | 13880 |
| Pittsburg | Iowa | 509 |

**Figure 2.3** A relation.

### An Alternative Formulation of Relations

The mathematical, or "set-of-lists" notion of a relation is not the only one of importance for database systems. If we attach attribute names to columns of a relation, then the order of the columns becomes unimportant. Thus, it is possible to view tuples as mappings from attributes' names to values in the domains of the attributes. This change in viewpoint makes certain tables represent the same relation, while representing different relations under the mathematical definition of a relation.

**Example 2.8:** Figure 2.4 shows two versions of the same relation in the set-of-mappings point of view. For example, as a mapping $\mu$, the tuple

(Buffalo, W. Va., 831)

is defined by $\mu(\text{CITY}) = $ Buffalo, $\mu(\text{STATE}) = $ W. Va., and $\mu(\text{POP}) = 831$. Note that the order in which the tuples are listed makes no difference in either viewpoint. However, in the traditional view of a tuple as a list of values, the tuples (Buffalo, W. Va., 831) and (W. Va., 831, Buffalo) would not be the same, and the two relations of Figure 2.4 would not be considered the same. □

| CITY | STATE | POP |
|------|-------|-----|
| Buffalo | W. Va. | 831 |
| Providence | Utah | 1608 |
| Las Vegas | N. M. | 13865 |

| STATE | POP | CITY |
|-------|-----|------|
| Utah | 1608 | Providence |
| W. Va. | 831 | Buffalo |
| N.M. | 13865 | Las Vegas |

**Figure 2.4** Two presentations of the same (set-of-mappings) relation.

As existing relational database systems allow the printing of columns of a relation in any order, we shall take the set-of-mappings definition of relations as the standard one. However, there are situations, such as when we discuss relational algebra in the next section, where we shall want to use the set-of-lists definition for relations. Fortunately, there is an obvious method for converting between the two viewpoints. Given a relation in the set-of-lists sense, we can give arbitrary attribute names to its columns, whereupon it can be viewed as a set of mappings. Conversely, given a relation in the set-of-mappings sense, we can fix an order for the attributes and convert it to a set of lists.

If $\mu$ is a tuple and $X$ is a set of attributes, we shall use $\mu[X]$ to stand for the components of $\mu$ in the attributes of $X$. Thus, if $\mu$ is the particular tuple from Example 2.8, then $\mu[\{CITY, POP\}]$ is the tuple (Buffalo, 831), or more properly, under the mapping interpretation of tuples, the tuple $\nu$ such that $\nu(CITY) = $ Buffalo and $\nu(POP) = 831$.

### Representing Entity-Relationship Diagrams in the Relational Model

The collection of relation schemes used to represent information is called a (*relational*) *database scheme*, and the current values of the corresponding relations form the (*relational*) *database*. We are, of course, free to create relations with any set of attributes as a relation scheme, and we can place any interpretation we wish on tuples. However, there is a typical usage pattern, which we observe when we convert entity-relationship diagrams to relational database schemes. The data of an entity-relationship diagram is represented by two sorts of relations.

1. An entity set $E$ can be represented by a relation whose relation scheme consists of all the attributes of the entity set. Each tuple of the relation represents one entity in the current instance of $E$. For example, the entity set CUSTOMERS in Figure 2.2 is represented by the relation

    CUSTOMERS(CNAME, CADDR, BALANCE)

If $E$ is an entity set whose entities are identified through a relationship with some other entity set $F$, then the relation scheme also has the attributes of $F$ that are needed for the key of $E$. Thus, in Figure 2.2, the relation for entity set MANAGERS has only one attribute, ENAME, which is the key for MANAGERS. The value of ENAME for a given manager is the name of the employee entity that *is* this manager.

2.   A relationship $\mathcal{R}$ among entity sets $E_1, E_2, \ldots, E_k$ is represented by a relation whose relation scheme consists of the attributes in the keys for each of $E_1, E_2, \ldots, E_k$. By renaming attributes if necessary, we make certain that no two entity sets in the list have attributes with the same name, even if they are the same entity set. A tuple $\mu$ in this relation represents a list of entities $e_1, e_2, \ldots, e_k$, where $e_i$ is a member of set $E_i$, for each $i$. That is, $e_i$ is the unique entity in $E_i$ whose attribute values for the key attributes of $E_i$ are found in the components of tuple $\mu$ for these attributes. The presence of tuple $\mu$ in the relation indicates that the list of entities

$$(e_1, e_2, \ldots, e_k)$$

is in the current relationship set for $\mathcal{R}$.

**Example 2.9:** Let us convert the entity-relationship diagram of Figure 2.2 to a relational database scheme. We shall here carry out the conversion mechanically. Later, we discuss some of the modifications one might make to simplify and improve the scheme. The following are the relation schemes for the entity sets; each comes from the entity set with the same name as the relation.

        EMPS(ENAME, SALARY)
        MANAGERS(ENAME)
        DEPTS(DNAME, DEPT#)
        SUPPLIERS(SNAME, SADDR)
        ITEMS(INAME, ITEM#)
        ORDERS(O#, DATE)
        CUSTOMERS(CNAME, CADDR, BALANCE)

The special case of MANAGERS, where the only attribute is the key borrowed from EMPS, was discussed above. In the other six relations we have simply taken the attributes of the entity set and made them the attributes of the relation.

Now let us consider the relationships in Figure 2.2. We shall not create a relation for the **isa** relationship, since it would just consist of the ENAME attribute repeated (and renamed in one repetition), and would hold exactly the same information as the MANAGES relation; that is, it would list the names of all those employees who are managers. The other six relationships yield the following relation schemes:

WORKS_IN(ENAME, DNAME)
MANAGES(ENAME, DNAME)
CARRIES(INAME, DNAME)
SUPPLIES(SNAME, INAME, PRICE)
INCLUDES(O#, INAME, QUANTITY)
PLACED_BY(O#, CNAME)

In each case, the set of attributes is the set of keys for the entity sets connected by the relationship of the same name as the relation. For example, SUPPLIES connects SUPPLIERS, ITEMS, and PRICE, which have keys SNAME, INAME, and PRICE, respectively, and it is these three attributes we see in the scheme for SUPPLIES. Fortunately, there were no coincidences among the names of the key attributes, so none had to have their names changed.

The two relations MANAGES and WORKS_IN have the same set of attributes, but of course their meanings are different. We expect that tuple $(e, d)$ in MANAGES means that $e$ manages department $d$, while the same tuple in WORKS_IN means that $e$ is an employee in department $d$.

These thirteen relations are not an ideal design for the YVCB relational database scheme. We shall consider how to improve the scheme in the remainder of this section. Chapter 7 covers the design of relational database schemes from a more formal point of view. □

## Keys of Relations

Like entity sets, relations have sets of one or more attributes that serve as keys. For relations we can give a definition of "key" that is more formal than the informal notion of a set of attributes that "distinguish" members of an entity set. We say that a set $S$ of attributes of a relation $R$ is a *key* if

1.  No instance of $R$ that represents a possible state of the world can have two tuples that agree in all the attributes of $S$, yet are not the same tuple, and
2.  No proper subset of $S$ has property (1).

**Example 2.10:** In the relation SUPPLIES, from Example 2.9, SNAME and INAME together form a key. If there were two tuples $(s, i, p_1)$ and $(s, i, p_2)$ in SUPPLIES, then supplier $s$ would apparently sell item $i$ both at price $p_1$ and at price $p_2$, a situation that means our data is faulty. This observation justifies condition (1). To check (2) we have to consider the proper subsets, that is, SNAME alone and INAME alone. Neither should satisfy condition (1). For example, it is quite possible that we find the two tuples

(Acme, Brie, 3.50)
(Acme, Perrier, 1.25)

in SUPPLIES at the same time, and although they agree on SNAME, they are not the same tuple. Similarly, we might find

(Acme, Brie, 3.50)
(Ajax, Brie, 3.95)

in the current instance of SUPPLIES, showing that INAME alone does not satisfy condition (1). □

It is important to remember that keyness depends on the scheme, not the current instance of a relation. Thus, INAME would not become a key for SUPPLIES just because at some moment in time, there was no item supplied by two different suppliers, provided there was no reason in principle why there could not in the future be an item supplied by two or more suppliers.

Also, observe that a relation may have more than one key. For example, consider DEPTS(DNAME, DEPT#) from Example 2.9. We do not expect to give two departments the same name, and we do not expect to give two departments the same number, so we may declare that DNAME is a key and DEPT# is a different key. Whether this expectation holds in practice, of course, depends on design decisions made by the database designer. If we believe DNAME and DEPT# are both keys, then the physical database scheme might be designed so that it is impossible to store two tuples that have the same DNAME or that have the same DEPT#; thus, such design decisions should not be taken lightly. Again, the reader should remember that assertions about keyness cannot be deduced or discovered from more basic principles; they are made by the designers of the database scheme after deliberation about their data and their beliefs about the constraints that data should obey.

Often, when a relation has two or more keys, it is useful to select one of them and regard it as the only key; for example, many physical storage structures expect there to be a unique key, or at least other keys are not supported by the structure. Therefore, the term *primary key* will be used to refer to the key selected from among several choices, all of which are called *candidate keys*.

When relations come from an entity-relationship diagram, it is usually easy to tell what the keys for the relations are. The following rules suffice if the keys selected for the entity sets are minimal; i.e., no subset of a chosen key would serve as a key.

1.  If a relation comes from an entity set, a set of attributes is a key for that relation if it is a key for the entity set.

2.  If a relation comes from a many-many relationship, then the key for the relation is normally the set of all the attributes.

3.  If a relation comes from a one-to-one relationship between entity sets $E$ and $F$, then the key for $E$ and the key for $F$ are both keys for the relation. Note that relations, like entity sets, can have more than one set of attributes that is a candidate key.

4.   If a relation comes from a relationship that is many-one from $E_1, \ldots, E_{k-1}$ to $E_k$, then the set of attributes that is the union of the keys for $E_1, \ldots, E_{k-1}$ is normally a key for the relation.

**Example 2.11:** Figure 2.5 lists the thirteen relations from Example 2.9. The set of attributes forming the primary key of each relation is indicated by bold-face letters. Where there is another candidate key, that is indicated by slanted letters. The reader should note the difference between a situation like that in SUPPLIES, where the lone key consists of two attributes, and that of DEPTS, where their are two candidate keys, each consisting of one attribute. The explanation for SUPPLIES is given by rule (4) above, since the relationship supplies is many-one from SUPPLIERS and ITEMS to PRICE, and the first two entity sets have keys SNAME and INAME, respectively. Thus, {SNAME, INAME} forms a key for relation SUPPLIES. The explanation regarding DEPTS is more ad-hoc. We know that DNAME is the key for entity set DEPTS, but we might well decide that DEPT# also should be a key, since the YVCB probably does not intend to give two departments the same number. □

(1)      EMPS(**ENAME**, SALARY)
(2)      MANAGERS(**ENAME**)
(3)      DEPTS(**DNAME**, *DEPT#*)
(4)      SUPPLIERS(**SNAME**, SADDR)
(5)      ITEMS(**INAME**, *ITEM#*)
(6)      ORDERS(**O#**, DATE)
(7)      CUSTOMERS(**CNAME**, CADDR, BALANCE)
(8)      WORKS_IN(**ENAME**, DNAME)
(9)      MANAGES(**ENAME**, *DNAME*)
(10)     CARRIES(**INAME**, DNAME)
(11)     SUPPLIES(**SNAME**, **INAME**, PRICE)
(12)     INCLUDES(**O#**, **INAME**, QUANTITY)
(13)     PLACED_BY(**O#**, CNAME)

**Figure 2.5**  Table of relations and keys.

## Relations with Common Keys

When two relations have a candidate key in common, we can combine the attributes of the two relation schemes and replace the two relations by one whose set of attributes is the union of the two sets. One advantage to doing so is that we save the storage space needed to repeat the key values in the two relations. A second is that queries talking about attributes of the two relations can sometimes be answered more quickly if the two relations are combined.

**Example 2.12:** Relations DEPTS and MANAGES from Figure 2.5 each have
DNAME as a candidate key; in one case it is the primary key and in the other
not. We may thus replace DEPTS and MANAGES by one relation

> DEPTS(DNAME, DEPT#, MGR)

Notice that we have decided to call the new relation DEPTS. The attributes
DNAME and DEPT# are intended to be the same as the attributes of the same
name in the old DEPTS relation, while MGR is intended to be the attribute
ENAME from MANAGES. There is nothing wrong with changing the names
of attributes, as long as we carry along their intuitive meaning.

In Figure 2.6(a) we see two possible instances for the old relation DEPTS
and MANAGES. Figure 2.6(b) shows them combined into one relation, the new
DEPTS. Notice that the twelve entries in the two relations have been combined
into nine in the single relation, saving a small amount of space. Also, a query
like "what is the number of the department that Harry Hamhock manages?"
can be answered by consulting the one relation in Figure 2.6(b), while in the
database of Figure 2.6(a) we would have to combine the two relations by a
possibly expensive operation called the join, discussed in the next section. □

| DNAME | DEPT# |
|---------|-------|
| Produce | 12 |
| Cheese | 31 |
| Meat | 5 |

DEPTS

| ENAME | DNAME |
|----------------|---------|
| Esther Eggplant | Produce |
| Larry Limburger | Cheese |
| Harry Hamhock | Meat |

MANAGES

(a) Old relations.

| DNAME | DEPT# | MGR |
|---------|-------|-----------------|
| Produce | 12 | Esther Eggplant |
| Cheese | 31 | Larry Limburger |
| Meat | 5 | Harry Hamhock |

(b) New relation DEPTS.

**Figure 2.6** Combination of relations with common keys.

**Dangling Tuples**

When we combine two or more relations like those in Example 2.12, there is a
problem that must be overcome, a problem that if not solved or defined away

prevents us from combining the relations despite the advantages to doing so. In Example 2.12 we made the hidden assumption that the set of departments was the same in both relations DEPTS and MANAGES. In practice that might not be the case. For example, suppose the YVCB has a Wine department, whose number is 16, but that temporarily has no manager. Then we could add the tuple (Wine, 16) to the old DEPTS relation, in Figure 2.6(a), but there seems to be no way to add a tuple to the new DEPTS in Figure 2.6(b), because such tuples need some value for the MGR attribute. Similarly, if Tanya Truffle were appointed to head the new Gourmet department, but we had not yet assigned that department a number, we could insert our new fact into MANAGES, but not into the DEPTS relation of Figure 2.6(b).

Tuples that need to share a value with a tuple in another relation, but find no such value, are called *dangling tuples*. One possible way to avoid the problem of dangling tuples is to add to the database scheme information about *existence constraints*, that is, conditions of the form "if a value $v$ appears in attribute $A$ of some tuple in relation $R$, then $v$ must also appear in attribute $B$ of some tuple in relation $S$." For example, if we guaranteed that every department appearing in the DNAME attribute of the old DEPTS appeared in the DNAME field of MANAGES, and vice-versa, then this problem of dangling tuples would be defined away. We would thus be free to combine the two relations, knowing that no information could be lost thereby.

Of course these existence constraints put some severe limitations on the way we insert new tuples into the two relations of Figure 2.6(a) or the one relation of Figure 2.6(b). In either case, we cannot create a new department name, number, or manager without having all three. If that is not satisfactory, we also have the option of storing *null values* in certain fields. We shall represent a null value by $\perp$. This symbol may appear as the value of any attribute that is not in the primary key,[5] and we generally take its meaning to be "missing value." When looking for common values between two or more tuples, we do not consider two occurrences of $\perp$ to be the same value; i.e., each occurrence of $\perp$ is treated as a symbol distinct from any other symbol, including other occurrences of $\perp$.

**Example 2.13:** If we added the Wine department and added manager Truffle of the Gourmet department, we could represent this data with null values in the relation DEPTS of Figure 2.6(b) by the relation of Figure 2.7. $\square$

If we assume that problems of dangling tuples are defined away by existence constraints or handled by allowing nulls in nonkey attributes, then we can combine relations whenever two or more share a common candidate key.

---

[5] In Chapter 6 we discuss storage structures for relations, and we shall then see why null values in the primary key often cause significant trouble.

| DNAME | DEPT# | MGR |
|---|---|---|
| Produce | 12 | Esther Eggplant |
| Cheese | 31 | Larry Limburger |
| Meat | 5 | Harry Hamhock |
| Wine | 16 | ⊥ |
| Gourmet | ⊥ | Tanya Truffle |

**Figure 2.7** Relation with nulls to preserve dangling tuples.

**Example 2.14:** The process of combining relations considerably simplifies the list of Figure 2.5. The new list appears in Figure 2.8. There, we indicate the relations of Figure 2.5 from which each combined relation was derived. Certain attribute names have been changed in an obvious way when the relations were combined.

| | |
|---|---|
| EMPS(**ENAME**, SALARY, DEPT) | 1, 8 |
| DEPTS(**DNAME**, DEPT#, MGR) | 2, 3, 9 |
| SUPPLIERS(**SNAME**, SADDR) | 4 |
| ITEMS(**INAME**, ITEM#, DEPT) | 5, 10 |
| ORDERS(**O#**, DATE, CUST) | 6, 13 |
| CUSTOMERS(**CNAME**, CADDR, BALANCE) | 7 |
| SUPPLIES(**SNAME**, **INAME**, PRICE) | 11 |
| INCLUDES(**O#**, **INAME**, QUANTITY) | 12 |

**Figure 2.8** Improved relational database scheme design.

We again indicate primary keys by boldface. The other candidate keys are generally not candidate keys for the combined relation, because the possibility of dangling tuples means that there could be a null in an attribute belonging to a candidate key. For example, in Figure 2.7 we saw nulls in both DEPT# and MGR, which prevents these attributes from being keys.

The selection of the DEPTS relation in Figure 2.8 requires some additional thought. We have chosen it to represent the unary relation MANAGERS, as well as the relations DEPTS and MANAGES from Figure 2.5, which shared the common candidate key DNAME. However, MANAGERS, with key (and only attribute) ENAME, does not share a common candidate key with these. First, we should note that the ENAME of MANAGERS is not the same as ENAME in the relations EMPS and WORKS_IN; in the latter two it represents the entity set of employees, while in MANAGERS it represents the subset of these employees that are managers. Thus, we clearly should not combine MANAGERS with EMPS and WORKS_IN. However, what is the justification for combining MANAGERS with DEPTS, with which it does not even share an attribute, let alone a key? In explanation, recall that MANAGES is a one-to-one relationship between ENAME (representing managers) and DNAME. Hence, these two attributes are in a sense equivalent, and we may regard MANAGERS as if its attribute were DNAME rather than ENAME.

There is, however, one special problem with our choice to combine relations in this way. Even with nulls, we cannot handle all situations with dangling tuples. For example, if there were a manager $m$ mentioned in MANAGERS, but not in MANAGES, we would want to insert into the new DEPTS relation a tuple $(\perp, \perp, m)$. But this tuple would have a null value in the key, DNAME, and as we mentioned, there are reasons concerning the physical storage of relations why this arrangement is frequently not acceptable.

Incidentally, one might wonder why one cannot further combine relations like SUPPLIES and SUPPLIERS, since the key of the latter is a subset of the key of the former. The reason is that in a combined relation with attributes SNAME, SADDR, INAME, and PRICE, we would find that each supplier's address was repeated once for each item that the supplier sold. That is not a fatal problem, but it does lead to wasted space and possible inconsistencies (Acme's address might be different according to the tuples for two different items Acme sells). The matter of relational database scheme design, called "normalization" provides considerable intellectual mechanics that can be brought to bear on issues like whether SUPPLIES and SUPPLIERS should be combined; we develop this theory in Chapter 7. $\square$

## 2.4 OPERATIONS IN THE RELATIONAL DATA MODEL

In the previous section we introduced the mathematical notion of a relation, which is the formalism underlying the relational data model. This section introduces the family of operations usually associated with that model. There are two rather different kinds of notations used for expressing operations on relations:

1. Algebraic notation, called *relational algebra*, where queries are expressed by applying specialized operators to relations, and
2. Logical notation, called *relational calculus*, where queries are expressed by writing logical formulas that the tuples in the answer must satisfy.

In this section, we shall consider relational algebra only. This algebra includes some familiar operations, like union and set difference of relations, but it also includes some that probably are not familiar. Logical notations will be introduced in Chapter 3, after we discuss logical languages for knowledge-base systems. One of the interesting facts about these notations for relational databases is that they are equivalent in expressive power; that is, each can express any query that the other can express, but no more.

## Limitations of Relational Algebra

The first thought we might have on the subject of operations for the relational model is that perhaps we should simply allow any program to be an operation on relations. There might be some situations where that makes sense, but there are many more where the advantages of using a well-chosen family of operations outweigh the restrictions on expressive power that result. Recall from Section 1.2 that one important purpose of a conceptual scheme, and hence of its data model, is to provide physical data independence, the ability to write programs that work independently of the physical scheme used. If we used arbitrary programs as queries, the programmer would

a)  Have to know everything about the physical data structures used, and

b)  Would have to write code that depended on the particular structure selected, leaving no opportunity for the physical structure to be tuned as we learned more about the usage of the database.

As a result, it is almost universally preferred in database systems that the query language should have dictions that speak only of the data model, not of any particular physical implementation of the model. But as soon as we agree to use a query language that operates only on relations, which is the structure that represents data in the relational model, we face another problem. We want the operations of the relational data model to have implementations that are efficient; they must be efficient, because people turn to DBMS's when they want fast response to queries on large quantities of data. Yet if we permit too rich a set of queries to ask, it is likely that we shall be able to ask queries for which the DBMS's query processor will be unable to find an efficient implementation, even though one exists.

For example, the language Prolog, whose syntactic style was introduced in Section 1.6, and which will be discussed in more detail in Chapter 3, is a logical language, whose predicates could well be thought of as relations. Thus, Prolog could be accepted as a language suitable for expressing the operations of the relational data model. However, Prolog, in its most general form, can simulate a Turing machine, like any other general-purpose programming language, so its optimization problem is undecidable. Thus, we cannot hope to find optimal implementations of arbitrary Prolog programs.

Hence, relational algebra and all the other languages for the relational model, whether real or abstract, have opted for limited expressive power, but chosen a subset of all possible queries (essentially the same subset in each case) that

1.  Allows the optimization problem to be solved satisfactorily, yet

2.   Provides a rich enough language that we can express enough things to make database systems useful.

We mentioned, in Section 1.4, the approximate point at which the power of relational languages fails; they cannot, in general, express the operation that takes a binary relation and produces the transitive closure of that relation.

Another limitation we face in relational languages, less cosmic perhaps, but of practical importance, is the finiteness of relations. Recall that we have assumed relations are finite unless we explicitly state otherwise; this convention is sound because infinite relations cannot be stored explicitly. The constraint of finiteness introduces some difficulties into the definition of relational algebra and other relational languages. For example, we cannot allow the algebraic operation of complementation, since the complement of $R$ is an infinite relation, the set of all tuples not in $R$.

## Operands and Operators of Relational Algebra

Recall that a relation is a set of $k$-tuples for some $k$, called the arity of the relation. In general, we give names (attributes) to the components of tuples, although some of the operations mentioned below, such as union, difference, product, and intersection, do not depend on the names of the components. These operations do depend on there being a fixed, agreed-upon order for the attributes; i.e., they are operations on the list style of tuples, rather than the mapping (from attribute names to values) style. Of course they can be applied to relations that are viewed in the mapping style (as most real relational DBMS's do) by fixing an order for the attributes before performing the operation and by specifying attribute names for the result relation.

The operands of relational algebra are either constant relations or variables denoting relations of a fixed arity. The arity associated with a variable will be mentioned only when it is important. There are five basic operations that serve to define relational algebra. After introducing them we shall mention a few more operations that do not add to the set of functions expressible in the language, but serve as useful shorthand.

1.   *Union.* The union of relations $R$ and $S$, denoted $R \cup S$, is the set of tuples that are in $R$ or $S$ or both. We may only apply the union operator to relations of the same arity, so all tuples in the result have the same number of components. As mentioned above, the attribute names for the operand relations are ignored when taking the union, and the result relation can be given attributes arbitrarily. The order of attributes in the operands is respected when taking the union. The same remarks apply to the other operators as well.

2.   *Set difference.* The difference of relations $R$ and $S$, denoted $R - S$, is the set of tuples in $R$ but not in $S$. We again require that $R$ and $S$ have the

same arity.

3.  *Cartesian product.* Let $R$ and $S$ be relations of arity $k_1$ and $k_2$, respectively. Then $R \times S$, the Cartesian product of $R$ and $S$, is the set of all possible $(k_1 + k_2)$-tuples whose first $k_1$ components form a tuple in $R$ and whose last $k_2$ components form a tuple in $S$.

4.  *Projection.* The idea behind this operation is that we take a relation $R$, remove some of the components (attributes) and/or rearrange some of the remaining components. If $R$ is a relation of arity $k$, we let $\pi_{i_1,i_2,\ldots,i_m}(R)$, where the $i_j$'s are distinct integers in the range 1 to $k$, denote the projection of $R$ onto components $i_1, i_2, \ldots, i_m$, that is, the set of $m$-tuples $a_1 a_2 \cdots a_m$ such that there is some $k$-tuple $b_1 b_2 \cdots b_k$ in $R$ for which $a_j = b_{i_j}$ for $j = 1, 2, \ldots, m$. For example, $\pi_{3,1}(R)$ is computed by taking each tuple $\mu$ in $R$ and forming a 2-tuple from the third and first components of $\mu$, in that order. If $R$ has attributes labeling its columns, then we may substitute attribute names for component numbers, and we may use the same attribute names in the projected relation. Thus, if relation $R$ is $R(A, B, C, D)$, then $\pi_{C,A}(R)$ is the same as $\pi_{3,1}(R)$, and the resulting relation has attribute $C$ naming its first column and attribute $A$ naming its second column.

5.  *Selection.* Let $F$ be a formula involving

    i)   Operands that are constants or component numbers; component $i$ is represented by $\$i$,

    ii)  The arithmetic comparison operators $<, =, >, \leq, \neq$, and $\geq$, and

    iii) The logical operators $\wedge$ (and), $\vee$ (or), and $\neg$ (not).

    Then $\sigma_F(R)$ is the set of tuples $\mu$ in $R$ such that when, for all $i$, we substitute the $i$th component of $\mu$ for any occurrences of $\$i$ in formula $F$, the formula $F$ becomes true. For example, $\sigma_{\$2>\$3}(R)$ denotes the set of tuples $\mu$ in $R$ such that the second component of $\mu$ exceeds its third component, while $\sigma_{\$1=\text{'Smith'}\vee\$1=\text{'Jones'}}(R)$ is the set of tuples in $R$ whose first components have the value 'Smith' or 'Jones'. As with projection, if a relation has named columns, then the formula in a selection can refer to columns by name instead of by number.

| $A$ | $B$ | $C$ |
|-----|-----|-----|
| $a$ | $b$ | $c$ |
| $d$ | $a$ | $f$ |
| $c$ | $b$ | $d$ |

| $D$ | $E$ | $F$ |
|-----|-----|-----|
| $b$ | $g$ | $a$ |
| $d$ | $a$ | $f$ |

(a) Relation $R$            (b) Relation $S$

**Figure 2.9**  Two relations.

**Example 2.15:** Let $R$ and $S$ be the two relations of Figure 2.9. In Figure 2.10(a) and (b), respectively, we see the relations $R \cup S$ and $R - S$. Note that we can take unions and differences even though the columns of the two relations have different names, as long as the relations have the same number of components. However, the resulting relation has no obvious names for its columns. Figure 2.10(c) shows $R \times S$. Since $R$ and $S$ have disjoint sets of attributes, we can carry the column names over to $R \times S$. If $R$ and $S$ had a column name in common, say $G$, we could distinguish the two columns by calling them $R.G$ and $S.G$. Figure 2.10(d) shows $\pi_{A,C}(R)$, and Figure 2.10(e) shows $\sigma_{B=b}(R)$. $\square$

| a | b | c |
|---|---|---|
| d | a | f |
| c | b | d |
| b | g | a |

(a) $R \cup S$

| a | b | c |
|---|---|---|
| c | b | d |

(b) $R - S$

| A | B | C | D | E | F |
|---|---|---|---|---|---|
| a | b | c | b | g | a |
| a | b | c | d | a | f |
| d | a | f | b | g | a |
| d | a | f | d | a | f |
| c | b | d | b | g | a |
| c | b | d | d | a | f |

(c) $R \times S$

| A | C |
|---|---|
| a | c |
| d | f |
| c | d |

(d) $\pi_{A,C}(R)$

| A | B | C |
|---|---|---|
| a | b | c |
| c | b | d |

(e) $\sigma_{B=b}(R)$

**Figure 2.10** Results of some relational algebra operations.

## Some Additional Algebraic Operations

There are some other useful operations on relations that can be expressed in terms of the five basic operations above. The simplest example is that any system closed under set difference is also closed under intersection, because

$R \cap S$ is equivalent to $R - (R - S)$. Thus, we can use intersection as if it were one of the basic relational algebra operators, knowing it can be replaced by two applications of the set difference operator. Some additional operations that can be expressed in terms of the five basic operators follow.

## Quotient

Let $R$ and $S$ be relations of arity $r$ and $s$, respectively, where $r > s$, and $S \neq \emptyset$. Then the *quotient* of $R$ and $S$, denoted $R \div S$, is the set of $(r - s)$-tuples $a_1, \ldots, a_{r-s}$ such that for all $s$-tuples $a_{r-s+1}, \ldots, a_r$ in $S$, the tuple $a_1, \ldots, a_r$ is in $R$. To express $R \div S$ using the five basic relational algebra operations, let $T$ stand for $\pi_{1,2,\ldots,r-s}(R)$. Then $(T \times S) - R$ is the set of $r$-tuples that are not in $R$, but are formed by taking the first $r - s$ components of a tuple in $R$ and following it by a tuple in $S$. Then let

$$V = \pi_{1,2,\ldots,r-s}\big((T \times S) - R\big)$$

$V$ is the set of $(r - s)$-tuples $a_1, \ldots, a_{r-s}$ that are the first $r - s$ components of some tuple in $R$, and for some $s$-tuple $a_{r-s+1}, \ldots, a_r$ in $S$, $a_1, \ldots, a_r$ is not in $R$. Hence, $T - V$ is $R \div S$. We can write $R \div S$ as a single expression in relational algebra by replacing $T$ and $V$ by the expressions they stand for. That is,

$$R \div S = \pi_{1,2,\ldots,r-s}(R) - \pi_{1,2,\ldots,r-s}\Big(\big(\pi_{1,2,\ldots,r-s}(R) \times S\big) - R\Big)$$

**Example 2.16:** Let $R$ and $S$ be the relations shown in Figure 2.11(a) and (b). Then $R \div S$ is the relation shown in Figure 2.11(c). Tuple $ab$ is in $R \div S$ because $abcd$ and $abef$ are in $R$, and tuple $ed$ is in $R \div S$ for a similar reason. Tuple $bc$, which is the only other pair appearing in the first two columns of $R$, is not in $R \div S$ because $bccd$ is not in $R$. $\square$

| $a$ | $b$ | $c$ | $d$ |
|---|---|---|---|
| $a$ | $b$ | $e$ | $f$ |
| $b$ | $c$ | $e$ | $f$ |
| $e$ | $d$ | $c$ | $d$ |
| $e$ | $d$ | $e$ | $f$ |
| $a$ | $b$ | $d$ | $e$ |

| $c$ | $d$ |
|---|---|
| $e$ | $f$ |

| $a$ | $b$ |
|---|---|
| $e$ | $d$ |

(a) Relation $R$        (b) Relation $S$        (c) $R \div S$

**Figure 2.11**  Example of a quotient calculation.

## Join

The $\theta$-join of $R$ and $S$ on columns $i$ and $j$, written $R \underset{i\theta j}{\bowtie} S$, where $\theta$ is an arithmetic comparison operator ($=$, $<$, and so on), is shorthand for $\sigma_{\$i\theta\$(r+j)}(R \times S)$, if $R$ is of arity $r$. That is, the $\theta$-join of $R$ and $S$ is those tuples in the Cartesian product of $R$ and $S$ such that the $i$th component of $R$ stands in relation $\theta$ to the $j$th component of $S$. If $\theta$ is $=$, the operation is often called an *equijoin*.

**Example 2.17:** Let $R$ and $S$ be the relations given in Figure 2.12(a) and (b). Then $R \underset{B<D}{\bowtie} S$ is given in Figure 2.12(c). As with all algebraic operations, when columns have names we are free to use them. Thus $\underset{B<D}{\bowtie}$ is the same as $\underset{2<1}{\bowtie}$ in this case.

Incidentally, note that tuple $(7,8,9)$ of $R$ does not join with any tuple of $S$, and thus no trace of that tuple appears in the join. Tuples that in this way fail to participate in a join are called dangling tuples. Recall that we first met the notion of "dangling tuples" in the previous section, when we discussed combining relations with a common key. What we tacitly assumed there was that the correct way to form the combined relation was to take the equijoin in which the key attributes were equated. There is a good reason for this assumption, which we shall cover in Chapter 7. $\square$

| A | B | C |
|---|---|---|
| 1 | 2 | 3 |
| 4 | 5 | 6 |
| 7 | 8 | 9 |

(a) Relation $R$

| D | E |
|---|---|
| 3 | 1 |
| 6 | 2 |

(b) Relation $S$

| A | B | C | D | E |
|---|---|---|---|---|
| 1 | 2 | 3 | 3 | 1 |
| 1 | 2 | 3 | 6 | 2 |
| 4 | 5 | 6 | 6 | 2 |

(c) $R \underset{B<D}{\bowtie} S$

**Figure 2.12** Example of a $<$-join.

## Natural Join

The *natural join*, written $R \bowtie S$, is applicable only when both $R$ and $S$ have columns that are named by attributes. To compute $R \bowtie S$ we

1. Compute $R \times S$.
2. For each attribute $A$ that names both a column in $R$ and a column in $S$ select from $R \times S$ those tuples whose values agree in the columns for $R.A$ and $S.A$. Recall that $R.A$ is the name of the column of $R \times S$ corresponding to the column $A$ of $R$, and $S.A$ is defined analogously.

3. For each attribute $A$ above, project out the column $S.A$, and call the remaining column, $R.A$, simply $A$.

Formally then, if $A_1, A_2, \ldots, A_k$ are all the attribute names used for both $R$ and $S$, we have

$$R \bowtie S = \pi_{i_1, i_2, \ldots, i_m} \sigma_{R.A_1 = S.A_1 \wedge \cdots \wedge R.A_k = S.A_k} (R \times S)$$

where $i_1, i_2, \ldots, i_m$ is the list of all components of $R \times S$, in order, except the components $S.A_1, \ldots, S.A_k$.

**Example 2.18:** Let $R$ and $S$ be the relations given in Figure 2.13(a) and (b). Then

$$R \bowtie S = \pi_{A,R.B,R.C,D} \sigma_{R.B = S.B \wedge R.C = S.C} (R \times S)$$

To construct $R \bowtie S$, we consider each tuple in $R$ to see which tuples of $S$ agree with it in both columns $B$ and $C$. For example, $abc$ in $R$ agrees with $bcd$ and $bce$ in $S$, so we get $abcd$ and $abce$ in $R \bowtie S$. Similarly, $dbc$ gives us $dbcd$ and $dbce$ for $R \bowtie S$. Tuple $bbf$ agrees with no tuple of $S$ in columns $B$ and $C$, so we obtain no tuple in $R \bowtie S$ that begins with $bbf$. Lastly, $cad$ matches $adb$, so we get tuple $cadb$. $\square$

| $A$ | $B$ | $C$ |
|---|---|---|
| $a$ | $b$ | $c$ |
| $d$ | $b$ | $c$ |
| $b$ | $b$ | $f$ |
| $c$ | $a$ | $d$ |

| $B$ | $C$ | $D$ |
|---|---|---|
| $b$ | $c$ | $d$ |
| $b$ | $c$ | $e$ |
| $a$ | $d$ | $b$ |

| $A$ | $B$ | $C$ | $D$ |
|---|---|---|---|
| $a$ | $b$ | $c$ | $d$ |
| $a$ | $b$ | $c$ | $e$ |
| $d$ | $b$ | $c$ | $d$ |
| $d$ | $b$ | $c$ | $e$ |
| $c$ | $a$ | $d$ | $b$ |

(a) Relation $R$          (b) Relation $S$          (c) $R \bowtie S$

**Figure 2.13** Example of a natural join.

## Semijoin

The *semijoin* of relation $R$ by relation $S$, written $R \ltimes S$, is the projection onto the attributes of $R$ of the natural join of $R$ and $S$. That is,

$$R \ltimes S = \pi_R(R \bowtie S)$$

Note the useful convention that a relation name, such as $R$, stands for the set of attributes of that relation in appropriate contexts, such as in the list of attributes of a projection. In other contexts, $R$ stands for the value of the relation $R$. An equivalent way of computing $R \ltimes S$ is to project $S$ onto the set of attributes that are common to $R$ and $S$, and then take the natural join of $R$ with the resulting relation. Thus, an equivalent formula for the semijoin is $R \ltimes S = R \bowtie \pi_{R \cap S}(S)$, as the reader may prove. Note that the semijoin is not symmetric; i.e., $R \ltimes S \neq S \ltimes R$ in general.

**Example 2.19:** Let $R$ and $S$ be the relations of Figure 2.13(a) and (b), respectively. Then $R \ltimes S$ is the projection of Figure 2.13(c) onto attributes $A$, $B$, and $C$, that is, the relation of Figure 2.14(a). Another way to obtain the same result is first to project $S$ onto $\{B, C\}$, the attributes shared by the relation schemes for $R$ and $S$, yielding the relation of Figure 2.14(b), and then joining this relation with $R$. $\square$

| $A$ | $B$ | $C$ |
|-----|-----|-----|
| $a$ | $b$ | $c$ |
| $d$ | $b$ | $c$ |
| $c$ | $a$ | $d$ |

(a) $R \ltimes S$

| $B$ | $C$ |
|-----|-----|
| $b$ | $c$ |
| $a$ | $d$ |

(b) $\pi_{B,C}(S)$

| $E$ | $F$ | $G$ | $H$ | $I$ |
|-----|-----|-----|-----|-----|
| $a$ | $d$ | $b$ | $c$ | $d$ |
| $a$ | $d$ | $b$ | $c$ | $e$ |

(c) $S(E, F, G) \bowtie S(G, H, I)$.

**Figure 2.14** Joins and semijoins.

When we use the natural join and semijoin operations, the attributes of the relations become crucial; that is, we need to see relations from the set-of-mappings viewpoint rather than the set-of-lists viewpoint. Thus, to make explicit what attributes we are assuming for a relation $R$, we shall write $R(A_1, \ldots, A_n)$ explicitly. We can even use the same relation in the mathematical sense as several arguments of a join with different attributes assigned to the columns in different arguments.

For example, suppose we had relation $S$ of Figure 2.13(b), but ignored the attributes $B$, $C$, and $D$ for the moment. That is, see $S$ only as a ternary relation with the three tuples $bcd$, $bce$, and $adb$. The natural join

$$S(E, F, G) \bowtie S(G, H, I)$$

takes this relation and joins it with itself, as an equijoin between the third column of the first copy and the first column of the second copy. The only value these columns have in common is $b$, so the result would be the relation of Figure 2.14(c).

We shall summarize the arguments made above, regarding extensions to the relational algebra, in our first theorem.

**Theorem 2.1:** If $R$ and $S$ are variables standing for relations, there are expressions of relational algebra using only $R$ and $S$ as operands and only the five basic operations of relational algebra ($\cup$, $-$, $\times$, $\sigma$, $\pi$) equivalent to the following operations: (a) $R \cap S$, (b) $R \div S$, (c) $R \underset{i\theta j}{\bowtie} S$, (d) $R \bowtie S$, and (e) $R \ltimes S$.
$\square$

## Algebraic Laws

Like many other algebras, there are laws that the operators of relational algebra obey. The reader is probably familiar with the fact that $\cup$ is associative

$$[R \cup (S \cup T) = (R \cup S) \cup T]$$

and commutative $[R \cup S = S \cup R]$. Likewise, Cartesian product is associative, but not commutative because the order in which the columns appear is important in the set-of-lists viewpoint. The natural join has a number of useful properties, including associativity and commutativity, which we prove as an example.

**Theorem 2.2:** In the set-of-mappings viewpoint:

a)    $R \bowtie (S \bowtie T) = (R \bowtie S) \bowtie T$.
b)    $R \bowtie S = S \bowtie R$.

**Proof:** The result depends on the fact that natural join is taken on relations with the database viewpoint; that is, tuples are regarded as mappings from attributes to values, and order of attributes is unimportant. To prove associativity, let $\mu$ be a tuple in $R \bowtie (S \bowtie T)$. Then there is a tuple $\mu_R$ in $R$ and a tuple $\nu$ in $S \bowtie T$, that each agree with $\mu$ on the attributes they have in common with $\mu$; i.e., $\mu_R = \mu[R]$ and $\nu = \mu[S \cup T]$. Similarly, there must be tuples $\mu_S$ and $\mu_T$ in $S$ and $T$ respectively, that agree with $\nu$ when they share attributes, and therefore they too agree with $\mu$ on attributes they share with $\mu$.

Since $\mu$ is defined on all the attributes in $R \cup S \cup T$, it follows that $\mu_R$, $\mu_S$, and $\mu_T$ agree whenever they have an attribute in common. Thus, when we compute $R \bowtie S$, we get a tuple $\rho$ that agrees with $\mu_R$ and $\mu_S$, and therefore agrees with $\mu$. When we then join $R \bowtie S$ with $T$, tuples $\rho$ and $\mu_T$ produce a tuple that agrees with $\mu$ on all attributes. Thus, assuming that $\mu$ is in $R \bowtie (S \bowtie T)$, we have shown that $\mu$ is also in $(R \bowtie S) \bowtie T$. That is, the left side of (a) is contained in the right side. An almost identical proof shows that the right side is contained in the left side, so we have proven equality (a), the associative law for $\bowtie$.

Part (b), the commutative law, is proven in a similar way, and we leave it as an exercise for the reader. $\square$

A consequence of Theorem 2.2 is that we can characterize the natural join of any set of relations quite simply; this result is stated in the following corollary.

**Corollary 2.1:** Suppose $R = R_1 \bowtie \cdots \bowtie R_n$.[6] Then $R$ is the set of tuples $\mu$ such that for all $i$, $1 \leq i \leq n$, $\mu$ restricted to the attributes of $R_i$, i.e., $\mu[R_i]$, is a tuple in relation $R_i$.

**Proof:** It is an easy induction on $n$ that any tuple in $R$ must have the property that it agrees with some tuple of each relation. For the converse, suppose that $\mu$ is such a tuple; i.e., it agrees with a tuple of $R_i$ for all $i$. If $n = 2$, $\mu$ is in $R$ by the definition of the natural join. For the induction, let $\nu$ be $\mu[R_1 \cup \cdots \cup R_{n-1}]$ and let $\rho$ be $\mu[R_n]$. Then by the inductive hypothesis, $\nu$ is in $R_1 \bowtie \cdots \bowtie R_{n-1}$, and by the definition of the join, $\mu$ is in $(R_1 \bowtie \cdots \bowtie R_{n-1}) \bowtie R_n$ since it agrees with $\nu$ and $\rho$ on the attributes it shares with them. By Theorem 2.2, this join is $R_1 \bowtie \cdots \bowtie R_n$. $\square$

The $\theta$-join is not commutative, because as we defined it, the order of columns matters. However, it is "associative," if we write the associativity law to take into account the fact that component numbers change as we apply the $\theta$-join operator. Specifically, if $\theta_1$ and $\theta_2$ are arithmetic comparison operators, $R$ is a relation of arity $r$, and $j$ is no larger than the arity of relation $S$, then

$$R \underset{i\theta_1 j}{\bowtie} (S \underset{k\theta_2 l}{\bowtie} T) = (R \underset{i\theta_1 j}{\bowtie} S) \underset{(r+k)\theta_2 l}{\bowtie} T$$

The proof of this and some other algebraic laws for relational algebra are left as exercises for the reader. Also, in Chapter 11, when we discuss query optimization, we shall catalog a number of other "laws" involving combinations of the relational operators.

## Relational Algebra as a Query Language

We can use selection and projection to ask many natural questions about single relations.

**Example 2.20:** Consider the relation SUPPLIES of Figure 2.8. If we want to know which suppliers supply Brie, we can say

$$\pi_{\text{SNAME}}\left(\sigma_{\text{INAME}=\text{'Brie'}} (\text{SUPPLIES})\right) \tag{2.1}$$

That is, the selection focuses us on those tuples that talk about item "Brie," and the projection lets us see only the supplier name from those tuples. The algebraic expression (2.1) thus evaluates to a relation of arity 1, and its value will be a list of all the suppliers of Brie.

---

[6] By Theorem 2.2, the order in which the $R_i$'s are joined does not affect the result and need not be specified.

If we wanted to know what items supplier "Acme" sells for less than \$5, and the prices of each, we could write:

$$\pi_{\text{INAME,PRICE}}\left(\sigma_{\text{SNAME='Acme'}\wedge\text{PRICE}<5.00}(\text{SUPPLIES})\right)$$

☐

## Navigation Among Relations

Many more queries are expressed by navigating among relations, that is, by expressing connections among two or more relations. It is fundamental to the relational data model that these connections are expressed by equalities (or sometimes inequalities) between the values in two attributes of different relations. It is both the strength and weakness of this model that connections are expressed that way. It allows more varied paths among relations to be followed than in other data models, where, as we shall see in the next sections, particular pathways are favored by being "built in" to the scheme design, but other paths are hard or impossible to express in the languages of these models.

**Example 2.21:** We again refer to the relations of Figure 2.8. Suppose we wish to determine which customers have ordered Brie. No one relation tells us, but INCLUDES gives us the order numbers for those orders that include Brie, and ORDERS tells us for each of those order numbers what customer placed that order. If we take the natural join of INCLUDES and ORDERS, we shall have a relation with set of attributes

(O#, INAME, QUANTITY, DATE, CUST)

and a tuple $(o, i, q, d, c)$ in this relation can be interpreted as saying that order $o$ includes quantity $q$ of item $i$, and the order was placed on date $d$ by customer $c$.[7] We are only interested in orders for Brie, so we can apply a selection to this relation for INAME = 'Brie'. Finally, we want only to know the customer's name, so we can project the result onto CUST. The algebraic expression for this query is thus:

$$\pi_{\text{CUST}}\left(\sigma_{\text{INAME='Brie'}}(\text{INCLUDES} \bowtie \text{ORDERS})\right) \tag{2.2}$$

☐

## Efficiency of Joins

Join is generally the most expensive of the operations in relational algebra. The "compare all pairs of tuples" method for computing the join, suggested by Example 2.18, is not the way to compute the join in reality; it takes $O(n^2)$

---

[7] We would not generally wish to have a relation with this set of attributes in the database scheme because of redundancy of the type discussed in Example 2.14. That is, we would have to repeat the date and customer for every item on the given order.

time on relations of size (number of tuples) $n$.[8] We shall discuss other methods in Chapter 11, but for the moment, observe one way to compute equijoins or natural joins is to sort both relations on the attribute or attributes involved in the equality, and then merge the lists, creating tuples of the join as we go. This approach takes time $O(m + n \log n)$ on relations of size $n$, where $m$ is the number of tuples in the result of the join. Typically $m$ is no more than $O(n \log n)$, although it could be as high as $n^2$.

However, a better idea in many cases is to avoid doing joins of large relations at all. By transforming an algebraic expression into an equivalent one that can be evaluated faster, we frequently save orders of magnitude of time when answering queries. It is the development of such *query optimization* techniques that made DBMS's using the relational model feasible.

**Example 2.22:** Consider expression (2.2) from Example 2.21. Rather than compute the large relation INCLUDES ⋈ ORDERS, then reduce it in size by selection and projection, we prefer to do the selection, and as much of the projection as we can as soon as we can. Thus, before joining, we select on the INCLUDES relation for those tuples with INAME = 'Brie' and then project this relation onto O#, to get only the set of order numbers that include Brie. Presumably, this will be a much smaller set than the entire INCLUDES relation.

Now we would like to select the tuples in ORDERS with this small set of order numbers, to get the desired set of customers. The whole process can be expressed by a semijoin:

$$\pi_{\text{CUST}}(\text{ORDERS} \ltimes \sigma_{\text{INAME='Brie'}}(\text{INCLUDES})) \qquad (2.3)$$

If there is an index on attribute INAME of INCLUDES, we can find the orders for Brie in time proportional to the number of these orders.[9] Then if this set is small and ORDERS has an index on O#, we can find the customers placing these orders in time proportional to their number. Thus, expression (2.3) can be evaluated in time that is typically much smaller than the size of the INCLUDES and ORDERS relations, and therefore much smaller than the time taken for even a sophisticated, but direct evaluation of (2.2). $\square$

## 2.5 THE NETWORK DATA MODEL

Roughly, the network data model is the entity-relationship model with all relationships restricted to be binary, many-one relationships. This restriction

---

[8] $O(f(n))$, for any function $f(n)$, is read "big oh of $f$ of $n$" and, informally, stands for "some function that is at most $cf(n)$ for some constant $c$ and all sufficiently large $n$." The reader not familiar with "big oh" notation should consult Aho, Hopcroft, and Ullman [1983].

[9] Index structures and the speed of access they provide are discussed in Chapter 6; for the moment, we simply assume that there is a magical way to find exactly the tuples we want from a relation in time proportional to the number of tuples retrieved.

allows us to use a simple directed graph model for data. In place of entity sets, the network model talks of *logical record types*.[10] A logical record type is a name for a set of records, which are called *logical records*. Logical records are composed of *fields*, which are places in which elementary values such as integers and character strings can be placed. The set of names for the fields and their types constitute the *logical record format*.

## Record Identity

One might suppose there is a close analogy between these terms for networks and the terms we used for relations, under the correspondence

| Logical record format | : | Relation scheme |
| Logical record | : | Tuple |
| Logical record type | : | Relation name |

However, there is an important distinction between tuples of relations and records of a record type. In the value-oriented relational model, tuples are nothing more than the values of their components. Two tuples with the same values for the same attributes are the same tuple. On the other hand, the network model is object-oriented, at least to the extent that it supports object identity. Records of the network model may be viewed as having an invisible key, which is in essence the address of the record, i.e., its "object identity." This unique identifier serves to make records distinct, even if they have the same values in their corresponding fields. In fact, it is feasible to have record types with no fields at all.

The reason it makes sense to treat records as having unique identifiers, independent of their field values, is that physically, records contain more data than just the values in their fields. In a database built on the network model they are given physical pointers to other records that represent the relationships in which their record type is involved. These pointers can make two records with the same field values different, and we could not make this distinction if we thought only of the values in their fields.

## Links

Instead of "binary many-one relationships" we talk about *links* in the network model. We draw a directed graph, called a *network*, which is really a simplified entity-relationship diagram, to represent record types and their links. Nodes correspond to record types. If there is a link between two record types $T_1$ and $T_2$, and the link is many-one from $T_1$ to $T_2$, then we draw an arc from the node

---

[10] We drop the word "logical" from "logical record," or "logical record type/format" whenever no confusion results.

for $T_1$ to that for $T_2$,[11] and we say the link is from $T_1$ to $T_2$. Nodes and arcs are labeled by the names of their record types and links.

### Representing Entity Sets in the Network Model

Entity sets are represented directly by logical record types; the attributes of an entity set become fields of the logical record format. The only special case is when an entity set $E$ forms its key with fields of some entity set $F$, to which $E$ is related through relationship $\mathcal{R}$. We do not need to place those fields of $F$ in the record format for $E$, because the records of $E$ do not need to be distinguished by their field values. Rather, they will be distinguished by the physical pointers placed in the records of $E$ to represent the relationship $\mathcal{R}$, and these pointers will lead from a record $e$ of type $E$ to the corresponding record of type $F$ that holds the key value for $e$.

Alternatively, when the relationship concerned is **isa**, and the subset has no field that the superset does not have, (as between MANAGERS and EMPS in Figure 2.2), we could eliminate the record type for the subset, e.g. MANAGERS, altogether, and let the relationships between MANAGERS and other entity sets (besides EMPS) be represented in the network model by links involving EMPS. The **isa** relationship itself could be represented by a one-bit field telling whether an employee is a manager. Another choice is to represent the **isa** implicitly; only EMPS records that represent managers will participate in relationships, such as MANAGES, that involve the set of managers.

### Representing Relationships

Among relationships, only those that are binary and many-one (or one-one as a special case) are representable directly by links. However, we can use the following trick to represent arbitrary relationships. Say we have a relationship $R$ among entity sets $E_1, E_2, \ldots, E_k$. We create a new logical record type $T$ representing $k$-tuples $(e_1, e_2, \ldots, e_k)$ of entities that stand in the relationship $R$. The format for this record type might be empty. However, there are many times when it is convenient to add information-carrying fields in the format for the new record type $T$. In any event, we create links $L_1, L_2, \ldots, L_k$. Link $L_i$ is from record type $T$ to the record type for entity set $E_i$, which we shall also call $E_i$. The intention is that the record of type $T$ for $(e_1, e_2, \ldots, e_k)$ is linked to the record of type $E_i$ for $e_i$, so each link is many-one.

As a special case, if the relationship is many-one from $E_1, \ldots, E_{k-1}$ to $E_k$, and furthermore, the entity set $E_k$ does not appear in any other relationships,

---

[11] Some works on the subject draw the arc in the opposite direction. However, we chose this direction to be consistent with the notion of functional dependency discussed in Chapter 7. Our point of view is that arrows mean "determines uniquely." Thus, as each record of type $T_1$ is linked to at most one record of type $T_2$, we draw the arrow into $T_2$.

then we can identify the record type $T$ with $E_k$, storing the attributes of $E_k$ in $T$. For example, the relationship SUPPLIES of Figure 2.2 is many-one from SUPPLIERS and ITEMS to PRICE, and PRICE participates in no relationship but this one. We may therefore create a type $T$ with links to ITEMS and SUPPLIERS, and containing PRICE as a field. We shall discuss this matter further when we convert the full entity-relationship diagram of Figure 2.2 to a network, in Example 2.24. For the moment, we consider a simpler example.

**Example 2.23:** We mentioned in Section 2.1 a common example of a purely many-many relationship, that between courses and students with the intended meaning that the student is taking the course. To represent this relationship in the network model, we would use two entity sets, COURSES and STUDENTS, each with appropriate fields, such as

> COURSES(DEPT, NUMBER, INSTRUCTOR)
> STUDENTS(ID#, NAME, ADDRESS, STATUS)

To represent the relationship between these entity sets, we need to introduce a new record type, say ENROLL, that represents single pairs in the relationship set, i.e., one course and one student enrolled in that course. There might not be any fields in ENROLL, or we might decide to use ENROLL records to store information that really does refer to the pair consisting of a course and a student, e.g., the grade the student receives in the course, or the section in which the student is enrolled. Thus, we might use record format

> ENROLL(SECTION, GRADE)

Notice that two or more enrollment records may look the same, in the sense that they have the same values in their SECTION and GRADE fields. They are distinguished by their addresses, i.e., by their "object identity."

We also need two links, one from ENROLL to COURSES, which we shall call E_COURSE, and one from ENROLL to STUDENTS, which we shall call E_STUDENT. The network for these record types and links is shown in Figure 2.15(a).

The link E_COURSE associates with each ENROLL record a unique COURSES record, which we take to be the course in which the enrollment is made. Likewise, E_STUDENT associates with each ENROLL record a unique STUDENTS record, that of the student who is thereby enrolled. As we shall discuss in Chapter 5, when we consider the DBTG network language in detail, the notion of *ownership* is used to help describe the relationship enforced by the links. If a link, such as E_STUDENT is from ENROLL to STUDENTS, then each student record is said to *own* the enrollment records which the link associates to that student.

In Figure 2.15(b) we see a simple example of three COURSES records, five ENROLL records, and four STUDENT records. The ENROLL records each

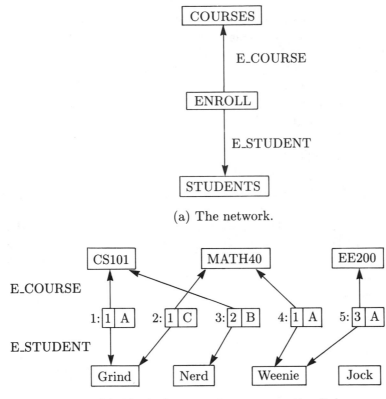

(a) The network.

(b) Physical connections representing links.

**Figure 2.15** Network for courses and students.

show fields for the section and grade; the fields of STUDENTS and COURSES are not shown. The unique identifiers for ENROLL records, which are in essence addresses, are shown as integers outside the records. The fact that records 1 and 4 have identical field values is of no concern. Evidently, they are distinguished by the differences in their links. For example, ENROLL record 1 represents only the fact that student Grind is enrolled in CS101.

We can say that the record for Grind owns ENROLL records 1 and 2. Weenie owns 4 and 5, while Jock owns no enrollment records. It is also true that CS101 owns ENROLL records 1 and 3. There is no conflict with the fact that Grind also owns record 1, because their ownership is through different links. That is, Grind is the owner of 1 according to the E_STUDENT link, and CS101 the owner of that record according to the E_COURSE link. □

**Example 2.24:** Let us design a network for the YVCB database scheme whose entity-relationship diagram was given in Figure 2.2. We start with logical record types for the six entity sets that remain after excluding MANAGERS, which as we mentioned above, can be represented by the logical record type for its superset, EMPS. Thus, we have logical record formats:

> EMPS(ENAME, SALARY)
> DEPTS(DNAME, DEPT#)
> SUPPLIERS(SNAME, SADDR)
> ITEMS(INAME, ITEM#)
> ORDERS(O#, DATE)
> CUSTOMERS(CNAME, CADDR, BALANCE)

These are, except for MANAGERS, the same as the relations we started with initially in Example 2.9.

We need two more record types, because two of the relationships, SUP-PLIES and INCLUDES, are not binary, many-one relationships. Let us use record type ENTRIES to represent order–item–quantity facts. It makes sense to store the quantity in the entry record itself, because the relationship IN-CLUDES is many-one from ORDERS and ITEMS to QUANTITY. Thus, we need only links from ENTRIES to ITEMS and ORDERS, which we call E_ITEM and E_ORDER, respectively.

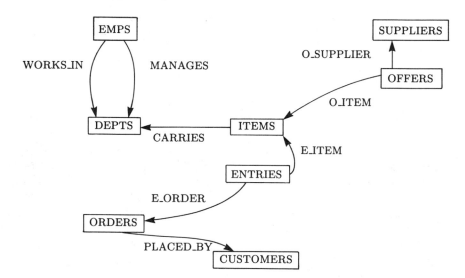

**Figure 2.16** Network for the YVCB database scheme.

Similarly, a new record type OFFERS can serve to represent the facts of the SUPPLIES relation. We prefer to store PRICE as a field of OFFERS, for the same reason as was discussed above concerning QUANTITY. We shall use O_ITEM and O_SUPPLIER, as the links from OFFERS to ITEMS and SUPPLIERS, respectively. The last two record types for our network are thus:

ENTRIES(QUANTITY)
OFFERS(PRICE)

The relationships in Figure 2.2, other than SUPPLIES and INCLUDES, are many-one and binary. Thus, they are directly representable by links. The only special remark needed is that the relationship MANAGES, originally between DEPTS and MANAGERS, will now be between DEPTS and EMPS, since we agreed to use EMPS to represent managers. Since this relationship is one-one, we could have it run in either direction, and we have chosen to have it run from EMPS to DEPTS. The complete network is shown in Figure 2.16. ☐

**Comparison of Networks and Relation Schemes: Link-Following Operations on Networks**

The distinction between tuples and records tells us a great deal about the ways in which each of the two data models, relational and network, excels. Recall that tuples are nothing but the values of their components but records can have built-in, invisible pointers that represent certain declared links. The relational model gives us the ability to use component values in arbitrary ways, whether or not they are the ways that were expected by the database designer when the scheme was first created. For example, one day YVCB owner Simon DeLamb gets curious and wants to know whether some customer has a balance that exactly equals the price of some item. He has only to say

$$\pi_{CNAME}(CUSTOMERS \underset{BALANCE=PRICE}{\bowtie} SUPPLIES)$$

in relational algebra. However, in the network model, whose languages only allow us to follow links, there is really no convenient way to compare customers' balances with items' prices.

On the other hand, when we do follow links, the network model provides a more succinct way to express these paths than does relational algebra. For example, if we had a language in which links could be followed, in either direction, by applying their names as functions to the record type at either end, we could relate customers to the items they have ordered by an expression like

PLACED_BY(E_ORDER(E_ITEM(ITEMS)))

In comparison, relational languages have to specify the equality of values needed to navigate between the relations INCLUDES and ORDERS. Line (2.2) in Example 2.21 was a similar query expressed in relational algebra. There, the requirement for equality of values between the O# fields of INCLUDES and ORDERS was hidden by our use of the natural join. However, natural join can only be used where, fortuitously, the attributes have the same name in the relation schemes; real relational DBMS's do not generally support the natural join directly, requiring it to be expressed as an equijoin, with the explicit equality of values spelled out.

It is probably a matter of taste which style one prefers: cascade of functions or equalities among values. However, there is one important advantage to the relational model that doesn't depend upon such matters of diction. The result of an operation on relations is a relation, so we can build complex expressions of relational algebra easily. However, the result of operations on networks is not generally a network, or even a part of one. It has to be that way, because the invisible pointers and unique identifiers for records cannot be referred to in network query languages. Thus, new networks cannot be constructed by queries; they must be constructed by the data definition language. While we can obtain some compounding of operations by following sequences of many links in one query, we are limited, in the network model, to following those links. Again, it is a matter of judgment whether the links we select for a database scheme design are adequate to the task of supporting all the queries we could reasonably wish to ask.

There is an additional distinction between the network and relational models in the way they treat many-many relationships. In the network model, these are forbidden, and we learned in Examples 2.23 and 2.24 how to replace many-many relationships by several many-one relationships. The reason framers of the network model forbade many-many relationships is that there is really no good way to store directly a many-many relationship between entity sets $E$ and $F$ so that given an entity of $E$ we can find the associated $F$'s efficiently and vice-versa. On the physical level, we are forced to build a structure similar to that implied by the breakup of a many-many relationship into some many-one relationships, although there are a substantial number of choices of structure available.

Presumably, the authors of the network model took the position that databases were so large that direct implementation of many-many relationships always lead to unacceptable performance. In relational systems, the philosophy is to provide the database designer with a DDL in which he can create the index structures needed to use a relation that is a many-many relationship with adequate efficiency. However, it is also permissible, and indeed may be preferable in small databases, to use a relation that is a many-many relationship (i.e., it has no key but its full set of attributes) without the data structure that supports efficient access.

## 2.6 THE HIERARCHICAL DATA MODEL

A *hierarchy* is simply a network that is a *forest* (collection of trees) in which all links point in the direction from child to parent. We shall continue to use the network terminology "logical record type," and so on, when we speak of hierarchies.

Just as any entity-relationship diagram can be represented in the relational and network models, such a diagram can always be represented in the hierarchical model. However, there is a subtlety embodied in our use of the vague term "represented." In the previous two models, the constructions used to convert entity-relationship diagrams had the property that relationships could be followed easily by operations of the model, the join in the relational case and link-following in the network case. The same is true in the hierarchical model only if we introduce "virtual record types."

### A Simple Network Conversion Algorithm

Let us first see what happens if we attempt to design hierarchies by simply splitting networks apart into one or more trees. Recall that in a hierarchy, all links run from child to parent, so we must start at a node with as many incoming links as possible and make it the root of a tree. We attach to that tree all the nodes that can be attached, remembering that links must point to the parent. When we can pick up no more nodes this way, we start with another, unattached node as root, and attach as many nodes to that as we can. Eventually, each node will appear in the forest one or more times, and at this point we have a hierarchy. The formal construction is shown in Figure 2.17.

```
procedure BUILD(n);
    make n selected;
    for each link from some node m to n do begin
        make m a child of n;
        if m is not selected then BUILD(m)
    end
end

/* main program */
make all nodes unselected;
while not all nodes are selected do begin
    pick an unselected node n;
    /* prefer a node n with no links to unselected nodes,
    and prefer a node with many incoming links */
    BUILD(n)
end
```

**Figure 2.17** Simple hierarchy-building procedure.

**Example 2.25:** Consider the network of Figure 2.16. DEPTS is a good candidate to pick as the first root, because it has three incoming links, two from EMPS and one from ITEMS. We then consider EMPS, but find it has no incoming links. However, ITEMS has incoming links from ENTRIES and OFFERS. These have no incoming links, so we are done building the tree with root DEPTS. All the above mentioned nodes are now selected.

The remaining nodes with no outgoing links are CUSTOMERS and SUPPLIERS. If we start with CUSTOMERS, we add ORDERS as a child and ENTRIES as a child of ORDERS, but can go no further. From SUPPLIERS we add OFFERS as a child and are done. Now, all nodes are selected, and we are finished building the forest. The resulting forest is shown in Figure 2.18. The only additional point is that of the two children of DEPTS that come from node EMPS, we have changed one, that representing the manager of the department, to MGR. $\square$

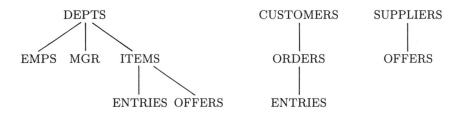

**Figure 2.18** First attempt at a hierarchy for the YVCB database scheme.

## Database Records

Hierarchies of logical record types, such as that in Figure 2.18, are scheme level concepts. The instances of the database corresponding to a scheme consist of a collection of trees whose nodes are records; each tree is called a *database record*. A database record corresponds to some one tree of the database scheme, and the root record of a database record corresponds to one entity of the root record type. If $T$ is a node of the scheme, and $S$ is one of its children, then each record of type $T$ in the database record has zero or more child records of type $S$.

**Example 2.26:** Figure 2.19(a) shows one database record for the DEPTS tree of Figure 2.18. This database record's root corresponds to the Produce Department, and it should be understood that the entire database instance has database records similar to this one for each department. The instance also includes a database record for each customer, with a structure that is an expansion of the middle tree in Figure 2.18, and it includes a database record for every supplier, with the structure implied by the rightmost tree of Figure

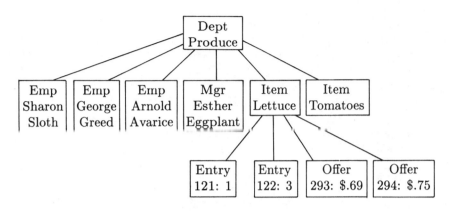

(a) One database record for DEPTS.

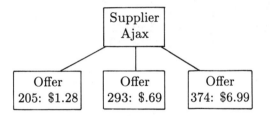

(b) One database record for SUPPLIERS.

**Figure 2.19** Example database records.

2.18. An example, for supplier Ajax, is shown in Figure 2.19(b).

Let us examine the database record of Figure 2.19(a). We see the Produce Department record at the root. Corresponding to the child EMPS of DEPTS in Figure 2.18, there are three children of the Produce Department record, for the three employees of that department, Sloth, Greed, and Avarice. Corresponding to the child MGR of DEPTS is one child of Produce, that for Esther Eggplant, the manager of the department. While we expect to find many employee children, there would normally be only one manager record, even though there is nothing in the scheme of Figure 2.18 that tells us the DEPTS-MGR relationship is one-to-one. Finally, we see two children of the produce record corresponding to items sold: lettuce and tomatoes. In reality, there would be more items, of course.

Each ITEMS record has some ENTRIES children and some OFFERS children. We have shown two of each for lettuce, but none for tomatoes, as much to save space in the figure as to remind the reader that a node in the hierarchical scheme can translate into zero records of that type in a given database record.

For records representing entries and offers, we have indicated the unique identifier that distinguishes each such record from all others of the same type; e.g.,
ENTRIES record 121 has QUANTITY 1. Recall that entries have only a quantity, and offers only a price as real data, and thus we cannot differentiate among
records of these types by field values alone. Other types of records must also
have unique identifiers, but we have not shown these because our assumptions
let us expect that records for departments, employees, and so on, are uniquely
identified by the values in their fields. As in networks, these unique identifiers
may be thought of as the addresses of the records. $\square$

## Record Duplication

As we may notice from Figure 2.18, certain record types, namely ENTRIES and
OFFERS, appear twice in the hierarchical scheme. This duplication carries over
to the instance, where an offer record by supplier $s$ to sell item $i$ appears both
as a child of the ITEMS record for $i$ and as a child of the SUPPLIER record for
$s$. For example, OFFERS record 293 appears twice in Figure 2.19, and we can
deduce thereby that this offer is an offer by Ajax to sell lettuce at $.69. This
duplication causes several problems:

1.   We waste space because we repeat the data in the record several times.
2.   There is potential inconsistency, should we change the price in one copy of
     the offer, but forget to change it in the other.

As we mentioned in Section 2.1, the avoidance of such problems is a recur-
ring theme in database design. We shall see how the network model deals with
it in Chapter 5, via the mechanism known as virtual fields, and in Chapter 7 we
shall investigate the response of the relational model, which is the extensive theory of database design known as "normalization." In the hierarchical model,
the solution is found in "virtual record types" and pointers, which we shall
discuss immediately after discussing another reason such pointers are needed.

## Operations in the Hierarchical Model

While the links in the network model were regarded as two-way, allowing us to
follow the link forward to the owner record or backward to the owned records,
in the hierarchical model, links are presumed to go only one way, from parent to
child, i.e., from owner to owned records. The reason for this difference will be
understood when we discuss the natural physical implementations of networks
and hierarchies in Chapter 6. For the moment, let us take for granted that one
can only follow links from parent to child unless there is an explicit pointer to
help us travel in the other direction.

For example, in Figure 2.19 we can, given a record for an item like lettuce,
find all its OFFERS children, but we cannot, given OFFERS record 293 determine that it is a child of the lettuce ITEMS record, and therefore it is an offer

to sell lettuce at the price, $.69, given in record 293. If that is so, how could we determine what items Ajax offers to sell? We can find the SUPPLIERS record for Ajax, because another operation generally found in hierarchical systems is the ability to find the root of a database record with a specified key, such as "Ajax." We can then go from Ajax to all its offers. But how do we find what items are offered for sale? In principle we can do so. Take a unique identifier for an OFFERS record, say 293, and examine the entire collection of DEPTS database records, until we find an item that has offer 293 as a child. However, that solution is evidently too time consuming, and we need to augment the hierarchical scheme by pointers that lead directly where we decide they are needed.

## Virtual Record Types

We can solve all three problems mentioned above, redundancy, potential inconsistency, and the inability to follow paths upwards in trees, by the same mechanism. In each scheme, we insist on having only one occurrence of any record type. Any additional places where we would like that record type to appear, we place instead a *virtual record* of that type. In an instance, instead of a physical record, we place a pointer to the one occurrence of that physical record in the database. For example, the ENTRIES node in the tree for CUSTOMERS and the OFFERS node in the tree for SUPPLIERS of Figure 2.18 will be replaced by virtual ENTRIES and virtual OFFERS, respectively, and in database trees, they will point to the corresponding record in the tree for DEPTS. Thus, in place of the record 293 in Figure 2.19(b) would be a pointer to the record 293 in Figure 2.19(a). This modification immediately removes the redundancy of records, and since we now have only one copy of any record to update, it removes the inconsistency, as well.

To avoid duplicating logical record types in hierarchical schemes we must modify the procedure *BUILD* of Figure 2.17 so it checks whether a new node *m* was previously selected, before adding *m* to a particular point in the hierarchical scheme. If it was selected already, then add a "virtual" *m* in the place it belongs. The details are given in Figure 2.20, and this version of *BUILD* must be coupled with the main routine in Figure 2.17 to make a complete program converting networks to hierarchies.

**Example 2.27:** Figure 2.21 shows the result of repeating Example 2.25 using the *BUILD* procedure of Figure 2.20 in place of that in Figure 2.17. One difference is that in the CUSTOMERS and SUPPLIERS trees, the nodes labeled ENTRIES and OFFERS in Figure 2.18 are replaced by virtual versions of themselves, because they represent the second time each of these logical record types was encountered in the forest. The nodes labeled ENTRIES and OFFERS in the DEPTS tree remain as they were, because those nodes represent the first

```
procedure BUILD(n)
    make n selected;
    for each link from some node m to n do
        if m is not selected then begin
            make m a child of n;
            BUILD(m)
        end
        else /* m was previously selected */
            make virtual m be a child of n
end
```

**Figure 2.20** Hierarchy-building procedure using virtual record types.

times these record types are encountered by the *BUILD* procedure.

A second difference is that we have replaced the MGR node by virtual EMPS. Recall that the node we called MGR in Figure 2.18 was really a second copy of EMPS, and we renamed it to help tell the difference between the DEPT children. Using a pointer to an employee record in place of a manager record makes excellent sense, since managers have no fields of their own; we merely need a reference to a particular employee record to mark which employee is the manager of the department. □

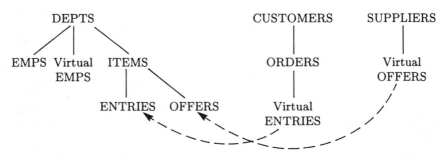

**Figure 2.21** Second attempt at a hierarchy for the YVCB database.

## Representation of Bidirectional Relationships

Virtual record types also solve the problem of traversing links in both directions. If we have a many-one relationship from record type $R$ to record type $S$, we can make $R$ be a child of $S$, and then make virtual $S$ be a child of $R$. If we have a many-many relationship between $R$ and $S$, we cannot make either a child of the other, but we can let $R$ and $S$ each take their natural position in the forest, and then create a child of each that is a virtual version of the other.

**Example 2.28:** Reconsider Example 2.23, which discussed a many-many relationship between courses and students. Instead of creating a new record type to interpose between COURSES and STUDENTS, as we did in that example, in the hierarchical model we may create a scheme with the two trees of Figure 2.22.

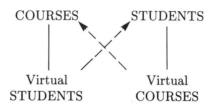

**Figure 2.22** Representing a many-many relationship.

In Figure 2.23 we see an instance of the scheme of Figure 2.22; this instance is the same one that was represented as a network in Figure 2.15. Given a course, such as CS101, we can find the students enrolled as follows.

1.  Find the courses record for CS101. Recall that finding a root record, given its key, is one of the typical operations of a hierarchical system.

2.  Find all the virtual STUDENTS children of CS101. In Figure 2.23, we would find pointers to the STUDENT records for Grind and Nerd, but at this point, we would not know the names or anything about the students to whose records we have pointers.

3.  Follow the pointers to find the actual student records and the names of these students.

Similarly, given a student, we could perform the analogous three steps and find the courses the student was taking. □

## Combined Record Types

To solve the third problem, that is, to navigate quickly along arbitrary paths that the database scheme designer believes will be taken in practice, we often need *combined records* consisting of some ordinary fields, holding data, and other fields that are pointers to other record types. As with all virtual record types, if we are at a record $r$ that contains a field of type "virtual $T$," we may follow that pointer as if a record of type $T$ were a child of $r$.

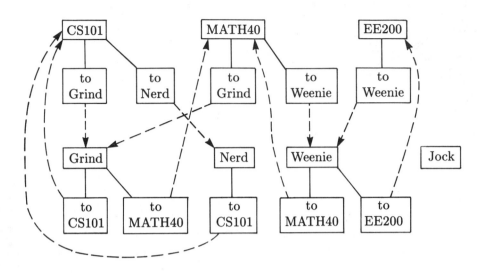

**Figure 2.23** Physical connections representing virtual records.

**Example 2.29:** Suppose we want to store grades in the enrollment records that interpose between student and course records. We can modify the scheme of Figure 2.22 by replacing the Virtual COURSE child of STUDENTS by a combined record that has a Virtual COURSE field as well as a GRADE field. The new scheme is shown in Figure 2.24, and to make matters clearer, we have shown the fields of the record types explicitly. We also adopt the convention that $*T$ stands for a virtual record of type $T$.

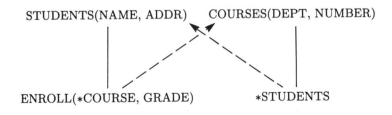

**Figure 2.24** Scheme with combined record type.

To find all the grades issued in CS101, we have to find the root of the COURSES database record for CS101, then follow all the virtual student pointers and from them, find their enrollment children. Only some of these enrollments will be for CS101, exactly one per student investigated.

If that is too inefficient, there are several other schemes we could use. One thing we don't want to do is duplicate enrollments as children of both STUDENTS and COURSES. However, we could use the scheme of Figure 2.25. There, we can go directly from the CS101 record to its enrollments, and find the grades directly. On the other hand, to find all the students taking CS101 we need to go first to ENROLL, then to STUDENTS, via two virtual record pointers. In comparison, Figure 2.24 lets us go from courses to students in one hop. Which is better depends on what paths are more likely to be followed. If we were willing to pay the space penalty, we could even use both sets of pointers. □

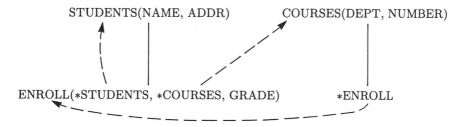

**Figure 2.25** Another scheme for courses and students.

**Example 2.30:** In Figure 2.26 we see a better design for the YVCB database. Entries, with their quantities, and offers, with their prices, are handled by the trick of the previous example, using combined records. We have also added virtual ORDERS as a child of ITEMS, to facilitate finding the orders for a given item, and we have similarly added virtual SUPPLIERS as a child of ITEMS to help find out who supplies a given item.

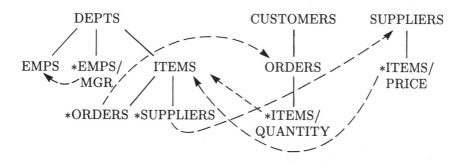

**Figure 2.26** Improved design for YVCB database.

We have not chosen to add virtual DEPTS as a child of either EMPS or MGR, even though that would help us find the department a given employee was in or what department a manager managed. We could have added these pointers if we chose, of course, paying additional space to speed navigation along a particular path. The reason we chose not to was that as the structure stands, the only way to reach EMPS or MGR records is through their DEPT, and therefore, we shall "know" the department anyway, without needing to follow a pointer. $\square$

## 2.7  AN OBJECT-ORIENTED MODEL

There are a large number of proposals, and some implementations, of models that capture the essentials of object-oriented query languages; they go by various names such as "semantic," "functional," or "format" data models, as well as by several other names. Their common thread is that they support

1. Object identity. The elements with which they deal are typically records with unique addresses, just as in the network and hierarchical models.
2. Complex objects. Typically, they allow construction of new types by record formation and set formation.
3. Type hierarchy. They allow types to have subtypes with special properties.

In what follows, we shall introduce a notation for defining object structures, i.e., the formats for types. We shall later discuss how type hierarchies can be constructed, and we shall give an example notation.

### Object Structure

The set of object structures definable in our model is very close to the set of possible schemes for database records in the hierarchical model. We can define the set of allowable *object types*, together with their intended physical implementation, recursively by:

1. A data item of an elementary type, e.g., integer, real, or character string of fixed or varying length, is an object type. Such a type corresponds to the data type for a "field" in networks or hierarchies.
2. If $T$ is an object type, then SETOF($T$) is an object type. An object of type SETOF($T$) is a collection of objects of type $T$. However, since objects must preserve their identity regardless of their connections to other objects, we do not normally find the member objects physically present in the collection; rather the collection consists of pointers to the actual objects in the set. It is as though every child record type in a hierarchy were a virtual record type, and every logical record type in the hierarchy were a root of its own tree.

3.   If $T_1, \ldots, T_k$ are object types, then RECORDOF$(T_1, \ldots, T_k)$ is an object type. As with sets, an object of this type really consists of pointers to one object of each of the $k$ types in the record. However, if object type $T_i$ is an elementary type, then the value of the object itself appears in the record.

**Example 2.31:** Let us translate our running example into the above terms. We shall, for simplicity, assume that the only elementary types are *string* and *int*. Then the type of an item can be represented by the record

```
ItemType = RECORDOF(name:string, I#:int)
```

Notice the convention that a field of a record is represented by the pair (<fieldname>: <type>).

To handle orders, we need to represent item/quantity pairs, as we did in Figure 2.26. Thus, we need another object type

```
IQType = RECORDOF(item:ItemType, quantity:int)
```

Here, the first field is an object of a nonelementary type, so that field should be thought of as a pointer to an item.

Now we can define the type of an order to be:

```
OrderType = RECORDOF(O#:int, includes:SETOF(IQType))
```

Here, we have embedded the definition of another object type, SETOF(*IQType*), within the definition of *OrderType*. That is equivalent to writing the two declarations:

```
SIQType = SETOF(IQType)
OrderType = RECORDOF(O#:int, includes:SIQType)
```

Either way, the field *includes* of *OrderType* is a representation of a set of pointers to objects of type *IQType*, perhaps a pointer to a linked list of pointers to those objects.

Customers can be represented by objects of the following type:

```
CustType = RECORDOF(name:string, addr:string,
     balance:int, orders:SETOF(OrderType))
```

while departments may be given the following declaration:

```
DeptType = RECORDOF(name:string, dept#:int,
     emps:SETOF(EmpType), mgr:EmpType,
     items:SETOF(ItemType))
```

Notice that this declaration twice makes use of a type *EmpType*, for employees, once as a set and once directly. In both cases, it is not the employees or manager of the department that appear there, but pointers to the actual employee objects. Those objects have the following type:

```
EmpType = RECORDOF(name:string,
    salary:int, dept:DeptType)
```

Here, we should notice that *DeptType* is the type of a field of *EmpType*, just as *EmpType* and SETOF(*EmpType*) are types of fields of *DeptType*. That apparent mutual recursion causes no problems because the references are by pointers, rather than physical presence, exactly as we used virtual record pointers in the hierarchical model to represent many-many relationships, e.g., in Figure 2.22.

The last feature of our YVCB example that we need to incorporate is suppliers and the prices of the items they sell. There, we need a type representing item-price pairs, analogous to the item-quantity pairs we used earlier. The entire definition of types for our example is given in Figure 2.27.

```
ItemType = RECORDOF(name:string, I#:int)

IQType = RECORDOF(item:ItemType, quantity:int)

OrderType = RECORDOF(O#:int, includes:SETOF(IQType))

CustType = RECORDOF(name:string, addr:string,
    balance:int, orders:SETOF(OrderType))

DeptType = RECORDOF(name:string, dept#:int,
    emps:SETOF(EmpType), mgr:EmpType,
    items:SETOF(ItemType))

EmpType = RECORDOF(name:string,
    salary:int, dept:DeptType)

IPType = RECORDOF(item:ItemType, price:int)

SupType = RECORDOF(name:string, addr:string,
    supplies:SETOF(IPType))
```

**Figure 2.27** Object types for the YVCB database.

The database scheme in Figure 2.27 is similar to, but not identical to the scheme of Figure 2.26. For example, Figure 2.27 includes a pathway from employees to their departments, since the field *dept* of *EmpType* is a pointer to the department. However, in Figure 2.27 we do not have a way to get from items to their orders or suppliers. There is nothing inherent in either model that forces these structures. We could just as well chosen to add a virtual pointer child of EMPS in Figure 2.26 that gave the department of the employee, and in Figure 2.27 we could have added the additional pointers to item records by declaring

```
ItemType = RECORDOF(name:string, I#:int,
       sups:SETOF(SupType), orders:SETOF(OrderType))
```

An additional difference between the two schemes is that in Figure 2.27, the manager of the department is an object, not a set, and therefore there can be only one manager of a department. However, in Figure 2.26, there could, in principle, be more than one manager for a department. □

## Classes and Methods

An object-oriented data model is not limited to the notion of an object type. The basic notion is really the *class*, which is an object type for the underlying data structure, and a set of *methods*, which are operations to be performed on the objects with the object-structure of that class.[12]

For example, we could construct a class of all objects with the structure of *EmpType* of Figure 2.27. For this class we might create a set of methods like those in Figure 2.28. In practice, there would probably be many more methods, since each field access must be performed by a declared method.

```
GetName:
    return(name)

Raise(X):
    salary := salary + X
```

**Figure 2.28**  Example methods.

## Class Hierarchies

Another essential ingredient in the object model is the notion of subclasses and hierarchies of classes, a formalization of "isa" relationships. There are two common approaches to the definition of class hierarchies.

1.  In addition to record and set constructors for types, allow a third constructor, *type union*. Objects of type $\cup(T_1, T_2)$ are either type $T_1$ objects or type $T_2$ objects.
2.  Define a notion of *subtype* for given types.

The first approach is used in programming languages like C and Pascal. In object-oriented database systems, it is preferable to use the second approach, because

---

[12] This book also uses the term "method" to refer to the body of an algorithm. The meanings are not the same, but not altogether unrelated either. We trust no confusion will result.

a)　It does not allow the union of unrelated types to be considered a type, a capability that is useful in programming languages when defining data structures, but is counterproductive when trying to develop a meaningful database scheme.

b)　It extends naturally from object structures to classes, i.e., from types to types with methods.

Suppose we have a class $C$, and we wish to define a subclass $D$. We begin with the same object structure for $D$ as for $C$, and with the same methods for $D$ as for $C$. We may then modify the class $D$ as follows.

1.　If the structure for $C$ is a record type, i.e., of the form

RECORDOF$(T_1, \ldots, T_k)$

then we may add additional components to the record structure.

2.　We may create new methods that apply only to subclass $D$.

3.　We may redefine methods of class $C$ to have a new meaning in $D$.

**Example 2.32:** Following our example in Figure 2.27, it would be natural to define $MgrType$ as a subclass of $EmpType$. We might give $MgrType$ the additional field $rank$, so the structure for $MgrType$ would be

```
MgrType = RECORDOF(name:string, salary:int,
        dept:DeptType, rank:int)
```

We might also create a method for $MgrType$ that returned the rank. We could even create a method for $MgrType$ that returned the department. If this method were not defined for the class of employees, then we could not use it on objects that were not of the manager class, even though the method "made sense," since all employee objects have a $dept$ field.

Notice that each employee, whether or not a manager, corresponds to exactly one object of class $EmpType$. If the employee happens to be a manager, then that object has extra fields and methods, but there are not two objects for this employee. □

### Operations in the Object Model

Methods, being arbitrary procedures, can perform any operation on data whatsoever. However, in order to access data efficiently, it is useful to limit the operations that may be performed to something like what is possible in the hierarchical model. It is essential to allow navigation from an object $O$ to the objects pointed to by fields of $O$; this operation corresponds to movement from parent to child, or along a pointer in a virtual field in the hierarchical model. It is also very useful to allow selection, as in the relational model, on fields that are sets of objects. Thus, we can navigate from an object $O$ to a designated subset of the objects found in some set-valued field of $O$.

In Chapter 5, we shall discuss OPAL, a language whose data model includes the features discussed in this section, as well as some generalizations. We shall see that OPAL allows arbitrary code in methods, but distinguishes between database objects and user objects. The former must be accessed only in limited ways, as outlined above, if access is to be efficient. User objects can be manipulated by arbitrary methods. In essence, the OPAL language serves as both the DML (when manipulating database objects) and as the host language (when manipulating user objects). As we discussed in Section 1.5, this integration of the DML and host language is one of the elements that give object-oriented languages like OPAL their power.

### Representing Entity-Relationship Diagrams in the Object Model

We mentioned above that the object model embeds the hierarchical model, in the sense that given any hierarchical scheme, one can mimic it in the object model by regarding children of a node $n$ (including children that are virtual record types) in a hierarchical scheme as fields in an object structure corresponding to $n$. The object structures for the children of $n$ have their children as fields, and so on. Thus, the object model can express whatever the entity-relationship model can express, at least in principle; as we saw in Section 2.6, direct constructions of hierarchies from entity-relationship diagrams, via networks, often present the user with awkward access paths, in which the information of the original entity-relationship diagram is present but not efficiently accessible. We shall leave as an exercise a translation from entity-relationship diagrams, networks, or hierarchies that makes the information of those schemes easily accessible in the object structures.

### EXERCISES

2.1: Many ordinary programming languages can be viewed as based on a particular data model. For example SNOBOL can be said to use a character string model of data. Can you think of any other programming languages that use a particular data model? What data models do they use? Are any of them well suited to database implementation?

2.2: Use the entity-relationship model to describe the data connected with an organization with which you are familiar, such as a school or business.

2.3: Give an entity-relationship diagram for a database showing fatherhood, motherhood, and spouse relationships among men and women.

2.4: Convert your answer to Exercise 2.3 into database schemes in the following models: (a) relational (b) network (c) hierarchical (d) object model (as in Section 2.7).

2.5: The *beer drinkers database* consists of information about drinkers, beers, and bars, telling

*i)*   Which drinkers like which beers.

*ii)*  Which drinkers frequent which bars.

*iii)* Which bars serve which beers.

Represent the scheme for the beer drinkers database in the (a) entity-relationship (b) relational (c) network (d) hierarchical (e) object models.

2.6: In Figure 2.29 we see the entity-relationship diagram of an insurance company. The keys for EMPLOYEES and POLICIES are EMP# and P#, respectively; SALESMEN are identified by their **isa** relationship to EMPLOYEES. Represent this diagram in the (a) relational (b) network (c) hierarchical (d) object models.

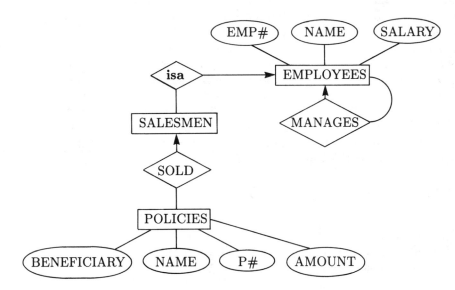

**Figure 2.29**  An insurance company database.

2.7: Figure 2.30 shows a genealogy database, with key attributes NAME and LIC#. The intuition behind the diagram is that a marriage consists of two people, and each person is the child of a marriage, i.e., the marriage of his mother and father. Represent this diagram in the (a) relational (b) network (c) hierarchical (d) object models.

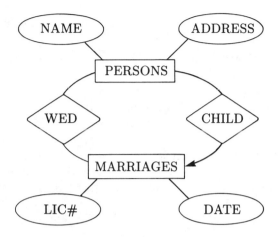

**Figure 2.30** A genealogy database.

2.8: The recipe for *moo shoo roe* includes bamboo shoots, sliced pork, wood ears, golden needles, and assorted vegetables. *Hot and sour soup* is made from wood ears, bean curd, and golden needles, while *family style bean curd* is made from bean curd, sliced pork, and assorted vegetables.

a)  Suppose we wish to store this information in a relation

   RECIPE(DISH, INGREDIENT)

   Show the current value of the relation as a table (use suitable abbreviations for the dishes and ingredients).

b)  Suppose we wish to represent the above information as a network with record types DISH, INGREDIENT and DUMMY, where a DUMMY record represents a pair consisting of one ingredient for one dish. Suppose also that there are links USES from DUMMY to DISH and PART_OF from DUMMY to INGREDIENT. Draw the INGREDIENT, DISH, and DUMMY record occurrences and represent the links USES and PART_OF for this database instance.

2.9: An "adventure" game is based on a map with a set of nodes representing locations. There is a set of directions (which you should not assume is limited to N, E, S, and W; there could be NE, UP, and so on). Given any node $n$ and any direction $d$, there is at most one other node that one reaches by going in direction $d$ from $n$.

a)  Give an entity-relationship diagram representing the map. Indicate the functionality of relationships.

b)  Design a network scheme for maps. Avoid redundancy whenever possible.

c)   Convert your network to a hierarchy using the algorithm of Figure
     2.17, but with the *BUILD* procedure of Figure 2.20.

d)   Does your answer to (c) allow you to find the next node, given a node
     and a direction, efficiently? If not, find another hierarchy that does.

* 2.10: Consider the entity-relationship diagram of Figure 2.31. The intent is that
   PART_OF is a ternary relationship among PARTS, PARTS, and QUAN-
   TITY, with $(p, s, q)$ in the relationship if and only if part $s$ appears $q \geq 1$
   times as a subpart of part $p$. It is to be expected that a given part appears in both the first and second components of this relationship; i.e., a
   subpart may itself have subparts. Note: since the entity set QUANTITY
   has only one attribute, we conventionally show this entity set as if it were
   an attribute of PART_OF.

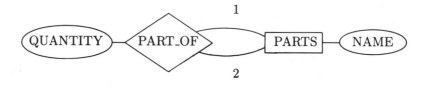

**Figure 2.31**  Part hierarchy database.

We wish to design database schemes in various data models that represent
the information in Figure 2.31. It is desired that the scheme avoids redundancy and that it is possible to answer efficiently the following two types
of queries.

*i*)   Given a part, find its subparts and the quantity of each (no recursion
      is implied; just find the immediate subparts).

*ii*)  Given a part, find all the parts of which it is a subpart.

Design suitable schemes in the (a) relational (b) network (c) hierarchical
(d) object models.

* 2.11: Suppose we wish to maintain a database of students, the courses they have
   taken, and the grades they got in these courses. Also, for each student, we
   want to record his name and address; for each course we record the course
   name and the department that offers it. We could represent the scheme in
   various models, and we have several options in each model. Some of those
   schemes will have certain undesirable properties, among which are

A)   The inability to determine, given a student, what courses he has taken,
     without examining a large fraction of the database.

B)   The inability to determine, given a course, what students have taken
     it, without examining a large fraction of the database.

C) The inability to determine, by any means, the grade a given student received in a given course.

D) Redundancy, such as the repetition of name-department facts for courses, student-course-grade facts, or name-address facts for students.

Below are several suggested schemes. For each indicate which subset of $\{A, B, C, D\}$ the scheme suffers from.

a) The relation scheme

(COURSE, DEPT, STUDENT, ADDR, GRADE)

with indices on STUDENT and COURSE that let us find the tuples for a given student or a given course without looking at other tuples.

b) The relation schemes (COURSE, DEPT, GRADE) and

(COURSE, STUDENT, ADDR)

with an index on course in each relation.

c) A network with logical record types COURSE(NAME, DEPT), giving a course name and its department, and

SAG(NAME, ADDR, GRADE)

giving the name of a student, his address, and a grade. The network has link CSG from SAG to COURSE, with the intent that a COURSE record owns a set of SAG records $(s, a, g)$, one for each student $s$ that took the course; $a$ is the student's address and $g$ is the grade he got in the course.

d) The hierarchy of Figure 2.32(a).

e) The hierarchy of Figure 2.32(b).

f) The object model scheme that has an object of type SETOF($Ctype$) to represent courses and an object of type SETOF($Stype$) to represent students. These types are defined by:

```
Ctype = RECORDOF(name:string, students:SETOF(Stype))
Stype = RECORDOF(name:string, transcript:Ttype)
Ttype = SETOF(RECORDOF(course:Ctype, grade:string))
```

* 2.12: We mentioned in Section 2.4 that two tables represent the same relation if one can be converted to the other by permuting rows and/or columns, provided the attribute heading a column moves along with the column. If a relation has a scheme with $m$ attributes and the relation has $n$ tuples, how many tables represent this relation?

2.13: Let $R$ and $S$ be the relations shown in Figure 2.33. Compute

a) $R \cup S$.

b) $R - S$ (ignore attribute names in the result of union and difference).

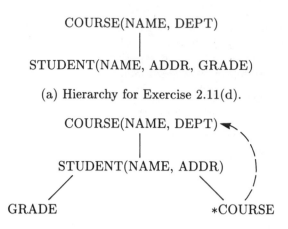

COURSE(NAME, DEPT)

|

STUDENT(NAME, ADDR, GRADE)

(a) Hierarchy for Exercise 2.11(d).

COURSE(NAME, DEPT)

|

STUDENT(NAME, ADDR)

GRADE                                            *COURSE

(b) Hierarchy for Exercise 2.11(e).

**Figure 2.32**  Two hierarchies.

c)   $R \bowtie S$.
d)   $\pi_A(R)$.
e)   $\sigma_{A=C}(R \times S)$.
f)   $S \ltimes R$.
g)   $S \div \{b, c\}$ (note $\{b, c\}$ is a unary relation, that is, a relation of arity
     1).
h)   $R \underset{B<C}{\bowtie} S$ (take $<$ to be alphabetic order on letters).

| $A$ | $B$ |
|-----|-----|
| $a$ | $b$ |
| $c$ | $b$ |
| $d$ | $e$ |

| $B$ | $C$ |
|-----|-----|
| $b$ | $c$ |
| $e$ | $a$ |
| $b$ | $d$ |

(a) $R$                                    (b) $S$

**Figure 2.33**  Example relations.

* 2.14: The *transitive closure* of a binary relation $R$, denoted $R^+$, is the set of
  pairs $(a, b)$ such that for some sequence $c_1, c_2, \ldots, c_n$:
  i)    $c_1 = a$.
  ii)   $c_n = b$.
  iii)  for $i = 1, 2, \ldots, n - 1$, we have $(c_i, c_{i+1})$ in $R$.

Prove that there is no expression of relational algebra equivalent to the transitive closure operation on finite relations. Note this result is easy for infinite relations, if we use the compactness theorem of first-order logic.

* 2.15: Show that the five relational algebra operators (union, difference, selection, projection, and Cartesian product) are *independent*, meaning that none can be expressed as a formula involving only the other four operators. *Hint:* For each operator you need to discover a property that is not possessed by any expression in the other four operators. For example, to show independence of union, suppose there were an expression $E(R, S)$ that used only difference, selection, projection, and product, but was equal to $R \cup S$ for any $R$ and $S$. Let $R_0$ consist of the single tuple $(a, b)$ and $S_0$ of the single tuple $(c, d)$, where $a, b, c$, and $d$ do not appear as constants in $E$. Show by induction on the number of operators used in any subexpression $F$ of $E$ that the relation that is the value of $F(R_0, S_0)$ cannot have a component in which one tuple has $a$ and another tuple has $c$. Since $R_0 \cup S_0$ has such a component, it follows that $E(R_0, S_0) \neq R_0 \cup S_0$.

* 2.16: Prove the following algebraic identities. In each case, assume the set-of-mappings viewpoint, in which columns of all relations have attribute names.

a)  $R \bowtie S = S \bowtie R$ (Theorem 2.2(b)).

b)  $\sigma_{F_1}\big(\sigma_{F_2}(R)\big) = \sigma_{F_1 \wedge F_2}(R)$.

c)  $\sigma_F(R \times S) = \big(\sigma_F(R) \times S\big)$, provided that condition $F$ mentions only attributes in the scheme for $R$.

d)  $\sigma_F\big(\pi_S(R)\big) = \pi_S\big(\sigma_F(R)\big)$, provided that $F$ mentions only attributes in the set $S$.

* 2.17: Show that, in the set-of-lists viewpoint,

$$R \underset{i\theta_1 j}{\bowtie} (S \underset{k\theta_2 l}{\bowtie} T) = (R \underset{i\theta_1 j}{\bowtie} S) \underset{(r+k)\theta_2 l}{\bowtie} T$$

where $r$ is the arity of $R$ and $j$ is at most the arity of $S$.

* 2.18: We defined the semijoin $R \ltimes S$ to be $\pi_R(R \bowtie S)$. Prove that $R \ltimes S$ can also be computed by the expression $R \bowtie \big(\pi_{R \cap S}(S)\big)$.

2.19: In relational algebra, the empty relation, $\emptyset$, and the relation $\{\epsilon\}$, which is the set containing only the empty tuple (tuple with no components), act very much like the constants 0 and 1, respectively, in ordinary arithmetic. Show the following laws.

a)  $R \cup \emptyset = \emptyset \cup R = R$.

b)  $R \times \emptyset = \emptyset \times R = \emptyset$.

c)  $R \times \{\epsilon\} = \{\epsilon\} \times R = R$.

d)  $\pi_\lambda(R)$ is $\{\epsilon\}$ if $R \neq \emptyset$ and is $\emptyset$ if $R = \emptyset$. Here, $\lambda$ stands for the empty list of attributes.

* 2.20: Show how every (a) network scheme and (b) hierarchical scheme can be translated into a collection of type definitions in the object model of Section 2.7, in such a way that traversing any link (in the network), or parent-to-child or virtual pointer (in the hierarchy) can be mimicked by following pointers in the fields of objects.
* 2.21: Show how every object model scheme can be expressed as an entity-relationship diagram.

## BIBLIOGRAPHIC NOTES

At an early time in the development of database systems, there was an established view that there were three important data models: relational, network, and hierarchical. This perspective is found in Rustin [1974], Sibley [1976], and the earliest edition of Date [1986], published in 1973; it is hard to support this view currently, although these models still have great influence. Kerschberg, Klug, and Tsichritzis [1977], Tsichritzis and Lochovsky [1982], and Brodie, Mylopoulos, and Schmidt [1984] survey the variety of data models that exist.

Bachman [1969] is an influential, early article proposing a data model, now called "Bachman diagrams." CODASYL [1971] is the accepted origin of the network model, and Chen [1976] is the original paper on the entity-relationship model.

### The Relational Model

The fundamental paper on the relational model, including the key issues of relational algebra and relational database design (to be discussed in Chapter 7), is Codd [1970].

There are a number of earlier or contemporary papers that contain some ideas of the relational model and/or relational algebra. The paper by Bosak et al. [1962] contains an algebra of files with some similarity to relational algebra. Kuhns [1967], Levien and Maron [1967], and Levien [1969] describe systems with relational underpinnings. The paper by Childs [1968] also contains a discussion of relations as a data model, while Filliat and Kranning [1970] describe an algebra similar to relational algebra.

### Extensions to the Relational Model

There is a spectrum of attempts to "improve" the relational model, ranging from introduction of null values, through structures that are closer to object-oriented models than they are to the value-oriented relational model.

Attempts to formalize operations on relations with null values have been made by Codd [1975], Lacroix and Pirotte [1976], Vassiliou [1979, 1980], Lipski [1981], Zaniolo [1984], Imielinski and Lipski [1984], Imielinski [1986], Vardi [1986], and Reiter [1986].

Some languages more powerful than relational algebra, for use with the relational model, have been considered by Aho and Ullman [1979], Cooper [1980], and Chandra and Harel [1980, 1982, 1985]. The complexity of such languages, i.e., the speed with which arbitrary queries can be answered, is discussed by Vardi [1982, 1985].

Some early attempts to enhance the relational model involve providing "semantics" by specializing the roles of different relations. Such papers include Schmid and Swenson [1970], Furtado [1979], Codd [1979], Sclore [1979], and Wiederhold and El Masri [1980].

## Object-Oriented Models

There is a large family of "semantic" data models that support object-identity; some of them also involve query languages with value-oriented features. Hull and King [1987] is a survey of such models. The semantic model of Hammer and McLeod [1981] and the functional model of Shipman [1981] are early efforts in this direction. More recent efforts are found in Abiteboul and Hull [1983], Heiler and Rosenthal [1985] and Beech [1987].

The paper by Bancilhon [1986] is an attempt to integrate an object-oriented data model with logic programming, but although it supports abstract data types, it finesses object-identity.

## Complex Objects

The fundamental paper on complex objects, built from aggregation (record formation) and generalization (type hierarchies) is Smith and Smith [1977].

Notations for complex objects have been developed in Hull and Yap [1984], Kuper and Vardi [1984, 1985], Zaniolo [1985], Bancilhon and Koshafian [1986], and Abiteboul and Grumbach [1987].

Minsky and Rozenshtein [1987] present a scheme for defining class hierarchies, including collections of classes that do not form a tree, but rather a class can have several incomparable superclasses.

There is also a family of papers that build complex objects in a value-oriented context, chiefly by allowing attributes of relations to have types with structure. These are called "non-first-normal-form" relations, following Codd [1970], who called a relation "in first-normal-form" if the types of attributes were elementary types, e.g., integers. Papers in this class include Jaeschke and Scheck [1982], Fischer and Van Gucht [1984], Roth, Korth, and Silberschatz [1984], Ozsoyoglu and Yuan [1985], and Van Gucht and Fischer [1986].

## Notes on Exercises

A solution to Exercise 2.14 can be found in Aho and Ullman [1979]. A result on operator independence similar to Exercise 2.15 was proved by Beck [1978].

# CHAPTER 3

Logic
as a
Data Model

We now begin a study of first-order (predicate) logic as a way to represent "knowledge" and as a language for expressing operations on relations. There is a hierarchy of data models, each with a notion of data like that of the relational model, but with progressively more powerful, logic-based languages for expressing the permitted operations on data. The simplest model, called "datalog," is introduced in Section 3.2. There and in Sections 3.3–3.5 we show how to implement this language as a sequence of steps in relational algebra. Section 3.6 introduces an extended form of datalog, in which the negation operator can be used. The extension that includes function symbols in arguments, as in Example 1.10, is deferred to Chapter 12 (Volume II).

In Section 3.7 we relate the expressive power of datalog to the power of relational algebra. The next two sections discuss two restricted forms of datalog, called "domain relational calculus" and "tuple relational calculus," that are equivalent in power to relational algebra and form the basis for most commercial query languages in relational systems. Finally, Section 3.10 mentions the "closed world assumption," which justifies some of the decisions we make about how logical rules relate to database operations.

## 3.1 THE MEANING OF LOGICAL RULES

Let us recall our informal introduction to if $\cdots$ then logical rules in Section 1.6. For example, we discussed the pair of rules

```
(1) boss(E,M) :- manages(E,M).
(2) boss(E,M) :- boss(E,N) & manages(N,M).
```

in Example 1.12. There we attributed an intuitive meaning to these rules, which is that whenever we substitute constants for the variables $E$, $N$, and $M$, if the substitution makes the right side true, then the left side must also be true. In general, rules define the true instances of certain predicates, *boss* in this case, in terms of certain other predicates that are defined by database relations, e.g., *manages*.

There are three alternative ways to define the "meaning" of rules. In simple cases, such as the one above, all these methods yield the same answer. As we permit more complicated kinds of logical rules, we are faced with different approaches that result in different answers, because logical rules, being declarative in nature, only state properties of the intended answer. In hard cases, there is no guarantee that a unique answer is defined, or that there is a reasonable way to turn the declarative program into a sequence of steps that compute the answer.

## Proof-Theoretic Interpretation of Rules

The first of the three interpretations we can give to logical rules is that of axioms to be used in a proof. That is, from the facts in the database, we see what other facts can be proved using the rules in all possible ways. This interpretation is the one we gave to the rules in Example 1.12, where we showed that the *boss* facts that could be proved from the rules (1) and (2) above, plus a given set of *manages* facts were exactly what one would expect if "boss" were given the interpretation "somewhere above on the management hierarchy."

In simple cases like Example 1.12, where all the axioms are if $\cdots$ then rules, and there are no negations in the rules or the facts, then it is known that all facts derivable using the rules are derivable by applying the rules as we did in that example. That is, we use the rules only by substituting proved or given facts in the right side and thereby proving the resulting fact on the left.[1] It turns out that when there are negations, the set of provable facts often is not what we intuitively want as a meaning for the logical rules anyway. Thus, we shall here define the "proof-theoretic meaning" of a collection of rules to be the set of facts derivable from given, or database facts, using the rules in the "forward" direction only, that is, by inferring left sides (consequents, or conclusions) from right sides (antecedents or hypotheses).

## Model-Theoretic Interpretation of Rules

In this viewpoint, we see rules as defining possible worlds or "models." An *interpretation* of a collection of predicates assigns truth or falsehood to every possible instance of those predicates, where the predicates' arguments are chosen from some infinite domain of constants. Usually, an interpretation is

---

[1] Note that if there are negations in our axioms or facts, this statement is false. For example, if we have rule $q :\text{-} p$ and the negative fact $\neg q$, we can derive $\neg p$ by applying the rule "backwards, i.e., given that the left side is false we can conclude that the right side is false.

represented by its set of true instances. To be a *model* of a set of rules, an interpretation must make the rules true, no matter what assignment of values from the domain is made for the variables in each rule.

**Example 3.1:** Consider the rules

   (1)  p(X)  :- q(X).
   (2)  q(X)  :- r(X).

and suppose the domain of interest is the integers. These rules say that whenever $r$ is true of a certain integer then $q$ is also true, and whenever $q$ is true, $p$ is true as well.

One possible model, which we call $M_1$, makes $r(1)$, $q(1)$, $p(1)$, $q(2)$, $p(2)$, and $p(3)$ true, and makes $p$, $q$, and $r$ false for all other arguments. To see that $M_1$ is a model, note that when we substitute $X = 1$ in rule (1), both the antecedent and consequent become true, so the statement "if $q(1)$ then $p(1)$" is true. Likewise, when we substitute $X = 1$ in rule (2), both sides are true. When we substitute $X = 2$ in rule (1), again both sides are true, but when we let $X = 2$ in rule (2), the antecedent is false and the consequent true. That is another way of making an if $\cdots$ then statement true, so again rule (2) is satisfied. The same observation applies if we substitute $X = 3$ in rule (1).

When we substitute $X = 3$ in rule (2), or we substitute any value besides 1, 2, or 3 in either rule, we get a situation where both antecedent and consequent are false. Again the if $\cdots$ then statement is made true. Thus whatever substitution we make, the rules are true, and therefore we have a model.

On the other hand, if we make $r(1)$ true and make the three predicates false for all other values, then we do not have a model. The reason is that when we substitute $X = 1$ in rule (2), we have a true antecedent and false consequent; that is the one combination that makes an if $\cdots$ then statement false. $\Box$

When we use rules to define operations on a database, we assume an instance of a database predicate is true if and only if the corresponding relation holds that fact as a tuple. We then try to extend the database to a model on all the predicates, and we may think of any such model as a possible world defined by the rules. For example, we might assume that $r$ is a database predicate in Example 3.1, while $p$ and $q$ are defined in terms of $r$. We might also suppose that $r(1)$ is true, while $r(X)$ is false for $X \neq 1$. Then the model

$$M_1 = \{r(1), q(1), p(1), q(2), p(2), p(3)\}$$

described in Example 3.1, is a possible world consistent with this database.

However, there is another consistent model $M_2 = \{r(1), q(1), p(1)\}$, in which $p(1)$, $q(1)$, and $r(1)$ are true and everything else is false; in fact there are an infinite number of models consistent with a database that has only $r(1)$ true. $M_2$ is special, because it is a *minimal model*; i.e., we cannot make any true fact false and still have a model consistent with the database $\{r(1)\}$. Note that $M_1$ does not have this property. For example, we could change $p(3)$ from true to false in $M_1$ and still have a model.

Moreover, $M_2$ is the unique minimal model consistent with the database $\{r(1)\}$. This model also happens to be what we get if we use the proof-theoretic definition of meaning for rules. That is, starting with the rules (1) and (2) of Example 3.1 and the one fact $r(1)$, we can prove $q(1)$, $p(1)$, and no other predicate instances. These happy coincidences will be seen true for "datalog" rules in general, as long as they do not involve negation. When negation is allowed as an operator, we shall see in Section 3.6, then there need not be a unique minimal model, and none of the minimal models necessarily corresponds to the set of facts that we can prove using the rules. For some rules we can get around this problem by defining a preferred minimal model, but in general, the issue of what sufficiently complicated rules mean gets murky very quickly.

## Computational Definitions of Meaning

The third way to define the meaning of logical rules is to provide an algorithm for "executing" them to tell whether a potential fact (predicate with constants for its arguments) is true or false. For example, Prolog defines the meaning of rules this way, using a particular algorithm that involves searching for proofs of the potential fact. Unfortunately, the set of facts for which Prolog finds a proof this way is not necessarily the same as the set of all facts for which a proof exists. Neither is the set of facts Prolog finds true necessarily a model. However, in many common cases, Prolog will succeed in producing the unique minimal model for a set of rules when those rules are run as a Prolog program.

In this book, we shall take another approach to treating rules as computation. We shall translate rules into sequences of operations in relational algebra, and for datalog rules without negation, we can show that the program so produced always computes the unique minimal model and (therefore) the set of facts that can be proved from the database. When negation is allowed, we shall consider only a limited case called "stratified" negation, and then we shall show that what our program produces is a minimal model, although it is not necessarily the only minimal model. There is, however, some justification for selecting our minimal model from among all possible minimal models.

## Comparison of "Meanings"

We might naturally ask which is the "best" meaning for a logic program. A logician would not even take seriously the computational meaning of rules, but for those wishing to implement knowledge-base systems, efficient computation is essential. We cannot use logical rules as programs unless we have a way of computing their consequences, and an efficient way of doing so, at that.

On the other hand, a purely operational definition of meaning for rules, "the program means whatever it is that this interpreter I've written does," is not acceptable either. We don't have a preference between the proof-theoretic and model-theoretic meanings, as long as these meanings are reasonably clear to the user of the logic-based language. In practice, it seems that the model-theoretic approach lets us handle more powerful classes of rules than the proof-theoretic approach, although we shall start out with the proof-theoretic meaning in Section 3.3. Whichever meaning we choose, it is essential that we show its equivalence to an appropriate computational meaning.

## 3.2 THE DATALOG DATA MODEL

In this section, we introduce the basic terminology needed to discuss the logic-based data model we call "datalog." The name "datalog" was coined to suggest a version of Prolog suitable for database systems. It differs from Prolog in several respects.

1.  Datalog does not allow function symbols in arguments. For example, the function symbol $s$ used to define addition in Example 1.10 is not permitted in datalog. Rather, datalog allows only variables and constants as arguments of predicates.

2.  The "meaning" of datalog programs follows the model-theoretic point of view discussed in the previous section, or when equivalent, the proof-theoretic approach. Prolog, however, has a computational "meaning," which, as we discussed, can deviate in some cases from either the model-theoretic or proof-theoretic meanings.

The underlying mathematical model of data for datalog is essentially that of the relational model. Predicate symbols in datalog denote relations. However, as in the formal definition of relational algebra, these relations do not have attributes with which to name their columns. Rather they are relations in the set-of-lists sense, where components appear in a fixed order, and reference to a column is only by its position among the arguments of a given predicate symbol. For example, if $p$ is a predicate symbol, then we may refer to $p(X, Y, Z)$, and variable $X$ will denote the first component of some tuple in the relation corresponding to predicate $p$.

### Extensional and Intensional Predicates

Another distinction between the relational and datalog models is that in datalog, there are two ways relations can be defined. A predicate whose relation is stored in the database is called an *extensional database* (EDB) relation, while one defined by logical rules is called an *intensional database* (IDB) relation. We assume that each predicate symbol either denotes an EDB relation or an IDB relation, but not both.

In the relational model, all relations are EDB relations. The capability to create views (see Section 1.2) in models like the relational model is somewhat analogous to the ability in datalog to define IDB relations. However, we shall see in Chapter 4 that the view-definition facility in relational DBMS's does not compare in power with logical rules as a definition mechanism.

## Atomic Formulas

Datalog programs are built from *atomic formulas*, which are predicate symbols with a list of arguments, e.g., $p(A_1, \ldots, A_n)$, where $p$ is the predicate symbol. An argument in datalog can be either a variable or a constant. As mentioned in Section 1.6, we use names beginning with lower case letters for constants and predicate names, while using names beginning with upper case letters for variables. We also use numbers as constants. We shall assume that each predicate symbol is associated with a particular number of arguments that it takes, and we may use $p^{(k)}$ to denote a predicate of arity $k$.

An atomic formula denotes a relation; it is the relation of its predicate restricted by

1.  Selecting for equality between a constant and the component or components in which that constant appears, and
2.  Selecting for equality between components that have the same variable.

For example, consider the YVCB database relations of Figure 2.8. The atomic formula

> $customers(joe, Address, Balance)$

represents the relation $\sigma_{\$1=\text{joe}}(\text{CUSTOMERS})$. Atomic formula

> $includes(X, Item, X)$

denotes $\sigma_{\$1=\$3}(\text{INCLUDES})$, that is, the tuples where the order number happens to be equal to the quantity ordered.

Notice that although there are no names for attributes in the datalog model, selecting suggestive variable names like *Address* help remind us what is going on. However, as in relational algebra, we must remember the intuitive meaning of each position in a list of arguments.

## Built-In Predicates

We also construct atomic formulas with the arithmetic comparison predicates, $=$, $\leq$, and so on; these predicates will be referred to as *built-in* predicates. Atomic formulas with built-in predicates will be written in the usual infix notation, e.g., $X < Y$ instead of $<(X, Y)$. Other atomic formulas and their predicates will be referred to as *ordinary* when a distinction needs to be made.

Built-in predicates do not necessarily represent finite relations. We could think of $X < Y$ as representing the relation of all tuples $(x, y)$ such that $x < y$, but this approach is unworkable because this set is infinite, and it is not even clear over what domain $x$ and $y$ should be allowed to range. We shall therefore require that whenever a rule uses an atomic formula with a built-in predicate, any variables in that formula are limited in range by some other atomic formula on the right side of the rule. For example, a variable might be limited by appearing in an atomic formula with an EDB predicate. We shall then find that built-in atomic formulas can be interpreted as selections on a single relation or on the join of relations. The details will be given when we discuss "safe" rules at the end of this section.

### Clauses and Horn Clauses

A *literal* is either an atomic formula or a negated atomic formula; we denote negated atomic formulas by $\neg p(A_1, \ldots, A_n)$ or $\bar{p}(A_1, \ldots, A_n)$. A negated atomic formula is a *negative literal*; one that is not negated is a *positive literal*. A *clause* is a sum (logical OR) of literals. A *Horn clause* is a clause with at most one positive literal. A Horn clause is thus either

1. A single positive literal, e.g., $p(X, Y)$, which we regard as a *fact*,
2. One or more negative literals, with no positive literal, which is an *integrity constraint*, and which will not be considered in our discussion of datalog, or
3. A positive literal and one or more negative literals, which is a *rule*.

The reason Horn clauses of group (3) are considered rules is that they have a natural expression as an inference. That is, the Horn clause

$$\bar{p}_1 \vee \cdots \vee \bar{p}_n \vee q \tag{3.1}$$

is logically equivalent to $p_1 \wedge \cdots \wedge p_n \rightarrow q$. To see why, note that if none of the $p$'s are false, then to make (3.1) true, $q$ is forced to be true. Thus, if $p_1, \ldots, p_n$ are all true (and therefore none of the $\bar{p}$'s are true), $q$ must be true. If at least one of the $p$'s is false, then no constraint is placed on $q$; it could be true or false.

We shall follow Prolog style for expressing Horn clauses, using

$$q \text{ :- } p_1 \text{ \& } \cdots \text{ \& } p_n.$$

for the Horn clause $p_1 \wedge \cdots \wedge p_n \rightarrow q$. We call $q$ the *head* of the rule and $p_1 \& \cdots \& p_n$ the *body*. Each of the $p_i$'s is said to be a *subgoal*. A collection of Horn clauses is termed a *logic program*.

When writing Horn clauses as implications, either in the style

$$p_1 \wedge \cdots \wedge p_n \rightarrow q$$

or in the Prolog style, variables appearing only in the body may be regarded as quantified existentially within the body, while other variables are universally quantified over the entire rule. For example, rule (1) in Figure 3.1 says "for all

$X$ and $Y$, $X$ is a sibling of $Y$ if there exists $Z$ such that $Z$ is a parent of both $X$ and $Y$, and $X$ and $Y$ are not the same individual." However, it is also correct and logically equivalent, to regard all the variables as universally quantified for the entire rule. Thus, rule (1) of Figure 3.1 may also be read as "for all $X$, $Y$, and $Z$, if $Z$ is a parent of both $X$ and $Y$, and $X$ is not $Y$, then $X$ is a sibling of $Y$."

(1)  `sibling(X,Y) :- parent(X,Z) & parent(Y,Z) & X≠Y.`

(2)  `cousin(X,Y) :- parent(X,Xp) & parent(Y,Yp) &`
     `              sibling(Xp,Yp).`

(3)  `cousin(X,Y) :- parent(X,Xp) & parent(Y,Yp) &`
     `              cousin(Xp,Yp).`

(4)  `related(X,Y) :- sibling(X,Y).`

(5)  `related(X,Y) :- related(X,Z) & parent(Y,Z).`

(6)  `related(X,Y) :- related(Z,Y) & parent(X,Z).`

**Figure 3.1** Example logic program.

### Dependency Graphs and Recursion

We frequently need to discuss the way predicates in a logic program depend on one another. To do so, we draw a *dependency graph*, whose nodes are the ordinary predicates. There is an arc from predicate $p$ to predicate $q$ if there is a rule with a subgoal whose predicate is $p$ and with a head whose predicate is $q$. A logic program is *recursive* if its dependency graph has one or more cycles. Note that a cycle consisting of one arc from a node to itself makes the program recursive, and in fact, one-node cycles are more common than multinode cycles.

All the predicates that are on one or more cycles are said to be *recursive predicates*. A logic program with an acyclic dependency graph is *nonrecursive*. Clearly, all predicates in a nonrecursive program are nonrecursive; we also call a predicate *nonrecursive* if it is in a recursive program but is not part of any cycle in the dependency graph.

**Example 3.2:** Suppose *parent* is an EDB relation, and *parent*$(C, P)$ means that $P$ is a parent of $C$. We define IDB relations *sibling*, *cousin*, and *related* in Figure 3.1. Siblings are persons with a common parent, but we must rule out the possibility that *sibling*$(a, a)$ is true for any individual $a$, which explains the subgoal $X \neq Y$ in rule (1). Cousins are people with a common ancestor who is the same number of generations away from each, and at least two generations away, i.e., they cannot be siblings or be the same individual.[2]

Rules (4)–(6) define $X$ and $Y$ to be "related" if they have a common ancestor that is neither $X$ nor $Y$. That is, rule (4) says that siblings are related in this sense, since their common parent is a common ancestor that cannot be either of the siblings themselves. Then rules (5) and (6) tell us that related persons are also related to each other's descendants.

The dependency graph for Figure 3.1 is shown in Figure 3.2. For example, rule (1) induces an arc from *parent* to *sibling*. Note that we do not use nodes for the built-in predicates like $\neq$. Rule (2) justifies the existence of an arc from *parent* to *cousin* and an arc from *sibling* to *cousin*. Rule (3) justifies arcs from *parent* to *cousin* and from *cousin* to *cousin*. The latter arc is a cycle and indicates that the logic program of Figure 3.1 is recursive. The remaining arcs are justified by rules (4)–(6).

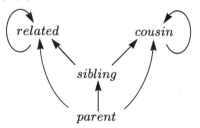

**Figure 3.2**  Dependency graph for Figure 3.1.

In Figure 3.2, there are two cycles, one involving only *cousin* and the other involving only *related*. Thus, these predicates are recursive, and the predicates *parent* and *sibling* are nonrecursive. Of course, every EDB relation, such as *parent*, must be nonrecursive. In fact, the EDB predicates are exactly those whose nodes have no incoming arc, which implies they cannot be recursive. The program of Figure 3.1 is recursive, because it has some recursive predicates. □

## Safe Rules

There are constraints that must be placed on the form of datalog rules if they are to make sense as operations on finite relations. One source of infiniteness is a variable that appears only in a built-in predicate, as we mentioned earlier. Another is a variable that appears only in the head of a rule. The following example illustrates the problems.

---

[2] Strictly speaking, rules (2) and (3) define a person to be his own cousin if his parents are brother and sister. Perhaps that's right, but if we're worried, we can add a subgoal $X \neq Y$ to the rules for *cousin*. Similarly, *related*($a, a$) can be true if certain unusual matings occur.

**Example 3.3:** The rule

```
biggerThan(X,Y) :- X>Y.
```

defines an infinite relation, if $X$ and $Y$ are allowed to range over the integers, or any infinite set. The rule

```
loves(X,Y) :- lover(Y).
```

i.e., "all the world loves a lover," also defines an infinite set of pairs $loves(X, Y)$, even if the relation *lover* is a finite set, as long as the first argument of *loves* ranges over an infinite set. $\square$

One simple approach to avoiding rules that create infinite relations from finite ones is to insist that each variable appearing in the rule be "limited." The intuitive idea is that we assume all the ordinary (non-built-in) predicates appearing in the body correspond to finite relations. After making that assumption, we need assurance that for each variable $X$, there is a finite set of values $V_X$ such that in any assignment of values to the variables that makes the body true, the value of $X$ must come from $V_X$. We formally define *limited* variables for a given rule as follows.

1. Any variable that appears as an argument in an ordinary predicate of the body is limited.
2. Any variable $X$ that appears in a subgoal $X = a$ or $a = X$, where $a$ is a constant, is limited.
3. Variable $X$ is limited if it appears in a subgoal $X = Y$ or $Y = X$, where $Y$ is a variable already known to be limited.

Note that (1) and (2) form a basis for the definition, and (3) can be applied repeatedly to discover more limited variables.

We define a rule to be *safe* if all its variables are limited. The critical issue is whether variables appearing in the head and variables appearing in subgoals with built-in predicates either appear in some subgoal with an ordinary predicate, are equated to constants, or are equated to other limited variables through the recursive use of (3).

**Example 3.4:** The first rule of Example 3.3 is not safe because none of its variables are limited. The second is not safe because, although $Y$ is limited by its occurrence in the subgoal $lover(Y)$, there is no way to limit $X$. In general, a variable appearing only in the head of a rule cannot be limited, so its rule cannot be safe.

Rule (1) of Figure 3.1 is safe because $X$, $Y$, and $Z$ are limited by their occurrences in the two *parent* subgoals. Note that the built-in predicate $X \neq Y$ cannot result in an infinite number of siblings, because $X$ and $Y$ are already limited to be individuals that appear in the first component of the *parent* relation. All the other rules in Figure 3.1 are likewise safe.

For a more complex example, consider the rule

```
p(X,Y) :- q(X,Z) & W=a & Y=W.
```

$X$ and $Z$ are limited by rule (1), because of the first subgoal in the body. $W$ is limited by the rule (2), because of the second subgoal, and therefore (3) tells us $Y$ is limited because of the third subgoal. As all variables are limited, the rule is safe. Note that it computes $p$ to be the relation $\pi_1(q) \times \{a\}$, which is surely finite if the relation corresponding to $q$ is finite. $\square$

## 3.3 EVALUATING NONRECURSIVE RULES

From here, until Section 3.6, we shall deal with only safe datalog rules that have no negation, and the term "datalog" will now refer only to rules in this class. We begin by studying nonrecursive datalog programs. For this simple class (and for the corresponding class of recursive programs as well), all three possible meanings mentioned in Section 3.1 coincide. We shall see that there is a way to convert nonrecursive datalog rules to expressions of relational algebra; these expressions yield relations for the IDB predicates that are at once the unique minimal model of the rules and the set of IDB facts deducible from the rules and the database. In this section we shall begin with the proof-theoretic point of view, but we shall see that the meaning we ascribe to rules is also the unique minimal model for the rules.

If our rules are not recursive, we may order the nodes of the dependency graph $p_1, \ldots, p_n$ so that if there is an arc $p_i \rightarrow p_j$ then $i < j$. Then, we may compute the relation for the predicates of $p_1, \ldots, p_n$ in that order, knowing that when we work on $p_i$ the relations for all predicates that appear in the bodies of the rules for $p_i$ have already been evaluated. The computation of the relation for $p_i$ will be divided into two steps.

1.  For each rule $r$ with $p_i$ at the head, compute the relation corresponding to the body of the rule. This relation has one component for each variable of $r$. To compute the relation for the body of $r$, we essentially take the natural join of the relations corresponding to the various subgoals of $r$, treating the attributes of these relations as the variables appearing in the corresponding positions of the subgoals. Because our rules are nonrecursive, we may assume that relations for the subgoals are already computed.

2.  We compute the relation for $p_i$ itself by, in essence, projecting the relation for each of $p_i$'s rules onto the components corresponding to the variables of the head, and taking the union over all rules with $p_i$ in the head.

In each of these steps, the computation is somewhat more complicated than joins and projections. We must take into account constants appearing as arguments, and we must consider situations in which one variable appears in several arguments of one subgoal or of the head. These details will be covered in Algorithms 3.1 and 3.2, below.

### The Relation Defined by a Rule Body

Our first step is to examine the set of values that we may substitute for the variables of a rule to make the body true. In proofs using the rule, it is exactly these substitutions that let us conclude that the head, with the same substitution, is true. Therefore, we define the *relation for a rule r* to have the scheme $X_1, \ldots, X_m$, where the $X_i$'s are the variables of the body of $r$, in some selected order. We want this relation to have a tuple $(a_1, \ldots, a_m)$ if and only if, when we substitute $a_i$ for $X_i$, $1 \le i \le m$, all of the subgoals become true.

More precisely, suppose that $p_1, \ldots, p_n$ is the list of all predicates appearing in the body of rule $r$, and suppose $P_1, \ldots, P_n$ are relations, where $P_i$ consists of all those tuples $(a_1, \ldots, a_k)$ such that $p(a_1, \ldots, a_k)$ is known to be true. Then a subgoal $S$ of rule $r$ is *made true* by this substitution if the following hold:

i)   If $S$ is an ordinary subgoal, then $S$ becomes $p(b_1, \ldots, b_k)$ under this substitution, and $(b_1, \ldots, b_k)$ is a tuple in the relation $P$ corresponding to $p$.

ii)   If $S$ is a built-in subgoal, then under this substitution $S$ becomes $b\theta c$, and the arithmetic relation $b\theta c$ is true.

**Example 3.5:** The following is an informal example of how relations for rule bodies are constructed; it will be formalized in Algorithm 3.1, to follow. Consider rule (2) from Figure 3.1. Suppose we have relations $P$ and $S$ computed for predicates *parent* and *sibling*, respectively. We may imagine there is one copy of $P$ with attributes $X$ and $Xp$ and another with attributes $Y$ and $Yp$. We suppose the attributes of $S$ are $Xp$ and $Yp$. Then the relation corresponding to the body of rule (2) is

$$R(X, Xp, Y, Yp) = P(X, Xp) \bowtie P(Y, Yp) \bowtie S(Xp, Yp) \qquad (3.2)$$

Recall that by Theorem 2.2, $\bowtie$ is an associative and commutative operator, so the order in which we group the predicates is irrelevant. Also, notice that when taking natural joins, it is important to indicate, as we have done in (3.2), what the attribute name corresponding to each component of each relation is. Finally, we should appreciate the close connection between attribute names for relation schemes and variables in logical rules, which we exploited in (3.2).

By Corollary 2.1, an equivalent way to express the formula (3.2) is by saying that we want a relation $R(X, Xp, Y, Yp)$, consisting of every tuple $(a, b, c, d)$ such that:

1.   $(a, b)$ is in $P$,
2.   $(c, d)$ is in $P$, and
3.   $(b, d)$ is in $S$.

This relation is exactly the set of tuples $(a, b, c, d)$ that, when substituted for $(X, Xp, Y, Yp)$ in that order, make the body of the rule true. Thus, (3.2) is the relation for the body of rule (2) of Figure 3.1.

For another example, consider rule (1) of Figure 3.1. Here, we need to join two copies of $P$ and then select for the arithmetic inequality $X \neq Y$. The algebraic expression for rule (1) is thus

$$Q(X, Y, Z) = \sigma_{X \neq Y}\big(P(X, Z) \bowtie P(Y, Z)\big) \tag{3.3}$$

The relation $Q(X, Y, Z)$ computed by (3.3) consists of all tuples $(x, y, z)$ such that:

1.  $(x, z)$ is in $P$,
2.  $(y, z)$ is in $P$, and
3.  $x \neq y$.

Again, it is easy to see that these tuples $(x, y, z)$ are exactly the ones that make the body of rule (1) true. Thus, (3.3) expresses the relation for the body of rule (1).

Finally, let us examine an abstract example that points out some of the problems we have when computing the relation for the body of a rule. Consider

```
p(X,Y)  :- q(a,X) & r(X,Z,X) & s(Y,Z)
```
(3.4)

Suppose we already have computed relations $Q$, $R$, and $S$ for subgoals $q$, $r$, and $s$, respectively. Since the first subgoal asks for only those tuples of $Q$ that have first component $a$, we need to construct a relation, with attribute $X$, containing only the second components of these tuples. Thus, define relation

$$T(X) = \pi_2\big(\sigma_{\$1=a}(Q)\big)$$

We also must restrict the relation $R$ so that its first and third components, each of which carries variable $X$ in the second subgoal, are equal. Thus define

$$U(X, Z) = \pi_{1,2}\big(\sigma_{\$1=\$3}(R)\big)$$

Then the relation for the body of rule (3.4) is defined by expression:

$$T(X) \bowtie U(X, Z) \bowtie S(Y, Z)$$

This expression defines the set of tuples $(x, y, z)$ that make the body of (3.4) true, i.e., the set of tuples $(x, y, z)$ such that:

1.  $(a, x)$ is in $Q$,
2.  $(x, z, x)$ is in $R$, and
3.  $(y, z)$ is in $S$.

□

We shall now describe how to construct an expression of relational algebra that computes the relation for a rule body.

**Algorithm 3.1:** Computing the Relation for a Rule Body, Using Relational Algebra Operations.

INPUT: The body of a datalog rule $r$, which we shall assume consists of subgoals $S_1, \ldots, S_n$ involving variables $X_1, \ldots, X_m$. For each $S_i = p_i(A_{i1}, \ldots, A_{ik_i})$ with an ordinary predicate, there is a relation $R_i$ already computed, where the $A$'s are arguments, either variables or constants.

OUTPUT: An expression of relational algebra, which we call

$$\text{EVAL-RULE}(r, R_1, \ldots, R_n)$$

that computes from the relations $R_1, \ldots, R_n$[3] a relation $R(X_1, \ldots, X_m)$ with all and only the tuples $(a_1, \ldots, a_m)$ such that, when we substitute $a_j$ for $X_j$, $1 \leq j \leq m$, all the subgoals $S_1, \ldots, S_n$ are made true.

METHOD: The expression is constructed by the following steps.

1.  For each ordinary $S_i$, let $Q_i$ be the expression $\pi_{V_i}\big(\sigma_{F_i}(R_i)\big)$. Here, $V_i$ is a set of components including, for each variable $X$ that appears among the arguments of $S_i$, exactly one component where $X$ appears. Also, $F_i$ is the conjunction (logical AND) of the following conditions:

    a)  If position $k$ of $S_i$ has a constant $a$, then $F_i$ has the term $\$k = a$.

    b)  If positions $k$ and $l$ of $S_i$ both contain the same variable, then $F_i$ has the term $\$k = \$l$.[4]

    As a special case, if $S_i$ is such that there are no terms in $F_i$, e.g., $S_i = p(X, Y)$, then take $F_i$ to be the identically true condition, so $Q_i = R_i$.

2.  For each variable $X$ not found among the ordinary subgoals, compute an expression $D_X$ that produces a unary relation containing all the values that $X$ could possibly have in an assignment that satisfies all the subgoals of rule $r$. Since $r$ is safe, there is some variable $Y$ to which $X$ is equated through a sequence of one or more $=$ subgoals, and $Y$ is limited either by being equated to some constant $a$ in a subgoal or by being an argument of an ordinary subgoal.

    a)  If $Y = a$ is a subgoal, then let $D_X$ be the constant expression $\{a\}$.

    b)  If $Y$ appears as the $j$th argument of ordinary subgoal $S_i$, let $D_X$ be $\pi_j(R_i)$.

---

[3] Technically, not all $n$ relations may be present as arguments, because some of the subgoals may have built-in predicates and thus not have corresponding relations.

[4] It is not necessary to add this term for all possible pairs $k$ and $l$, just for enough pairs that all occurrences of the same variable are forced to be equal. For example, if $X$ appears in positions 2, 5, 9, and 14, it suffices to add terms $\$2 = \$5$, $\$5 = \$9$, and $\$9 = \$14$.

3.  Let $E$ be the natural join of all the $Q_i$'s defined in (1) and the $D_X$'s defined in (2). In this join, we regard $Q_i$ as a relation whose attributes are the variables appearing in $S_i$, and we regard $D_X$ as a relation with attribute $X$.[5]

4.  Let EVAL-RULE$(r, R_1, \ldots, R_n)$ be $\sigma_F(E)$, where $F$ is the conjunction of $X\theta Y$ for each built-in subgoal $X\theta Y$ appearing among $p_1, \ldots, p_n$, and $E$ is the expression constructed in (3). If there are no built-in subgoals, then the desired expression is just $E$. $\square$

    Example 3.5 illustrates the construction of this algorithm. For instance, the expression $T(X) = \pi_2\big(\sigma_{\$1=a}(Q)\big)$ is what we construct by step (1) of Algorithm 3.1 from the first subgoal, $q(a, X)$, of the rule given in (3.4); that is, $T(X)$ in Example 3.5 is $Q_1$ here. Similarly, $U(X, Z) = \pi_{1,2}\big(\sigma_{\$1=\$3}(R)\big)$ in Example 3.5 is $Q_2$, constructed from the second subgoal, $r(X, Z, X)$. $Q_3$, constructed from the third subgoal, $S(Y, Z)$, is $S(Y, Z)$ itself. There are no built-in subgoals, so no extra domains need be constructed in step (2), and no selection is needed in step (4). Thus, the expression $T(X) \bowtie U(X, Z) \bowtie S(Y, Z)$ is the final expression for the body of the rule (3.4). In Example 3.7 we shall give a more extensive example of how EVAL-RULE is computed when there are built-in subgoals.

**Theorem 3.1:** Algorithm 3.1 is correct, in the sense that the relation $R$ produced has all and only those tuples $(a_1, \ldots, a_m)$ such that, when we substitute each $a_j$ for $X_j$, every subgoal $S_i$ is made true.

**Proof:** Suppose $(a_1, \ldots, a_m)$ makes every $S_i$ true. By $(i)$ in the definition of "made true"[6] and step (1) of Algorithm 3.1, there is a tuple $\mu_i$ in $Q_i$ that has $a_j$ in its component for $X_j$, for every variable $X_j$ appearing in subgoal $S_i$. Step (2) tells us there is a (unary) tuple $\nu_{X_i} = a_i$ in $D_{X_i}$, for every variable $X_i$ that appears in no ordinary subgoal. Then step (3) of the algorithm takes the natural join of the $Q_i$'s and $D_X$'s. At each step of the join, the tuples $\mu_i$ agree on any variables in common, so they join together into progressively larger tuples, each of which agrees with $(a_1, \ldots, a_m)$ on the attributes they have in common.

Finally, the join of all the $\mu_i$'s and $\nu$'s is $(a_1, \ldots, a_m)$ itself. Furthermore, by $(ii)$ in the definition of "made true," the tuple $(a_1, \ldots, a_m)$ satisfies condition $F$ in step (4), so Algorithm 3.1 puts $(a_1, \ldots, a_m)$ in relation $R$.

Conversely, suppose $(a_1, \ldots, a_m)$ is put in $R$ by the algorithm. Then this tuple must satisfy $F$ of step (4), and therefore condition $(ii)$ of "made true" is met. Also, $(a_1, \ldots, a_m)$ must be in the relation defined by $E$ of step (3), so each $Q_i$ has a tuple $\mu_i$ whose component for variable $X_j$ has value $a_j$, for each $X_j$ that appears in subgoal $S_i$. An examination of step (1) tells us that the

---

[5]  Since any $X$ for which $D_X$ is constructed cannot be an attribute of any $Q_i$, the natural join really involves the Cartesian product of all the $D_X$'s, if any.

[6]  The formal definition of "made true" appears just before Example 3.5.

only way $\mu_i$ could be in $Q_i$ is if there is a tuple $\rho_i$ in $R_i$ that:

a)  Has constant $a$ in position $k$ if $S_i$ has $a$ in position $k$, and

b)  Has $a_j$ in all positions where $S_i$ has variable $X_j$.

But $p_i(\rho_i)$ is exactly what $S_i$ becomes when we substitute $a_j$ for $X_j$, $1 \le j \le m$. Since $\rho_i$ is in $R_i$, condition $(i)$ of the "made true" definition is satisfied. $\square$

### Rectified Rules

We must now consider how the relations for rule bodies are combined into relations for predicates. As we mentioned, the basic idea is that we consider all the rules with $p$ in the head, compute the relations for these rules, project onto the variables appearing in the heads, and take the union. However, we have trouble when some of the heads with predicate $p$ have constants or repeated variables, e.g., $p(a, X, X)$. Thus, we define the rules for predicate $p$ to be *rectified* if all their heads are identical, and of the form $p(X_1, \ldots, X_k)$ for distinct variables $X_1, \ldots, X_k$.

It is easy to rectify rules; the "trick" is to introduce new variables for each of the arguments of the head predicate, and introduce built-in subgoals into the body to enforce whatever constraints the head predicate formerly enforced through constants and repetitions of variables. Suppose we have a rule $r$ with head $p(Y_1, \ldots, Y_k)$, where the $Y$'s may be variables or constants, with repetitions allowed. We replace the head of $r$ by $p(X_1, \ldots, X_k)$, where the $X$'s are each distinct, new variables, and to $r$ we add the subgoals $X_i = Y_i$ for all $i$. If $Y_i$ is a variable, we may eliminate the subgoal $X_i = Y_i$ and instead substitute $X_i$ for $Y_i$ wherever it is found.[7]

**Example 3.6:** All of the rules in Figure 3.1 are already rectified. For another example, consider the predicate $p$ defined by the rules

```
p(a,X,Y)  :- r(X,Y).
p(X,Y,X)  :- r(Y,X).
```

We rectify these rules by making both heads be $p(U, V, W)$ and adding subgoals as follows.

```
p(U,V,W)  :- r(X,Y) & U=a & V=X & W=Y.
p(U,V,W)  :- r(Y,X) & U=X & V=Y & W=X.
```

If we substitute for $X$ and $Y$ one of the new variables $U$, $V$, or $W$, as appropriate, we get

```
p(U,V,W)  :- r(V,W) & U=a.
p(U,V,W)  :- r(V,U) & W=U.
```

---

[7] Note that when we make such a substitution for $Y_i$, we cannot later make another substitution for the same variable $Y_i$.

That is, in the first rule, $X$ is replaced by $V$ and $Y$ is replaced by $W$, while in the second, $X$ is replaced by $U$ and $Y$ is replaced by $V$. $\square$

**Lemma 3.1:** Suppose $r$ is a rule, and the result of rectifying $r$ is a rule $r'$. Then

a)  If $r$ is safe, so is $r'$.

b)  Rules $r$ and $r'$ are equivalent, in the sense that, given relations for the predicates of their subgoals, there is a substitution for the variables of $r$ that makes all its subgoals true and makes the head become $p(c_1, \ldots, c_n)$ if and only if there is some substitution for the variables of $r'$ that makes the head of $r'$ become $p(c_1, \ldots, c_n)$.

**Proof:** First, assume that when transforming $r$ to $r'$, we do not eliminate any variables by substituting $X$ for $Y$ if $X = Y$ is a subgoal. Then (a) is easy; the variables of $r$ are limited since $r$ is safe, and the introduced variables $X_1, \ldots, X_k$ are limited because they are all equated to variables of $r$.

Part (b) is also straightforward. If an assignment of constants to the variables of $r$ makes the head of $r$, which is $p(Y_1, \ldots, Y_k)$, become $p(a_1, \ldots, a_k)$, then we can find an assignment to the variables of $r'$ that yields the same head. Recall that the head of $r'$ is $p(X_1, \ldots, X_k)$, and the $X$'s are all new variables. Choose the same value for $X_i$ as the given assignment of constants uses for $Y_i$. Then the subgoal $X_i = Y_i$ will be made true, and the head of $r'$ will become $p(a_1, \ldots, a_n)$. Conversely, if an assignment of constants to the variables of $r'$ yields head $p(b_1, \ldots, b_k)$, then this assignment must give the same value to $X_i$ and $Y_i$ for all $i$, or else the subgoal $X_i = Y_i$ of $r'$ is not made true. Thus, the same assignment, restricted to the variables that appear in $r$, will also yield head $p(b_1, \ldots, b_k)$ when applied to $r$.

The final step in the proof is to observe that if we modify $r'$ by substituting some $X$ for $Y$, where $X = Y$ is a subgoal, then we do not make the rule unsafe if it was safe, and we do not change the set of facts that the head of the rule yields. These observations are left as an exercise. $\square$

In all that follows, we shall assume rules are rectified without formally stating that presumption.

## Computing the Relations for Nonrecursive Predicates

Once we have rectified the rules, we have only to project the relation for each rule body onto the variables of the head and, for each predicate, take the union of the relations produced from each of its rules.

**Algorithm 3.2:** Evaluating Nonrecursive Rules Using Relational Algebra Operations.

INPUT: A nonrecursive datalog program and a relation for each EDB predicate appearing in the program.

OUTPUT: For each IDB predicate $p$, an expression of relational algebra that gives the relation for $p$ in terms of the relations $R_1, \ldots, R_m$ for the EDB predicates.

METHOD: Begin by rectifying all the rules. Next, construct the dependency graph for the input program, and order the predicates $p_1, \ldots, p_n$, so that if the dependency graph for the program has an arc from $p_i$ to $p_j$, then $i < j$. We can find such an order because the input program is nonrecursive, and therefore the dependency graph has no cycles. Then for $i = 1, 2, \ldots n$, form the expression for relation $P_i$ (for $p_i$) as follows.

If $p_i$ is an EDB predicate, let $P_i$ be the given relation for $p_i$. In the opposite case, suppose $p_i$ is an IDB predicate. Then:

1. For each rule $r$ having $p_i$ as its head, use Algorithm 3.1 to find an expression $E_r$ that computes the relation $R_r$ for the body of rule $r$, in terms of relations for the predicates appearing in $r$'s body.

2. Because the program is nonrecursive, all the predicates appearing in the body of $r$ already have expressions for their relations in terms of the EDB relations. Substitute the appropriate expression for each occurrence of an IDB relation in the expression $E_r$ to get a new expression $F_r$.

3. Renaming variables, if necessary, we may assume that the head of each rule for $p_i$ is $p_i(X_1, \ldots, X_k)$. Then take the expression for $P_i$ to be the union over all rules $r$ for $p_i$, of $\pi_{X_1, \ldots, X_k}(F_r)$. $\square$

**Example 3.7:** Let us take an abstract example that illustrates the mechanics of Algorithm 3.2. Suppose we have the four rules:

```
(1)  p(a,Y)  :- r(X,Y).
(2)  p(X,Y)  :- s(X,Z) & r(Z,Y).
(3)  q(X,X)  :- p(X,b).
(4)  q(X,Y)  :- p(X,Z) & s(Z,Y).
```

Here, $r$ and $s$ are EDB predicates, which we may suppose have given relations $R$ and $S$. Predicates $p$ and $q$ are IDB predicates, for which we want to compute relations $P$ and $Q$.

We begin by rectifying the rules, which requires modification to (1) and (3). Our new set of rules is:

```
(1)  p(X,Y)  :- r(Z,Y) & X=a.
(2)  p(X,Y)  :- s(X,Z) & r(Z,Y).
(3)  q(X,Y)  :- p(X,b) & X=Y.
(4)  q(X,Y)  :- p(X,Z) & s(Z,Y).
```

The proper order is to work on $p$ first, then $q$, because $q$ depends on $p$, but not vice-versa. The relation for the body of rule (1) is, by Algorithm 3.1, $R(Z,Y) \bowtie D_X(X)$, where $D_X = \{a\}$; that for rule (2) is $S(X,Z) \bowtie R(Z,Y)$. Both these expressions must be projected onto the list of attributes $X, Y$ before the union is taken. As a special case, no projection is needed for the first of these. Thus, the expression for $P$ is

$$P(X,Y) = \pi_{X,Y}\big(R(Z,Y) \bowtie \{a\}(X)\big) \ \cup \ \pi_{X,Y}\big(S(X,Z) \bowtie R(Z,Y)\big)$$

Next, we consider $q$. The relation for rule (3) is computed as follows. By Algorithm 3.1, the expression for the subgoal $p(X,b)$ is

$$\pi_X\Big(\sigma_{Z=b}\big(P(X,Z)\big)\Big)$$

Here, $Z$ is an arbitrarily chosen variable that disappears in the projection. This expression yields a relation over attribute $X$ only, and we need an expression that generates all the possible values of $Y$, since $Y$ appears nowhere else. As $Y$ is equated to $X$, we know that only values of $X$ can be values of $Y$, so we can take an argument where $X$ appears, namely the first argument of $P$, as the domain for $Y$. This domain is thus expressed by $\pi_Y\big(P(Y,W)\big)$; $W$ is another arbitrarily chosen variable. After we take the cross product of the expression for $p(X,b)$ with the domain for $Y$, we select for $X = Y$ because of the subgoal $X = Y$ in rule (3). Thus, the expression for the body of rule (3) is

$$\sigma_{X=Y}\left( \pi_X\Big(\sigma_{Z=b}\big(P(X,Z)\big)\Big) \times \pi_Y\big(P(Y,W)\big) \right)$$

Finally, the expression for rule (4) is $P(X,Z) \bowtie S(Z,Y)$ so the expression for $Q$ is

$$Q(X,Y) = \sigma_{X=Y}\left( \pi_X\Big(\sigma_{Z=b}\big(P(X,Z)\big)\Big) \times \pi_Y\big(P(Y,W)\big) \right) \cup$$
$$\pi_{X,Y}\big(P(X,Z) \bowtie S(Z,Y)\big)$$

Technically, we must first substitute for $P$ the expression we constructed for $P$, in order to get $Q$ in terms of the database relations $R$ and $S$ only. $\square$

**Theorem 3.2:** Algorithm 3.2 correctly computes the relation for each predicate, in the sense that the expression it constructs for each IDB predicate yields both:

1.   The set of facts for that predicate that can be proved from the database, and

2.   The unique minimal model of the rules.

**Proof:** Recall our comment at the end of Section 3.1 that, when our axioms are all datalog rules with no negation, and our given facts are nonnegated literals (the EDB facts), then the only IDB facts that can be proven are those that can be derived by applying rules the way we have, i.e., from antecedent to consequent. Given this fact, it is an easy induction on the order in which the expressions for the predicates are constructed, that each expression yields all and only the facts that are provable from the EDB facts and rules.

To see that the set of EDB and IDB facts thus constructed is the unique minimal model, we again perform an induction on the order in which the predicates are handled. The claim this time is that any model for the facts and rules must contain all the facts constructed by the expressions. Thus, the model consisting of the union of the relations for each of the predicates produced by Algorithm 3.2 is a subset of any model whatsoever. It is itself a model, since any substitution into one of the rules that makes the body true surely makes the head true. Thus, what we construct is the only possible minimal model. □

## 3.4 COMPUTING THE MEANING OF RECURSIVE RULES

Algorithm 3.2 does not apply to recursive datalog programs, because there is no order for the predicates that allows the algorithm to be applied. That is, whenever there is a cycle in the dependency graph, the first predicate on that cycle which we try to evaluate will have a rule with a subgoal whose expression is not yet available.

However, the proof-theoretic approach still makes sense if we remember that it is permissible to derive some facts using a rule, and later use newly derived facts in the body to derive yet more facts. If we start with a finite database, and we use only datalog rules, then there are only a finite number of different facts that could possibly be derived; they must be of the form $p(a_1, \ldots, a_k)$, where $p$ is an IDB predicate mentioned in the rules, and $a_1, \ldots, a_k$ are constants appearing in the database.

Consider a datalog program with given EDB relations $R_1, \ldots, R_k$ and with IDB relations $P_1, \ldots, P_m$ to be computed. For each $i$, $1 \le i \le m$, we can express the set of provable facts for the predicate $p_i$ (corresponding to IDB relation $P_i$) by the assignment

$$P_i := \text{EVAL}(p_i, R_1, \ldots, R_k, P_1, \ldots, P_m)$$

where EVAL is the union of EVAL-RULE (as defined in Algorithm 3.1) for each of the rules for $p_i$, projected onto the variables of the head. If we start with all $P_i$'s empty, and we execute an assignment such as this for each $i$, repeatedly, we shall eventually reach a point where no more facts can be added to any of the $P_i$'s.[8] Now, the assignment symbol becomes equality; that is, the set of IDB facts that can be proved satisfies the equations

$$P_i = \text{EVAL}(p_i, R_1, \ldots, R_k, P_1, \ldots, P_m)$$

---

[8] We shall show later in this section that when the rules have no negative subgoals, EVAL is "monotone"; that is, the $P_i$'s can only grow, and once in $P_i$, a fact will continue to be there every time $P_i$ is recomputed.

for all $i$. We shall call equations derived from a datalog program in this manner *datalog equations*.

**Example 3.8:** The rules of Figure 3.1 can be viewed as the following equations. We use $P$, $S$, $C$, and $R$ for the relations corresponding to *parent*, *sibling*, *cousin*, and *related*, respectively.

$$S(X,Y) = \pi_{X,Y}\Big(\sigma_{X \neq Y}\big(P(X,Z) \bowtie P(Y,Z)\big)\Big)$$

$$C(X,Y) = \pi_{X,Y}\big(P(X,Xp) \bowtie P(Y,Yp) \bowtie S(Xp,Yp)\big) \cup$$
$$\pi_{X,Y}\big(P(X,Xp) \bowtie P(Y,Yp) \bowtie C(Xp,Yp)\big)$$

$$R(X,Y) = S(X,Y) \cup \pi_{X,Y}\big(R(X,Z) \bowtie P(Y,Z)\big) \cup$$
$$\pi_{X,Y}\big(R(Z,Y) \bowtie P(X,Z)\big)$$

□

## Fixed Points of Datalog Equations

The replacement of the "if" symbol, :-, in datalog rules by an equality to form datalog equations is justified by the intuition that the "meaning" of the rules is no more nor less than what can be proved using the rules. It would be nice if there were a unique solution to a set of datalog equations, but generally there are many solutions. Given a set of relations for the EDB predicates, say $R_1, \ldots, R_k$, a *fixed point* of the datalog equations (*with respect to $R_1, \ldots, R_k$*), is a solution for the relations corresponding to the IDB predicates of those equations.

A fixed point $P_1, \ldots, P_m$, with respect to given EDB relations $R_1, \ldots, R_k$, together with those relations, forms a model of the rules from which the datalog equations came. In proof, let $M$ be the model in which only the facts that are tuples in $P_1, \ldots, P_m$ and $R_1, \ldots, R_k$ are true. Then any assignment of constants to the variables that makes the body of some rule $r$ true must also make the head of $r$ true. For if that head is, say, $p(a_1, \ldots, a_n)$, then tuple $(a_1, \ldots, a_n)$ must be in the relation for IDB predicate $p$, or else the chosen IDB relations are not a fixed point of the equations.

However, it is not true that every model of a set of datalog rules is a fixed point of the corresponding datalog equations, because the model may have "too many" facts, and some of them appear on the left sides of equations but not on the right. We shall see an example of this phenomenon shortly. On the other hand, we shall continue to be interested primarily in fixed points and models that are minimal, in the sense that they have no proper subset of facts that is also a fixed point. We leave as an exercise the observation that the IDB portions of minimal models are always fixed points, and in fact, minimal fixed points.

It turns out that datalog programs each have a unique minimal model containing any given EDB relations, and this model is also the unique minimal fixed point, with respect to those EDB relations, of the corresponding equations. Moreover, as we shall see, just as in the nonrecursive case, this "least fixed point" is exactly the set of facts one can derive, using the rules, from a given database.

More formally, let the variables of the equations be $P_1, \ldots, P_m$, corresponding to IDB predicates $p_1, \ldots, p_m$, and let us focus our attention on particular relations $R_1, \ldots, R_k$ assigned to the EDB predicates $r_1, \ldots, r_k$. A solution, or fixed point, for the EDB relations $R_1, \ldots, R_k$ assigns to $P_1, \ldots, P_m$ particular relations $P_1^{(1)}, \ldots, P_m^{(1)}$, such that the equations are satisfied. If $S_1 = P_1^{(1)}, \ldots, P_m^{(1)}$ and $S_2 = P_1^{(2)}, \ldots, P_m^{(2)}$ are two solutions to a given set of equations, we say that $S_1 \leq S_2$ if relation $P_i^{(1)}$ is a subset of relation $P_i^{(2)}$ for all $i$, $1 \leq i \leq m$. Then $S_0$ is the *least fixed point* of a set of equations, with respect to the EDB relations $R_1, \ldots, R_k$, if for any solution $S$, we have $S_0 \leq S$. More generally, $S_0$ is a *minimal fixed point* if there is no other fixed point $S$ such that $S \leq S_0$. Notice that if there is a least fixed point, then that is the only minimal fixed point. However, there may be several minimal fixed points that are not comparable by $\leq$, and in that case there is no least fixed point.

**Example 3.9:** Let us consider the common problem of computing the transitive closure of a directed graph. If the graph is represented by an EDB predicate *arc* such that $arc(X, Y)$ is true if and only if there is an arc from node $X$ to node $Y$, then we can express the paths in the graph by rules:

(1) `path(X,Y) :- arc(X,Y).`
(2) `path(X,Y) :- path(X,Z) & path(Z,Y).`

That is, the first rule says that a path can be a single arc, and the second says that the concatenation of any two paths, say one from $X$ to $Z$ and another from $Z$ to $Y$, yields a path from $X$ to $Y$. This pair of rules is not necessarily the best way we can define paths, but they are probably the most natural way. Note the analogy between *path* and *arc* here and the predicates *boss* and *manages* in Example 1.12. There, we used another, simpler way of computing the transitive closure of a relation.

We can turn these rules into a single equation for the relation $P$ that corresponds to the *path* predicate. The equation assumes there is a given relation $A$ corresponding to predicate *arc*.

$$P(X,Y) = A(X,Y) \cup \pi_{X,Y}\big(P(X,Z) \bowtie P(Z,Y)\big) \tag{3.5}$$

Suppose that the nodes are $\{1, 2, 3\}$ and $A$ represents the arcs $1 \to 2$ and $2 \to 3$; that is, $A = \{(1,2), (2,3)\}$. The first rule for *path* tells us that $(1,2)$ and $(2,3)$ are in $P$, and the second rule implies that $(1,3)$ is in $P$. However, we are not required to deduce the existence of any more paths, because $P = \{(1,2), (2,3), (1,3)\}$ is a solution to Equation (3.5). That is,

$$\{(1,2), (2,3), (1,3)\} = \{(1,2), (2,3)\} \cup$$
$$\pi_{X,Y}\big(\{(1,2), (2,3), (1,3)\} \bowtie \{(1,2), (2,3), (1,3)\}\big)$$

is an equality. In interpreting the above, we have to remember that the left operand of the join is a relation over attribute list $X, Z$, and its right operand is a relation over attributes $Z, Y$. Thus, the expression $\pi_{X,Y}\big(P(X,Z) \bowtie P(Z,Y)\big)$ can be thought of as the composition of the relation $P$ with itself, and its value here is $\{(1,3)\}$.

This solution is the proof-theoretic meaning of the rules, because we derived from the EDB relation $A$ exactly what the rules allowed us to prove. It is also easy to see it is the minimal model of the rules or least fixed point of the equation (3.5) [with respect to the given relation $A$], because every derived fact can be shown to be in every model or fixed point containing the EDB relation $A$.

However, there are other solutions to (3.5). Suppose we arbitrarily decided that $(1,1)$ was also in $P$. The rules do not imply any more paths, given that $A = \{(1,2), (2,3)\}$ and $P = \{(1,1), (1,2), (2,3), (1,3)\}$. Notice how $(1,1)$ "proves" itself if we let $X = Y = Z = 1$ in rule (2). Thus, another solution to (3.5) is:

$$\{(1,1), (1,2), (2,3), (1,3)\} = \{(1,2), (2,3)\} \cup$$
$$\pi_{X,Y}\big(\{(1,1), (1,2), (2,3), (1,3)\} \bowtie \{(1,1), (1,2), (2,3), (1,3)\}\big)$$

Similarly, we could let $P$ consist of all nine pairs $(i,j)$, where $1 \leq i,j \leq 3$, and that value would also satisfy (3.5). On the other hand, not every value of $P$ satisfies (3.5). For example, still assuming $A = \{(1,2), (2,3)\}$, we cannot let $P = \{(1,2), (2,3), (1,3), (3,1)\}$, because the resulting substitution into (3.5), which is

$$\{(1,2), (2,3), (1,3), (3,1)\} = \{(1,2), (2,3)\} \cup$$
$$\pi_{X,Y}\big(\{(1,2), (2,3), (1,3), (3,1)\} \bowtie \{(1,2), (2,3), (1,3), (3,1)\}\big)$$

is not an equality. The join on the right yields, for example, tuple $(3,1,2)$ over attribute list $X, Z, Y$, which after projection is $(3,2)$, a tuple that is not on the left.

As a final example, let us see a model that is not a fixed point. Let $A = \emptyset$ and $P = \{(1,2)\}$. Then the rules are made true. In rule (1), there is no way to make the body, $arc(X,Y)$ true, so the rule is true no matter what constants are substituted for the variables. In rule (2), there is no value we can substitute for $Z$ that will make both $(X,Z)$ and $(Z,Y)$ be tuples of $P$, so again the body cannot be made true and the rule must always be true. We conclude that the set of facts consisting of $path(1,2)$ alone is a model of the given datalog rules.

However, (3.5) is not made true; its left side is $\{(1,2)\}$ and its right side is $\emptyset$ for the given $A$ and $P$. Thus, $P = \{(1,2)\}$ is not a fixed point of the equations with respect to EDB $A = \emptyset$. $\square$

### Solving Recursive Datalog Equations

We can solve a set of datalog equations by assuming initially that all the $P_i$'s are empty, and the $R_i$'s are whatever is given. We then apply EVAL to the current values of the IDB relations and the permanent values of the EDB relations, to get new values for the IDB relations. This process repeats, until at some point, none of the $P_i$'s change. We know the IDB relations must *converge* in this sense, because the EVAL operation is "monotone," a property that we shall define more formally later, but which essentially means that when you add more tuples to some of the arguments of the operation, the result cannot lose tuples.

**Algorithm 3.3:** Evaluation of Datalog Equations.

INPUT: A collection of datalog rules with EDB predicates $r_1, \ldots, r_k$ and IDB predicates $p_1, \ldots, p_m$. Also, a list of relations $R_1, \ldots, R_k$ to serve as values of the EDB predicates.

OUTPUT: The least fixed point solution to the datalog equations obtained from these rules.

METHOD: Begin by setting up the equations for the rules. These equations have variables $P_1, \ldots, P_m$ corresponding to the IDB predicates, and the equation for $P_i$ is $P_i = \text{EVAL}(p_i, R_1, \ldots, R_k, P_1, \ldots, P_m)$. We then initialize each $P_i$ to the empty set and repeatedly apply EVAL to obtain new values for the $P_i$'s. When no more tuples can be added to any IDB relation, we have our desired output. The details are given in the program of Figure 3.3. $\square$

```
for i := 1 to m do
    Pᵢ := ∅;
repeat
    for i := 1 to m do
        Qᵢ := Pᵢ; /* save old values of Pᵢ's */
    for i := 1 to m do
        Pᵢ := EVAL(pᵢ, R₁, ..., Rₖ, Q₁, ..., Qₘ);
until Pᵢ = Qᵢ for all i, 1 ≤ i ≤ m;
output Pᵢ's
```

**Figure 3.3** Simple evaluation algorithm.

**Example 3.10:** Consider the rules of Figure 3.1 and the particular relation $P$ for the EDB predicate *parent* shown in Figure 3.4. In that figure, an edge downward from $x$ to $y$ means that $x$ is a parent of $y$; i.e., $parent(y, x)$ is true. The EVAL formulas for predicates *sibling, cousin,* and *related*, or equivalently their relation variables $S$, $C$, and $R$, are the formulas given on the right sides of the equations in Example 3.8. When we apply Algorithm 3.3, the relation $P$ remains fixed; it contains the tuples $ca$, $da$, and so on, indicated by Figure 3.4. [Note we use the compact notation for tuples here, $ca$ instead of $(c, a)$, and so on.]

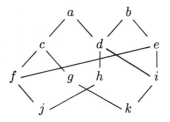

**Figure 3.4** The relation $P$ for predicate *parent*.

We see in Figure 3.5 the tuples added to the relations $S$, $C$, and $R$, for *sibling, cousin,* and *related*, respectively. The tuples are grouped by the round (of the repeat-loop of Figure 3.3) in which they are added. After each round, the value of each relation is the set of tuples added at that round and at previous rounds. However, as all three relations are symmetric, i.e., they contain tuple $xy$ if and only if they contain $yx$, we have listed only those tuples whose first component precedes the second component alphabetically. Thus, after round 1, the relation $S$ really contains ten tuples, $cd$, $dc$, and so on.

Initially, $S = C = R = \emptyset$, so on the first round, only $S$ can get some tuples. The reason is that for the other two relations, each join includes one of the IDB relations, which are currently empty. For instance, as we saw in Example 3.8, the expression EVAL($cousin, P, S, C, R$) contains two joins, the first involving two copies of $P$ and one occurrence of $S$, the second involving two $P$'s and a $C$. Since $S$ and $C$ are each currently empty, and the join of anything with an empty relation is empty, the new value of $C$ is $\emptyset$.

On the second round, $S$ will get no more tuples, because the relation $P$ on which it depends is an EDB relation and therefore has not changed. Rule (2) of Figure 3.1, for *cousin*, now has nonempty relations for each of its subgoals, so on the second round it gets some tuples. For example, the sibling pair $cd$ implies that all the children of $c$, namely $f$ and $g$, are cousins of the children of $d$, namely $h$ and $i$. Thus, we add $fh$, $fi$, $gh$, and $gi$ to $C$. By symmetry, the

| | $S$ | $C$ | $R$ |
|---|---|---|---|
| 1 | cd de<br>fg hi<br>fi | ∅ | ∅ |
| 2 | | fh fi ii<br>gh gi<br>hi jk | cd de<br>fg hi<br>fi |
| 3 | | jj kk | df dg ch di<br>ci eh ei gj<br>fk hk ij |
| 4 | | | fh dj gh jk<br>gi dk cj ii<br>ck ej ek |
| 5 | | | fj hj gk ik |
| 6 | | | jj kk |

**Figure 3.5** Application of the algorithm of Figure 3.3.

sibling pair $dc$ causes the reverses of each of these pairs to be placed in $C$, but we don't list these pairs because of our convention (just as we did not explicitly show that $dc$ is in $S$).

In the third round, rule (3) for *cousin* causes $jj$ and $kk$ to be added to $C$. For example, the fact that $f$ and $h$ were discovered to be cousins in round 2 (they are children of siblings $c$ and $d$) tells us in round 3 that $j$ is his own cousin, an unintuitive but technically correct result.

Rules (4)–(6) for *related* are similarly applied starting at round 2. It takes until round 6 for all the tuples in $R$ to be deduced. For example, the fact that $j$ is related to himself is not deduced until that round.[9] □

## Monotonicity

To prove that Algorithm 3.3 converges at all, let alone that it converges to the least fixed point, requires establishing that repeated application of EVAL produces for each IDB predicate a sequence of relations that are progressively larger, until at some point they stop growing and remain fixed. We need the

---

[9] Note that $j$ is related to himself because $c$ and $d$ are siblings, $j$ is a descendant of $c$ and $j$ is also a descendant of $d$.

terminology of "monotonicity" to express formally this property of functions such as EVAL: when you give them arguments no smaller than you gave them before, they give you no less as a result.

Formally, let $f(P_1, \ldots, P_m)$ be a function whose arguments and result are each relations. Let

$$S_1 = P_1^{(1)}, \ldots, P_m^{(1)} \text{ and } S_2 = P_1^{(2)}, \ldots, P_m^{(2)}$$

be two assignments of relations to the relation variables of $f$. Suppose $S_1 \leq S_2$; that is, each relation $P_i^{(2)}$ is a superset (not necessarily proper) of the corresponding relation $P_i^{(1)}$. Then we say $f$ is *monotone* if for any $S_1$ and $S_2$ as above, $f(S_1) \subseteq f(S_2)$. Monotone functions are quite common in relational database theory, since of the basic relational algebra operations, only difference fails to be monotone.

**Theorem 3.3:** The operations union, select, project, and product are monotone.

**Proof:** The proof in each case is very simple; we shall give the proof for selection only, leaving the rest for an exercise. Consider a selection $\sigma_F$, where $F$ is an arbitrary condition, and let $R^{(1)} \subseteq R^{(2)}$ be two relations to which $\sigma_F$ applies. Let $\mu$ be a tuple in $\sigma_F(R^{(1)})$. Then $\mu$ must be in $R^{(1)}$, and therefore $\mu$ is in $R^{(2)}$. Moreover, $\mu$ satisfies condition $F$, so we conclude $\mu$ is in $\sigma_F(R^{(2)})$. Since this reasoning applies to an arbitrary tuple in $\sigma_F(R^{(1)})$, we conclude that $\sigma_F(R^{(1)}) \subseteq \sigma_F(R^{(2)})$. $\square$

**Corollary 3.1:** Natural joins and $\theta$-joins are monotone functions.

**Proof:** These operations are compositions of operations we proved monotone in Theorem 3.3. The reader may, as an easy exercise, show that the composition of monotone functions is itself monotone.

**Corollary 3.2:** The operation EVAL is a monotone function.

**Proof:** An inspection of Algorithms 3.1 and 3.2 confirms that we use only the operations of union, natural join, selection, projection, and product in computing the function EVAL. Since these are monotone functions, so is EVAL. $\square$

We are now able to prove the correctness of Algorithm 3.3. We show that it produces the least fixed point of the equations. As we observed, this solution is also the unique minimal model of the corresponding datalog program. It is also easy to observe that the least fixed point is the set of facts provable from the database given the rules; we leave this proof as an exercise.

**Theorem 3.4:** Algorithm 3.3 produces the least fixed point of the equations to which it is applied, with respect to the given EDB relations.

**Proof:** We need to do several inductions on the number of times we go through the repeat-loop of Figure 3.3. We refer to these iterations as "rounds."

The first observation is that the tuples placed in $P_i$ consist of symbols that are either in the EDB relations or in the rules themselves. The proof is by induction on the rounds. Before round 1, each $P_i = \emptyset$, so surely the claim holds. For the induction, each application of EVAL uses only union, selection, natural join, projection, and product. None of these operations introduce symbols not present in their arguments.

Next, we observe that for each $i$, the value of $P_i$ produced on round $j$ is a superset (not necessarily proper) of the value for that relation produced on the previous round. Again, the result is an induction on the round. For round 1, the previous value is $\emptyset$, so the claim holds. For the induction, note that EVAL is monotone, by Corollary 3.2. On round $j > 1$, the arguments of EVAL in the algorithm of Figure 3.3 are the $R$'s, which do not change, and the $Q$'s, which are the values of the $P$'s that were produced on round $j - 1$. In comparison, the arguments of EVAL on round $j - 1$ were the same $R$'s and the values of the $P$'s produced on round $j - 2$ (if $j = 2$, these $P$'s are all $\emptyset$). By the inductive hypothesis, the values of the $P$'s produced on round $j - 1$ are supersets of the corresponding values produced on round $j - 2$. By monotonicity of EVAL, the value of each $P_i$ produced on round $j$ is a superset of the value of $P_i$ on round $j - 1$. That observation gives us the induction, and we conclude that each $P_i$ takes on a sequence of values $V_{i1}, V_{i2}, \ldots$ that is a nondecreasing sequence; i.e., $V_{i1} \subseteq V_{i2} \subseteq \cdots$.

Now, notice that for a given set of rules, there is an upper limit on the arity of the IDB predicates, say $a$. Also, for a given list of relations for the EDB predicates, there are a finite number of symbols that appear in the database and the rules, say $b$. Then there are at most $b^a$ different tuples that can appear in any relation. Consequently, no one of the $P_i$'s can increase in size on more than $b^a$ different rounds. As there are $m$ IDB predicates, there can be no more than $mb^a$ rounds on which some $P_i$ increases in size. Thus, after no more than $mb^a$ rounds there will be a round on which no $P_i$ changes, and hence Algorithm 3.3 will halt.

We must now show that when the algorithm halts, it does so at the least fixed point. First, it is an easy induction on the number of rounds that if a tuple $\mu$ is ever put into any $P_i$, then $\mu$ is in $P_i$ in every solution to the equations. The reason is that the equation for $P_i$ is exactly the assignment to $P_i$ in Figure 3.3, that is,

$$P_i = \text{EVAL}(p_i, R_1, \ldots, R_k, Q_1, \ldots, Q_m)$$

If every tuple in every relation on the right has already been proven to be there in every solution, then any tuple appearing on the left must likewise be in $P_i$ in every solution.

Thus, if $S_0$ is the list of relations produced by Algorithm 3.3, we have shown that $S_0 \leq S$ for any solution $S$. To complete the proof that $S_0$ is the least fixed point, we have only to observe that $S_0$ is a solution. That claim follows from the fact that when the algorithm terminates, the $P_i$'s are equal to their corresponding $Q_i$'s. Hence, the assignments to the $P_i$'s in Figure 3.3 can be replaced by equalities, and therefore, the $P_i$'s form a solution to the equations. $\square$

## 3.5 INCREMENTAL EVALUATION OF LEAST FIXED POINTS

Notice from Example 3.10 that when computing new values of the $P_i$'s in Figure 3.3 we instinctively focussed on the question of what tuples had been added to IDB relations on the previous round, and we asked what new tuples these yielded for their own relation or for another IDB relation. That restriction of the problem is valid, because when we evaluate the assignment

$$P_i := \mathrm{EVAL}(p_i, R_1, \ldots, R_k, Q_1, \ldots, Q_m)$$

we care only about the tuples in the expression on the right that are not already known to be in $P_i$.

It is important to notice that when we perform the EVAL procedure, for each tuple $\mu$ that is produced we can identify one particular rule for $p_i$, from which $\mu$ comes.[10] Moreover, for each subgoal of that rule, we can identify one tuple of the relation for that subgoal that is used to help produce $\mu$.

**Example 3.11:** Let us reconsider the data of Example 3.10. The tuple $fh$ added to $C$ in round 2 comes from rule (2) of Figure 3.1 for *cousin*, and in particular, from the tuples $fc$ in $parent(X, Xp)$, $hd$ in $parent(Y, Yp)$, and $cd$ in $sibling(Xp, Yp)$. No tuple in the relation for *sibling* besides $cd$ is needed, and the only reason we care about two different tuples in the relation for *parent* is because there are two subgoals in rule (2) with the *parent* predicate. Only one tuple for each subgoal contributes to the proof that $fh$ is in $C$. $\square$

The new tuples produced by each rule can thus be found if we substitute the full relation for all but one of the subgoals and substitute only the incremental tuples, i.e., the tuples found on the previous round, for the remaining subgoal. The reason is that if tuple $\mu$ is not added until the $i$th round, then there must be at least one subgoal $S$, with a tuple $\nu$ that $\mu$ needs, such that $\nu$ was not added to the relation for $S$ until round $i - 1$. Hence, $\nu$ is an incremental tuple on round $i$, and when we use the incremental tuples for $S$ (and the full relations for the other subgoals) we shall generate $\mu$.

In principle, we must do this substitution using each subgoal in turn as the subgoal with the incremental relation, and then take the union of the resulting

---

[10] There may be more than one rule that produces this tuple. We shall focus on any one of these rules.

relations. However, since there can be no incremental tuples for EDB relations, we may take the union over the subgoals with IDB predicates only, except on the first round. On the first round, we must use the full relations for all predicates. However, since the IDB predicates have empty relations on round 1, we in effect use only the EDB relations on round 1.

Let us define more formally the operation of incremental evaluation of the relations associated with rules and predicates. Let $r$ be a rule with ordinary subgoals $S_1, \ldots, S_n$; we exclude from this list any subgoals with built-in predicates. Let $R_1, \ldots, R_n$ be the current relations associated with subgoals $S_1, \ldots, S_n$, respectively, and let $\Delta R_1, \ldots, \Delta R_n$ be the list of corresponding *incremental relations*, the sets of tuples added to $R_1, \ldots, R_n$ on the most recent round. Recall that EVAL-RULE$(r, T_1, \ldots, T_n)$ is the algebraic expression used by Algorithm 3.1 to compute the relation for the body of rule $r$, when that algorithm uses relation $T_i$ as the relation for subgoal $S_i$ ($T_i$ is $R_i$ in Algorithm 3.1). Then the *incremental relation for rule $r$* is the union of the $n$ relations

$$\text{EVAL-RULE}(r, R_1, \ldots, R_{i-1}, \Delta R_i, R_{i+1}, \ldots, R_n)$$

for $1 \leq i \leq n$. That is, in each term, exactly one incremental relation is substituted for the full relation. Formally, we define:

$$\text{EVAL-RULE-INCR}(r, R_1, \ldots, R_n, \Delta R_1, \ldots, \Delta R_n) =$$
$$\cup_{1 \leq i \leq n} \text{EVAL-RULE}(r, R_1, \ldots, R_{i-1}, \Delta R_i, R_{i+1}, \ldots, R_n)$$

Remember that all rules are assumed rectified, so the union is appropriate here, just as it was in Algorithm 3.3.

Now, suppose we are given relations $R_1, \ldots, R_k$ for the EDB predicates $r_1, \ldots, r_k$. For the IDB predicates $p_1, \ldots, p_m$ we are given associated relations $P_1, \ldots, P_m$ and associated incremental relations $\Delta P_1, \ldots, \Delta P_m$. Let $p$ be an IDB predicate. Define:

$$\text{EVAL-INCR}(p, R_1, \ldots, R_k, P_1, \ldots, P_m, \Delta P_1, \ldots, \Delta P_m)$$

to be the union of what EVAL-RULE-INCR produces for each rule for $p$. In each application of EVAL-RULE-INCR, the incremental relations for the EDB predicates are $\emptyset$, so the terms for those subgoals that are EDB predicates do not have to appear in the union for EVAL-RULE-INCR.

**Example 3.12:** Consider the rules of Figure 3.1 again. Let $P$, $S$, $C$, and $R$ be the relations for *parent*, *sibling*, *cousin*, and *related*, as before, and let $\Delta S$, $\Delta C$, and $\Delta R$ be the incremental relations for the last three of these predicates, which are the IDB relations. Since *sibling* is defined only in terms of the EDB relation *parent*, we find

$$\text{EVAL-INCR}(sibling, P) = \emptyset$$

That is, EVAL-RULE-INCR for rule (1) is a union over an empty set of subgoals that have IDB predicates. This situation is not alarming, since we saw in Example 3.10 that $S$ will get all the tuples it is ever going to get on the first round [and incremental evaluation starts by applying EVAL($sibling, P$) once].

Predicate *cousin* is defined by rules (2) and (3), and these rules each have only one IDB predicate: *sibling* in (2) and *cousin* in (3). Thus, for each of these rules EVAL-RULE-INCR has only one term, and the formula for *cousin* has the union of the terms for each of the two rules:

$$\text{EVAL-INCR}(cousin, P, S, C, \Delta S, \Delta C) =$$
$$\pi_{X,Y}\big(P(X, Xp) \bowtie P(Y, Yp) \bowtie \Delta S(Xp, Yp)\big) \cup$$
$$\pi_{X,Y}\big(P(X, Xp) \bowtie P(Y, Yp) \bowtie \Delta C(Xp, Yp)\big)$$

Finally, the incremental evaluation formula for *related* is built in a similar way from rules (4)–(6); it is:

$$\text{EVAL-INCR}(related, P, R, S, \Delta R, \Delta S) = \Delta S(X, Y) \cup$$
$$\pi_{X,Y}\big(\Delta R(X, Z) \bowtie P(Y, Z)\big) \cup \pi_{X,Y}\big(\Delta R(Z, Y) \bowtie P(X, Z)\big)$$

$\square$

## Semi-Naive Evaluation

These definitions are used in the following improvement to Algorithm 3.3. The algorithm below, taking advantage of incremental relations, is sometimes called "semi-naive," compared with the simpler but less efficient Algorithm 3.3, which is called "naive." In Chapter 13 (Volume II) we shall examine some algorithms that are more efficient still, and do not warrant the approbation "naive."

**Algorithm 3.4:** Semi-Naive Evaluation of Datalog Equations.

INPUT: A collection of rectified datalog rules with EDB predicates $r_1, \ldots, r_k$ and IDB predicates $p_1, \ldots, p_m$. Also, a list of relations $R_1, \ldots, R_k$ to serve as values of the EDB predicates.

OUTPUT: The least fixed point solution to the relational equations obtained from these rules.

METHOD: We use EVAL once to get the computation of relations started, and then use EVAL-INCR repeatedly on incremental IDB relations. The computation is shown in Figure 3.6, where for each IDB predicate $p_i$, there is an associated relation $P_i$ that holds all the tuples, and there is an incremental relation $\Delta P_i$ that holds only the tuples added on the previous round. $\square$

**Example 3.13:** Let us continue with Example 3.12. On the first round, which is the initial for-loop of Figure 3.6, we use the ordinary EVAL operation. As we saw in Example 3.10, only relation $S$ for *sibling* gets any tuples on this round, because only that predicate has a rule without IDB predicates in the body. Thus, on the second round, $S$ and $\Delta S$ are both the complete relation for *sibling*, while all other IDB relations and incremental relations are empty.

```
for i := 1 to m do begin
    ΔP_i := EVAL(p_i, R_1, ..., R_k, ∅, ..., ∅);
    P_i := ΔP_i
end;
repeat
    for i := 1 to m do
        ΔQ_i := ΔP_i; /* save old ΔP's */
    for i := 1 to m do begin
        ΔP_i := EVAL-INCR(p_i, R_1, ..., R_k, P_1, ..., P_m,
            ΔQ_1, ..., ΔQ_m);
        ΔP_i := ΔP_i − P_i /* remove "new" tuples
            that actually appeared before */
    end;
    for i := 1 to m do
        P_i := P_i ∪ ΔP_i
until ΔP_i = ∅ for all i;
output P_i's
```

**Figure 3.6** Semi-naive evaluation of datalog programs.

On the second round, i.e., the first time through the repeat-loop of Figure 3.6, $\Delta S$ becomes equal to $\emptyset$, since this is what EVAL-INCR returns, as discussed in Example 3.12. The terms from rules (2) and (4) now contribute some tuples to $\Delta C$ and $\Delta R$, respectively, and these tuples then find their way into $C$ and $R$ at the end of the repeat-loop. That is, on round 2 we compute:

$$C = \Delta C = \pi_{X,Y}\big(P(X, Xp) \bowtie P(Y, Yp) \bowtie \Delta S(Xp, Yp)\big)$$
$$R = \Delta R = \Delta S$$

On the third round, since $\Delta S$ is empty, rules (2) and (4) can no longer yield new tuples, but as $\Delta C$ and $\Delta R$ now have some tuples, rules (3), (5), and (6) may. We thus compute:

$$\Delta C = \pi_{X,Y}\big(P(X, Xp) \bowtie P(Y, Yp) \bowtie \Delta C(Xp, Yp)\big)$$
$$\Delta R = \pi_{X,Y}\big(\Delta R(X, Z) \bowtie P(Y, Z)\big) \cup \pi_{X,Y}\big(\Delta R(Z, Y) \bowtie P(X, Z)\big)$$

The values of $\Delta C$ and $\Delta R$ are accumulated into $C$ and $R$, respectively, and provided both were not empty, we repeat another round in the same way. $\square$

**Theorem 3.5:** Algorithm 3.4 correctly computes the least fixed point of its given rules and given EDB relations.

**Proof:** We shall show that Algorithms 3.3 and 3.4 compute the same sets of tuples for each of the IDB relations on each round. Since Algorithm 3.3 was shown to compute the least fixed point, we shall thus conclude that Algorithm

3.4 does so too. The actual inductive hypothesis we need is that a tuple added to some IDB relation $P$ in round $j$ by Algorithm 3.3, not having been placed in that relation on any prior round, will be placed in both $P$ and $\Delta P$ on round $j$ by Algorithm 3.4. The basis, round 1, is immediate, since the same formulas, given by EVAL, are used by both algorithms.

For the induction, one has only to notice that if a tuple $\mu$ is added to some IDB relation $P$ on round $i$, and $\mu$ was not previously in $P$, then there must be some rule $r$ for predicate $p$ (the predicate corresponding to relation $P$) and tuples in the relations for all the subgoals of $r$ such that

1.   The tuples for the subgoals together yield $\mu$, and
2.   At least one of these tuples, say $\nu$, was added to its relation, say $T$, on round $i - 1$.

By the inductive hypothesis with $j = i - 1$ and observation (2) above, $\nu$ is in $\Delta T$ when we start round $i$ of Algorithm 3.4. Therefore the term of EVAL-INCR that uses $\Delta T$ (or rather its copy into some $\Delta Q_j$) will produce $\mu$, since that term uses full relations for subgoals other than the one that supplies $\nu$, and $\nu$ will be supplied by $\Delta T$. $\square$

## 3.6 NEGATIONS IN RULE BODIES

There are frequent situations where we would like to use negation of a predicate to help express a relationship by logical rules. Technically, rules with negated subgoals are not Horn clauses, but we shall see that many of the ideas developed so far apply to this broader class of rules. In general the intuitive meaning of a rule with one or more negated subgoals is that we should complement the relations for the negated subgoals, and then compute the relation of the rule exactly as we did in Algorithm 3.1.

Unfortunately, the "complement" of a relation is not a well-defined term. We have to specify the relation or domain of possible values with respect to which the complement is taken. That is why relational algebra uses a set-difference operator, but not a complementation operator. But even if we specify the universe of possible tuples with respect to which we compute the complement of a relation, we are still faced with the fact that this complement will normally be an infinite relation. We cannot, therefore, apply operations like selection or join to the complement, and we cannot perform Algorithm 3.1 on a rule with negation in a straightforward manner.

It turns out that one critical issue we face when trying to define the meaning of rules with negated subgoals is whether the variables appearing in the negated subgoals also appear in nonnegated, ordinary (non-built-in) subgoals. In the next example, we see what happens when things work right, and then we see where problems arise when variables appear only in negated subgoals. Later, we examine another problem that comes up when some subgoals are negated:

there is not necessarily a least fixed point for a logic program. Furthermore, since we have no mechanism for proving negated facts, the proof-theoretic point of view does not help us, and we are forced to select one of the minimal models as the "meaning" of the logic program.

**Example 3.14:** Suppose we want to define "true cousins" to be individuals who are related by the *cousin* predicate of Figure 3.1 but who are not also related by the *sibling* relationship. We might write

```
trueCousin(X,Y) :- cousin(X,Y) & ¬sibling(X,Y).
```

This rule is very much like an application of the difference operator of relational algebra, and indeed we can compute $T = C - S$, where $T$ is the relation for *trueCousin*, and $C$ and $S$ are the relations for *cousin* and *sibling*, computed as in the previous section.

The formula $T = C - S$ is easily seen to give the same relation as

$$C(X,Y) \bowtie \bar{S}(X,Y)$$

where $\bar{S}$ is the "complement" of $S$ with respect to some universe $U$ that includes at least the tuples of $C$.[11] For example, we might let $U$ be the set of individuals that appear in one or more tuples of the *parent* relation, i.e., those individuals mentioned in the genealogy. Then, $\bar{S}$ would be $U \times U - S$, and surely $C$ is a subset of $U \times U$. □

Unfortunately, not all uses of negation are as straightforward as the one in Example 3.14. We shall investigate some progressively harder problems concerning what rules with negation mean, and then develop a set of restraints on the use of negation that allow datalog rules with this limited form of negation to be given a sensible meaning. The first problem we encounter is what happens when variables appear only in negated subgoals.

**Example 3.15:** Consider the following rule:

```
bachelor(X) :- male(X) & ¬married(X,Y).                    (3.6)
```

Here, we suppose that *male* is an EDB relation with the obvious meaning, and *married*$(X,Y)$ is an EDB relation with the meaning that $X$ is the husband of $Y$.

One plausible interpretation of (3.6) is that $X$ is a bachelor if he is male and there does not exist a $Y$ such that $Y$ is married to $X$. However, if we computed the relation for this rule by joining the relation *male*$(X)$ with the "complement" of *married*, that is, with the set of $(X,Y)$ pairs such that $X$ is not married to $Y$, we would get the set of pairs $(X,Y)$ such that $X$ is male and $Y$ is not married to $X$. If we then project this set onto $X$, we find that "bachelors" are

---

[11] Notice that the natural join is an intersection when the sets of attributes are the same, and intersection with the complement is the same as set difference.

males who are not married to absolutely everybody in the universe; that is, there exists some $Y$ such that $Y$ is not married to $X$.

To avoid this apparent divergence between what we intuitively expect a rule should mean and what answer we would get if we interpreted negation in the obvious way (complement the relation), we shall forbid the use of a variable in a negated subgoal if that variable does not also appear in another subgoal, and that subgoal is neither negated nor a built-in predicate. This restriction is not a severe one, since we can always rewrite the rule so that such variables do not appear.[12] For example, to make the attributes of the two relations involved in (3.6) be the same, we need to project out $Y$ from *married*; that is, we rewrite the rules as:

```
husband(X)  :- married(X,Y).
bachelor(X) :- male(X) & ¬husband(X).
```

These rules can then have their meaning expressed by:

$$husband(X) = \pi_X\big(married(X,Y)\big)$$
$$bachelor(X) = male(X) - husband(X)$$

or just:

$$bachelor(X) = male(X) - \pi_X\big(married(X,Y)\big)$$

☐

While we shall forbid variables that appear only in negated subgoals, the condition found in Example 3.14 and in the rewritten rules of Example 3.15, which is that the set of variables in a negated subgoal exactly match the variables of a nonnegated subgoal, is not essential. The next example gives the idea of what can be done in cases when there are "too few" variables in a negated subgoal.

**Example 3.16:** Consider:

```
canBuy(X,Y) :- likes(X,Y) & ¬broke(X).
```

Here, *likes* and *broke* are presumed EDB relations. The intention of this rule evidently is that $X$ can buy $Y$ if $X$ likes $Y$ and $X$ is not broke. Recall the relation for this rule is a join involving the "complement" of *broke*, which we might call *notBroke*. The above rule can then be expressed by the equivalent relational algebra equation:

$$canBuy(X,Y) = likes(X,Y) \bowtie notBroke(X) \tag{3.7}$$

The fact that *notBroke* may be infinite does not prevent us from computing

---

[12] Provided, of course, that we take the interpretation of $\neg q(X_1, \ldots, X_n)$ to be that used implicitly in (3.6): "there do not exist values of those variables among $X_1, \ldots, X_n$ that appear only in negated subgoals such that these values make $q(X_1, \ldots, X_n)$ true."

the right side of (3.7), because we can start with all the $likes(X,Y)$ tuples and then check that each one has an $X$-component that is a member of $notBroke$, or equivalently, is not a member of $broke$.

As we did in the previous two examples, we can express (3.7) as a set difference of finite relations if we "pad" the $broke$ tuples with all possible objects that could be liked. But there is no way to say "all objects" in relational algebra, nor should there be, since that is an infinite set.

We have to realize that we do not need all pairs $(X,Z)$ such that $X$ is broke and $Z$ is anything whatsoever, since all but a finite number of the possible $Z$'s will not appear as a second component of a $likes$ tuple, and therefore could not possibly be in the relation $canBuy$ anyway. The set of possible $Z$'s is expressed in relational algebra as $\pi_2(likes)$, or equivalently, $\pi_Y(likes(X,Y))$. We may then express $canBuy$ in relational algebra as:

$$canBuy(X,Y) = likes(X,Y) - \Big(broke(X) \times \pi_Y\big(likes(X,Y)\big)\Big)$$

Finally, we can derive from the above expression a way to express $canBuy$ with rules where the only negated literal appears in a rule with a positive literal that has exactly the same set of variables, as we derived in Example 3.15. Such rules can naturally be interpreted as straightforward set differences. The general idea is to use one rule to obtain the projection onto the needed set of values, $\pi_2(likes)$ in this case, then use another rule to pad the tuples in the negated relation. The rules for the case at hand are:

```
liked(Y) :- likes(X,Y).
brokePair(X,Y) :- broke(X) & liked(Y).
canBuy(X,Y) :- likes(X,Y) & ¬brokePair(X,Y).
```

☐

### Nonuniqueness of Minimal Fixed Points

Adjusting the attribute sets in differences of relations is important, but it does not solve all the potential problems of negated subgoals. If $S_1$ and $S_2$ are two solutions to a logic program, with respect to a given set of EDB relations, we say $S_1 < S_2$ if $S_1 \leq S_2$ and $S_1 \neq S_2$. Recall that fixed point $S_1$ is said to be minimal if there is no fixed point $S$ such that $S < S_1$. Also, $S_1$ is said to be a least fixed point if $S_1 \leq S$ for all fixed points $S$. When rules with negation are allowed, there might not be a least fixed point, but several minimal fixed points. If there is no unique least fixed point, what does a logic program mean?

**Example 3.17:** Consider the rules:

```
(1) p(X) :- r(X) & ¬q(X).
(2) q(X) :- r(X) & ¬p(X).
```

Let $P$, $Q$, and $R$ be the relations for IDB predicates $p$ and $q$, and EDB predicate $r$, respectively. Suppose $R$ consists of the single tuple 1; i.e., $R = \{1\}$. Let $\mathcal{S}_1$ be the solution $P = \emptyset$ and $Q = \{1\}$; let $\mathcal{S}_2$ have $P = \{1\}$ and $Q = \emptyset$. Both $\mathcal{S}_1$ and $\mathcal{S}_2$ are solutions to the equations $P = R - Q$ and $Q = R - P$.[13]

Observe that $\mathcal{S}_1 \leq \mathcal{S}_2$ is false, because of the respective values of $Q$, and $\mathcal{S}_2 \leq \mathcal{S}_1$ is false because of $P$. Moreover, there is no solution $\mathcal{S}$ such that $\mathcal{S} < \mathcal{S}_1$ or $\mathcal{S} < \mathcal{S}_2$. The reason is that such an $\mathcal{S}$ would have to assign $\emptyset$ to both $P$ and $Q$. But then $P = R - Q$ would not hold.

We conclude that both $\mathcal{S}_1$ and $\mathcal{S}_2$ are fixed points, and that they are both minimal. Thus, the set of rules above has no least fixed point, because if there were a least fixed point $\mathcal{S}$, we would have $\mathcal{S} < \mathcal{S}_1$ and $\mathcal{S} < \mathcal{S}_2$. $\square$

## Stratified Negation

To help deal with the problem of many minimal fixed points, we shall permit only "stratified negation." Formally, rules are *stratified* if whenever there is a rule with head predicate $p$ and a negated subgoal with predicate $q$, there is no path in the dependency graph from $p$ to $q$.[14] Restriction of rules to allow only stratified negation does not guarantee a least fixed point, as the next example shows. However, it does allow a rational selection from among minimal fixed points, giving us one that has become generally accepted as "the meaning" of a logic program with stratified negation.

**Example 3.18:** Consider the stratified rules:[15]

```
(1) p(X) :- r(X).
(2) p(X) :- p(X).
(3) q(X) :- s(X) & ¬p(X).
```

The above set of rules is stratified, since the only occurrence of a negated subgoal, $\neg p(X)$ in rule (3), has a head predicate, $q$, from which there is no path to $p$ in the dependency graph. That is, although $q$ depends on $p$, $p$ does not depend on $q$.

Let EDB relations $r$ and $s$ have corresponding relations $R$ and $S$, and let IDB relations $p$ and $q$ have relations $P$ and $Q$. Suppose $R = \{1\}$ and $S = \{1, 2\}$.

---

[13] Note that rules (1) and (2) are logically equivalent, but these two set-valued equations are not equivalent; certain sets $P$, $Q$, and $R$ satisfy one but not the other. This distinction between logically equivalent forms as we convert logic into computation should be seen as a "feature, not a bug." It allows us, ultimately, to develop a sensible semantics for a large class of logical rules with negation.

[14] The construction of the dependency graph does not change when we introduce negated subgoals. If $\neg q(X_1, \ldots, X_n)$ is such a subgoal, and the rule has head predicate $p$, we draw an arc from $q$ to $p$, just as we would if the $\neg$ were not present.

[15] If one does not like the triviality of the rule (2), one can develop a more complicated example along the lines of Example 3.9 (paths in a graph) that exhibits the same problem as is illustrated here.

Then one solution is $\mathcal{S}_1$ given by $P = \{1\}$ and $Q = \{2\}$, while another is $\mathcal{S}_2$ given by $P = \{1, 2\}$ and $Q = \emptyset$. That is, both $\mathcal{S}_1$ and $\mathcal{S}_2$ are solutions to the equations $P = P \cup R$ and $Q = S - P$.[16]

One can check that both $\mathcal{S}_1$ and $\mathcal{S}_2$ are minimal. Thus, there can be no least fixed point for the rules of this example, by the same reasoning we used to conclude there is none for the rules of Example 3.17. On the other hand, $\mathcal{S}_1$ is more "natural," since its tuples each can be obtained by making substitutions of known facts in the bodies of rules and deducing the fact that appears at the head. We shall see later how the proper attribution of "meaning" to stratified rules produces $\mathcal{S}_1$ rather than $\mathcal{S}_2$. $\Box$

### Finding Stratifications

Since not every logic program with negations is stratified, it is useful to have an algorithm to test for stratification. While this test is quite easy, we explain it in detail because it also gives us the *stratification* of the rules; that is, it groups the predicates into *strata*, which are the largest sets of predicates such that

1.   If a predicate $p$ is the head of a rule with a subgoal that is a negated $q$, then $q$ is in a lower stratum than $p$.
2.   If predicate $p$ is the head of a rule with a subgoal that is a nonnegated $q$, then the stratum of $p$ is at least as high as the stratum of $q$.

The strata give us an order in which the relations for the IDB predicates may be computed. The useful property of this order is that following it, we may treat any negated subgoals as if they were EDB relations.

**Algorithm 3.5:** Testing For and Finding a Stratification.

INPUT: A set of datalog rules, possibly with some negated subgoals.

OUTPUT: A decision whether the rules are stratified. If so, we also produce a stratification.

METHOD: Start with every predicate assigned to stratum 1. Repeatedly examine the rules. If a rule with head predicate $p$ has a negated subgoal with predicate $q$, let $p$ and $q$ currently be assigned to strata $i$ and $j$ respectively. If $i \leq j$, reassign $p$ to stratum $j + 1$. Furthermore, if a rule with head $p$ has a nonnegated subgoal with predicate $q$ of stratum $j$, and $i < j$, reassign $p$ to stratum $j$. These laws are formalized in Figure 3.7.

If we reach a condition where no strata can be changed by the algorithm of Figure 3.7, then the rules are stratified, and the current strata form the output of the algorithm. If we ever reach a condition where some predicate is assigned a stratum that is larger than the total number of predicates, then the rules are not stratified, so we halt and return "no." $\Box$

---

[16] If we did not have rule (2), then the first equation would be $P = R$, and there would be a unique solution to the equations.

```
for each predicate p do
    stratum[p] := 1;
repeat
    for each rule r with head predicate p do begin
        for each negated subgoal of r with predicate q do
            stratum[p] := max(stratum[p], 1+stratum[q]);
        for each nonnegated subgoal of r with predicate q do
            stratum[p] := max(stratum[p], stratum[q])
    end
until there are no changes to any stratum
    or some stratum exceeds the number of predicates
```

**Figure 3.7** Stratification computation.

**Example 3.19:** If there are no negated subgoals, then Algorithm 3.5 immediately halts with all predicates in stratum 1, which is correct.

For a less trivial example, consider the rules of Example 3.17. Initially, $p$, $q$, and $r$ each have stratum 1. Rule (1) forces us to increase the stratum of $p$ to 2, and then the rule (2) forces us to increase the stratum of $q$ to 3. The first rule then requires the stratum of $p$ to be 4. We now have a stratum higher than the number of predicates, and so conclude the rules are not stratifiable. That conclusion is correct. For example, $q$ appears as a negated subgoal in the first rule, which has head predicate $p$, yet $q$ depends on $p$.

For another example, consider the rules of Example 3.18. Starting with all four predicates in stratum 1, rule (3) forces us to increase $q$ to stratum 2. However, there are no further adjustments that need to be made. We conclude $p$, $r$, and $s$ are in stratum 1; $q$ is in stratum 2. That makes sense, because $r$ and $s$ are EDB relations, while $p$ is an IDB relation that can be computed from these by Algorithm 3.3 or 3.4, without any uses of negation. After we have computed $p$, we can then pretend the negation of $p$ is an EDB relation. Since $q$ is not recursive, we can compute the relation for $q$ by Algorithm 3.2. $\square$

The correctness of Algorithm 3.5 is proved by the following lemmas and theorem.

**Lemma 3.2:** If a logic program has a stratification, then it is stratified.

**Proof:** The reader should not be lulled by the similarity of the terms "stratified" and "has a stratification" into thinking that they are easy to prove equivalent. In fact they are equivalent, but the proof requires some work. Recall that a program is stratified if whenever there is a negated subgoal with predicate $q$ in the body of a rule for predicate $p$, there is no path in the dependency graph from $p$ to $q$. It is easy to see from the definition of a "stratification" that the stratum of predicates along any path in the dependency graph can never decrease, because those paths go from subgoal to head, and the stratum of a head predicate is never less than the stratum of one of its subgoals.

Suppose a program had a stratification, but was not stratified. Then there would be a path in the dependency graph to some $q$ from some $p$, such that negated $q$ was a subgoal of a rule $r$ for $p$. The existence of the path says that the stratum of $q$ is at least as high as the stratum of $p$, yet the rule $r$ requires that the stratum of $q$ be less than that of $p$. $\square$

**Lemma 3.3:** If a logic program is stratified, then Algorithm 3.5 halts on that program without producing a stratum higher than $n$, the number of predicates in the program.

**Proof:** Each time we increase the stratum of some predicate $p$ because of some predicate $q$ in the algorithm of Figure 3.7, it must be that $q$ is a subgoal (negated or not) of a rule for $p$. If we increase $stratum[p]$ to $i$, and $q$ is not negated, then write $q \xrightarrow{i} p$; if $q$ is negated, write $q \overset{i}{\Rightarrow} p$. For example, the sequence of stratum changes discussed in Example 3.19 for the nonstratified rules of Example 3.17 is $q \overset{2}{\Rightarrow} p \overset{3}{\Rightarrow} q \overset{4}{\Rightarrow} p$.

For technical reasons, it is convenient to add a new symbol $start$, which is assumed not to be a predicate. We then let $start \overset{1}{\Rightarrow} p$ for all predicates $p$.

It is an easy induction on the number of times Algorithm 3.5 changes a stratum that if we set the stratum of a predicate $p$ to $i$, then there is a chain of $\rightarrow$ and $\Rightarrow$ steps from $start$ to $p$ that includes at least $i \Rightarrow$ steps. The key point in the proof is that if the last step by which Algorithm 3.5 makes the stratum of $p$ reach $i$ is $q \overset{i}{\Rightarrow} p$, then there is a chain with at least $i-1 \Rightarrow$ steps to $q$, and one more makes at least $i \Rightarrow$'s to $p$. If the step by which Algorithm 3.5 makes the stratum of $p$ reach $i$ is $q \xrightarrow{i} p$, then there is already a chain including at least $i \Rightarrow$'s to $q$, and this chain can be extended to $p$.

Now, notice that if the stratum of some predicate reaches $n+1$, there is a chain with at least $n+1 \Rightarrow$'s. Thus some predicate, say $p$, appears twice as the head of a $\Rightarrow$. Thus, a part of the chain is

$$q_1 \overset{i}{\Rightarrow} p \cdots q_2 \overset{j}{\Rightarrow} p$$

where $i < j$. Also, observe that every portion of the chain is a path in the dependency graph; in particular, there is a path from $p$ to $q_2$ in the dependency graph.

The fact that $q_2 \overset{j}{\Rightarrow} p$ is a step implies that there is a rule with head $p$ and negated subgoal $q_2$. Thus, there is a path in the dependency graph from the head, $p$, of some rule to a negated subgoal, $q_2$, of that rule, contradicting the assumption that the logic program is stratified. We conclude that if the program is stratified, no stratum produced by Algorithm 3.5 ever exceeds $n$, and therefore, Algorithm 3.5 must eventually halt and answer "yes." $\square$

**Theorem 3.6:** Algorithm 3.5 correctly determines whether a datalog program with negation is stratified.

**Proof:** Evidently, if Algorithm 3.5 halts and says the program is stratified, then it has produced a valid stratification. Lemma 3.2 says that if there is a stratification, then the program is stratified, and Lemma 3.3 says that if the logic program is stratified, then Algorithm 3.5 halts and says "yes" (the program is stratified). We conclude that the algorithm says "yes" if and only if the given logic program is stratified. $\square$

**Corollary 3.3:** A logic program is stratified if and only if it has a stratification.

**Proof:** The three-step implication in the proof of Theorem 3.6 incidentally proves that the three conditions "stratified," "has a stratification," and "Algorithm 3.5 says 'yes'," all are equivalent. $\square$

## Safe, Stratified Rules

In order that a sensible meaning for rules can be defined we need more than stratification; we need safety. Recall that we defined rules to be "safe" in Section 3.2 if all their variables were limited, either by being an argument of a nonnegated, ordinary subgoal, or by being equated to a constant or to a limited variable, perhaps through a chain of equalities. When we have negated subgoals, the definition of "safe" does not change. We are not allowed to use negated subgoals to help prove variables to be limited.

**Example 3.20:** The rules of Examples 3.16, 3.17, and 3.18 are all safe. The rule of Example 3.15 is not safe, since $Y$ appeared in a negated subgoal but in no nonnegated subgoal, and therefore could not be limited. However, as we saw in that example, we can convert that rule to a pair of safe rules that intuitively mean the same thing. $\square$

When rules are both safe and stratified, there is a natural choice from among possible fixed points that we shall regard as the "meaning" of the rules. We process each stratum in order, starting with the lowest first. Suppose we are working on a predicate $p$ of stratum $i$. If a rule for $p$ has a subgoal with a predicate $q$ of stratum less than $i$, we can obtain $q$'s relation, because that relation is either an EDB relation or has been computed when we worked on previous strata. Of course, no subgoal can be of stratum above $i$, if we have a valid stratification. Moreover, if the subgoal is negated, then stratum of $q$ must be strictly less than $i$.

As a consequence of these properties of a stratification, we can view the set of rules for the predicates of stratum $i$ as a recursive definition of the relations for exactly the stratum-$i$ predicates, in terms of relations for the EDB relations and all IDB relations of lower strata. As the equations for the IDB predicates of stratum $i$ have no negated subgoals of stratum $i$, we may apply Algorithm 3.3 or 3.4 to solve them.

The only technicality concerns how we create the relation for a negated subgoal $\neg q(X_1, \ldots, X_n)$ of a rule $r$, so that we may pretend it is the finite relation belonging to some nonnegated subgoal. Define $DOM$ to be the union of the symbols appearing in the EDB relations and in the rules themselves. As we argued, in safe rules, no symbol not in the EDB or the rules can appear in a substitution that makes the body of a rule true. Therefore, we lose nothing by restricting the relation for a negated subgoal to consist only of tuples whose values are chosen from $DOM$.

Thus, let $Q$ be the relation already computed for $q$ (or given, if $q$ is an EDB predicate). Let the relation $\bar{Q}$ for subgoal $\neg q(X_1, \ldots, X_n)$ be

$$DOM \times \cdots \times DOM \ (n \text{ times}) - Q$$

If we make the analogous substitution for each negated subgoal in the rules for stratum $i$, and then apply Algorithm 3.3 to compute the least fixed point for the IDB predicates of that one stratum, $i$, then we shall obtain the same result as if we had managed to use the infinite relation of all tuples not in $Q$ in place of $\bar{Q}$. The reason is that we can prove, in an easy induction on the number of rounds of Algorithm 3.3, that every tuple we add to an IDB relation of stratum $i$ consists of tuples whose components are all in $DOM$. The proof depends only on the observation that, as the rules are safe, every variable appearing in a negated subgoal appears also in a nonnegated subgoal. Given that, we can invoke the inductive hypothesis to show that at each round the relation for any rule will be a subset of $DOM \times \cdots \times DOM$. We can thus offer the following algorithm for computing the "perfect" fixed point of a datalog program with safe, stratified negation.

**Algorithm 3.6:** Evaluation of Relations for Safe, Stratified Datalog Programs.

INPUT: A datalog program whose rules are safe, rectified, and stratified. Also, relations for all the EDB predicates of the program.

OUTPUT: Relations for all the IDB predicates, forming a minimal fixed point of the datalog program.

METHOD: First, compute the stratification for the program by Algorithm 3.5. Compute $DOM$ by projecting all EDB relations onto each of their components and then taking the union of these projections and the set of constants appearing in the rules, if any.

Then for each stratum $i$, in turn, do the following steps. When we reach stratum $i$, we have already computed the relations for the IDB predicates at lower strata, and of course we are given the relations for the EDB predicates. Thus, in particular, if a rule at stratum $i$ has a negated subgoal, the relation for that subgoal is known.

1.  Consider each nonnegated subgoal in a rule for stratum $i$. If that subgoal is an EDB predicate or an IDB predicate at a stratum below $i$, use the relation already known for that predicate.
2.  For each negated subgoal in a rule for stratum $i$, let $Q$ be the relation for its predicate; $Q$ must have been computed, because the stratum of the predicate for the negated subgoal is less than $i$. If this subgoal has arity $n$, use the relation $DOM \times \cdots \times DOM - Q$ in place of this subgoal, where $DOM$ appears $n$ times in the product.
3.  Use Algorithm 3.3 or 3.4 to compute the relations for the IDB predicates of stratum $i$, treating all the subgoals whose relations were obtained in either step (2) or step (3), as if they were EDB relations with the values given by those steps. $\square$

**Example 3.21:** Consider the rules of Example 3.18. Recall from Example 3.19 that $p$, $r$, and $s$ are in stratum 1, and $q$ is in stratum 2. The relations $R$ and $S$ for $r$ and $s$ are given EDB relations. Since all EDB relations are of arity 1, and there are no constants in the rules, $DOM$ is just $\pi_1(R) \cup \pi_1(S)$, or $R \cup S$.

We first work on stratum 1, and we merely need one round to find that $P$, the relation for $p$ is equal to $R$. Now, we proceed to stratum 2. Since $p$ appears negated, we must compute $\bar{P}$, a relation that includes all tuples that could possibly be in the relation $Q$ for $q$, yet are not in $P$. This relation is $DOM - P = R \cup S - P$. Since $R = P$ was just established, $\bar{P} = S - R$ here. Since there is no recursion in stratum 2, we immediately get

$$Q(X) = S(X) \bowtie \bar{P}(X) = S(X) \cap \bar{P}(X) = \\ S(X) \cap \big(S(X) - R(X)\big) = S(X) - R(X)$$

That is, $Q(X) = S(X) - R(X)$.[17]

In Example 3.18, we observed that there could be more than one minimal fixed point. The fixed point produced by Algorithm 3.6 corresponds to the fixed point $\mathcal{S}_1$ of that example. $\square$

## Perfect Fixed Points

Let us call the fixed point computed by Algorithm 3.6 the *perfect* fixed point or model. There is little we can prove about Algorithm 3.6, since as we understand from Example 3.18, it simply computes one of a number of minimal fixed points for a set of safe, stratified rules with negation. Technically, we never proved that what Algorithm 3.6 produces *is* a minimal fixed point. However, the fact that we have a fixed point follows from Theorem 3.4 (the correctness of Algorithm

---

[17]  The reader should not assume from this example that the result of Algorithm 3.6 is always a formula in relational algebra for the IDB relations. Generally, when the rules are recursive, there is no such formula, and the only reason we have one in this case is that the recursion of rule (2) in Example 3.18 is trivial.

3.3 for computing least fixed points when there is no negation) and a simple induction on the strata. That is, we show by induction on $i$ that the equations derived from the rules with heads of stratum $i$ are satisfied.

As for showing we have a minimal fixed point, we can actually show more. The perfect fixed point $S$ has the following properties:

1. If $S_1$ is any other fixed point, then for every predicate $p$ of stratum 1, $p$'s relation in $S$ is a subset (not necessarily proper) of $p$'s relation in $S_1$.
2. For all $i > 1$, if $S_1$ is any fixed point that agrees with $S$ on the relations for all predicates of strata less than $i$, then the relations for the predicates of stratum $i$ are subsets in $S$ of their relations in $S_1$.

It follows from (1) and (2) that $S$ is a minimal fixed point. In fact, $S$ is "least" of all minimal fixed points if one puts the most weight on having small relations at the lowest strata. All the results mentioned above are easy inductions on the strata, and we shall leave them as exercises for the reader.

## 3.7 RELATIONAL ALGEBRA AND LOGIC

We can view relational algebra expressions as defining functions that take given relations as arguments and that produce a value, which is a computed relation. Likewise, we know that datalog programs take EDB relations as arguments and produce IDB relations as values. We might ask whether the functions defined by relational algebra and by logic programs are the same, or whether one notation is more expressive than the other.

The answer, as we shall prove in this section, is that without negation in rules, relational algebra and datalog are incommensurate in their expressive power; there are things each can express that the other cannot. With negation, datalog is strictly more expressive than relational algebra. In fact, the set of functions expressible in relational algebra is equivalent to the set of functions we can express in datalog (with negation) if rules are restricted to be safe, nonrecursive, and have only stratified negation. In this section, "nonrecursive datalog" will be assumed to refer to rules of this form unless stated otherwise. Note that since the rules are nonrecursive, it is easy to see that they must be stratified.

### From Relational Algebra to Logical Rules

Mimicking the operations of relational algebra with datalog rules is easy except for selections that involve complex conditions. Thus, we begin with two lemmas that let us break up selections by arbitrary formulas into a cascade of unions and selections by simpler formulas. Then we give a construction of rules from arbitrary relational algebra formulas.

**Lemma 3.4:** Every selection is equivalent to a selection that does not use the NOT operator.

**Proof:** Suppose we have an arbitrary selection $\sigma_F(E)$, where the formula $F$ contains occurrences of $\neg$. We can push all negations inside the AND and OR operators by *DeMorgan's laws*:

$$\neg(F \wedge G) = (\neg F) \vee (\neg G) \text{ and } \neg(F \vee G) = (\neg F) \wedge (\neg G)$$

Repeating these transformations from left to right, as often as needed, and canceling double negations by $\neg\neg F = F$, we eventually reach a point where all negations apply to comparisons $X\theta Y$. However, since $\theta$ is one of the comparisons $=, \neq, <, \leq, >$, or $\geq$, we can always write $\neg X\theta Y$ as $X\theta' Y$, where $\theta'$ is the "opposite" of $\theta$; e.g., if $\theta$ is $<$, then $\theta'$ is $\geq$. Thus, all traces of $\neg$ are removed. $\square$

**Lemma 3.5:** Every relational algebra expression produces the same relation (as a function of its argument relations) as some relational algebra expression whose only selections are of the form $\sigma_{X\theta Y}$, where $X$ and $Y$ are attributes or constants, and $\theta$ is an arithmetic comparison operator.

**Proof:** Call selections of the form stated in the lemma *simple* selections, and call selections whose formulas involve AND, OR, or NOT *complex* selections. By Lemma 3.4, we shall assume our formulas have no occurrences of the NOT operator.

Suppose we have an expression $\sigma_F(E)$, where $F$ is a complex selection without NOT's. We assume that any complex selections in $E$ have already been replaced, so any selections found there are simple. We show by induction on the number of AND's and OR's in $F$, that we can replace $\sigma_F(E)$ by an expression whose selections are all simple. The basis, zero logical operators, is trivial; $\sigma_F(E)$ will serve.

For the induction, suppose that we can write $F$ as $F_1 \wedge F_2$. Then we can write $\sigma_F(E) = \sigma_{F_2}(\sigma_{F_1}(E))$. $F_1$ and $F_2$ each have fewer AND's and OR's than $F$, so by the inductive hypothesis, there is an expression $E_1$ equivalent to $\sigma_{F_1}(E)$ with only simple selections. Also by the inductive hypothesis, there is an expression using only simple selections that is equivalent to $\sigma_{F_2}(E_1)$. This expression is equivalent to $\sigma_F(E)$.

If the outer operator of $F$ is not $\wedge$, then it must be $\vee$; i.e., $F$ is of the form $F_1 \vee F_2$. Then we can write $\sigma_F(E) = \sigma_{F_1}(E) \cup \sigma_{F_2}(E)$. The inductive hypothesis tells us that expressions $E_1$ and $E_2$, free of complex selections and equivalent to $\sigma_{F_1}(E)$ and $\sigma_{F_2}(E)$, respectively, exist. Then $E_1 \cup E_2$ is an expression equivalent to $\sigma_F(E)$ and having only simple selections. $\square$

**Example 3.22:** Consider the expression

$$E = \sigma_{\neg\left(\$1=\$2 \wedge (\$1<\$3 \vee \$2 \leq \$3)\right)}(R)$$

We use DeMorgan's laws twice to replace the selection condition by

$$\neg(\$1 = \$2) \vee \neg(\$1 < \$3 \vee \$2 \le \$3)$$

then by $\neg(\$1 = \$2) \vee \big(\neg(\$1 < \$3) \wedge \neg(\$2 \le \$3)\big)$. Next, we absorb the $\neg$'s into the comparisons, leaving

$$E = \sigma_{\$1 \neq \$2 \vee (\$1 \ge \$3 \wedge \$2 > \$3)}(R)$$

Now we apply the construction of Lemma 3.5. The outermost operator is $\vee$, so we can write:

$$E = \sigma_{\$1 \neq \$2}(R) \ \cup \ \sigma_{\$1 \ge \$3 \wedge \$2 > \$3}(R)$$

The first argument of the union is simple, but the second requires an application of Lemma 3.5 to the $\wedge$, leaving

$$E = \sigma_{\$1 \neq \$2}(R) \ \cup \ \sigma_{\$1 \ge \$3}\big(\sigma_{\$2 > \$3}(R)\big)$$

$\square$

**Theorem 3.7:** Every function expressible in relational algebra is expressible as a nonrecursive datalog program.

**Proof:** The theorem is an easy induction on the size of the algebraic expression. Formally, we show that if an expression has $i$ occurrences of operators, then there is a nonrecursive datalog program that produces, as the relation for one of its predicates, the value of the expression. The basis is $i = 0$, that is, a single operand. If this operand is a given relation $R$, then $R$ is an EDB relation and thus "available" without the need for any rules. The only other possibility is that the operand is a set of tuples. Then we invent a name, say $P$, for this set, and for each of the tuples in the set, say $a_1 a_2 \cdots a_n$, we have a (bodyless) rule:

$$p(a_1, a_2, \ldots, a_n).$$

For the induction, consider an expression whose outermost operator is one of union, difference, selection, projection, and product. Recall that all the other operators we introduced, such as intersection and various forms of join, are expressible in terms of these five basic operators.

*Case 1:* The expression is $E = E_1 \cup E_2$. Then by the inductive hypothesis, there are predicates $e_1$ and $e_2$ defined by nonrecursive datalog rules, whose relations are the same as the relations defined by expressions $E_1$ and $E_2$. Let these relations have arity $n$; their arities must be the same, or the union operator cannot be applied. Then for expression $E$ we have rules:

$$e(X_1, \ldots, X_n) :\!\!- e_1(X_1, \ldots, X_n).$$
$$e(X_1, \ldots, X_n) :\!\!- e_2(X_1, \ldots, X_n).$$

Thus, the tuples in the relation for $e$ are exactly those tuples that are in the relation for $e_1$ or in the relation for $e_2$, or both, as we can see by applying Algorithm 3.2.

*Case 2:* $E = E_1 - E_2$. Assume, as in Case 1, that the relations for $E_1$ and $E_2$ are each of arity $n$, and that there are predicates $e_1$ and $e_2$ whose rules define their relations to be the same as the relations for $E_1$ and $E_2$, respectively. Then we use rule:

$$e(X_1, \ldots, X_n) :- e_1(X_1, \ldots, X_n) \ \& \ \neg e_2(X_1, \ldots, X_n).$$

to define a predicate $e$ whose relation is the same as the relation for $E$. We can easily check that Algorithm 3.6, which we must use because there is a negation, assigns the proper relation to $e$.

*Case 3:* $E = \pi_{i_1, \ldots, i_k}(E_1)$. Let $E_1$'s relation have arity $n$, and let $e_1$ be a predicate whose rules produce the relation for $E_1$. Then the rule for $e$, the predicate corresponding to expression $e$, is:

$$e(X_{i_1}, \ldots, X_{i_k}) :- e_1(X_1, \ldots, X_n).$$

*Case 4:* $E = E_1 \times E_2$. Let $E_1$ and $E_2$ have predicates $e_1$ and $e_2$ whose rules define their relations, and assume their relations are of arities $n$ and $m$, respectively. Then define $e$, the predicate for $E$, by:

$$e(X_1, \ldots, X_{n+m}) :- e_1(X_1, \ldots, X_n) \ \& \ e_2(X_{n+1}, \ldots, X_{n+m}).$$

*Case 5:* $E = \sigma_F(E_1)$. By Lemma 3.5 we may assume that $F$ is a simple selection, say $\$i \ \theta \ \$j$; the case where one of the operands of $F$ is a constant is similar and left for the reader. Let $e_1$ be a predicate whose relation is the same as the relation for $E_1$, and suppose $e_1$ has arity $n$. Then the rule for $e$ is:

$$e(X_1, \ldots, X_n) :- e_1(X_1, \ldots, X_n) \ \& \ X_i \theta X_j.$$

$\square$

**Example 3.23:** Let us consider the algebraic expression

$$canBuy(X, Y) = likes(X, Y) - \Big(broke(X) \times \pi_Y\big(likes(X, Y)\big)\Big)$$

developed in Example 3.16. The outermost operator is $-$, with left operand $likes(X, Y)$ and right operand equal to an expression that we shall name for convenience:

$$brokePair(X, Y) = broke(X) \times \pi_Y\big(likes(X, Y)\big)$$

The left operand, being an EDB relation, requires no rules. The right operand has outermost operator $\times$, with a left operand that is an EDB relation and right operand $\pi_Y\big(likes(X, Y)\big)$. The latter expression can be transformed into a rule by Case 3 of Theorem 3.7; it is:

```
liked(Y)  :- likes(X,Y).
```

Here we have invented the predicate name *liked* for the predicate whose relation is the same as that of the expression $\pi_Y\big(likes(X, Y)\big)$.

Now, we can write the rule for the expression *brokePair*, using Case 4 of Theorem 3.7:

```
brokePair(X,Y) :- broke(X) & liked(Y).
```

Finally, we use Case 2 of Theorem 3.7 to produce the rule for *canBuy*:

```
canBuy(X,Y) :- likes(X,Y) & ¬brokePair(X,Y).
```

Notice that the three rules developed here are the same as the rules produced by an ad-hoc argument in Example 3.16. □

## From Logic to Algebra

Now, we shall prove the converse of Theorem 3.7; for every nonrecursive datalog program, every IDB relation can be computed by an equivalent expression of relational algebra. Essentially all the ideas for constructing the desired algebraic expression from a collection of nonrecursive rules have been given; we only have to put them together properly.

**Theorem 3.8:** Let $\mathcal{R}$ be a collection of safe, nonrecursive datalog rules, possibly with negated subgoals. Then for each predicate $p$ of $\mathcal{R}$ there is an expression of relational algebra that computes the relation for $p$.

**Proof:** Since $\mathcal{R}$ is nonrecursive, we can order the predicates according to a topological sort of the dependency graph; that is, if $q$ appears as a subgoal in a rule for $p$, then $q$ precedes $p$ in the order. Essentially, we apply Algorithm 3.2 to evaluate the relation for each predicate in its turn. However, as we now have the possibility of negated subgoals, we first use the trick of Algorithm 3.6 to replace relations $R$ for negated subgoals by complementary relations $\bar{R} = DOM^k - R$, where $k$ is the arity of $R$, and $DOM$ is the set of all symbols appearing in $\mathcal{R}$ and in the EDB relations.

The set $DOM$ can always be expressed in relational algebra; it is the union of a constant set and projections of the EDB relations. Also, the construction of Algorithm 3.2 uses only the operators of relational algebra. As we may compose these algebraic operations into expressions with as many operators as we need, we can easily show by induction on the order in which the predicates are considered that each has a relation defined by some expression of relational algebra. □

**Example 3.24:** Consider the rules

```
p(X) :- r(X,Y) & ¬s(Y).
q(Z) :- s(Z) & ¬p(Z).
```

Assume $r$ and $s$ are EDB predicates with relations $R$ and $S$; we shall derive expressions for relations $P$ and $Q$, which correspond to IDB predicates $p$ and $q$, respectively. The algebraic expression for $DOM$ is the projection of $R$ onto its first and second components, plus the unary relation $S$ itself; that is:

$$DOM = \pi_1(R) \cup \pi_2(R) \cup S$$

We must use the topological order $p, q$. Predicate $p$ is defined by the first rule. For the first subgoal we can use the EDB relation $R(X, Y)$, and for the second subgoal we use the complementary relation $[DOM - S](Y)$, i.e., the unary relation $DOM - S$ regarded as a relation over attribute $Y$. As required by Algorithm 3.2, we take the join of these relations and project onto attribute $X$, the sole attribute of the head. The resulting expression is:

$$P(X) = \pi_X \Big( R(X, Y) \bowtie [DOM - S](Y) \Big) \tag{3.8}$$

Next we construct the expression for $Q$ according to rule (2). For the first subgoal of rule (2) we use relation $S(Z)$. For the second subgoal we need $[DOM - P](Z)$. Thus, the relation $Q$ is $S(Z) \bowtie [DOM - P](Z)$, or, since the join is an intersection in this case,

$$Q(Z) = [S \cap (DOM - P)](Z)$$

Since $S$ is a subset of $DOM$, the above simplifies to $Q(Z) = S(Z) - P(Z)$, or, substituting (3.8), with $Z$ in place of $X$, for $P(Z)$,

$$Q(Z) = S(Z) - \pi_Z \Big( R(Z, Y) \bowtie [DOM - S](Y) \Big)$$

One can further argue that $DOM$ can be replaced by $\pi_2(R)$ in the above expression. The reason is that $[DOM - S](Y)$ is joined with $R(Z, Y)$, so only those elements of $DOM$ that are derived from the second component of $R$ could contribute to the join. $\square$

## Monotone Relational Algebra

Recall from Theorem 3.3 that of the five basic relational algebra operations, all but set difference are monotone. The operations union, product, selection, and projection form the *monotone subset* of relational algebra. We also include in the monotone subset any operation derivable from these four operators, such as natural join. Finally, intersection, even though it was defined using set difference, is in fact a monotone operator.

Examination of the constructions in Theorems 3.7 and 3.8 tells us that when there are no set difference operators in the algebraic expression, the rules constructed by Theorem 3.7 use no negated subgoals, and when there are no negated subgoals, Theorem 3.8 provides an expression using only the monotone subset of relational algebra. Thus, we have the following equivalence.

**Theorem 3.9:** The set of functions from relations to relations expressible in the monotone subset of relational algebra is the same as the functions expressible by nonrecursive datalog programs with no negated subgoals. $\square$

### Comparing Datalog and Relational Algebra

It is not hard to show that without negated subgoals, but with recursion permitted, datalog programs are monotone. Corollary 3.2 showed that any step of Algorithm 3.3, which evaluates such datalog programs, is an operation in the monotone subset of relational algebra. We have only to show that an arbitrary composition of monotone functions is still monotone, which we leave as an easy exercise.

If we accept the monotonicity of datalog without negation, then we can easily see that there are expressions of relational algebra, such as $R - S$, that are not equivalent to any datalog program without negation. That is, $R - S$ is not monotone, because adding tuples to $S$ will decrease the set of tuples in $R - S$, if any of the added tuples are in $R$.

Similarly, there are functions that can be expressed in recursive datalog, even without negation, that cannot be expressed in relational algebra. An example is the transitive closure of a relation, such as the predicate *path* defined from the *arc* predicate of a graph in Example 3.9 (see Exercise 2.14).

## 3.8 RELATIONAL CALCULUS

A form of logic called "relational calculus" underlies most commercial query languages that are based on the relational model. Essentially, relational calculus is what you get when you take a nonrecursive datalog program and substitute the logical OR of the rule bodies for all the predicates but the one predicate that represents the answer to a query. In this section we shall define the notation of relational calculus in one of its two forms, called "domain" relational calculus, and in the next section, we define "tuple" relational calculus.

When we introduce the appropriate notion of "safety," these two versions of calculus can be shown equivalent in expressive power to nonrecursive datalog, and therefore, to relational algebra. The ubiquity of this class of queries is reinforced strongly by the fact that commercial relational database languages also have essentially the same expressivity, although they usually add certain capabilities such as aggregation (taking averages, counts, and so on) and arithmetic (select those tuples for which $X = Y + Z$, e.g.). Therefore, it has become common to call a language that is able to express at least all the queries of relational algebra *complete*.

### Formulas of Relational Calculus

Formulas are expressions that denote relations, possibly infinite ones. Each formula has a set of "free" variables, which are analogous to variables declared global to the procedure (i.e., the formula) at hand. Other variables appearing in a formula are "bound," by a mechanism we shall describe, and correspond to local variables of a procedure. The *relation scheme* for a formula is a set of attributes corresponding to the free variables of the formula.

As with local and global variables of procedures, it is possible for two occurrences of the same variable name $X$ to refer to two different declarations of $X$, and it is possible that one occurrence is bound while another is free. That is, in general we must distinguish between bound *occurrences* of variables and free occurrences of a variable. Thus, as we recursively define the allowable formulas of relational calculus, we shall at the same time distinguish those occurrences of variables that are free from those that are bound.

1.   Every literal $p(X_1, \ldots, X_n)$, where $p$ is a predicate symbol and $X_1, \ldots, X_n$ are variables or constants, is a formula. The predicate $p$ represents a relation, and the relation defined by this literal is exactly the same as the relation defined by Algorithm 3.1 for a rule whose body consists of the single subgoal $p(X_1, \ldots, X_n)$. All occurrences of variables among $X_1, \ldots, X_n$ are free.

2.   Every arithmetic comparison $X \theta Y$ is a formula, where $X$ and $Y$ are variables or constants, and $\theta$ is one of the six arithmetic comparison operators, $=$, $>$, and so on. We regard the occurrences of $X$ and $Y$, if they are variables, as free in the formula $X \theta Y$. In many cases, $X \theta Y$ represents an infinite relation, the set of all $(X, Y)$ pairs that stand in relation $\theta$. Thus, as in datalog rules, we shall require that such formulas are attached by logical AND to another formula that defines a finite relation; in that case, the formula $X \theta Y$ can be viewed as a selection operator.

Items (1) and (2) above form the basis of the definition of "formulas"; the formulas they describe are often called *atomic formulas*. In items (3)–(6) below, we give the inductive parts of the definition.

3.   If $F_1$ and $F_2$ are formulas, then $F_1 \land F_2$ is a formula, with the intuitive meaning "both $F_1$ and $F_2$ are true." Also, $F_1 \lor F_2$ is a formula meaning "at least one of $F_1$ and $F_2$ is true," and $\neg F_1$ is a formula, meaning "$F_1$ is not true." Occurrences of variables are free or bound in $F_1 \land F_2$, $F_1 \lor F_2$, and $\neg F_1$ if and only if they are free or bound in whichever of $F_1$ and $F_2$ they occur. Note that a variable $X$ could be bound in some occurrences and free in others. In particular, we might find that $X$ is free in $F_1$ and bound in $F_2$, and the binding of $X$ in $F_2$ has no influence on the status of occurrences of $X$ in $F_1$ (or vice-versa).

4.   If $F$ is a formula in which $X$ appears free in at least one occurrence,[18] then $(\exists X)F$ is a formula with the intuitive meaning that there is at least one

---

[18]   The condition that $X$ actually appears free in $F$ is generally not made here or in item (5) below. However, the cases where $X$ does not appear free in $F$ are trivial, and we simplify matters by ruling them out from the start.

value of $X$ that when substituted for all free occurrences of $X$ in $F$ makes the resulting formula true. We read $(\exists X)$ as "there exists an $X$." $(\exists X)$ and $(\forall X)$, defined below, are called *quantifiers*. Quantifiers play the role of declarations as far as the bound/free distinction is concerned. All free occurrences of $X$ in $F$ are bound by the quantifier $(\exists X)$ and are considered bound in the formula $(\exists X)F$.

5.  If $F$ is a formula with at least one free occurrence of $X$, then $(\forall X)F$ is a formula with the intuitive meaning that whatever value we pick, if we substitute that value for all free occurrences of $X$ in $F$, then the resulting formula becomes true. We read $(\forall X)$ as "for all $X$." Like $(\exists X)$, quantifier $(\forall X)$ binds all free occurrences of $X$ in $F$, so these occurrences are bound in $(\forall X)F$.

6.  If $F$ is a formula, so is $(F)$, and its meaning is the same as that of $F$. Occurrences of variables are bound or free in $(F)$ exactly as they are bound in $F$. We need parentheses for grouping of operands in formulas exactly as we do in other kinds of expressions. The order of evaluation we shall use in the absence of parentheses is

    *i)*   The unary prefix operators, $\neg$, $(\forall X)$, and $(\exists X)$ are of highest precedence and are grouped rightmost first when they appear consecutively.

    *ii)*  $\wedge$ is of next highest precedence and groups from the left.

    *iii)* $\vee$ is of lowest precedence and groups from the left.

    Thus, for example, the formula $(\forall X)\neg p(X, Y) \vee q(Y) \wedge r(X)$ is grouped as if parenthesized

    $$\Big((\forall X)\big(\neg p(X, Y)\big)\Big) \vee \big(q(Y) \wedge r(X)\big)$$

    Notice that the occurrence of $X$ in $r(X)$ is free, rather than bound by the quantifier $(\forall X)$.

**Example 3.25:** In Example 2.21 we discussed the relational algebra formula

$$\pi_{\text{CUST}}\big(\sigma_{\text{INAME}=\text{'Brie'}}(\text{INCLUDES} \bowtie \text{ORDERS})\big)$$

involving relations INCLUDES(O#, INAME, QUANTITY) and

    ORDERS(O#, DATE, CUST)

In relational calculus, the join operator is reflected by logical AND, with variables chosen to correspond to the attributes of the relations being joined; this is the same idea that is used to express join in datalog rules. Thus, we may start with the formulas $includes(N, I, Q)$ and $orders(N, D, C)$, corresponding to the relations INCLUDES and ORDERS, respectively, with the variable $N$ used in both occurrences of the attribute O#. Then

    INCLUDES $\bowtie$ ORDERS

is represented by the formula

$$includes(N, I, Q) \land orders(N, D, C)$$

The selection for ITEM='Brie' is handled by the logical AND of the above with a third atomic formula, $I = $'Brie'. Then, the projection onto attribute CUST tells us that we are interested only in the existence of some value for each of the variables $N$, $I$, $Q$, and $D$ that make the formula

$$includes(N, I, Q) \land orders(N, D, C) \land I = \text{'Brie'}$$

true. Thus, we may existentially quantify those four variables, leaving $C$, or "customer," as the only free variable:

$$(\exists N)(\exists I)(\exists Q)(\exists D)\big(includes(N, I, Q) \land$$
$$orders(N, D, C) \land I = \text{'Brie'}\big) \tag{3.9}$$

Since one of the conjuncts in (3.9) requires that $I$ be equal to 'Brie', the only $I$ that could possibly exist to make the formula true is 'Brie'. Thus, we can remove the quantifier $(\exists I)$ if we replace occurrences of $I$ by the constant 'Brie'. With a small effort, we can thus prove that (3.9) is equivalent to:

$$(\exists N)(\exists Q)(\exists D)\big(includes(N, \text{'Brie'}, Q) \land orders(N, D, C)\big) \tag{3.10}$$

in the sense that (3.9) and (3.10) produce the same relation over $C$, i.e., the same sets of customers, when given the same INCLUDES and ORDERS relations. $\square$

### Domain Relational Calculus

Formulas can be used to express queries in a simple way. Each formula with one or more free variables defines a relation whose attributes correspond to those free variables. Conventionally, we shall write $F(X_1, \ldots, X_n)$ to mean that formula $F$ has free variables $X_1, \ldots, X_n$ and no others. Then the query, or expression, denoted by $F$ is

$$\{X_1 \cdots X_n \mid F(X_1, \ldots, X_n)\} \tag{3.11}$$

that is, the set of tuples $a_1 \cdots a_n$ such that when we substitute $a_i$ for $X_i$, $1 \leq i \leq n$, the formula $F(a_1, \ldots, a_n)$ becomes true.

The query language consisting of expressions in the form of (3.11) is called *domain relational calculus* (DRC). The adjective "domain" seems odd in this context, but it refers to the fact that variables are components of tuples, i.e., variables stand for arbitrary members of the domain for their components. This form of logic should be distinguished from "tuple" relational calculus, which we take up later in this section, where variables stand for whole tuples.

It should be observed that the relations defined by DRC expressions need not be finite. For example,

$$\{XY \mid \neg p(X,Y)\}$$

is a legal DRC expression defining the set of pairs $(X,Y)$ that are not in the relation of predicate $p$. To avoid such expressions, we shall later introduce a subset of DRC formulas called "safe," in analogy with safe datalog rules introduced in Section 3.2.

### From Relational Algebra to Domain Relational Calculus

Before dealing with the question of safety, we can show how to express relational algebra in DRC. The ideas are close to those of Theorem 3.7, where we translated the algebra into datalog rules. Only the union operator needs to be handled in a different way, because while datalog allows us to use several rules to express an "or" of possibilities, in relational calculus we need the logical OR operator.

**Theorem 3.10:** Every query expressible in relational algebra is expressible in domain relational calculus.

**Proof:** As in Theorem 3.7, the proof is an induction on the number of operators in the algebraic expression. We show that for every expression $E$ of relational algebra defining a $k$-ary relation, there is a formula $F(X_1, \ldots, X_k)$ of DRC defining the same relation. The basis, zero operators, covers the case where $E$ is either a single relation $R$, or a constant relation. If it is a relation name $R$, then $R$ must be $k$-ary, and we may use predicate $r$ to represent $R$ in DRC formulas. Then the desired formula is just $r(X_1, \ldots, X_k)$.

The other part of the basis is more complex to state, but the idea is simple. Suppose for convenience that the constant relation has only two tuples: $a_1 \cdots a_k$ and $b_1 \cdots b_k$. The generalization to any finite number of tuples should be obvious when we observe that membership in the above finite set is expressed by the formula

$$(X_1 = a_1 \wedge \cdots \wedge X_k = a_k) \vee (X_1 = b_1 \wedge \cdots \wedge X_k = b_k)$$

For the induction, we consider the five cases corresponding to the five basic operators of relational algebra.

*Case 1:* $E = E_1 \cup E_2$. We may assume that $E$, $E_1$, and $E_2$ are all of arity $k$. By the inductive hypothesis there are DRC formulas $F_1$ and $F_2$ that define the relations of $E_1$ and $E_2$, respectively. By substituting for free variables in one of the formulas, we may assume that $F_1$ and $F_2$ both have $X_1, \ldots, X_k$ as their free variables, and that these variables correspond to the components of the tuples in $E$, $E_1$, and $E_2$ in that particular order, $X_1, \ldots, X_k$. Then the formula for $E$ is $F_1 \vee F_2$.

*Case 2:* $E = E_1 - E_2$. As in Case 1, assume there are formulas $F_1(X_1, \ldots, X_k)$ and $F_2(X_1, \ldots, X_k)$ that produce the relations of $E_1$ and $E_2$, respectively. Then the formula for $E$ is $F_1 \wedge \neg F_2$.

*Case 3:* $E = \pi_{i_1,\ldots,i_k}(E_1)$. Let $E_1$'s relation have arity $n$. By the inductive hypothesis there is a formula $F_1(X_1,\ldots,X_n)$ that produces the same relation as $E_1$. Let $j_1,\ldots,j_{n-k}$ be the list of $\{1,\ldots,n\}$ that do not appear among $i_1,\ldots,i_k$. Then a tuple $\mu$ is in the relation of $E$ if and only if there exist values of the components $j_1,\ldots,j_{n-k}$ with which we can extend $\mu$ and thereby produce a tuple of $E_1$. In relational calculus terms, we say:

$$F(X_{i_1},\ldots,X_{i_k}) = (\exists X_{j_1})(\exists X_{j_2})(\cdots)(\exists X_{j_{n-k}})F_1(X_1,\ldots,X_n)$$

to obtain the formula $F$ for $E$.

*Case 4:* $E = E_1 \times E_2$. Let $F_1(X_1,\ldots,X_n)$ and $F_2(Y_1,\ldots,Y_m)$ be formulas for $E_1$ and $E_2$, respectively. Renaming variables, if necessary, we shall assume that the $X$'s and the $Y$'s have no variables in common. Then

$$F(X_1,\ldots,X_n,Y_1,\ldots,Y_m) = F_1(X_1,\ldots,X_n) \wedge F_2(Y_1,\ldots,Y_m)$$

is a formula for $E$.

*Case 5:* $E = \sigma_A(E_1)$. By Lemma 3.5, we shall assume $A$ is a simple selection, of the form $\$i\theta\$j$ or $\$i\theta a$. By the inductive hypothesis, there is a formula $F_1(X_1,\ldots,X_k)$ for $E_1$. Then formula $F_1 \wedge X_i\theta X_j$ or $F_1 \wedge X_i\theta a$ serves for $E$, depending on the form of $A$. $\square$

**Example 3.26:** Let us follow the steps of Example 3.23, to produce a DRC expression for the algebraic expression

$$likes(X,Y) - \left(broke(X) \times \pi_Y\big(likes(X,Y)\big)\right)$$

For the left operand of the difference, we have the DRC formula $likes(X,Y)$.

We must work on the right operand of $-$, whose outer operator is $\times$. That operator, in turn, has a left operand with DRC formula $broke(X)$. Its right operand is obtained by applying Case 3 to the formula $likes(X,Y)$, yielding $(\exists X)likes(X,Y)$.

The latter formula has free variable $Y$, and the formula $broke(X)$ for the left operand of $\times$ has free variable $X$, so they may be combined without renaming to obtain the formula for the right operand of $-$, which is

$$broke(X) \wedge (\exists X)likes(X,Y) \tag{3.12}$$

The reader should appreciate that in (3.12) the occurrence of $X$ in $broke$ is free, while the occurrence of $X$ in $likes$ is bound by the existential quantifier.

The formula for the entire algebraic expression is obtained by Case 2 from $likes(X,Y)$ and the above formula (3.12). We can turn it into a query by inserting it in a set former, as:

$$\{XY \mid likes(X,Y) \wedge \neg\big(broke(X) \wedge (\exists Z)likes(Z,Y)\big)\}$$

For clarity, we have replaced the bound occurrence of $X$ by $Z$. As with local variables in programs, we can replace all occurrences of a single bound variable like $X$ by any other variable, like $Z$, that does not appear free in the scope of the quantifier that declares $X$ (i.e., in the line above, we could not use $Y$ in place of $X$, but any other variable would do). $\Box$

### Domain-Independent Formulas

To get at the concept of "safety" of formulas, we shall first consider what we really would like concerning relational calculus expressions. This property, called "domain independence," is a semantic notion; it will be seen that it is impossible to tell, given a formula, whether the formula satisfies the property. After defining "domain independence," we shall therefore look for approximations to the ideal, and that is where we shall find our notion of "safety."

For each free variable of a formula, we can imagine that there is some domain of possible values this variable can assume. There are certain values that it would not make sense to exclude from the domain: the values that appear in the formula itself and the values that appear in the given relations. We call this set $DOM(F)$, where $F$ is the formula at hand. Note that $DOM(F)$ is not a constant depending only on $F$, but rather a function of the relations that are given for each predicate of $F$. $DOM(F)$ is a simple function; it can always be expressed in relational algebra as the union of the set of constants appearing in $F$ and the projections of all the relations that are arguments of $F$, projected onto each of their components. Of course, the relation $DOM(F)$ is of arity 1; i.e., it is a set of symbols.

**Example 3.27:** Consider the formula

$$F = p(X, Y) \land q(Y, Z) \lor X > 10$$

Let predicates $p$ and $q$ have relations $P$ and $Q$, respectively. Then

$$DOM(F) = \{10\} \cup \pi_1(P) \cup \pi_2(P) \cup \pi_1(Q) \cup \pi_2(Q)$$

$\Box$

Intuitively, if the relation defined by a formula $F$ includes tuples with symbols not in $DOM(F)$, then somehow the formula is not paying attention to the data it is given, but is materializing data from "somewhere else." Notice that neither relational algebra nor safe datalog rules can cause the invention of new symbols. The property that the formula "pays attention" to its data can be formalized by the notion of "domain independence."

Let $F(X_1, \ldots, X_n)$ be a formula, and let $D \supseteq DOM(F)$ be a set of values. The *relation for $F$ with respect to $D$* is the set of tuples $a_1 \cdots a_n$ in

$$D \times \cdots \times D \ (n \text{ times})$$

such that when each $a_i$ is substituted for $X_i$, $F(a_1, \ldots, a_n)$ becomes true. In evaluating $F$, any quantified variables are assumed to range over the set $D$, and the negation of a subformula $G$ is satisfied only by values in $D$ that do not make $G$ true. We say $F$ is *domain independent* if the relation for $F$ with respect to $D \supseteq DOM(F)$ does not actually depend on $D$. If $F$ is domain independent, then its relation with respect to any domain $D \supseteq DOM(F)$ is the same as its relation with respect to $DOM(F)$.

**Example 3.28:** The formula $F_1 = \neg r(X, Y)$ is not domain independent. Let $R$ be the relation given for predicate $r$; therefore $DOM(F_1) = \pi_1(R) \cup \pi_2(R)$. However, if $D$ is any set that contains $DOM(F_1)$, then the relation for $F_1$ with respect to $D$ is $(D \times D) - R$. In particular, if $a$ is any symbol in $D$ that is not in $DOM(F_1)$, then the tuple $(a, a)$ is in the relation of $F_1$ with respect to $D$, but is not in the relation of $F_1$ with respect to $DOM(F_1)$.

For another, more complex example, consider

$$F_2 = (\exists Y)\big(p(X, Y) \vee q(Y, Z)\big)$$

Let $P = \{ab, cd\}$ and $Q = \{ef\}$ be the relations given for $p$ and $q$, respectively. Then $DOM(F_2) = \{a, b, c, d, e, f\}$. Let $D = \{a, b, c, d, e, f, g\}$. Then the relation for $F_2$ with respect to $D$, which is a relation over $X$ and $Z$, the free variables of $F_2$, includes the tuple $(a, g)$. The reason is that there exists a value of $Y$ in the domain $D$, namely $Y = b$, that makes $p(a, Y) \vee q(Y, g)$ true. Naturally, $q(b, g)$ isn't true, because $bg$ is not in $Q$, but $p(a, b)$ is true because $ab$ is in $P$. Since eliminating $g$ from $D$ surely yields a different relation for $F_2$, we conclude that $F_2$ is not domain independent.

On the other hand, consider $F_3 = (\exists Y)\big(p(X, Y) \wedge q(Y, Z)\big)$. As with $F_2$, the relation for $F_3$ is a relation over $X$ and $Z$. However, suppose $(a, b)$ is a tuple in the relation for $F_3$ with respect to some $D$. Then there must be some value $c$ in $D$ such that when $c$ is substituted for $Y$, the formula $p(a, Y) \wedge q(Y, b)$ becomes true. That is, if $P$ and $Q$ are the relations for $p$ and $q$, then $ac$ is in $P$ and $cb$ is in $Q$. Therefore, $a$ is in $\pi_1(P)$, and thus $a$ is in $DOM(F_3)$. Similarly, $b$ is in $\pi_2(Q)$ and therefore in $DOM(F_3)$. We conclude that whatever $D \supset DOM(F_3)$ we choose, the set of $(a, b)$ pairs in the relation for $F_3$ with respect to $D$ will be the same as the relation for $F_3$ with respect to $DOM(F_3)$; therefore, $F_3$ is domain independent. $\square$

## Safe DRC Formulas

As we mentioned, there is no algorithm to tell whether a given DRC formula is domain independent. Thus, real query languages based on relational calculus use only a subset of the DRC formulas, ones that are guaranteed to be domain independent. We shall define "safe" formulas to be a subset of the domain independent formulas. The important properties of safety are:

a)    Every "safe" formula must be domain independent.
b)    We can tell easily, just by inspecting a formula, whether or not it is "safe."
c)    The formulas that are expressible in real query languages based on relational calculus are "safe."

With these criteria in mind, we introduce the following definition of *safe DRC formulas*. Intuitively, these conditions force DRC formulas to look like the result of applying a sequence of (safe) nonrecursive datalog rules. Rule (2) below says that logical OR is used in the same way that two rectified rules for the same predicate may be used, and rule (3) is analogous to the requirement that all variables in the body of a rule be limited.

1.    There are no uses of the $\forall$ quantifier. This constraint does not affect the expressiveness of the language, because $(\forall X)F$ is logically equivalent to $\neg(\exists X)\neg F$. That is, $F$ is true for all $X$ if and only if there does not exist an $X$ for which $F$ is false. By applying this transformation wherever we find a $\forall$, we can eliminate all universal quantifiers.

2.    Whenever an OR operator is used, the two formulas connected, say $F_1 \lor F_2$, have the same set of free variables; i.e., they are of the form

$$F_1(X_1, \ldots, X_n) \lor F_2(X_1, \ldots, X_n)$$

3.    Consider any maximal subformula consisting of the conjunction of one or more formulas $F_1 \land \cdots \land F_m$. Then all variables appearing free in any of these $F_i$'s must be *limited* in the following sense.
      a)    A variable is limited if it is free in some $F_i$, where $F_i$ is not an arithmetic comparison and is not negated.
      b)    If $F_i$ is $X = a$ or $a = X$, where $a$ is a constant, then $X$ is limited.
      c)    If $F_i$ is $X = Y$ or $Y = X$, and $Y$ is a limited variable, then $X$ is limited.

      It is important to note that this rule applies to atomic formulas if they do not appear in a larger group of formulas connected by logical AND. For example, if our entire formula is $X = Y$, it is not safe because it is the "conjunct" of one formula, and the variables $X$ and $Y$ are not limited. Likewise, the formula $X = Y \lor p(X, Y)$ is not safe because the left operand of the OR violates rule (3). However, $X = Y \land p(X, Y)$ is safe, because $p(X, Y)$ limits both $X$ and $Y$ by (a).

4.    A $\neg$ operator may only apply to a term in a conjunction of the type discussed in rule (3). In particular, a subformula $\neg G$ violates the "safety" definition unless it is part of a larger subformula

$$H_1 \land \cdots \land H_i \land \neg G \land I_1 \land \cdots \land I_j$$

satisfying (3), such that at least one of the $H$'s and $I$'s is positive (not negated).

**Example 3.29:** Every formula generated in Theorem 3.10 is a safe formula. For a more complex example, consider

$$r(X, Y, Z) \wedge \neg\big(p(X, Y) \vee q(Y, Z)\big) \tag{3.13}$$

Subformula $p(X, Y) \vee q(Y, Z)$ may have an infinite relation, over scheme $\{X, Y, Z\}$. The reason is that whenever $p(X, Y)$ is true, $q(Y, Z)$ need not be true, so $Z$ could take on any value, and yet $p(X, Y) \vee q(Y, Z)$ would be true for the tuple $(X, Y, Z)$. Likewise, $\neg\big(p(X, Y) \vee q(Y, Z)\big)$ can be seen to have an infinite relation. Yet the complete formula (3.13) has a finite relation, in particular, one that is a subset of the relation for $r$. Thus, (3.13) is a domain independent formula. However, it is not safe; in particular, condition (2) is violated by the subformula $p(X, Y) \vee q(Y, Z)$.

One way to convert (3.13) to a safe formula is to use DeMorgan's law on the negated subformula to yield

$$r(X, Y, Z) \wedge \neg p(X, Y) \wedge \neg q(Y, Z)$$

Then, all three variables are limited by the positive conjunct $r(X, Y, Z)$, so this formula satisfies condition (3). $\square$

### Safe DRC to Relational Algebra

We can prove that every safe formula has a relational algebra expression defining the same relation. Of course, there are many nonsafe formulas that also have equivalent relational algebra expressions, such as the formula of Example 3.29, but we cannot in general tell which ones do and which do not.

**Theorem 3.11:** The sets of functions computed by expressions of relational algebra, by safe, nonrecursive datalog programs, and by safe formulas of domain relational calculus are the same.

**Proof:** Theorems 3.7 and 3.8 proved the equivalence of relational algebra and safe, nonrecursive datalog rules. Theorem 3.10, when we check the form of each constructed formula, tells us that the functions expressible in relational algebra are all expressible in safe DRC. We complete the proof by showing that safe DRC formulas define functions that are expressible in safe, nonrecursive datalog.

The proof proceeds by induction on the number of operators in the safe DRC formula. However, because rule (3) applies to maximal sets of formulas connected by logical AND, we have to state the inductive hypothesis carefully, to avoid considering subformulas that appear unsafe only because they are a proper subpart of a conjunct that does satisfy rule (3). For example, we do not want to consider $X = Y$ separately in the formula $X = Y \wedge p(X, Y)$. Thus, the inductive hypothesis we shall prove is the following. Let $F$ be a safe DRC formula. Then for every subformula $G$ such that $F$ does not apply the AND operator to $G$ (i.e., there is no larger subformula $G \wedge H$ or $H \wedge G$ in $F$), if $G$ has free variables $X_1, \ldots, X_n$, then there is a safe, nonrecursive datalog program that defines the relation for some predicate $p_G(X_1, \ldots, X_n)$ to be equal to the set of tuples $(a_1, \ldots, a_n)$ that make $G$ true, when $a_i$ is substituted for $X_i$, $1 \leq i \leq n$.

*Basis*: $G$ is a maximal conjunct of atomic formulas $G_1 \wedge \cdots \wedge G_k$. The basis includes the case $k = 1$, where $G$ is an atomic formula not part of any conjunct. Then each $G_i$ has the form of a subgoal, either ordinary or built-in. If $k \geq 2$, define the predicate $p_G$ for $G$ by

$$p_G(X_1, \ldots, X_m) \coloneq G_1 \ \& \ \cdots \ \& \ G_k.$$

where $X_1, \ldots, X_m$ are all the free variables in $G$. Rule (3) in the definition of safety for DRC implies that the above rule is a safe datalog rule.

If $k = 1$, then $G$ must be an ordinary atomic formula of the form $p(X_1, \ldots, X_k)$. In this case, use the EDB relation name $p$ for $p_G$, and do not generate any rules.

*Induction*: Since universal quantifiers are forbidden in safe formulas, and negations can only appear within conjunctions, we can break the induction into three cases, for $\exists$, $\vee$, and $\wedge$.

1.  $G = (\exists X_i)H$, where the free variables of $H$ are $X_1, \ldots, X_k$. Then the rule

    $$p_G(X_1, \ldots, X_{i-1}, X_{i+1}, \ldots, X_k) \coloneq p_H(X_1, \ldots, X_k).$$

    defines the desired predicate $p_G$.

2.  $G = H \vee I$. Then the free variables of $H$ and $I$ must be the same, by rule (2) in the definition of "safety"; let these variables be $X_1, \ldots, X_k$. Then we use the two rules

    $$p_G(X_1, \ldots, X_k) \coloneq p_H(X_1, \ldots, X_k).$$
    $$p_G(X_1, \ldots, X_k) \coloneq p_I(X_1, \ldots, X_k).$$

3.  $G = G_1 \wedge \cdots \wedge G_n$. Here, we may assume that $G$ is a maximal conjunct, because the inductive hypothesis does not apply to nonmaximal ones.

    a)  For all those $G_i$'s that are not arithmetic atomic formulas (i.e., of the form $X\theta Y$, where $\theta$ is $=$, $<$, etc.), let subgoal $S_i$ be $p_{G_i}(Y_{i1}, \ldots, Y_{im_i})$, where $Y_{i1}, \ldots, Y_{im_i}$ are all the free variables in $G_i$. By the inductive hypothesis, $p_{G_i}$ has already been defined by the appropriate rules.

    b)  If $G_i$ is an arithmetic atomic formula, then let $S_i$ be $G_i$ itself.

    Let $X_1, \ldots, X_k$ be all the variables appearing among the $G_i$'s. Then the rule for $G$ is

    $$p_G(X_1, \ldots, X_k) \coloneq S_1 \ \& \ \cdots \ \& \ S_n.$$

□

**Example 3.30:** Let us treat the DRC formula constructed in Example 3.26:

$$likes(X, Y) \land \neg (broke(X) \land (\exists Z)likes(Z, Y))$$

Of the three atomic formulas, only $likes(Z, Y)$ is not part of a larger conjunct; it is part of an existentially quantified formula. We thus use $likes$ as the predicate for this subformula and create no rules.

For the expression $(\exists Z)likes(Z, Y)$ we create a new predicate, say $p$ and give it the rule

```
p(Y) :- likes(Z,Y).
```

Next we work on the maximal conjunct $broke(X) \land (\exists Z)likes(Z, Y)$, which is $broke(X) \land p(Y)$. The rule for this conjunct is thus

```
q(X,Y) :- broke(X) & p(Y).
```

where $q$ is used as the predicate name. Finally, the outer conjunct is translated into a rule

```
r(X,Y) :- likes(X,Y) & ¬q(X,Y).
```

Notice that the rules we obtain are essentially those of Example 3.23. What we called $p$, $q$, and $r$ here are $liked$, $brokePair$, and $canBuy$ there. □

## 3.9 TUPLE RELATIONAL CALCULUS

Tuple relational calculus, or TRC, is a variant of relational calculus where variables stand for tuples rather than components of tuples. To refer to the $i$th component of a tuple $\mu$ we use $\mu[i]$. If an attribute $A$ for that component is known, we may also write $\mu[A]$. The formulas of TRC are defined recursively, and the structure of TRC formulas is quite close to the structure of DRC formulas. The basis, atomic formulas, is:

1.  If $p$ is a predicate name and $\mu$ a tuple variable, then $p(\mu)$ is an atomic formula. Its meaning is that "tuple $\mu$ is in the relation for $p$."
2.  $X\theta Y$ is an atomic formula if $\theta$ is an arithmetic comparison operator and $X$ and $Y$ are each either constants or component references; the latter are of the form $\mu[i]$ for some tuple variable $\mu$ and component number or attribute $i$.

The inductive definition proceeds as in domain relational calculus. If $F_1$ and $F_2$ are formulas of TRC and $\mu$ is a tuple variable appearing free in $F_1$, then the following are TRC formulas, with the obvious meanings and sets of free and bound variables.

|   |   |   |   |
|---|---|---|---|
| a) | $F_1 \land F_2$ | d) | $(\exists \mu)F_1$ |
| b) | $F_1 \lor F_2$ | e) | $(\forall \mu)F_1$ |
| c) | $\neg F_1$ |   |   |

The relation associated with a formula of TRC is defined in the same way as for DRC. The relation for $F$ has one component for each component of each free tuple variable of $F$ that actually is mentioned in $F$.[19] The value of the relation for $F$ is the set of tuples whose values, when substituted for their corresponding components of tuple variables, makes $F$ true. A *query* of TRC is an expression of the form $\{\mu \mid F(\mu)\}$, where $\mu$ is the only free variable of $F$. Naturally, this expression defines the relation of all tuples $\mu$ such that $F(\mu)$ is true.

On occasion, the arity of a tuple variable will not be clear from context. We shall use the notation $\mu^{(i)}$ to denote a tuple variable $\mu$ that is of arity $i$. Frequently, we use the superscript when the tuple variable is quantified and leave it off in other places.

**Example 3.31:** The DRC query derived in Example 3.26 can be turned into TRC if we use the tuple $\mu$ for $(X, Y)$, $\nu$ for $X$ in *broke*, and $\rho$ for $(Z, Y)$ in *likes*. The query is:

$$\{\mu^{(2)} \mid \mathit{likes}(\mu) \wedge \neg\Big((\exists\nu^{(1)})(\mathit{broke}(\nu) \wedge \nu[1] = \mu[1])\wedge$$
$$(\exists\rho^{(2)})(\mathit{likes}(\rho) \wedge \rho[2] = \mu[2])\Big)\} \tag{3.14}$$

Notice how the atomic formula $\nu[1] = \mu[1]$ replaces the connection that in DRC was expressed by using the same variable $X$ in *likes* and in *broke*. We cannot use $\mu$ as the argument of *broke*, because *broke* takes a unary tuple, while *likes* takes a binary tuple. Similarly, $\rho[2] = \mu[2]$ substitutes for the double use of $Y$. Also notice that $\nu$ must be existentially quantified, or else it would be a free variable of the query that did not appear to the left of the bar in the set former (3.14). Although it looks like $\nu$ could therefore be anything, the formula $\nu[1] = \mu[1]$ completely defines the unary tuple $\nu$. The relation for the formula $\mathit{broke}(\nu) \wedge \nu[1] = \mu[1]$ is

$$\{(X, X) \mid X \text{ is in } \mathit{broke}\}$$

The two components correspond to $\nu[1]$ and $\mu[1]$. They have the same value in each tuple, because in order for the formula to be satisfied, the subformula $\nu[1] = \mu[1]$ must be satisfied.

In the formula $(\exists\nu^{(1)})(\mathit{broke}(\nu) \wedge \nu[1] = \mu[1])$ there is only one free component, $\mu[1]$. The relation for this formula is thus $\{X \mid X \text{ is in } \mathit{broke}\}$; i.e., it is the same as *broke*. $\square$

### Safe Tuple Relational Calculus

As in DRC, we can write TRC formulas, such as $\neg r(\mu)$, that denote infinite relations. We want to avoid them in real query languages, and as with DRC,

---

[19] Note that in TRC it is possible that a subformula could mention $\mu[2]$, say, without mentioning $\mu[1]$.

the most useful approach is to define a restricted form of TRC called "safe TRC." Again in analogy with DRC, we shall be rather more restrictive than we have to be, when defining "safety," because all we really need to do is define a class that reflects what is found in commercial TRC-based languages and that is equivalent in expressive power to relational algebra.

Since the arity of a tuple variable is not always clear from context in a TRC formula, we shall assume that the arity of each variable is given and that the arity of one variable does not change from occurrence to occurrence, even if the two occurrences are bound by different quantifiers. The safety of a TRC formula is defined as follows, in close analogy with the definition of safe DRC.

1.  There are no uses of the $\forall$ quantifier.
2.  Whenever an $\vee$ operator is used, the two formulas connected, say $F_1 \vee F_2$, have only one free tuple variable, and it is the same variable.
3.  Consider any subformula consisting of a maximal conjunction of one or more formulas $F_1 \wedge \cdots \wedge F_m$. Then all components of tuple variables that are free in any of these $F_i$'s are *limited* in the following sense.
    a)  If $F_i$ is not negated, not an arithmetic comparison, and has free tuple variable $\mu$, then all components of $\mu$ are limited.
    b)  If $F_i$ is $\mu[j] = a$ or $a = \mu[j]$, where $a$ is a constant, then $\mu[j]$ is limited.
    c)  If $F_i$ is $\mu[j] = \nu[k]$ or $\nu[k] = \mu[j]$, and $\nu[k]$ is a limited variable, then $\mu[j]$ is limited.
4.  A $\neg$ operator may only apply to a term in a conjunction of the type discussed in rule (3).

### From Relational Algebra to Safe Tuple Relational Calculus

We shall show that safe TRC is equivalent in expressive power to relational algebra, and therefore to the other languages of Theorem 3.11. The proof is in two lemmas, one converting relational algebra to TRC and the other converting TRC to DRC. These two results, together with the equivalences of Theorem 3.11 will show the equivalence between safe TRC and the three other abstract query languages shown equivalent in that theorem.

Our first step is to show how relational algebra expressions can be converted into TRC formulas. The proof is quite similar to that of Theorem 3.10, where we turned the algebra into domain calculus.

**Lemma 3.6:** Every query expressible in relational algebra is expressible in safe tuple relational calculus.

**Proof:** We show by induction on the number of operators in the relational algebra expression $E$ that there is a TRC formula, with a single free tuple variable, that defines the same relation as $E$. The basis, zero operators, requires that we consider two cases, where $E$ is a relation variable $R$ or a constant relation. If $E$ is a relation name $R$, then formula $R(\mu)$ suffices. If $E$ is a constant, say $\{\mu_1, \ldots, \mu_n\}$, consisting of tuples of arity $k$, then we use one free variable, say $\nu$, and we write the TRC formula

$$\nu[1] = \mu_1[1] \wedge \nu[2] = \mu_1[2] \wedge \cdots \wedge \nu[k] = \mu_1[k] \vee$$
$$\nu[1] = \mu_2[1] \wedge \nu[2] = \mu_2[2] \wedge \cdots \wedge \nu[k] = \mu_2[k] \vee$$
$$\cdots$$
$$\nu[1] = \mu_n[1] \wedge \nu[2] = \mu_n[2] \wedge \cdots \wedge \nu[k] = \mu_n[k]$$

Note that for all $i$ and $j$, $\mu_i[j]$ is a constant here. Thus, the above formula is safe, by rules (2) and (3b) of the safety definition.

For the induction, we consider the five cases.

1. $E = E_1 \cup E_2$. Then there are TRC formulas $F_1$ and $F_2$ for $E_1$ and $E_2$. By renaming if necessary, we may assume that the lone free tuple variable in $F_1$ and $F_2$ is $\mu$. Because $E_1$ and $E_2$ have the same arity, the free tuple variables of $F_1$ and $F_2$ must also have the same arity, so the renaming is permitted. Then $F_1 \vee F_2$ is a TRC formula for $E$.

2. $E = E_1 - E_2$. As in (1), assume there are formulas $F_1(\mu)$ and $F_2(\mu)$ for $E_1$ and $E_2$, respectively. Then $F_1 \wedge \neg F_2$ is a TRC formula for $E$.

3. $E = \pi_{i_1,\ldots,i_k}(E_1)$. Let $F_1(\nu)$ be a TRC formula for $E_1$. Then a formula for $E$, with free variable $\mu$, is

$$(\exists \nu)\big(F_1(\nu) \wedge \mu[1] = \nu[i_1] \wedge \mu[2] = \nu[i_2] \wedge \cdots \wedge \mu[k] = \nu[i_k]\big)$$

4. $E = E_1 \times E_2$. Let $F_1(\nu^{(m)})$ and $F_2(\rho^{(n)})$ be TRC formulas for $E_1$ and $E_2$. Then the TRC formula for $E$, with lone free variable $\mu^{(m+n)}$, is

$$(\exists \nu)(\exists \rho)\big(F_1(\nu) \wedge F_2(\rho) \wedge$$
$$\mu[1] = \nu[1] \wedge \cdots \wedge \mu[m] = \nu[m] \wedge$$
$$\mu[m+1] = \rho[1] \wedge \cdots \wedge \mu[m+n] = \rho[n]\big)$$

5. $E = \sigma_A(E_1)$. By Lemma 3.5, we may assume $A$ is a simple selection of the form $\$i \; \theta \; \$j$ or $\$i \; \theta \; a$, for constant $a$. Let $F_1(\mu)$ be a TRC formula for $E_1$. Then for $E$ we have TRC formula

$$F_1(\mu) \wedge \mu[i] \; \theta \; \mu[j] \quad \text{or} \quad F_1(\mu) \wedge \mu[i] \; \theta \; a$$

depending on the form of $A$. $\square$

**Example 3.32:** Let us convert the algebraic expression of Example 3.26:

$$likes(X, Y) - \big(broke(X) \times \pi_Y(likes(X, Y))\big)$$

into tuple calculus. To begin, the three occurrences of predicates will be translated to $likes(\lambda)$, $broke(\mu)$, and $likes(\nu)$, in order of appearance in the expression above. For $\pi_Y(likes(X, Y))$, we must introduce a new, unary tuple variable $\rho$, and write $(\exists \nu)(likes(\nu) \wedge \rho[1] = \nu[2])$. Notice that this formula is safe, since the subformula $likes(\nu) \wedge \rho[1] = \nu[2]$ has all its components of free variables limited; the components of $\nu$ are limited by $likes(\nu)$, and $\rho[1]$ is limited by being equated to $\nu[2]$.

For $broke(X) \times \pi_Y(likes(X,Y))$ we must again introduce a new variable, this time a binary variable whose first component is equated to the lone component of $\mu$ and whose second component is equated to the lone component of $\rho$. While we could call this new variable what we liked, it makes sense to call it $\lambda$. The reason is that, at the next step, we must subtract the formula we construct now from the formula $likes(\lambda)$, and to make the resulting formula safe, the free tuple variable of each formula must be the same. Therefore, we construct TRC formula

$$(\exists\mu)(\exists\rho)\Big(broke(\mu) \wedge \big((\exists\nu)(likes(\nu) \wedge \rho[1] = \nu[2])\big)\big) \wedge$$
$$\lambda[1] = \mu[1] \wedge \lambda[2] = \rho[1]\Big) \tag{3.15}$$

Finally, for the entire expression we have

$$\{\lambda^{(2)} \mid likes(\lambda) \wedge \neg\Big((\exists\mu^{(1)})(\exists\rho^{(1)})\big(broke(\mu) \wedge$$
$$\big((\exists\nu^{(2)})(likes(\nu) \wedge \rho[1] = \nu[2])\big) \wedge$$
$$\lambda[1] = \mu[1] \wedge \lambda[2] = \rho[1]\big)\Big)\} \tag{3.16}$$

☐

## From TRC to DRC

The conversion from safe TRC to safe DRC is straightforward; we replace each tuple variable by a collection of domain variables, one for each component of the tuple variable.

**Lemma 3.7:** For every safe formula of TRC there is a safe formula of DRC that defines the same relation.

**Proof:** The idea, as stated above, is to replace each tuple variable $\mu^{(k)}$ by $k$ domain variables $X_1, \ldots, X_k$, and let $X_j$ be used exactly where $\mu[j]$ is used. The existential quantification of a tuple variable, say $(\exists\mu^{(k)})F$, is replaced by $(\exists X_1)(\exists X_2)(\cdots)(\exists X_k)F'$, where $F'$ is the translation of $F$ into DRC. The straightforward proof that this transformation produces safe formulas from safe formulas, and preserves the defined relation, is left for an exercise. ☐

**Example 3.33:** Let us consider the TRC query (3.16) from Example 3.32. For the two components of $\lambda$ we shall use domain variables $L_1$ and $L_2$. We use $N_1$ and $N_2$ for the two components of $\nu$, and we use $M$ and $R$ for the lone components of $\mu$ and $\rho$, respectively. Thus, the TRC formula

$$likes(\nu) \wedge \rho[1] = \nu[2]$$

is replaced by the DRC formula $likes(N_1 N_2) \land R = N_2$.

Then, for the TRC formula $(\exists \nu)(likes(\nu) \land \rho[1] = \nu[2])$ we have DRC formula

$$F_1 = (\exists N_1)(\exists N_2)(likes(N_1 N_2) \land R = N_2)$$

Notice that $F_1$, which has only $R$ as a free variable, defines the same relation as $(\exists N_1)(likes(N_1 R))$, because of the subformula equating $R$ to $N_2$ in $F_1$.

Progressing outwards, the negated subformula of (3.16), which appeared in Example 3.32 as (3.15), is converted to

$$F_2 = (\exists M)(\exists R)(broke(M) \land F_1 \land L_1 = M \land L_2 = R)$$

where $F_1$ is the formula above.

Finally, the entire query (3.16) can be expressed in DRC as:

$$\{L_1 L_2 \mid likes(L_1 L_2) \land \neg(F_2)\}$$

This formula, like $F_1$, can be simplified by taking advantage of the equalities between domain variables to eliminate one of them. $\square$

The above relationships and Theorem 3.11 can be summarized as follows.

**Theorem 3.12:** The following four languages define the same class of functions:

1. Relational algebra expressions.
2. Safe, nonrecursive datalog programs with negation.
3. Safe domain relational calculus formulas.
4. Safe tuple relational calculus formulas. $\square$

## 3.10 THE CLOSED WORLD ASSUMPTION

We have seen in this chapter how logic can be used to define operations on a database, and how the process of obtaining answers to a query is one of proving that certain facts follow logically from the facts in the extensional database. However, to follow through consistently with the point of view that operations on data are proofs, we ought to be able to prove that certain facts are *not* part of the answer to a query by proving that their negation follows from the given EDB and rules.

Unfortunately, there is nothing in the logic we have developed that lets us conclude a negative fact. For example, let us recall our genealogy rules of Figure 3.1, and suppose we are given an EDB relation $P$ for predicate *parent*. We might well suppose that there do not exist in $P$ tuples that let us use rule (1), which is

    sibling(X,Y) := parent(X,Z) & parent(Y,Z) & X≠Y.

to deduce $sibling(superman, henry\_viii)$. Can we therefore deduce the truth of the logical formula

$$\neg(sibling(superman,\ henry\_viii)) \tag{3.17}$$

If we assume that there is no $Z$ for which $parent(superman, Z)$ and $parent(henry\_viii, Z)$ are both true, then there is no way

$$sibling(superman,\ henry\_viii)$$

could be deduced by rule (1) of Figure 3.1. But that is not a proof that (3.17) is true. For example, there might be parent-child facts that are not in the relation $P$, or there might be a way to deduce $sibling(X, Y)$ other than by rule (1).

Rather than get paranoid about the matter, we can make the *closed world assumption* (CWA). The CWA says that whenever an atomic formula $p(a_1, \ldots, a_k)$ with no variables (such a formula is often called a *ground atom*) is not deducible from your EDB and your rules, then you may assume $\neg p(a_1, \ldots, a_k)$. Thus, the CWA is a powerful rule for inferring new formulas. We are used to one kind of deduction, where we are given some facts that match the body of a rule, and we thereby deduce the head of the rule as a new fact. But the CWA acts as a "metarule," which talks about the deductions themselves. The CWA lets us "deduce" facts of the form $\neg p(a_1, \ldots, a_k)$ whenever the usual form of deduction does not yield $p(a_1, \ldots, a_k)$.

## Validity of the Closed World Assumption

It turns out that there are circumstances where the CWA leads to logical contradictions, and we therefore may not assume it. Before giving such an example, let us see an important special case where the CWA is logically consistent.

First, we need to assume that different constants are distinct. For example, in our rule for siblings, we have no trouble believing that $superman \neq henry\_viii$, so if these two individuals had a common parent, surely it would make sense to accept that the third subgoal of rule (1), $X \neq Y$, is satisfied, and therefore, $sibling(superman,\ henry\_viii)$ could be deduced. However, if instead, our database had $P$ facts

$$parent(superman,\ jor\_el)\ \text{and}\ parent(clark\_kent,\ jor\_el)$$

we would be less comfortable about accepting $superman \neq clark\_kent$, thus deducing $sibling(superman,\ clark\_kent)$. The consequence is that in order to rely on the CWA we must assume that distinct constants are not somehow "the same"; i.e., use $superman$ in your database to denote the man of steel, or use $clark\_kent$ if you wish, but pick one consistently.

A second essential is that we assume there are no more constants than actually appear in the database and the rules. Without this *domain closure* assumption, we could not conclude

$$\neg sibling(superman,\ henry\_viii)$$

just because we found no common parent in the database; there could be a common parent of *superman* and *henry_viii* that was not mentioned in the database.

The final necessary assumption is that our rules are all Horn clauses (with no negated subgoals, of course).[20] Formally, what we can show is the following.

**Theorem 3.13:** Let $\mathcal{R}$ be a set of Horn-clause rules, and $E$ be the set of EDB facts (tuples) of the EDB relations of $\mathcal{R}$. Let $I$ be the set of IDB facts deducible by Algorithm 3.3; that is, $I \cup E$ is the set of tuples in all the relations of the least fixed point of $\mathcal{R}$. Let $J$ be the set of ground atoms $\neg p(a_1, \ldots, a_k)$ such that $p$ is a predicate of $\mathcal{R}$, and $a_1, \ldots, a_k$ are constants, but $p(a_1, \ldots, a_k)$ is not in $I \cup E$. Then $I \cup E \cup J$ is logically consistent (no contradiction can be derived).

**Proof:** Suppose $K = I \cup E \cup J$ yielded a contradiction. Then there would be some rule $r$ and some substitution for the variables of $r$ such that each of the subgoals of the body of $r$ becomes a member of $K$, but the head does not become a member of $K$. But the subgoals are all unnegated literals, and therefore they must be in $I \cup E$ after the substitution. That is, because we have Horn clauses, a subgoal, after substitution, cannot be in $J$. Then since $I$ is computed by taking a fixed point, as in Algorithm 3.3, the head of $r$ after substitution is also placed in $I$ by Algorithm 3.3, and therefore, the head is also in $K$, contrary to assumption. $\square$

### Problems with the Closed World Assumption

As we just saw, while we stay within the realm of Horn clauses, the CWA makes good sense. However, logic as a data model allows more general modes of reasoning. With Horn clauses, we can only deal with facts that are true and facts that are not true. We cannot make statements like $p(0) \vee p(1)$, i.e., either the (unary) tuple 0 is in relation $P$, or 1 is, or both, but we don't know which of these three cases applies. This sort of reasoning is of a kind that we might hope a knowledge-base system could support. Unfortunately, the CWA does not interact well with this kind of reasoning; it leads to a contradiction.

**Example 3.34:** Suppose we have only the EDB relation $R$ corresponding to predicate $r$, and our rules are $p(X) \text{ :- } r(X)$ and $p(0) \vee p(1)$. Note that the latter rule is not a Horn clause, because it has two literals that are not negated. We may write it in our usual notation as $p(0) \text{ :- } \neg p(1)$, but that is still not, strictly

---

[20] The subgoal $X \neq Y$ in rule (1) of Figure 3.1 might give us pause, since it is in a sense negated. However, we can think of it as a nonnegated subgoal $n(X, Y)$, where the relation $N$ for predicate $n$ consists of the infinite set of pairs $(a, b)$ such that $a \neq b$. Since variables $X$ and $Y$ each appear in other subgoals of this rule, the infiniteness of $N$ does not bother us. Notice how the assumption that distinct constants are unequal is important here too, or else we could not tell what pairs belonged in $N$.

speaking, a Horn clause, because it has a negated subgoal.

Let us suppose that $R$ does not contain either 0 or 1. Then there is no way to deduce $p(0)$ and there is no way to deduce $p(1)$. Therefore, the CWA allows us to assert $\neg p(0)$ and $\neg p(1)$. However, the three formulas $\neg p(0)$, $\neg p(1)$, and $p(0) \vee p(1)$ clearly yield a logical contradiction. Thus, when we have non-Horn clauses among our rules, we may not make the CWA, and it is unsafe to conclude that something is not true just because you cannot deduce it from the database and rules. $\square$

### Generalizations of the Closed World Assumption

There have been proposed some more restrictive rules that let us infer some negated facts, but not enough to lead to the contradiction in Example 3.34. Such generalizations are needed whenever we have inference rules that are not Horn clauses. For example, we might add to the set of accepted facts (our selected fixed point) the negated ground atom $\neg p(a_1, \ldots, a_k)$ as long as there is no formula $F$ such that:

1. $F$ is the logical OR of ground atoms.
2. $p(a_1, \ldots, a_k) \vee F$ is deducible by the application of rules to the EDB.
3. $F$ itself is not deducible by application of rules to the EDB.

This law would protect against adding either $p(0)$ or $p(1)$ to the fixed point in Example 3.34, because each serves as $F$ for the other. That is, we cannot add $\neg p(0)$, because we can derive $p(0) \vee F$, where $F = p(1)$, and similarly for $\neg p(1)$.

The matter of what may be assumed from negative evidence is an active area for research in the theory of reasoning. Generalizations of the CWA, such as the one just mentioned, suffer from the problem that there do not appear to be efficient algorithms to tell whether a negated ground atom $\neg p(a_1, \ldots, a_k)$ meets the condition. The references contain pointers to the research on the subject.

### EXERCISES

3.1: In Example 1.13 we gave datalog rules for a simple black/white cell definition system. Generalize the system to allow $n$ colors, $1, 2, \ldots, n$. That is, EDB relation $contains(I, J, X, Y)$ has the same meaning as in Example 1.13, and EDB relation $set(I, X, Y, C)$ says that cell $I$ has color $C$ at point $(X, Y)$. Define $color(I, X, Y, C)$ to mean that cell $I$ has color $C$ at point $(X, Y)$, either directly or through the presence of some subcell. If a point is defined to have more than one color, then $color$ will be true for each.

* 3.2: Modify your answer to Exercise 3.1 so at most one color is defined for any point, using the rules:

   *i)*   If $I$ has two subcells that each define a color for a given point, the higher-numbered color predominates.

   *ii)*  If $I$ has a subcell $J$, then whatever color a point has in $J$ (including both directly defined colors and colors required by subcells of $J$) predominates over a color defined for that point directly in $I$ [i.e., via $set(I, X, Y, C)$].

   *Hint:* Simplify life by ignoring the translation of coordinates. Start by assuming there is only one point per cell, and the EDB predicates are $set(I, C)$ and $contains(I, J)$.

3.3: Are your rules from Exercise 3.2 (a) safe? (b) stratified?

** 3.4: Show that

   a)  Your rules from Exercise 3.2 can have more than one minimal fixed point for some values of $set$ and $contains$.

   b)  Relation $contains$ is *acyclic*, if the graph whose nodes correspond to cells and that has an arc from $I$ to $J$ if $contains(I, J, X, Y)$ is true for some $X$ and $Y$, is acyclic. Show that if $contains$ is acyclic, then your rules from Exercise 3.2 have a unique least fixed point.

* 3.5: The following is a simplification of a calculation that must be performed in an optimizing compiler. We shall assume that all procedures of the hypothetical language being compiled have a single parameter, and an EDB relation $param(P, X)$ says that $X$ is the formal parameter of procedure $P$. Another EDB predicate $calls(P, Q, Y)$ says that procedure $P$ calls procedure $Q$ with actual parameter $Y$. It is possible that $Y$ is a local variable of $P$, the formal parameter of $P$, or a constant. For example, the procedures in Figure 3.8 are characterized by the EDB facts

$$\begin{array}{ll} param(p, x) & calls(p, q, a) \\ param(q, y) & calls(p, q, x) \\ & calls(q, p, y) \\ & calls(q, q, 3) \end{array}$$

Write datalog rules that compute the "transitive closure" of $calls$, that is, an IDB predicate $calls\_star(P, Q, Z)$ that says when procedure $P$ executes, it results in a call to $Q$ with argument $Z$, perhaps through a sequence of calls to procedures. For example, in the procedures of Figure 3.8, $calls\_star(p, p, a)$ is true, because $p$ calls $q$ with argument $a$, and $q$ calls $p$ with its own formal parameter as argument. Try to avoid the use of negated subgoals in your answer.

```
procedure p(x);
    local a;
    call q(a);
    call q(x);
end

procedure q(y);
    call p(y);
    call q(3);
end
```

**Figure 3.8** Example program for Exercise 3.5.

3.6: Suppose we have EDB relations

    *frequents(Drinker, Bar)*
    *serves(Bar, Beer)*
    *likes(Drinker, Beer)*

The first indicates the bars a drinker visits; the second tells what beers each bar serves, and the last indicates which beers each drinker likes to drink. Define the following predicates using safe datalog rules.

  a)  *happy(D)* that is true if drinker $D$ frequents at least one bar that serves a beer he likes.

  b)  *shouldVisit(D, B)* if bar $B$ serves a beer drinker $D$ likes.

\* c)  *veryHappy(D)* if every bar that drinker $D$ frequents serves at least one beer he likes. You may assume that every drinker frequents at least one bar.

\* d)  *sad(D)* if drinker $D$ frequents no bar that serves a beer he likes.

3.7: Write each of the queries of Exercise 3.6 in (*i*) relational algebra (*ii*) safe DRC (*iii*) safe TRC.

3.8: Assuming $R$ and $S$ are of arity 3 and 2, respectively, convert the expression $\pi_{1,5}\big(\sigma_{\$2=\$4\vee\$3=\$4}(R \times S)\big)$ to

  a)  Safe, nonrecursive datalog rules.

  b)  Safe DRC.

  c)  Safe TRC.

\* 3.9: Consider the TRC expression

$$\{\mu^{(2)} \mid r(\mu) \wedge (\exists\nu^{(2)})\big(s(\nu) \wedge \nu[1] \neq \mu[2]\big)\}$$

  a)  Show that the expression is domain independent but not safe.

  b)  Find an equivalent safe TRC formula.

3.10: Convert the DRC expression

$$\{AB \mid r(AB) \wedge r(BA)\}$$

    a)    To an English statement.
    b)    To a datalog rule.
    c)    To TRC.
    d)    To relational algebra.

3.11: Show that over the domain of the integers, there are an infinite number of models for the rules of Example 3.1 that are consistent with the EDB consisting of $\{r(1)\}$ only.

* 3.12: A *generalized projection* of a relation $R$ is denoted $\pi_L(R)$, where $L$ is a list of component numbers and constants. Unlike ordinary projection, components may appear more than once, and constants as components of the list $L$ are permitted. In generalized projection, use $\$i$ for component $i$ to distinguish it from the constant $i$. For example, if $R = \{abc, def\}$, then

$$\pi_{\$2,a,\$1,\$2}(R) = \{baab, eade\}$$

    a)    Show that there is a relational algebra expression equivalent to each generalized projection.
    b)    Give a construction alternative to that of Algorithm 3.2 that uses generalized projections but does not require that the rules be rectified.

```
p(X,X)  :- q(X,Y) & r(Y,Z).
p(X,Y)  :- q(X,X) & r(Y,Y).

q(a,X)  :- s(X).
q(X,Y)  :- r(X,Z) & r(Z,b) & r(Y,c).

r(X,Y)  :- s(X) & s(Y).
```

**Figure 3.9** Rules for Exercise 3.13.

3.13: Consider the rules in Figure 3.9. Here, $s$ is the only EDB predicate.

    a)    Rectify the rules.
    b)    Write relational algebra expressions for the relations defined by the IDB predicates $p$, $q$, and $r$. To simplify, you may use the result for one predicate as an argument of the expression for other predicates.
    c)    Produce algebraic expressions directly from the rules (without rectification) by using the extended projection operator.
    d)    Write a safe DRC expression for the relation of $q$.

3.14: Verify that the expression $T(X) \bowtie U(X,Z) \bowtie S(Y,Z)$ in Example 3.5 defines the relation for the body of the rule (3.4) from that exercise.

* 3.15: Complete the proof of Lemma 3.1 by showing that substituting $X$ for $Y$ in a rule that has $X = Y$ as a subgoal does not make the rule unsafe if it was safe and does not change the set of facts that the head of the rule yields.

3.16: Complete the proof of Theorem 3.2 by showing that the set of facts produced by Algorithm 3.2 is a subset of any model of the rules, and therefore is the unique minimal model.

3.17: Complete the proof of Theorem 3.3 by showing that the operations union, projection, and product are monotone.

3.18: Show that intersection is monotone.

* 3.19: Is $\div$ a monotone operator?

3.20: Show Corollary 3.1: the composition of monotone operators is monotone.

3.21: Show that Algorithm 3.3 computes the proof-theoretic meaning of datalog rules, i.e., the set of facts that can be inferred by applying the rules in the forward direction (from body to head).

3.22: Rules are said to be *linear* if they each have at most one subgoal with an IDB predicate. Give a simplification of Algorithm 3.4 (semi-naive evaluation) for the case that rules are linear.

* 3.23: A logic program is said to be *metalinear* if we can partition the predicates into "strata" such that a rule whose head is in stratum $i$ can have no subgoals of strata above $i$ and at most one subgoal at stratum $i$. Note these "strata" have nothing to do with negated subgoals; we assume there are none.

    a)    Give an example of a datalog program that is metalinear but not linear.

    b)    Simplify Algorithm 3.4 for the case that the rules are metalinear.

* 3.24: Extend Algorithm 3.4 to the case that the rules are stratified rules (in the sense of Section 3.6, not Exercise 3.23) with negations.

3.25: Consider the rules:

```
p(X,Y) :- q(X,Y) & ¬r(X).
r(X) :- s(X,Y) & ¬t(Y).
r(X) :- s(X,Y) & r(Y).
```

    a)    Determine the stratum of each predicate. Is the program stratified?

    b)    Suppose the relations for the EDB predicates $s$, $t$, and $q$ are, respectively, $S = \{ab, bc, ca\}$, $T = \{a, b, c\}$, and $Q = \{ab, bc, cd, de\}$. Find the perfect fixed point for the IDB predicates $p$ and $r$, given this EDB.

    c)    Find another minimal model for the rules and the EDB given in (b).

* 3.26: Consider the rules

```
p(X) :- r(X) & ¬s(X).
p(X) :- t(X,Y) & p(Y).
q(X) :- r(X) & ¬p(X).
q(X) :- t(X,Y) & q(Y).
```

Suppose the EDB predicates $r$, $s$, and $t$ have, respectively, the relations $R = \{2, 3\}$, $S = \{2\}$, and

$$T = \{(1,1),\ (2,2),\ (3,3),\ (4,4),\ (2,1),\ (3,2),\ (4,3)\}$$

Find, for the IDB predicates $p$ and $q$:

a)   The perfect fixed point.
b)   Another minimal fixed point.
c)   A fixed point that is not minimal.

*Hint*: For the value of $T$ given, we can think of the second rule as saying "if $p(i)$ is true, then $p(j)$ is true for all $j$, $i \leq j \leq 4$," and we can understand the fourth rule similarly.

* 3.27: Consider the rules:

```
p(X) :- q(X) & ¬r(X).
s(X) :- q(X) & ¬p(X).
t(X) :- q(X) & ¬s(X).
```

Assume $q$ and $r$ are EDB predicates with unary relations $\{1, 2, 3\}$ and $\{1\}$, respectively; other predicates are IDB.

a)   Find the perfect fixed point for these rules and the given EDB relations.
b)   Are there any other minimal fixed points for the given EDB relations? If so, find one; if not, prove it.
c)   Are there any nonminimal fixed points for the given EDB relations? Find one or prove none exist.

* 3.28: In Example 3.15 we suggested that there was a transformation to eliminate variables appearing only in negated subgoals by rewriting the rules without changing the IDB relations defined. Give a general algorithm to eliminate such variables, using the intuitive semantics of Example 3.15 and assuming that a variable occurring in two or more negated subgoals, and no positive subgoal, actually represents different variables, each local to one of the negated subgoals.

* 3.29: In Example 3.16 we showed how negated subgoals in safe rules could be replaced by set differences; i.e., we could transform the rules so that if there is a negated subgoal $\neg p(X_1, \ldots, X_n)$, then there is some positive subgoal $q(X_1, \ldots, X_n)$ with an identical list of arguments in the same rule. Give

an algorithm to implement this transformation.

* 3.30: Show that perfect fixed points, as produced by Algorithm 3.6, are minimal fixed points.

* 3.31: Show that the IDB portion of any minimal model for datalog rules without negated subgoals is a minimal fixed point of the corresponding datalog equations. What happens if there are negated subgoals?

* 3.32: Show that it is undecidable whether a given formula of domain relational calculus is domain independent.

  3.33: Verify that all the DRC formulas constructed from relational algebra expressions in Theorem 3.10 are safe.

* 3.34: One might get the impression, from examples and constructions in Section 3.9, that tuple calculus is always less succinct than domain calculus. Show that is not the case by exhibiting an infinite family of queries whose expressions in TRC are much more succinct than their shortest expressions in DRC. That is, give a "big-oh" upper bound on the growth in size of your TRC formulas and a larger "big-omega" lower bound on the growth of your DRC formulas.

  3.35: Complete the proof of Lemma 3.7, that every safe TRC formula can be converted to a safe DRC formula.

  3.36: Consider the rules of Example 3.1, and assume that the domain from which values are taken is the integers. If $R$ is the EDB relation corresponding to predicate $r$, describe (in terms of $R$) what negative ground atoms the closed-world assumption allows us to conclude.

* 3.37: Consider the rules:

$$q(X) \ :- \ r(X).$$
$$p(X) \ \lor \ r(X)$$

  Notice that the second is not a Horn clause; it says that for all $X$, either $p(X)$ or $q(X)$ (or both) is true. Suppose we are given a relation $R$ for EDB predicate $r$, and also assume that the domain from which values are chosen is the integers.

  a) Under the closed world assumption, what negative facts for IDB predicates $p$ and $q$ can be inferred?

  b) Under the generalized closed world assumption, what negative facts for $p$ and $q$ can be derived?

  c) Are there contradictory facts deduced in your answers to (a) and/or (b)?

3.38: Some definitions of logical rules allow predicates that are mixed EDB/IDB predicates. That is, a predicate $p$ may have a stored relation with some tuples for which $p$ is true, and there may be rules that define additional tuples for which $p$ is true. Show that any such collection of rules can be replaced by another collection, defining the same relations, in which each predicate is either EDB or IDB, but not both.

## BIBLIOGRAPHIC NOTES

The basic concepts of logic are found in Manna and Waldinger [1984], and the elements of logic programming appear in Lloyd [1984] and Apt [1987].

There have been two directions from which applications of logic to database systems have been approached. One, often called "deductive databases," emphasizes issues of expressibility of languages, and semantic issues, such as the closed world assumption. Gallaire and Minker [1978] is a compendium of basic results in this area, and later surveys were written by Gallaire, Minker, and Nicolas [1984] and Minker [1987]. Minker [1988] is a collection of recent papers on the subject. A critique of this area is found in Harel [1986].

The second direction emphasizes the optimization of queries expressed as logic programs. We shall cover this area in detail in Chapter 13 (Volume II). Bancilhon and Ramakrishnan [1986] is a survey of results in this class.

### Relational Calculus

Codd [1972b] is the basic paper on relational calculus, including the equivalence with relational algebra. Pirotte [1978] classifies query languages into domain-calculus and tuple-calculus languages.

Levien and Maron [1967] and Kuhns [1967] were early papers on the use of similar forms of logic as a query language.

Klug [1981] extends the logic and the algebra-logic correspondence to aggregate operators (sum, average, etc.). Kuper and Vardi [1984] develop a calculus for a model more general than the relational model; it is similar to the "object model" discussed in Section 2.7.

### Fixed-Point Semantics of Logic Programs

The fixed point semantics for datalog that we developed in Section 3.5 was explored in the context of logic programming by Van Emden and Kowalski [1976] and Apt and Van Emden [1982], and in the database context by Chandra and Harel [1982]. The basic mathematics, relating monotonicity to the existence of least fixed points goes back to Tarski [1955].

Reiter [1984] compares the proof-theoretic and model-theoretic approaches to defining semantics.

**Semi-Naive Evaluation**

The notion of "semi-naive" evaluation of logic, based on the "derivatives" of set-valued expressions, has been rediscovered many times in recent years. The concept dates back at least as far as the study of an optimization technique in set-theoretic languages called "reduction in strength," by Fong and Ullman [1976] and Paige and Schwartz [1977]. Bancilhon and Ramakrishnan [1986] attribute it to unpublished work of Bancilhon; the term "semi-naive" is from there. The same idea appears independently in Bayer [1985], Balbin and Ramamohanarao [1986], and Gonzalez-Rubio, Rohmer, and Bradier [1987].

**Safety**

The notion of domain independence is from DiPaola [1969], where it was called "definiteness." The undecidability of domain independence (Exercise 3.28) was shown there. Codd [1972b] has a definition of a subclass of tuple relational calculus roughly corresponding to what we have called "safe" formulas.

The definition of safety we have used here, based on "limiting" the domains of the variables in a formula, follows Zaniolo [1986] and Ramakrishnan, Bancilhon, and Silberschatz [1987]. More general notions of "safety" that are decidable are discussed in Van Gelder and Topor [1987].

Extensions of the "safety" concept to entire logic programs were made by Ramakrishnan, Bancilhon, and Silberschatz [1987] and Shmueli [1987]. Beeri, Naqvi, Ramakrishnan, Shmueli, and Tsur [1987], Kuper [1987], and Ozsoyoglu and Wang [1987] discuss the issue in the context of languages with set-valued variables.

**Logic with Negation**

A basic paper on the meaning of negation is Clark [1978], which proposes "negation by failure," a concept similar to the closed-world assumption, defining negated subgoal $\neg p(a)$ to be true whenever we cannot prove $p(a)$ itself is true. This is the approach taken by Prolog implementations, e.g., and it is what justifies our replacing the "if" operator :- by equality in Section 3.4, to form datalog equations.

Various other approaches to defining appropriate models for logical rules containing negated subgoals have been proposed, such as Le [1985], Naish [1986], Naqvi [1986], Bidiot and Hull [1986], Ross and Topor [1987], Gelfond and Lifschitz [1988], Lifschitz [1988], and Ross and Van Gelder [1988].

Ginsberg [1988] is a collection of articles on the general subject of coping with negation in logical rules.

**Stratified Logic**

Chandra and Harel [1982] defined a class of logic programs equivalent to what we call stratified datalog and defined their meaning to be the "perfect" fixed point. Immerman [1982] proved the surprising result that any query expressible in this language can be expressed with a single level of negation, i.e., with two strata. However, the number of arguments in predicates in the two-strata program may be very much larger than in the original, so this technique is not generally useful as an optimization.

Apt, Blair, and Walker [1985] considered the multiplicity of minimal fixed points for logic programs and argued that for stratified programs the "perfect" fixed point is the preferred one. Van Gelder [1986] independently argued the same and gave a relatively efficient algorithm for testing whether a given fact is in the perfect model of a stratified datalog program. Additional application of the "stratified" concept appears in Apt and Pugin [1987] and Przymusinski [1988].

### The Closed World Assumption

The fundamental paper on the CWA is Reiter [1978]; also see Reiter [1980] for a discussion of the domain closure and unique-value axioms. Minker [1982] introduces the generalized CWA.

There is a close connection between the CWA and the "negation as failure" idea in Clark [1978]; see Shepherdson [1984].

McCarthy [1980] defines a more general metarule for inferring negative information, called "circumscription." Lifschitz [1985] and Gelfond, Przymusinska, and Przymusinski [1986] relate circumscription and the CWA.

A fundamental problem with all attempts to define metarules for negative information is the complexity of answering queries according to these rules. Przymusinski [1986] attempts to provide an algorithm for answering queries in the presence of circumscriptions, but the question whether the circumscription approach can be made computationally tractable remains open.

# CHAPTER 4

Relational
Query
Languages

We got acquainted with relational algebra in Section 2.4, and in Chapter 3 we met the two forms of logic, tuple and domain calculus, commonly used for querying relational databases. Now let us consider some of the real query languages that have been used in systems built upon the relational model of data. Section 4.2 discusses ISBL, an almost pure embodiment of relational algebra. Section 4.3 is devoted to QUEL, which is primarily a tuple calculus language, and Section 4.4 covers Query-by-Example, a domain calculus language. The data definition language for Query-by-Example is briefly described in Section 4.5. Then in Section 4.6 we introduce SQL, or "Sequel," a language that combines features from all three of the abstract languages and is today very influential. The data definition language of SQL is covered in Section 4.7, and in Section 4.8 we describe how SQL is embedded in the host language C. The treatments of these languages varies, so the reader is exposed to essentially all of the features found in relational query languages, without covering each feature in each of the languages studied.

## 4.1 GENERAL REMARKS REGARDING QUERY LANGUAGES

As we saw in Theorem 3.12, the three abstract relational query languages, relational algebra and the safe versions of domain and tuple relational calculus, are all equivalent in their expressive power. Historically, Codd [1972b] first proposed tuple relational calculus (in a formulation somewhat different from that given in Section 3.9) as a benchmark for evaluating data manipulation languages based on the relational model. That is, a language without at least the expressive power of the safe formulas of relational calculus, or equivalently of relational algebra, was deemed inadequate. A language that can (at least) simulate safe tuple calculus, or equivalently, relational algebra or safe domain calculus, is said to be *complete*. We shall, in this chapter, consider some important relational query languages and show their completeness.

## Additional Features of Data Manipulation Languages

Data manipulation languages generally have capabilities beyond those of relational algebra or calculus. Of course, all data manipulation languages include insertion, deletion, and modification commands, which are not part of relational algebra or calculus. Some additional features frequently available are:

1. *Arithmetic capability.* Often, atoms in calculus expressions or selections in algebraic expressions can involve arithmetic computation as well as comparisons, e.g., $A < B + 3$. Note that $+$ and other arithmetic operators appear in neither relational algebra nor calculus, but the extension of those notations to include arithmetic should be obvious.

2. *Assignment and Print Commands.* Languages generally allow the printing of the relation constructed by an algebraic or calculus expression and the assignment of a computed relation to be the value of a relation name.

3. *Aggregate Functions.* Operations such as average, sum, min, or max can often be applied to columns of a relation to obtain a single quantity.

For these reasons, the languages we shall discuss are really "more than complete"; that is, they can do things with no counterpart in relational algebra or calculus. Many, but not all, become equivalent to relational calculus when we throw away arithmetic and aggregate operators. Some languages, like Query-by-Example (Section 4.4), may be called "more than complete" even after eliminating arithmetic and aggregation. The original design for Query-by-Example allows computation of the transitive closure of a relation, although not all implementations support this feature, and we do not discuss it here. Recall that transitive closure is not something that can be expressed by nonrecursive logic, and therefore, by Theorem 3.12, cannot be expressed in relational algebra or the two forms of relational calculus.

## Comparison of Algebraic and Calculus Languages

It is sometimes said that relational calculus-based languages are "higher-level" or "more declarative" (recall our discussion of declarativeness and its importance in Sections 1.4 and 1.7.) than the algebraic languages because the algebra (partially) specifies the order of operations while the calculus leaves it to a compiler or interpreter to determine the most efficient order of evaluation. For instance, Example 2.21 discussed a typical query form, line (2.2), which we shall here abstract for succinctness. That is, suppose we have relations $R(A, B)$ and $S(B, C)$, and we want to ask the algebraic query

$$\pi_C\Big(\sigma_{A=a}\big(R(A,B) \bowtie S(B,C)\big)\Big) \tag{4.1}$$

This query says: "print the $C$-values associated with $A$-value $a$ in the joined relation $[R \bowtie S](A,B,C)$. An equivalent domain calculus expression is

$$\{C \mid (\exists B)\big(r(a,B) \wedge s(B,C)\big)\} \tag{4.2}$$

If we compare (4.1) and (4.2) we see that the calculus expression does in fact tell only what we want, not how to get it; that is, (4.2) only specifies the properties of the desired values $C$. In comparison, (4.1) specifies a particular order of operations. It is not immediately obvious that (4.1) is equivalent to:

$$\pi_C\Big(\pi_B\big(\sigma_{A=a}R(A,B)\big) \bowtie S(B,C)\Big) \tag{4.3}$$

To evaluate (4.3) we need only look for the tuples in $R$ that have $A$-value $a$ and find the associated $B$-values. This step computes $R_1(B) = \pi_B\big(\sigma_{A=a}R(A,B)\big)$. Then we look for the tuples of $S$ whose $B$-values are in $R_1$, i.e., we compute $R_1(B) \bowtie S(B,C)$. Finally, we project this relation onto $C$ to get the desired answer.

As we suggested in Example 2.22, this operation can be quite efficient if we have the proper indices. An index on attribute $A$ for relation $R$ allows us to find those tuples with $A$-value $a$ in time that is proportional to the number of tuples retrieved. The set of $B$-values in these tuples is the set $R_1$. If we also have an index on $B$ for relation $S$, then the tuples with $B$-values in $R_1$ can likewise be retrieved in time proportional to the number of tuples retrieved. From these, the $C$-values in the answer may be obtained. The time to do these steps could be proportional to the sizes of $R$ and $S$, since in the worst case, all tuples in these relations have the desired $A$-values or $B$-values. However, in typical cases, the size of $R_1$ and the size of the answer will be much smaller than the sizes of the relations, so the time to perform the query by following (4.3) is much less than the time to look at $R$ and $S$.

In comparison, (4.1) requires that we evaluate the natural join of $R$ and $S$, which could involve sorting both relations on their $B$-values and running through the sorted relations. The resulting relation could be very large compared to $R$ and $S$. Under no circumstances could (4.1) be evaluated in less time than it takes to scan at least one of $R$ and $S$, no matter how we choose to do the join. Thus, the time to evaluate (4.1) exceeds the time to evaluate (4.3), often by a wide margin, even though the relations computed by the two expressions are always the same.

In principle, we can always evaluate (4.2) like (4.3) rather than (4.1), which appears to be an advantage of calculus over algebra, especially as (4.1) is simpler, and therefore more likely to be written than is (4.3). However, an optimization pass in an algebra-based query language compiler can convert (4.1) into (4.3) immediately, and relational calculus expressions require optimization as well if we are to receive the full benefit of their declarativeness.

We shall consider such optimization in Chapter 11. Thus, we feel it is specious to regard calculus as higher-level than algebra, if for no other reason than that the first step in the optimization of an algebraic expression could be to convert it, by Theorem 3.10 or Lemma 3.6, to an equivalent calculus expression. We must admit, however, that calculus-based languages are today more prevalent than algebraic languages. We prefer to attribute the dominance of calculus languages to the desirability of their declarativeness from the programmer's point of view, rather than from the point of view of efficiency or ease of compilation.

## Select-Project-Join Expressions

While we expect a query language to be complete, there is a subset of the expressions of relational algebra that appear with great frequency, and it is important to consider how easily a language handles these expressions. This class is formed from the operators select, project, and join. Intuitively, many queries can be viewed as taking an entity (described by the selection clause), connecting it to an entity of another type, perhaps through many relationships (the join expresses the connection), and then printing some attributes of the latter entity (the projection determines the attributes printed). We call such expressions *select-project-join* expressions. For example, all single datalog rules without negated subgoals define relations (for their bodies) that are expressed by select-project-join queries. The reader is encouraged to observe how the query languages to be described each handle select-project-join queries in a succinct way.

## 4.2 ISBL: A "PURE" RELATIONAL ALGEBRA LANGUAGE

ISBL (Information System Base Language) is a query language developed at the IBM United Kingdom Scientific Center in Peterlee, England, for use in the PRTV (Peterlee Relational Test Vehicle) system. It closely approximates the relational algebra given in Section 2.4, so the completeness of ISBL is easy to show. The correspondence of syntax is shown in Figure 4.1. In both ISBL and relational algebra, $R$ and $S$ can be any relational expressions, and $F$ is a Boolean formula. Components of a relation are given names (the attributes of the relation), and we refer to components by these names in $F$.

To print the value of an expression, precede it by LIST. To assign the value of an expression $E$ to a relation named $R$, we write $R = E$. An interesting feature of assignment is that we can delay the binding of relations to names in an expression until the name on the left of the assignment is used. To delay evaluation of a name, precede it by N!. The N! calls for evaluation "by name."

| Relational algebra | ISBL |
|---|---|
| $R \cup S$ | $R + S$ |
| $R - S$ | $R - S$ |
| $R \cap S$ | $R \cdot S$ |
| $\sigma_F(R)$ | $R : F$ |
| $\pi_{A_1,\ldots,A_n}(R)$ | $R \% A_1, \ldots, A_n$ |
| $R \bowtie S$ | $R * S$ |

**Figure 4.1** Correspondence between ISBL and relational algebra.

**Example 4.1:** Suppose we want to use the composition of binary relations $R(A, B)$ and $S(C, D)$ from time to time. This composition, in relational algebra, is:

$$\pi_{A,D}\left(R(A, B) \underset{B=C}{\bowtie} S(C, D)\right)$$

If we write

    T = (R*S): B=C % A,D

the composition of the current relations $R$ and $S$ would be computed and assigned to relation name $T$. Note that as $R$ and $S$ have attributes with different names, the *, or natural join operator, is here a Cartesian product.

However, suppose we wanted $T$ to stand not for the composition of the current values of $R(A, B)$ and $S(C, D)$ but for the formula for composing $R$ and $S$. Then we could write

    T = (N!R*N!S): B=C % A,D

The above ISBL statement causes no evaluation of relations. Rather, it defines $T$ to stand for the formula

    (R*S): B=C % A,D

If we ever use $T$ in a statement that requires its evaluation, such as

    LIST T

or

    U = T+V

the current values of $R$ and $S$ are at that time substituted into the formula for $T$ to get a value for $T$. $\square$

The delayed evaluation operator N! serves two important purposes. First, large relational expressions are hard to write down correctly the first time. Delayed evaluation allows the programmer to construct an expression in easy stages, by giving temporary names to important subexpressions. More importantly, delayed evaluation serves as a rudimentary facility for defining views. By defining a relation name to stand for an expression with delayed evaluation, the programmer can use this name as if the defined relation really existed. Thus, a set of one or more defined relations forms a view of the database.

## Renaming of Attributes

In ISBL, the purely set theoretic operators, union, intersection, and difference, have definitions that are modified from their standard definitions in relational algebra, to take advantage of the fact that components have attribute names in ISBL. The union and intersection operators are only applicable when the two relations involved have the same set of attribute names. The difference operator, $R - S$, is the ordinary set-theoretic difference when $R$ and $S$ have the same set of attribute names. More generally, if some of the attributes of $R$ and $S$ differ, then $R - S$ denotes the set of tuples $\mu$ in $R$ such that $\mu$ agrees with no tuple in $S$ on those attributes that $R$ and $S$ have in common. Thus, in ISBL the expression $R - S$, if $R$ is $R(A, B)$ and $S$ is $S(A, C)$, denotes the relational algebra expression

$$R - \big(\pi_A(S) \times \pi_B(R)\big)$$

To allow these operators to be used at will, a special form of projection permits the renaming of attributes. In a list of attributes following the projection (%) operator, an item $A \to B$ means that the component for attribute $A$ is included in the projection but is renamed $B$. For example, to take the union of $R(A, B)$ with $S(A, C)$ we could write

    (R % A, B→C) + S

The resulting relation has attributes $A$ and $C$.

We can also use renaming to take the Cartesian product of relations whose sets of attributes are not disjoint. Observe that in ISBL notation, the natural join $R(A, B) * S(C, D)$ is really a Cartesian product, but $R(A, B) * S(B, C)$ is a natural join in which the $B$-components of $R$ and $S$ are equated. If we want to take the Cartesian product of $R(A, B)$ with $S(B, C)$ we can write

    (R % A, B→D) * S

As the left operand of the $*$ has attributes $A$ and $D$, while $S$ has attributes $B$ and $C$, the result is a Cartesian product.

With attribute renaming, we have a way to simulate any of the five basic relational algebra operations in ISBL. Thus, it is immediately obvious that ISBL is complete.

## Some Sample Queries

Recall that the Yuppie Valley Culinary Boutique (YVCB) keeps a database with information about its business. The design for a relational database with this information was shown in Figure 2.8. Of the eight relations of that scheme, we shall deal with four that will serve for most of our examples. These relations tell about customers, the orders for delivery that they place, the items on each order, and the suppliers of those items. The schemes for these relations, with some attributes renamed from Figure 2.8 to allow the use of the same attribute, e.g., NAME, with different meanings in different relations, are:

```
CUSTOMERS(NAME, ADDR, BALANCE)
ORDERS(O#, DATE, CUST)
INCLUDES(O#, ITEM, QUANTITY)
SUPPLIES(NAME, ITEM, PRICE)
```

In Figure 4.2 we see sample data that will serve as the "current instance" of this database.

We shall now consider some typical queries on the YVCB database and their expression in ISBL. For comparison, we shall use these same queries as examples for several other languages as well.

**Example 4.2:** The simplest queries often involve a selection and projection on a single relation. That is, we specify some condition that tuples must have, and we print some or all of the components of these tuples. The specific example query we shall use is

*Print the names of customers with negative balances.*

In ISBL we can write

**LIST CUSTOMERS: BALANCE<0 % NAME**

The clause **BALANCE<0** selects the first and second tuples, because their values in column 3 (BALANCE) is negative. The projection operator leaves only the first column, NAME, so LIST causes the table

Zack Zebra
Judy Giraffe

to be printed. □

**Example 4.3:** A more complicated type of query involves taking the natural join, or perhaps a more general join or Cartesian product of several relations, then selecting tuples from this relation and printing some of the components. Our example query is:

*Print the suppliers who supply at least one
item ordered by Zack Zebra.*

This query asks us to go to the ORDERS relation to find the numbers of all the orders placed by Zack Zebra. Then, armed with those numbers, we go to the INCLUDES relation to find the items ordered by Zebra, which are the items associated with these order numbers. Lastly, we go to the SUPPLIES relation

| NAME | ADDR | BALANCE |
|------|------|---------|
| Zack Zebra | 74 Family Way | −200 |
| Judy Giraffe | 153 Lois Lane | −50 |
| Ruth Rhino | 21 Rocky Road | +43 |

(a) CUSTOMERS

| O# | DATE | CUST |
|----|------|------|
| 1024 | Jan 3 | Zack Zebra |
| 1025 | Jan 3 | Ruth Rhino |
| 1026 | Jan 4 | Zack Zebra |

(b) ORDERS

| O# | ITEM | QUANTITY |
|----|------|----------|
| 1024 | Brie | 3 |
| 1024 | Perrier | 6 |
| 1025 | Brie | 5 |
| 1025 | Escargot | 12 |
| 1025 | Endive | 1 |
| 1026 | Macadamias | 2048 |

(c) INCLUDES

| NAME | ITEM | PRICE |
|------|------|-------|
| Acme | Brie | 3.49 |
| Acme | Perrier | 1.19 |
| Acme | Macadamias | .06 |
| Acme | Escargot | .25 |
| Ajax | Brie | 3.98 |
| Ajax | Perrier | 1.09 |
| Ajax | Endive | .69 |

(d) SUPPLIES

**Figure 4.2** Example YVCB database.

to find the suppliers of those items. While we could write the query directly, it is conceptually simpler to begin by defining the join that follows these connections from ORDERS to INCLUDES to SUPPLIES. This connection happens to be a natural join, since the connecting attributes, O# and ITEM, have the same names in each of the connected relations; if that were not the case we would have to use renaming to adjust the attributes. We define the natural join by:

    OIS = N!ORDERS * N!INCLUDES * N!SUPPLIES

In this way, OIS is defined to be a relation with scheme

    OIS(O#, DATE, CUST, ITEM, QUANTITY, NAME, PRICE)

Note that evaluation of OIS is deferred. When evaluated, it would consist of all those $(o, d, c, i, q, n, p)$ tuples such that customer $c$ placed order $o$ on date $d$, order $o$ includes an order for quantity $q$ of item $i$, and supplier $n$ supplies $i$ at price $p$. To complete the query, we have only to select from this relation the tuples for customer Zack Zebra and project onto the name attribute, to produce the set of all suppliers for the items ordered by Zebra. This step is:

    OIS: CUST="Zack Zebra" % NAME

Since Zack Zebra placed orders 1024 and 1026; the first includes Brie and Perrier and the latter includes Macadamias, and both Ajax and Acme supply at least one of these, the answer to the query is { "Ajax", "Acme"}.  □

**Example 4.4:** A still more complicated sort of query involves what amounts to a "for all" quantifier. The particular query we shall consider is:

> *Print the suppliers that supply every*
> *item ordered by Zack Zebra.*

Such queries are easier in calculus languages than algebraic languages. That is, in domain calculus we can write the query as

$$\left\{ N \ \middle| \ (\forall I)\left( ((\exists P)supplies(N, I, P)) \ \lor \right.\right.$$
$$\neg\left( (\exists O)(\exists D)(\exists Q)(orders(O, D, \text{``Zack Zebra''}) \ \land \right.$$
$$\left.\left.\left. includes(O, I, Q)) \right) \right) \right\} \tag{4.4}$$

That is, print the set of supplier names $N$ such that for all items $I$, either $N$ supplies $I$ [there exists a price $P$ such that $(N, I, P)$ is a tuple of SUPPLIES] or there exists no order by Zack Zebra for item $I$. The latter condition is expressed by the negation of the condition that there is an order number $O$, a date $D$, and a quantity $Q$ such that $orders(O, D, \text{``Zack Zebra''})$, i.e., Zebra placed order $O$, and $includes(O, I, Q)$, i.e., item $I$ is included in that order. Notice also that $p \lor \neg q$ is logically equivalent to $p \to q$, i.e., $p$ implies $q$, so we are saying that if

Zebra placed an order for the item $I$, then supplier $N$ supplies it.

To convert (4.4) to algebra, it helps to eliminate the universal quantifier. Recall that we can always do so by

$$(\forall X)p(X) = \neg\big((\exists X)(\neg p(X))\big)$$

Then, we can use DeMorgan's law to move the generated negation inside the OR: $\neg(P \lor Q) = (\neg P) \land (\neg Q)$. The resulting expression is:

$$\Big\{N \;\Big|\; \neg\Big((\exists I)\big(\neg((\exists P)supplies(N, I, P))\big) \land$$
$$(\exists O)(\exists D)(\exists Q)\big(orders(O, D, \text{"Zack Zebra"}) \land$$
$$includes(O, I, Q)\big)\Big)\Big)\Big\} \tag{4.5}$$

Equation (4.5) is not safe; it is not even domain independent [if Zebra hasn't ordered any items, then both (4.4) and (4.5) define the set of all suppliers in the domain]. However, if we make the closed world assumption, that the only suppliers that exist are those that appear in the SUPPLIES relation, we can work with (4.5) to produce an algebraic expression.[1] We first compute the set of all suppliers, and then subtract those that satisfy the body of (4.5), that is, there is an item that Zebra orders but which the supplier doesn't sell. The set of all suppliers is

```
ALLSUPS = SUPPLIES % NAME
```

For the database of Figure 4.2, ALLSUPS is { "Ajax", "Acme"}.

In a manner similar to the previous example, we can find all of the items ordered by Zebra by:

```
ZEBRAITEMS = (ORDERS * INCLUDES):
    CUST="Zack Zebra" % ITEM
```

For our example database, ZEBRAITEMS is

{ "Brie", "Perrier", "Macadamias"}

Next, we use a trick that was introduced in Example 3.16. To find the suppliers that fail to supply some item in the set ZEBRAITEMS, we take from SUPPLIES the set of pairs $(n, i)$ such that supplier $n$ does supply item $i$, and subtract it from the set of pairs consisting of any supplier and any item in ZEBRAITEMS. The difference is the set of pairs $(n, i)$ such that $n$ is some

---

[1] Perhaps we should also consult the SUPPLIERS relation, mentioned in Figure 2.8 but not used in this section, since that relation, holding supplier names and addresses, might mention a supplier that does not appear in the SUPPLIES relation, presumably because it sells nothing now. If Zebra ordered nothing, then such a supplier would satisfy the query.

supplier, $i$ is an item Zack Zebra ordered, but $n$ doesn't supply $i$. This set of pairs can be obtained by the sequence of steps:

```
NIPAIRS = SUPPLIES % NAME, ITEM
NOSUPPLY = (ALLSUPS * ZEBRAITEMS) - NIPAIRS
```

In our example database, NOSUPPLY has only the pair

{ ("Ajax", "Macadamias") }

Finally, if we project NOSUPPLY onto NAME, we get the set of suppliers that fail to supply some item that Zebra ordered. The difference between ALLSUPS and this set is the set of suppliers that do supply everything Zebra ordered. Thus, the last step in our ISBL program is

```
LIST (ALLSUPS - (NOSUPPLY % NAME))
```

The result is that only "Acme" is printed. The entire ISBL program is shown in Figure 4.3, where we have treated all the assignments as view definitions, to be executed only when the answer is called for by the last statement. □

```
ALLSUPS = N!SUPPLIES % NAME
ZEBRAITEMS = (N!ORDERS * N!INCLUDES):
    CUST="Zack Zebra" % ITEM
NIPAIRS = N!SUPPLIES % NAME, ITEM
NOSUPPLY = (N!ALLSUPS * N!ZEBRAITEMS) - N!NIPAIRS
LIST (ALLSUPS - (NOSUPPLY % NAME))
```

**Figure 4.3** Solution to query of Example 4.4.

## ISBL Extensions

The ISBL language is fairly limited, when compared with query languages to be discussed in the next sections. For example, it has no aggregate operators (e.g., average, min), and there are no facilities for insertion, deletion, or modification of tuples. However, there exists in the surrounding PRTV system the facility to write arbitrary PL/I programs and integrate them into the processing of relations. The simplest use of PL/I programs in ISBL is as tuple-at-a-time processors, which serve as generalized selection operators.

**Example 4.5:** We could write a PL/I program $LOWADDR(S)$ that examines the character string $S$ and determines whether $S$, as a street address, has a number lower than 100, returning "true" if so. We can then apply LOWADDR to an attribute in an ISBL expression, with the result that the component for that attribute in each tuple is passed to LOWADDR, and the tuple is "selected" if LOWADDR returns "true." The syntax of ISBL calls for the join operator to be used for these generalized selections. Thus

    `LIST (CUSTOMERS * LOWADDR(ADDR)) % NAME`

prints the names of customers whose street number does not exceed 99,

    { "Zack Zebra", "Ruth Rhino" }

for the example database of Figure 4 ?  □

PL/I programs that operate on whole relations, rather than tuples, can also be defined. To facilitate such processing, the PRTV system allows relations to be passed to PL/I programs, either as *relational read files*, or *relational write files*. These are ordinary files in the PL/I sense, opened for reading or writing, respectively. A PL/I program can read or write the next record, which is a tuple of the underlying relation, into or from a PL/I record structure. The reader should be able to envision how to write PL/I programs to compute aggregate operators like sums or averages, to delete or modify tuples in arbitrarily specified ways, or to read tuples from an input file (not necessarily a relational read file; it could be a terminal, for example) and append them to a relation.

## 4.3 QUEL: A TUPLE RELATIONAL CALCULUS LANGUAGE

QUEL is the query language of INGRES, a relational DBMS developed at Berkeley, and marketed by Relational Technology, Inc. In viewpoint and style, QUEL most closely resembles tuple relational calculus, although the correspondence is less close than ISBL's resemblance to relational algebra.

### The Retrieve Statement

The most common form of query in QUEL is:

$$
\begin{aligned}
&\texttt{range of } \mu_1 \texttt{ is } R_1\\
&\quad \cdots\\
&\texttt{range of } \mu_k \texttt{ is } R_k\\
&\texttt{retrieve } (\mu_{i_1}.A_1,\ldots,\mu_{i_r}.A_r)\\
&\quad\texttt{where } \Psi(\mu_1,\ldots,\mu_k)
\end{aligned}
\tag{4.6}
$$

The intuitive meaning of a range-statement such as

    `range of` $\mu$ `is` $R$

is that any subsequent operations, such as retrieval, are to be carried out once for each tuple in relation $R$, with $\mu$ equal to each of these tuples in turn. Thus, the $\mu_i$'s in (4.6) are tuple variables, and each range-statement corresponds to an atomic formula $R_i(\mu_i)$ of TRC. It is possible to redeclare a tuple variable to range over another relation, but until one does, the relation corresponding to a tuple variable does not change. It is unnecessary to include the range statement for $\mu$ in every query, if the relation for $\mu$ is the one already declared for $\mu$, but we shall do so for clarity in the examples to follow.

The condition $\Psi$ is a formula involving components of the $\mu_i$'s. QUEL uses $\mu_i.B$ to designate the component for attribute $B$ of the relation $R_i$, over which $\mu_i$ ranges. Component designators and constants can be related by comparison operators, as in the language C (<= for $\leq$, != for $\neq$, and so on). Comparisons can be connected by the logical connectives, and, or, and not for $\wedge$, $\vee$, and $\neg$.

As each of the $\mu_i$'s ranges over the tuples of its relation, the QUEL interpreter determines whether the current $\mu_i$'s make $\Psi$ true. If so, certain components of the $\mu_i$'s are printed. The components of the tuple to be printed are computed from component designators in the retrieve-clause. That is, the first component printed is the component of tuple variable $\mu_{i_1}$ corresponding to attribute $A_1$ of relation $R_{i_1}$, and so on.

The retrieve statement thus prints a table whose columns are headed $A_1, \ldots, A_r$. If we wish a different name, say TITLE, for column $m$, use

$$\text{TITLE} = \mu_{i_m}.A_m$$

in place of the simple component designator $\mu_{i_m}.A_m$.

The QUEL statement form above is thus equivalent to the TRC query:

$$\{\nu^{(r)} \mid (\exists \mu_1) \cdots (\exists \mu_k)(R_1(\mu_1) \wedge \cdots \wedge R_k(\mu_k)$$
$$\wedge \; \nu[1] = \mu_{i_1}[j_1] \wedge \cdots \wedge \nu[r] = \mu_{i_r}[j_r]$$
$$\wedge \; \Psi')\} \tag{4.7}$$

In (4.7), the formula $\Psi'$ is $\Psi$ translated from the QUEL notation into the TRC notation. That is:

1. Some comparison and logical operators are changed; e.g., and becomes $\wedge$, and == becomes =.

2. A component designator $\mu_i.B$ becomes $\mu_i[j]$, where $B$ is the $j$th attribute of relation $R_i$, assuming some fixed order for the attributes of each relation.

Thus, in the first line of (4.7) we have the existential quantification of the $\mu_i$'s, which in effect says "let the $\mu_i$'s range over all possible values." We also have the atomic formulas $R_i(\mu_i)$, which restrict each tuple variable $\mu_i$ to range only over the tuples of its corresponding relation $R_i$. Note, incidentally, that there is no prohibition against two or more tuple variables ranging over the same relation, and it is sometimes essential that they do.

In the second line of (4.7) we see the equalities that say the tuple $\nu$ to be printed consists of certain components of the $\mu_i$'s, namely those components that are indicated in the retrieve-clause. Finally, the condition $\Psi'$ on the third line of (4.7) enforces the where-clause, only allowing the printing of a tuple $\nu$ if the $\mu_i$'s satisfy $\Psi$.

While the form of a QUEL query is clearly patterned after tuple relational calculus, it is also convenient to see the same query as an expression of relational algebra:

$$\pi_N\big(\sigma_F(R_1 \times \cdots \times R_k)\big)$$

where $N$ is the list of components corresponding to the tuple variable $\nu$ in (4.7), and $F$ is the condition $\Psi'$, with component designators translated to refer to their position in the product $R_1 \times \cdots \times R_k$.

**Example 4.6:** The query of Example 4.2 is written in QUEL:

```
range of c is CUSTOMERS
retrieve (c.NAME)
     where c.BALANCE < 0
```

Here there is only one tuple variable, $c$. To answer the query, the QUEL interpreter allows $c$ to assume as a value each tuple in its relation, CUSTOMERS. If the where-clause is satisfied for that tuple, i.e., the BALANCE component is negative, then the NAME component of that tuple is printed.

The query of Example 4.3 can be written as shown in Figure 4.4. Lines (1)–(3) declare $o$, $i$, and $s$ to be tuple variables, and also represent the atomic formulas $ORDERS(t)$, $INCLUDES(i)$, and $SUPPLIES(s)$, as was implied by Formula (4.7). The natural join of ORDERS, INCLUDES, and SUPPLIES is expressed in the where-clause by equating, in lines (6) and (7), the two pairs of components of the three tuple variables that correspond to the same attribute. The additional condition, that the customer must be Zack Zebra, is expressed by line (5). Finally, line (4) indicates that the resulting relation is projected onto the component NAME of relation SUPPLIES, to print the desired supplier names.

```
(1)  range of o is ORDERS
(2)  range of i is INCLUDES
(3)  range of s is SUPPLIES
(4)  retrieve (s.NAME)
(5)      where o.CUST = "Zack Zebra"
(6)         and o.O# = i.O#
(7)         and i.ITEM = s.ITEM
```

**Figure 4.4**  Print the suppliers of an item ordered by Zebra.

To execute the query of Figure 4.4, the QUEL interpreter considers each choice of a tuple $o$ from ORDERS, $i$ from INCLUDES, and $s$ from SUPPLIES.[2]

---

[2] Technically, the optimization performed by the QUEL processor will cause it to take a rather different approach to answering this query, but the result will be the same as the algorithm described here, which follows the definition of the "meaning" of the query. See Chapter 11 (Volume II) for details of the actual QUEL processing algorithm.

Whenever all the conditions of lines (5)–(7) are satisfied, the NAME component of the tuple $s$ is printed. The conditions of lines (6) and (7) say that $o$, $i$, and $s$ fit together to form a tuple of the natural join

$$ORDERS \bowtie INCLUDES \bowtie SUPPLIES$$

The condition of line (5) says that the tuple refers to an order placed by Zack Zebra, so the supplier name printed will surely supply some item, the one in the ITEM components of $i$ and $s$, that Zebra ordered. $\Box$

**Example 4.7:** A third example illustrates how we can use several tuple variables ranging over the same relation. Consider the query:

> *Print the name and address of each customer whose*
> *balance is lower than Judy Giraffe's.*

In QUEL, this query is written:

```
range of c1 is CUSTOMERS
range of c2 is CUSTOMERS
retrieve (c1.NAME, c1.ADDR)
    where c1.BALANCE < c2.BALANCE
        and c2.NAME = "Judy Giraffe"
```

Tuple variables $c1$ and $c2$ range independently over the relation CUSTOMERS. To trigger the printing of the NAME and ADDR components of $c1$, the NAME component of $c2$ must be "Judy Giraffe," and the balance in $c1$ must be less than the balance in $c2$; i.e., $c1$ is now the tuple for a customer who owes more than Judy Giraffe. $\Box$

### Safety of QUEL Retrieve Queries

The TRC query (4.7) is easily seen to be domain independent. The reason is that the initial group of atomic formulas $R_1(\mu_1) \wedge \cdots \wedge R_k(\mu_k)$ together with the second group, which equate each component of $\nu$ to some component of the $\mu_i$'s, guarantees that no value appearing in the answer can fail to appear in the EDB, that is, in one of the $R_i$'s.

Whether a QUEL query representing (4.7) meets our definition of "safety" for TRC queries depends on the exact form of $\Psi'$. If $\Psi'$ is the logical AND of arithmetic comparisons, such as the where-clause of Figure 4.4, then the formula is safe. For, as just mentioned, the atomic formulas $R_i(\mu_i)$ in the first line of (4.7) limit all components of all the $\mu$'s. Then the second line equates the components of $\nu$ to components of the $\mu$'s, thereby limiting all components that appear in the conjunct.

If $\Psi'$ is a more complex formula, (4.7) may not be a conjunction of atomic formulas, and therefore may violate one of the rules for safety of TRC formulas, e.g., there may be a logical OR of subformulas that have more than one free tuple variable. Expression (4.7) is still domain independent, of course, which is really what we need to assure that QUEL queries have finite answers. Moreover, as we already observed, there is a relational algebra formula equivalent to (4.7). Thus, we can use Lemma 3.6 to convert this expression to a safe TRC formula. We leave it as an exercise for the reader to give an algorithm that converts any $\Psi'$ satisfying the restrictions mentioned in connection with (4.6) to an equivalent formula so that (4.7) satisfies the definition of safety.

### Union and Difference

The retrieve-where form of QUEL statement introduced above is not powerful enough to express the union or difference of relations. Our first instinct might be to think that we can, in fact, write retrieve-where programs to do these jobs.

**Example 4.8:** Suppose $R(A, B)$ and $S(A, B)$ are relations. We might suppose that the QUEL program of Figure 4.5 should produce the union of $R$ and $S$; however, *it is erroneous for two reasons*. The first reason is a syntactic matter: the elements of the retrieve list must be components of tuple variables, not new domain variables. This rule of QUEL is essential to guarantee safety of general queries, although the query of Figure 4.5 is, in fact, safe.

```
range of r is R
range of s is S
retrieve (x, y)
      where (x=r.A and y=r.B)
         or (x=s.A and y=s.B)
```

**Figure 4.5** Erroneous "union" program.

The second matter is more serious. The OR in QUEL[3] does not behave as one might intuitively expect. The translation between TRC and QUEL, defined in connection with expression (4.6), suggests that Figure 4.5 should correspond to the TRC query

$$\{\nu \mid (\exists\mu)(\exists\rho)\Big(R(\mu) \wedge S(\rho) \wedge$$
$$((\nu[1] = \mu[1] \wedge \nu[2] = \mu[2]) \ \vee \ (\nu[1] = \rho[1] \wedge \nu[2] = \rho[2]))\Big)\} \quad (4.8)$$

However, consider what happens if $S$ is empty. Then the atomic formula $S(\rho)$ is never satisfied, and therefore no values of $\nu$ can ever be found to satisfy the body of (4.8). Similarly, the result is the empty set whenever $R$ is empty. It is easy to check that if neither $R$ nor $S$ is empty, then (4.8) produces $R \cup S$, as one would

---

[3] The same is true in SQL, to be discussed in Section 4.6.

expect. However, it produces $\emptyset$ when $R$ is empty ($S$ is the expected answer, of course), and when $S$ is empty (when $R$ would be the expected answer).

The problem, incidentally, is not limited to "incorrect" examples, like Figure 4.5. For example, the QUEL query

```
range of r is R
range of s is S
range of t is T
retrieve (r.A)
    where r.A=s.A or r.A=t.A
```

Produces $\pi_A(R) \cap \big(\pi_A(S) \cup \pi_A(T)\big)$ as long as neither $S$ nor $T$ is empty, but produces the empty set when either $S$ or $T$ is empty. The reason, again, is that the formal semantics of QUEL retrieve queries of the form (4.6) is given by the corresponding TRC formula (4.7), and when we follow the definition we find that is exactly the answer defined by the TRC query

$$\{\nu \mid (\exists\mu)(\exists\rho)(\exists\phi)\Big(R(\mu) \wedge S(\rho) \wedge T(\phi) \wedge$$
$$\nu[1] = \mu[1] \wedge \big(\mu[1] = \rho[1] \vee \mu[1] = \phi[1]\big)\Big)\}$$

☐

## Delete Statements

In order to perform unions and differences properly, QUEL provides two other statement forms. To delete from a relation, one can write

```
range of μ₁ is R₁
    ...
range of μₖ is Rₖ
delete μᵢ
    where Ψ(μ₁,...,μₖ)
```

Here, $\Psi(\mu_1,\ldots,\mu_k)$ is a QUEL expression like those that can follow "where" in the retrieve statement. The effect of this statement is to delete from $R_i$ all tuples $\mu_i$ for which there exist, for all $j = 1,2,\ldots,k$ other than $j = i$, tuples $\mu_j$ in $R_j$ such that $\Psi(\mu_1,\ldots,\mu_k)$ holds. Note that $\mu_i$ and the $\mu_j$'s are found before any deletions occur, so the order in which tuples are deleted does not matter.

**Example 4.9:** The QUEL command

```
range of o is ORDERS
range of i is INCLUDES
delete o
    where o.O# = i.O# and i.ITEM = "Brie"
```

deletes from the ORDERS relation all orders that include Brie among their items. The deletion occurs only from ORDERS; the information is left in the INCLUDES relation, where it constitutes a collection of "dangling" tuples, no longer connected to an existing order. Probably, we should also issue a command to delete from INCLUDES all tuples whose order number is the same as the order number of some (perhaps other) tuple whose ITEM component is "Brie." $\square$

## Append Statements

Similarly, QUEL has an append statement to perform unions, among other tasks. We can write

> range of $\mu_1$ is $R_1$
>      . . .
> range of $\mu_k$ is $R_k$
> append to $S(A_1 = \mathcal{E}_1, \ldots, A_n = \mathcal{E}_n)$
>      where $\Psi(\mu_1, \ldots, \mu_k)$

Here $\Psi$ is a QUEL expression as above, and the $\mathcal{E}_i$'s are expressions involving components of the $\mu_i$'s and/or constants, connected by arithmetic operators, if needed. For each assignment of values to the $\mu_j$'s such that $\Psi(\mu_1, \ldots, \mu_k)$ is true, we add to relation $S$ the tuple whose component for attribute $A_p$ is the value of $\mathcal{E}_p$, for $p = 1, 2, \ldots, n$.

**Example 4.10:** We could insist that every order in the YVCB database include ten pounds of Brie by writing:

> range of o is ORDERS
> append to INCLUDES(O#=o.O#, ITEM="Brie", QUANTITY=10)

Note that the where-clause is not required in the append statement, and it is possible, indeed more usual, for the append statement to be used without tuple variables like $o$ above, for the purpose of appending a single tuple to a relation. Thus, we can add Sammy Snake to the list of YVCB customers, with

> append to CUSTOMERS(NAME="Sammy Snake",
>     ADDR="56 Allina Row", BALANCE=0)

$\square$

## Retrieval into a Relation

We are still not ready to simulate any relational algebra expression in QUEL; we need the capability to assign values to new relations. If $S$ is the name of a new relation we can write

```
range of μ₁ is R₁
    ...
range of μₖ is Rₖ
retrieve into S(A₁ = ℰ₁, ..., Aₙ = ℰₙ)
    where Ψ(μ₁, ..., μₖ)
```

This statement will find all lists of tuples $\mu_1, \ldots, \mu_k$ such that $\mu_i$ is in $R_i$ for all $i = 1, 2, \ldots, k$, and $\Psi(\mu_1, \ldots, \mu_k)$ is true. It then creates for relation $S$ a tuple whose $i$th component is $\mathcal{E}_i$. Here, $\mathcal{E}_i$ is a formula as in the append statement.[4] The attribute names $A_1, \ldots, A_n$ become the names of the components of $S$. We may omit "$A_i =$" if $\mathcal{E}_i$ is of the form $\mu_j$.NAME, whereupon NAME becomes the $i$th attribute of $S$.

**Example 4.11:** QUEL, like most relational query languages, does not automatically remove duplicates when it computes a relation, because doing so is a very expensive operation. However, there are times when allowing duplicates explodes the size of a relation, and we need to cleanse it of its duplicates. Also, we frequently do not want duplicate information printed.

Suppose, for example, that we wanted to print the names of all the suppliers appearing in the SUPPLIES relation. We could write

```
range of s is SUPPLIES
retrieve (s.NAME)
```

but then each supplier would be printed once for each item it supplies. QUEL provides a sort command to eliminate duplicates while it sorts a relation, initially on the first component, then on the second component among tuples with the same first component, and so on. To print each supplier only once, and incidentally print them in alphabetical order, we could write

```
range of s is SUPPLIES
retrieve into JUNK(NAME=s.NAME)
sort JUNK
print JUNK
```

JUNK has one column headed NAME. We could have eliminated the "NAME=" from the retrieve-clause, since the attribute of $s$ used to form the one column of JUNK is called NAME. □

## Completeness of QUEL

Since we now know how to create temporary relations, all we must do to evaluate any relational algebra expression is to apply the five basic operators of relational algebra to given and temporary relations. That is, we work bottom-up

---

[4] Note that the use of formulas, the $\mathcal{E}_i$'s, to compute the components of tuples is permitted in all retrieve statements, not just those that have an "into" keyword.

through the algebraic expression, computing relations for progressively larger subexpressions, and storing these results in temporary relations.

It therefore suffices to show how we can compute the result of any one of the five basic operators of relational algebra in QUEL and store the result in a new relation. Suppose in what follows that $R(A_1, \ldots, A_n)$ and $S(B_1, \ldots, B_m)$ are relations, and $T$ is a new relation name. To compute $T = R \cup S$ (assuming $m = n$) we could write

```
range of r is R
append to T(C₁ = r.A₁,...,Cₙ = r.Aₙ)
range of s is S
append to T(C₁ = s.B₁,...,Cₙ = s.Bₙ)
```

Note that tuples appearing in both $R$ and $S$ appear twice in $T$, since duplicates are not eliminated automatically in QUEL.

To compute $T = R - S$ (assuming $m = n$) write

```
range of r is R
append to T(C₁ = r.A₁,...,Cₙ = r.Aₙ)
range of s is S
range of t is T
delete t
    where s.B₁ = t.C₁ and ··· and s.Bₙ = t.Cₙ
```

For $T = R \times S$ write

```
range of r is R
range of s is S
append to T(C₁ = r.A₁,...,Cₙ = r.Aₙ,
    Cₙ₊₁ = s.B₁,...,Cₙ₊ₘ = s.Bₘ)
```

To compute the selection $T = \sigma_F(R)$, write

```
range of r is R
append to T(C₁ = r.A₁,...,Cₙ = r.Aₙ)
    where F′
```

Here $F'$ is the formula $F$ translated into QUEL notation (component $i$ of $R$ becomes $r.A_i$, $\wedge$ becomes **and**, and so on). Finally, to express the projection $T = \pi_{i_1, \ldots, i_k}(R)$ we can write

```
range of r is R
append to T(C₁ = r.A_{i₁},...,Cₖ = r.A_{iₖ})
```

**Example 4.12:** Let us express the query of Example 4.4 in QUEL. The strategy we use is to translate the steps of relational algebra into QUEL, using one command for each of the steps in Figure 4.3. The QUEL program is shown in Figure 4.6, and the explanation follows that of Example 4.4, because we have

```
range of s is SUPPLIES
retrieve into ALLSUPS(s.NAME)

range of o is ORDERS
range of i is INCLUDES
retrieve into ZEBRAITEMS(i.ITEM)
    where o.O# = i.O#
        and o.CUST = "Zack Zebra"

range of a is ALLSUPS
range of z is ZEBRAITEMS
retrieve into NOSUPPLY(a.NAME, z.ITEM)
/* temporarily, we have set NOSUPPLY to the product
of ALLSUPS and ZEBRAITEMS; we now delete all tuples
that are in NIPAIRS, i.e., they are the NAME and
ITEM components of a SUPPLIES tuple */

range of n is NOSUPPLY
range of s is SUPPLIES
delete n
    where n.NAME = s.NAME
        and n.ITEM = s.ITEM

range of a is ALLSUPS
range of n is NOSUPPLY
delete a
    where a.NAME = n.NAME
/* above computes the answer into ALLSUPS */

print ALLSUPS
```

**Figure 4.6** Print the supplies who supply everything Zebra ordered.

used the same names for each of the intermediate relations. ☐

## Aggregate Operators

QUEL uses the aggregate functions sum, avg, count, min, and max. The argument of such a function can be any expression involving the components of a single relation, constants, and arithmetic operators. The components must all be referred to as $\mu.A$ for some one tuple variable $\mu$ and various attributes $A$.

**Example 4.13:** The net balance of all the YVCB customers can be calculated by

```
range of c is CUSTOMERS
retrieve (sum(c.BALANCE))
```

☐

We can also partition the tuples of a relation according to the value of one or more expressions computed from each tuple. We then take an aggregate separately for each set of tuples having values in common for each of the expressions. This partitioning is achieved by writing

$$\text{agg\_op}(E \text{ by } F_1, F_2, \ldots, F_k) \tag{4.9}$$

where $E$ and the $F$'s are expressions whose operands are chosen from among constants and terms $\mu.A$ for one tuple variable $\mu$ only. The operands in an expression may be connected by arithmetic operators. If $\mu$ ranges over $R$, the value of (4.9) for a given value of $\mu$ is computed by finding the set $S_\mu$ of all those tuples $\nu$ of $R$ such that $\nu$ and $\mu$ give the same value for each of the formulas $F_1, \ldots, F_k$. Then, apply the aggregate operator $agg\_op$ to the value of $E(\nu)$, as $\nu$ ranges over all the tuples in $S_\mu$.

**Example 4.14:** To print the items supplied with their average prices, we could write

```
range of s is SUPPLIES
retrieve into DUMMY(ITEM=s.ITEM,
    AP = avg(s.PRICE by s.ITEM))
sort DUMMY
print DUMMY
```

For example, suppose SUPPLIES is the relation of Figure 4.2(d). When $\mu$ is the first tuple, (Acme, Brie, 3.49), we look for all tuples with the same ITEM value, "Brie," finding the first and fifth tuples. For each of these tuples, we evaluate the expression PRICE, i.e., we obtain the third field. These values are 3.49 and 3.98, respectively. We then take the average of these values, which is 3.74, rounding up. Thus, from the first tuple of SUPPLIES, we get the tuple of relation DUMMY that has first component equal to the ITEM, i.e., "Brie," and the second component, AP, equal to 3.74. Note that when $\mu$ is the fifth tuple of SUPPLIES, we get an identical tuple of DUMMY.

We sort DUMMY to remove duplicates, as DUMMY will have, for each item, as many tuples as the SUPPLIES relation has for that item. The result of running the above program on relation SUPPLIES of Figure 4.2 is shown in Figure 4.7. ☐

## 4.4 QUERY-BY-EXAMPLE: A DRC LANGUAGE

Query-by-Example (*QBE*) is a language developed in Yorktown Heights by IBM. It contains a number of features not present in relational algebra or cal-

| ITEM | AP |
|------|------|
| Brie | 3.74 |
| Perrier | 1.14 |
| Macadamias | .06 |
| Escargot | .25 |
| Endive | .69 |

**Figure 4.7** Average prices of items.

culus, or in any of the other query languages discussed in this chapter. Among its interesting features is that QBE is designed to be used through a special screen editor that helps compose queries. A key on the terminal allows the user to call for one or more *table skeletons,* as shown in Figure 4.8, to be displayed on the screen. The user then names the relations and attributes represented by the skeleton, using the screen editor.

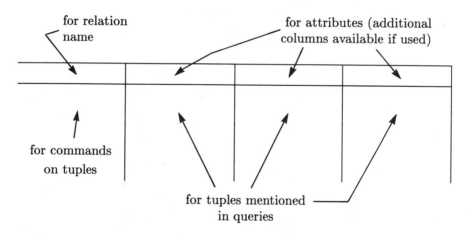

**Figure 4.8** A QBE table skeleton.

Queries are posed by using domain variables and constants, as in domain relational calculus, to form tuples that we assert are in one of the relations whose skeletons appear on the screen. Certain of the variables, those prefixed by the operator P., are printed.[5] When a tuple or combination of tuples matching the conditions specified by the query are found, the components for those attributes preceded by P. are printed.

---

[5] All operators in QBE end in dot, and the dot is not itself an operator.

Before going into detail regarding the form and meaning of queries in QBE, let us take an example of what a typical query looks like. Suppose we want to answer the query of Example 4.3, to print the suppliers of items ordered by Zack Zebra, and we have the ORDERS, INCLUDES, and SUPPLIES relations available in the database. We call for three table skeletons to be displayed. In the box reserved for the relation name, in one skeleton, we type ORDERS P.. In response to the P., the attributes of ORDERS will appear along the first row of that skeleton, as shown in Figure 4.9. Similarly, we type INCLUDES P. in the upper left corner of the second skeleton to get the attributes of the INCLUDES relation, and we type SUPPLIES P. to get the attributes of the SUPPLIES relation, in the third skeleton.

| ORDERS | O# | DATE | CUST |
|--------|------|------|------------|
|        | _123 |      | Zack Zebra |

| INCLUDES | O# | ITEM | QUANTITY |
|----------|------|---------|----------|
|          | _123 | _banana |          |

| SUPPLIES | NAME | ITEM | PRICE |
|----------|------|---------|-------|
|          | P.   | _banana |       |

**Figure 4.9** Print the suppliers of an item ordered by Zebra.

In Figure 4.9 we see this query expressed in QBE. In each of the skeletons is a tuple of the relation for that variable, with the important features shown. For example, the customer name in the ORDERS skeleton is specified to be Zack Zebra. The order number in the ORDERS and INCLUDES relations are required to be the same, indicated by the fact that the domain variable _123 appears in both places. Likewise, the ITEM in the INCLUDES and SUPPLIES tuples must be the same, because the one domain variable _banana appears in both places. The entry Zack Zebra appears with no quotation marks or underscore, to indicate it is a literal, while all variables in QBE must have names that begin with an underscore.[6]

---

[6] Note that this convention, preceding names of domain variables by an underscore and leaving literals unadorned, is diametrically opposed to the usual style of query languages and programming languages, where character string literals are adorned with quotes,

The occurrence of P. in the NAME component for the SUPPLIES tuple indicates that this component is to be printed. The QBE query of Figure 4.9 corresponds to the domain relational calculus expression

$$\{N \mid (\exists O)(\exists D)(\exists I)(\exists Q)(\exists P)\big(customers(O, D, \text{"Zack Zebra"}) \wedge$$
$$includes(O, I, Q) \wedge supplies(N, I, P)\big)\} \qquad (4.10)$$

The variable $O$ of (4.10) appears in Figure 4.9 as _123, and $I$ is replaced by _banana. Further, the other existentially quantified variables, $D$, $Q$, and $P$, appear only once in (4.10), so in QBE we need not give them names at all. That is, a blank in any position of a QBE skeleton is assumed to be a domain variable that appears nowhere else, not even in other places that are blank.

A large family of QBE queries correspond to domain calculus expressions of the form

$$\{A_1, A_2, \ldots, A_n \mid (\exists B_1)(\exists B_2) \cdots (\exists B_m)\big(r_1(C_{11}, \ldots, C_{1k_1}) \wedge$$
$$\cdots \wedge r_p(C_{p1}, \ldots, C_{pk_p})\big)\}$$

where each $C_{ij}$ is an $A_l$, a $B_l$, or a constant, and each $A_l$ and $B_l$ appears at least once among the $C$'s. To express any such query, we display the table skeletons for all the relations $R_1, \ldots, R_p$ corresponding to predicates $r_1, \ldots, r_p$, and create a variable name for each of the $A$'s and $B$'s.

In general, it is a good mnemonic to use variable names that are examples of objects actually found in the appropriate domains, but any character string preceded by an underscore will do. Now, for each atomic formula $r_i(C_{i1}, \ldots, C_{ik_i})$ write a tuple in the skeleton for $R_i$. If $C_{ij}$ is a constant, place that constant in the $j$th component. If $C_{ij}$ is one of the $A$'s or $B$'s, place the variable corresponding to that symbol there instead. However, if one of the $A$'s or $B$'s appears only once among all the terms, then we can leave the corresponding component blank if we wish.

It will often be the case that all the $A$'s appear as components of one atomic formula $r_i(C_{i1}, \ldots, C_{ik_i})$. If so, in the tuple for this term we prefix each of the $A$'s by the operator P., and we are done. However, if no such term exists, we can create another table skeleton, whose components we can optionally name, and enter into the table skeleton the tuple

P._A1 P._A2 $\cdots$ P._An

where _A$i$ is the variable name for $A_i$.

---

and variables are unadorned. Also observe that Query-by-Example takes its name from the suggestion that variable names be chosen to be examples of the object desired. However, as with variables of other languages, the name "banana" has no semantic meaning, and it could be replaced in all its occurrences by "junk," "a," or "xyz."

**Example 4.15:** Suppose we wish to print the order number and quantity ordered, for all orders for brie. We can express this query in domain calculus as

$$\{A_1 A_2 \mid includes(A_1, \text{"Brie"}, A_2)\}$$

and in QBE as

| INCLUDES | O# | ITEM | QUANTITY |
|----------|------|------|----------|
|          | P._123 | Brie | P. |

Here variable _123 replaces $A_1$. We could have omitted _123 altogether, since it appears only once. We have taken our option not to create a variable for $A_2$, since it also appears only once.

Let us consider another query: print the name, address, order number, and date for all current orders. In domain calculus this query is:

$$\{A_1 A_2 A_3 A_4 \mid (\exists B_1)(customers(A_1 A_2 B_1) \wedge orders(A_3 A_4 A_1))\}$$

As no term has all the $A$'s, we call for a new table skeleton, as well as the skeletons of CUSTOMERS and ORDERS. The query is shown in Figure 4.10.

| CUSTOMERS | NAME | ADDR | BALANCE |
|-----------|-------|-------|---------|
|           | _Snake | _Rock |         |

| ORDERS | O# | DATE | CUST |
|--------|------|--------|--------|
|        | _123 | _today | _Snake |

|   |   |   |   |   |
|---|---|---|---|---|
|   | P._Snake | P._Rock | P._123 | P._today |

**Figure 4.10** Print names, addresses, orders, and dates.

It would also have been permissible to write the unnamed relation of Figure 4.10 as

|   |   |   |   |   |
|---|---|---|---|---|
|   | P. | _Snake | _Rock | _123 | _today |

since a command such as P. in the first column (the column corresponding to the relation name) applies to all components of the tuple. □

## Implementation of QBE Queries

The general rule for implementing a query in QBE is that the system creates a tuple variable for each row that was entered into the table skeletons for the existing relations.[7] For the second query of Example 4.15 we would create a tuple variable $\mu$ for the row (_Snake, _Rock, ) of CUSTOMERS and a tuple variable $\nu$ for the row (_123, _today, _Snake) of ORDERS. Note that no variable is created for the row of the unnamed relation in Figure 4.10, since that relation does not exist in the database.

If there are $k$ such tuple variables we create $k$ nested loops; each loop causes one of the variables to range over all tuples in its relation. For each assignment of values to the tuple variables (each "value" is a tuple in the corresponding relation), we check whether the domain variables of the query can be given consistent values. In the above example, we only have to check that

$$\mu[\text{NAME}] = \nu[\text{CUST}]$$

so we can give a consistent value to domain variable _Snake. Other domain variables appear only once in CUSTOMERS or ORDERS, and thus can take whatever value $\mu$ or $\nu$ gives them.

Each time we are successful in obtaining consistent values for the domain variables, we take whatever action the query calls for. For example, if one or more rows of the query has some print commands, we print the values of the domain variables to which P. is prefixed. In Figure 4.10, only the tuple in the unnamed relation has P. operators, so we obtain the values for the variables mentioned in that tuple and print them. If more than one row has print commands, whether or not the rows are in the same relation, we print the values for those rows in separate tables. Other actions that might be taken when we find a successful match include the insertion or deletion of tuples, which we shall discuss shortly.

## Entries Representing Sets

An entry in a skeleton can be made to match more than one, but less than all, of the elements in some domain. A primary example is an entry $\theta c$, where $\theta$ is an arithmetic comparison and $c$ a constant. For example, >=3 matches any value three or greater. We can also write $\theta v$, where $v$ is a domain variable. For example, <_amount matches any value less than the value of _amount. Presumably, the value of _amount is determined by some other entry of the query, and

---

[7] That is not to say that QBE must be implemented this way. Rather, the procedure to be described serves as a definition of queries in QBE.

that value changes as we allow tuple variables to range over all tuples, as in the implementation procedure just described.

**Example 4.16:** The query of Figure 4.11(a) asks for all supplier-item-price triples for which the price is at least a dollar. Figure 4.11(b) asks for all items such that at least one supplier sells the item at a price greater than the lowest price for Perrier.

| SUPPLIES | NAME | ITEM | PRICE |
|----------|------|------|-------|
| P. | | | > 1.00 |

(a)

| SUPPLIES | NAME | ITEM | PRICE |
|----------|------|------|-------|
| | | P. | _x |
| | | Perrier | < _x |

(b)

**Figure 4.11** Queries using inequalities.

The query of Figure 4.11(b) is implemented by creating tuple variables $\mu$ and $\nu$ for the two rows of the skeleton. As we allow $\mu$ and $\nu$ to range over the various tuples in SUPPLIES, we check for matches. Tuple $\mu$ must have some PRICE component, which defines a value for _x. For example, _x = 3.49 when $\mu$ is the first tuple of SUPPLIES in Figure 4.2(d). We then look at the PRICE and ITEM components of $\nu$. If $\nu$[PRICE] is less than the value of _x, and $\nu$[ITEM] is "Perrier," then we have a match. We therefore perform the action indicated by tuple $\mu$, that is, we print $\mu$[ITEM]. For example, if $\mu$ is the first tuple and $\nu$ the second tuple in the relation of Figure 4.2(d), then the conditions are met, and we print "Brie," which is $\mu$[ITEM].

Note that QBE, unlike QUEL, eliminates duplicates automatically. Thus "Brie" would be printed only once, even though there are, in Figure 4.2(d), two tuples for Brie and two for Perrier, and the price of Brie exceeds the price of Perrier in all four combinations. □

Another way to designate a set is to use an entry that is part constant and part variable. Juxtaposition represents concatenation, so if the domain for this entry is character strings, we can try to match any constant character strings in the entry to substrings of the string that forms the corresponding component of some tuple. If we find such a match, we can assign pieces of the remainder of the string to the variables in the entry.

**Example 4.17:** To print all the orders placed in January we could write

| ORDERS | O# | DATE | CUST |
|--------|-----|--------|------|
| P. |  | Jan _32 |  |

If the date component of a tuple begins with "Jan" then the remainder of that date matches variable _32, and the entire tuple is printed. For the relation of Figure 4.2(b), all tuples would be printed, since all are dated January. □

## Negation of Rows

We may place the symbol ¬ in the first column (the column with the relation name $R$) of any row. Intuitively, the query then requires that any tuple matching the row not be a tuple of $R$. We shall try to be more precise later, but first let us consider an example.

**Example 4.18:** Suppose we wish to print the order or orders with the largest quantity. We could use the aggregate function **MAX.**, to be described later, but we can also do it with a negation. Rephrase the query as: "print an order if there is no order with a larger quantity." This condition is expressed in QBE in Figure 4.12. □

| INCLUDES | O# | ITEM | QUANTITY |
|----------|-----|------|----------|
|  | P. |  | _x |
| ¬ |  |  | > _x |

**Figure 4.12** Print orders such that no order has a larger quantity.

The implementation of queries with a negation requires that we modify the query-evaluation algorithm described earlier. If in Figure 4.12 we created tuples $\mu$ and $\nu$ for the two rows ($\mu$ for the first row), and we considered all possible values of $\mu$ and $\nu$, we would not want to print the order number in $\mu$ just because we found a tuple $\nu$ whose QUANTITY component was not greater than $\mu$[QUANTITY]. This approach would cause each tuple in INCLUDES, whose QUANTITY was not the minimum, to be printed eventually. Rather, we must arrange our loops for the tuple variables so that the tuple variables corresponding to negated rows vary in the innermost loops. Then for each set of values for the tuple variables corresponding to unnegated rows, we check that all values of the tuple variables for negated rows fail to produce a consistent assignment of values for the domain variables in the query.

For the query of Figure 4.12, the outer loop is on tuple variable $\mu$, and the inner loop is on $\nu$. For a fixed $\mu$, we print $\mu[O\#]$ only if, while considering all values of $\nu$, we never find a quantity larger than $\mu[\text{QUANTITY}]$. If we followed this procedure on the data of Figure 4.2(c), then when $\mu$ was any tuple but the last, the quantity in $\nu$, when $\nu$ was the last tuple, would be greater than the quantity in $\mu$. When $\mu$ is the last tuple, no value of $\nu$, including the last tuple, has a greater quantity, so $\mu[O\#]$, which is 1026, would be the only order number printed.

## Aggregate Operators

QBE has the usual five aggregate operators, denoted SUM., AVG., MAX., MIN., and CNT. (count). There are two other operators, ALL. and UN. (unique) that often are used in conjunction with aggregate operators. ALL. applied to a domain variable produces the list of values that the variable takes on as we run through all the tuples in the relevant relation. The list may have duplicate elements; it is not the same as a set. Thus, the ALL. operator effectively leaves duplicates in, while most other QBE operations eliminate duplicates.

**Example 4.19:** To compute the average balance of YVCB customers we write

| CUSTOMERS | NAME | ADDR | BALANCE |
|-----------|------|------|---------|
|           |      |      | P.AVG.ALL._x |

The tuple variable $\mu$ for this row ranges over all customers, and for each one, domain variable _x takes on the value $\mu[\text{BALANCE}]$.

The expression ALL._x produces the list of values assumed by _x. Should two customers have the same balance, that balance will appear twice. To compute the average balance, we want duplicates left in, or else balances appearing in the tuples for two or more customers would receive less weight than they deserve when we take the average.

The expression AVG.ALL._x then produces the average of all the elements on the list that was produced by ALL._x. Duplicates are not eliminated prior to taking the average, which we just argued is what we want in this example. Finally, the P. causes the average to be printed. □

The operator UN. converts a list into a set, by eliminating duplicates.

**Example 4.20:** Suppose we wanted to know how many suppliers there are in the YVCB database. If we (incorrectly) wrote

| SUPPLIES | NAME | ITEM | PRICE |
|----------|------|------|-------|
|          | P.CNT.ALL._x |      |       |

and applied it to the relation of Figure 4.2(d) we would get the answer 7, since variable _x takes on a list of seven values, one for each tuple in the relation. The correct way to pose the query is

| SUPPLIES | NAME | ITEM | PRICE |
|----------|------|------|-------|
| | P.CNT.UN.ALL._x | | |

In this way, before counting the set of suppliers produced by the expression ALL._x, the operator UN. removes duplicates. The value of the expression UN.ALL._x is the set {"Acme", "Ajax"}. Then the operator CNT. computes the size of this set, and P. prints the correct answer, 2. □

## Insertion and Deletion

If a row in a query has the operator I. or D. in the first column, then when implementing the query we do not create a tuple variable for this row. Rather, when a match for all the tuple variables is found, we insert (I.) or delete (D.) into or from the relation in whose skeleton one of these commands is found. Variables in the row or rows to be inserted, deleted, or updated take their values from the appropriate components of the tuple variables.

**Example 4.21:** If Ajax starts selling Escargot at \$.24 each, we can insert this information into the SUPPLIES relation by:

| SUPPLIES | NAME | ITEM | PRICE |
|----------|------|------|-------|
| I. | Ajax | Escargot | .24 |

Notice that this query is implemented by a special case of the QBE implementation rule. Since there are no tuple variables on which to loop, we simply execute the insert operation once. The row to be inserted has no variables, so the components of the inserted tuple are well defined.

If instead, Ajax wants to sell Escargot for the same price that Acme sells them, we could retrieve Acme's price as we perform the insertion:

| SUPPLIES | NAME | ITEM | PRICE |
|----------|------|------|-------|
| I. | Ajax | Escargot | _ripoff |
| | Acme | Escargot | _ripoff |

A tuple variable $\mu$ for the second row ranges over all tuples in SUPPLIES. Assuming the data of Figure 4.2(d), the only value of $\mu$ that contains the constants "Acme" and "Escargot" for NAME and ITEM, respectively, also has .25 in its PRICE component. Thus, the value .25 is given to the variable _ripoff when $\mu$ reaches this tuple. At that time, the insert action of the first row is taken, with variable _ripoff bound to .25, so the tuple ("Ajax", "Escargot", .25) is inserted into SUPPLIES. □

### Updates

The update operation can only be understood if we are aware that the QBE system allows us to define *key* and *nonkey* attributes of relations, by a mechanism to be discussed shortly. The set of key attributes must uniquely determine a tuple; that is, two different tuples in a relation cannot agree on all key attributes. If we place the update (U.) operator in the first column of a row, then entries in key fields must match the tuple updated, and any tuple of the relation that does match the row of the skeleton in the key attributes will have its nonkey attributes updated to match the values in the row with the U. operator.

**Example 4.22:** In the SUPPLIES relation, NAME and ITEM are key attributes and PRICE is nonkey. That is, NAME and ITEM together form a key for the relation. If Acme decides to lower its price for Perrier to one dollar, we may update the YVCB database by:

| SUPPLIES | NAME | ITEM | PRICE |
|----------|------|------|-------|
| U. | Acme | Perrier | 1.00 |

If Acme instead decides to lower all its prices by 10%, we can write:

| SUPPLIES | NAME | ITEM | PRICE |
|----------|------|------|-------|
| U. | Acme | _spam | .9*_ripoff |
| | Acme | _spam | _ripoff |

Note the use of an arithmetic expression in the row to be updated. The use of arithmetic is permitted where it makes sense, such as in rows to be updated or inserted, and in "condition boxes," a concept to be described next. The execution of the above command follows the general rules we have been following. A tuple variable for the second row is allowed to range over all SUPPLIES tuples. Whenever the tuple has supplier name Acme, the variable _spam gets bound to the item, and _ripoff gets bound to the price. We then update the unique tuple with NAME equal to "Acme" and ITEM equal to the value of variable _spam, by changing the PRICE component to .9×_ripoff, that is, to 90% of its former value. □

### Condition Boxes

There are times when we wish to include a condition on a query, insertion, deletion, or update that is not expressed by simple terms such as <3 in the rows of the query. We can then call for a *condition box* to be displayed and enter into the box any relationships we wish satisfied. Entries of a condition box are essentially conditions as in a language like Pascal, but without the use of the "not" operator, ¬. Either AND or & can be used for logical "and," while OR or | is used for "or." When the query is implemented, a match is deemed to occur only when the current values of the tuple variables allow a consistent assignment of values to the domain variables in the query, and these values also satisfy the conditions.

**Example 4.23:** Suppose we want to find all the suppliers whose price for Brie and Perrier together is no greater than \$5.00. We can express this query with a condition box, as shown in Figure 4.13. The two tuple variables $\mu$ and $\nu$ range over all SUPPLIES tuples. When we find a pair of tuples with the same supplier name, with $\mu$[ITEM] equal to "Brie" and $\nu$[ITEM] equal to "Perrier," the variables _x and _y get bound to the prices of these items charged by the supplier in question. If the condition in the condition box is satisfied, i.e., the sum of _x and _y is no more than five dollars, then consistent values of $\mu$ and $\nu$ have been found, and we perform the print action indicated in $\mu$. If the condition box is not satisfied, then we do not have a match, even though $\mu$ and $\nu$ agree on the value of the variable _bmw.

| SUPPLIES | NAME | ITEM | PRICE |
|----------|------|------|-------|
|          | P._bmw | Brie | _x |
|          | _bmw | Perrier | _y |

| CONDITIONS |
|------------|
| _x + _y <= 5.00 |

**Figure 4.13** Suppliers who sell a Brie and Perrier for under \$5.

For example, using the data of Figure 4.2(d), when _bmw has value "Acme," the sum of _x and _y is 4.68, which satisfies the condition, so "Acme" is printed. However, when the variable _bmw has value "Ajax," the sum is 5.07, which does not satisfy the condition, and we do not print "Ajax." □

### Completeness of QBE

As with the other languages we have studied, it appears simplest to prove completeness by showing how to apply each of the five basic relational algebra operations and store the result in a new relation. For instance, to compute

$T = R \cup S$ we can execute the QBE command shown in Figure 4.14, assuming $T$ is initially empty. The operation of set difference is achieved with an insertion command, then a deletion command; Cartesian product and projection are performed with an insertion. We leave these commands as exercises. For selection, we invoke Lemma 3.5, which says that all selections can be broken into simple selections of the form $\sigma_{X\theta Y}$. Thus, a condition box can be used to implement any selection.[8]

| $R$ | | | | |
|-----|-----|-----|-------|------|
|     | _a1 | _a2 | $\cdots$ | _a$n$ |

| $S$ | | | | |
|-----|-----|-----|-------|------|
|     | _b1 | _b2 | $\cdots$ | _b$n$ |

| $T$ | | | | |
|-----|-----|-----|-------|------|
| I.  | _a1 | _a2 | $\cdots$ | _a$n$ |
| I.  | _b1 | _b2 | $\cdots$ | _b$n$ |

**Figure 4.14** QBE command for $T = R \cup S$.

## 4.5 DATA DEFINITION IN QBE

Like each of the languages studied in this section, QBE has an associated data definition language. The QBE DDL uses the same format and graphical interface as does the query language. We shall mention two important aspects: how relations are declared and how views are declared.

### The Table Directory

The QBE system maintains a list, called the *table directory*, of all the relation names in the database, their attributes and certain information about the attributes. One can query, insert, or delete from this list using the same notation as for general queries. For example, typing P._relname, or just P., in the upper left hand box of a table skeleton will cause the system to print the current list of relation names. Typing P._relname P. in that box will print the relation

---

[8] Lemma 3.5 is essential here, because condition boxes forbid the $\neg$ operator, and therefore, one cannot implement arbitrary selections with condition boxes alone.

names and their attribute names. The second P. refers to the attribute names. To insert a new relation REL into the table directory, type I.REL I. in the upper left box and then type the attributes of REL along the top of the skeleton. Again, the second I. refers to the attributes, while the first I. refers to the relation name.

The attributes may be declared to have certain properties. These properties are:

1. KEY, telling whether or not the attribute is part of the key (recall that updates require the system to distinguish between key and nonkey fields). The values of this property are Y (key) and N (nonkey).

2. TYPE, the data type of the attribute, such as CHAR (variable length character string), CHAR($n$) (character string of length $n$), FLOAT (real number), or FIXED (integer).

3. DOMAIN, a name for the domain of values for this attribute. If a domain variable in a query appears in two different columns, those columns must come from the same domain. The system rejects queries that violate this rule, a useful check on the meaningfulness of queries.

4. INVERSION, indicating whether an index on the attribute is (Y) or is not (N) to be created and maintained.

**Example 4.24:** To create the SUPPLIES relation we might fill a table skeleton with some of its properties, as shown in Figure 4.15. The first row indicates the key for the relation; recall that NAME and ITEM together determine a unique price, so the key for SUPPLIES is {NAME, ITEM}. The second row indicates the data type for each ATTRIBUTE. We suppose that the NAME and ITEM components are character strings, while PRICE is a real number, presumably one that is significant to two decimal places.

In the row for domains we have indicated a distinct domain for each attribute. That would prevent us, for example, from asking a query about suppliers who provide an item with the same name as the supplier, because the same variable would not be allowed to appear in the NAME and ITEM fields. In the last row we have declared that there are no indices to be created. Recall that an index on an attribute, such as NAME, allows us to find tuples with a given name very fast; we do not have to search the entire relation. Particular structures that could be used to create indices will be discussed in Chapter 6. □

### Views

QBE contains a delayed-evaluation feature similar to ISBL. When we wish to create a view $V$, we insert $V$ into the table directly as a relation, prefixing the name $V$ by the keyword VIEW. We then formulate in QBE the method whereby $V$ is to be calculated. $V$ is not actually computed at the time. Rather, it is

| I. SUPPLIES | I. | NAME | ITEM | PRICE |
|---|---|---|---|---|
| KEY | I. | Y | Y | N |
| TYPE | I. | CHAR | CHAR | FLOAT |
| DOMAIN | I. | NAMES | ITEMS | AMOUNTS |
| INVERSION | I. | N | N | N |

**Figure 4.15** Creation of SUPPLIES relation.

computed whenever $V$ is used in a subsequent query, and its value is computed then, from the current relations mentioned in the formula for $V$.

**Example 4.25:** Suppose we wish to take the natural join of ORDERS and IN-CLUDES, projecting out the order number, to obtain a view OI, with attributes NAME, DATE, ITEM, and QUANTITY, whose tuples $(n, d, i, q)$ indicate a customer $n$ who placed an order on date $d$ for quantity $q$ of item $i$. This view can be defined as in Figure 4.16.

| I.VIEW OI I. | NAME | DATE | ITEM | QUANTITY |
|---|---|---|---|---|
| I. | _Snake | _today | _hotdogs | _somuch |

| ORDERS | O# | DATE | CUST |
|---|---|---|---|
| | _123 | _today | _Snake |

| INCLUDES | O# | ITEM | QUANTITY |
|---|---|---|---|
| | _123 | _hotdogs | _somuch |

**Figure 4.16** Definition of View OI.

We can later use the view OI as if it were an EDB relation, by formulating queries such as:

| OI | NAME | DATE | ITEM | QUANTITY |
|---|---|---|---|---|
| | Ruth Rhino | P. | P. | P. |

which prints the date, item and quantity for everything ordered by Ruth Rhino.

The value of relation OI, or rather its relevant part—the tuples with NAME equal to "Ruth Rhino"—is computed from ORDERS and INCLUDES when the above query is executed. $\square$

## 4.6 THE QUERY LANGUAGE SQL

SQL, formerly known as SEQUEL, is a language developed by IBM in San Jose, originally for use in the experimental database system known as System R. The language is now used in a number of commercial database systems, and in some cases, the entire database system is marketed under the name SQL. The particular version we shall discuss here is SQL/RT, implemented for the IBM PC/RT by Oracle Corp.

Because SQL is the most commonly implemented relational query language, we shall discuss it in more detail than the other languages of this chapter. This section discusses the query language. Section 4.7 covers the data definition facilities of the SQL system, and Section 4.8 introduces the reader to the way SQL's query language interfaces with a host language.

### The Select Statement

The most common form of query in SQL is a select statement of the form:

SELECT $R_{i_1}.A_1, \ldots, R_{i_r}.A_r$
FROM $R_1, \ldots, R_k$
WHERE $\Psi$;                                                              (4.11)

Here, $R_1, \ldots, R_k$ is a list of distinct relation names, and $R_{i_1}.A_1, \ldots R_{i_r}.A_r$ is a list of component references to be printed; $R.A$ refers to the attribute $A$ of relation $R$. If only one relation in the list following the keyword FROM has an attribute $A$, then we may use $A$ in place of $R.A$ in the select-list.

$\Psi$ is a formula involving logical connectives AND, OR, and NOT, and comparison operators =, <=, and so on, essentially as in QUEL. Later, we shall discuss more general conditions that can appear in place of $\Psi$.

The meaning of query (4.11) is most easily expressed in relational algebra, as:

$$\pi_{R_{i_1}.A_1,\ldots,R_{i_r}.A_r}\left(\sigma_{\Psi'}(R_1 \times \cdots \times R_k)\right)$$

That is, we take the product of all the relations in the from-clause, select according to the where-clause ($\Psi$ is replaced by an equivalent expression $\Psi'$, using the operators of relational algebra, i.e., $\wedge$ in place of AND, and so on), and finally project onto the attributes of the select-clause. Note the unfortunate notational conflict: the keyword SELECT in SQL corresponds to what is called "projection" in relational algebra, not to "selection."

**Example 4.26:** The query of Example 4.2, to list the customers with negative balances, is expressed in SQL by:

```
SELECT NAME
FROM CUSTOMERS
WHERE BALANCE < 0;
```

Here, since there is only one relation in the from-clause, there can be no ambiguity regarding what the attributes refer to. Thus, we did not have to prefix attributes by their relation names. However, we could have written

```
SELECT CUSTOMERS.NAME
```

if we wished, or similarly adorned BALANCE in the third line.

In either style, the result would be a one column relation whose attribute is the one in the select-clause, that is, NAME. Had we wanted another header for the column, we could have provided an alias for NAME by writing that alias immediately after NAME in the select-clause, with no punctuation.[9] Thus,

```
SELECT NAME CUSTOMER
FROM CUSTOMERS
WHERE BALANCE < 0;
```

Prints the table

| CUSTOMER |
| --- |
| Zack Zebra |
| Judy Giraffe |

Had we wished to print the entire tuple for customers with a negative balance, we could have written

```
SELECT NAME, ADDR, BALANCE
FROM CUSTOMERS
WHERE BALANCE < 0;
```

or just

```
SELECT *
FROM CUSTOMERS
WHERE BALANCE < 0;
```

since $R.*$ is SQL's way of saying "all the attributes of relation $R$." In this example, since CUSTOMERS is the only relation in the from-clause, we do not even need to mention that relation, and hence used $*$ instead of CUSTOMERS.$*$. □

---

[9] In the SQL style, $A$ $B$ written with no punctuation implies that $B$ is an alias, or renaming, of $A$, while $A, B$ means that $A$ and $B$ are elements of a list, e.g., a list of attributes.

**Example 4.27:** The query of Example 4.3, to print the suppliers of the items Zack Zebra ordered, is expressed in SQL by the program of Figure 4.17. Here, we take the natural join of ORDERS, INCLUDES and SUPPLIES, using equalities in the where-clause to define the join, just as we did in QUEL in Example 4.6 or in QBE in Figure 4.9. The where-clause also contains the condition that the customer be Zack Zebra, and the select-clause causes only the supplier name to be printed.

```
SELECT NAME
FROM ORDERS, INCLUDES, SUPPLIES
WHERE CUST = 'Zack Zebra'
    AND ORDERS.O# = INCLUDES.O#
    AND INCLUDES.ITEM = SUPPLIES.ITEM;
```

**Figure 4.17** Print the suppliers of an item ordered by Zebra.

We should notice the way attributes are referenced in Figure 4.17. CUST and NAME unambiguously refer to attributes of ORDERS and SUPPLIES, respectively, so they do not have to be prefixed by a relation name. However, O# is an attribute of both ORDERS and INCLUDES, so its two occurrences on the fourth line of Figure 4.17 have to be prefixed by the relations intended. A similar handling of the two occurrences of ITEM appears on the last line.

One other nuance is that SQL, like most real query languages, does not remove duplicates automatically. Thus, in the query of Figure 4.17, "Acme" would be printed three times, because it supplies each of the three items ordered by Zebra, and "Ajax" would be printed twice. To remove duplicates, we use the keyword DISTINCT following SELECT; i.e., the first line of Figure 4.17 would become

```
SELECT DISTINCT NAME
```

☐

**Tuple Variables**

Sometimes we need to refer to two or more tuples in the same relation. To do so, we define several tuple variables for that relation in the from clause and use the tuple variables as aliases of the relation. The effect is exactly the same as was achieved by the range-statement in QUEL, so SQL, which appeared at first to be a "syntactically sugared" form of relational algebra, is now revealed to resemble tuple relational calculus.

**Example 4.28:** The query of Example 4.7, to print the names and addresses of customers whose balance is less than that of Judy Giraffe may be expressed:

```
SELECT c1.NAME, c1.ADDR
FROM CUSTOMERS c1, CUSTOMERS c2
WHERE c1.BALANCE < c2.BALANCE
    AND c2.NAME = 'Judy Giraffe';
```

Recall that in the style of SQL, a name followed with no punctuation by another name makes the second be an alias for the first. Thus, the above from-clause declares both $c1$ and $c2$ to be aliases of CUSTOMERS, in effect making them tuple variables that range over CUSTOMERS. With that understanding, the above SQL program is only a syntactic variation on the QUEL program that we gave in Example 4.7. □

### Pattern Matching

In addition to the usual arithmetic comparisons in where-clauses, we can use the operator LIKE to express the condition that a certain value matches a pattern. The symbol % in character strings stands for "any character string," while the underscore _ stands for "any one character."

**Example 4.29:** The following code prints those items that begin with "E."

```
SELECT ITEM
FROM SUPPLIES
WHERE ITEM LIKE 'E%';
```

The next program prints those orders whose number is in the range 1000–1999, i.e., those whose order numbers are a "1" followed by any three characters. For this code to make sense, we have to assume that order numbers are stored as character strings, rather than integers.[10]

```
SELECT *
FROM ORDERS
WHERE O# LIKE '1___';
```

□

### Set Operations in the Where-Clause

While we have imagined the expression in a where-clause to resemble the selection conditions of relational algebra, these expressions are actually far more general. One minor point is that arithmetic is allowed in comparisons, so we can write conditions like

---

[10] It is often desirable to store numerical data as character strings anyway, because the data becomes more easily transported between computers with different internal formats for numbers.

```
WHERE A > B+C-10
```

Far more important is that SQL allows sets as operands; these sets are defined by complete select-from-where statements nested within a where-clause, and are called *subqueries*. The operators IN, NOT IN, ANY, and ALL are used, respectively, to denote membership in a set, nonmembership, existential quantification over a set, and universal quantification over a set.

**Example 4.30:** One use of subqueries is to replace a sequence of joins by semijoins. Consider the query of Example 4.3 again, which we wrote using joins in Example 4.27. Another way to implement the query is:

1. Find the set $S_1$ of orders placed by Zebra, using the ORDERS relation.
2. Find the set $S_2$ of items in set of orders $S_1$, using the INCLUDES relation.
3. Find the set $S_3$ of suppliers of the items in set $S_2$ by using the SUPPLIES relation.

The result desired is $S_3$. We express $S_3$ by a query on SUPPLIES only, but with a where-clause containing the condition that the item should be in the set $S_2$. $S_2$ is then defined by a subquery on INCLUDES, with a where-condition that the order should be in set $S_1$, and $S_1$ is defined by a subquery on ORDERS. The query is shown in Figure 4.18. Notice that the parenthesis surrounding the subqueries of lines (4)–(9) and (7)–(9) are essential. □

```
(1)  SELECT NAME
(2)  FROM SUPPLIES
(3)  WHERE ITEM IN
(4)      (SELECT ITEM
(5)      FROM INCLUDES
(6)      WHERE O# IN
(7)          (SELECT O#
(8)          FROM ORDERS
(9)          WHERE CUST = 'Zack Zebra'));
```

**Figure 4.18** Query of Example 4.3, using subqueries.

Notice that in Figure 4.18 there is no ambiguity regarding the relation to which ITEM belongs at line (3), since SUPPLIES is the only relation defined at line (3). Formally, the *scope* of a relation defined in a from-clause (or of an alias for that relation) consists of the preceding select-clause and the following where-clause. Thus, the scope of SUPPLIES, defined in the from-clause on line (2) is lines (1)–(9), while the scope of INCLUDES, defined on line (5), is lines (4)–(9) and the scope of ORDERS, from line (8), is (7)–(9). It follows that (3)

is only in the scope of SUPPLIES, and it is to that relation ITEM on line (3)
refers.

The occurrence of ITEM on line (4) might refer to SUPPLIES or IN-
CLUDES, since it is in the scope of both. However, SQL follows a "most
closely nested" rule to resolve ambiguities, so the scope of INCLUDES, being
nested within the scope of SUPPLIES, yet including line (4), is deemed to be
the relation to which ITEM at line (4) refers. Had we wanted to refer to the
ITEM component of SUPPLIES anywhere within lines (4)–(9), we could have
said SUPPLIES.ITEM. Similar remarks apply to the occurrences of O# on lines
(6) and (7), which refer to the O# components of INCLUDES and ORDERS,
respectively, for the same reasons that ITEM refers to SUPPLIES on line (3)
and to INCLUDES on line (4).

The keyword **ANY** is used like an existential quantifier. If $S$ is some expression denoting a set, then the condition

$A \ \theta \ $**ANY**$ \ S$

is equivalent to the logical expression

$(\exists X)(X$ is in $S \ \wedge \ A\theta X)$

Presumably, $A$ is an attribute, whose value is taken from some tuple of some
relation, $S$ is a set defined by a subquery, and $\theta$ is an arithmetic comparison
operator. Similarly,

$A \ \theta \ $**ALL**$ \ S$

means

$(\forall X)($ if $X$ is in $S$ then $A\theta X)$

**Example 4.31:** We can print each item whose price is as large as any appearing
in the SUPPLIES relation by using a subquery to form the set $S$ of all prices,
and then saying that the price of a given item is as large as any in the set $S$.
This query is shown in Figure 4.19. Notice that the scope rules described above
disambiguate which of the two uses of relation SUPPLIES [lines (2) and (5)]
the attribute PRICE refers to at lines (3) and (4). Line (3) is only in the scope
of the SUPPLIES of line (2), while at line (4), PRICE refers to the relation
with a PRICE attribute whose scope most closely surrounds line (4); that is
the relation SUPPLIES declared at line (5) and used in the subquery of lines
(4)–(5). Notice also that a where-clause is not essential in a query or subquery,
and this subquery creates a list of all prices by having a missing, or always-true,
where-clause. □

If we are sure that the set of values produced by a subquery will be a
singleton, then we can treat it as an ordinary value, and it may appear in arithmetic comparisons. However, if the data is such that the set $S$ in a condition
like $A = S$ is not a singleton, then the condition makes no sense, and an error

```
(1)  SELECT ITEM
(2)  FROM SUPPLIES
(3)  WHERE PRICE >= ALL
(4)       (SELECT PRICE
(5)        FROM SUPPLIES);
```

**Figure 4.19** Finding the most costly item.

occurs when the query is executed.

**Example 4.32:** If we are sure that Ruth Rhino has placed exactly one order, then we can get its number in a subquery and use it to select from INCLUDES all the items ordered by Rhino. The query is shown in Figure 4.20, and on the data of Figure 4.2 the subquery returns {1025} and the items

{"Brie", "Escargot", "Endive"}

are printed. If we replace "Ruth Rhino" by "Zack Zebra" in Figure 4.20, the query will fail because Zebra placed two orders. □

```
SELECT ITEM
FROM INCLUDES
WHERE O# =
    (SELECT O#
    FROM ORDERS
    WHERE CUST = 'Ruth Rhino');
```

**Figure 4.20** Find the items ordered by Ruth Rhino.

## Aggregate Operators

SQL provides the usual five aggregate operators, AVG, COUNT, SUM, MIN, and MAX. It also provides the operators STDDEV and VARIANCE to provide the standard deviation and variance of a list of numbers. A select-from-where statement can print the result of applying one or more of these aggregate operators to the attributes of a single relation, by placing the relation in the from-clause and placing in the select-clause the list of aggregate terms, $agg\_op(A)$, where $agg\_op$ is an aggregate operator and $A$ is an attribute. The where-clause may have a condition $\Psi$, and if so, only those tuples that satisfy $\Psi$ are included in the computation of the aggregate. The keyword DISTINCT may precede the attribute $A$ in $agg\_op(A)$, in which case duplicates are eliminated before $agg\_op$ is applied.

**Example 4.33:** Let us consider the queries of Examples 4.19 and 4.20, which were to compute the average balance and the total number of suppliers in the YVCB database. For the first of these we write

```
SELECT AVG(BALANCE)
FROM CUSTOMERS;
```

This query would print the average balance, which is −69 for the data of Figure 4.2(a). The column header would be AVG(BALANCE). If we wanted another column header, say AV_BAL, we could specify an alias, as in:

```
SELECT AVG(BALANCE) AV_BAL
FROM CUSTOMERS;
```

For the query of Example 4.20, to count the number of suppliers, we can examine the SUPPLIES relation but, recall from that example, we must eliminate duplicates before we count. That is, we write

```
SELECT COUNT(DISTINCT NAME) #SUPPS
FROM SUPPLIES;
```

to print the number of different suppliers, in a column headed by #SUPPS.

If we wished to know only how many suppliers sell Brie, we could ask:

```
SELECT COUNT(NAME) #BRIE_SUPPS
FROM SUPPLIES
WHERE ITEM = 'Brie';
```

Note it is unnecessary to remove duplicates here, because the fact that a supplier sells Brie appears only once, assuming {NAME, ITEM} is a key for SUPPLIES in the YVCB database. □

## Aggregation by Groups

As in QUEL, we can partition the tuples of a relation into groups and apply aggregate operators to the groups individually. To do so, we follow the select-from-where statement with a "group-by" clause, consisting of the keywords GROUP BY and a list of attributes of the relation mentioned in the from-clause that together define the groups. That is, if we have clause

$$\text{GROUP BY } A_1, \ldots, A_k$$

then we partition the relation into groups, such that two tuples are in the same group if and only if they agree on all the attributes $A_1, \ldots, A_k$. For the result of such a query to make sense, the attributes $A_1, \ldots, A_k$ must also appear in the select-clause, although they could be given aliases for printing, if desired.[11]

---

[11] This situation is the only one where it is permitted to have both attributes of a relation and aggregations of other attributes of the same relation appearing in the same select-clause; otherwise, the combination of, say, NAME and AVG(BALANCE) from relation

**Example 4.34:** Let us reconsider the query of Example 4.13, to print a table, which was shown in Figure 4.7, of all the items and their average prices. In SQL we write

```
SELECT ITEM, AVG(PRICE) AP
FROM SUPPLIES
GROUP BY ITEM;
```

The alias AP for AVG(PRICE) is used to conform with the table of Figure 4.7.
□

A where-clause can follow the from-clause if we wish only a subset of the tuples to be considered as we form the groups. We can also arrange to have only a subset of the groups printed, independently of any filtering that goes on in the where-clause before we construct the groups. The keyword HAVING introduces a clause that may follow the group-by clause. If we write

```
GROUP BY A₁,...,Aₖ
HAVING Ψ
```

then the condition $\Psi$ is applied to each relation $R_{a_1,...,a_k}$ that consists of the group of tuples with values $a_1,...,a_k$ for attributes $A_1,...,A_k$, respectively. Those groups for which $R_{a_1,...,a_k}$ satisfies $\Psi$ are part of the output, and the others do not appear.

**Example 4.35:** Suppose we wanted to restrict the groups in the query of Example 4.34 to those items that were sold by more than one supplier. We could then write

```
SELECT ITEM, AVG(PRICE) AP
FROM SUPPLIES
GROUP BY ITEM
HAVING COUNT(*) > 1;
```

Recall that * stands for all the attributes of the relation referred to, which in this case can only be SUPPLIES. Thus, COUNT(*) counts the distinct tuples, but since it appears in a having-clause, it does so independently for each group. It finds that only the groups corresponding to Brie and Perrier have more than one tuple, and only these two groups have their averages printed. The resulting output is a subset of the tuples of Figure 4.7, that is,

| ITEM | AP |
|------|------|
| Brie | 3.74 |
| Perrier | 1.14 |

If we had wanted to consider only those groups with two or more distinct prices, we could have used the following having-clause:

---

CUSTOMERS does not make sense.

```
HAVING COUNT(DISTINCT PRICE) > 1
```

The answer would not change for the data of Figure 4.2(d), but we would notice a difference if an item had several suppliers, all of whom charged the same price. Such an item would not be printed if we used the above having-clause. □

### Insertion

To insert new tuples into a relation we use the statement form:

```
INSERT INTO R
VALUES (v₁,...,vₖ);
```

Here, $R$ is a relation name and $v_1, \ldots, v_k$ is a list of values for the attributes of $R$. These attributes are given a particular order when the relation $R$ is declared; we shall discuss data definition in the next section. The values are assumed to correspond to the attributes of $R$ in the same order. For example, if Ajax starts selling Escargot at \$.24 each, we can say:

```
INSERT INTO SUPPLIES
VALUES ('Ajax', 'Escargot', .24);
```

Under certain circumstances, we do not have to specify values for all the attributes of the relation. As discussed in the next section, certain attributes may permit null values, and for these attributes a value in the insert command is optional. If a value is not provided, NULL will be the assumed value. In some senses, NULL is an ordinary value; one can select for it in a where-clause, for example. On the other hand, NULL does not match itself in joins.

We introduce null values by listing a subset of the attributes of the relation into which we are inserting, and by providing values for only these attributes. Attributes not listed are given value NULL, provided those attributes permit nulls; if not it is an error.

**Example 4.36:** Suppose that attribute PRICE of SUPPLIES may have nulls. Then we could create a tuple that says "Ajax sells Escargot, but we don't know the price," by:

```
INSERT INTO SUPPLIES(NAME, ITEM)
VALUES ('Ajax', 'Escargot');
```

□

Instead of inserting one tuple at a time, we can replace the value-clause of an insert-statement by a select-from-where statement that produces a relation of values, say $R$. The arity of $R$ must match the arity of the relation into which insertion occurs.

**Example 4.37:** Suppose we wanted a new relation

    ACME_SELLS(ITEM, PRICE)

that listed just the item and price components of the SUPPLIES tuples with
NAME equal to "Acme." We create this new relation by a mechanism discussed
in the next section. Then we can issue the insert command:

```
INSERT INTO ACME_SELLS
    SELECT ITEM, PRICE
    FROM SUPPLIES
    WHERE NAME = 'Acme';
```

Whatever the attributes of ACME_SELLS, provided there are exactly two of
them and they are of appropriate type, the first will receive the ITEM component and the second will receive the PRICE component of every tuple in
SUPPLIES with the name component "Acme." □

## Deletion

The form of a deletion command in SQL is

```
DELETE FROM R
WHERE Ψ;
```

$R$ is a relation name and $\Psi$ is a condition as is normally associated with where-
clauses. The effect, naturally, is that every tuple of $R$ for which $\Psi$ is true is
deleted from $R$.

**Example 4.38:** Let us reconsider Example 4.8, which showed how to delete
from the ORDERS relation all orders that included Brie. Recall that we must
use the INCLUDES relation to tell whether a given order includes Brie. The
SQL form of this deletion is:

```
DELETE FROM ORDERS
WHERE O# IN
    (SELECT O#
    FROM INCLUDES
    WHERE ITEM = 'Brie');
```

Of course, most deletions will not need a subquery. If we wish to delete
a particular tuple, we simply specify all its values, or at least the values of its
key. For example, if Acme no longer sells Perrier, we can write:

```
DELETE FROM SUPPLIES
WHERE NAME = 'Acme'
    AND ITEM = 'Perrier';
```

□

## Update

The general form of an update command is

```
UPDATE R
SET A₁ = ℰ₁,...,Aₖ = ℰₖ
WHERE Ψ;
```

Here, $R$ is a relation, some of whose tuples are to be updated. The updated tuples are those that satisfy the condition $\Psi$, and the changes are specified by the set-clause. For each tuple $\mu$ satisfying $\Psi$, we set component $\mu[A_i]$ to $\mathcal{E}_i$, for each $i = 1, 2, \ldots, k$.

**Example 4.39:** Let us reconsider the updates of Example 4.22, which concerned QBE. The first update is to change the price Acme charges for Perrier to \$1.00. In SQL this change is:

```
UPDATE SUPPLIES
SET PRICE = 1.00
WHERE NAME = 'Acme'
    AND ITEM = 'Perrier';
```

The second update was to lower all of Acme's prices by 10%. In SQL we write:

```
UPDATE SUPPLIES
SET PRICE = .9*PRICE
WHERE NAME = 'Acme';
```

Notice how the above query applies to any tuple whose NAME component is "Acme," independent of the item. Also observe that the assignment in the set-clause is like an ordinary assignment, computing the new value of PRICE in terms of the old value. □

## Completeness of SQL

As with QUEL and QBE, in order to simulate an arbitrary expression of relational algebra in SQL, we must assume that a relation for each subexpression has been defined.[12] We then compute the relation for each subexpression, from smallest to largest expression, culminating in the evaluation of the entire expression. Thus, as with the other languages, we have only to show how to apply the five basic operators of relational algebra.

Assume we have relations $R(A_1, \ldots, A_n)$ and $S(B_1, \ldots, B_m)$. In the case that we need to take the union or difference of $R$ and $S$, we also assume $m = n$ and $A_i = B_i$ for all $i$. Of course, if the arities of $R$ and $S$ disagree, we cannot take their union or difference. However, if we need to rename the attributes of

---

[12] Creation of new relations is explained in the next section.

$S$, we can create a new relation $Snew$ with the same attributes, $A_1, \ldots, A_n$, as $R$. We then copy $S$ into $Snew$ by:

```
INSERT INTO Snew
SELECT *
FROM S;
```

Now, we may use $Snew$ in place of $S$.

Finally, we assume in what follows that relation $T$ is declared to have the appropriate number of attributes for each of the five operations, and that the attributes of all three relations are $A_1, \ldots, A_n$ in the cases of union and difference.

To compute $T = R \cup S$ we write

```
INSERT INTO T
SELECT *
FROM R;
```

followed by

```
INSERT INTO T
SELECT *
FROM S;
```

To compute the set difference $T = R - S$, we start with the first insertion into $T$, as above, and follow it with:

```
DELETE FROM T
WHERE (A₁,...,Aₙ) IN
    (SELECT *
    FROM S);
```

Recall we assume that the attributes of $R$, $S$, and $T$ are the same when we take a set difference, and we may assume so because attributes can be renamed if necessary. The list $A_1, \ldots, A_n$ in the where-clause above refers to the attributes of $T$, while the subquery produces all the tuples of $S$, which are each matched with the attribute list for $T$ and deleted from $T$ if they are present.

For the Cartesian product $T = R \times S$ we say:

```
INSERT INTO T
SELECT R.A₁,...,R.Aₙ,S.B₁,...,S.Bₘ
FROM R, S;
```

while the selection $T = \sigma_F(R)$ is written

```
INSERT INTO T
SELECT *
FROM R
WHERE F';
```

Here, $F'$ is the selection condition $F$ translated into SQL notation.

Finally, the projection $T = \pi_{i_1,\ldots,i_k}(R)$ is expressed in SQL by:

```
INSERT INTO T
SELECT A_{i_1}, ..., A_{i_k}
FROM R;
```

## 4.7 DATA DEFINITION IN SQL

The SQL data definition commands are issued to the same interpreter that accepts the queries and updates described in the previous section. Thus, the DML and DDL are really two sets of commands that are part of a single language.

The most fundamental DDL command is the one that creates a new relation. We say

```
CREATE TABLE R
```

followed by a parenthesized list of attributes and their data types.

**Example 4.40:** We can define the SUPPLIES relation scheme from our YVCB example by

```
CREATE TABLE SUPPLIES
    (NAME CHAR(20) NOT NULL,
    ITEM CHAR(10) NOT NULL,
    PRICE NUMBER(6,2));
```

The three attributes are seen to be NAME, ITEM, and PRICE. The data type of NAME is a string of up to 20 characters, while ITEM is a string of up to 10 characters. PRICE is a number, and the specification $(6,2)$ says that prices may have up to six digits, and two of them are to the right of the decimal point.

The specification NOT NULL for the NAME and ITEM attributes says that nulls will not be permitted in these components. This choice makes sense because these two attributes together form a key for SUPPLIES, and it might be awkward if null values were permitted in a key. On the other hand, there might be no harm if a price were temporarily null, so we have elected not prohibit nulls in the PRICE component. □

The opposite of CREATE is DROP. If we wanted to delete the relation SUPPLIES from the database entirely, we would write:

```
DROP TABLE SUPPLIES
```

### Creation of Indices

Indices are used to speed up access to a relation. Recall that if relation $R$ has an index on attribute $A$, then we can retrieve all the tuples with a given value $a$ for attribute $A$, in time roughly proportional to the number of such tuples, rather than in time proportional to the size of $R$. That is, in the absence of an index on $A$, the only way to find the tuples $\mu$ in $R$ such that $\mu[A] = a$ is to look at all the tuples in $R$. We devote Chapter 6 to a discussion of data structures that give indices the capability to focus on only the desired tuples. For the moment, let us consider only how indices are created and used in SQL.

The basic index creation command is:

```
CREATE INDEX I
ON R(A);
```

The effect is to create an index named $I$ on attribute $A$ of relation $R$.

**Example 4.41:** We can say

```
CREATE INDEX O#_INDEX
ON ORDERS(O#);
```

to create an index on attribute O# of relation ORDERS. The name of the index is O#_INDEX, and it allows the retrieval of the tuple for a given order number in time that does not depend (significantly) on the size of the ORDERS relation. □

An index can also enforce the condition that a certain attribute is a key. If in Example 4.41 we had said

```
CREATE UNIQUE INDEX O#_INDEX
ON ORDERS(O#);
```

then the index O#_INDEX would not only speed up access given an order number, but it would make sure, as tuples were inserted into ORDERS, that we never had two tuples with the same order number.

It makes sense to use the UNIQUE keyword in the declaration of the index on O# for ORDERS, but if we declared an index on O# for INCLUDES, we would not want to declare it UNIQUE, because it is normal for orders to include more than one item, and therefore several tuples in INCLUDES may have the same order number.

To remove an index $I$ from a relation $R$, without affecting the data in $R$ itself, we issue command

```
DROP INDEX I;
```

### Views

A third group of commands of the SQL language functions as a subschema DDL, or view definition mechanism. In general, we create a view by the command

```
CREATE VIEW V(A₁,...,Aₖ) AS
    Q;
```

where $V$ is the name of the view, $A_1,\ldots,A_k$ are its attributes, and $Q$ is the query that defines the view. The view $V$ does not exist, but it can be queried, and when we do so, $V$, or its relevant part, is constructed. To construct $V$, we evaluate the query $Q$, and whatever tuples $Q$ produces are the tuples in $V$.

**Example 4.42:** We can construct a view consisting of those items Acme sells and their prices, by:

```
CREATE VIEW ACME_SELLS(ITEM, PRICE) AS
    SELECT ITEM, PRICE
    FROM SUPPLIES
    WHERE NAME = 'Acme';
```

Since the attributes of the view ACME_SELLS are the same as the attributes of the query that returns its tuples, we do not even have to list attributes for the view, and the first line above could have been written simply:

```
CREATE VIEW ACME_SELLS AS
```

A second example is the view OI constructed in Example 4.25. This view is the join of ORDERS and INCLUDES, with the common O# attribute projected out. We can create this view as

```
CREATE VIEW OI(NAME, DATE, ITEM, QUANTITY) AS
    SELECT CUST, DATE, ITEM, QUANTITY
    FROM ORDERS, INCLUDES
    WHERE ORDERS.O# = INCLUDES.O#;
```

Note how the attribute CUST of ORDERS becomes NAME in view OI, because we have chosen to specify attributes for that view explicitly. □

Finally, should we want to destroy a view $V$ we say

```
DROP VIEW V;
```

This statement has no effect on the database, but queries on view $V$ will no longer be accepted.

## Database Catalogs

There are four database *catalogs*, called TABLES, VIEWS, INDEXES, and COLUMNS, and we may obtain information about the current database scheme by issuing queries that refer to these catalogs as if they were relations. There is only one major syntactic difference: the name of the table, view, etc., which we might assume is an attribute of TABLES and VIEWS, respectively, is not specified in a where-clause, but rather by appending the object name, in brackets, to the catalog name. We shall not enumerate all the attributes of the four catalogs, but rather give some examples of the information available, and how it is requested.

Suppose we wanted to find the definition of the view ACME_SELLS introduced in Example 4.42. We could ask:

```
SELECT VIEW$TEXT
FROM VIEWS[ACME_SELLS];                                          (4.12)
```

Here, VIEW$TEXT is an attribute of catalog VIEWS. The name of the view we are interested in is indicated by the bracketed ACME_SELLS in the second line. It is as though there were an attribute NAME of VIEWS, and we had followed FROM VIEWS by

```
WHERE NAME = 'ACME_SELLS'
```

However, we must follow the form given in (4.12) if we are to query database catalogs. The answer to the query (4.12) is the single string

```
SELECT ITEM, PRICE FROM SUPPLIES WHERE NAME = 'Acme'
```

To get information about the attributes of a relation or view, we query the COLUMNS catalog. Some of the attributes of this catalog are:

1. COL$NAME, the attribute's name.
2. COL$ID, the position of the attribute in the list of attributes for its relation. For example, relation SUPPLIES, defined in Example 4.40, has attribute NAME in position 1, ITEM in position 2, and PRICE in position 3. It is important to know the positions of these attributes if we use a subquery like SELECT * FROM SUPPLIES, since that order affects the interpretation of the "*."
3. COL$DATATYPE, tells whether the attribute is of type number, char, or date. We have not discussed data of the latter type, but the idea should be obvious; a day, month, year, and time of day is represented and may be printed externally in a variety of formats, e.g., 14-MAY-1948 (here the time of day is not printed).
4. COL$LENGTH, the number of bytes or decimal places of char and number data, respectively. The value of this attribute is 20 for the attribute NAME of Example 4.40 and 6 for the attribute PRICE.
5. COL$SCALE, the number of digits to the right of the decimal point, for number data only. The value of this attribute is 2 for PRICE in Example 4.40.
6. COL$NULL, tells whether or not nulls are permitted in a column.

For example, if we wanted to examine some of these attributes for the view ACME_SELLS of Example 4.42 we would write:

```
SELECT COL$NAME, COL$ID, COL$DATATYPE
FROM COLUMNS[ACME_SELLS];
```

Much of the information for view ACME_SELLS is inherited from the declarations we made when we created relation SUPPLIES in Example 4.40. In particular, the data types of attributes ITEM and PRICE are inherited, because they correspond to the attributes of the same names in the view definition.

Their order, as far as COL$ID is concerned, comes from the order in which they appeared in the create-view statement. Thus, the information printed by the above query is:

| COL$NAME | COL$ID | COL$DATATYPE |
|----------|--------|--------------|
| ITEM     | 1      | CHAR         |
| PRICE    | 2      | NUMBER       |

We can use the TABLES catalog to find out the date on which a relation such as SUPPLIES was created, by a query like:

```
SELECT TAB$TIME
FROM TABLES[SUPPLIES];
```

If we want to know the same thing about a view, we refer to the attribute VEW$CTIME of catalog VIEWS.

Finally, we can query the catalog INDEXES to find out information about the indices declared for a given relation. Some of the attributes of indices are:

1. IDX$NAME, the name of the index.
2. IDX$COLUMN, the attribute that is indexed.
3. IDX$UNIQUE tells whether the index is "unique," i.e., whether the attribute IDX$COLUMN serves as a key for the relation.

Thus, we could ask about the index O$_INDEX created in Example 4.41, by:

```
SELECT IDX$NAME, IDX$COLUMN, IDX$UNIQUE
FROM INDEXES[ORDERS];
```

Since there is only the one index for ORDERS, the following single tuple:

| IDX$NAME | IDX$COLUMN | IDX$UNIQUE |
|----------|------------|------------|
| O#_INDEX | O#         | NON UNIQUE |

would be the only one printed.

## 4.8 EMBEDDING SQL IN A HOST LANGUAGE

We shall now sketch the way SQL/RT interfaces the SQL language with the host language C. We try to avoid details of the C language itself, using a "Pidgin" version that should make clear what functions the code written in the host language is performing, without getting bogged down in the details of C or of the UNIX operating system that surrounds it. While the interfaces between other hosts and/or other database languages differ in many details, the treatment given here is representative of the capabilities found in such interfaces.

The process of creating an executable program *prog* that accesses an SQL database is shown in Figure 4.21. We begin with a source program *prog.pc*, that is mainly C code, but also includes special statements, each on a line beginning EXEC SQL, that are translated by the SQL *precompiler* into C code, mostly calls to library routines that perform the various SQL commands and pieces of commands.

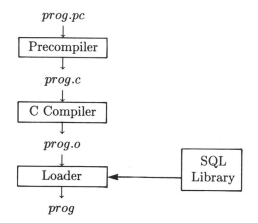

**Figure 4.21** SQL/C interface.

The resulting C program *prog.c* is then compiled, in the ordinary manner, into a relocatable object code program *prog.o*. Finally, *prog.o* is loaded, along with library routines that perform the SQL operations, creating an executable program *prog*.

### Data of the Interface

The basic idea behind the connection of C programs and their variables to the world of SQL and its data is that the names of C variables are treated like constants in SQL commands. We have only to prefix a colon to the C variable name, to have its current value treated as a constant whenever the SQL command containing it is executed. Further, we must enclose the declarations of all C variables that are so used, within an SQL *declare section*, which serves to declare their data types both to the C compiler and to the SQL precompiler.

**Example 4.43:** The following code declares some variables that we shall use in a subsequent example, which is to write a program that accepts an order, determines the items and their quantities, and inserts the necessary tuples into the relations ORDERS and INCLUDES of our YVCB example database.

```
EXEC SQL BEGIN DECLARE SECTION;
    int ordno, quant;
    char date[10], name[20], item[10];
EXEC SQL END DECLARE SECTION;
```

The first and last statement are endmarkers for the declarations that the SQL precompiler must know about. Notice the use of EXEC SQL to warn the precompiler to take notice of what follows

The middle two statements are ordinary C declarations. Variables *ordno* and *quant* are defined to be integers, and variables *date*, *name*, and *item* are declared to be arrays of 10, 20, and 10 characters, respectively, which is the way C represents character strings. □

Another device to connect SQL and C is the *communication* area. This is a C data structure, defined in the SQL library, that allows SQL commands to indicate when any of a wide variety of errors have occurred during the time the command was executing. We shall not discuss the structure of the communication area or the details regarding the types of errors and their representation. One kind of "error" that is reported in the communication area is the failure to find a desired tuple. That event occurs ordinarily during queries, as we repeatedly ask for a tuple matching some where-clause, until SQL can find no more and reports "error." As we shall see below, we do not, in this case, need to examine the communication area directly, as there is a special SQL precompiler statement that will do the examination for us; that is, the precompiler generates the C code that tests the appropriate part of the communication area.

## Execute-Immediate Statements

The simplest way to have a C program influence an SQL database is to embed within the C program an *execute-immediate* statement, of the form

```
EXEC SQL EXECUTE IMMEDIATE S;
```

Here, $S$ is an SQL statement that is not a query; i.e., $S$ may not be a select-from-where statement. For example, $S$ might be a command to insert a particular tuple into the ORDERS relation, as in:

```
EXEC SQL EXECUTE IMMEDIATE
    INSERT INTO ORDERS
    VALUES(1027, 'Jan 4', 'Sally Squirrel');             (4.13)
```

There is, however, little use in placing such a statement in a C program, since every time the program is executed, the same tuple will be inserted into ORDERS. What we really want is an application program that can be run every time the YVCB accepts a new order. The program must therefore ask the user for the order number,[13] name, and date, place the user-supplied values into C variables, which we call *ordno*, *name*, and *date*, and then execute the statement:

```
EXEC SQL EXECUTE IMMEDIATE
    INSERT INTO ORDERS
    VALUES(:ordno, :date, :name);
```

Notice how the C variables preceded by colons are used exactly as constants were used in (4.13).

## Prepare-and-Execute

An alternative to immediate execution of statements is to prepare statements prior to their execution, giving each a name known to the SQL precompiler only, and then executing the statement, by referring to it by its name. The advantage to this arrangement is that the time spent by the SQL system processing a command occurs only once, when we prepare the statement, and executions of the statement can then proceed more rapidly. In contrast, if we use execute-immediate statements, the cost of processing the command is paid every time the statement is executed.

The form of a prepare-statement is

```
EXEC SQL PREPARE S FROM S;
```

Here, $S$ is an SQL statement, which is still not permitted to be a query, and $S$ is the name chosen for this statement. $S$ may be an SQL command written out, perhaps with C variables, preceded by colons, in place of some constants. $S$ may also be the name of a C variable (again preceded by a colon) that is a character string in which the command appears.[14] Thus, we could write

```
EXEC SQL PREPARE stat FROM :com;
```

and store the text of the desired command in variable *com* prior to executing the above statement. Subsequently, *stat* will refer to the statement that was in *com* when the prepare-statement above was executed.

We may then execute a statement $S$ by issuing a command of the following form:

```
EXEC SQL EXECUTE S USING :A₁,...,:Aₖ;
```

where $A_1,\ldots,A_k$ are the C variables that appear in the text from which $S$ was prepared.

---

[13] Perhaps the program would generate a new order number from a C variable representing the "next order number," which in turn might come from a UNIX file accessible from C programs, or from a one-tuple SQL relation accessible through SQL commands.

[14] We would need a variable like *com* if we read commands from a terminal and executed them; the matter is discussed further at the end of the section.

```
read ordno, date, and name;
insert (ordno, date, name) into ORDERS;
read item;
while item ≠ 'end' do begin
    read quant;
    insert (ordno, item, quant) into INCLUDES;
    read item;
end
```

**Figure 4.22**  Sketch of order processing algorithm.

**Example 4.44:** Let us write the code to read orders and insert the appropriate tuples into the ORDERS and INCLUDES relations. Figure 4.22 is a sketch of the algorithm we want to follow. Then, in Figure 4.23 we offer a more detailed rendition of the algorithm, showing the SQL statements explicitly and using a "Pidgin" form of C. For input/output we use a hypothetical function $write(X)$ to print $X$ and $read(X)$ to read a value of the appropriate type and assign it to variable $X$.

In Figure 4.23, lines (1)–(4) are the declarations discussed in Example 4.43. Line (5) is a statement that must appear before any executable SQL statements, to initialize the connection between the database and the program. Lines (6) and (7) prepare the insertion statements. Lines (8) and (9) request that the data for the order be entered by the user and read his response; the data supplied is entered into the database by line (10). The remainder of the program instructs the user to enter a sequence of the form $i_1, q_1, i_2, q_2, \ldots, i_n, q_n, end$, where $i_j$ is an item and $q_j$ the quantity of that item. These entries are then read, and each $(i_j, q_j)$ pair is inserted into the INCLUDES relation at line (15). Note the use of != as the C "not equal" operator and brackets in place of a begin-end pair. □

### Embedding Queries in C

We should remember that the embedded SQL statements described so far are not capable of handling select-from-where statements. In order to retrieve tuples from the database, there must be an arrangement that allows the tuples to be supplied one at a time to the host language program. To do so, we declare a *cursor* corresponding to each query statement. A cursor is a variable that, like a statement name, is of concern only to the SQL precompiler. We can think of it as a tuple variable that ranges over all the tuples of the relation that is the answer to the query.

We begin the query by opening the cursor. We then fetch one tuple at a time; the components of each tuple are copied into a list of C variables that

```
(1)  EXEC SQL BEGIN DECLARE SECTION;
(2)      int ordno, quant;
(3)      char date[10], name[20], item[10];
(4)  EXEC SQL END DECLARE SECTION;
(5)  EXEC SQL CONNECT;
(6)  EXEC SQL PREPARE ord_insert FROM
          INSERT INTO ORDERS
          VALUES(:ordno, :date, :name);
(7)  EXEC SQL PREPARE incl_insert FROM
          INSERT INTO INCLUDES
          VALUES(:ordno, :item, :quant);
(8)  write("Please enter order number, date, and customer");
(9)  read(ordno); read(date); read(name);
(10) EXEC SQL EXECUTE ord_insert USING :ordno, :date, :name;
(11) write("Please enter a list of item-quantity pairs,
          terminated by the item 'end'");
(12) read(item);
(13) while(item != "end") {
(14)     read(quant);
(15)     EXEC SQL EXECUTE incl_insert
              USING :ordno, :item, :quant;
(16)     read(item);
     }
```

**Figure 4.23** Order program using prepare and execute.

correspond to these components. Eventually, no tuples remain and we break out of the tuple-reading loop. Figure 4.24 is a sketch of this process.

Line (1) of Figure 4.24 is an ordinary preparation statement for the statement named $S$. As before, $S$ is an SQL statement, but now it is a select-from-where statement. $S$ can be written explicitly or it can be a reference to a string variable holding the query. C variables, preceded by a colon, can appear in place of constants in the where-clause of $S$.

At line (2), the cursor $C$ is declared to be the cursor for statement $S$, and at line (3), $C$ is opened, or initialized to refer to the first tuple of the answer. Line (4) tells the SQL precompiler that when the "error" condition of no more tuples occurs, we must go to the statement *nomore*; the latter name is an ordinary C label.

Lines (5)–(7) form a loop, in which a tuple is read by line (6). Presumably, the tuple has $k$ components, and the values of these components are read into variables $A_1, \ldots, A_k$, in the proper order; i.e., the $i$th component becomes the

```
(1)        EXEC SQL PREPARE S FROM S;
(2)        EXEC SQL DECLARE C CURSOR FOR S;
(3)        EXEC SQL OPEN C;
(4)        EXEC SQL WHENEVER NOTFOUND GOTO nomore;
(5)        while(1) { /* repeat forever */
(6)            EXEC SQL FETCH C INTO :A₁,...,:Aₖ;
(7)            /* do something with this tuple */
           }

(8)  nomore:
(9)        EXEC SQL CLOSE C;
(10)       /* Continue with program following query S */
```

**Figure 4.24**  Prepare-open-fetch-close pattern.

value of $A_i$. Line (7) suggests that something must happen with each tuple, and in practice, line (7) will be replaced by code that accesses some of the variables $A_1, \ldots, A_k$, thereby using the tuple retrieved in some calculation.

We break out of the loop of lines (5)–(7) when line (6) fails to find a new tuple, after each tuple of the answer has been retrieved. At that time, the "whenever" clause of line (4) applies, taking us to line (8). Line (9) closes the cursor $C$, so it can be reopened if we repeat this query, and we then continue with the program after the query. A small technical note is that lines (8) and (9) may not be combined, because the EXEC SQL must be the first characters, other than white space, on any line in which it appears.

**Example 4.45:** Let us write a program determine the total number of pounds of Brie on order. Of course we could do this job with an ordinary SQL command:

```
SELECT SUM(QUANTITY)
FROM INCLUDES
WHERE ITEM = 'Brie';
```

but the problem will still serve for an illustration. The program is shown in Figure 4.25.

Notice that the declaration of variable *sum* does not have to appear in the SQL declare section, because it is not used as an interface variable. Also, == is C's equality operator, and += is an accumulation operator; sum += quant is what would be written

```
sum := sum + quant
```

in most other languages. Procedure *equalstrings*, not written here, tests whether two strings are identical. □

```
    EXEC SQL BEGIN DECLARE SECTION;
        int quant;
        char item[10];
    EXEC SQL END DECLARE SECTION;
    int sum;
    EXEC SQL CONNECT;
    EXEC SQL PREPARE incl_get FROM
        SELECT ITEM, QUANTITY
        FROM INCLUDES;
    EXEC SQL DECLARE cur CURSOR FOR incl_get;
    EXEC SQL OPEN cur;
    EXEC SQL WHENEVER NOTFOUND GOTO printsum;
    sum = 0;
    while(1) {
        EXEC SQL FETCH cur INTO :item, :quant;
        if(equalstrings(item, "Brie"))
            sum += quant;
    }

printsum:
    EXEC SQL CLOSE cur;
    write("Amount of Brie ordered = "); write(sum);
```

**Figure 4.25**  Printing the amount of Brie ordered.

## More General Queries

There is one other method of interfacing queries with C programs that we shall
not cover here. The limitation of the method just described is that the form of
the query must be known when the C program is written; the only things that
may be left unspecified are the values of certain constants in the where-clause,
which may be represented by variables and changed each time we execute the
query. There are situations where we cannot know the form of the statement
before we write the program. A simple example is the command interpreter
itself, described in Section 4.6. This program must be able to read and execute
an arbitrary SQL command, which could be a query, an insertion, or one of a
number of other forms. Suffice it to say that a complex but completely general
method for reading arbitrary SQL statements and executing them is provided
by the SQL/C precompiler.

## EXERCISES

4.1: Suppose we have the beer drinkers' database from Example 3.6 with relations

        FREQUENTS(DRINKER, BAR)
        SERVES(BAR, BEER)
        LIKES(DRINKER, BEER)

Write the following queries in (*i*) ISBL (*ii*) QUEL (*iii*) Query-by-Example (*iv*) SQL.

  a)    Print the bars that serve a beer drinker Charles Chugamug likes.
  b)    Print the drinkers that frequent at least one bar that serves a beer that they like.
 * c)    Print the drinkers that frequent only bars that serve some beer that they like (assume each drinker frequents at least one bar).
 * d)    Print the drinkers that frequent no bar that serves a beer that they like.

4.2: Write in (*i*) QUEL (*ii*) Query-by-Example (*iii*) SQL:

  a)    The DRC expression of Exercise 3.10.
 * b)    The TRC expression of Exercise 3.9.

4.3: Using (*i*) QUEL (*ii*) Query-by-Example (*iii*) SQL, write programs to perform the following operations on the beer drinkers' database of Exercise 4.1.

  a)    Delete from SERVES all tuples for Potgold Beer.
  b)    Insert the fact that drinker Charles Chugamug likes Potgold.
  c)    Insert the facts that Chugamug likes all beers served at the Bent Elbow Bar and Grill.

4.4: Suppose that the beer drinkers' database has relation

        SELLS(BAR,BEER,AMOUNT)

Write in (*i*) QUEL (*ii*) Query-by-Example (*iii*) SQL queries to print the

  a)    Total amount of each beer sold.
  b)    Average amount of each beer sold per per bar, excluding bars that do not sell the beer.
 * c)    Maximum amount of each beer sold, provided at least two bars sell the beer.

4.5: Suppose that we want a view of the beer drinkers' database

        WHERE(DRINKER, BEER, BAR)

containing those tuples $(d, b, r)$ such that drinker $d$ likes beer $b$, bar $r$ serves beer $b$, and drinker $d$ frequents bar $r$. Write in $(i)$ ISBL $(ii)$ Query-by-Example $(iii)$ SQL a view definition for this view.

4.6: Write or sketch a simple command interpreter that interfaces with the beer drinkers' database through calls to SQL. The commands are of the forms

    $i)$    $i$ <bar name> <beer name>, meaning "insert into SERVES the fact that the bar serves the beer."

    $ii)$   $d$ <bar name> <beer name>, meaning "delete from SERVES the fact that the bar serves the beer."

    $iii)$  $q$ *bar* <bar name>, meaning "print the beers served by the bar."

    $iv)$  $q$ *beer* <beer name>, meaning "print the bars that serve the beer."

* 4.7: Suppose we have a relation

        MANAGES(EMPLOYEE, MANAGER)

Write a C program interfacing with SQL that prompts for an employee name and prints all the people this employee manages, either directly or indirectly (i.e., of whom he is the "boss" in the sense of Example 1.12).

4.8: Suppose we have relations $FSO(F, S, O)$, meaning that file $F$ is of size $S$ and has owner $O$, and $FTD(F, T, D)$, meaning that file $F$ is of type $T$ and appears in directory $D$. Write the following queries in $(i)$ QUEL $(ii)$ Query-by-Example $(iii)$ SQL.

    a)    Print the owner and type of all files that are of size at least 10,000.

    b)    Print all those directories that have a file owned by *root*.

    c)    Print the average size of files in the directory *bin* (QUEL and SQL only).

    d)    Print all the files in directory *foo* whose name contains the substring *bar* (SQL only).

4.9: Translate the queries of Figure 4.26 (a), (b), and (c) into relational algebra. Each refers to the database of Exercise 4.8.

4.10: Complete Example 4.9 by writing the query to delete tuples from the INCLUDES relation if they are part of an order that includes Brie as one of its items.

4.11: In the following questions, we shall assume that conditions in the various query languages do not involve aggregate operators and do not involve arithmetic; e.g. $A < B + 1$ is forbidden. We want to show that various classes of queries are equivalent to safe domain relational calculus formulas, by direct constructions (not by going through relational algebra). Give algorithms to convert the following to safe DRC (or safe TRC if it is more convenient).

```
SELECT OWNER
FROM FSO
WHERE FILE IN
     SELECT FILE
     FROM FTD
     WHERE TYPE = 'tex'
```

(a) SQL query.

| FTD | FILE | TYPE | DIRECTORY |
|-----|------|------|-----------|
|     | _foo |      | _root     |
|     | _bar |      | _root     |

|     |      |      |
|-----|------|------|
| P.  | _foo | _bar |

(b) QBE query.

```
range of t is FSO
range of s is FSO
retrieve(t.File, s.File)
    where t.Size > s.Size
        and t.Owner == 'joe'
```

(c) Quel query.

**Figure 4.26**  Queries for Exercise 4.9.

    a)   QUEL retrieve queries in which the where-condition is a conjunction.

 * b)   QUEL queries in which the where condition can involve OR and NOT.

 * c)   Query-by-Example queries without condition boxes, I., D., U., or ¬ operators.

 * d)   SQL queries without subqueries, **ANY**, or **ALL** operators, but with AND, OR, and NOT operators permitted in where-conditions.

** e)   SQL queries as in (d), but with subqueries, **ANY**, and **ALL** permitted.

4.12: Show how to express the relational algebra operators $-$, $\times$, and $\pi$ in Query-by-Example.

4.13: Suppose we wish to declare the relations FSO and FTD mentioned in Example 4.8, and we wish to have indices on $F$ in each relation, and on $O$ in FSO. In FTD, $F$ and $D$ together form a key, while in FSO $F$ and $O$ form the key. Assume nonkey attributes can be null, but key attributes cannot.

a)   Show the Query-by-example table directory entries for FSO and FTD. Invent suitable types and domains for the attributes.

b)   Show the entries in the SQL database catalog TABLES for FSO and FTD. Indicate the values of the fields COL$NAME, COL$ID, COL$DATATYPE, COL$LENGTH, COL$SCALE, and COL$NULL. Where no value can be deduced, give suitable values, making them consistent with your choices for (a), when possible.

## BIBLIOGRAPHIC NOTES

The notion of completeness for query languages is from Codd [1972b]. Kim [1979] is a survey of relational systems, while Kent [1979] argues the inadequacy of such systems. Greenblatt and Waxman [1978] compare several relational languages for ease-of-use by naive users.

### ISBL

Todd [1976] is the principal source of information.

### QUEL

The description of QUEL given here is based on Stonebraker, Wong, Kreps, and Held [1976] and Zook et al. [1977]. An overview of the surrounding INGRES system can be found in Stonebraker [1980].

### Query-by-Example

Development of the system is described in Zloof [1975, 1977]. A description of the commercial version is in IBM [1978a].

### SQL

A definition of the SQL language (formerly called SEQUEL) can be found in Chamberlin et al. [1976]; earlier versions are described in Boyce, Chamberlin, King, and Hammer [1975] (called SQUARE) and Astrahan and Chamberlin [1975].

System/R, which included the original implementation of SQL, is surveyed in Astrahan et al. [1976, 1979], Blasgen et al. [1981], and Chamberlin et al. [1981]. The VM commercial implementation of SQL is covered in IBM [1984], while the PC/RT version of Sections 4.6–4.8 is from IBM [1985a, b].

## AWK

There is a UNIX tool called AWK that we have not covered here, but which, along with the join command of UNIX can serve as a rudimentary relational database system for small files. See Aho, Kernighan, and Weinberger [1979, 1988].

## View Update

An unresolved technical problem for relational database systems is how one properly translates update operations on views into operations on the actual database relations. Dayal and Bernstein [1982] and Keller [1985] present techniques for managing part of this problem.

# CHAPTER 5

Object-Oriented
Database
Languages

In this chapter we consider some object-oriented database languages, mirroring the treatment of value-oriented languages in the previous chapter. Many would disagree with our use of the term "object-oriented" when applied to the first two languages: the CODASYL DBTG language, which was the origin of the network model, and IMS, an early database system using the hierarchical model. However, these languages support object identity, and thus present significant problems and significant advantages when compared with relational languages. The third language covered in this chapter, OPAL, is a modern example of an object-oriented language, whose pedigree few would dispute.

## 5.1 THE DBTG DATA DEFINITION LANGUAGE

The dominant influence in the development of the network data model and database systems using that model has been a series of proposals put forth by the Data Base Task Group (DBTG) of the Conference on Data Systems Languages (CODASYL), the group responsible for the standardization of the programming language COBOL. In addition to proposing a formal notation for networks (the *Data Definition Language* or *DDL*), the DBTG has proposed a *Subschema Data Definition Language* (*Subschema DDL*) for defining views and a *Data Manipulation Language* (*DML*) suitable for writing applications programs that manipulate the conceptual scheme or a view.

This section discusses the data definition language and the concept of "DBTG sets," which are equivalent to the links, or many-one relationships, mentioned in Section 2.5. The next section covers the data manipulation language.

240

## Records

What we called logical record types in Section 2.5 are referred to as *record types* in the DBTG proposal. The fields in a logical record format are called *data items,* and what we called logical records are known simply as *records.* We shall use the terms "record" and "record type," since we are inclined to drop the term "logical" anyway, when no confusion results. However, let us continue to use "field," rather than "data item," since the latter term is rarely used outside the DBTG proposal itself. The database can, naturally, contain many occurrences of records of the same type. There is no requirement that records of the same type be distinct, and indeed, record types with no fields are possible; they would be used to connect records of other types, and in the implementation, the seemingly empty records would have one or more pointers.

## DBTG Sets

By an unfortunate turn of fate, the concept of a link, that is, a many-one relationship from one record type to another, is known in the DBTG world as a *set.* To avoid the obvious confusions that would occur should the term "set" be allowed this meaning, many substitute names have been proposed; the term *DBTG set* is a common choice, and we shall adopt it here.

When we have a many-one relationship $m$ from records of type $R_2$ to records of type $R_1$, we can associate with each record $r$ of type $R_1$ the set $S_r$, consisting of those records $s$ of type $R_2$ such that $m(s) = r$. Since $m$ is many-one, the sets $S_{r_1}$ and $S_{r_2}$ are disjoint if $r_1 \neq r_2$. If $S$ is the name of the DBTG set representing the link $m$, then each set $S_r$, together with $r$ itself, is said to be a *set occurrence* of $S$. Record $r$ is the *owner* of the set occurrence, and each $s$ such that $m(s) = r$ is a *member* of the set occurrence. Record type $R_1$ is called the *owner type* of $S$, and $R_2$ is the *member type* of $S$.

The DBTG model requires that the owner and member types of a DBTG set be distinct. This requirement produces some awkwardness, but it is considered necessary because many DBTG operations assume that we can distinguish the owner from members in a set occurrence. We can get around the requirement by introducing dummy record types, as in the following example.

**Example 5.1:** Suppose we have a record type PEOPLE, which we would like to be both the owner and member types of DBTG set MOTHER_OF, where the owner record in a set occurrence is intended to be the mother of all its member records. Since we cannot have PEOPLE be both the owner and member types for MOTHER_OF, we instead create a record type DUMMY, with the following DBTG sets.

1. IS, with owner DUMMY and member PEOPLE. The intention is that each DUMMY record owns an IS set occurrence with exactly one PEOPLE record. Thus, each DUMMY record $d$ is effectively identified with the

person represented by the PEOPLE record owned by $d$.

2.    MOTHER_OF, with owner PEOPLE and member DUMMY. The intention is that a PEOPLE record $p$ owns the DUMMY records that own (in the IS set occurrence) the PEOPLE records of which $p$ is the mother. □

It is useful to visualize a DBTG set as a ring of records, consisting of the owner record and the member records in some order. For example, a common operation is to visit each member record in turn, stopping when we come back to the owner record.

**Example 5.2:** Let us consider the link E_STUDENT, an instance of which was shown in Figure 2.15. The DBTG set occurrences for that instance are:

1.    Grind owns enrollment records 1 and 2.
2.    Nerd owns enrollment record 3.
3.    Weenie owns entrollment records 4 and 5.
4.    Jock owns no enrollment records.

These sets, drawn as rings, are shown in Figure 5.1. □

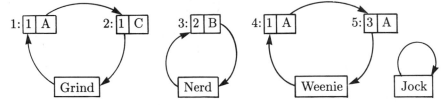

**Figure 5.1** Ring representation of DBTG sets.

## Declaring Record Types and DBTG Sets

The data definition language allows us to describe record types and their fields, and it allows us to describe DBTG sets, their member type and their owner type. We are also able to define details of the physical structure that will be used to store these records and sets, but we shall not discuss the options available until Chapter 6. Therefore, we shall here use a "Pidgin" version of the DBTG data definition language, sketching only part of the declarations for records and sets.

A record type $R$ is defined by

    RECORD $R$

followed by a list of the fields of record type $R$. A field declaration consists of a level number, a field name, and a data type. Level numbers up to 99 are permitted, allowing fields to have structure. A typical use of such structure is to declare, within a field such as ADDRESS at level 1, subfields like STREET, CITY, and ZIP at level 2.

```
RECORD EMPS
    1 ENAME CHAR(20)
    1 SALARY REAL;

RECORD DEPTS
    1 DNAME CHAR(10)
    1 DEPT# INTEGER;

RECORD SUPPLIERS
    1 SNAME CHAR(10)
    1 SADDR CHAR(50);

RECORD ITEMS
    1 INAME CHAR(10)
    1 ITEM# INTEGER;

RECORD ORDERS
    1 O# INTEGER
    1 DATE CHAR(10);

RECORD CUSTOMERS
    1 CNAME CHAR(20)
    1 CADDR CHAR(50)
    1 BALANCE REAL;

RECORD ENTRIES
    1 QUANTITY INTEGER;

RECORD OFFERS
    1 PRICE REAL;
```

**Figure 5.2** Record type declarations for YVCB database.

**Example 5.3:** The YVCB network database scheme was described in Example 2.24. There are eight record types. In Figure 5.2 we see the declarations for each of these. □

We declare DBTG set $S$, with owner type $O$ and member type $M$ by the following statement form:

```
DBTG SET S
    OWNER IS O
    MEMBER IS M;
```

**Example 5.4:** The YVCB database also has eight links, as indicated in Figure 2.16. In Figure 5.3 we see them listed with their owner and member types. □

```
DBTG SET WORKS_IN
     OWNER IS DEPTS
     MEMBER IS EMPS;

DBTG SET MANAGES
     OWNER IS DEPTS
     MEMBER IS EMPS;

DBTG SET O_ITEM
     OWNER IS ITEMS
     MEMBER IS OFFERS;

DBTG SET O_SUPPLIER
     OWNER IS SUPPLIERS
     MEMBER IS OFFERS;

DBTG SET E_ITEM
     OWNER IS ITEMS
     MEMBER IS ENTRIES;

DBTG SET E_ORDER
     OWNER IS ORDERS
     MEMBER IS ENTRIES;

DBTG SET CARRIES
     OWNER IS DEPTS
     MEMBER IS ITEMS;

DBTG SET PLACED_BY
     OWNER IS CUSTOMERS
     MEMBER IS ORDERS;
```

**Figure 5.3** DBTG set declarations for YVCB database.

## Virtual Fields and Redundancy Avoidance

There are situations where it is convenient to imagine that fields of one record type were duplicated in another record type. For example, the OFFERS logical record type has only a PRICE field, but we might wish that it were like the relation SUPPLIES discussed in our running example of Chapter 4, with fields (supplier) NAME and ITEM, as well as PRICE. However, if we added these fields to OFFERS, we would have at least the following two problems.

1.   The NAME and ITEM fields would waste space, because they duplicated data that could be obtained without them. That is, given an OFFERS record, we could find the value of NAME by finding the owner of that

record according to the O_SUPPLIER link and taking the SNAME field of the owner record. Similarly, we could find the owner of the OFFERS record according to the O_ITEM link, and take the INAME field of that record in place of the ITEM field of the OFFERS record.

2. There is a potential for inconsistency. Perhaps, because of careless updating of the database, when we follow the links described in (1) to get SNAME or INAME values, they do not agree with the NAME and ITEM fields of the OFFERS record.

The way the DBTG proposal copes with the problems of redundancy and potential inconsistency is to allow us to declare *virtual fields*, which are fields defined to be logically part of a record, but not physically present in the record. Rather, when we declare the virtual field, we define a *source* for the field, which is a field of some owner record. When we refer to the virtual field in a query, the database system obtains its value by following a link to the proper owner record and obtaining the source field from that record. By having only one physical copy of each field, we not only save space, but we also render impossible the inconsistency mentioned in (2) above. Of course, we trade increased access time for the privileges of consistency and space conservation, since instead of finding the virtual field in the record where we imagine it resides, we have to go to the database to obtain the source field from another record.

**Example 5.5:** If we wished to have virtual NAME and ITEM fields in OFFERS records we could have defined that record type by the DDL code in Figure 5.4. Note that we use the notation $A.B$ for field $B$ of record type $A$.[1] $\Box$

```
RECORD OFFERS
    1 PRICE REAL
    1 NAME VIRTUAL
        SOURCE IS SUPPLIERS.SNAME OF OWNER OF O_SUPPLIER
    1 ITEM VIRTUAL
        SOURCE IS ITEMS.INAME OF OWNER OF O_ITEMS;
```

**Figure 5.4** Virtual fields for OFFERS records.

Incidentally, the reader should note that each of the models discussed has a method, roughly equivalent to "virtual fields," for solving the redundancy and consistency problems. The virtual record types used in the hierarchical model are quite similar in spirit to the virtual fields of the DBTG proposal, and they serve the same purpose. The object model provides the same facility, since an object $O_1$ that is part of another object $O_2$ never appears physically within

---

[1] The DBTG proposal uses the notation $B$ IN $A$ for the more common $A.B$.

$O_2$. Rather, $O_1$ is pointed to, or referenced by, $O_2$. In Chapter 7 we shall see how these problems are dealt with in the relational model through the schema design process known as "normalization."

## View Definition

The DBTG proposal calls for a subschema data definition language, in which one can define views. In a view, one is permitted to use a different name for any record type, field, or DBTG set. We can omit from the view fields that are present in a record type, we can eliminate record types altogether, and we can eliminate DBTG sets from the view.

   As the view facility of the DBTG proposal contains no concepts not present in the data definition language for the conceptual scheme, we shall, in the following sections, write programs that act on the conceptual scheme directly, as if it were a complete view of itself. Thus, views play no role in what follows.

## 5.2 THE DBTG QUERY LANGUAGE

In this section we shall consider the query aspects of the DML that is defined by the CODASYL proposal. The next section covers the commands that update the database.

   In the DBTG approach, all programs are written in a host language (COBOL in the DBTG proposal) augmented by the commands of the data manipulation language, such as FIND (locate a described record), GET (read a record from the database), and STORE (put a record into the database). This arrangement is essentially the one illustrated in the second column of Figure 1.4, although statements of the extended language are not marked explicitly for a preprocessor as they were in Figure 1.4.

## The Program Environment

The environment in which a program operates is depicted in Figure 5.5. There is a workspace, called the *user working area*, in which is found space for three kinds of data.

1.   Variables defined by the program.
2.   *Currency pointers*, which are pointers, or references, to certain records in the database; we shall describe currency pointers in more detail next.
3.   *Templates* for the various record types. The template for a record type $T$ consists of space for each field $F$ of the record type, and that space is referred to as $T.F$ (or just $F$ if the field name is unique) in programs. A record is stored into the database only after assembling the record in the template for its type, and the STORE command copies the contents of the template into the database. Similarly, the GET command reads a record from the database into the appropriate template. We also use the template

as a way of "passing parameters" to certain commands that at first glance
do not appear to have parameters, especially to the FIND command.

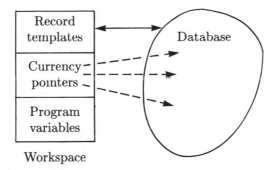

**Figure 5.5** The program environment.

## Currency Pointers

As a program runs, it is necessary for it to locate various records by a FIND
command, and to operate upon them by other commands. To keep track of
recently accessed records, a collection of currency pointers is maintained automatically by the database system, and the values of these pointers are made
available to the program. The currency pointers with which we deal are:

1. The *current of run-unit*. The term "run-unit" means "program" in the
   DBTG proposal. The most recently accessed record, of any type whatsoever, is referenced by a currency pointer called the "current of run-unit."
2. The *current of record type*. For each record type $T$, the most recently
   accessed record of this type is referred to as the "current of $T$."
3. The *current of set type*. For each DBTG set $S$, consisting of owner record
   type $T_1$ and member record type $T_2$, the most recently accessed record of
   type $T_1$ or $T_2$ is called the "current of $S$." Note that sometimes the current
   of $S$ will be an owner, and sometimes it will be a member. Also understand
   that the current of $S$ is a record, rather than a set occurrence. Sometimes
   it is convenient to talk of the set occurrence containing the record "current
   of $S$" as if this set occurrence itself were the "current $S$ occurrence," but
   there is no such thing as a pointer to a set occurrence.

**Example 5.6:** Suppose that the data about suppliers from the relation of
Figure 4.2 is now represented according to the network of Figures 5.2 and 5.3.
In particular, let us focus on the set occurrence of the O_SUPPLIER set owned
by Ajax, in which the Ajax SUPPLIERS record owns three OFFERS records,
corresponding to items Brie, Perrier, and Endive. Each of these is owned by

an ITEMS record, according to the O_ITEM DBTG set. If we assume that the virtual fields described in Figure 5.4 are not present in OFFERS records, then to find the items supplied by Ajax, we must visit each OFFERS record Ajax owns. Only the prices are found in OFFERS records, but they are linked in rings to their owner according to the O_ITEM set, and by following that link we can find the owning item, which is one of the items sold by Ajax. The structure is suggested by Figure 5.6.

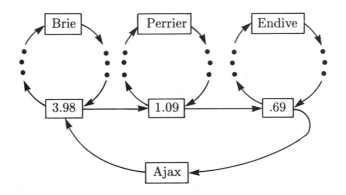

**Figure 5.6** Set occurrences connecting suppliers to items sold.

We have not described yet the commands whereby we can follow the links suggested in Figure 5.6. However, in order to discuss currency pointers, let us outline the steps such a sequence of commands would take.

1.  Find the SUPPLIERS record for Ajax.
2.  Find the first member of Ajax's O_SUPPLIER set occurrence, marked 3.98 in Figure 5.6.
3.  Go from the latter record to its owner in the O_ITEM set, that is, the ITEMS record for Brie.
4.  Find the second member of Ajax's O_SUPPLIER set occurrence, the record 1.09.
5.  Find its item owner, Perrier.
6.  Find the third member of Ajax's O_SUPPLIER set occurrence, that is, .69.
7.  Find its item owner, Endive.

As we execute these seven steps, we change the pointers for the current of run-unit, the current of the SUPPLIERS, OFFERS, and ITEMS record types, and the current of the O_SUPPLIER and O_ITEM sets. For example, the first step makes the Ajax record be the current of run-unit, of the SUPPLIERS record type, and of the O_SUPPLIER set. The other currency pointers are undefined, or retain values they held previously. When we move, at the second step, to the record 3.98, that record becomes the current of run-unit, the current OFFERS record, and the current of both the O_SUPPLIER and O_ITEM sets; other currency pointers are not changed. The history of the currency pointers is summarized in Figure 5.7. □

Current of:

| | SUPPLIERS | OFFERS | ITEMS | O_SUPPLIER | O_ITEM | run-unit |
|---|---|---|---|---|---|---|
| 1. | Ajax | – | – | Ajax | – | Ajax |
| 2. | Ajax | 3.98 | – | 3.98 | 3.98 | 3.98 |
| 3. | Ajax | 3.98 | Brie | 3.98 | Brie | Brie |
| 4. | Ajax | 1.09 | Brie | 1.09 | 1.09 | 1.09 |
| 5. | Ajax | 1.09 | Perrier | 1.09 | Perrier | Perrier |
| 6. | Ajax | .69 | Perrier | .69 | .69 | .69 |
| 7. | Ajax | .69 | Endive | .69 | Endive | Endive |

**Figure 5.7** A program's effect on currency pointers.

### Navigation Within the Database

Reading a record from the database to the workspace is a two stage process. First, using a sequence of FIND statements, we locate the desired record; that is, the desired record must become the current of run-unit. At this point, nothing has been copied into the template for the record type. To copy the record into the template in the workspace, we simply execute the command GET. This command always copies the current of run-unit into the template for whatever record type is the current of run-unit. If we wish to copy only a subset of the fields of the current of run-unit, we can list the desired fields after GET, as in

```
GET <record type>; <list of fields>
```

**Example 5.7:** Suppose that the OFFERS record type is defined as in Figure 5.4, with the virtual fields NAME and ITEM, as well as the field PRICE. If the current of run-unit is an OFFERS record, we can read the ITEM and PRICE fields by:

```
GET OFFERS; ITEM, PRICE
```

The NAME field in the template for offers is not affected.

Notice that even though ITEM is a virtual field of OFFERS, we can program as though it actually existed. We rely on the system to get the correct

value from the ITEMS.INAME field of the owner of the OFFERS record in its
O_ITEM set occurrence. □

For debugging purposes, we can append the record type to the command
GET, even if we want all fields of the record. For example

> `GET OFFERS`

will copy the current of run-unit into the OFFERS template, if the current of
run-unit is a OFFERS record. Otherwise, the system will warn the user of an
error when the `GET OFFERS` command is executed. Let us emphasize that one
cannot use GET to read a record other than the current of run-unit, even if we
follow GET by the type of that record.

### CALC-Keys and Database Keys

Frequently, record types in DBTG databases are stored in such a way that given
values for a certain subset of the fields, one can get all the records with those
values quickly, i.e., without scanning the entire set of records of that type; this
set of fields is called the *CALC-key* for the record type. In effect, there is an
index on the CALC-key for a record type. This index could be implemented by
any of a number of forms discussed in Chapter 6, although the DBTG proposal
visualizes the index as a hash table, where records are grouped according to the
hash value of the fields of the CALC-key.[2]

We should understand that a CALC-key is not a "key" in the usual sense.
Rather, there can be more than one record with the same value of the fields
in the CALC-key. Thus, for example, we could choose CADDR, or {CADDR,
BALANCE} as the CALC-key for CUSTOMERS, even though it is conceivable
that there are two or more customers with the same address, or even the same
address and balance. However, it would be more normal to use CNAME, which
we suppose is a key, as the CALC-key.[3]

The DBTG proposal also uses the term *database key* to mean a pointer
to, or physical address of, a record. Database keys therefore always refer to a
unique record, and they are not related to CALC-keys.

### The FIND Statement

The FIND command in the DBTG proposal is really a collection of different
commands, distinguished by the keywords following FIND. These commands
have the common purpose of locating a particular record by some designated

---

[2] Readers not familiar with hashing should consult Section 6.3.

[3] Recall that we have agreed to pretend that "names" of things are unique identifiers.
In practice, customers are given ID numbers to distinguish two or more with the same
name, and there would be an additional field of CUSTOMERS, say ID#, which would
really be the key and would be the normal choice for the CALC-key.

strategy. The variety of FIND statements is extensive, and we shall here consider only the following useful subset of the possibilities.

1. Find a record given its database key, i.e., a pointer to the record.
2. Find a record given a value for its CALC-key.
3. From the file of records of a given type, find (one-at-a-time) all the records with a given value in the CALC-key field or fields.
4. Visit all the members of a set occurrence in turn.
5. Scan a set occurrence for those member records having specified values in certain of the fields.
6. Find the owner of a given record according to a given DBTG set.
7. Find the current of any record or DBTG set.

At first, (7) seems paradoxical, since if a record is "current of something" it is, in principle, "found." However, recall that GET operates only on the current of run-unit, not on a current of set or record. Most other commands also require the current of run-unit as the sole possible operand. Thus the purpose of this FIND statement is to make a "current of something" record be the current of run-unit, for further processing.

## Finding a Record Directly

Let us now introduce the commands for executing the FIND statement. We shall use a "Pidgin" version of the DBTG data manipulation language throughout, which differs from the proposal in two ways.

1. The proposal calls for many optional "noise words" in its syntax. We have arbitrarily chosen to include or exclude them, with an eye toward maximizing clarity.
2. We have inserted the words RECORD, SET, and other explanatory words, in certain places where they help to remind the reader of what the variables represent.

The first two kinds of FIND statement access records by a "key," either the database key or the CALC-key. To access by database key we write:

> FIND <record type> RECORD BY DATABASE KEY <variable>

where the <variable> is a variable in the workspace that has previously been given a database key as value.

**Example 5.8:** We can store a database key into a variable of the workspace by an instruction such as

> XYZ := CURRENT OF ITEMS

Later, we could retrieve this particular ITEMS record by saying:

```
FIND ITEMS RECORD BY DATABASE KEY XYZ
GET ITEMS
```

☐

To find a record given values for its CALC-key fields, we "pass" those values to FIND by placing the values in the corresponding fields of the template; then we issue the command

```
FIND <record type> RECORD BY CALC-KEY
```

**Example 5.9:** Suppose CUSTOMERS records have field CNAME as CALC-key. Then we could find the balance for Zack Zebra by:

```
CUSTOMERS.CNAME := "Zack Zebra"
FIND CUSTOMERS RECORD BY CALC-KEY
GET CUSTOMERS; BALANCE
```

Note that CUSTOMERS.CNAME and CUSTOMERS.BALANCE could have been written CNAME and BALANCE, respectively, as no ambiguity would arise in our example database. ☐

## Scanning a Record Type

To find all the records of a given type with a given value for the CALC-key, we can find the first such record as in Example 5.9, and then find additional records with the same CALC-key by executing, in a loop,

```
FIND DUPLICATE <record type> RECORD BY CALC-KEY
```

Assuming the current of run-unit is of the type <record type>, and its value in the CALC-key field or fields equals the corresponding value in the template for <record type>, then the next <record type> record with that value is found.

When performing any sort of scan, we must be prepared to find no record matching the specifications. In the DBTG proposal, there is a global *error-status* word that indicates when a FIND operation fails to find a record, among other abnormal conditions. We shall here assume for convenience that a variable FAIL becomes true if and only if a FIND operation fails to find a record.

**Example 5.10:** Suppose we wish to print all the suppliers of Brie and the prices they charge. Suppose for convenience that OFFERS has virtual fields NAME and ITEM, as in Figure 5.4, and that the CALC-key for OFFERS is ITEM. Then the desired table could be printed by the routine shown in Figure 5.8. ☐

## Scanning a Set Occurrence

To begin, suppose we have a current set occurrence for some DBTG set $S$. Recall that the set occurrence can be viewed as a ring consisting of the owner

```
print "SUPPLIER", "PRICE" /* print header */
OFFERS.ITEM := "Brie"
FIND OFFERS RECORD BY CALC-KEY
while ¬FAIL do begin
    GET OFFERS; NAME, PRICE
    print OFFERS.NAME, OFFERS.PRICE
    FIND DUPLICATE OFFERS RECORD BY CALC-KEY
end
```

**Figure 5.8** Print suppliers and prices for Brie.

and each of the members. If we get to the owner, we can scan around the ring and come back to the owner, causing FAIL to become true when we do. The FIND statement

```
FIND OWNER OF CURRENT <set name> SET
```

finds the owner of the current of <set name>, making it the current of run-unit and the current of <set name>.

The statement

```
FIND NEXT <record type> RECORD IN
    CURRENT <set name> SET
```

goes one position around the ring from the current of <set name>, setting FAIL[4] to true if the next record is not of the <record type>. Normally, the <record type> is the member type of the <set name>, so we fail when we get back to the owner. The FIND NEXT command can be repeated as many times as we like, taking us around the ring for the set occurrence.

An alternative way to scan around the ring is to issue the command

```
FIND FIRST <record type> RECORD IN
    CURRENT <set name> SET
```

to get the first member record of the current <set name> DBTG set. If there are no members of this set, FAIL becomes true. Otherwise, we can continue around the ring with a loop containing a FIND NEXT command, as above.

**Example 5.11:** Figure 5.9 prints the items ordered by Zack Zebra. We begin by finding the CUSTOMERS record for Zebra. This record owns the PLACED_BY set occurrence we wish to scan, and in that set occurrence are all the orders placed by Zebra. We find the first member record of this set occurrence, and in the body of the outer while-loop we check whether we have

---

[4] Technically, the error-status word treats reaching the last member of a set occurrence as a different "abnormality" from failing to find a record, but we trust no confusion will occur if we use FAIL to indicate all abnormalities.

gone around the ring already. If not, we "process" an order and move to the next order.

To "process" an order, we must treat the ORDERS record as the owner of an E_ORDER set occurrence, and scan each of the ENTRIES records in that set occurrence by a similar loop, the inner while-loop. For each ENTRIES record, we use a FIND OWNER command to reach the owner of that record according to the E_ITEM set. That owner is one of the items ordered by Zack Zebra, and we print it. Note that duplicates, that is, items found on more than one order, will be printed several times. ☐

```
CNAME := "Zack Zebra"
FIND CUSTOMERS RECORD BY CALC-KEY
/* CALC-key for CUSTOMERS is CNAME */
FIND FIRST ORDERS RECORD IN CURRENT PLACED_BY SET
while ¬FAIL do begin
    FIND FIRST ENTRIES RECORD IN CURRENT E_ORDERS SET
    while ¬FAIL do begin
        FIND OWNER OF CURRENT E_ITEM SET
        GET ITEMS; INAME
        print INAME
        FIND NEXT ENTRIES RECORD IN CURRENT E_ORDERS SET
    end
    FIND NEXT ORDERS RECORD IN CURRENT PLACED_BY SET
end
```

**Figure 5.9** Print the items ordered by Zebra.

### Singular Sets

There are times when we would like to scan all the records of a certain type, for example, to find all customers with negative balances. We cannot directly access all the CUSTOMERS records by CALC-key or database key, unless we know the name of every customer of the YVCB, or if we know all the database keys for these records, which are two unlikely situations. Scanning set occurrences for CUSTOMERS records won't work either, unless we have some way of locating every set occurrence of some DBTG set.

We may define, for a given record type, what is known as a *singular* DBTG set. A singular set has two special properties.

1.   The owner type is a special record type called SYSTEM. Having SYSTEM as the owner distinguishes singular DBTG sets.

2.  There is exactly one set occurrence, and its members are all the records of
    the member type. The records are made members automatically, with no
    specific direction required from the user.

**Example 5.12:** If we wish the capability of searching all the CUSTOMERS
records conveniently, we could add to the DBTG set declarations in Figure 5.3
the definition of the following singular set.

```
DBTG SET ALLCUST
    OWNER IS SYSTEM
    MEMBER IS CUSTOMERS;
```

To print all the customers with negative balances we could then execute the
program of Figure 5.10. □

```
print "NAME", "BALANCE"
FIND FIRST CUSTOMERS RECORD IN CURRENT ALLCUST SET
/* the lone set occurrence of ALLCUST is always current */
while ¬FAIL do begin
    GET CUSTOMERS
    if BALANCE < 0 then
        print CNAME, BALANCE
    FIND NEXT CUSTOMERS RECORD IN CURRENT ALLCUST SET
end
```

**Figure 5.10** Print YVCB customers with negative balances.

### Scanning a Set Occurrence for Fields of Specified Value

The next type of FIND statement also scans the members of a set occurrence,
but it allows us to look at only those records with specified values in certain
fields. The values for these fields are stored in the template for the member
record type before using the FIND. To get the first member record having the
desired values, we can write

```
FIND <record type> RECORD IN CURRENT
    <set name> SET USING <field list>
```

Here, <record type> is the member type for the DBTG set whose name is
<set name>, and the <field list> is a list of fields of the <record type> whose
values, stored in the template for <record type>, must match the values of
these fields in the selected record. To get subsequent records in the same set
occurrence with the same values we say

```
FIND DUPLICATE <record type> RECORD IN CURRENT
    <set name> SET USING <field list>
```

**Example 5.13:** To find the price charged by Ajax for Perrier, we could use the program of Figure 5.11. It assumes that OFFERS records have the virtual fields NAME and ITEM, and it assumes that SNAME is the CALC-key for SUPPLIERS. After finding the SUPPLIERS record for Ajax, we scan the O_SUPPLIER set occurrence it owns for an OFFER record that has ITEM equal to "Perrier," and we print the price when and if such a record is found.

```
SNAME := "Ajax"
FIND SUPPLIERS RECORD USING CALC-KEY
ITEM := "Perrier"
FIND OFFERS RECORD IN CURRENT O_SUPPLIER SET USING ITEM
GET OFFERS; PRICE
print PRICE
```

**Figure 5.11** Find the price charged by Ajax for Perrier.

As an example of a situation where we might wish to scan for several matching records, consider Figure 5.12, where we scan the singular set ALLCUST, introduced in Example 5.11, for all customers with zero balance. □

```
BALANCE := 0
FIND CUSTOMERS RECORD IN CURRENT ALLCUST
  SET USING BALANCE
while ¬FAIL do begin
    GET CUSTOMERS; CNAME
    print CNAME
    FIND DUPLICATE CUSTOMERS RECORD IN
      CURRENT ALLCUST SET USING BALANCE
end
```

**Figure 5.12** Find customers with zero balance.

### Establishing a Current of Run-Unit

The last type of FIND we shall cover is a FIND statement whose purpose is to make a current of record or set become the current of run-unit. The syntax is:

```
FIND CURRENT OF <set name> SET
```

or

        FIND CURRENT OF  <record type> RECORD

**Example 5.14:** Suppose we wish to find out how much Brie Zack Zebra ordered. We begin by scanning the E_ITEM set occurrence owned by Brie, and
for each ENTRIES record, we need to determine whether it is an entry in an
order placed by Zebra. If so, we shall accumulate the quantity found in that
ENTRIES record, in a workspace variable named *zbtotal*

        When we find each ENTRIES record, we could immediately read it into
the workspace. However, that would waste time, since we only need to read
the record if it turns out to be part of a Zack Zebra order. One solution is to
reestablish this ENTRIES record as the current of run-unit when we find that
we want to read it.[5] We test that we want to read the entry by following the
E_ORDER and PLACED_BY links to their owners, thus finding the appropriate CUSTOMERS record. If the customer in this record is Zebra, then and
only then do we wish to read the ENTRIES record that is still the current of
ENTRIES. The program that implements these ideas is shown in Figure 5.13.
It assumes INAME is the CALC-key for ITEMS. □

```
zbtotal := 0
INAME := "Brie"
FIND ITEMS RECORD USING CALC-KEY
FIND FIRST ENTRIES RECORD IN CURRENT E_ITEM SET
while ¬FAIL do begin
    FIND OWNER OF CURRENT E_ORDER SET
    FIND OWNER OF CURRENT PLACED_BY SET
    /* now we have arrived at the customer */
    GET CUSTOMERS; CNAME
    if CNAME = "Zack Zebra" then begin
        FIND CURRENT OF ENTRIES RECORD
        /* now we can read the quantity */
        GET ENTRIES; QUANTITY
        zbtotal := zbtotal + QUANTITY
    end
    FIND NEXT ENTRIES RECORD IN CURRENT E_ITEM SET
end
print zbtotal
```

**Figure 5.13** Finding how much Brie Zack Zebra ordered.

---

[5] Recall that we can only GET the current of run-unit.

## 5.3 THE DBTG DATABASE MODIFICATION COMMANDS

In addition to FIND and GET, the DBTG proposal includes commands to in-sert or delete the current of run-unit from set occurrences and from the list of records of a type, and a command to modify the current of run-unit. Database modification is complex, because the user is given, in the DDL, a variety of *existence constraints* that he may choose to have the system enforce. For example, if there is a DBTG set $S$ with owner type $T_1$ and member type $T_2$, we may wish that whenever we create a $T_2$ type record, it has some $S$ set occurrence to which it belongs. To do so, when the DBTG set $S$ is declared, we add:

        INSERTION IS AUTOMATIC

and give a *set selection* clause, to be illustrated shortly, that tells how to select the set occurrence into which the $T_2$ record should be placed. One use of such constraints is to check that we do not perform meaningless operations, such as inserting an order from a nonexistent customer.

   Another form of constraint we may place on DBTG set members is to de-clare a *retention class* for them. If we declare retention to be MANDATORY, then once a record is a member of some set occurrence, it cannot be removed from that occurrence and placed in another; we must copy the record into the working area, delete it from the database, and then store it in the desired set occurrence. If, however, retention is declared OPTIONAL, then by INSERT and REMOVE commands to be discussed, we can shift it from one set occur-rence to another. The purpose of mandatory retention is not to make things difficult, but to offer the user a check on possible program bugs.

### The STORE Command

To store a new record of type $T$ into the database, we create the record $r$ in the template for record type $T$ and then issue the command

        STORE $T$

This command adds $r$ to the collection of records of type $T$ and makes $r$ be the current of run-unit, the current of $T$, and the current of any DBTG set of which $T$ is the owner or member type.

   As mentioned above, if $T$ is the member type of any DBTG sets in which it is declared to have automatic insertion, then $r$ becomes a member of one set occurrence for each of these sets; exactly which occurrences depends on the set selection clauses that are part of the DDL database description.

   The opposite of AUTOMATIC is MANUAL. If DBTG set $S$ is declared this way, then member records are not inserted into any set occurrence of $S$ when the records are stored, and we must "manually" insert records into set occurrences of $S$ by an INSERT command, to be discussed later in this section.

## Set Selection

Granted that we have declared insertion of records of type $T$ into set occurrences of $S$ to be AUTOMATIC, we need a mechanism for deciding which set occurrence of $S$ gets the new record. The STORE command itself cannot specify the correct set occurrence. Rather, when we declare DBTG set $S$, we include a SET SELECTION clause that tells how to select the set occurrence of $S$ into which a newly stored member record is to be placed. There are many different ways in which the set occurrence could be chosen. We shall describe only the two simplest kinds of set selection clauses. Remember that each of the following statements belongs in the declaration for a set $S$; i.e., they would be added to declarations such as those of Figure 5.3. They are not part of the data manipulation language. Also note that we use a "Pidgin" syntax to make the meaning of the clauses more apparent.

1. SET SELECTION IS THRU CURRENT OF $S$ SET. Here, before storing a record, the program itself establishes a current set occurrence for DBTG set $S$, and when the record is stored, it becomes a member of that occurrence.

2. SET SELECTION IS THRU OWNER USING <field list>. The <field list> must be the CALC-key for the owner type of $S$. The current values of these fields in the template for the owner type must determine a unique record of the owner type for $S$, and the stored record goes into the set occurrence of $S$ owned by that record.

**Example 5.15:** Suppose we wish to store ENTRIES records and insert them automatically into E_ORDER and E_ITEM set occurrences when we do. If O# is the CALC-key for ORDERS, we can use an order number to select the set occurrence for E_ORDER, by including in the declaration for E_ORDER the clause

    SET SELECTION IS THRU OWNER USING O#

We might choose to select the E_ITEM occurrence through the owner identified by INAME, but for variety, let us select the E_ITEM occurrence by placing

    SET SELECTION IS THRU CURRENT OF E_ITEM SET

in the declaration of E_ITEM. The clause

    INSERTION IS AUTOMATIC

must be placed in the declarations of both E_ORDER and E_ITEM. The program in Figure 5.14 reads an order number, item, and quantity, creates an ENTRIES record with the quantity, and stores that record into the database. Because of the set-selection declarations we have made, this ENTRIES record is automatically inserted into the correct set occurrences of E_ORDER and E_ITEM. □

```
read O, I, Q /* the name, item, and quantity */
ORDERS.O# := O /* prepare E_ORDER set selection */
ITEMS.INAME := I
FIND ITEMS RECORD BY CALC-KEY
/* above prepares E_ITEM set selection */
ENTRIES.QUANTITY := Q
/* above creates a new ENTRIES record in the template */
STORE ENTRIES /* automatically places the record in the
    E_ORDER set occurrence owned by O and in the current
    E_ITEM set, which is that owned by I */
```

**Figure 5.14** Read and store an entry in an order.

## Manual Insertion into Set Occurrences

If we do not wish to use set selection to place records in set occurrences, we can do insertion by an explicit command. A record type can be declared an AUTOMATIC member of some DBTG sets, in which case set selection is used, and the same record type can be declared

**INSERTION IS MANUAL**

for some other DBTG set of which it is a member, in which case a record, when stored, is not made a member of any set occurrence for this DBTG set.

To insert a record $r$ (which already exists in the database) of the member type $T$ for DBTG set $S$, into a designated set occurrence of $S$, we first make this set occurrence be the current of $S$, by whatever means we find suitable. Then we make $r$ be the current of run-unit and issue the command

**INSERT $T$ INTO $S$**

Note that $r$ must be the current of run-unit, not just the current of $T$. It is permissible to follow INTO by a list of DBTG sets, and if so, insertion of $r$ into the current of each set will occur.

**Example 5.16:** In Example 5.15 we read an ENTRIES record and inserted it automatically into ORDERS and ITEMS set occurrences. If we instead declare ENTRIES to be a MANUAL member of the E_ORDER and E_ITEM DBTG sets, we can do the insertion manually by the procedure of Figure 5.15. □

## Manual Deletion from Set Occurrences

To remove the current of run-unit, which is a record of type $T$, from its set occurrence for DBTG set $S$, we issue the command

**REMOVE $T$ FROM $S$**

As with insertion, $S$ could be replaced by a list of DBTG sets. Remember,

```
read O, I, Q
ORDERS.O# := O
FIND ORDERS RECORD BY CALC-KEY
/* establishes the correct current of E_ORDER */
ITEMS.INAME := I
FIND ITEMS RECORD BY CALC-KEY
/* establishes the correct current of E_ITEM */
ENTRIES.QUANTITY := Q
STORE ENTRIES /* new order is now the current of run-unit,
   but not a member of any set occurrences */
INSERT ENTRIES INTO E_ORDER, E_ITEM
```

**Figure 5.15** Manual insertion of a new ENTRIES record.

the record removed must be the current of run-unit, not just the current of $T$. Also, we are not permitted to execute the REMOVE statement if mandatory retention has been specified for $S$.

**Record Modification**

The command

MODIFY <record type>

has the effect of copying the template for <record type> into the current of run-unit. If the current of run-unit is not of the designated record type, it is an error. We can also modify a selected subset of the fields in the current of run-unit by writing

MODIFY <record type>; <field list>

If $T$ is the record type for the current of run-unit, the values of the fields in the list are copied from the template for $T$ into the fields of the current of run-unit. Other fields in the current of run-unit are unchanged.

**Example 5.17:** Suppose Ruth Rhino moves to 62 Cherry Lane. Assuming that CNAME is the CALC-key for CUSTOMERS, we could change her CUSTOMERS record by:

```
CUSTOMERS.CNAME := "Ruth Rhino"
FIND CUSTOMER RECORD BY CALC-KEY
CUSTOMERS.CADDR := "62 Cherry Lane"
MODIFY CUSTOMERS; CADDR
```

□

## Deletion of Records from the Database

The command

        DELETE <record type>

deletes the current of run-unit, which must be of the specified <record type>, from the file of records of that type. Naturally, if the current of run-unit is a member of any set occurrences, it is removed from those occurrences. If the current of run-unit is the owner of any set occurrences, those occurrences must presently have no members, or it is an error, and the deletion cannot take place.

    Another form of DELETE statement is

        DELETE <record type> ALL

This instruction is applicable even if the current of run-unit is the owner of some nonempty set occurrences. The DELETE ALL statement not only erases the current of run-unit, as the simple DELETE does, but recursively, DELETE ALL is applied to any members of set occurrences owned by the deleted record. Thus it is conceivable that DELETE ALL could destroy the entire database.

**Example 5.18:** We can delete the current ENTRIES record by simply saying:

        DELETE ENTRIES

Since ENTRIES records are not owners in any DBTG set, the given entry is simply deleted from the file of ENTRIES records and from whatever E_ORDER and E_ITEM set occurrences it belongs to.

    As another example, suppose O# is the CALC-key for ORDERS. We can delete order number 1024 from the database by:

        ORDERS.O# := 1024
        FIND ORDERS RECORD BY CALC-KEY
        DELETE ORDERS ALL

This erasure has the effect of deleting the record for order 1024 from the ORDERS file and deleting the entire E_ORDER set occurrence of which it is the owner. The members of this set occurrence are the entries for order 1024. Recursively, each entry in the deleted set occurrence is itself deleted from the ENTRIES file and from the E_ITEM set occurrence of which it is a member. Since ENTRIES records do not own any set occurrences, the recursion stops here, and no further alterations to the database are made. □

## 5.4 DATA DEFINITION IN IMS

In this section we shall begin the study of a language for the hierarchical model. The data manipulation language we shall describe in the next section is a "Pidgin" version of the language DL/I (data language one) used by the IMS database management system, marketed by IBM since the early 1960's. Here, we shall illustrate the important features of IMS's data definition language for defining the structure of hierarchies; the syntax is again a "Pidgin" language chosen for clarity. In Chapter 6 we shall discuss some of the options for declaring physical layout of hierarchies that IMS provides.

There are three essential features that define structure in a hierarchy: trees, nodes (logical record types), and fields within nodes. We shall declare trees by:

> **TREE** <name> <list of logical record types>

Each logical record type is then declared by:

> **RECORD** <name> <information>

The information associated with records includes the following.

1. Fields. We shall use the same notation as in Section 5.1 for declaring fields within a record type.
2. The position of the record type within the hierarchy. We use the word **ROOT** to indicate the record type is at the root of the tree, and otherwise, we shall include a clause

> **PARENT** = <parent name>

   to indicate the parent record type for the record type being declared.
3. Virtual record types present as fields within the record. We use the clause

> **VIRTUAL** <record name> **IN** <tree name>

   to indicate which node in which tree the pointer field points to.

There are a number of other aspects to the IMS data definition language. They allow us to declare additional pointers, for example, to parent records, to the leftmost child, or to the next record in a preorder traversal of the database. Unlike the pointers resulting from virtual record type declarations, these pointers are not accessible to the data manipulation commands, and are only used by the query-processing algorithms to speed up access to data.

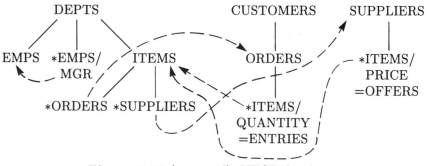

**Figure 2.26** (repeated) YVCB database.

**Example 5.19:** Let us express the hierarchy of Figure 2.26 in the above notation. (Figure 2.26 is repeated here, for convenience.) We use the same set of fields for the logical record types as was found in Figure 5.2, when we declared the network structure for the YVCB database. To these we must add the pointer fields representing virtual record types. The structure is shown in Figure 5.16. For consistency with Figure 5.2, we use the record name OFFERS for the node in Figure 2.26 that has a PRICE and a virtual ITEMS field, and we use ENTRIES for the node consisting of a QUANTITY and a virtual ITEMS field. □

## 5.5 A HIERARCHICAL DATA MANIPULATION LANGUAGE

We shall now introduce the reader to a hierarchical query language that is based on IMS's data manipulation language called DL/I. As with the network DML described in Sections 5.2 and 5.3, DL/I is a language with a great number of complex features, and we shall simplify it significantly, in order to give the flavor of, and concepts behind, the language without getting bogged down in details. We shall refer to our language as "Pidgin DL/I." This language is a collection of commands that are embedded in a host language. In IMS, these commands actually have the form of procedure calls, and we can regard them as such here.

### The Program Environment

The database consists of a collection of trees, as discussed in Sections 2.6 and 5.4. As in the DBTG model, we may assume there is a workspace in which a template for each logical record type is kept. These templates can be filled by particular records of the correct type chosen from the database by the GET command. Also in analogy with the DBTG proposal, it is convenient to assume that there is a "current record" of each tree. This record could be of any type in the scheme for that tree. We shall also have some use for the notion of a "current parent," the parent of the current record.

Additionally, we assume that there is a variable FAIL, accessible both to the host language program and to the commands of the query language. FAIL will be used to indicate whether or not certain database searches have found a record meeting the desired conditions.

### The GET Command

The basic retrieval command, called GET LEFTMOST, specifies a path from a root record occurrence to a (*target*) record of a particular type, not necessarily a leaf record type. The reader should remember that the trees on which this and other commands operate is not the scheme trees, as in Figure 2.26, but trees that represent instances of the database, as was suggested by Figure 2.19.

```
TREE DEPTS_TREE
    RECORD DEPTS ROOT
        1 DNAME CHAR(10)
        1 DEPT# INTEGER
    RECORD EMPS PARENT=DEPTS
        1 ENAME CHAR(20)
        1 SALARY REAL
    RECORD MGR PARENT=DEPTS
        VIRTUAL EMPS IN DEPTS_TREE
    RECORD ITEMS PARENT=DEPTS
        1 INAME CHAR(10)
        1 ITEM# INTEGER
    RECORD VIRT_ORDERS PARENT=ITEMS
        VIRTUAL ORDERS IN CUST_TREE
    RECORD VIRT_SUPPS PARENT=ITEMS
        VIRTUAL SUPPLIERS IN SUPPS_TREE


TREE CUST_TREE
    RECORD CUSTOMERS ROOT
        1 CNAME CHAR(20)
        1 CADDR CHAR(50)
        1 BALANCE REAL
    RECORD ORDERS PARENT=CUSTOMERS
        1 O# INTEGER
        1 DATE CHAR(10)
    RECORD ENTRIES PARENT=ORDERS
        1 QUANTITY INTEGER
        VIRTUAL ITEMS IN DEPTS_TREE


TREE SUPPS_TREE
    RECORD SUPPLIERS ROOT
        1 SNAME CHAR(10)
        1 SADDR CHAR(50)
    RECORD OFFERS PARENT=SUPPLIERS
        1 PRICE REAL
        VIRTUAL ITEMS IN DEPTS_TREE
```

**Figure 5.16** Hierarchical database for YVCB.

The GET LEFTMOST command causes a certain record to be retrieved and placed in the template for the target record type. This record is the leftmost record occurrence of that type to satisfy whatever conditions are placed on it and on its ancestors by the GET LEFTMOST command.

The syntax we shall use in our "Pidgin DL/I" for GET LEFTMOST is

```
GET LEFTMOST <target record name>
    WHERE <condition list>
```

The <condition list> consists of a sequence of conditions of the form

<record name> . <field name> $\theta$ <value>

possibly connected by "and" and "or." Each <record name> is an ancestor (not necessarily proper) of the target record type. The <field name> is a field of the <record name>, and $\theta$ is one of the arithmetic comparison operators, $=$, $<$, and so on. The <value> can be a constant or a variable of the host language program; the latter option helps us pass "parameters" to the calls represented by the DL/I commands. We can omit the <record name> if it is uniquely determined by the <field name>.

**Example 5.20:** Let us suppose that we have opened access to the tree with root CUSTOMERS, of the database described as a diagram in Figure 2.26 and as a formal declaration in Figure 5.16. The Pidgin DL/I command

```
GET LEFTMOST CUSTOMERS
    WHERE CUSTOMERS.BALANCE < 0
```
                                                                          (5.1)

finds the leftmost customer record whose BALANCE field has a negative value.
□

## Order of Records

To understand what "leftmost" means in this context, recall that for each tree of a database scheme, such as Figure 2.26, there is a collection of trees, one for each database record in the current instance of the scheme. A database record consists of one record of the root type and all its descendant records in the database, as we discussed in Section 2.6. The order of database records of a given type might be a sort based on some key field, or it might be random, perhaps based on a hash function; the actual order depends on the physical structure chosen when the database scheme is declared. Whatever order of the database records there is, getting the "leftmost" means getting the first eligible database record in this order. For example, the "leftmost" CUSTOMERS database record might be the one whose customer name comes first in alphabetical order. If there is a condition to be satisfied, such as BALANCE<0 in (5.1), then we would scan CUSTOMERS records in their order, until we find one meeting the condition.

If we are looking for a record type $R$ that is not the root, then we examine the database records in order from the left. Within a tree, the nodes have a natural "from the left" order, with order among records of the same type that are children of the same node determined in some specified manner, e.g., sorted according to some key value, or random. We consider all records of type $R$, in this order, until we find one meeting the conditions of the where-clause.

**Example 5.21·** Referring again to the tree CUST_TREE, we could ask:

```
GET LEFTMOST ORDERS
    WHERE CUSTOMERS.BALANCE < 0
    AND ORDERS.DATE = "Jan 3"
```

The effect of this query is that customer database records are examined, in order "from the left," until we find one that has a root CUSTOMERS record with a BALANCE less than zero and an ORDERS child with a DATE field of "Jan 3." To find this ORDERS record we may skip over many database records with BALANCE less than zero. If the desired database record has two or more ORDERS children with the date "Jan 3," we stop at the leftmost such child.

We can access virtual record types as if they were physically present in the database at the point where the virtual record (pointer) appears. Thus, we could imagine that the ITEMS children of ORDERS in the CUST_TREE database records are physically part of that tree, and treat them as grandchildren of CUSTOMERS records. Thus, we could write

```
GET LEFTMOST ITEMS
    WHERE ORDERS.O# = 1024
```

to find the first item on order 1024. To execute this command, we scan all of the CUST_TREE database records in order, until we find one with an ORDERS child having order number 1024. Then we find the first (virtual) ITEMS child of this ORDERS record. Note that the "ITEMS child" of an orders record is technically part of an ENTRIES record, which includes a physical field, QUANTITY, as well as the fields of a virtual ITEMS record.

As a final variant, we could use, instead of a constant, 1024, an order number that was read by the host language and passed to the GET command, in a host-language variable we shall call *order*.

```
read order
GET LEFTMOST ITEMS
    WHERE ORDERS.O# = order
```

☐

## Scanning the Database

Another version of the GET command allows us to scan the entire database for all records satisfying certain conditions. We use the word NEXT in place of

LEFTMOST to cause a scan rightward from the last record accessed (i.e., from the "current record") until we next meet a record of the same type satisfying the conditions in the GET NEXT statement. These conditions could differ from the conditions that established the "current record," but in practice they are usually the same.

**Example 5.22:** Suppose we want to find all the items ordered by Zack Zebra. We again go to CUST_TREE, and we execute the program of Figure 5.17. In principle, we examine all the customer database records, but only the one with CNAME equal to "Zack Zebra" will satisfy the condition in the where-clause. We find the first item in the first order placed by Zebra, with the GET LEFTMOST statement. Then we scan to the right, from order to order, and within each order, from item to item, printing the name of each item.

Eventually, we find no more items that Zebra ordered. At that time, the variable FAIL will become true, indicating that the GET NEXT statement has failed to find a record. It is also possible that there are no items ordered by Zebra, in which case the initial GET LEFTMOST statement will cause FAIL to become true. In general, any GET statement that does not find a record sets FAIL to true. □

```
GET LEFTMOST ITEMS
    WHERE CUSTOMERS.CNAME = "Zack Zebra"
while ¬FAIL do begin
    print ITEMS.INAME /* "print" refers to the template
        for the appropriate record type in the workspace */
    GET NEXT ITEMS
        WHERE CUSTOMERS.CNAME = "Zack Zebra"
end
```

**Figure 5.17** Print the items Zack Zebra ordered.

### Scanning the Descendants of a Given Node

A third form of GET, written GET NEXT WITHIN PARENT, permits us to visit all the children of a particular record occurrence in the actual database. It utilizes the informal concept of "current parent," which is the record occurrence most recently accessed by any variety of GET other than GET NEXT WITHIN PARENT. The record type accessed by a GET NEXT WITHIN PARENT command need not be a child record type for the type of the current parent; it could be any descendant record type. The difference between GET NEXT and GET NEXT WITHIN PARENT is that the latter fails when it has scanned all the descendants of the current parent; the former searches rightward for any record occurrence such that it and its ancestors satisfy the associated conditions.

**Example 5.23:** Another way to print all the items ordered by Zebra is to find the root of his database record by

```
GET LEFTMOST CUSTOMERS
    WHERE CUSTOMERS.CNAME = "Zack Zebra"
```

This statement makes the customer record for Zebra be the "current parent" as well as the "current record" for the CUST_TREE tree. Then, we scan all the ITEMS descendants of this one record by repeatedly executing GET NEXT WITHIN PARENT, as shown in Figure 5.18. We never look for any item that is not a descendant of the customer record for Zebra, even though there is no

```
WHERE CUSTOMERS.CNAME = "Zack Zebra"
```

clause constraining us from jumping to other database records. Notice that the "parent" record in this case is really a grandparent of the ITEMS records being found. The "current parent" remains the Zack Zebra record, since all retrievals but the first use GET NEXT WITHIN PARENT. □

```
GET LEFTMOST CUSTOMERS
    WHERE CUSTOMERS.CNAME = "Zack Zebra"
GET NEXT WITHIN PARENT ITEMS
while ¬FAIL do begin
    print ITEMS.INAME
    GET NEXT WITHIN PARENT ITEMS
end
```

**Figure 5.18** Using get-next-within-parent.


**Insertions**

An INSERT command, for which we use the same "Pidgin" syntax as for the varieties of GET, allows us to insert a record of type $S$, first created in the workspace, as a child of a designated record occurrence of the parent type for $S$. If the "current record" is either of the parent type for $S$, or any descendant of the parent type, simply writing

```
INSERT S
```

will make the record of type $S$ sitting in the workspace a child of that occurrence of the parent type that is the current record or an ancestor of the current record.

The position of the new child among its siblings is a matter to be declared when the database scheme is specified. We shall not discuss the syntax for specifying order, but the options include making each record the rightmost or leftmost child of its parent at the time it is inserted, or keeping children in sorted order according to a key field or fields.

If the desired parent record is not the current record or an ancestor of that record, we can make it be so by including a where-clause in the INSERT statement, with syntax and meaning exactly as for the GET statement.

**Example 5.24:** If the Produce Department starts selling Cilantro, which we give product number 99, we can insert this fact into the database by the steps of Figure 5.19. If the Produce Department's DEPTS record, or some descendant of that record such as the EMPS record for an employee of the Produce Department, were already the current record, then we could omit the where-clause of Figure 5.19. □

```
ITEMS.INAME := "Cilantro"
ITEMS.ITEM# := 99
/* the above assignments take place in the ITEMS
   template of the workspace */
INSERT ITEMS
   WHERE DEPTS.DNAME = "Produce"
```

**Figure 5.19**  The Produce Department now sells Cilantro.

### Deletion and Modification

In order to delete or modify a record we must first "hold" it by issuing some variety of GET command that will make the desired record be the current record. However, we add the word HOLD after GET in the command. The requirement for holding a record before deleting or modifying it is motivated by the possibility that there is concurrent processing of the database by two or more application programs. Upon executing GET HOLD, any other program is prevented from accessing the record. See Chapter 9 for a description of the need for "holding" a record before modifying it. "Hold" here corresponds to "lock" or "write-lock" in Chapter 9.

To delete a record after finding and holding it, simply issue the command

```
DELETE
```

The effect of this statement is to delete the current record and also to delete any of its children in the underlying database. Virtual records would not be deleted, of course.

To modify a record after finding and holding it, we first change the copy of the record found in the workspace. When we issue the command

REPLACE

the version of the current record in the workspace replaces the corresponding record in the database.

**Example 5.25:** Suppose we wish to double the amount of Brie on order number 1024. We first get the ENTRIES child of the ORDER record for 1024, and hold it. Then we double the QUANTITY field of the record, in the workspace, and finally store the new ENTRIES record by a REPLACE command. The steps are.

```
GET HOLD LEFTMOST ENTRIES
    WHERE ITEMS.INAME = "Brie" AND ORDERS.O# = 1024
ENTRIES.QUANTITY := 2 * ENTRIES.QUANTITY
REPLACE
```

Aas another example, we can delete order 1024 by the following code.

```
GET HOLD LEFTMOST ORDERS
    WHERE ORDERS.O# = 1024
DELETE
```

The effect of this sequence of steps is to delete not only the ORDERS record for 1024, but all the ENTRIES children of that record. Those records include the QUANTITY field and the pointer to an ITEMS record that represents the virtual ITEMS child of ENTRIES. We do not, of course, delete any ITEMS records or any of their children. □

## 5.6 DATA DEFINITION IN OPAL

The object-oriented language OPAL presents a contrast to all of the languages we have studied in this chapter and the previous one. OPAL is the language of the Gemstone database system marketed by Servio Logic Corp. Its data definition and data manipulation facilities are present in one language, whose style borrows heavily from the language Smalltalk. We shall sketch the most important features of this language, and then discuss the way the language lets us define database schemes. The next section talks about other aspects of OPAL that are more important for data manipulation.

### Classes

A *class* is an abstract data type, consisting of

1.  A data structure definition for the class, and
2.  A collection of operations, called "methods," that apply to objects in the class.

In Section 2.7 we saw a simple example of a language for defining data structures for classes; OPAL has a considerably more general mechanism. The way one defines methods in OPAL will be discussed below.

Objects that are members of a given class $C$ are *instances* of $C$; they each have the data structure of that class, and the methods for class $C$ can be applied to any instance of $C$.

Classes are arranged in a hierarchy. If class $C$ is a descendant of class $D$, then the methods of class $D$ can (usually) be applied to instances of $C$, but not vice versa. The details of subclass creation and inheritance of methods will be described near the end of this section.

## Methods

A procedure in OPAL is called a *method*. Each method is defined for a particular class, and it applies to instances of that class and instances of its subclasses, if any. The form of a method definition is:

```
method <class name>
    <message format>
    <body of method>
%
```

The <class name> is the class to which the method applies. The <message format> is the name of the method and/or the names of its parameters, and the body is the code that is executed whenever the method is called.

The format of messages requires some explanation. In the simplest form, a message format consists of only a name for the method. Such a method has only one argument, the *receiver* object to which the method is applied. The receiver of a method always appears to the left of the method's name, and the receiver must be an instance of the class for which the method is defined.

**Example 5.26:** Any class understands the built-in (predefined) method *new*. The message format for this method is simply the word *new*. For our first OPAL examples, let us draw upon Example 2.31, where we defined certain types of structures, roughly equivalent to OPAL classes, that were used to build the YVCB database. For example, *ItemType* is a class, and if we wished to create a new instance of that class, i.e., a record for an item, we could say:

```
ItemType new
```

This OPAL statement produces a new instance of the *ItemType* class. As it is, nothing is done with that instance, but we could assign it to a variable, say *NewItem*, by the statement

```
NewItem := ItemType new
```

Here, the receipt of the message **new** by the class name *ItemType* causes a new instance of that class to be generated, and the assignment symbol := causes the variable on the left of the assignment to become a name for that instance. □

## Methods with Parameters

A more general message format has one or more parameters, in addition to the implicit parameter that is the receiver of the message. We should appreciate that a method with parameters has no "name"; rather the list of parameter names serves as a name for the method. While in most programming languages, parameters of a procedure are identified only by their argument positions, in OPAL parameters also have names.[6] The format in which parameters are passed is

<receiver> <parm1>: <val1> ⋯ <parm$n$>: <val$n$>

Here, <receiver> is the object to which the method is applied; <parm$i$> is the name of one of the parameters of this method, and <val$i$> is the value passed for that parameter.

**Example 5.27:** Let us write a method that, given the name of an item, tests whether a given object of class *ItemType* has *name* field equal to that item name, and returns the item number if so. If not, the method returns a character string that serves as an error message. The method is shown in Figure 5.20.

```
(1)  method:  ItemType
(2)     checkItem:  i
(3)     ((self getName) = i)
(4)         ifTrue:  [^self getNumber]
(5)         ifFalse:  [^'error:  wrong item name']
(6)  %
```

**Figure 5.20** Accessing an item record.

The code of Figure 5.20 uses a number of constructs we have not yet explained, so let us consider the program line-by-line. Line (1) tells us that we are declaring a method for class *ItemType*. Line (2) says that this method is distinguished by one parameter, called *checkItem*, and it introduces $i$ as the formal parameter of the method; $i$ represents the actual value that will be passed when this method is applied to a particular *ItemType* object. For example, if we use this method with variable *CurrentItem* as receiver we could write

```
CurrentItem checkItem:  'Brie'
```
(5.2)

---

[6] The use of attribute names in relational query languages frequently serves a similar purpose: naming the components of tuples. In contrast, logical rules, as in Chapter 3, follow the syntax of traditional programming languages, since the arguments of a predicate are known only by their order and have no names.

Then the formal parameter $i$ would have the value "Brie" when we executed the code of Figure 5.20 on the object that *CurrentItem* represents.

Line (3) introduces the special object designator *self*, which always denotes the receiver of the method. That is, when executing (5.2), *self* denotes the same object that *CurrentItem* denotes. Notice that without the word *self*, we would have no way to refer to the receiver of a method, because methods have no formal parameter name to represent their receiver.

We also see in line (3) a method *getName*, which we suppose has already been defined. The presumed effect of *getName*, when applied to an object $O$ of class *ItemType*, is to return the *name* field of $O$. Thus, when *getName* is applied to *self* during the execution of (5.2), it has the effect of returning the name of the item *CurrentItem*. That value becomes the receiver of the second method on line (3), the built-in method =.[7] This method tests whether the value of its receiver equals the value of its parameter. For example, in (5.2), we test whether the item *CurrentItem* has *name* field equal to "Brie."

Lines (4) and (5) represent a test on the Boolean value (true or false) created by the expression on line (3). Think of *ifTrue*: and *ifFalse*: as parameter names for a built-in method whose receiver is a Boolean value. The effect of applying the method is that the block of code following *ifTrue*: is executed if the message is sent to the value *true*, and the block of code following *ifFalse*: is executed if the message is sent to *false*.

Blocks of code are surrounded by square brackets, which function as begin–end pairs. Thus, line (4) says that if *CurrentItem* is indeed the item object for Brie, then we return the item number for Brie. In explanation, ^ is the symbol for "return." We suppose that the method *getNumber* was previously defined and, when applied to an *ItemType* object, produces the value of the *I#* field of that object, which is then returned by the method *checkItem*. Finally, line (5) says that if the item name in *CurrentItem* doesn't match the parameter $i$, "Brie" in the case of (5.2), then we return the string `'error: wrong item name'` as a value. □

## Creating Record Types

The language OPAL allows us to define classes of objects in many different categories: bags (multisets), arrays, strings, and others. We shall concentrate on only two kinds of classes here:

1.  General "objects" used as record types and
2.  Sets, whose members are objects of some fixed class.

Classes of these two types correspond to the type constructors RECORDOF and SETOF, respectively, discussed in Section 2.7. To create the type for a relation,

---

[7] Note that methods are applied from left-to-right, so the inner parentheses are redundant. We shall continue to show the correct grouping, for clarity.

we define a class $C_1$ of type (1) whose instances are the tuples, and we create a class $C_2$ of type (2) to be the type of the relation itself, that is, a set of objects of class $C_1$. That relation may be the only instance of class $C_2$.

To create a record type, we send to the built-in "variable" *Object* the message *subclass*. More exactly, there is a built-in method with a number of parameters, most of which we shall not discuss, whose function is to define a new class. The three important parameters of the class-creation method, as far as we are concerned here, are:

1.   *subclass*: <class name>. This parameter's value is the name of the new class, given as a quoted string.
2.   *instVarNames*: <field names>. The objects of a given class can have *instance variable names*, which function as names of fields. These variables are called "instance variables" because they occur in every instance of the class.
3.   *constraints*: <data types>. We may, optionally, place a constraint on the class to which the value of one or more of the instance variables must belong. It is worth noting that OPAL, as a default, is typeless, and objects belonging to any class can be stored in instance variables or anywhere else objects are permitted.

**Example 5.28:** Let us create a class *ItemType* corresponding to the declaration in Example 2.31, where this class was defined to consist of an item name field and an item number field. The message we send to *Object* is shown in Figure 5.21.

```
Object
    subclass:  'ItemType'
    instVarNames:  #['name', 'number']
    constraints:  #[
        #[ #name, String],
        #[ #number, Integer]
    ].
```

**Figure 5.21** Declaration of *ItemType* class.

There are some syntactic matters concerning Figure 5.21 that we have not yet discussed. The instance variables are specified by an array of string constants; here, 'name' and 'number' are used. Such an array is delimited by #[...]. The constraints are also indicated by an array, whose elements are pairs (i.e., arrays of length two) consisting of a *symbol*, which is the instance variable name preceded by a #, and a class name, such as the built-in classes *String* and *Integer* used in Figure 5.21. Note that 'number' appears as a string when it is defined to be the name of an instance variable, but when we refer to the instance variable itself, in the constraint, we must use the "symbol" #number. □

## Creating Set Types

In order to define a class that will behave like a set, we send the *subclass* message to the built-in class *Set*. Generally, these subclasses of *Set* will not have instance variables, but we shall wish to constrain a set to contain objects of only one class; as a default, OPAL permits sets to have objects of mixed types. Thus, a typical definition of a set would have the following form (as usual, we omit certain parameters whose role in the message will not be discussed):

```
Set
     subclass: <set name>
     constraints: <element class>.
```

**Example 5.29:** We can now do all of the definitions in Example 2.31. Corresponding to Figure 2.27 we have Figure 5.22, with the comparable OPAL declarations. In addition to the classes of sets required for Example 2.31, we have added declarations for sets of customers, suppliers, and departments, to serve as types for the relations (or record types) CUSTOMERS, SUPPLIERS, and DEPTS, found in the databases defined for the other languages we have studied in Chapters 4 and 5. □

## Subclasses

Every class is created as a subclass of some previously existing class; we can use the most general class, *Object*, if there is nothing more suitable for a superclass. Each subclass *inherits* all of the methods of its superclass. For example, *ItemType*, being a subclass of *Object*, inherits the method *new*, which creates a new object of class *ItemType* when sent to the variable *ItemType*.[8] While we have seen subclasses created only from the built-in classes of OPAL, there is often a use for creating subclasses of user-defined classes. Such subclasses can have extra instance variables, which is equivalent to adding extra fields to records in the subclass. Subclasses can also have methods that apply only to them, and we can redefine for the subclass methods that are already defined for the superclass.

**Example 5.30:** We might wish to define managers to be a subclass of employees; that is, we create a subclass *MgrType* from class *EmpType*. For example,

---

[8] The reader should note a difference between methods like *new*, which are sent to the name of a class, and methods like *getName* in Figure 5.20, which are sent to instances of that class. The former are called *class methods*, and the latter *instance methods*, or just "methods." Both kinds of methods are inherited by subclasses.

```
Object subclass:  'Itemtype'
   instVarNames:  #['name', 'number']
   constraints:  #[#[ #name, String],
      #[ #number, Integer]].
Set subclass:  'ItemSet'
   constraints:  ItemType.
Object subclass:  'IQType'
   instVarNames:  #['item', 'quantity']
   constraints:  #[#[ #item, ItemType],
      #[ #quantity, Integer]].
Set subclass:  'IQset'
   constraints:  IQType.
Object subclass:  'OrderType'
   instVarNames:  #['ordno', 'includes']
   constraints:  #[#[ #ordno, Integer],
      #[ #includes, IQset]].
Set subclass:  'OrderSet'
   constraints:  OrderType.
Object subclass:  'CustType'
   instVarNames:  #['name', 'addr', 'balance', 'orders']
   constraints:  #[#[ #name, String],
      #[ #addr, String],
      #[ #balance, Integer],
      #[ #orders, OrderSet]].
Object subclass:  'DeptType'
   instVarNames:  #['name', 'deptno',
      'emps', 'mgr', 'items']
   constraints:  #[#[ #name, String],
      #[ #deptno, Integer],
      #[ #emps, EmpSet],
      #[ #mgr, EmpType],
      #[ #items, ItemSet]].
Object subclass:  'EmpType'
   instVarNames:  #['name', 'salary', 'dept']
   constraints:  #[#[ #name, String],
      #[ #salary, Integer],
      #[ #dept, DeptType]].
```

**Figure 5.22(a)** OPAL classes for the YVCB database (begin).

```
Set subclass:  'EmpSet'
   constraints:  EmpType.

Object subclass:  'IPType'
   instVarNames:  #['item', 'price']
   constraints:  #[#[ #item, String],
       #[ #price, Integer]].

Set subclass:  'IPset'
   constraints:  IPType.

Object subclass:  'SupType'
   instVarNames:  #['name', 'addr', 'supplies']
   constraints:  #[#[ #name, String],
       #[ #addr, String],
       #[ #supplies, IPSet]].

Set subclass:  'CustSet'
   constraints:  CustType.

Set subclass:  'SuppSet'
   constraints:  SupType.

Set subclass:  'DeptSet'
   constraints:  DeptType.
```

**Figure 5.22(b)**  OPAL classes for the YVCB database (continued).

we could then declare the *mgr* instance variable of *DeptType* of Figure 5.22(a) constrained to be of type *MgrType*, rather than *EmpType*. Managers will have an additional instance variable (field) *rank*, which is a character string, along with all of the instance variables that employees possess. We can express this situation by declaring class *MgrType*, as follows.

```
EmpType subclass:  'MgrType'
   instVarNames:  #['rank']
   constraints:  #[#[ #rank, String]].
```

Then, objects of type *MgrType* have the instance variables, or "fields," *name*, *salary*, and *dept*, as well as *rank*. The methods we define for *EmpType* in the next section are also applicable to objects of type *MgrType*. □

## 5.7  DATA MANIPULATION IN OPAL

In all of the other languages we have discussed so far, once the database scheme is declared, we immediately have available certain data manipulation operations. For example, relational languages give us relational algebra or calculus, plus insertion, deletion, and modification operations; DBTG and IMS databases provide FIND and GET, respectively, to do search and retrieval from the database, as well as providing insert, delete, and modify operations. In OPAL, however, even the most primitive operations must be declared for each class we define.

For example, it would be normal that for each instance variable, we should have a way of obtaining the value of that variable given an instance. It would also be typical that we should have a way of changing the value of that variable, given an instance. We shall, in what follows, assume that for each instance variable $X$ in any class, there is a method $getX$ that returns the value of $X$, when the message with that name is sent to an object of the appropriate class. Also, there is a method

$storeX: v$

that sets $X$ to value $v$ when sent to an object with an instance variable $X$.[9]

**Example 5.31:** For class $ItemType$ we could declare the methods of Figure 5.23. $\square$

```
method:  ItemType
    getName
            ^name
%

method:  ItemType
    getNumber
            ^number
%

method:  ItemType
    storeName:  n
        name := n
%

method:  ItemType
    storeNumber:  n
        number := n
%
```

**Figure 5.23** Methods for $ItemType$.

---

[9] It is possible to create methods like these automatically by sending the class name the message $compileAccessMethodsFor:$, followed by a list of instance variables.

## Insertion

As we saw in Section 5.6, sets can be used as if they were relations. We might therefore want to define a method for some class that was a set of "tuples," to allow us to create new tuple objects and insert them.[10] The scenario is as follows. Suppose we have a class $T$ that serves as "tuples," e.g., *ItemType* in Figure 5.22(a). Suppose also that $S$ is the class defined to be a set of $T$'s, as *ItemSet* in Figure 5.22(a). Then we would ordinarily create one instance of class $S$, say $r$, to serve as the "relation" of type $T$. We create $r$ by sending the message *new* to $S$, which understands this message because all classes do. That is, we execute:

```
r := S new.
```

Now, we can create a method, which we shall refer to as *insert*, for objects of type $S$. This method takes a value for each of the instance variables (fields or components) of class $T$. It creates a new object of type $T$, and sends that object an appropriate storeX message for each instance variable $X$. Finally, *insert* sends the *add* message to $r$, to add the new object; *add* is another built-in method that all sets understand.

**Example 5.32:** Suppose we have executed

```
Items := ItemSet new.
```

to create a "relation" *Items* that is a set of objects of class *ItemType*. We can then define the method *insert* as in Figure 5.24. Notice that "insert" does not appear as the name of the method; we only used that name informally. Rather, the method is identified by its two parameter names, *insertName:* and *insertNumber:*. Also note that surrounding *NewItem* with bars, as in line (4), is OPAL's way of declaring *NewItem* to be a local variable for the method.

Line (5) makes *NewItem* an object of class ItemType, and line (6) sets its instance variables to the desired values, *na* and *num*, which are the values of the parameters for this method. Note that two different methods, *storeName* and *storeNumber* are applied to the object *NewItem* in line (6), and the semicolon is punctuation to separate the two methods. Finally, line (7) adds the new tuple to the set to which the method being defined is applied; hence the receiver *self* for the method *add*.

Having declared *Items* to be the set of items for the YVCB database, we can add Cilantro, which is item 99, by sending it the message:

```
Items insertName:  'Cilantro' insertNumber:  99.
```

---

[10] We talk as if all actions had to be defined as methods. While it would be usual for something as fundamental as insertion into a set to be defined for that set's type, it is also possible to write all of the operations we describe here as parts of ordinary OPAL programs.

```
(1)  method:  ItemSet
(2)      insertName:  na
(3)      insertNumber:  num
(4)         | NewItem |
(5)         NewItem := ItemType new.
(6)         NewItem storeName:  na; storeNumber:  num.
(7)         self add:  NewItem.
(8)  %
```

**Figure 5.24** "Insert" method for items.

In the method of Figure 5.24, `'Cilantro'` will be the value of *na*, 99 will be the value of *num*, and *self* on line (7) refers to *Items*. $\square$

### Retrieval

Access to the database is obtained by following the paths that are implicit in the structure of the various classes. For example, one of the instance variables of each customer object is *orders*, which is constrained to be of class *OrderSet*, that is, a set of orders. By sending message *getOrders* to an object of type *CustType*, we are returned this set of orders; actually we get a pointer to a representative of the set, so this retrieval operation can be carried out cheaply, without copying large sets unless forced to do so.

Given this pointer, which OPAL sees as a set-valued object, we can visit each order in the set. From each order object we can reach, through its *includes* instance variable, an object that is an *IQset*, i.e., a set of item-quantity pairs. Similarly, from this object, we can reach each of the items in that order, and the quantity of each that was ordered.

We should notice the similarity between this way of exploring the objects in the database and the way we explored a tree in the hierarchical model. What we just described is very much like exploring a database record of the tree CUST_TREE in Figure 5.16, which has a customer record at the root, orders records for children of the root, and children of each order record consisting of a (virtual) item and its corresponding quantity. The principal difference is that in OPAL, all objects other than constants are "virtual." For example, orders records appear physically as children of customer records in the hierarchical database, but in the OPAL database, only pointers to orders appear in the object that is a set of orders. Furthermore, that set of orders does not appear physically in the customer record; only a pointer to that set-valued object does.[11]

---

[11] Of course, physical layout of either kind of database may allow the orders placed by a

There is also an analogy between the customer-order-item structure in Figure 5.22(a) and the DBTG record types (CUSTOMERS, ORDERS, ENTRIES, and ITEMS) and DBTG sets (PLACED_BY, E_ORDER, and E_ITEM) found in Figures 5.2 and 5.3. That is, the presence, in each customer object, of an object that is a set of orders, mirrors the PLACED_BY set, in which each customer owns a set of orders. The fact that each order object contains a set of item-quantity pairs is analogous to each order owning, via the E_ORDER set, a set of ENTRIES, each of which is effectively an item-quantity pair. The only apparent difference is that an ENTRIES record contains only the quantity, and we have to find its owner in the E_ITEM set to find the item. That is not really different from the arrangement in Figure 5.22(a), since there, the item object, while in principle present in the $IQType$ object, is actually represented there by a pointer to an object of class $ItemType$. On the other hand, the quantity in an $IQType$ object, being a constant, is physically present in the object, just as it was in the ENTRIES records of the DBTG database.

## The "Select" Method

OPAL provides several ways of exploring all the members of an object that is a set. One is by a method whose parameter name is *select:*. The parameter of a selection is a block of code with a single local variable that takes on, in turn, each of the members of the set as its value. The form of the message is

$$\text{select:} \quad [:X \mid <\text{code involving } X \text{ and}$$
$$\text{returning } true \text{ or } false>] \tag{5.3}$$

Here, :$X$, followed by a bar, declares $X$ to be a local variable. A block of code used as the parameter of a *select:* message must have exactly one local variable; this variable takes on each member of the receiver set as its value, in turn. A block such as that found in (5.3) will be called a *one-argument block*.

When a message of the form (5.3) is sent to an object $O$ of class $S$, which is a subclass of *Set*, a new object of class $S$ is returned. That object is the set of all objects $X$ in the set $O$ such that the body of the selection, evaluated for $X$, returns value *true*.

**Example 5.33:** Suppose we want to find the set of customers with balances less than 0. Let us suppose that our database contains an object *Customers*, of class *CustSet*, whose members are the objects for all the customers in the YVCB database. Then we can find the subset of these customers with negative balances by

---

customer to appear close to the record for that customer, which is what we really want if we are to retrieve the orders for a given customer quickly. In general, when we refer to "pointers," we really mean "some convenient representation that lets us locate the physical copy of the object easily"; physical contiguity could serve this purpose well.

```
Deadbeats := Customers select:   [:c | (c getBalance) < 0]
```

Here, variable $c$ takes on each customer object in turn. Sending the *getBalance* message to $c$ returns the balance of the customer, and if that value is less than 0, the block has value *true*. In that case, a pointer to the customer object represented by $c$ is placed in the set being formed by the selection, and when that set is complete, it is assigned to the new variable *Deadbeats*, which, like *Customers*, is of class *CustSet*. □

## The "Detect" Method

We can also send a set $S$ the message *detect:* followed by a one-argument block. The block is executed with its local variable equal to each member of $S$, in some order, until a member $x$ that makes the block true is found. Then, $x$ is produced as a value. Note that unlike the *select:* method, which produces a subset as value, *detect:* produces an element of the set that is its receiver.

**Example 5.34:** If we want to obtain the object for customer Zack Zebra, we could send the *Customers* set, mentioned in Example 5.33, the message

```
Zebra := Customers detect:
    [:c | (c getName) = 'Zack Zebra']
```

When $c$ takes on the object for customer Zebra, the body of the one-argument block will be true for the first time, so variable *Zebra* is assigned this object as its value. □

The *detect:* method can take a second parameter, *ifNone:*, which is followed by a (not necessarily one-argument) block. If a message of this type is sent to a set, none of whose elements satisfy the one-argument block following *detect:*, then the result of executing the block following *ifNone:* is returned.

**Example 5.35:** Let us attempt to answer the query "who has ordered Brie?" As in the previous examples, we assume the set of all customers is available in object *Customers*. While we could write the entire query as code, it is convenient to create two methods, which apply to sets of item-quantity pairs and to sets of orders, respectively, and are useful as subroutines.

The first applies to objects of class $IQSet$ and tells whether some member of the set has a given item. The code is shown in Figure 5.25(a). The method is identified by the parameter name *testFor:*, and it takes a parameter, $i$, which is the item we are looking for. We attempt to detect an item-quantity pair with item equal to $i$, by sending the *detect:* message to *self*, i.e., to the set of item-quantity pairs that received the *testFor:* message. The message *getItem:* retrieves the item object part of a typical item-quantity pair, $iq$. The message *getName* sent to that object produces the name of the item; i.e., it retrieves the *name* instance variable from the item object.

If the name equals *i*, this item-quantity object *iq* is the value produced by the detection. If there is no such object, then the block following *ifNone*: is executed, and this block simply returns the value *nil*, a built-in constant. The result of the detection is passed the message *notNil*. This built-in method returns *true* if passed to a value that is not *nil*. Thus, *testFor*: returns *true* if an item with name *i* is found and returns *false* if not.

```
method:  IQSet
   testFor:  i
      ^((self detect:  [:iq | ((iq getItem) getName) = i]
         ifNone:  [nil]) notNil)
%
```

(a) testFor applied to sets of item-quantity pairs.

```
method:  OrderSet
   testFor:  i
      ^((self detect:  [:o | (o getIncludes) testFor:  i]
         ifNone:  [nil]) notNil)
%
```

(b) testFor applied to order sets.

**Figure 5.25** Methods to find an item within orders.

The method of Figure 5.25(b) is also called *testFor*. Note that there is no reason the same name cannot be used for methods that apply to different classes, even if they are radically different, because objects know the class to which they belong, and therefore we can tell which method of a given name applies to a given object. The ideas behind this method are very similar to those behind Figure 5.25(a). However, here, instead of testing equality between an item name and the parameter value *i*, we apply the *testFor* method defined in Figure 5.25(a) to an object that is the entire set of entries for an order.

Finally, we can find who ordered Brie by saying:

```
BrieLovers := Customers select:
   [:c | (c getOrders) testFor:  'Brie']
```

☐

## Deletion

Let us reflect briefly on the different ways different types of systems perform deletion. Each of the relational systems, being value-oriented, deletes one or more tuples from a relation by specifying values in certain fields that the victim tuples must possess. On the other hand, network and hierarchical systems, being object-oriented, first locate the victim by making it the "current of run-unit" or the equivalent, and then delete the record independently of any values it may have. OPAL, being object-oriented, also needs to locate victim objects before it can delete them. However, in OPAL we have no currency pointers to keep track of objects automatically; rather we need to store the victim objects in variables used for that purpose.

If variable $O$'s value is an object in set $S$, then sending $S$ the message

$S$ remove: $O$

will delete that object from $S$.

There are several ways we could arrange that $O$ denotes an object in $S$. One approach is to use the *do*: method described below.

**The "Do" Method**

The method *do*: applies a block of code to each element of a set. This code is essentially a one-argument block, but it does not have to produce a Boolean value. The form of the *do*: method is:

do:  [: $X$  |  <code involving $X$>]

**Example 5.36:** Suppose we wish to delete all the orders that include Brie. One way to do this task is shown in Figure 5.26. There are two "do-loops"; the first lets variable $c$ range over all customers, that is, members of the object *Customers*, which we suppose is the relation that holds data about customers. In this loop we do two things. First, we assign the set of orders in each customer object to the local variable *OrdersForCust*. Then we use the inner do-loop to let variable $o$ range over all orders in this current set of orders.

The method *testFor* of Figure 5.25(b) is used to test whether an order includes Brie. If so, then we send the *remove*: message to *OrdersForCust*. The effect of that message is to remove the object $o$, which is an order that includes Brie, from the object that *OrdersForCust* denotes; that object is the value of the *orders* "field" of the current customer.

The reader should observe carefully how the object-oriented approach to data differs from the value-oriented approach. In OPAL, the value of *OrdersForCust* is not a copy of the set of orders for the customer; rather it is that set itself. Thus, deletions to *OrdersForCust* apply to the data of the database. In a relational system, *OrdersForCust* would be a view or a relation separate from *Customers*, and deletion from the former would either be prohibited or have no effect on the latter. □

**Index Creation**

To this point, we have described OPAL as if it were a general-purpose language,

```
| OrdersForCust |
Customers do:
    [:c |
        OrdersForCust := c getOrders.
        OrdersForCust do:
            [:o |
                ((o getIncludes) testFor:  'Brie')
                ifTrue:  [OrdersForCust remove:  o]
            ]
    ]
```

**Figure 5.26**  Delete all orders for Brie.

rather than a database language. In fact, OPAL provides the features of a DBMS outlined in Chapter 1, such as security (see Section 8.6) and concurrency control. Also very important for a database language is the ability to support efficient access to data. We shall now give a brief description of how one can create and use indices to speed up certain operations on large sets of objects.

Suppose $S$ is a set whose elements are of class $C$. Suppose also that objects of class $C$ have an instance variable $I$ whose values are constrained to be of a type with comparable values, e.g., numbers or character strings (an *elementary* type). Then we can create an index on $S$ by sending it the message

$S$ `createEqualityIndexOn:`  '$I$'

From then, certain uses of methods with one-argument blocks, such as *select*: will be executed in such a way that we do not have to examine all members of $S$ to perform the selection; this matter is discussed later in the section.

If $I$ is not constrained to be an elementary type, we cannot create an index on $I$, but we might be able to create such an index on a subfield of $I$. That is, suppose $I$ is constrained to have a value that is an object of class $D$, and $J$ is an instance variable of $D$, constrained to be of a particular elementary type. We can create the index for $S$ on the *path $I.J$*. This idea generalizes to paths $I_1.I_2.\cdots.I_n$ of any length, as long as:

1.  $S$ is a set constrained to have elements of some class $C$, and $C$'s objects have instance variable $I_1$.
2.  For $j = 1, 2, \ldots, n-1$, $I_j$ is an instance variable constrained to be of some class whose members have instance variable $I_{j+1}$.
3.  $I_n$ is an instance variable constrained to be of elementary type.

Then we can send $S$ the message

$S$ `createEqualityIndexOn:`  $I_1.I_2.\cdots.I_n$

to speed up accesses to elements of $S$ whose $I_1$ "field" has a value in its $I_2$ "field" that has $\cdots$ that has a given value in its $I_n$ "field."

**Example 5.37:** Suppose *IQPs* is a variable whose value is a set of item-quantity pairs. Its elements are of class *IQtype* [see Figure 5.22(a)], and one of the instance variables for *IQtype* is *item*, which is constrained to be of class *ItemType*. That class, in turn, has instance variable *name*, which is of elementary type *String*. Thus, we may create an index for *IQPs* based on the path *item.name*, that is, on the actual name of the item in the pair. The command is

```
IQPs createEqualityIndexOn:  'item.name'
```

☐

### Identity Indices

We can also create indices on subparts of the elements of a set, even if those subparts are not of elementary type. We base these indices on the object identity of the objects found in those fields. The paths referring to such fields are of the same form $I_1.I_2.\cdots.I_n$ as for equality indices, but condition (3) does not necessarily hold; that is, $I_n$ does not have to be constrained to be of an elementary type.

**Example 5.38:** We could have based an index for *IQPs* of Example 5.37 on the object identity of the item objects themselves. That is, we could say

```
IQPs createIdentityIndexOn:  'item'
```

Note that the parameter name mentions "identity" rather than "equality." ☐

### Using Indices

When we create one or more indices on an object that is a set, that object functions like a database object, for example, as a relation or as a logical record type. To take advantage of efficient retrieval from such sets, we must use a *selection block*, which is a one-argument block whose body is a conjunction (logical AND) of comparisons. Each comparison must relate two variables or constants by one of the arithmetic comparison operators.

If we wish to take advantage of an equality index, we can use any of the usual six comparisons on values, which are written =, ~=, <, >, <=, and >= in OPAL. If we wish to use an identity index, which we should recall is on the objects' identities (i.e., pointers to objects) themselves, then the last four of these make no sense, and we are restricted to the two comparisons on object identities, == (the same object) and ~~ (different objects).

Selection blocks are distinguished from ordinary one-argument blocks by the use of curly brackets {} rather than square brackets []. If there is no appropriate index to use, the effect of a selection block does not differ from that of the corresponding one-argument block. However, if there is an index that can help, retrieval takes time roughly proportional to the number of objects found, rather than to the size of the whole set.

**Example 5.39:** Suppose we have the set *IQPs* from Example 5.37, and we also have the index on *item.name* for this set. Then we can find all the item-quantity pairs where the item name is "Brie" by using the following selection block.

```
BriePairs := IQPs select:  {:p | p.item.name = 'Brie'}
```

Note that the path *p.item.name* takes us to the *name* field of the *item* field of a typical item-quantity pair object *p*, and it is on the *name* field that the index for *IQPs* is organized. Moreover, the value in this field is compared with a constant, "Brie." It is in exactly this situation, where the field used for the index is compared with a constant, that the index can be of use. Thus, the pairs with item name "Brie" are found directly, without searching the whole set *IQPs*.

If we had the identity index of Example 5.38 instead, then we could also use it to find certain item-quantity pairs. Now, suppose we want those pairs for which the item is Brie. We are now looking for pairs with a particular object as item, so we need a name for this object to use in a comparison. Suppose that we obtain, perhaps by a *detect:* operation on the set of items, the Brie object, which becomes the value of variable *BrieObject*. Then we can obtain the members of *IQPs* that have Brie as the item by

```
BriePairs := IQPs select:  {:p | p.item == BrieObject}
```

Notice that the symbol == is used to require that the values being compared be the same object, not merely objects with the same value, as = requires. As with the previous selection, the identity index on *item* helps us find all the desired pairs quickly. □

## EXERCISES

5.1: In Exercise 2.8 we discussed information about the ingredients of certain dishes.
   a)   Define a network to represent the data, using the DBTG DDL.
   b)   Show the links in your network for the particular data given in Exercise 2.8.

5.2: Suppose we have the following record types:

    COMPANY(CNAME, CADDR)
    STOCK(SH_NO, QUANTITY)
    PERSON(PNAME, PADDR)

Let there also be the following DBTG sets.

*i*)   EMP, with member PERSON and owner COMPANY, indicating the employees of a company.

*ii*)  OWNS, with member STOCK and owner PERSON, indicating which person owns which stock certificates.

*iii*) ST_CO, with member STOCK and owner COMPANY, indicating the company to which a stock certificate pertains.

You may assume the location mode for each record is CALC, with keys CNAME, SH_NO, and PNAME, respectively. Write programs in the "Pidgin" DBTG data manipulation language of this chapter, to do the following:

a)   Read a share number and print the name and address of the person owning the share.

b)   List all persons owning stock in IBM. You may list a person owning two certificates twice.

c)   List all persons owning stock in the company they work for. (Assume a singular set of persons exists.)

d)   Determine the total quantity of stock in IBM owned by its employees.

5.3:  Suppose we wish to enter new shares into the database of Exercise 5.2, and we want a new share to be entered into the correct OWNS and ST_CO set occurrences when the stock record is stored.

a)   Suggest set selection clauses that will enable the automatic insertion to be performed.

b)   Write a program to read the necessary data and store the new stock record correctly.

c)   Suppose we wish to use manual insertion instead of automatic. Write a program to store STOCK records and insert them in the proper OWNS and ST_CO occurrences manually.

5.4:  In Figure 5.27 is a hierarchical database scheme representing the navies of the world. Assume for convenience that each record type has a field NAME that serves as a key. Write queries in Pidgin DL/I to do the following:

a)   Print all squadrons that have at least one submarine.

b)   Print all countries that have a squadron with at least two cruisers.

* c) Print all countries that have a fleet with at least two cruisers.

* d) Read a naval base and print the country to which it belongs.

e)   Read a country, fleet, squadron, and the name of a submarine and enter the submarine into the proper squadron.

5.5:  What additional structure added to the database scheme would make it possible to execute the query of Exercise 5.4(d) efficiently?

5.6:  Express the hierarchy of Figure 2.32(b) in the Pidgin DDL for IMS that was described in Section 5.4.

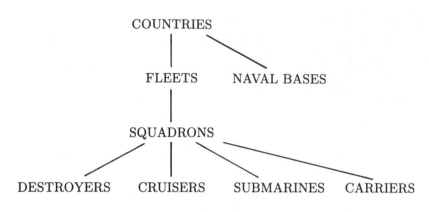

**Figure 5.27** Naval database.

5.7: In Figure 5.28(a) is a hierarchy for a real estate corporation's database, and in Figure 5.28(b) are the fields in each of the logical record types. Write Pidgin DL/I queries to answer the following questions:

a)   Find the addresses of all listings selling for over one million dollars.

b)   Find an agent in the Princeton, NJ office whose sales are over one million dollars. You may assume that there is only one city named Princeton in the Northeast region, although there may be cities with that name in other regions.

c)   Find all the clients of agent Sam Slick. Assume that there is only one agent with that name among all the offices.

5.8: Perform the following updates on the hierarchical database of Figure 5.28, using the Pidgin DL/I of Section 4.5.

a)   Add the fact that Joe Nebbish, who lives at 74 Family Way, is now a client of agent Sam Slick.

b)   Add 100,000 to the sales of Sam Slick.

c)   Delete all listings of the Princeton (Northeast region) office.

5.9: We wish to define an OPAL object that looks like the relation

$$FSO(F, S, O)$$

which was discussed in Exercise 4.8.

a)   Write the commands to define the appropriate class for such an object.

b)   Write the command to create an object $FSO$ of the desired class.

c)   Write a command that can be used to insert a "tuple" into $FSO$, given its file name, size, and owner.

d)   Write a query to find all the files owned by Sally Hacker.

e)   Declare an index that will speed up the answer to query (d).

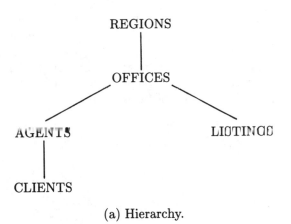

(a) Hierarchy.

REGIONS(RNAME)
OFFICES(CITY, OADDR)
AGENTS(ANAME, SALES)
LISTINGS(LADDR, PRICE)
CLIENTS(CNAME, CADDR)

(b) Record formats.

**Figure 5.28** Real estate database.

5.10: In Exercise 2.11(f) we defined a scheme for courses, students, and grades in the object model of Section 2.7. Translate that scheme into data definitions of OPAL.

5.11: Write the following queries in (*i*) the DBTG DML (*ii*) DL/I (*iii*) OPAL. Refer to the databases defined in (*i*) Figures 5.2 and 5.3 (*ii*) Figure 5.16 (*iii*) Figure 5.22, respectively.

    a)   Find all the employees of the Produce department.

    b)   Find the items supplied by Acme.

    c)   Find the suppliers of the items sold by the Produce department.

  * d)   Find the manager of the department Arnold Avarice works for.

5.12: Give OPAL data definitions for the beer drinkers' database of Exercise 4.1. Create suitable classes for drinkers, bars, and beers, that make all the important connections accessible. For example, the object for a bar consists of a field (instance variable) for the name of the bar, a field for the set of drinkers who frequent the bar, and a field for the set of beers sold at the bar. Also, declare OPAL variables *Drinkers*, *Bars*, and *Beers* to represent the sets of objects of the three classes.

* 5.13: Write OPAL programs to answer the queries of Exercise 4.1, using the database you defined in answer to Exercise 5.12. Assume that *getX* has been defined for every instance variable $X$ of every class. As we have not discussed printing in OPAL, assign the results of the queries to suitable variables. *Hint:* The following methods that were not covered in the text may prove useful here and in following exercises:

   *i*)   $B$ *not* produces the complement of the Boolean value $B$.

   *ii*)  $S$ *includes*: $O$ produces the value *true* if object $O$ is a member of set $S$ and *false* if not.

   *iii*) $S$ *isEmpty* produces *true* if $S$ is an empty set and *false* otherwise.

  5.14: Write the queries of Exercise 4.3 in OPAL, referring to the database of Exercise 5.12.

* 5.15: Write an OPAL program to find the sum of all the customers' balances in the YVCB database.

* 5.16: Suppose we have defined employee-manager pair objects with the following OPAL declaration:

```
Object subclass:  'EMpair'
    instVarNames:  #['emp', 'mgr']
    constraints:  #[ #[#emp, String], #[#mgr, String]]
```

Also suppose that *Manages* is a set of employee-manager pairs. Write an OPAL method that finds, in *Manages*, all the subordinates of a given individual $i$, that is, all the individuals of whom $i$ is the "boss" in the sense of Example 1.12.

## BIBLIOGRAPHIC NOTES

A number of references concerning object-oriented systems and models were given in the bibliographic notes for Chapters 1 and 2. Here, we shall add references to particular database management systems.

### Network-Model Systems

As was mentioned, the DBTG proposal comes from CODASYL [1971, 1978]. Olle [1978] is a tutorial on the proposal.

   Among the important systems based on this proposal are TOTAL (Cincom [1978]), IDMS (Cullinane [1978]), and ADABAS (Software AG [1978]). Each of these systems is described in Tsichritzis and Lochovsky [1977], and TOTAL is also described in Cardenas [1979].

## IMS

The material in Sections 5.4 and 5.5 is based on IBM [1978b]. More extensive descriptions of the system can be found in Date [1986], Tsichritzis and Lochovsky [1977], and Cardenas [1979].

## System 2000

Another important system based on the hierarchical model is System 2000 (MRI [1978]). For descriptions, see Tsichritzis and Lochovsky [1977], Cardenas [1979], or Wiederhold [1983].

## OPAL

The description of the language in Sections 5.6 and 5.7 is taken from Servio Logic [1986]. The underlying Smalltalk language is defined in Goldberg and Robson [1980]. The Gemstone database management system, of which OPAL is the user interface, is described in Maier, Stein, Otis, and Purdy [1986].

# CHAPTER 6

## Physical
## Data
## Organization

We have alluded many times to the need to make operations like selection from a relation or join of relations run efficiently; for example, selections should take time proportional to the number of tuples retrieved, rather than the (typically much larger) size of the relation from which the retrieval is made. In this chapter we cover the basic techniques of storage organization that make these goals realistic.

We begin by discussing key-based organizations, or "primary index" structures, in which we can locate a record quickly, given values for a set of fields that constitute a key. These organizations include hashing, indexed-sequential access, and B-trees. Then we consider how these structures are modified so we can locate records, given values for fields that do not constitute a key and whose values do not, in principle, influence the location of the record. These structures are called "secondary indices."

Then, we explore what happens when the objects stored, which we think of as records, have variable-length. This situation includes both true variable-length records, e.g., those containing fields that are strings of arbitrary length, and structures that are more complex than records, such as a record for a department followed by records for all of the employees of that department. We next show how these techniques are used to support efficient access in the database systems that we discussed in Chapters 4 and 5.

In the last sections, we discuss partial-match queries and range queries, two classes of database operations that are increasing in importance as database systems tackle the new kinds of applications discussed in Section 1.4. We offer two data structures to support systems where these types of queries are common: partitioned hashing and k-d-trees.

294

## 6.1 THE PHYSICAL DATA MODEL

The physical database is a stored collection of *records*, each consisting of one or more fields. The values of fields are of an elementary type, such as integers, reals, and fixed-length character strings. We also include among our elementary types the *pointer*, which is a reference to a record; we shall discuss the nature of a pointer in more detail later in this section. At times, certain other types, such as variable-length character strings, will be treated as elementary.

Records are used to store physically each of the basic data objects found in the various data models we have discussed. For example:

1.  A tuple can be stored as a record; each component of the tuple is stored in one field.

2.  A logical record, as used in the network and hierarchical models, can be stored as a record. The fields of the logical record are fields of the physical record. In the case that a field of a logical record in a hierarchy is a virtual record of some type $T$, its corresponding field in the physical record is a pointer to a record of type $T$.

3.  An OPAL object can be stored as a record. Instance variables whose values are elementary objects, e.g., integers, have their values stored physically in fields, while instance variables whose values are objects of a user-defined class are represented by fields containing pointers to objects (i.e., pointers to the records representing these objects).

### Files

As with the higher-level data models, it is normal to see records as being instances of a scheme. That is, normally we deal with collections of records that have the same number of fields, and whose corresponding fields have the same data type, field name, and intuitive meaning. For example, records representing the tuples of a single relation have a field for each attribute of that relation, and the field for each attribute has the data type associated with that attribute. Let us term the list of field names and their corresponding data types the *format* for a record.

We shall use the term *file* for a collection of records with the same format. Thus, for example, a file is an appropriate physical representation for a relation. This notion of a file differs from the common notion of a "file" as a stream of characters, or perhaps other types of elements, accessible only by scanning from beginning to end. In practice, we shall find that files are normally accessible in many different ways, and their records often are not stored as a single stream or sequence.

### Two-Level Storage

The physical storage medium in which records and files reside can normally be thought of as a large array of bytes numbered sequentially. For example, storage may be a virtual memory space whose bytes are numbered from 0 up to some large number, probably in the range $2^{24}$ to $2^{30}$. This virtual memory would be stored physically on secondary storage devices, such as disks. On a computer system that does not support virtual memory, the physical storage might be thought of as the sequence of bytes on a disk or collection of disks, ordered in some simple way.

When the amount of data in our database is large, we should not picture storage as the main memory of the computer. Rather, we must take into account the fact that in order to operate upon any of the data in the database, that data must be moved from the secondary storage device upon which it resides, into main memory. Further, this transfer of data from secondary to main memory, or back, is very slow, compared with the typical things that one does with the data once it is brought to main memory.

## Blocks

Another factor that influences the way we account for costs in database operations is that it is normal for storage to be partitioned into *blocks* of some substantial number of bytes, say $2^9$ through $2^{12}$, and for transfers of data between secondary and main memory to occur only in units of a full block. This constraint applies whether we have a system that supports virtual memory, in which case that memory is partitioned into blocks of consecutive bytes, or whether our secondary storage is thought of as the bytes of a disk, in which case a block might be a sector of a single track.

It is common that records are significantly smaller than blocks, so we frequently find several records on one block. Since our costs are so closely tied to the number of blocks we move between main and secondary memory, it becomes very important to arrange that, when we have to access several records of a file, they tend to lie on a small number of different blocks. Ideally, when we access a block, we need to access all, or almost all, the records on that block.

## The Cost of Database Access

We shall define the unit of cost for operations on physical blocks to be the *block access*, which is either the reading from or writing into a single block. We assume that computation on the data in a block does not take as much time as transferring a block between main and secondary memory, so the cost of computation will generally be neglected.

In reality, not every time we need to read or write the contents of a block will the block be transferred to or from secondary memory. The operating system or the DBMS itself will *buffer* blocks, keeping copies around in main memory as long as there is room and remembering they are there. However, we often cannot predict whether a block will be available in main memory when we need it, since it may depend on factors beyond our control, such as what other jobs are running on the system at the time, or what other database operations are being executed as a result of requests from other users.

Conversely, the time to access a particular block on a disk depends on the place where the last access on that disk was made, because of the time to move the heads from cylinder to cylinder and the time it takes a disk to rotate from one angular position to another. Systems that deal with the largest amounts of data often need to take into account the exact sequence in which block accesses are made and design the layout of blocks on the disk units accordingly. These systems are often quite limited in the class of operations on data that they perform, compared with the data manipulation languages discussed in Chapters 4 and 5. We shall, therefore, not consider access costs at this level of detail.

In summary, we assume there is some fixed probability that the need to use a block will actually result in a transfer of data between main and secondary memory. We also suppose that the cost of an access does not depend on what accesses were made previously. With that agreed, we can assume each block access costs the same as any other, and thus we justify the use of block accesses as our measure of running time.

## Pointers

In essence, a pointer to a record $r$ is data sufficient to locate $r$ "quickly." Because of the variety of data structures used to store records, the exact nature of a pointer can vary. The most obvious kind of pointer is the absolute address, in virtual memory or in the address system of a disk, of the beginning of record $r$.

However, absolute addresses are often undesirable; for several reasons, we might permit records to move around within a block, or perhaps within a group of blocks. If we moved record $r$, we would have to find all pointers to $r$ and change them. Thus, we often prefer to use as a pointer a pair $(b, k)$, where $b$ is the block on which a record $r$ is found, and $k$ is the key value for $r$, that is the value of the field or fields serving as a key for records in the file to which $r$ belongs. If we use such a scheme, then in order to find $r$ within block $b$ we need to rely on the organization of blocks so that we can find $r$ within $b$. The matter of block formats is discussed below, but as an example, in order to find $r$ in block $b$, given its key $k$, it is sufficient to know that:

1.  All records in block $b$ have the same record format as $r$ (and therefore, none can agree with $r$ in its key fields),
2.  The beginnings of all the records in block $b$ can be found (so we can examine each in turn, looking for key $k$), and
3.  Each record in block $b$ can be decoded into its field values, given the beginning of the record (so we can tell if a record has key $k$).

## Pinned Records

When records may have pointers to them from unknown locations, we say the records are *pinned*; otherwise they are *unpinned*. If records are unpinned, they can be moved around within blocks, or even from block to block, with no adverse consequences, as long as the movement of blocks makes sense from the point of view of the data storage structure. However, when records are pinned, we cannot move them at all, if pointers are absolute addresses, and we can move them only within their block if a block-key-pair scheme is used for pointers.

Another constraint we face when records are pinned is that we cannot delete them completely. If there were a pointer $p$ to record $r$, and at some time we deleted $r$, we might, at a later time place some other record $r'$ in the space formerly occupied by $r$. Then, if we followed pointer $p$, we would find record $r'$ in place of $r$, yet have no clue that what we found was not the record $r$ to which $p$ was intended to refer. Even if we use block-key pairs for pointers, we are not completely safe from this problem, known as *dangling pointers* or *dangling references*. The reason is that $r'$ might have the same key value as $r$, since it was inserted into the file after $r$ had left, and therefore, caused no violation of the principle of unique key values.

To avoid dangling pointers, each record must have a bit called the *deleted bit*, that is set to 1 if the record is deleted. The space for the record can never again be used, but if we go searching for a record, say by following a pointer, and we come upon the deleted record, we know the record isn't really there and ignore it.

## Record Organizations

When we arrange the fields in a record, we must place them in such a way that their values can be accessed. If all fields have fixed length, then we have only to choose an order for those fields. Each field will thus begin at a fixed number of bytes, called its *offset*, from the beginning of the record. Then, whenever we come upon a record known to have the format in question, we can find a field, given the beginning of the record, by moving forward a number of bytes equal to the offset for that field.

There may be several bytes, not devoted to data fields, that are required in each record. For example, under some circumstances we need:

1.  Some bytes that tell us what the format of the record is. For example, if we are storing records belonging to several record types or several relations, we may wish to store a code indicating the type or relation of each. Alternatively, we can store only one type of record in any block, and let the block indicate the type of all of its records.
2.  One or several bytes telling how long the record is. If the record is of a type that has only fixed-length fields, then the length is implicit in the type

information.

3. A byte in which a "deleted" bit, as described above, is kept.

4. A "used/unused" bit, kept in a byte by itself, or sharing a byte with other information such as the "deleted" bit. This bit is needed when blocks are divided into areas, each of which can hold a record of some fixed length. We need to know, when we examine an area, whether it really holds a record, or whether it is currently empty space, with some random data found therein.

5. Waste space. We might put useless bytes in a record's area is so that all fields can begin on a byte whose address is a convenient number. For example, many machines operate on integers more efficiently if they begin at an address divisible by 4, and we shall assume this requirement here.

**Example 6.1:** Let us introduce a simple, running example for this chapter. We suppose that records of the type *numbers* consist of the following fields:

1. Field NUMBER, of type integer, which serves as a key. It is intended that this field always holds a positive integer.

2. Field NAME, which is a single byte indicating the first letter of the English name for the number in the first field. All positive integers have names that begin with one of the letters in the word *soften*, but there is no known significance to this fact.

3. Field SQUARE, which holds the square of the number in the first field. In this example, SQUARE is of type integer. In other examples, we shall let SQUARE be a character string holding the digits of the number in question; the purpose of the latter arrangement is so this field can vary in length.

On the assumption that integers take four bytes, the three fields above take a total of nine bytes. To this quantity, we shall add another byte, at the beginning of the record, which holds a used/unused bit and a "deleted" bit. We shall call this the *INFO* byte.

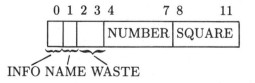

**Figure 6.1** A fixed-length record format.

However, recall we suppose integers must begin at an address that is a multiple of 4. Thus, it makes the most efficient use of space if we choose as our record organization the order: INFO, NAME, NUMBER, SQUARE, placing two waste bytes after NAME so the last two fields can be properly aligned. The arrangement is suggested in Figure 6.1, and it uses 12 bytes per record. □

## Variable-Length Records

When fields can vary in length, we have additional record-formating problems, because we cannot rely on fields being at the same offset in each record with a given format. There are two general strategies:

1. Let each field of variable length start with a *count*, that tells how many bytes the field value uses. If there is more than one variable-length field, it is sometimes useful to have in the beginning of the record a count of the total length of the record, although that information is, in principle, redundant.

2. Place, in the beginning of each record, pointers to the beginning of each variable-length field. We also need a pointer to the end of the last such field. Furthermore, it is necessary to have all the fixed-length fields precede the variable-length fields, so the end of one is the beginning of the next.

Scheme (1) uses less space, but it is time-consuming to locate fields beyond the first variable-length field, since we can only calculate the offset of a field if we examine all previous variable-length fields, in turn, to determine how long they are. We shall give a simple example of (1) below. Scheme (2) can be used not only for storing fields within records but for storing records within blocks, and we shall give an example of such an arrangement when we cover block formats.

**Example 6.2:** Let us consider *numbers* records, as introduced in Example 6.1, but with the field SQUARE stored as a character string composed of its decimal digits. The bytes of this field will be preceded by a single byte whose value is the number of (additional) bytes used by the SQUARE field. Thus, character strings for this field are limited to the range 0 to 255, which is a common treatment for variable-length character strings. The fields and information bytes of the record are:

1. Byte 0 holds the length of the entire record, including the variable-length field. Thus, the limit on field SQUARE is somewhat more stringent than 255 bytes, since the whole record must use no more than 255 bytes.
2. Byte 1 holds the INFO bits, discussed in Example 6.1.
3. Byte 2 holds the field NAME.
4. Byte 3 is waste.
5. Bytes 4–7 hold the field NUMBER.
6. Byte 8 holds the length of the field SQUARE.
7. Bytes 9 and following hold the value of SQUARE, as a character string.

The contents of two records, for numbers 2 and 13, are shown in Figure 6.2.

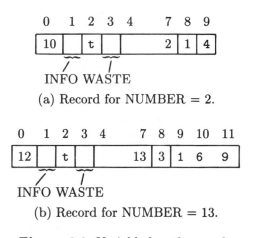

(a) Record for NUMBER = 2.

(b) Record for NUMBER = 13.

**Figure 6.2** Variable-length records.

Notice that because there is only one variable-length field, the length of the record and the length of that field are easily related, and we can dispense with either byte 0 or byte 8, but not both. That is, the value of byte 0 is always nine more than the value of byte 8.

Also note that if there were fields following SQUARE in this format, then we would have to consult byte 8 to find them. For example, the offset of a hypothetical field following SQUARE would have offset equal to nine plus the contents of byte 8. □

## Block Formats

Just as we need to locate fields within a record, we must be able to locate records within a block. As records require some space for format information, such as a length or a "deleted" bit, so do blocks often require some extra space for special purposes. For example, blocks often have pointers in fixed positions to link blocks into lists of blocks.

If integers and pointers within the records are required to start at "convenient" bytes, which we have taken (as a plausible example) to mean "divisible by 4," then we must be careful how we place records within a block. While many variations are possible, the simplest scheme is to assume that the offsets of integers and pointers within a record are always divisible by 4, and then require that records start with an offset within their block that is also divisible by 4. Since blocks themselves will begin at bytes that are multiples of some large power of 2, it follows that the *address* (first byte) of a block will also be divisible by 4, and thus, all fields that need to be aligned will start at bytes divisible by 4.

If a block holds fixed-length records, then we have only to partition the block into as many areas, each holding one record, as will fit on the block. Of course, if there are special fields belonging to the block, such as pointers among blocks, then space for these pointers must be reserved in a known place in each block. Any byte not usable either in a special field or as part of the area for a record, is waste space.

**Example 6.3:** In our examples we shall assume blocks of length 64, a number that is much too small to be realistic, but which will make our examples easier to follow. Suppose we wish to store records of the fixed-length format discussed in Example 6.1, and we also want blocks to have a pointer of 4 bytes, for use as a link to another block. Then the block layout of Figure 6.3 will serve and has no waste space. $\square$

```
0      11 12    23 24    35 36    47 48    59 60 63
┌─────────┬─────────┬─────────┬─────────┬─────────┬──────┐
│Record 1 │Record 2 │Record 3 │Record 4 │Record 5 │ Link │
└─────────┴─────────┴─────────┴─────────┴─────────┴──────┘
```

**Figure 6.3**  Block format for fixed-length records.

Incidentally, the format of Figure 6.3 assumes that a used/unused bit appears in each record, so we can find an empty area in which to insert a record, if one exists on the block. That scheme is time consuming, since we must visit each record area to see if it is unused. Instead, we could put all the used/unused bits for the record areas in a byte or bytes at the beginning of the block. That arrangement facilitates finding an empty area in which to place a newly inserted record.

**Example 6.4:** For the format of Example 6.3, grouping the used/unused bits happens to waste a lot of space. Because of our constraints about aligning records and integer- or pointer-valued fields at bytes divisible by 4, we could not reduce the length of records below 12, even if there were no need for an information byte in the records themselves. We would need only byte 0 of the block for all the used/unused bits, but we could not start the first record area until byte 4. Then, since we need the last four bytes for a link, we could only fit four record areas in the block, in bytes 4–15, 16–27, 28–39, and 40–51. Bytes 1–3 and 52–59 are now waste space. $\square$

### Blocks with Variable-Length Records

If we pack variable-length records into a block, with no special fields to help locate the beginnings of records, we can, in principle, still find each record. We assume the first record starts in byte 0, and there we can find the length of the record. Increasing that length to the next multiple of 4, we find the beginning of the second record; the length field in that record tells us where to find the third record, and so on.

Evidently, that is a cumbersome way to search the block, so a more desirable approach is to place at the beginning of the block a *directory*, consisting of an array of pointers to the various records in the block. These "pointers" are really offsets in the block, that is, the number of bytes from the beginning of the block to the place where the record in question starts.

The directory can be represented in several ways, depending on how we determine the number of pointers in the directory. Some choices are:

1.  Precede the directory by a byte telling how many pointers there are.

2.  Use a fixed number of fields at the beginning of the block for pointers to records. Fields that are not needed, because there are fewer records in the block than there are pointers, are filled with 0, which could not be the offset of a record under this scheme.

3.  Use a variable number of fields for pointers to records, with the last field so used holding 0, to act as an endmarker for the list of pointers.

**Example 6.5:** In Figure 6.4 we see a block holding variable-length records in the format of Example 6.2. The scheme for managing pointers to records could be either (2) or (3) above, since only the last of the four fields holds 0. The three records found are for numbers 2, 13, and 100; these have lengths 10, 12, and 14, respectively. Note that bytes 26–27 are waste, because of our need to start the second record at an offset that is a multiple of 4. Bytes 54–59 are waste because we cannot find a record, of the format discussed in Example 6.2, that fits in so small a space.

```
 0  3 4  7 8 11  12 15  16      25 26 27 28      39 40      53 54 59 60 63
┌────┬────┬────┬─────┬────────┬────┬──────────┬──────────┬────┬──────┐
│ 16 │ 28 │ 40 │  0  │Record 2│////│Record 13 │Record 100│////│ Link │
└────┴────┴────┴─────┴────────┴────┴──────────┴──────────┴────┴──────┘
```

**Figure 6.4** Block format for variable-length records.

We could have been more economical about the storage of offsets in the first four fields. Rather than using four bytes for each, we could have used a single byte for each offset, since in these tiny blocks, offsets are numbers in the range 0–63. In fact, even if blocks were of length 1024, which is a common choice, we still could have stored offsets in a single byte, assuming that offsets had to be divisible by 4 and storing the offset divided by 4, in the byte. □

### Semi-Pinned Records

Another reason for adopting the scheme of Figure 6.4 is that it has the effect of "unpinning" pinned records. If there are pointers to a record $r$ from outside the block, we make that pointer point to the field of the directory that holds the offset of $r$. We may then move $r$ around within the block, changing its offset in the directory as we do, and we never create a dangling reference.

Incidentally, when we have variable-length records, there is frequently a good reason why we would move these records around in the block. For example, the data in a record may grow or shrink, and we wish to make space by moving all following records to the right, or we wish to consolidate space and move subsequent records left. The number of records on the block may change, requiring us to create additional directory fields, and move records around to make the room.

Another advantage of the scheme of Figure 6.4 is that we can, in effect, delete pinned records. We move the "deleted" bit from the record itself to the directory, assuming there is room. Then, if we wish to delete a record $r$, we can reuse its space. We set the "deleted" bit in $r$'s directory entry, so if we ever follow a pointer to that entry, we shall know the record is no longer there. Of course, the directory entry is now dedicated to the deleted record permanently, but that is preferable to retaining the space for a large, deleted record.

## 6.2 THE HEAP ORGANIZATION

In the three following sections we shall consider data structures that are useful for *primary indices*, that is, for structures that determine the location of the records of a file. Generally, a primary index is based on a key for the file, and the location of a record is determined by its key value. It is also important that given the value for the key of a record, one can quickly find that record. In some of the organizations we shall discuss, the field or fields used as a "key" need not uniquely identify a record. However, if there are too many records with the same "key" value, then the time to find records may be much larger than expected.

In this section, we define the operations normally permitted on records within files. As a baseline for performance, we then examine the *heap* file organization, the most trivial organization, in which records are packed into blocks in no special order, and with no special organization to the blocks. We assume only that pointers to all of the blocks of the file are available, and we shall suppose that these pointers are stored in main memory. If there are too many blocks to store even these pointers in main memory, then the pointers themselves can be stored in blocks of secondary storage and retrieved when needed.

We shall consider how long it takes to do the three basic operations:

1. *Lookup.* Given a "key" value, find the record(s) with that value in its "key" fields. We put quotation marks around "key" because we need not assume that values for the field or fields forming a "key" uniquely determine a record.

2. *Insertion.* Add a record to the file. We assume that it is known that the record does not already exist in the file, or that we do not care whether or not an identical record exists. If we do wish to avoid duplication of records, then the insertion must be preceded by a lookup operation.

3. *Deletion.* Delete a record from the file. We assume it is not known whether the record exists in the file, so deletion includes the process of lookup.

4. *Modification.* Change the values in one or more fields of a record. In order to modify a record, we must find it, so we assume that modification includes lookup.

## Efficiency of Heaps

Suppose there are $n$ records, and that $R$ is the number of records that can fit on one block. If records are pinned, and deleted records cannot have their space reused, then we should understand $n$ to be the number of records that have ever existed; otherwise, $n$ is the number of records currently in the file. If records are of variable length, then take $R$ to be the average number of records that can fit in a block, rather than the exact number. Then the minimum number of blocks needed to store a file is $\lceil n/R \rceil$, or, since $n$ is normally much greater than $R$, about $n/R$.

Recall that the time to perform operations such as insertion, deletion, and lookup is measured by the number of blocks that must be retrieved or stored, between secondary and main memory. We shall assume, for uniformity among all our data structures, that initially, the entire file is in secondary memory. To look up a record in a heap, given its key, we must retrieve $n/2R$ blocks on the average, until we find the record, and if there is no record with that key, then we must retrieve all $n/R$ blocks.

To insert a new record, we have only to retrieve the last record of the heap, which is the one that has empty space within it. If the last block has no more room, then we must start a new block. In either case, we must write the block to secondary storage after we insert the record. Thus, insertion takes two block accesses, one to read and one to write.

Deletion requires us to find the record, i.e., perform a lookup, and then rewrite the block containing the record, for a total of $n/2R + 1$ accesses, on the average when the record is found, and $n/R$ accesses when the record is not found. If records are pinned, then the process of deletion is only the setting of the "deleted" bit. If records are not pinned, then we have the option of reclaiming the space of the record.

For deletions from files of fixed-length records, we can reclaim space by finding a record on the last block of the file, and moving it into the area of the deleted record. With luck, we can dispense with the last block altogether, if we have removed its last record. In general, compacting the file in this way minimizes the number of blocks over which it is spread, thereby reducing the number of blocks that must be retrieved in lookups and further deletions.

If records are of variable length, we can still do some compaction. If we use a format like that of Figure 6.4, we can slide records around in the block, making sure the pointers to those records, which are at the beginning of the block, continue to point to their records. If we create enough space in one block to move in a record from the last block, we might do so. However, when records vary in length, it is wise to keep some of the space in each block free, so when records on that block grow, we are unlikely to have to move a record to another block.

Finally, modification takes time similar to deletion. We need $n/2R$ block accesses for a successful lookup, followed by the writing of the one block containing the modified record. If records are of variable length, then we may want to, or be required to, read and write a few more blocks to consolidate records (if the modified record is shorter than the old record), or to find another block on which the modified record can fit, if that record has grown.

**Example 6.6:** Suppose we have a file of 1,000,000 records, of 200 bytes each. Suppose also that blocks are $2^{12} = 4096$ bytes long. Then $R = 20$; i.e., we can fit 20 records on a block. Thus, a successful lookup takes $n/2R = 25,000$ block accesses, and an unsuccessful one takes 50,000 block accesses. On the optimistic assumption that the retrieval of any block from disk takes .01 second, even successful lookups take over four minutes. The time to do modification and deletion are essentially the same as for lookup. Only insertion, which assumes no search of the file is necessary, can be done at "computer speed," that is, in a fraction of a second.

The directory of blocks takes a significant amount of space, perhaps so much that we would not want to keep it in main memory. Suppose that block addresses are four bytes long. Then we need 200,000 bytes, or 50 blocks, to hold the addresses of all the blocks. □

## 6.3 HASHED FILES

The basic idea behind the *hashed* file organization is that we divide the records in the file into *buckets*, according to the value of the key.[1] For each file stored in this manner there is a *hash function* $h$ that takes as argument a value for the key and produces an integer in the range 0 to $B - 1$, where $B$ is the number

---

[1] As in the previous section, we do not require that what we call a key field or fields uniquely determine a record, although for the sake of efficiency it is desirable that there not be many records with the same "key" value.

of buckets used for this file. The integer $h(v)$ is the *bucket number* for the key value $v$.

Each bucket consists of some (presumably small) number of blocks, and the blocks of each bucket are organized as a heap. There is an array of pointers, indexed from 0 to $B - 1$, which we call the *bucket directory*. The entry for $i$ in the bucket directory is a pointer to the first block for bucket $i$; we call this pointer the *bucket header*. All of the blocks in bucket $i$ are linked in a list by pointers, with a *null pointer*, some value that cannot be the address of a block, appearing in the last block of the list (or in the bucket header if the bucket is currently empty). It is common for $B$ to be sufficiently small that the entire bucket directory can reside in main memory, but if that is not the case, then the directory is spread over as many blocks as necessary, and each is called into main memory as needed.

### Hash Functions

There are many different kinds of functions one can use for the hash function $h$. It is essential that the range be $0, \ldots, B - 1$, and it is highly desirable that $h$ "hashes" keys; that is, $h(v)$ takes on all its possible values with roughly equal probability, as $v$ ranges over all possible key values. A great deal has been said about hash functions, and we do not intend to go into the subject deeply here; see Knuth [1973], for example.

A simple kind of hash function converts each key value to an integer, and then takes the remainder of that integer modulo $B$. If key values are integers to begin with, we simply compute $h(v) = v \bmod B$. If keys are character strings, we can convert strings to integers as follows. Divide a string into groups of characters, perhaps one or two characters per group, treat the bits representing the character group as an integer, and sum these integers.

If key values consist of values from several fields, convert each field's value to an integer, by a method such as the ones just mentioned, and take their sum, and divide the result by $B$, the number of buckets. A variety of other ways to produce "random" integers from data of other types exist, and good methods are not hard to discover.

**Example 6.7:** In Figure 6.5 we see a file of *numbers* records with the format introduced in Example 6.1, organized as a hashed file with four buckets; i.e., $B = 4$. We assume the parameters of Example 6.3, that is, records twelve bytes long, with up to five of these and a link packed into one block, as in Figure 6.3. We have stored a set of prime numbers, using the hash function $h(v) = v \bmod 4$.

Storing keys that are primes is one of the few foolish things one can do with a hash function that chooses buckets by taking remainders divided by $B$, the number of buckets. There can never be a prime that goes into bucket 0, except for $B$ itself, if $B$ is a prime. In Figure 6.5, there will never be a prime

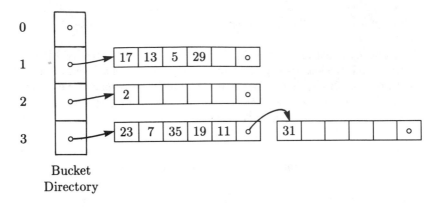

**Figure 6.5**  Hashed file organization.

in bucket 0, and only the prime 2 belongs in bucket 2. Thus, all the records for primes, except for 2, will distribute themselves in buckets 1 and 3, so we only get the benefit of two buckets, while paying for four buckets. $\square$

### Operations on Hashed Files

To look up a record with key value $v$, we compute $h(v)$, find the bucket header for that hash value, and examine the list of blocks in that bucket, as if the bucket were a heap. If the desired record is not found, there is no point in examining other buckets, because records whose keys have hash value $h(v)$ could not be placed in any other bucket. The lookup process does not depend on there being a unique record with "key" $v$, although if there is more than one, we must keep searching through bucket $h(v)$ to find them all, or we must be content with the first one we find.

To insert a record with key value $v$, we compute $h(v)$ and go to bucket $h(v)$. Presumably, only the last block of the bucket has room, so we must find that block.[2] We could search from the bucket header, down the list of blocks for the bucket, but there are two situations in which that would not be necessary:

1.    The insertion was preceded by a search through the bucket to check that the record we are inserting is not already there. In this case, we are already at the last block of the bucket.
2.    The data structure of Figure 6.5 is enhanced by an array of pointers to the last blocks of each bucket. Then we can find the desired block directly.

---

[2]  We might link blocks in the reverse order from that shown in Figure 6.5, i.e., with the last block to be added placed at the front of the list rather than at the end. However, if buckets tend to have few blocks, say one or two, then we would prefer to have a full block or blocks at the beginning of the list, so the number of blocks retrieved in a successful lookup is as small as possible.

Having found the last block, we place the inserted record therein, if there is room. If there is no room, we must obtain another block and link it to the end of the list for bucket $h(v)$.

Deletions are executed similarly. We find the record to be deleted as in a lookup. If records are pinned, then we simply set the "deleted" bit in the record. If records are unpinned, we have the option of compacting the blocks of the bucket, as we did for a heap in the previous section. So doing may reduce the number of blocks needed for this bucket, thereby reducing the average number of block accesses needed for subsequent operations.

**Example 6.8:** It is discovered that 35 is not a prime, so we wish to delete its record from the structure of Figure 6.5. We compute $h(35) = 35 \bmod 4$, which is 3, and so look in bucket 3, where we find the record for 35 in the first block on the list. Assuming records are unpinned, we can go to the last (second) block in bucket 3 and move a record from that block into the third area in the first block for bucket 3. In this case, the record for 31 is the only candidate, and it empties its block. We can thus remove the second block for bucket 3, leaving the situation in Figure 6.6. □

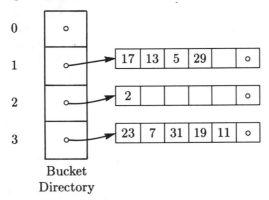

**Figure 6.6** Effect of deleting 35.

Finally, modifications are performed by doing a lookup. We then change the field or fields in those records that are to be modified. If records are variable-length, there is the possibility that records will have to be moved among the blocks of the bucket, as discussed in connection with heaps.

**Efficiency of Hashing**

The central point is that a hashed file with $B$ buckets behaves as if it were a heap approximately $1/B$th as long. Thus, we can speed up our operations by almost any desired factor, $B$, that we want. The limiting considerations are:

1.  Buckets must have at least one block, so we cannot lower the average
    lookup cost below one access per lookup, no matter how large we make $B$.
2.  We have to store the bucket directory, either in main memory or on blocks
    of secondary storage. Making $B$ too large forces us to use secondary storage
    and increase the number of block accesses by one per operation (to retrieve
    the block with the needed bucket header).

Thus, if we have a file of $n$ records, of which $R$ fit on a block, and we
use a hashed file organization with $B$ buckets, whose headers are kept in main
memory, we require on the average:

a)  $\lceil n/2BR \rceil$ accesses for a successful lookup, deletion of an existing record,
    or modification of an existing record.
b)  $\lceil n/BR \rceil$ accesses for an unsuccessful lookup, or for checking that a record
    is not in the file (during the attempted deletion of a nonexistent record or
    during a check for existence prior to an insertion).

The reason these relationships hold is that the average bucket has $n/B$
records, and we can apply the analysis for heaps from the previous section. It
should be emphasized that these estimates assume random records in our file.
If the hash function does not distribute records evenly among the buckets, or
if by bad luck, our file has an atypical collection of records, then the average
number of accesses per operation could rise considerably.

To these estimates, we must add one if the bucket directory is not in
main memory, and we must add an additional one for operations that require
modification and writing of one of the blocks of the bucket (i.e., for anything
but a lookup). If records are of variable length, and it may be necessary to move
records among blocks of the bucket, then a fraction of an access per operation
should be added.

**Example 6.9:** Let us consider the file with $n = 1,000,000$ and $R = 20$ discussed
in Example 6.6. If we choose $B = 1,000$, then the average bucket has $n/B =$
$1,000$ records, which would be distributed over $n/BR = 50$ blocks. On the
assumption block addresses require four bytes, the bucket directory requires
4,000 bytes, and could easily be kept in main memory. The operations requiring
examination of an entire bucket, such as lookup of a record that is not in the file,
take 50 block accesses, plus another one if writing of a block is needed, e.g., if
the operation is insertion preceded by a check that the record does not already
exist. Operations requiring search of only half the bucket on the average are
expected to require 25 or 26 accesses. Using our previous estimate of .01 second
per access, any of these operations can be performed in under a second. $\square$

## 6.4 INDEXED FILES

We now consider a second representation for files that are to be accessed via
a key. This organization is often called *isam*, standing for *indexed sequential*

*access method.* The description of isam files that we shall give here assumes that keys are true keys, each belonging to a unique record of the file, rather than "keys" that determine a small number of records, as in the previous two sections. We leave as an exercise the generalization of the lookup technique to the case where keys are really "keys." For the isam representation, we are required to sort the records of a file by their key values, so let us first consider how data of arbitrary format is to be sorted.

## Sorting Keys

No matter what the domain of values for a field, we can, in principle, compare values from the domain, and therefore we can sort these values. The justification is that to be stored in a file, the values must be representable as bit strings, which can be ordered if we treat them as integers and use numerical order.

The usual domains of values, such as character strings, integers, and reals have conventional orders placed on them. For integers and reals we have numerical order. For character strings we have *lexicographic,* or *dictionary* order defined by $X_1 X_2 \cdots X_k < Y_1 Y_2 \cdots Y_m$, where the $X$'s and $Y$'s represent characters, if and only if either

1. $k < m$ and $X_1 \cdots X_k = Y_1 \cdots Y_k$, or
2. For some $i \leq min(k, m)$, we have $X_1 = Y_1, X_2 = Y_2, \ldots, X_{i-1} = Y_{i-1}$, and the binary code for $X_i$ is numerically less than the binary code for $Y_i$.

In ASCII or any other character code in common use, the order of the codes for letters of the same case is alphabetical order and the order of the codes for digits is the numerical order of the digits. Thus, for example, 'an' < 'and' by rule (1), and 'banana' < 'bandana' by rule (2) with $i = 4$.

If we have a key of more than one field, we can sort key values by first arbitrarily picking an order for the key fields. Records are sorted by the first field, which will result in an ordered sequence of clusters; each cluster consists of records with the same values in the first field. Each cluster is sorted by the value of the second field, which will result in clusters of records with the same values in the first two fields. These clusters are sorted on the third field, and so on. Note that this ordering is a generalization of lexicographic ordering for character strings where, instead of ordering lists of characters, we order lists of values from arbitrary domains.

**Example 6.10:** Suppose we have a key with two fields, both with integer values, and we are given the list of key values (2,3), (1,2), (2,2), (3,1), (1,3). We sort these on the value of the first field to get (1,2), (1,3), (2,3), (2,2), (3,1). The first cluster, with 1 in the first field, is by coincidence already sorted in the second field. The second cluster, consisting of (2,3) and (2,2), needs to be interchanged to sort on the second field. The third cluster, consisting of one record, naturally is sorted already. The sorted order is

$(1,2)$, $(1,3)$, $(2,2)$, $(2,3)$, $(3,1)$

☐

## Accessing Sorted Files

If we are willing to maintain a file of records sorted by key values, we can take advantage of the known order to find a record quickly, given its key value. We are probably familiar with at least two examples of searching for key values in a sorted list: using the dictionary and using the phone book. In both cases each page has in the upper left corner the first word or name on the page.[3] By scanning these first words, we can determine the one page on which our word (if a dictionary) or name (if a phone book) could be found.[4] This strategy is far better than looking at every entry on every page. Except for one page, which we must scan completely, we need only look at one entry per page.

To help speed access to a sorted file, (which we call the *main* file), we create a second file called a (*sparse*) *index*, consisting of pairs

(<key value>, <block address>)

For each block $b$ of the main file, there is a record $(v, b)$ in the index file; $v$ is a key value that is at least as low as any key value on block $b$, but higher than any key on any block that precedes $b$. Often, we initially pick $v$ to be the lowest key on block $b$, but as time goes on, $v$ could be strictly less than any of the keys remaining on that block. Also, it is convenient to use $v = -\infty$ if $b$ is the first block, where $-\infty$ is a value smaller than any real key.

The first field of $(v, b)$ is a key for the index file, and the index file is kept sorted by its key value. In a sense, an index file is like any other file with a key, but we may take advantage of the fact that in an index file, records are never pinned down by pointers from elsewhere. However, there is an important difference between index files and the general files we have been discussing. In addition to (possibly) wishing to do insertions, deletions, and modifications on index files, we wish to obtain the answer to questions of the form: given a key value $v_1$ for the file being indexed, find that record $(v_2, b)$ in the index such that $v_2 \leq v_1$ and either $(v_2, b)$ is the last record in the index, or the next record $(v_3, b')$ has $v_1 < v_3$. (Say that $v_2$ *covers* $v_1$ in this situation.) This is how we find the block $b$ of the main file that contains a record with key value $v_1$, since the index file is guaranteed to be sorted.

Operations of the above type rule out certain organizations for index files.

---

[3] The upper right contains the last word/name, but this information is redundant, since the first word/name of the next page provides equivalent information.

[4] In practice we use our intuitive feeling about the distribution of words/names to take an educated guess as to where our goal lies, and we do not search stolidly starting at page 1. We shall have more to say about adapting this idea to computer search later.

For example, it would not be convenient to use the hashed file organization of Section 6.3 for index files, since there is no way to find the value $v_2$ that covers $v_1$ in a hashed file without searching the entire file.

## Searching an Index

Let us assume the index file is stored over a known collection of blocks, and we must find that record $(v_2, b)$ such that $v_2$ covers a given key value $v_1$. The simplest strategy is to use *linear search*. Scan the index from the beginning, looking at each record until the one that covers $v_1$ is found. This method is undesirable for all but the smallest indices, as the entire index may be called into main memory, and on the average, half the index blocks will be accessed in a successful lookup. Yet even linear search of an index is superior to linear search of the main file; if the main file has $R$ records per block, then the index has only $1/R$th as many records as the main file. In addition, index records are usually shorter than records of the main file, allowing more to be packed on one block.

## Binary Search

A better strategy is to use *binary search* on the keys found in the index file. Suppose that $B_1, \ldots, B_n$ are the blocks of the index file (not main file), and $v_1, \ldots, v_n$ are the first keys found on $B_1, \ldots, B_n$, respectively. Let us look for the block of the main file where a record with key $v$ could be found. We first retrieve index block $b_{\lceil n/2 \rceil}$ and compare $v$ with its first key, say $w$. If $v < w$, repeat the process as if the index were on blocks $B_1 \cdots B_{\lceil n/2 \rceil - 1}$. If $v \geq w$, repeat the process as if the index were on $B_{\lceil n/2 \rceil} \cdots B_n$. Eventually, only one index block will remain. Use linear search on that block to find the key value in the index that covers $v$. There is a pointer to a block $B$ of the main file associated with this key, and if there is a record with key $v$, it will be on block $B$.

As we divide the number of blocks by two at each step, in $\lceil \log_2(n + 1) \rceil$ steps at most we narrow our search to one index block. Thus the binary search of an index file requires that about $\log_2 n$ blocks be brought into main memory. Once we have searched the index, we know exactly which block of the main file must be examined and perhaps must be rewritten to perform an operation on that file. The total number of block accesses, about $2 + \log_2 n$, is not prohibitive, as an example will show.

**Example 6.11:** Let us again consider the hypothetical file of 1,000,000 records described in Example 6.6. We assumed blocks were 4,096 bytes long, and records 200 bytes long. Since the length of the key matters here, let us assume the key field or fields use 20 bytes. As $R = 20$, i.e., 20 records fit on a block, the main file uses 50,000 blocks. We thus need the same number of records in the index file.

An index record uses 20 bytes for the key and 4 bytes for the pointer to a block of the main file. As many as 170 records of 24 bytes each could fit on one block, but that would leave no room for used/unused bits. Let us suppose 150 records are placed on one block of the index file. We would then require $50,000/150 = 334$ blocks for the index file; that is, $n = 334$ in the above calculation.

Linear search would require about 168 index block accesses on the average for a successful lookup, in addition to two accesses to read and write a block of the main file. However, if we use a binary search, accessing and rewriting a record of the main file requires $2 + \log_2 334$, or about 11 block accesses. In comparison, the hashed organization requires only three accesses, on the average, provided we use about as many buckets as there are blocks of the main file (one access to read the bucket directory, and two to read and write the lone block of the bucket).

However, there are some advantages of the sorted organization over the hashed file. In response to a query asking for records with keys in a given range, we would have to examine almost all the buckets of the hash table, if the range were substantial, so the hash table offers little help. On the other hand, the sorted organization allows us to look almost exclusively at those blocks of the index and the main file that contain relevant records. The only extra work we have to do is use binary search to find the first relevant index block, and look at some records outside the desired range in the first and last index blocks and the first and last blocks of the main file that we access. $\square$

### Interpolation Search

A method of searching an index that can be superior to binary search is known as *interpolation* or *address calculation* search. This method is predicated on our knowing the statistics of the expected distribution of key values, and on that distribution being fairly reliable. For example, if we are asked to look up John Smith in the phone book, we do not open it to the middle, but to about 75% of the way through, "knowing" that is roughly where we find the $S$'s. If we find ourselves among the $T$'s, we go back perhaps 5% of the way, not halfway to the beginning, as we would for the second step of a binary search.

In general, suppose we have an algorithm that given a key value $v_1$, tells us what fraction of the way between two other key values, $v_2$ and $v_3$, we can expect $v_1$ to lie. Call this fraction $f(v_1, v_2, v_3)$. If an index or part of an index lies on blocks $B_1, \ldots, B_n$, let $v_2$ be the first key value in $B_1$ and $v_3$ the last key value in $B_n$. Look at block $B_i$, where $i = \lceil nf(v_1, v_2, v_3) \rceil$ to see how its first key value compares with $v_1$. Then, as in binary search, repeat the process on either $B_1, \ldots, B_{i-1}$ or $B_i, \ldots, B_n$, whichever could contain the value that covers $v_1$, until only one block remains.

It can be shown that if we know the expected distribution of keys, then we can expect to examine about $1 + \log_2 \log_2 n$ blocks of the index file (Yao and Yao [1976]). When we add to this number the two accesses to read and write a block of the main file, we get $3 + \log_2 \log_2 n$. Under the assumptions of Example 6.11, this number is a little over 6, compared with 11 for binary search.

## Operating on a Sorted File with Unpinned Records

Let us consider how to do the operations of lookup, insertion, deletion, and modification on a sorted file with records that are not pinned down, by pointers, to a fixed location. These four operations will require insertions, deletions, and modifications to the index file, so it is important to bear in mind that the index file itself is sorted and has unpinned records. Thus in describing operations on the main file, we may call for the same operations to be done to the index file, assuming that the reader sees how to implement these operations on the index. Note that since the index file has no index, and lookup strategies for the index file have been described already, we are not using circular reasoning.

The original sorted file is kept on a sequence of blocks $B_1, B_2, \ldots, B_k$, with the records of each block in sorted order, and the records of $B_i$ preceding those of $B_{i+1}$ in the ordering, for $i = 1, 2, \ldots, k - 1$. We assume that bytes at the beginning of the file give used/unused information for each of the records areas of the file, or if records are variable-length, then the beginning of the block tells us, by offsets, where the records are and where unused space, if any, begins.

## Initialization

First, we sort the initial file of records and distribute them among blocks. Since files tend to grow, we often find it convenient to distribute the initial records in such a way that there is a small fraction, say 20%, of the total space unused on each block.

The second step of initialization is to create the index file, by examining the first record on each block of the main file. The keys of each of these records are paired with the addresses of their blocks to form the records of the index file. One useful exception is to replace the key value in the first index record by $-\infty$, a value that is less than any real key value. Then, should we insert a record with a key that precedes any key in the current file, we do not have to treat it specially. When we apportion the index records among blocks, we might again want to leave a small fraction of the space available, because when we are forced to increase the number of blocks of the main file we also have to increase the number of records of the index file.

The final step of initialization is to create a directory containing the addresses of the index blocks. Often, this directory is small enough to put in main memory. If that is not the case, the directory may itself be put on blocks and moved in and out of main memory as needed. If we must do so, we are getting very close to the multilevel index structure known as "B-trees," discussed in Section 6.5.

## Lookup

Suppose we want to find the record in the main file with key value $v_1$. Examine the index file to find the key value $v_2$ that covers $v_1$. The index record containing $v_2$ also contains a pointer to a block of the main file, and it is on that block that a record with key value $v_1$ will be found, if it exists.

The search for the index record with key $v_2$ covering $v_1$ can be performed by any of the techniques discussed above—linear search, binary search, or interpolation search—whichever is most appropriate.

## Modification

To modify a record with key value $v_1$, use the lookup procedure to find the record. If the modification changes the key, treat the operation as an insertion and deletion. If not, make the modification and rewrite the record.

## Insertion

To insert a record with key value $v_1$, use the lookup procedure to find the block $B_i$ of the main file, on which a record with key value $v_1$ would be found. Place the new record in its correct place in block $B_i$, keeping the records sorted and moving records with key values greater than $v_1$ to the right, to make room for the new record.[5]

If block $B_i$ had at least one empty record area, all records will fit, and we are done. However, if $B_i$ was originally full, the last record has no place to go, and we must follow one of several strategies for creating new blocks. In the next section we shall discuss a strategy ("B-trees"), in which $B_i$ is split into two half-empty blocks. An alternative is to examine $B_{i+1}$. We can find $B_{i+1}$, if it exists, through the index file, since a pointer to $B_{i+1}$ is in the record of the index file that follows the record just accessed to find $B_i$. If $B_{i+1}$ has an empty record area, move the excess record from $B_i$ to the first record area of $B_{i+1}$, shifting other records right until the first empty record area is filled. Change the used/unused information in the header of $B_{i+1}$ appropriately, and modify the index record for $B_{i+1}$ to reflect the new key value in its first record. If $B_{i+1}$ has many empty record areas, we can shift enough records from $B_i$ to $B_{i+1}$ to equalize the amount of empty space on each; the number of block accesses is not increased, and in fact, very little extra computation is needed.

---

[5] Remember, we assume that the most significant cost of operations is the block access time, and simple computations on the block, like moving data left or right, do not dominate the total cost.

If $B_{i+1}$ does not exist, because $i = k$, or $B_{i+1}$ exists but is full, we could consider obtaining some space from $B_{i-1}$ similarly. If that block is also full, or doesn't exist, we must get a new block, which will follow $B_i$ in the order. Divide the records of $B_i$ between $B_i$ and the new block. Then insert a record for the new block in the index file, using the same strategy as for inserting a record into the main file.

## Deletion

As for insertion, a variety of strategies exist, and in the next section we shall discuss one in which blocks are not allowed to get less than half full. Here, let us mention only the simplest strategy, which is appropriate if relatively few deletions are made. To delete the record with key value $v_1$, use lookup to find it. Move any records to its right one record area left to close the gap,[6] and adjust the used/unused bits in the header. If the block is now completely empty, return it to the file system and delete the record for that block in the index, using the same deletion strategy.

**Example 6.12:** Suppose we have a file of *numbers* records, and initially our file consists of records for the following list of "random" numbers, which were generated by starting with 2, and repeatedly squaring and taking the remainder modulo 101. Our initial sorted list is:

   2, 4, 5, 16, 25, 37, 54, 56, 68, 79, 80, 88

We can fit five records on a block, but let us initially place only four on each to leave some room for expansion. The initial layout is shown in Figure 6.7. Each of the three blocks of the main file has one empty record area and four bytes of waste space at the end, one byte of which could be occupied by used/unused bits for the five record areas of the block. The one block of the index file has three records, $(-\infty, b_1)$, $(25, b_2)$, and $(68, b_3)$, where $b_1$, $b_2$, and $b_3$ are the addresses of the three blocks of the main file. The directory of index blocks is not shown, but would contain the address of the one index block.

   Now, let us consider what happens when the next four numbers in this random sequence, 19, 58, 31, and 52, are inserted. We place 19 in the first block, and it happens to follow all the numbers already in that block. We thus place it in the fifth record area, the one that is empty, and there is no need to slide records to the right in this block. Number 58 similarly goes in the second block, and its proper place is in the fifth record area, so no rearrangement is necessary.

   The third insertion, 31, also belongs in block 2, and its proper place is in

---

[6] This step is not essential. If we do choose to close up gaps, we can use a count of the full record areas in the header in place of a used/unused bit for each record area. The reader should again be reminded that if records are pinned we do not even have the option of moving records into record areas whose records have been deleted.

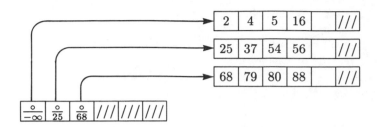

**Figure 6.7** Initial index file.

the second record area, after 25. We must thus slide 37, 54, 56, and 58 to the right to make room. However, there is not room for six records, and we must find a place for one of them. In this case, the third block has space, so we can shift 58 into the first record area of the third block, and shift the four records already in that block to the right. Since 58 is now the lowest key in the third block, we must change the index record for that block. These modifications are shown in Figure 6.8.

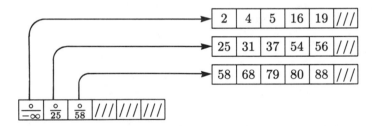

**Figure 6.8** After inserting 19, 58, 31.

Our final insertion is 52, which also belongs in block 2, following 37. Again there is no room in block 2, but now, the following and preceding blocks are also full. Thus, we split the second block into two, each of which will take three of the records: 25, 31, and 37 in one, and 52, 54, and 56 in the other. The first of these two blocks can be identified with the block being split, since its index record $(25, b_2)$ is the same. The second requires a new index record, with key 52, and this record must be inserted in the proper order into the index file. The resulting structure is shown in Figure 6.9. $\square$

## Sorted Files with Pinned Records

If records are pinned down to the place in which they are first stored, we cannot, in general, keep records sorted within a block. One solution is to start the file

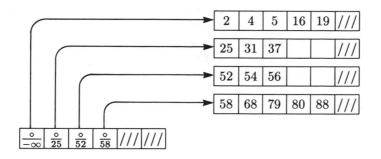

**Figure 6.9**  After inserting 52.

with essentially the same organization as if records were unpinned, as in Figure 6.7. However, we view each block of the main file as the first block of a bucket. As records are inserted, additional blocks will be added to the bucket, and new blocks are chained by a series of pointers extending from the original block for that bucket.

The index never changes in this organization, and the first records of each block of the initial file determine the distribution of records into buckets forever, or at least until the file has gotten so large that it is worthwhile reorganizing it into a larger number of buckets. Let us now describe the way in which operations are performed on a file with this organization.

### Initialization

Sort the file and distribute its records among blocks. Consider filling each block to less than its capacity to make room for expected growth and to avoid long chains of blocks in one bucket. Create the index with a record for each block. As in the previous organization, it is important to use key $-\infty$ for the first block, so keys smaller than any seen before will have a bucket in which they belong.

### Operations

The operations on files with this organization are performed with a combination of the ideas found in Section 6.3, concerning hashed files, and the organization just discussed, concerning sorted files with unpinned records. The salient features are mentioned below:

1.  *Lookup.* Find the index record whose key value $v_2$ covers the desired key value $v_1$. Follow the pointer in the selected index record to the first block of the desired bucket. Scan this block and any blocks of the bucket chained to it to find the record with key $v_1$.

2. *Insertion*. Use the lookup procedure to find the desired bucket. Scan the blocks of the bucket to find the first empty place. If no empty record area exists, get a new block and place a pointer to it in the header of the last block of the bucket. Insert the new record in the new block.

3. *Deletion*. Use the lookup procedure to find the desired record. We might consider setting the used/unused bit for its record area to 0. However, as discussed in Section 6.1, if there may exist pointers to the record being deleted, another deletion strategy must be used. The used/unused bit is kept at 1, and to indicate removal of the record, a deletion bit in the record itself is set to 1.

4. *Modification*. Perform a lookup with the given key. If only nonkey fields are to be changed, do so. If one or more fields of the key change, treat the modification as a deletion followed by an insertion. However, if records are pinned and modification of key fields is permitted, we must not simply set the deleted bit of the old record to 1. If we did nothing else, then old pointers to that record would "dangle," and we would not be able to find the modified record by following those pointers. Thus, we must not only set the deleted bit for the deleted record, but we must leave in that record a "forwarding address," pointing to the new incarnation of the record.

**Example 6.13:** Suppose we begin with the file shown in Figure 6.7 and add the numbers 19, 58, 31, 52, 78, and 24. As in Example 6.12, the first two of these go in blocks 1 and 2, and they accidentally maintain the sorted order of the blocks, as they are placed in the fifth record area of each block. When we insert 31, we must create a new block for the second bucket and place it in the first record area. Similarly, 52 goes in the second record area of the new block, 78 fills the block of the third bucket, and 24 requires us to create a second block for bucket 1. The final organization is shown in Figure 6.10. □

## Additional Links

As records are not placed in a bucket in sorted order after the initialization, we may have difficulty if we wish to examine records in sorted order. To help, we can add a pointer in each record to the next record in sorted order. These pointers are somewhat different from the pointers we have been using, since they not only indicate a block, but they also indicate an offset within the block; the offset is the number of the byte that begins the stored record, relative to the beginning of the block. The algorithms needed to maintain such pointers should be familiar from an elementary study of list processing.

**Example 6.14:** The second bucket of Figure 6.10 with pointers indicating the sorted order is shown in Figure 6.11. □

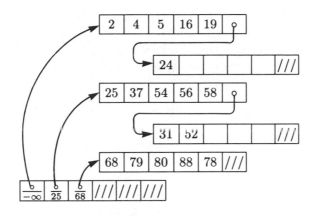

**Figure 6.10** Inserting into file of pinned records.

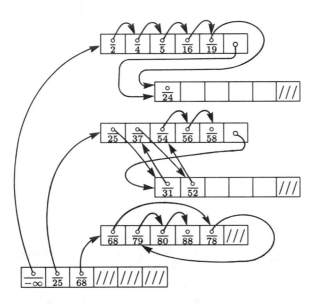

**Figure 6.11** Linking records in sorted order.

## 6.5 B-TREES

An index being nothing more than a file with unpinned records, there is no reason why we cannot have an index of an index, an index of that, and so on, until an index fits on one block, as suggested in Figure 6.12. In fact, such an arrangement can be considerably more efficient than a file with a single level of indexing. In the structure of Figure 6.12, the main file is sorted by key value. The first level index consists of pairs $(v, b)$, where $b$ is a pointer to a block $B$ of the main file and $v$ is the first key on block $B$. Naturally, this index is also sorted by key value. The second level of index has pairs $(v, b)$, where $b$ points to a first-level index block and $v$ is its first key, and so on.

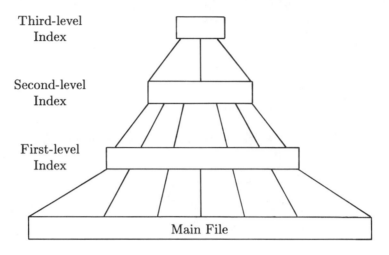

Third-level
Index

Second-level
Index

First-level
Index

Main File

**Figure 6.12** Multilevel index.

There are many forms that multilevel index structures can take, and they are collectively referred to as *B-trees* (balanced trees). The particular structure suggested in Figure 6.12 keeps the main file as part of the B-tree itself and assumes that the main file has unpinned records. This style does not use space as efficiently as possible, and we introduce the subject of B-trees this way only because of its simplicity. A superior approach, which saves space in most situations and is also suitable for storing pinned records, is described in Section 6.6. There we keep the main file packed tightly on blocks with records in no particular order, as a heap. Then the leaves of the B-tree contain not the main file records, but pointers to those records.

For insertion and deletion on a B-tree, we could use the same strategy as was described in the previous section, applying the insertion and deletion operations to the nodes (blocks) of the tree at all levels. This strategy would result in nodes having between one and the maximum possible number of records. Rather, B-trees are usually defined to use a particular insertion/deletion strategy that ensures no node, except possibly the root, is less than half full. For convenience, we assume that the number of index records a block can hold is an odd integer $2d - 1 \geq 3$, and the number of records of the main file a block can hold is also an odd integer $2e - 1 \geq 3$.

Before proceeding, we must observe one more difference between B-trees and the index hierarchy suggested by Figure 6.12. In index blocks of a B-tree, the key value in the first record is omitted, to save space. During lookups, all key values less than the value in the second record of a block are deemed to be covered by the (missing) first key value.

## Lookup

Let us search for a record with key value $v$. We find a path from the root of the B-tree to some leaf, where the desired record will be found if it exists. The path begins at the root. Suppose at some time during the search we have reached node (block) $B$. If $B$ is a leaf (we can tell when we reach a leaf if we keep the current number of levels of the tree available) then simply examine block $B$ for a record with key value $v$.

If $B$ is not a leaf, it is an index block. Determine which key value in block $B$ covers $v$. Recall that the first record in $B$ holds no key value, and the missing value is deemed to cover any value less than the key value in the second record; i.e., we may assume the missing key value is $-\infty$. In the record of $B$ that covers $v$ is a pointer to another block $B'$. In the path being constructed, $B'$ follows $B$, and we repeat the above steps with $B'$ in place of $B$.

Since the key value in record $i$ of $B$ is the lowest key of any leaf descending from the $i$th child of $B$, and the main file's records are sorted by key value, it is easy to check that $B'$ is the only child of $B$ at which a record with key $v$ could exist. This statement also holds for $i = 1$, even though there is no key in the first record of $B$. That is, if $v$ is less than the key in the second record, then a main-file record with key $v$ could not be a descendant of the second or subsequent children of $B$.

## Modification

As with the other organizations discussed, a modification involving a key field is really a deletion and insertion, while a modification that leaves the key value fixed is a lookup followed by the rewriting of the record involved.

## Insertion

To insert a record with key value $v$, apply the lookup procedure to find the block $B$ in which this record belongs. If there are fewer than $2e - 1$ records in $B$, simply insert the new record in sorted order in the block. One can show that the new record can never be the first in block $B$, unless $B$ is the leftmost leaf. Thus, it is never necessary to modify a key value in an ancestor of $B$.

If there are already $2e - 1$ records in block $B$, create a new block $B_1$ and divide the records of $B$ and the inserted record into two groups of $e$ records each. The first $e$ records go in block $B$ and the remaining $e$ go in block $B_1$.

Now let $P$ be the parent block of $B$. Recall that the lookup procedure finds the path from the root to $B$, so $P$ is already known. Apply the insert procedure recursively, with constant $d$ in place of $e$, to insert a record for $B_1$ to the right of the record for $B$ in index block $P$. Notice that if many ancestors of block $B$ have the maximum $2d-1$ records, the effects of inserting a record into $B$ can ripple up the tree. However, it is only ancestors of $B$ that are affected. If the insertion ripples up to the root, we split the root, and create a new root with two children. This is the only situation in which an index block may have fewer than $d$ records.

**Example 6.15:** Nontrivial examples of B-trees are hard to show on the page. Let us therefore take the minimum possible values of $d$ and $e$, namely two. That is, each block, whether interior or a leaf, holds three records. Also to save space, we shall use small integers as key values and shall omit any other fields, including used/unused bits in the header. In Figure 6.13 we see an initial B-tree.

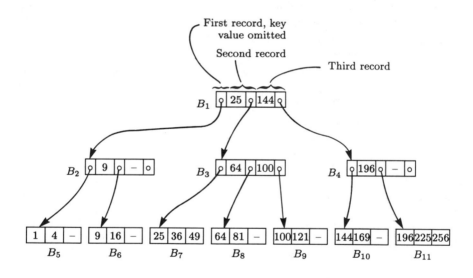

**Figure 6.13** Initial B-tree.

Suppose we wish to insert a record with key value 32. We find a path to the block in which this record belongs by starting at the root, $B_1$. We find that 32 is covered by 25, the key value in the second record of $B_1$. We therefore progress to $B_3$, the block pointed to by the second record of $B_1$. At $B_3$ we find that 32 is less than 64, the value in the second record of $B_3$, so we follow the first pointer in $B_3$, to arrive at $B_7$. Clearly 32 belongs between 25 and 36 in

$B_7$, but now $B_7$ has four records. We therefore get a new block, $B_{12}$, and place 25 and 32 in $B_7$, while 36 and 49 go in $B_{12}$.

We now must insert a record with key value 36 and a pointer to $B_{12}$ into $B_3$. Value 36 is selected because that is the lowest key value on the block $B_{12}$. This insertion causes $B_3$ to have four records, so we get a new block $B_{13}$. The records with pointers to $B_7$ and $B_{12}$ go in $B_3$, while the records with pointers to $B_8$ and $B_9$ go in $B_{13}$. Next, we insert a record with key value 64 and a pointer to $B_{13}$ into $B_1$. Now $B_1$ has four records, so we get a new block $B_{14}$, and place the records with pointers to $B_2$ and $B_3$ in $B_1$, while the records with pointers to $B_{13}$ and $B_4$ go in $B_{14}$. As $B_1$ was the root, we create a new block $B_{15}$, which becomes the root and has pointers to $B_1$ and $B_{14}$. The resulting B-tree is shown in Figure 6.14.

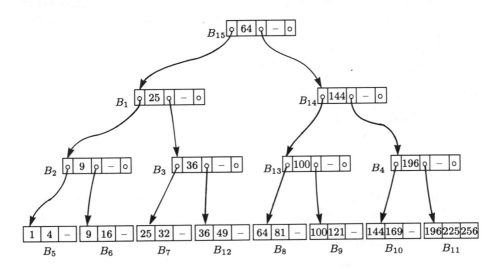

**Figure 6.14** B-tree after insertion of 32.

## Deletion

If we wish to delete the record with key value $v$, we use the lookup procedure to find the path from the root to a block $B$ containing this record. If after deletion, block $B$ still has $e$ or more records, we are usually done. However, if the deleted record was the first in block $B$, then we must go to the parent of $B$ to change the key value in the record for $B$, to agree with the new first key value of $B$. If $B$ is the first child of its parent, the parent has no key value for $B$, so we must go to the parent's parent, the parent of that, and so on, until we find an ancestor $A_1$ of $B$ such that $A_1$ is not the first child of its parent $A_2$. Then the new lowest key value of $B$ goes in the record of $A_2$ that points to $A_1$. In this manner, every record $(v_1, p_1)$ in every index block has key value $v_1$ equal to the lowest of all those key values of the original file found among the leaves that are descendants of the block pointed to by $p_1$.[7]

If, after deletion, block $B$ has $e - 1$ records, we look at the block $B_1$ having the same parent as $B$ and residing either immediately to the left or right of $B$. If $B_1$ has more than $e$ records, we distribute the records of $B$ and $B_1$ as evenly as possible, keeping the order sorted, of course. We then modify the key values for $B$ and/or $B_1$ in the parent of $B$, and if necessary, ripple the change to as many ancestors of $B$ as have their key values affected. If $B_1$ has only $e$ records, then combine $B$ with $B_1$, which will then have exactly $2e - 1$ records, and in the parent of $B$, modify the record for $B_1$ (which may require modification of some ancestors of $B$) and delete the record for $B$. The deletion of this record requires a recursive use of the deletion procedure, with constant $d$ in place of $e$.

If the deletion ripples all the way up to the children of the root, we may finish by combining the only two children of the root. In this case, the node formed from the combined children becomes the root, and the old root is deleted. This is the one situation in which the number of levels decreases.

**Example 6.16:** Let us delete the record with key value 64 from the B-tree of Figure 6.14. The lookup procedure tells us the path to the block that holds this record is $B_{15}$, $B_{14}$, $B_{13}$, $B_8$. We delete the record from $B_8$ and find that it was the first record of that block. We therefore must propagate upwards the fact that the new lowest key value in $B_8$ is 81. As $B_8$ is the leftmost child of $B_{13}$, we do not change $B_{13}$, nor do we change $B_{14}$, since $B_{13}$ is its leftmost child. However, $B_{14}$ is not the leftmost child of $B_{15}$, so there is a key value in $B_{15}$ that must be changed, and we change 64 to 81 there. Notice that a deletion never causes more than one key value to be changed.

We have another problem when we delete 64. Block $B_8$ now has only one record. We go to its parent, $B_{13}$, and find that $B_8$ has no sibling to its left. We therefore examine $B_8$'s sibling to the right, $B_9$. As $B_9$ has only two records, we can combine $B_9$ with $B_8$. Now we discover that $B_{13}$ has only one child, and we must combine $B_{13}$ with its sibling, $B_4$. Block $B_{13}$ will now have pointers to $B_8$, $B_{10}$, and $B_{11}$. The key value 196 to go with the pointer to $B_{11}$ is found in $B_4$, while the key value 144 to go with $B_{10}$ is found in $B_{14}$. In general, when we merge blocks in a deletion, the necessary key values are found either in the merged blocks or in their common parent. We leave it as an exercise for the reader to develop an algorithm to tell where the desired key values are found.

---

[7] This property is not essential, and we could dispense with the modification of keys in index blocks. Then $v_1$ would be a lower bound on the keys of descendants of the block pointed to by $p_1$. The descendants to the left of that block will still have keys less than $v_1$, as they must for the B-tree to be useful for finding records.

On combining $B_{13}$ and $B_4$, we find $B_{14}$ has only one child, and so we combine $B_{14}$ with $B_1$. At this time, $B_{15}$ has only one child, and since it is the root, we delete it, leaving the B-tree of Figure 6.15. $\square$

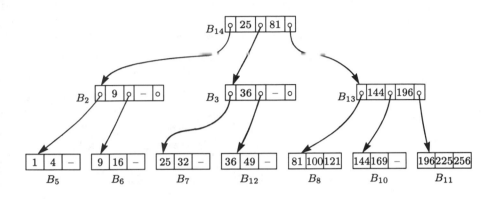

**Figure 6.15** B-tree after deleting 64.

## Time Analysis of B-tree Operations

Suppose we have a file with $n$ records organized into a B-tree with parameters $d$ and $e$. The tree will have no more than $n/e$ leaves, no more than $n/de$ parents of leaves, $n/d^2e$ parents of parents of leaves, and so on. If there are $i$ nodes on paths from the root to leaves, then $n \geq d^{i-1}e$, or else there would be fewer than one node at the level of the root, which is impossible. It follows that

$$i \leq 1 + \log_d(n/e)$$

To perform a lookup, $i$ read operations on blocks suffices. For an insertion, deletion, or modification, usually only one block (the leaf holding the record involved) needs to be written, although in pathological cases, about $i$ additional reads and $i$ additional writes may be necessary. Exact analysis of the probability of finding blocks with too many records in an insert or too few records in a deletion is very difficult. However, it is not hard to show that even for $d = e = 2$, the expected number of extra reads and writes (in excess of the $i$ reads to find the leaf and one write to store the leaf) is a proper fraction. We shall thus neglect this fraction and estimate the number of read/writes at $2 + \log_d(n/e)$. Even this figure is conservative, since in the average case many blocks will have more than the minimum number of records, and therefore the height of the tree may well be less than $1 + \log_d(n/e)$.

**Example 6.17:** Let us reconsider our running example of a file, which we discussed in relation to single-level indices in Example 6.11. Records are assumed 200 bytes long, and if we want an odd number on 4,096-byte blocks, we must choose $2e - 1 = 19$; i.e., $e = 10$. We assumed in Example 6.11 that keys were 20 bytes long, and pointers took 4 bytes. Since we omit the first key, we can fit 171 index records on a 4,096-byte block, since $170 \times 20 + 171 \times 4 = 4,084$. Thus, $d = 86$. The expected number of block accesses per operation is thus

$$2 + \log_d(n/e) = 2 + \log_{86}(1,000,000/10) < 5$$

This figure is greater than the best for hashed access (about 3 read/writes), but is superior to methods using a single level of indexing, except perhaps in those situations where an interpolation search can be performed. The B-tree shares with the methods of Section 6.4 the advantage over hashed access of permitting the file to be listed or searched conveniently in sorted order. $\square$

## 6.6 FILES WITH A DENSE INDEX

In the schemes discussed so far, hashing, sparse indices, and B-trees, most blocks of the main file are only partially filled. For example, a hash structure with an adequate number of buckets will have only one or two blocks in most buckets, and at least one block per bucket will be only partially filled. In the B-tree scheme discussed in the previous section, all the leaf blocks are between half-full and completely full, with the average block around three-quarters full.

In contrast, the heap, mentioned in Section 6.2, keeps all main file blocks but the last full, which saves a significant amount of space.[8] The problem with using a heap, of course, is that we must have an efficient way of finding a record, given its key value. To do so, we need another file, called a *dense index*, that consists of records $(v, p)$ for each key value $v$ in the main file, where $p$ is a pointer to the main file record having key value $v$. The structure of the dense index may be any of the ones discussed in Sections 6.3–6.5; i.e., we only require that we can find the record $(v, p)$ quickly, given the key $v$. Note, incidentally, that a "dense" index stores a pointer to every record of the main file, while the "sparse" indices discussed previously stored the keys for only a small subset of the records of the main file, normally only those that were the first on their blocks.

To look up, modify, or delete a record of the main file, given its key, we perform a lookup on the dense index file, with that key, which tells us the block of the main file we must search for the desired record. We must then read this block of the main file. If the record is to be modified, we change the record and

---

[8] There is the detail that if records are pinned, we cannot physically delete records but must set a "deleted" bit. However, this extra space cost occurs with all storage structures when records are pinned.

rewrite its block onto secondary storage. We thus make two more block accesses (one to read and one to write) than are necessary to perform the corresponding operation on the dense index file.

If we are to delete the record, we again rewrite its block and also delete the record with that key value from the dense index file. This operation takes two more accesses than a lookup and deletion from the dense index.

To insert a record $r$, we place $r$ at the end of the main file and then insert a pointer to $r$, along with $r$'s key value, in the dense index file. Again this operation takes two more accesses than does an insertion on the dense index file.

It would thus seem that a file with a dense index always requires two more accesses than if we used, for the main file, whatever organization (e.g., hashed, indexed, or B-tree) we use on the dense index file. However, there are two factors that work in the opposite direction, to justify the use of dense indices in some situations.

1.  The records of the main file may be pinned, but the records of the dense index file need not be pinned, so we may use a simpler or more efficient organization on the dense index file than we could on the main file.
2.  If records of the main file are large, the total number of blocks used in the dense index may be much smaller than would be used for a sparse index or B-tree on the main file. Similarly, the number of buckets or the average number of blocks per bucket can be made smaller if hashed access is used on the dense index than if hashed access were used on the main file.

**Example 6.18:** Let us consider the file discussed in Example 6.17, where we used a B-tree with $d = 86$ and $e = 10$ on a file of $n = 1,000,000$ records. Since dense index records are the same size as the records in the interior nodes of a B-tree, if we use a B-tree organization for the dense index, we may take $d = 86$ and $e = 85$.[9] Thus, the typical number of accesses to search the dense index is $2 + \log_{86}(1,000,000/85)$, or slightly more than 4. To this we must add two accesses of the main file, so the dense index plus B-tree organization takes between one and two more block accesses [the actual figure is $2 - \log_{86}(85/10)$] than the simple B-tree organization.

There are, however, compensating factors in favor of the dense index. We can pack the blocks of the main file fully if a dense index is used, while in the B-tree organization, the leaf blocks, which contain the main file, are between half full and completely full; thus, we can save about 25% in storage space for the main file. The space used for the leaves of the B-tree in the dense index is only 12% of the space of the main file, since index records are 24 bytes

---

[9] Technically, the leaf blocks of the B-tree used as a dense index must have key values in all the records, including the first. This difference means that we can fit only 170 records in leaf blocks, and so must take $e = 85$.

long and main file records are 200 bytes. Thus, we still have a net savings of approximately 13% of the space. Perhaps more importantly, if the main file has pinned records, we could not use the B-tree organization described in Section 6.5 at all. $\square$

## Methods for Unpinning Records

Another use for a dense index is as a place to receive pointers to records. That is, a pointer to record $r$ of the main file may go instead to the record in the dense index that points to $r$. The disadvantage is that to follow a pointer to $r$ we must follow an extra pointer from the dense index to the main file. The compensation is that now records of the main file are not pinned (although the records of the index file are). When we wish to move a record of the main file, we have only to change the one pointer in the dense index that points to the moved record. We may thus be able to use a more compact storage organization for the main file, and the storage savings could more than cover the cost of the dense index. For example, if the main file is unpinned, we can reuse the subblocks of deleted records.

Another technique for making files unpinned is to use the key values of records in place of pointers. That is, instead of storing the address of a record $r$, we store the value of the key for $r$, and to find $r$ we do a standard lookup given the key value. The IMS database system (IBM [1978b]), for example, makes use of this technique, as discussed in Section 6.10. In this way, both the dense index file and the main file can be unpinned. The disadvantage of this implementation of pointers is that to follow a "pointer" to the main file, we must search for the key value of that record in the dense index, or in whatever structure is used for accessing the main file, which will probably take several block accesses. In comparison, we would need only one block access if we could go directly to the record of the main file, or two accesses if we went directly to the record in the dense index and then to the record in the main file.

## Summary

In Figure 6.16 we list the four types of organizations for files allowing lookup, modification, insertion, and deletion of records given the key value. In the timing analyses, we take $n$ to be the number of records in the main file and, for uniformity with B-trees, we assume the records of the main file are packed about $e$ to a block on the average, and records of any index files can be packed about $d$ to a block on the average.

## 6.7 NESTED RECORD STRUCTURES

Frequently, we are interested in doing more than retrieving records, given their key value. Instead, we want to find a subset of the records in a file based

| Organization | Time per Operation | Advantages and Disadvantages | Problems with Pinned Records |
|---|---|---|---|
| Hashed | $\approx 3$ if buckets average one block. | Fastest of all methods. If file grows, access slows, as buckets get large. Cannot access records easily in order of sorted key values. | Must search buckets for empty space during insertion or allow more blocks per bucket than optimal |
| Isam index | $\approx 2 + \log(n/de)$ for binary search $\approx 3 + \log\log(n/de)$ if address calculation is feasible and is used. | Fast access if address calculation can be used. Records can be accessed in sorted order. | Same as above. |
| B-tree | $\approx 2 + \log_d(n/e)$ | Fast access. Records can be accessed in sorted order. Blocks tend not to be solidly packed. | Use B-tree as dense index. |
| Dense index | $\leq 2 +$ time for operation on dense index file. | Often slower by one or two block accesses than if same access method used for index file were used for the main file. May save space. | None. |

**Figure 6.16** Summary of access methods.

on their value in a nonkey field or fields, or we want to retrieve a subset of records because of their relationship to a record in another file. For example, consider the hierarchical structure of Figure 2.26, and particularly the tree with root CUSTOMERS, intermediate node ORDERS, and leaf ENTRIES (which consist of an item plus a quantity of that item ordered). We might wish to find a given customer, examine all of the orders placed by that customer, and all of the entries within some or all of those orders.

When we are interested in retrieving related collections of records, we can minimize block accesses in a way that does not even enter into consideration when we assume the basic operation is the retrieval of a single record, as in Sections 6.1–6.6. For example, we might hope that all the orders and entries for a given customer are located on the same block or, at worst, among a few consecutive blocks. Then having found the customer, perhaps reading several blocks of an index or hash structure to find his record, we could retrieve all of his orders and entries from the block on which the customer record was found plus the immediately following blocks, if necessary.

When we interleave records of two or more types, it is useful to have a notation to describe the common patterns that arise. We define *patterns* and their *instances*, i.e., the sequences of records they denote, as follows.

1.   If $R$ is a record type, then $R$ is a pattern whose instances are all the occurrences of a single record of type $R$.
2.   If $P_1, \ldots, P_n$ are patterns, then $P_1 \cdots P_n$ is a pattern. This pattern's instances are all those sequences of records of the form $I_1 \cdots I_n$, where $I_j$ is an instance of pattern $P_j$, for $j = 1, 2, \ldots, n$.
3.   If $P$ is a pattern, then $(P)^*$ is a pattern. Its instances are all those sequences of records of the form $I_1 \cdots I_n$, where each $I_j$ is an instance of pattern $P$. Here, $1 \leq j \leq n$, and $n$ may be 0, in which case the instance is the "sequence" of zero records. The parentheses may be omitted if no ambiguity results. We call an instance of a starred pattern such as $(P)^*$ a *repeating group*.

**Example 6.19:** Let us consider the hierarchy of Figure 2.26 again. An entry consists of a virtual item and a quantity. We may regard the virtual item pointer as a record type, say VITEM, and the quantity likewise as a one-field record, which we shall call QUANTITY. Then we could define the pattern ENTRIES to consist of a VITEM record followed by a QUANTITY record, as

> ENTRIES = VITEM QUANTITY

Note that there is no significant distinction between two records concatenated, as we have done here, and a single record with two fields; we could have regarded ENTRIES as a fundamental record type, rather than the name of a pattern.

We may then regard an order as an ORDERS record followed by a sequence of zero or more "entries," that is, an alternation of virtual items pointers and quantities. These sequences are exactly the instances of the pattern

$$\text{ORDERS (VITEM QUANTITY)*} \tag{6.1}$$

Then, we might represent the entire tree rooted at CUSTOMERS by saying that a customer is a collection of records with pattern

$$\text{CUSTOMERS (ORDERS (VITEM QUANTITY)* )*} \tag{6.2}$$

The instances of this pattern are the preorder traversals of the possible database records.[10] A file consisting of any number of these database records would have the pattern

$$\text{(CUSTOMERS (ORDERS (VITEM QUANTITY)* )* )*}$$

For a more complex example, a database record for DEPTS in Figure 2.26 can be described by

$$\text{DEPTS EMPS* MGR (ITEMS VORDERS* VSUPPLIERS*)*}$$

That is, in preorder traversals of database records for departments, we find one DEPTS record followed by records for all the employees of the department, followed by a record for the one manager of the department, and zero or more groups of records, one group for each item the department sells. Each group consists of the ITEMS record for the item, a sequence of virtual ORDERS records, one for each order including that item, and a sequence of virtual SUPPLIERS records, one for each supplier of the item. □

**Storage by Preorder Sequence**

One common way to store nested or hierarchical structures is in the preorder sequence as we traverse tree-structured "database records." That is, we store the records in exactly the order implied by the pattern that describes the hierarchy.

**Example 6.20:** Suppose we have a collection of CUSTOMERS database records, each with the structure of (6.2) above. Also assume that the data in this database record is what we find in the sample database for the YVCB of Figure 4.2. Then the preorder traversal of the database record for Zack Zebra visits records in the order shown in Figure 6.17.

If we take the data type definitions of Figure 5.16 as a guide, we might suppose that CUSTOMERS records require 80 bytes, ORDERS require 20, and virtual ITEMS and QUANTITY records require 8 each. These figures assume that fields must begin at a multiple of 4, and there is a 4-byte region of every record holding a code that identifies the record type, as well as other information such as a "deleted" bit. With these estimates, the entire database

---

[10] Recall from Section 2.6 that a "database record" in a hierarchical system is an instance $r$ of the record type of some root, together with all the descendant records in the tree of the actual database whose root is (physical) record $r$.

CUSTOMERS record for Zack Zebra
   ORDERS record for order 1024
      Virtual ITEM pointer to "Brie"
      QUANTITY 3
      Virtual ITEM pointer to "Perrier"
      QUANTITY 6
   ORDERS record for order 1026
      Virtual ITEM pointer to "Macadamias"
      QUANTITY 2048

**Figure 6.17** Order of records in one database record.

record takes 168 bytes, and it is very likely that it fits on one block. Thus, if we search for and find the Zack Zebra CUSTOMERS record, we often require no additional retrievals to find the orders and entries within those orders for this customer, although additional block retrievals are necessary if we follow the virtual pointers and actually retrieve the items ordered.

With bad luck, the records of Figure 6.17 will be distributed over two consecutive blocks, and both will have to be retrieved to get all the orders for Zack Zebra. However, even two block accesses is much better than what we might have to face if we stored customers, orders, and item-quantity pairs in separate files, with no clustering of orders or entries for the same customer. Then we might find each of the nine records of Figure 6.17 on a different block. □

## Separate Storage of Repeating Groups

Another way to store a nested structure is to replace each of the outermost repeating groups (those that are not inside any other repeating group) by a pointer that indicates a place on another block or group of blocks where the repeating group itself may be found in consecutive space. Also needed is information about how to tell when the list of records in the repeating group ends. For example, we might attach to the pointer a count of the number of occurrences of the repeating group, or the records of the repeating group itself might be linked in a list, with a null pointer to indicate the end of the repeating group.

**Example 6.21:** In the structure for a single CUSTOMERS database record, given by (6.2) above, there is one outermost repeating group, which is the structure for a single order that was given by (6.1). We could replace this repeating group by a pointer, which we could think of as a "virtual list of orders." The structure of a CUSTOMERS database record thus becomes

CUSTOMERS VORDERS

This structure is equivalent to a simple, fixed-length record, like CUSTOMERS records, with an additional field for a pointer and perhaps a count of orders.

The structures for the orders can then be stored in preorder sequence, or they can be further broken down by replacing the outermost repeating group of (6.1), which is

(VITEM QUANTITY)*

by a pointer to a list of "entries," which are item-quantity pairs. If we take this option, then the CUSTOMERS, ORDERS, and ENTRIES records are spread over three files, and therefore, over three groups of blocks, as is suggested by the structure of Figure 6.18. There, we have linked together records belonging to a single repeating group. □

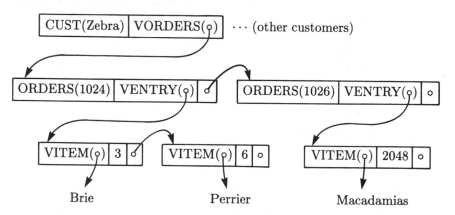

**Figure 6.18** Representing repeating groups by pointers.

## Operations on Nested Record Structures

Some of the operations that we want to perform on nested record structures are the usual ones: lookup, insert, delete, or modify a record of one of the record types involved in the structure. In previous sections, we assumed that these record accesses were performed with a key value, and that value determined where the record was located. In this more complex situation, where we are trying to store nested structures to keep "related" records close together, we cannot allow the records also to be positioned according to the demands of some primary index structure, such as a hashed file or a sorted file.[11]

---

[11] There are some exceptions. For example, under the separate-storage technique illus-

In general, if we want to access records of a given type by their key value, we need to create a dense index, as was discussed in Section 6.6, to take us from key values to the locations of the records. For example, if ORDERS records are stored near the customer who placed the order, as in Figure 6.17, then we might create a hash table or B-tree that stored records consisting of a key value, which is an order number, and a pointer to an ORDERS record. But we could not store the ORDERS records themselves in buckets, because then they would not be close to their customer, as in Figure 6.17. If orders are not placed near their customer, we cannot retrieve all of the orders for a given customer by accessing just one or a few blocks, on which all of those orders were found; we would have to retrieve about one block per order.

However, as indicated above, the reason for using a nested structure is not to assist with simple record accesses; it is to support operations that access related records. We have suggested that structures such as (6.2) are suitable for operations in which we scan a tree of a hierarchy, and indeed that is so, since the descendants of any node appear on a number of blocks that is not too much greater than the smallest number on which they are physically capable of fitting. Thus, we can see them all with a number of block accesses that is proportional to the space taken by the records (measured in blocks), rather than proportional to the number of records, which is usually much larger, since typically many records fit on a block.

**Example 6.22:** Let us use the estimates of record sizes given in Example 6.20 and assume that a typical customer has four orders with five entries each. Then an average database record uses

$$80 + 4 \times (20 + 5 \times (8 + 8)) = 480 \text{ bytes}$$

Moreover, since this database record consists of 45 separate records of differing lengths,[12] we need a block directory or an equivalent structure to help us find the records. At four bytes per pointer, we need another 180 bytes per database record for directory space, or 660 bytes per customer. If blocks are 4,096 bytes long, we can store about six customers per block. Thus, the probability is approximately 83% that the records for a single customer will be found on one block; in the remaining 17% of the cases, two blocks need to be retrieved.

Suppose our query is: given a customer, find his order numbers. With the nested structure stored in preorder, we must find the record for the customer. If we use a dense index on customer name, stored as a hash table with an

---

trated in Example 6.21, we could store CUSTOMERS records in a hash table or sorted file if we kept the pointers to orders structures along with the corresponding customer's record.

[12] That is probably an overestimate, since we would naturally group entries, consisting of a virtual item and a quantity, into a single record, reducing the number of different records per customer to 25.

adequate number of buckets, we need about 2 block accesses, one for the block of the bucket and one for the block on which the customer record is stored. To that, we add another sixth of an access in the case the orders are spread over two blocks.

It is hard to make an exact comparison of this performance with a structure in which orders are not nested close to their customers, because, given the structures seen so far, we do not even have a way of finding orders records given a customer name. In fact, in the hierarchy of Figure 2.26, ORDERS records do not contain the name of the customer, and it was assumed implicitly that the name is found in the parent record whenever we reach an ORDERS record.

However, if we adopt the approach of the relational model, where ORDERS records are tuples containing the name of the customer, as in Figure 2.8, then we can find the orders, given a customer, provided we use a "secondary index" on customer name for the ORDERS relation. Secondary indices are discussed further in the next section, but, for example, we might build a hash table whose records have a "key" field, which is a customer name, and a second field, which is a pointer to one of the orders for that customer. Of course these "keys" are not true keys, but since we assume only four orders per customer on the average, the records will distribute fairly well among buckets, and we might expect to discover the locations of all orders for a given customer in about two block accesses. There is no reason to expect two of these orders to be on the same block, if they are in a file sorted by order number, for example. Thus, six accesses (two for hashing and four for finding the orders themselves) are needed for an "ordinary" structure, while the nested structure needs only 2.17 on the average. $\square$

Another natural use of nested structures is for storing two record types connected by a DBTG set. For example, the structure of Figure 6.17 could be thought of as one where CUSTOMERS records "own" the following ORDERS records, which in turn "own" their following ENTRIES records, each consisting of a pointer to an item and a quantity. Then the nested structure facilitates queries that ask for the orders owned by a given customer, or the entries owned by a given order. It also facilitates moving from member records to their owners, e.g., from an order to the customer that placed the order, since it is likely that the owner is on the same block as the member record in question.

## Block Formats for Nested Structures

In order for the operations described above to be done at all, we need to design record and block formats carefully, so blocks can be broken apart into their constituent records. Since records of various types are mixed on one block:

1.   Blocks must be formatted for records of variable length.
2.   We must be able to tell what type a given record is.

For example, we might use the format of Figure 6.4 for blocks, where at the beginning of each block is a directory of the records contained therein. To satisfy (2), we might include in the directory a code, stored in one or more bytes, that indicates the type of the record being stored. Alternatively, we might insist that all records begin with a byte or several bytes that indicate the type of the record.

If we have a format meeting these conditions, then we can search forward from a given record $r$ to find all its descendant records. We know we have seen the last of $r$'s descendants when we meet another record of type $r$. As another example, if we store DBTG sets as nested structures, in the manner just mentioned, then we can scan backwards from record $r$ of a member type, to find its owner. The reason is that the owner of $r$ is the record of the owner type that most closely precedes $r$.

### Performing Insertions and Deletions

When several record types are intertwined, as in Figure 6.17, insertions or deletions of records of any of these types affect records of the other types. In essence, the records appearing in a nested structure are sorted, not by key value, but by their need to appear in a particular position relative to a record or records of other types. For example, in Figure 6.17, all the orders placed by Zack Zebra must appear after his record and before the record of the next customer. Each order record must also precede its entries records but follow the entries of previous orders. On the other hand, the sort is not rigid, because, for example, we could place order 1024 and its two entries after order 1026 and its entry (unless we wanted orders sorted by order number).

It is, on balance, easiest to treat the blocks storing a nested structure as if their records were in a fixed order. Thus, if records are unpinned, we can use the method illustrated in Figures 6.7–6.9 to create additional blocks in the middle of a sequence of blocks.

### Insertion of Pinned Records

However, it is likely that records are pinned, since we often need a dense index to records of each type in the nested structure. In that case, we must adopt a strategy like that of Figure 6.10, where we dealt with pinned records in a sorted file. We should start with records spread among blocks in such a way that a fraction of available space is found on each block. Deletions must be made by setting a "deleted" bit.

There are two cases to consider for insertions. In one case, pointers go to the records themselves, and we may not move them around within their block.

Then, inserted records are placed in available space at the end of the block in which they belong, and records can be linked in the proper order, as was suggested by Figure 6.11. In the second case, we have a block directory for our variable-length records, and pointers go to the directory itself. Then, we can slide records around within the block, making sure the directory pointers continue to point to the correct records. Therefore, we can insert records into their proper order in the block, and need not link the records.

However, we must consider what happens when blocks overflow. If records are pinned to fixed locations within blocks, the best we can do is what was done in Figure 6.10. We consider each original block the first block of a "bucket," and we link to it additional blocks containing the newly inserted records. To preserve the correct order of records we need links as in Figure 6.11.

If pointers to records are really pointers to the block directory, then we have some options. The block directory itself cannot move, so we cannot split blocks into two blocks and distribute records simply. We still must think of the overflowing block as the beginning of a chain for a bucket. We must keep the directory on that block or, as the bucket grows, on the first and subsequent blocks of its bucket. However, we can keep the records of the bucket in their proper order, distributed among the blocks of the bucket.

## 6.8 SECONDARY INDICES

Prior to Section 6.7, we were concerned with structures for primary indices, those that allow us to find a record given the value of its key. Often, the organization of the file was determined by the needs of the primary index. Then in Section 6.7 we saw that there are reasons why we might want to organize the records of a file in a way that is not compatible with the desired primary index structure. That problem can be handled by using a dense index, with one of the structures discussed in Sections 6.3–6.5, to hold pointers to the records of the file, which are then distributed to meet some other need, such as fitting into a nested structure. We also saw in Section 6.7 that structures can be designed to make efficient certain operations other than lookup, insertion, and deletion of a record with a given key value; in particular, we considered how to support queries that follow relationships between two or more record types.

In this section, we shall consider another type of operation: given the value $v$ of a field other than the key, find all records of a certain type that have value $v$ in that field. This problem reduces to the one we considered in the previous section, because we can use a *secondary index*, which is a nested structure with pattern

VALUE (REFERENCE)*

A REFERENCE, in this sense, is a way of getting to one of the records having the given VALUE. Two reasonable interpretations of references are:

1.   A pointer to the record in question.

2.   The key value of the record in question.

If we use pointers, we can get to the intended records faster than if we use key values, since with a key value we have to use the primary index structure to get at the record. On the other hand, using key values rather than pointers prevents the records from becoming pinned, thus allowing us several opportunities for primary index structures that are forbidden when records are pinned, as discussed in Sections 6.1 and 6.4, for example.

**Example 6.23:** Recall that *numbers* records, first introduced in Example 6.1, have a nonkey field NAME, which is the first letter of the English name of the number. If our main file stores the twelve numbers of the initial file from Example 6.12 (Figure 6.7), then the instance of the nested structure representing the secondary index on NAME is

$$e, 80, 88, f, 4, 5, 54, 56, s, 16, 68, 79, t, 2, 25, 37$$

Here, the letters are the different values of the NAME field that actually appear in the twelve chosen *numbers* records, and the numbers themselves can be thought of either as key values or as pointers to the records with those keys.

We can store this secondary index by packing its elements into blocks in the order shown and then creating another structure that serves as a dense index for the values of the NAME field. We show this structure in Figure 6.19, assuming that six elements of any type can fit on one block. Since there are only six different values of NAME that are possible, we use a simple heap structure for that index. In fact, since we have the dense index, it is not necessary to repeat the letters in the nested structure itself (right side of Figure 6.19), and we could have pointers from the dense index go directly to the first of the references for the corresponding letter.

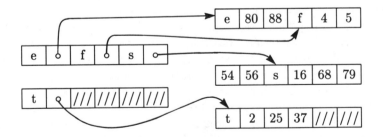

**Figure 6.19** Secondary index structure for NAME.

Fortuitously, the references for each letter but $f$ fall on one block. Thus, assuming the dense index for letters is kept in main memory, we need only a little more than one block access per letter to find references to all the numbers with a given NAME value. Of course, we must still retrieve the records for these numbers if we want to access them, and this step would take one access per number if pointers were stored in the secondary index, and several accesses per number if keys (i.e., the numbers themselves) were stored in the secondary index and some appropriate structure were used for a primary index. If the size of the *numbers* file were very large, and the numbers for each NAME value covered several blocks, we could still retrieve references to all of the numbers with a given first letter with about as many block accesses as the references themselves could fit in.

Instead of storing the secondary index in preorder, with a dense index on letters, we could use separate storage of the repeating group of references, as in Figure 6.18. Then the secondary index itself would consist of only the (up to) six letters that are possible values of NAME, each paired with a pointer to a chain of blocks that hold of all the references for that letter. The index itself becomes a short file with at most six letter-pointer records, which we might store as a linked list of blocks. An example, using the data of Figure 6.7, with our tiny blocks holding six elements each, is shown in Figure 6.20. There, each of the lists of references fits on one block, but in general, these lists would cover many blocks. □

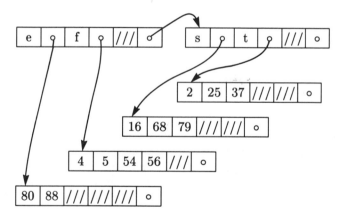

**Figure 6.20** Separate-storage structure for secondary index.

## Dense Indices as Secondary Indices

The importance of storing the references for a given value close to that value and close to each other goes up as the number of references associated with each value increases. Only then can we minimize the number of blocks that need to be retrieved when using the secondary index. On the other hand, if the expected number of records with a given value in the field of the secondary index is small, then we have the option of treating the secondary index as if it were a dense index for a key value. Some of the structures for primary indices need some modification. A hashed file, as we have mentioned, does not depend on the keyness of the values it hashes. However, sorted files and index structures can present some pitfalls if used as a dense index on values that do not serve as keys.

Suppose we have a secondary index on field $F$, which we store as a dense index. That is, our secondary (dense) index is a file of pairs $(v, p)$, where $p$ is a pointer to a record with value $v$ in field $F$. Let us sort the file on the first component and use the (sparse) isam index structure of Section 6.4 to find, given a value $v$, those pairs with first component $v$. There may, in fact, be two or more records, say $(v, p_1)$ and $(v, p_2)$, in the secondary index file. With bad luck, the first of these comes at the end of one block and the second at the beginning of the next, as

If we followed the lookup strategy of Section 6.4, with value $v$ we would be directed only to the second of these blocks (unless the first were entirely filled with pairs of first component $v$). Thus, on finding the first block with a given value $v$, if we find no value less than $v$ on that block, we must check the previous block in case it too contains a pair with value $v$. A similar warning applies if we use a B-tree as the structure for the secondary index.

## 6.9 DATA STRUCTURES IN DBTG DATABASES

Now, let us consider how the data structure ideas seen so far in this chapter are made available to the designer of the physical scheme of a CODASYL database. There are certain options that the DBTG proposal, introduced in Sections 5.1–5.3, makes available to the designer of a particular database, and others that might be provided by the implementer of the database system. In this section, we shall cover the options regarding the representation of links and then discuss data structures for logical record types.

### Representing Links

There are several ways we can represent links so that we can travel efficiently from owner to members or vice versa. Suppose we have a link from member record type $T_2$ to owner record type $T_1$. The most efficient implementation of the link is generally to store the files corresponding to both of these record types as a nested structure $T_1(T_2)^*$. Then, if we implement this structure as suggested in Section 6.7, we can easily go from an owner of type $T_1$ to all of its members, and we can go easily from a member to its owner, if we use the preorder sequence.[13]

If there is another link from record type $T_3$ to $T_1$, we can list the occurrences of $T_3$ records with the corresponding $T_1$ records, using a nested structure such as $T_1(T_2)^*(T_3)^*$. Again, the methodology of Section 6.7 can be used to implement such structures.

However, suppose there is another link from $T_2$ to some record type $T_4$. We cannot list $T_2$ records after $T_1$ records and also list them after $T_4$ records, or at least, it would hardly be efficient or convenient to do so. If we duplicated $T_2$ records and placed them after both $T_1$ and $T_4$ records owning them, we would introduce the redundancy and potential for inconsistency that we always wish to avoid.

## Multilist Structures

We therefore need another way of representing links, one that does not force records of one type to be adjacent to records of another type. In this organization, called a *multilist*, each record has one pointer for each link in which it is involved, although we do have the option of eliminating the pointer for one link and representing that link by a nested structure, as discussed above.

Suppose we have a link $L$ from $T_2$ to $T_1$. For each record $R$ of type $T_1$ we create a ring beginning at $R$, then to all of the records $R_1, R_2, \ldots, R_k$ of type $T_2$ linked to $R$ by $L$, and finally back to $R$. The pointers for link $L$ in records of types $T_2$ and $T_1$ are used for this purpose. Such rings were suggested in Figure 5.1.

It is important to remember that in a multilist organization, each record has as many pointers as its record type has links. As the pointers are fields in the records, and therefore appear in fixed positions, we can follow the ring for a particular link without fear of accidentally following some other link. Another essential, if we are to navigate through multilists is that each record must have, in a fixed location such as the first byte, a code that indicates its record type. If we didn't have that code, we couldn't tell when we had reached the owner record in a ring. If the owner and member types of a link kept their pointer for the link in different positions,[14] then we could not find that pointer without knowing whether we were at a member or owner.

**Example 6.24:** Multilist structures involving two or more links can look quite complex, although logically, they are only implementing physically several many-one mappings, as we illustrated in Figure 2.15. There, we showed

---

[13] If we store the repeating group of $T_2$ records separately, as in Figure 6.18, then we also need pointers back from the $T_2$ records to their $T_1$ "owner."

[14] In general, it is not possible to avoid having the pointer position for at least one link differ between its owner and member types, without wasting substantial space.

the many-many relationship between courses and students, represented by two
many-one relationships and an intermediate "enrollment" record type. In Figure 2.15, ENROLL records have fields SECTION and GRADE. We now give
them two additional pointer fields, one for the link E_COURSE from ENROLL
to COURSES and the other for link E_STUDENT, which goes from ENROLL
to STUDENTS. The STUDENTS and COURSES records are given one pointer
field, for the one link in which each of these records participates. The multilist
structure corresponding to Figure 2.15 is shown in Figure 6.21. That figure can
also be viewed as a physical realization of the rings of Figure 5.1. □

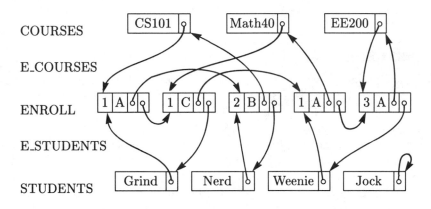

**Figure 6.21** A multilist structure for courses and students.

We may choose a multilist structure when we do not want to, or cannot,
store the member type of a link with its owner type as a nested structure. While
the multilist structure does allow us to traverse the rings, and thus, to perform
the FIND operations on DBTG sets described in Section 5.2 (e.g., finding owners
given members and vice-versa), the cost of doing so tends to be much greater
than with the nested structure discussed earlier in the section. The reason is
that on almost every step around the ring we shall have to retrieve a new block
into memory; the difference in performance between the multilist and nested
structure is similar to that illustrated in Example 6.23 of the previous section.

**Location Modes**

The DBTG data definition language allows us to declare data structures, called
*location modes*, for logical record types, and by implication, for the links involving those record types. One important location mode is called *CALC*; it was
mentioned in Section 5.2 because it is used for certain kinds of FIND statement.
This mode is declared by the clause

LOCATION MODE IS CALC <procedure> USING <field list>

in the declaration of the record type. For example, in Figure 5.2 we could include with the declaration for the SUPPLIERS record type the information

LOCATION MODE IS CALC PROC1 USING SNAME

Presumably, PROC1 is the name of a procedure that takes values for the SNAME field, producing a "hash value." In general, the CALC location mode suggests, but does not require, that the file for a record type declared this way be stored in buckets, one for each value produced by the "hashing" <procedure> applied to the values of the fields in the <field list>, as described in Section 6.3. As a perfectly reasonable alternative, the <procedure> could examine a sparse index to find the bucket in which a record belongs, as described in Section 6.4, or it could examine a dense index organized as a $B$-tree, as suggested in Sections 6.5 and 6.6.

There are no fundamental limits on what the <procedure> can do, but the user of the database is entitled to expect that, given values for the <field list>, locating some record (there may be several, because CALC-keys are not true keys) with those values in the <field list> can be done efficiently; it is the responsibility of the system to provide built-in procedures that make this search efficient.

A second location mode is *DIRECT*, declared by

LOCATION MODE IS DIRECT

This mode declares that records of the type are found only by their addresses in the file system, which are called "database keys" in the DBTG proposal. In principle, the file of records of this type can be kept in any order; a record will be accessed by providing a database key, that is, the location of the record.

A third location mode, *VIA*, is declared for a record type $T_1$ by

LOCATION MODE IS VIA <set name> SET

This declaration implies that type $T_1$ is the member type of the designated <set name>, $S$, and each record of type $T_1$ will be grouped with the owner of the $S$ occurrence of which it is a member. That is, if the owner type for $S$ is $T_2$, the $T_2$ records and the $T_1$ records are stored as a nested structure with format $T_2(T_1)^*$.

The VIA location mode leads to some very complex structures. For example, it is possible that record type $T_2$ is given declaration

LOCATION MODE IS VIA $R$ SET

where $T_2$ is the member type for DBTG set $R$, whose owner type is $T_3$. Then records of types $T_1$, $T_2$, and $T_3$ are organized as if in variable length records with format $T_3(T_2(T_1)^*)^*$.

## Comparison of Location Modes

Each location mode makes certain operations efficient but not others. The direct mode, corresponding to the heap organization of Section 6.2, allows us to use minimum area for a file, but makes search for records, given values for certain fields, almost impossible. The CALC mode is very good for lookup of records given their CALC-key, but navigation through links involving a member type stored in CALC mode may be inefficient. That is, to get all members of a given set occurrence we must follow the multilist structure, which requires that we make almost as many block accesses as there are members in the occurrence.

One the other hand, the VIA mode makes navigation between owners and members efficient, while lookup of a record is difficult if we don't know its owner. We can, however, create a secondary index (called a *search key* in the DBTG proposal) on the key values for some record type that was stored VIA a set and thus have the advantage of fast lookup inherent in the CALC mode.

As always, we can only decide what organization to use for a physical database if we have a clear idea of what sorts of operations we shall do most frequently; e.g., shall we be doing more lookup or more navigation through sets?

## Set Modes

There are also options regarding how DBTG sets are to be stored. The DBTG proposal allows us to declare *set modes* for DBTG sets. While the proposal is somewhat vague about what all of the options should be, it includes the multilist structure, called *chain mode*, and an arrangement called *pointer array mode*, in which each owner record has an array of pointers to its members. Presumably, any DBMS implementing the proposal would also allow users to declare other set modes, such as some of those discussed in Section 6.7 to implement variable length records.

## 6.10 DATA STRUCTURES FOR HIERARCHIES

The nested structures of Section 6.7 are the natural implementation of a hierarchy. That is, the structure for a leaf node with record type $R$ is just $R$, and the record structure for an interior node with record type $T$ and children of record types $S_1, \ldots, S_n$ is $R(S_1)^* \cdots (S_n)^*$. We gave several examples of this construction in Example 6.19, although we did take advantage of the fact that we expected there to be only one manager of a department, as we used MGR instead of (MGR)* in constructing the nested structure for departments database records.

Another way to view this structure for hierarchies is that each logical record type except for the root is stored "via" the implicit DBTG set of which its parent is the owner and it is the member type. As we pointed out in Section 6.7, a feature of such an organization is that given a node, we can find its descendants in the tree in very few block accesses on the average, since they collectively follow the node in the preorder sequence. It is this property of the preorder listing, together with the assumption that the most frequent type of query will ask for the descendants of a given node, that justifies the preorder sequence as an important organization for hierarchical data.

## Data Structures in IMS

The IMS hierarchical database system offers the database designer certain options that combine nested structures, stored in preorder, with some of the access techniques described earlier in this chapter. Specifically, we are given the option to have the collection of database records corresponding to a single tree in the hierarchical scheme stored in a sequence of blocks, with each database record kept together and stored in the preorder sequence. To help access root records quickly, we create a primary index on the key of the root record type. This index can be either:

1. A hash table, used as a dense index, or
2. An isam index, as described in Section 6.4, used as a dense index.

That is, we create a pair $(v, p)$ for each root record, where $v$ is its key value and $p$ is a pointer to that record. These pairs are stored either in a hash table or an isam index, with the first component as key for the pairs. In analogy with the DBTG options, we store the root record type by CALC-key and the other record types $R$ "via" the link between $R$ and its parent.

A third strategy, called *HISAM* (hierarchical, indexed-sequential access method) partitions database records into buckets, using an isam index based on the keys of the root records. The buckets each hold keys in some range, and the ranges do not change as the database evolves. We can view each bucket as arranged in a two-dimensional way. The rows correspond to single database records, and each database record will be, in general, spread over some linked list of blocks. We shall assume that no block holds data from more than one database record and that, as usual, records are not spread over more than one block. The former constraint is for implementation convenience; if we select the block size to be somewhat smaller than the typical database record, there will be little waste space because of it.

**Example 6.25:** Figure 6.22(a) shows a simple hierarchy and Figure 6.22(b) shows three database records that might form a tiny instance of the database. We have made assumption about the relative sizes of $A$, $B$, and $C$ records, which can be deduced from Figure 6.23. For convenience, the key value for an $A$-type record $a_i$ is taken to be $i$ itself. We suppose that the database records whose roots have key values 10 and 20 belong in one bucket and the one with key value 30 belongs in a second bucket.

Figure 6.23 shows the three database records stored among blocks. Each

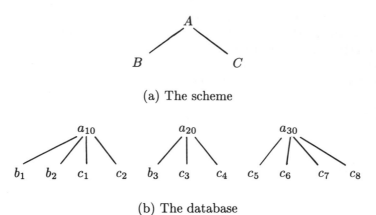

(a) The scheme

(b) The database

**Figure 6.22** Example database and its scheme.

block has a pointer in the front to the first block of the next database record in the same bucket. This pointer is unused if the block is not the first block for its database record. We also show a pointer at the end of each block, linking the block to the next block for the same database record if there is one. □

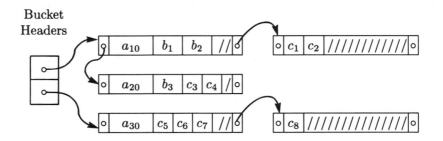

**Figure 6.23** Two-dimensional organization of database records.

In the HISAM organization, records can be moved around within the blocks of one database record, because pointers to the descendant records consist of:

1. The address of the first block of the database record, and
2. The value of the key field or fields for the record in question.

Note that this type of "pointer" will not support the movement of records among different database records. It does, however, allow us to insert new records into their proper place within a database record, moving other records among the various blocks holding that database record, if necessary.

**Example 6.26:** Suppose that in the database of Figure 6.23 we insert $b_4$ as a child of $a_{30}$. Using our relative size assumptions it is necessary to move $c_7$ to the block now occupied by $c_8$, while shifting $c_5$, $c_6$, and $c_8$ to the right. If we then delete $c_6$, we simply set a deletion bit in that record; no motion of records is made.

Now, imagine that we insert a database record with root $a_{12}$ and children $b_5$ and $c_9$, then insert a database record with root $a_{15}$ and children $b_6$, $b_7$, and $b_8$. Each of these database records belongs in the first bucket, and we can place them in sorted order within the bucket. The resulting arrangement of blocks and records is shown in Figure 6.24. □

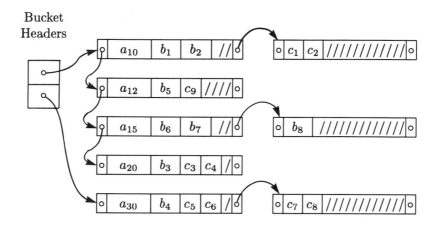

**Figure 6.24** Database records after some insertions and deletions.

### Pointer Networks

In some queries, we do not want to see the entire database record, and if so, we can often speed our access to the relevant parts if we use a network of pointers to connect the records that belong to one database record. For example, if all the children of the root were linked by a chain of pointers, we could visit each child in turn, even though many blocks holding the descendants of those children appear between them.

IMS uses two types of pointer networks. The first is the obvious one: each record points to the next record in the preorder listing. This arrangement is called *preorder threads*. The second arrangement is for each record to have a pointer to its leftmost child and a pointer to its right sibling. The *right sibling* of a node $n$ is that child of the parent of $n$ that is immediately to the right of *n*. For example, in Figure 6.25(a), *g* is the right sibling of *b*, and *g* has no right sibling.

**Example 6.27:** Figure 6.25(a) shows a tree; Figure 6.25(b) shows that tree with preorder threads, and Figure 6.25(c) shows the same tree with leftmost child (solid) and right sibling (dashed) pointers. □

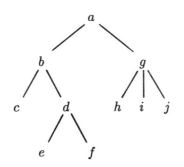

(a) A tree.

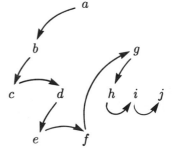

(b) Preorder threads

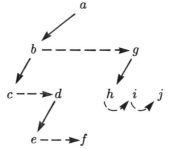

(c) Leftmost child/right sibling pointers

**Figure 6.25** Pointer arrangements.

Each method has its advantages. Preorder threads need only one pointer per record, while leftmost child/right sibling pointers require space for two pointers per record, even though many of these pointers are null (for example, no leaf node has a leftmost child). On the other hand, leftmost child/right sibling pointers enable us to travel from left to right through the children of a node quickly, even though many descendants intervene in the preorder sequence. Observe, for example, how we can go from *b* to *g* directly in Figure 6.25(c), while we must travel through *c*, *d*, *e*, and *f* in Figure 6.25(b).

## 6.11 DATA STRUCTURES FOR RELATIONS

A relation has an obvious representation as a file of records, with one record for each tuple. However, many data structures can be used to make access to relations more efficient than the obvious organization. In this section we shall examine some of the options that have been used in relational database systems.

### Storage of Relations in INGRES

INGRES was one of the first relational database systems; its query language, Quel, was introduced in Section 4.3. In its original implementation there were three options for organization of relations. Later, B-trees became available, as well. When a relation $R$ is created, it has a "heap" organization; that is, the tuples are in any order, with no access structure. Tuples of such a relation can be found only by scanning the file.

We can arrange for hashed access to the file for relation $R$ by saying

> modify $R$ to hash on $A_1, \ldots, A_k$

where $A_1, \ldots, A_k$ is the list of attributes of $R$ whose values are hashed to determine the bucket for a given record. The INGRES implementation of the file for $R$ becomes that of Section 6.3; records may be pinned because of secondary indices, as mentioned below.

An ISAM index can be created for the file $R$, by writing

> modify $R$ to isam on $A_1, \ldots, A_k$

Again, $A_1, \ldots, A_k$ is the assumed key for $R$.

We can create a secondary index for $R$ by the statement

> index on $R$ is $S(A_1, \ldots, A_k)$

The relation $S$ becomes a secondary index on attributes $A_1, \ldots, A_k$ for $R$. That is, associated with each list of values $v_1, \ldots, v_k$ for $A_1, \ldots, A_k$, respectively, is a set of pointers to those records of relation $R$ that have value $v_i$ for attribute $A_i$, for $i = 1, 2, \ldots, k$. The relation $S$ has $k + 1$ components, the first $k$ being $A_1, \ldots, A_k$, and the last being a pointer to a record of $R$; the last component has no attribute name, so the user cannot access its values or change them. The file for secondary index $S$ can be given a structure by the modify command, just as any other relation can.

### Storage Organization in System R

System R is the original relational database system from which the language SQL, introduced in Section 4.5, derives. This system used a number of data structure ideas that mirror the techniques found in the DBTG proposal, although some more recent implementations of SQL do not use all these options. In System R one can:

1. Store one relation "VIA" another,
2. Create a multilist structure to connect the tuples of two relations, and
3. Create an index for any relation on any set of attributes; this index is a dense index, as described in Section 6.6, with a B-tree structure.

### Indices in System R

The B-tree indices mentioned in (3) above make no distinction between a primary and secondary index. That is, it doesn't matter to the system whether the set of attributes for an index forms a key for the relation. Suppose we have an index on attributes $A_1, \ldots, A_k$. Then the interior nodes of the B-tree are blocks filled, as much as the B-tree scheme allows, with records consisting of a pointer to another block and a list of values, one for each of the attributes of the index. These records are essentially the same as the pairs consisting of a pointer and a key value that we discussed in connection with B-trees in Section 6.5; the difference is that there is no presumption of keyness.

Leaf nodes of the B-tree consist of values for attributes $A_1, \ldots, A_k$ and associated lists of *tuple identifiers*; there is one tuple identifier for each tuple having the given values for $A_1, \ldots, A_k$. Actually, tuple identifiers point not to the tuple, but to a place near the end of the block, where a pointer to the tuple itself can be found. This double indirection, through a block directory, does not cost us extra block accesses, and it has the advantage that tuples may be moved around within blocks, as was mentioned in Section 6.1.

The reader should note that this arrangement differs somewhat from the B-tree schemes we discussed in Sections 6.5 and 6.6. In the terms of Section 6.7, there is a nested structure with the pattern

VALUE (RECORD)*

serving as a secondary index into the main file. This structure is implemented by storing its instance in preorder, among a sequence of blocks. These blocks, which are the "leaves of the B-tree" mentioned above, are managed by splitting overfull blocks into two, and merging blocks less than half full, according to the B-tree style of handling insertions and deletions.

### "Via Set" Structures in System R

As we mentioned above, System R also allows the tuples of one relation to be stored as a nested structure with the tuples of another relation, thus imitating storage "via set" as defined by the DBTG proposal. This storage option gives us the advantage of nested structures discussed in Section 6.7. For example, the relations CUSTOMERS, ORDERS, and INCLUDES from Figure 4.2 can be stored in preorder, as an instance of the nested structure

CUSTOMERS (ORDERS (INCLUDES)*)*

The resulting sequence of tuples beginning with the CUSTOMERS record for Zack Zebra and including all its "owned" ORDERS records and INCLUDES records "owned" by them, is shown in Figure 6.26.

CUSTOMERS record for Zack Zebra
ORDERS record for order 1024
INCLUDES record:
    O# = 1024; ITEM = "Brie"; QUANTITY = 3
INCLUDES record:
    O# = 1024; ITEM = "Perrier"; QUANTITY = 6
ORDERS record for order 1026
INCLUDES record:
    O# = 1026; ITEM = "Macadamias"; QUANTITY = 2048

**Figure 6.26** Tuples stored "via set."

The similarity of Figure 6.26 to Figure 6.17 should be observed. The INCLUDES tuples correspond to what we called "entries," which consist of a virtual item and a quantity. However, one should appreciate the fact that in the hierarchical and network models, we do not have to place the customer name in both CUSTOMERS and ORDERS, or the order number in both ORDERS and INCLUDES. The structure of the network or hierarchy allows us to determine the customer for an order by its owner (in networks) or parent (in hierarchies). In a relational system, it is the common values between CUSTOMERS and ORDERS, and between ORDERS and INCLUDES, that determines the positions of ORDERS and INCLUDES records; e.g., an ORDERS record follows the CUSTOMERS record with the same customer name.

The formal requirements for storing the tuples of a relation $R$ nested within a relation $S$, according to the pattern $SR^*$ are as follows.

1. We can establish a correspondence between a set of attributes $X$ of $R$ and $Y$ of $S$. For example, $R$ could be ORDERS, $S$ could be CUSTOMERS, $X$ could consist of the single attribute CUST, and $Y$ could be the single attribute NAME. Note that CUST in ORDERS and NAME in CUSTOMERS "mean" the same thing, but of course there is no requirement for a similarity of "meaning."

2. $Y$ is a key for $S$.

3. Whenever we have a tuple $\mu$ in $R$, there is a tuple $\nu$ in $S$ such that $\mu[X] = \nu[Y]$; that is, the $X$-value of every tuple in $R$ occurs as a $Y$-value in some tuple of $S$.

Under these conditions, we can store, after each tuple $\nu$ of $S$, all the tuples $\mu$ of $R$ such that $\mu[X] = \nu[Y]$. Every tuple of $R$ will have a unique tuple of $S$ to follow.

### Multilist Structures in System R

We can also have, in System R, a multilist structure linking tuples of two relations according to common values in a field of each. Suppose that two relations $R$ and $S$ satisfy (1)–(3) above. Then we may create new attributes PTR for both relation schemes; these new attributes are not accessible to the user. The values for these two attributes are used to form rings connecting each tuple $\nu$ of $S$ to the tuples of $R$ that it "owns," that is, the tuples of $R$ whose $X$-values agree with $\nu[Y]$.

| O# | DATE | CUST | PTR | | PTR | O# | ITEM | QUANT. |
|------|-------|-------|-----|---|-----|------|-----------|--------|
| 1024 | Jan 3 | Zebra | | | | 1024 | Brie | 3 |
| 1025 | Jan 3 | Rhino | | | | 1024 | Perrier | 6 |
| 1026 | Jan 4 | Zebra | | | | 1025 | Brie | 5 |
| | | | | | | 1025 | Escargot | 12 |
| | | | | | | 1025 | Endive | 1 |
| | | | | | | 1026 | Macad-amias | 2048 |

**Figure 6.27** Ring Structure for ORDERS and INCLUDES.

**Example 6.28:** In Figure 6.27 we see the ORDERS and INCLUDES relations of Figure 4.2 stored as a multilist structure based on the commonality of values between the attributes CUST and NAME, respectively. □

## 6.12 RANGE QUERIES AND PARTIAL-MATCH QUERIES

Classical database systems are designed to handle the type of query that appears repeatedly in Chapters 4 and 5, one in which a value for one attribute or field is given and values of related attributes or fields are desired. The index structures covered so far in this chapter are well suited to such queries. However, in some modern applications, such as those discussed in the second half of Chapter 1—graphics databases, computer aided design databases, and VLSI databases—we are often faced with queries for which the index structures described so far are inadequate. These queries may involve inequalities, rather than equalities, and they may have many simultaneous conditions.

**Figure 6.28** Representation of a rectangle.

**Example 6.29:** A fundamental object in a graphics or VLSI database is a rectangle, which we may suppose is represented by a record with four fields, giving the coordinates of the lower-left and upper-right corners, as suggested in Figure 6.28. Some typical queries about a relation

RECTANGLES(X1, Y1, X2, Y2)

are shown in Figure 6.29. Part (a) asks for all the rectangles that contain the point $(3, 4)$, while (b) asks for the rectangles that have lower-left corner at point $(5, 6)$. Query (c) asks for all rectangles whose lower-left corner is in the square bounded by the $x$- and $y$-axes, and the lines $x = 10$ and $y = 10$. $\square$

```
SELECT X1, Y1, X2, Y2
FROM RECTANGLES
WHERE X1 <= 3 AND X2 >= 3 AND Y1 <= 4 AND Y2 >= 4
```
          (a) Rectangles that contain the point $(3, 4)$.

```
SELECT X1, Y1, X2, Y2
FROM RECTANGLES
WHERE X1 = 5 AND Y1 = 6
```
          (b) Rectangles with lower-left corner at $(5, 6)$.

```
SELECT X1, Y1, X2, Y2
FROM RECTANGLES
WHERE X1 >= 0 AND X1 <= 10 AND Y1 >= 0 and Y1 <= 10
```
          (c) Lower-left corner in square of side 10.

**Figure 6.29** Some range and partial-match queries.

## Range Queries

A query in which fields are restricted to a range of values rather than a single value is called a *range query*. Figure 6.29(a) and (c) are range queries; in (a), $x_1$ is restricted to the range $-\infty \le x_1 \le 3$, and in (c) $x_1$ is restricted to the range $0 \le x_1 \le 10$, for example.

## Partial-Match Queries

A query in which several fields (but not all fields) are restricted to single values is often called a *partial-match query*. Figure 6.29(b) is a partial-match query, since values for two of the fields, $x_1$ and $y_1$ are specified, and the other two fields are left unspecified.

Usually, but not necessarily, range queries and partial-match queries are applied to files with the property that no proper subset of the fields of a record is a key. For example, a rectangle is uniquely determined only by the four coordinates used in Example 6.29; any subset of three or fewer cannot determine a unique rectangle. It is also normal that the query asks for the entire record, as did the queries in Figure 6.29, rather than for a subset of the fields.

## Performance of Index Structures on Partial-Match Queries

Let us consider a partial-match query such as Figure 6.29(b). Suppose we placed a secondary index on each of the fields in Example 6.29. The query of Figure 6.29(b) could then be answered as follows:

1. Use the index on $x_1$ to find all those rectangles with $x_1 = 5$.
2. Select from among those records retrieved in (1) the records that have $y_1 = 6$.

That method is better than searching the entire file of rectangles, but it is not as good as the theoretical optimum. If we were to group the rectangles to answer that one query, we would put all answers on as few blocks as would hold them. Instead, if we have a secondary index on $x_1$, we have to access as many blocks as there are rectangles with $x_1 = 5$, because no two of these rectangles are likely to appear on the same block. That is many more blocks than there are answers (since most rectangles with $x_1 = 5$ will not have $y_1 = 6$), and it is far more than the number of blocks on which the answers could be held under some ideal organization.

In reality, we cannot expect to have an organization that is ideal for any partial-match query. If we choose to organize the file of rectangles with a primary index on $x_1$, such as a hash, isam, or B-tree index, then rectangles with the same $x_1$ value will be close physically, and we can retrieve, say, the rectangles having $x_1 = 5$ with a number of accesses close to the number of blocks on which they all fit, rather than the (much larger) number of such rectangles.

However, even that is not as good as the ideal, because on the average, few of these rectangles will have $y_1 = 6$. Furthermore, the primary index would only help if the query specifies a value for $x_1$ (or whichever field we chose for the primary index).

Another alternative is to get pointers to all of the possible solution records from dense indices on all of the fields for which the query provides a value. Then we intersect these sets of pointers. If these sets are sufficiently small, the intersection can take place in main memory. The pointers in the intersection tell us where to find the records in the solution. In our running example, the cost is proportional to the number of index blocks that point to records with either $x_1 = 5$ or $y_1 = 6$, plus the number of blocks on which solution records are found, which can still be much larger than the theoretical ideal.

## Performance of Index Structures on Range Queries

We have similar, or even worse, problems with range queries. If we use hashing for our indices, then we get no help for queries with large ranges. For example, if field $X$ is restricted to range $a \leq X \leq b$, then we must look in the buckets for every value between $a$ and $b$ inclusive for possible values of $X$. There may easily be more values in this range than there are buckets, meaning that we must look in all, or almost all, the buckets.

Structures like isam indices and B-trees do support range queries to an extent. We can find all $X$ values in the range $a \leq X \leq b$ with a number of block accesses that is close to the number of records whose $X$ field is in that range. However, isam or B-tree secondary indices on each of the fields still leave us with the problem we encountered with partial-match queries: the number of blocks retrieved is proportional to the number of records that satisfy one of the conditions, not to the number of answers. For example, in the query of Figure 6.29(c), we would retrieve either all the rectangles with $0 \leq x_1 \leq 10$ or all the rectangles with $0 \leq y_1 \leq 10$.

The data structures we propose in the next two sections are more efficient on some but not all of the partial-match and range queries. However, they allow us to avoid maintaining indices on all the fields,[15] which is expensive because all insertions and deletions must deal with each of the indices we create. The structures we propose next are often superior in retrieval time, are simpler and faster to update, and require less space than keeping secondary indices on all the fields.

---

[15] If we omitted an index on one field $F$, then a query that specified a range or a value only for $F$ would receive no help from the structure.

## 6.13 PARTITIONED HASH FUNCTIONS

Partitioned hashing is a technique that can be used for partial-match queries and, if we know something about the distribution of values in the various fields, for range queries as well. Let us assume we have a file with fields $F_1, F_2, \ldots, F_k$, and suppose that they are all regarded as part of the key for purposes of hashing. If we used a typical hash function such as those suggested in Section 6.3, we could not locate a record without being given values for all the fields. However, if we design the hash function carefully, we can limit the number of buckets to be searched in response to any partial-match query; the more fields that are specified, the fewer buckets we must search.

The "trick" is to divide the bits of the bucket number into several pieces and let each field determine one of the pieces. Then, whenever we know one or more fields, we know something about the bucket numbers in which the desired record or records could be found. We assume for convenience that the number of buckets is a power of two; i.e., $B = 2^b$. Then a bucket number is a string of $b$ bits. If the fields are $F_1, \ldots, F_k$, we assign $b_i$ bits to field $F_i$, in such a way that $\sum_{i=1}^{k} b_i = b$. It is not necessary that all the $b_i$'s be the same, or even close to each other in value, but that is often a sensible thing to do. As with all hash tables, we want $B$ to approximate the number of blocks needed to hold the file, so the number of blocks per bucket is about one.

For each $i = 1, 2, \ldots, k$ there is a hash function $h_i$ whose range is the integers from 0 through $2^{b_i} - 1$, inclusive. We may think of $h_i(v)$ as a sequence of exactly $b_i$ bits, by padding small integers with 0's on the left, if necessary. To determine the bucket in which a record $(v_1, \ldots, v_k)$ belongs, we apply $h_i$ to $v_i$ for each $i$. The bucket for this record is then the integer whose bit string is $h_1(v_1)h_2(v_2) \cdots h_k(v_k)$. Note this string is of length $b$, and therefore represents a bucket number in the correct range, from 0 to $B - 1$, inclusive.

**Example 6.30:** Instead of storing rectangles as we did in Example 6.29, let us consider the simpler problem of storing points, that is, $(x, y)$ pairs. The following is the sample database we shall use, consisting of nine points.

$$(3,6) \qquad (6,7) \qquad (1,1)$$
$$(5,6) \qquad (4,3) \qquad (5,0)$$
$$(6,1) \qquad (0,4) \qquad (7,2)$$

Let us choose $B = 4$, and pick $b_1 = b_2 = 1$. For both the hash functions $h_1$ and $h_2$ we shall use the high-order bit in the three-bit representation of the number; i.e., $h_1(i) = h_2(i) = 0$ for $0 \le i \le 3$ and $h_1(i) = h_2(i) = 1$ for $4 \le i \le 7$. The reason for using this function will become clear when we take up range queries. The sample data above divides into the four buckets with numbers $b_1 b_2$ as shown in Figure 6.30. For example, the point $(4, 3)$ has $b_1 = h_1(4) = 1$, and $b_2 = h_2(3) = 0$, so it goes in bucket $b_1 b_2 = 10$, i.e., the

$$b_2 =$$

|  | 0 | 1 |
|---|---|---|
| 0 | $(1,1)$ | $(3,6)$ $(0,4)$ |
| 1 | $(4,3)$ $(5,0)$ $(6,1)$ $(7,2)$ | $(6,7)$ $(5,6)$ |

$b_1 =$

**Figure 6.30**  Distribution of points into buckets.

bucket whose number is 2. $\Box$

### Answering Partial-Match Queries

If we are given values for a subset of the fields $F_1, \ldots, F_k$, We use the hash functions for the fields whose values were given, to compute whatever bits of the bucket number are determined by those fields. The only buckets that could hold records to be retrived are those whose numbers, treated as binary strings, match all of the computed bits; values in other bits can be either 0 or 1.

**Example 6.31:** Continuing with Example 6.30, suppose we ask for all those points with $x = 5$. Then we know bit $b_1$ is 1, but we do not know $b_2$. Thus, we must look in buckets whose numbers are bit strings 10 and 11; i.e., in buckets number 2 and 3. In those buckets we find points $(5,0)$ and $(5,6)$, as well as several points that do not match the query (see Figure 6.30). $\Box$

### Answering Range Queries

We can also adapt the partitioned hash function structure to answer range queries if our data obeys a "uniformity" assumption. In general, one of the advantages of hashing is that it randomizes the distribution of keys into buckets, so even if keys were chosen in some regular pattern, it is very likely that records would distribute themselves fairly evenly among buckets. However, if we want to answer range queries, we also want to know that records whose values in a given field are close have a high probability of being in the same bucket, or scattered over relatively few buckets. Put another way, we want a hash function $h$ that respects the linear order on the values in each field, i.e., if $v \leq w$ we want $h(v) \leq h(w)$.

That condition is not compatible with the requirement that $h$ divide "random" sets of values evenly among buckets. In effect, we must partition values so the lowest numbers, up to some fixed value $a_0$, go in bucket 0, values bigger than $a_0$, up to some larger value $a_1$, go in bucket 1, and so on. If we can find a sequence of numbers $a_0, \ldots, a_{B-2}$ such that the number of values in each of the ranges $-\infty$ to $a_0$, $a_0$ to $a_1, \ldots, a_{B-2}$ to $+\infty$ are expected to be about equal, then the hash function that sends these ranges to buckets $0, 1, \ldots, B-1$, respectively, serves both purposes: it preserves order and it "randomizes." However, to use this approach to hashing requires that we know quite accurately the distribution of values in each of the fields on which we hash.

**Example 6.32:** The partitioned hash function of Example 6.30 respects order, since it uses the most significant bits of its values. To justify its use, we must assume that points are chosen at random from the square of side 8 with lower-left corner at the origin, i.e., the set of points $(x, y)$ defined by $0 \leq x \leq 7$ and $0 \leq y \leq 7$. Actually, in this simple case it is sufficient to assume that the expected numbers of points in each of the four quadrants of this square are about the same; the exact distribution within quadrants does not matter. Even this assumption requires accurate knowledge of the nature of the data. It would be terrible, for example, if 90% of the points turned out to be in one quadrant.

With bad luck, even a small range in $x$ and $y$ will force us to look at all four buckets. That happens, for example, if the query asks for $3 \leq x \leq 4$ and $3 \leq y \leq 4$. However, some ranges for $x$ or $y$ that are smaller than half of the entire range (0 to 7) allow us to restrict bit $b_1$ (if the range is for $x$) or bit $b_2$ (if for $y$) of the bucket number. In that case, we need only look at a subset of the buckets. For example, the query $1 \leq x \leq 3$ and $2 \leq y \leq 5$ requires us to look only at the two buckets with $b_1 = 0$, i.e., buckets 0 and 1. For the data of Figure 6.30, no matching points are found. $\square$

### Performance of Partitioned Hashing

The small size of our running example may not allow the general rule to be seen. Thus, let us consider general partial-match queries, with fields $F_1, \ldots, F_k$ and with $b_i$ bits of the bucket address devoted to field $F_i$, for $i = 1, 2, \ldots, k$. If a query specifies values for set of fields $S$, let $\bar{S}$ be the set of fields for which a value is not specified. Then the number of buckets we must examine is $2^c$, where

$$c = \sum_{i \text{ in } \bar{S}} b_i$$

In justification, note that $c$ bits are left unspecified, and these bits can be replaced by any of $2^c$ bit strings.

For example, if $b_i = b/k$ for each $i$, and $m$ out of the $k$ fields are specified, then the number of buckets searched is $2^{b(k-m)/k}$. As a more specific example, if $m = k/2$, then we search $2^{b/2}$ buckets, or the square root of the total number of buckets.

When we have range queries to evaluate, we need to make the simplifying assumption that the number of bits devoted to each field is large. Then, we can neglect "edge effects" due to small ranges that hash to two different values, as was illustrated in Example 6.32. That is, we assume that if a field $F_i$ is restricted to a range that is fraction $r$ of its total domain, then the number of different hash values $h_i(v)$ resulting from given values $v$ in this range will be fraction $r$ of the total number of values that $h_i$ can produce, that is, $r2^{b_i}$.

Thus, let us suppose that for $i = 1, 2, \ldots, k$, field $F_i$ is restricted by our query to a range whose length is fraction $r_i$ of its total range; if the query does not restrict $F_i$, then take $r_i$ to be 1. Then the number of buckets that must be retrieved is

$$\prod_{i=1}^{k} r_i 2^{b_i} = B \prod_{i=1}^{k} r_i$$

The above equality follows because $\prod_{i=1}^{k} 2^{b_i} = 2^b$, and $2^b$ is $B$, the number of buckets. Thus, we have shown that, neglecting edge effects, the fraction of the buckets that must be examined is the same as the product of the $r_i$'s, which is the fraction of all possible records that match the query. That is the least possible cost, since almost all the retrieved blocks consist of answer records only, and any retrieval algorithm must access at least that many blocks.

In summary, partitioned hashing offers essentially best-possible performance on range queries. It offers good performance on partial-match queries, but the comparison with the multiple-indices structure considered in Section 6.12 could go either way depending on the data. In favor of partitioned hashing is the fact that update of records is almost as simple as possible, while a possible problem is that the good performance on retrieval depends on our having a priori knowledge of the statistics of the data.

## 6.14 A SEARCH TREE STRUCTURE

There are a variety of tree structures that one can use to support range and partial-match queries. B-trees, for example, can be modified so that at different levels, different fields are used to divide records among the subtrees descending from a single node. If we had a value (in a partial-match query) or a small range (in a range query) for a field $F$, and the level we are at during our search branched according to the value of $F$, then we could restrict our search significantly at levels below. If a value or range were unspecified for $F$, then at this level we would have to look at all the children of each node $N$ at that level, such that prior levels of search brought us to $N$.

The problem is that B-trees often have very few levels, so frequently it would not be possible to devote even one level to each field. We shall instead consider a similar structure, called a k-d-tree, which is really designed for main-memory operation. We shall then mention how it can be adapted to our model of costs, where only block accesses are counted.

A k-d-tree is a variant of a *binary search tree*, which is a tree whose nodes each hold a record and have (optional) left and right children. In an ordinary binary search tree, there is one key field for records, and if node $N$ has key $x$, then the left child of $N$ and all its descendants have keys less than $x$, while the right child of $N$ and all its descendants have keys greater than $x$.

To find the record with key value $v$, we start at the root. In general, during the search we shall be at some node $M$. If the key at $M$ is $v$ we are done. If $v$ is less than the key of $M$ we go to $M$'s left child, and if $v$ is greater, we go to $M$'s right child. Thus, we follow only one path from the root to a place where the record is found, or we try to move to a missing child, in which case we know there is no record with key $v$ in the tree. If we wish to insert a record, we search for its key and insert the record at the place where we find a missing child. Deletion is a bit trickier; if we find the record with key $v$, say at node $N$:

1.    If $N$ has no children, delete $N$.
2.    If $N$ has only one child, $M$, replace $N$ by $M$.
3.    If $N$ has two children, find the leftmost descendant of the right child of $N$, and move that node to replace $N$.

These techniques, and the reason they work, are fairly common knowledge, and we shall not elaborate on them further. The reader interested in the details can consult Aho, Hopcroft, and Ullman [1983].

A k-d-tree differs from a binary search tree only in that the levels of the tree are assigned to fields in round-robin fashion; that is, if there are $k$ fields, $F_1, \ldots, F_k$, then level $i$ is assigned $F_i$, for $i = 1, 2, \ldots, k$, level $k + 1$ is assigned $F_1$, and so on. If $N$ is a node at a level to which $F_i$ is assigned, and the value of field $F_i$ in the record at $N$ is $x$, then the left child of $N$ and all its descendants must have $F_i < x$, while the right child of $N$ and its descendants must have $F_i \geq x$.

**Example 6.33:** Let us store the nine points of Example 6.30 in a k-d-tree. In general, many different k-d-trees can be used for the same set of records; which one we get depends on the order in which we insert. The one we get by inserting the nine points in order, row by row and left-to-right within rows, is shown in Figure 6.31; we shall see how this tree is obtained shortly. $\square$

## Lookup in k-d-Trees

As above, we assume our k-d-tree stores records with fields $F_1, \ldots, F_k$, and the levels are assigned fields in round-robin fashion. Suppose we are asked to

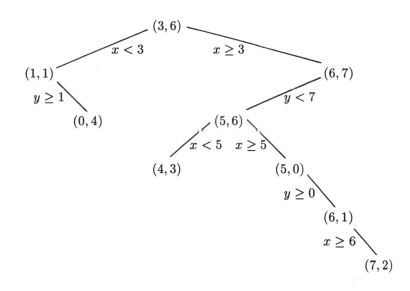

**Figure 6.31** k-d-tree.

find the record $(v_1, \ldots, v_k)$. The search procedure is applicable to any node $N$; initially, we start with $N$ equal to the root.

1. If $N$ holds record $(v_1, \ldots, v_k)$, we are done.
2. Otherwise, let $N$ be at level $j$, and let $F_i$ be the field assigned to $N$'s level. Let $x$ be the value of field $F_i$ in the record at $N$; we call $x$ the *dividing value* for $N$. If $v_i < x$, and there is no left child of $N$, then we have failed to find the desired record. If $v_i < x$ and $N$ has a left child $M$, then repeat the search process at $M$.
3. If $v_i \geq x$ and $N$ has no right child, then the search has failed. If $v_i \geq x$ and $N$ has right child $M$, repeat the search at $M$

Thus, the lookup procedure is little different from lookup in an ordinary binary search tree. The only modification is that at each node along the search path, we must compare the proper fields of the desired record and the record at the node; in the binary search tree, it is always the key fields that are compared.

To insert a record $r$, we perform the lookup procedure, and when we come to a missing child, we insert the record in the place for that child, knowing that should we come looking for $r$ we shall be directed from the root to that child and thus find $r$. Deletion is performed as described for binary search trees in general. In fact, we have some additional options regarding the choice of the record that replaces the deleted record; this matter is left as an exercise.

**Example 6.34:** We mentioned that the k-d-tree of Figure 6.31 was constructed by inserting each of the nine data points in turn. The last to be inserted is $(7, 2)$, so let us imagine the tree missing that node and see how insertion takes place. We start at the root, which is level one and, therefore, is assigned the first field $(x)$ for its branching. We compare the first field of $(7, 2)$ with the first field of the record at the root, which is $(3, 6)$. Thus, the dividing value at the root is 3. As $7 \geq 3$, we go to the right child of the root.

At the second level, we deal with field two, i.e., the $y$ components. The second field of our record, 2, is less than the second field of the record $(6, 7)$ which we found at the right child of the root. Thus, we move to the left child of that node, where record $(5, 6)$ is found. At the third level, we again compare first fields, we find that $7 \geq 5$, and so we move to the right child, where record $(5, 0)$ lives. We compare second fields, find $2 \geq 0$, and again move to the right child, which holds record $(6, 1)$. As this node is at level five, we compare first fields again, and we find $7 \geq 6$, so we move to the right child. However, there is no right child, so we place the record $(7, 2)$ in that position, making it the right child of $(6, 1)$. $\square$

### Partial-Match Retrieval from k-d-Trees

If we are given values for a subset of the fields, we search as outlined above, as long as we are at a node whose assigned field is one for which we have a value. If we have no value for the field of our current node, then we must go both left and right, and the search algorithm is applied to both children of the node. Thus, the number of paths we follow from the root can double at each level for which no value is given by the partial-match query.

**Example 6.35:** Suppose we want to find, in the tree of Figure 6.31, the set of points with $y = 1$. Then at even-numbered levels, we can use the $y$-value 1 to guide our search to the left or right, while at odd-numbered levels we have no $x$-value to use, and so must search both left and right.

We begin at the root, and since $x$ is the field assigned to this level, we must examine both the left and right subtrees of the root. Of course, we must also check the point at the root itself, but that point, $(3, 6)$ does not have $y = 1$, so we do not select it. At the left child of the root we find point $(1, 1)$, which we select because of its $y$-value. As this node is assigned field $y$, we can restrict the search. We need only move to the right child, because no point with $y = 1$ can be found in the left subtree, where all $y$-values must be less than 1 (the left subtree is empty, here, so by coincidence we haven't saved any work). The right child has point $(0, 4)$, which we do not select. Since $x$ is the assigned field, we must look at both subtrees, but they are empty trees, and we are done with the left subtree of the root.

Now, we search the right subtree of the root, starting at $(6, 7)$. As $y$ is the assigned field at this level, and $7 > 1$, we need only search the left subtree of

$(6, 7)$. That takes us to $(5, 6)$, where because the branch is on $x$, we are forced to look at both subtrees. The left subtree has only point $(4, 3)$, so we are done with the left side. For the right side, we examine $(5, 0)$. Since $y$ is the assigned field, and $1 \geq 0$, we have only to search right.

The next move takes us to $(6, 1)$, which we select because it has $y = 1$. As $x$ is the assigned field, we must examine both subtrees. As the left is empty, and the right contains only $(7, 2)$, we are done. The two points with $y = 1$, namely $(1, 1)$ and $(6, 1)$, have been found.

In the above example, each time we were able to restrict the search to one subtree, it turned out that the other subtree was empty anyway; thus we did not save any time. However, had we asked a partial-match query like $x = 4$, we would have quickly followed one path:

$$(3, 6), \quad (6, 7), \quad (5, 6), \quad (4, 3)$$

thereby finding the one point with $x = 4$. □

### Range Queries on k-d-Trees

A similar idea allows us to restrict the search in a k-d-tree when given a range query. Suppose we are at a node $N$ that is assigned the field $F$, and the query specifies a range from $a$ to $b$ for that field (possibly $a = -\infty$ or $b = \infty$, or both). Let the value of field $F$ at $N$ be $x$. If $b < x$, then any descendant of $N$ with an $F$-value in the range would have to be in the left subtree, so we do not have to search the right subtree of $N$. Likewise, if $a \geq x$, then we need not search the left subtree. Otherwise, we must search both left and right.

**Example 6.36:** Suppose we again have the k-d-tree of Figure 6.31 and we ask the range query with $2 \leq x \leq 4$ and $2 \leq y \leq 4$.[16] Begin at the root and note that the point there is not selected because its $y$-value is outside the range for $y$. As the dividing value, $x = 3$, is inside the range for $x$, we must search both left and right from the root.

Following the left path, we come to $(1, 1)$, which is outside the range in both $x$ and $y$. The dividing value, $y = 1$, is below the lower limit for $y$'s range, so we need only search right. That takes us to $(0, 4)$, which is not selected because $x$ is outside the range.

Now, let us follow the right path from the root. We come to $(6, 7)$, whose dividing value is $y = 7$. As this number exceeds the top end of the range for $y$, we need search only left. That takes us to $(5, 6)$, and the dividing value, $x = 5$, again sends us only left, because the top of $x$'s range is less than 5. We thus come to $(4, 3)$, which is the only point selected, and we are done, because the node of $(4, 3)$ has no children. The entire subtree rooted at $(5, 0)$ is not searched because we know that any point found there would have to have a

---

[16] We use the same range for $x$ and $y$ only for convenience in remembering the query.

$x$-value larger than the top of the desired range for $x$. $\square$

## Performance of k-d-Trees for Partial-Match Queries

As k-d-trees assume many shapes, even for a given set of records, it is hard to generalize about the lengths of paths that must be searched or the frequency with which the search must examine both subtrees of a node. We shall make the assuption that trees are *complete*; that is, all interior nodes down to some level have both their children, and all the leaves are at the same level. Then in a tree of $n$ nodes, all paths from the root to a leaf have length $\log n$.

While this assumption minimizes the average path length, and thus appears to underestimate the cost of searching, in compensation, whenever we are forced to look at both subtrees of a node, we find they are both nonempty; we do not get the fortuitous help that we did because of empty subtrees in the previous two examples.

Consider a partial match query in which $m$ out of $k$ fields are specified. Then $k - m$ times out of $k$, when we reach a node we shall have to search both subtrees. Thus, starting at the root, and traveling downward for $\log n$ levels, we shall split the path at $((k - m)/k) \log n$ levels, thereby reaching a total of

$$2^{((k-m)/k)\log n} = n^{(k-m)/k}$$

leaves.

## Performance of k-d-Trees for Range Queries

The performance of k-d-trees on range queries is harder to estimate precisely. The following argument offers a reasonable approximation. Suppose that our query restricts field $F_i$ to fraction $r_i$ of its total domain. In particular, consider a node $N$ with assigned field $F_i$. If the range for $F_i$ is $a$ to $b$, and the dividing value at $N$ is $x$, where $a \leq x \leq b$, then we must search both subtrees of $N$. However, on the left, we shall only encounter records with $F_i < x$. Thus, in the search of the left subtree, the range for $F_i$ is from $a$ to $x$, and the set of possible values for $F_i$ we might encounter in the left subtree of $N$ is that portion of the set of possible values for $F_i$ that is less than $x$. A similar statement holds for the right subtree of $x$, but the range and set of possible values are restricted to the portion $\geq x$.

As a result, on the average, both the range and the set of possible values are divided in half when we must search both subtrees, keeping $r_i$ effectively the same as it was at $N$. On the other hand, if we are fortunate to need to search only one subtree, then the range does not change size, but the set of possible values for $F_i$ that we might encounter is divided by 2 on the average. Thus, on the average, $r_i$ doubles when we need to search only one subtree.

The consequence is that we cannot expect to search only one of the subtrees too often. If we start with a range for $F_i$ that is fraction $r_i$ of the total domain for $F_i$, and at $j$ nodes that have $F_i$ as the assigned field, we need to search only one subtree, then the effective range for $F_i$ has become fraction $r_i 2^j$ of the set of possible values. As this fraction cannot exceed 1, we find that, on the average, we cannot expect to search only one subtree more than $j \leq \log(1/r_i)$ times due to $F_i$.

When we consider the possible savings due to each of the $k$ fields, we find that the number of levels at which we might expect that any path falls to bifurcate is

$$\sum_{i=1}^{k} \log(1/r_i) = \log\left(\frac{1}{\prod_{i=1}^{k} r_i}\right) \tag{6.3}$$

The fraction of leaves reached is $1/2$ raised to the power given by quantity (6.3), which simplifies to fraction $\prod_{i=1}^{k} r_i$. For example, if each range in the query is half the total domain for its field, and there are $n$ records in the file, we shall have to look at about $n/2^k$ of the records. In general, the fraction of nodes we look at will be close to the fraction of the entire file that we expect to meet the conditions of the range query. Thus, like partitioned hashing, k-d-trees are approximately as efficient as possible for range queries.

## Minimizing Block Accesses for k-d-Trees

The k-d-tree was conceived of as a main-memory data structure, and it is not well tuned to the cost measure that is appropriate for large databases: the number of block accesses. To minimize block accesses, we must apportion nodes to blocks in such a way that when we access a block, we are likely to need many of the records (nodes) found on that block.

Let us suppose that blocks and records are related in size so that a node and all its descendants for $m$ levels can fit on one block; that is, blocks can hold $2^m - 1$ records. Then we can allow every node at levels $1$, $m + 1$, $2m + 1$, and so on, to be the "root" of a block, and use that block for all its descendants for $m$ levels down the tree.

**Example 6.37:** The tree of Figure 6.31 is shown partitioned into blocks on the assumption that $m = 2$; i.e., blocks can hold three records. That number of records is too low to be typical, but will illustrate the idea. Notice that the node $(0, 4)$ is in a block by itself, and the block with root $(6, 1)$ is missing one of its descendants. It is inevitable for all but the most regular trees that gaps like these will occur. $\square$

Partitioning the nodes into blocks as described above will tend to minimize the number of block accesses, because whenever a search reaches the root node $N$ of a block, thereby causing the block to be read into main memory, we shall be following at least one path of descendants of $N$, and we shall follow many

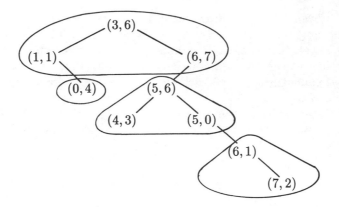

**Figure 6.32** Partition into blocks.

paths from $N$ through the block, if the query forces the search to branch at $N$ or some of its descendants within the block.

However, we are still faced with the problem that many blocks will be only partially full, and some may be very sparse. All structures we have studied tend to leave a fraction of each block empty. However, in a k-d-tree partitioned into blocks this way, it will be fairly common for a node that is the root of a block to be missing both its children, and thus be the only node on the block. Call such a node a *singleton*.

We can treat singletons specially. Instead of allocating a block for each, place a notation in it parent that the node is stored not on its own block, but on a block used to hold many singletons. The singleton's parent holds a pointer to the location of that node. If we insert any child of the singleton, then the singleton is moved to its own block, where it becomes the root.

Similarly, we could devise a more complicated scheme where nodes with only one descendant, or only some small number of descendants, are packed into special blocks. A node only becomes the root of its own block when it has acquired a sufficent number of descendants.

## EXERCISES

6.1: Suppose we have a file of 100,000 records. Each record takes 200 bytes, of which 50 are for fields of the key. A block has room for 1000 bytes. A pointer to a block takes five bytes, and an offset requires two bytes.

    a) If we use a hashed file organization with 1000 buckets, how many blocks are needed for the bucket directory?

    b) How many blocks are needed for the buckets, assuming all buckets have the average number of records?

c)   On the assumption of (b), what is the average number of block accesses to lookup a record that is actually present in the file?

d)   If we assume pinned records and use a sparse isam index that has just been created for the file (all file blocks are full, with no overflow), how many blocks are used for the index?

e)   If we use binary search for the index, how many block accesses are needed to lookup a record?

f)   If we use a D-tree and assume all blocks are as full as possible, how many index blocks are used (among all nonleaf levels)?

6.2:  Suppose keys are integers, and we have a file consisting of records with keys $1, 4, 9, \ldots, 15^2 = 225$. Assume that three records will fit in one block.

a)   If we use the hashed organization of Section 6.3, with the hash function "divide by 7 and take the remainder," what is the distribution of records into buckets?

** b)   Explain why the perfect squares hash so nonuniformly in part (a).

c)   Suppose we begin a sparse index organization as in Section 6.4 by packing the odd perfect squares into blocks as tightly as possible. Assuming the records are unpinned, show the file organization after inserting the even perfect squares.

d)   Repeat part (c) assuming pinned records.

e)   Show a B-tree organization of the file if the fifteen records are inserted in order of their keys. Assume the parameters of the B-tree are

$$d = e = 2$$

f)   Suppose we use a B-tree with d=2 as a dense index on the file. Show the organization if the records are inserted even squares first, in numerical order, then odd squares in numerical order.

6.3:  Suppose records have four fields, $A$, $B$, $C$, and $D$, which are of type integer, byte, variable-length character string, and character string of length 10, respectively. Also assume that a used/unused bit and a deleted bit are required in each record. Suggest an appropriate record format for such records assuming:

a)   Integers must start at a byte that is a multiple of 4.

b)   Integers (and other fields) may start at any byte.

6.4:  Assume blocks are 1000 bytes long and pointers require four bytes (offsets within a block are not pointers). Suppose all blocks have two pointer fields linking them to other blocks, and we wish to store variable-length records within a block. Suggest an appropriate block format on the assumption that

a)   All records must begin at offsets that are divisible by 4.

b)   Records may begin at any offset.

* 6.5: Give an algorithm that takes definitions for complex objects, as in Section 2.7, and produces appropriate record formats.

  6.6: Give algorithms to allocate and deallocate records using the block formats of

  a)  Figure 6.3.
  * b)  Figure 6.4.

  6.7: What advantage is there to using key values as pointers (rather than block addresses), if a hash table is used as the primary index?

* 6.8: In Section 6.5 we claimed that when deleting from a B-tree, the keys for the new interior nodes are found either in the blocks being merged or in their common parent. Show this claim is true by giving an algorithm to find the needed keys.

* 6.9: In Section 6.4 we defined "covering" of a key value by an entry in an isam index; that definition is appropriate if the key is a true key, guaranteed to determine a unique record in the main file. Modify the definition of "covers" so we can obtain the first (of perhaps many) records of the main file with a given "key" value, in the case that "keys" do not determine unique records.

* 6.10: Modify the B-tree lookup procedure for the case (as in System R), where "keys" can determine more than one record, and we need to find all records with a given "key" value.

* 6.11: Modify the B-tree lookup, insertion, and deletion algorithms if we do not insist that a key value at an interior node be the exact minimum of the keys of the descendants for one of the children of that node (just that it be a lower bound on the keys of the descendants of that child).

* 6.12: What happens to the distribution of nodes in a B-tree if keys only increase? For example, consider a file of employees where ID numbers are never reused as employees leave the company, and a new number, higher than any used before, is assigned to each new employee.

  6.13: Suppose we keep a file of information about states. Each state has a variable-length record with a field for the state name and a repeating group for the counties of the state. Each county group has fields for the name and population, a repeating group for township names, and a repeating group for city names. Give the nested structure for state records.

* 6.14: Suppose we have a nested structure of format $A(B)^*$. An $A$ record takes 20 bytes and a $B$ record 30 bytes. A pointer requires 4 bytes. Each $A$ has associated with it from 2 to 8 $B$'s with probabilities .05, .1, .2, .3, .2, .1, and .05, respectively. If blocks are 100 bytes long, compare the average number of blocks per instance of the structure used if we adopt

the following organizations.

a)   Store records in preorder, as in Figure 6.17.
b)   Allocate space for eight $B$ records regardless of how many there are.
c)   Represent the repeating group of $B$'s by a pointer, as in Figure 6.18.
d)   Allocate room for $p$ $B$ records along with each $A$ record, and include a pointer to additional $B$ records; the pointer is null if there are $p$ or fewer $B$ records in the repeating group.

In (d), what is the optimal value of $p$?

6.15: Express the following hierarchies as nested structures.

a)   The tree of Figure 5.27.
b)   The tree of Figure 5.28.

6.16: Show how to express the structures of complex objects, as in Section 2.7, as nested structures.

6.17: Explain the differences between the terms ($i$) primary index ($ii$) secondary index ($iii$) dense index, and ($iv$) sparse index.

6.18: Give an algorithm to maintain sorted order within a bucket by linking records, as in Figure 6.11.

* 6.19: In Section 6.9 we discussed the formatting of records in a DBTG database, and we claimed that it was not always possible to keep the pointer fields associated with a link at the same offset in both member and owner types of a given link, without wasting space. Show that this claim is true by giving an example of a network in which at least one record type has unnecessary, unused space, or at least one link has its pointers in different positions in owner and member records. *Hint:* Assume that all nonpointer fields are too large to fit in space unoccupied by a pointer.

* 6.20: Continuing with the problem of Exercise 6.19, suppose that we reserve $k$ fields of all record formats to hold link pointers, that no record type is involved in more than $m$ links, and that in the entire network of $n$ record types, we are willing to tolerate up to $p$ links that do not have the same position in owner and member types. For given $m$, $n$, and $p$, what is the smallest $k$ such that we can find record formats for any network meeting the above conditions.

6.21: Suppose blocks hold 1000 bytes of data, in addition to a few pointers, and there are records of three types, $A$, $B$, and $C$, of length 300, 200, and 400 bytes, respectively. Let $C$ be a child of $B$, and $B$ a child of $A$ in the hierarchy. Suppose that the key for record $a_i$ of type $A$ is taken to be $i$, and that database records are to be distributed into three buckets, based on the key value of their root records. The three buckets take keys ($i$) below 10 ($ii$) 10–20, and ($iii$) above 20, respectively. Show the structure

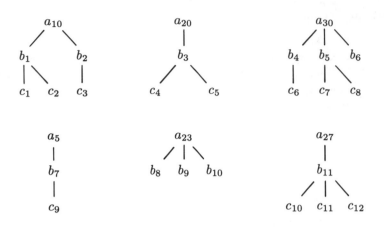

**Figure 6.33** Database records.

of blocks if the database records of Figure 6.33 are inserted, in the order shown, assuming the "two-dimensional" organization of Figure 6.23.

6.22: Show (a) preorder threads, and (b) leftmost-child/right-sibling pointers on the database records of Exercise 6.21.

6.23: Show the effect of deleting $c_7$ and inserting $c_{13}$ as the rightmost child of $b_2$

a)   Assuming records are unpinned and can slide within a bucket.

b)   Assuming records are pinned and preorder threads are maintained.

* 6.24: Give algorithms to update (a) preorder threads (b) leftmost-child/right-sibling pointers when a record is inserted or deleted.

* 6.25: Show that in any $n$ node tree, the number of nonnull leftmost-child pointers plus the number of nonnull right-sibling pointers is exactly $n - 1$. What does this relationship say about the space efficiency of leftmost-child/right-sibling pointers?

6.26: Suppose we store a file of rectangles, as discussed in Example 6.29. Let the particular rectangles in the file be:

$$(1, 2, 10, 5) \quad (3, 4, 7, 6) \quad (2, 4, 9, 6)$$
$$(5, 1, 7, 8) \quad (1, 6, 3, 8) \quad (4, 2, 7, 10)$$
$$(5, 6, 9, 10) \quad (8, 2, 10, 7) \quad (9, 3, 10, 9)$$

a)   Show the effect of storing these in turn, into an empty k-d-tree.

b)   Assume that we use a partitioned hash function with one bit from each field, and that bit is the least significant bit in each case. Show the distribution of rectangles into buckets. Would this structure be useful for range queries?

6.27: Write an SQL query saying that two rectangles, represented as in Example 6.29, intersect. Is this a partial-match query? A range query? Would the structures of Sections 6.13 and 6.14 be of use answering the query?

6.28: If all partial-match queries specify values for at least $m$ out of the $k$ fields, how many indices are needed so that there will be at least one index to answer each query, using the method outlined in Section 6.12?

0.29. Suppose we ask a range query that specifies a range for the key equal to 1/10th of the total domain for the key in the isam-indexed file of Example 6.11. On the average, how many block accesses does it take to answer the query?

* 6.30: More generally than was discussed in Section 6.13, we can use a partitioned hash function whose individual $h_i$'s have ranges that are not powers of 2. If the range of $h_i$ is 0 to $n_i - 1$, then the number of buckets is $\prod_{i=1}^{k} n_i$. Prove that for any distribution of partial-match queries with the property that when a value for field $F$ is specified, any possible value for $F$ is equally likely, we can minimize the average number of buckets examined if we use a partitioned hash function that stores record $(v_1, \ldots, v_k)$ in the bucket numbered

$$h_k(v_k) + n_k \Big( h_{k-1}(v_{k-1}) + n_{k-1} \big( h_{k-2}(v_{k-2}) + \cdots + n_2 h_1(v_1) \big) \Big) \quad (6.4)$$

for some values $n_1, \ldots, n_k$. Note that $n_1$ is not explicitly involved in the formula.

6.31: Suppose we use the scheme described in Exercise 6.30 to store the rectangle data of Exercise 6.26 in nine buckets, with $n_1 = n_2 = 3$ and $n_3 = n_4 = 1$; i.e., only the coordinates of the lower-left corner determine the bucket. Show the distribution into buckets of the data in Exercise 6.26.

* 6.32: Consider the population of partial-match queries that each specify a value for exactly one of the $k$ fields, and the probability that field $F_i$ is specified is $p_i$, where $\sum_{i=1}^{k} p_i = 1$. Show that the optimum value of $n_i$ to choose in the bucket address formula (6.4) is $cp_i$, where $c$ is a constant that is the same for all $i$ and depends only on the desired number of buckets. As a function of $B$, the number of buckets, what is $c$?

* 6.33: Consider the population of partial match queries in which the probabilities of any field having a specified value is independent of what other fields are specified. Let the probability that $F_i$ has a specified value be $q_i$, for $i = 1, 2, \ldots, k$. Show that the optimum value of $n_i$ in (6.4) for this class of queries is $dq_i/(1 - q_i)$, for some $d$ that is independent of $i$. Give a method of calculating $d$ as a function of the $q_j$'s and the desired number of buckets.

6.34: Suppose we use a partitioned hashing scheme for partial-match retrieval, and bucket addresses have 12 bits. If there are four fields, and each query specifies exactly one of them, with probabilities 1/2, 1/4, 1/8, and 1/8, what is the optimum distribution of bits in the bucket addresses to the fields? *Hint*: Find the optimum values of the $n_i$'s by the formula of Exercise 6.32 and "round" so each $n_i$ becomes a power of 2.

6.35: Let all be as in Exercise 6.34, but queries specify any number of fields independently, and the probability that values are specified for the four fields are 8/9, 1/2, 1/9, and 1/17. What is the optimal distribution of bits in the bucket address?

* 6.36: Suppose keys have three fields, $A$, $B$, and $C$, and we attempt to handle range queries by using a partitioned hash function with 2, 3, and 4 bits devoted to $A$, $B$, and $C$, respectively. Let the number of values in the total allowable range for these fields be 100, 200, and 500, respectively, and suppose that a particular query specifies ranges of size 10, 20, and 30, for $A$, $B$, and $C$, respectively. Taking into account the edge effects resulting from the fact that entire buckets must be searched if they may contain even one record in the desired set, estimate the total number of buckets that must be retrieved.

6.37: Suppose we are again handling range queries, and our file consists of a million records. All queries specify a range for $A$ equal to 1/10th of the total range for that field, and also specify a range for either field $B$ or field $C$, but not both, equal to half the total range for the field specified.

&ast;&ast; a) If we use a partitioned hash function with 16 bit addresses, how many bits should we devote to each of the fields $A$, $B$, and $C$?

&ast; b) Compare the performance in average number of blocks retrieved of a partitioned hash table with 6, 5, and 5 bits devoted to $A$, $B$, and $C$, respectively, against a B-tree organization. You may assume each bucket fits on two blocks, and in the B-trees, each block contains 100 (key, pointer) pairs.

* 6.38: When deleting a node from a k-d-tree, we can get the replacing node from many different places. Describe all the places where a suitable node can be found.

## BIBLIOGRAPHIC NOTES

General information about data structures can be found in Knuth [1968, 1973] and Aho, Hopcroft, and Ullman [1974, 1983]. Wiederhold [1987] covers file structures for database systems. The selection of physical database schemes is discussed by Gotlieb and Tompa [1973].

## Hashing

Two surveys of techniques for hashing are Morris [1968] and Maurer and Lewis [1975]; Knuth [1973] also treats the subject extensively.

Some recent developments involve variations of hashing that adapt to changing conditions, especially growth in file size. Larson [1978], Fagin, Nievergelt, Pippenger, and Strong [1979], Litwin [1980], and Larson [1982] describe these structures.

## Interpolation Search

The $O(\log \log n)$ complexity of interpolation search appears in Yao and Yao [1976] and Perl, Itai, and Avni [1978].

## B-trees

The B-tree is from Bayer and McCreight [1972], where it was presented as a dense index, as in Section 6.6. Comer [1978] surveys the area.

The performance of B-trees as a data structure for database systems is discussed by Held and Stonebraker [1978], Snyder [1978], Gudes and Tsur [1980], and Rosenberg and Synder [1981]. Also see the references to Chapter 9 for articles on concurrent access to B-trees.

## Secondary Indices

Optimal selection of secondary indices is discussed by Lum and Ling [1970] and Schkolnick [1975]. Comer [1978] shows the problem to be $\mathcal{NP}$-complete.

## Partial-Match and Range Queries

The use of partitioned hash functions was considered in its generality by Rivest [1976], and the design of such functions was also investigated by Burkhard [1976] and Bolour [1979].

The k-d-tree is from Bentley [1975]. Finkel and Bentley [1974], Bentley and Stanat [1975], Lueker [1978], Willard [1978a, b], Culik, Ottmann, and Wood [1981], Robinson [1981], Scheuermann and Ouksel [1982], Willard and Lueker [1985], and Robinson [1986] consider related structures for range queries. Bentley and Friedman [1979] and Samet [1984] survey the area.

There is a well-developed theory of how fast range queries can be answered. See Burkhard, Fredman, and Kleitman [1981] and Fredman [1981].

## Notes on Exercises

Exercise 6.30 is from Bolour [1979]. Exercise 6.32 is by Rothnie and Lozano [1974] and 6.33 from Aho and Ullman [1979].

# CHAPTER 7

# Design Theory
# for
# Relational Databases

Our study of database scheme design in Chapter 2 drew heavily on our intuition regarding what was going on in the "real world," and how that world could best be reflected by the database scheme. In most models, there is little more to design than that; we must understand the options and their implications regarding efficiency of implementation, as was discussed in Chapter 6, then rely on skill and experience to create a good design.

In the relational model, it is possible to be somewhat more mechanical in producing our design. We can manipulate our relation schemes (sets of attributes heading the columns of the relation) according to a well-developed theory, to produce a database scheme (collection of relation schemes) with certain desirable properties. In this chapter, we shall study some of the desirable properties of relation schemes and consider several algorithms for obtaining a database scheme with these properties.

Central to the design of database schemes is the idea of a *data dependency*, that is, a constraint on the possible relations that can be the current instance of a relation scheme. For example, if one attribute uniquely determines another, as SNAME apparently determines SADDR in relation SUPPLIERS of Figure 2.8, we say there is a "functional dependency" of SADDR on SNAME, or "SNAME functionally determines SADDR."

In Section 7.2 we introduce functional dependencies formally, and in the following section we learn how to "reason" about functional dependencies, that is, to infer new dependencies from given ones. This ability to tell whether a functional dependency does or does not hold in a scheme with a given collection of dependencies is central to the scheme-design process. In Section 7.4 we consider lossless-join decompositions, which are scheme designs that preserve all the information of a given scheme. The following section considers the preservation of given dependencies in a scheme design, which is another desirable

376

property that, intuitively, says that integrity constraints found in the original design are also found in the new design.

Sections 7.6–7.8 study "normal forms," the properties of relation schemes that say there is no, or almost no, redundancy in the relation. We relate two of these forms, Boyce-Codd normal form and third normal form, to the desirable properties of database schemes as a whole—lossless join and dependency preservation—that were introduced in the previous sections.

Section 7.9 introduces multivalued dependencies, a more complex form of dependency that, like functional dependencies, occurs frequently in practice. The process of reasoning about multivalued and functional dependencies together is discussed in Section 7.9, and Section 7.10 shows how fourth normal form eliminates the redundancy due to multivalued dependencies that is left by the earlier normal forms. We close the chapter with a discussion of more complex forms of dependencies that, while not bearing directly on the database design problem as described here, serve to unify the theory and to relate the subject of dependencies to logical rules and datalog.

## 7.1 WHAT CONSTITUTES A BAD DATABASE DESIGN?

Before telling how to design a good database scheme, let us see why some schemes might present problems. In particular let us suppose that we had chosen, in Example 2.14, to combine the relations SUPPLIERS and SUPPLIES of Figure 2.8 into one relation SUP_INFO, with scheme:

SUP_INFO(SNAME, SADDR, ITEM, PRICE)

that included all the information about suppliers. We can see several problems with this scheme.

1.  *Redundancy.* The address of the supplier is repeated once for each item supplied.

2.  *Potential inconsistency (update anomalies).* As a consequence of the redundancy, we could update the address for a supplier in one tuple, while leaving it fixed in another. Thus, we would not have a unique address for each supplier as we feel intuitively we should.

3.  *Insertion anomalies.* We cannot record an address for a supplier if that supplier does not currently supply at least one item. We might put null values in the ITEM and PRICE components of a tuple for that supplier, but then, when we enter an item for that supplier, will we remember to delete the tuple with the nulls? Worse, ITEM and SNAME together form a key for the relation, and it might be impossible to look up tuples through a primary index, if there were null values in the key field ITEM.

4.  *Deletion anomalies*. The inverse to problem (3) is that should we delete all of the items supplied by one supplier, we unintentionally lose track of the supplier's address.

The reader should appreciate that the problems of redundancy and potential inconsistency are ones we have seen before and dealt with in other models. In the network model, virtual fields were introduced for the purpose of eliminating redundancy and inconsistency. In the hierarchical model, we used virtual record types for the same purpose. The object model encourages references to objects to be made by pointers rather than by copying the object.

In the present example, all the above problems go away if we replace SUP_INFO by the two relation schemes

> SUPPLIERS(SNAME, SADDR)
> SUPPLIES(SNAME, ITEM, PRICE)

as in Figure 2.8. Here, SUPPLIERS, gives the address for each supplier exactly once; hence there is no redundancy. Moreover, we can enter an address for a supplier even if it currently supplies no items.

Yet some questions remain. For example, there is a disadvantage to the above decomposition; to find the addresses of suppliers of Brie, we must now take a join, which is expensive, while with the single relation SUP_INFO we could simply do a selection and projection. How do we determine that the above replacement is beneficial? Are there other problems of the same four kinds present in the two new relation schemes? How do we find a good replacement for a bad relation scheme?

## Dependencies and Redundancy

The balance of the chapter is devoted to answering these questions. Before proceeding though, let us emphasize the relationship between dependencies and redundancy. In general, a dependency is a statement that only a subset of all possible relations are "legal," i.e., only certain relations reflect a possible state of the real world. If not all relations are possible, it stands to reason that there will be some sort of redundancy in legal relations. That is to say, given the fact that a relation $R$ is legal, i.e., satisfies certain dependencies, and given certain information about the current value of $R$, we should be able to deduce other things about the current value of $R$.

In the case that the dependencies are functional, the form of the redundancy is obvious. If, in our relation SUP_INFO we saw the two tuples:

| SNAME | SADDR | ITEM | PRICE |
|-------|-------|------|-------|
| Acme | 16 River St. | Brie | 3.49 |
| Acme | ??? | Perrier | 1.19 |

we may use the assumption that SNAME functionally determines SADDR to deduce that the ??? stands for "16 River St." Thus, the functional dependency makes all but the first SADDR field for a given supplier redundant; we know what it is without seeing it. Conversely, suppose we did not believe the functional dependency of SADDR on SNAME holds. Then there would be no reason to believe that the ??? had any particular value, and that field would not be redundant.

When we have more general kinds of dependencies than functional dependencies, the form redundancy takes is less clear. However, in all cases, it appears that the cause and cure of the redundancy go hand-in-hand. That is, the dependency, such as that of SADDR on SNAME, not only causes the redundancy, but it permits the decomposition of the SUP_INFO relation into the SUPPLIERS and SUPPLIES relations in such a way that the original SUP_INFO relation can be recovered from the SUPPLIERS and SUPPLIES relations. We shall discuss these concepts more fully in Section 7.4.

## 7.2 FUNCTIONAL DEPENDENCIES

In Section 2.3 we saw that relations could be used to model the "real world" in several ways; for example, each tuple of a relation could represent an entity and its attributes or it could represent a relationship between entities. In many cases, the known facts about the real world imply that not every finite set of tuples could be the current value of some relation, even if the tuples were of the right arity and had components chosen from the right domains. We can distinguish two kinds of restrictions on relations:

1. *Restrictions that depend on the semantics of domain elements.* These restrictions depend on understanding what components of tuples mean. For example, no one is 60 feet tall, and no one with an employment history going back 37 years has age 27. It is useful to have a DBMS check for such implausible values, which probably arose because of an error when entering or computing data. The next chapter covers the expression and use of this sort of "integrity constraint." Unfortunately, they tell us little or nothing about the design of database schemes.

2. *Restrictions on relations that depend only on the equality or inequality of values.* There are other constraints that do not depend on what value a tuple has in any given component, but only on whether two tuples agree in certain components. We shall discuss the most important of these constraints, called functional dependencies, in this section, but there are other types of value-oblivious constraints that will be touched on in later sections. It is value-oblivious constraints that turn out to have the greatest impact on the design of database schemes.

Let $R(A_1, \ldots, A_n)$ be a relation scheme, and let $X$ and $Y$ be subsets of $\{A_1, \ldots, A_n\}$. We say $X \to Y$, read "$X$ functionally determines $Y$" or "$Y$

functionally depends on $X$" if, whatever relation $r$ is the current value for $R$, it is not possible that $r$ has two tuples that agree in the components for all attributes in the set $X$ yet disagree in one or more components for attributes in the set $Y$. Thus, the functional dependency of supplier address on supplier name, discussed in Section 7.1, would be expressed

$$\{SNAME\} \rightarrow \{SADDR\}$$

## Notational Conventions

To remind the reader of the significance of the symbols we use, we adopt the following conventions:

1. Capital letters near the beginning of the alphabet stand for single attributes.
2. Capital letters near the end of the alphabet, $U, V, \ldots, Z$, generally stand for sets of attributes, possibly singleton sets.
3. $R$ is used to denote a relation scheme. We also name relations by their schemes; e.g., a relation with attributes $A$, $B$, and $C$ may be called $ABC$.[1]
4. We use $r$ for a relation, the current instance of scheme $R$. Note this convention disagrees with the Prolog convention used in Chapter 3, where $R$ was used for the instance of a relation and $r$ for a predicate, i.e., the name of the relation.
5. Concatenation is used for union. Thus, $A_1 \cdots A_n$ is used to represent the set of attributes $\{A_1, \ldots, A_n\}$, and $XY$ is shorthand for $X \cup Y$. Also, $XA$ or $AX$, where $X$ is a set of attributes and $A$ a single attribute, stands for $X \cup \{A\}$.

## Significance of Functional Dependencies

Functional dependencies arise naturally in many ways. For example, if $R$ represents an entity set whose attributes are $A_1, \ldots, A_n$, and $X$ is a set of attributes that forms a key for the entity set, then we may assert $X \rightarrow Y$ for any subset $Y$ of the attributes, even a set $Y$ that has attributes in common with $X$. The reason is that the tuples of each possible relation $r$ represent entities, and entities are identified by the value of attributes in the key. Therefore, two tuples that agree on the attributes in $X$ must represent the same entity and thus be the same tuple.

Similarly, if relation $R$ represents a many-one relationship from entity set $E_1$ to entity set $E_2$, and among the $A_i$'s are attributes that form a key $X$ for $E_1$ and a key $Y$ for $E_2$, then $X \rightarrow Y$ would hold, and in fact, $X$ functionally

---

[1] Unfortunately, there are cases where the natural symbol for a single attribute, e.g., $Z$ for "zip code" or $R$ for "room" conflicts with these conventions, and the reader will be reminded when we use a symbol in a nonstandard way.

determines any set of attributes of $R$. However, $Y \rightarrow X$ would not hold unless the relationship were one-to-one.

It should be emphasized that functional dependencies are statements about all possible relations that could be the value of relation scheme $R$. We cannot look at a particular relation $r$ for scheme $R$ and deduce what functional dependencies hold for $R$. For example, if $r$ is the empty set, then all dependencies appear to hold, but they might not hold in general, as the value of the relation denoted by $R$ changes. We might, however, be able to look at a particular relation for $R$ and discover some dependencies that did not hold.

The only way to determine the functional dependencies that hold for relation scheme $R$ is to consider carefully what the attributes mean. In this sense, dependencies are actually assertions about the real world; they cannot be proved, but we might expect them to be enforced by a DBMS if told to do so by the database designer. As we saw in Chapter 4, many relational systems will enforce those functional dependencies that follow from the fact that a key determines the other attributes of a relation.

**Example 7.1:** Let us consider some of the functional dependencies that we expect to hold in the YVCB database of Example 2.14 (Figure 2.8). The most basic dependencies are those that say a key determines all the attributes of the relation scheme. Thus, in SUPPLIERS we get

> SNAME $\rightarrow$ SADDR

and in SUPPLIES we get

> SNAME ITEM $\rightarrow$ PRICE

In CUSTOMERS we have

> CNAME $\rightarrow$ CADDR BALANCE

and similar functional dependencies hold in the other relations of Figure 2.8.

We can also observe many trivial dependencies, like

> SNAME $\rightarrow$ SNAME

and some that are less trivial, such as

> SNAME ITEM $\rightarrow$ SADDR PRICE

which is obtained by combining the dependencies from SUPPLIERS and SUPPLIES, and realizing that attribute SNAME represents the same concept (the supplier name) in each relation. The reason we believe this functional dependency holds is that given a supplier's name and an item, we can uniquely determine an address; we ignore the item and take the address of the supplier. We can also determine a unique price, the price the given supplier charges for the given item.

The reader should understand, however, that the above dependency, unlike the others we have mentioned in this example, is not associated with a particular relation; it is rather something we deduce from our understanding about the "semantics" of suppliers, items, addresses, and prices. We expect that this dependency will have influence on any relation scheme in which some or all of the attributes mentioned appear, but the nature of that influence, which we discuss in Section 7.4, is often subtle.

One might wonder whether a dependency like

$$\text{CADDR} \rightarrow \text{CNAME}$$

holds. Looking at the sample data of Figure 4.2(a), we do not find two tuples that agree on the address but disagree on the name, simply because there are no two tuples with the same address. However, in principle, there is nothing that rules out the possibility that two customers have the same address, so we must not assert this dependency, even though it appears to hold in the only sample relation we have seen. $\square$

### Satisfaction of Dependencies

We say a relation $r$ *satisfies* functional dependency $X \rightarrow Y$ if for every two tuples $\mu$ and $\nu$ in $r$ such that $\mu[X] = \nu[X]$, it is also true that $\mu[Y] = \nu[Y]$. Note that like every "if $\cdots$ then" statement, it can be satisfied either by $\mu[X]$ differing from $\nu[X]$ or by $\mu[Y]$ agreeing with $\nu[Y]$. If $r$ does not satisfy $X \rightarrow Y$, then $r$ *violates* that dependency.

If $r$ is an instance of scheme $R$, and we have declared that $X \rightarrow Y$ holds for $R$, then we expect that $r$ will satisfy $X \rightarrow Y$. However, if $X \rightarrow Y$ does not hold for $R$ in general, then $r$ may coincidentally satisfy $X \rightarrow Y$, or it might violate $X \rightarrow Y$.

## 7.3  REASONING ABOUT FUNCTIONAL DEPENDENCIES

Suppose $R$ is a relation scheme and $A$, $B$, and $C$ are some of its attributes. Suppose also that the functional dependencies $A \rightarrow B$ and $B \rightarrow C$ are known to hold in $R$. We claim that $A \rightarrow C$ must also hold in $R$. In proof, suppose $r$ is a relation that satisfies $A \rightarrow B$ and $B \rightarrow C$, but there are two tuples $\mu$ and $\nu$ in $r$ such that $\mu$ and $\nu$ agree in the component for $A$ but disagree in $C$. Then we must ask whether $\mu$ and $\nu$ agree on attribute $B$. If not, then $r$ would violate $A \rightarrow B$. If they do agree on $B$, then since they disagree on $C$, $r$ would violate $B \rightarrow C$. Hence $r$ must satisfy $A \rightarrow C$.

In general, let $F$ be a set of functional dependencies for relation scheme $R$, and let $X \rightarrow Y$ be a functional dependency. We say $F$ *logically implies* $X \rightarrow Y$, written $F \models X \rightarrow Y$, if every relation $r$ for $R$ that satisfies the dependencies in $F$ also satisfies $X \rightarrow Y$. We saw above that if $F$ contains $A \rightarrow B$ and $B \rightarrow C$, then $A \rightarrow C$ is logically implied by $F$. That is,

$$\{A \rightarrow B, B \rightarrow C\} \models A \rightarrow C$$

### Closure of Dependency Sets

We define $F^+$, the *closure* of $F$, to be the set of functional dependencies that are logically implied by $F$; i.e.,

$$F^+ = \left\{ X \rightarrow Y \mid F \models X \rightarrow Y \right\}$$

**Example 7.2:** Let $R = ABC$ and $F = \{A \rightarrow B, B \rightarrow C\}$. Then $F^+$ consists of all those dependencies $X \rightarrow Y$ such that either

1. $X$ contains $A$, e.g., $ABC \rightarrow AB$, $AB \rightarrow BC$, or $A \rightarrow C$,
2. $X$ contains $B$ but not $A$, and $Y$ does not contain $A$, e.g., $BC \rightarrow B$, $B \rightarrow C$, or $B \rightarrow \emptyset$, and
3. $X \rightarrow Y$ is one of the three dependencies $C \rightarrow C$, $C \rightarrow \emptyset$, or $\emptyset \rightarrow \emptyset$.

We shall discuss how to prove the above contention shortly. $\square$

### Keys

When talking about entity sets we assumed that there was a key, a set of attributes that uniquely determined an entity. There is an analogous concept for relations with functional dependencies. If $R$ is a relation scheme with attributes $A_1 A_2 \cdots A_n$ and functional dependencies $F$, and $X$ is a subset of $A_1 A_2 \cdots A_n$, we say $X$ is a *key* of $R$ if:

1. $X \rightarrow A_1 A_2 \cdots A_n$ is in $F^+$. That is, the dependency of all attributes on the set of attributes $X$ is given or follows logically from what is given, and
2. For no proper subset $Y \subseteq X$ is $Y \rightarrow A_1 A_2 \cdots A_n$ in $F^+$.

We should observe that minimality, condition (2) above, was not present when we talked of keys for entity sets in Section 2.2 or keys for files in Chapter 6. The reason is that without a formalism like functional dependencies, we can not verify that a given set of attributes is minimal. The reader should be aware that in this chapter the term "key" does imply minimality. Thus, the given key for an entity set will only be a key for the relation representing that entity set if the given key was minimal. Otherwise, one or more subsets of the key for the entity set will serve as a key for the relation.

As there may be more than one key for a relation, we sometimes designate one as the "primary key." The primary key might serve as the file key when the relation is implemented, for example. However, any key could be the primary key if we desired. The term *candidate key* is sometimes used to denote any minimal set of attributes that functionally determine all attributes, with the term "key" reserved for one designated ("primary") candidate key. We also use the term *superkey* for any superset of a key. Remember that a key is a special case of a superkey.

**Example 7.3:** For relation $R$ and set of dependencies $F$ of Example 7.2 there is only one key, $A$, since $A \to ABC$ is in $F^+$, but for no set of attributes $X$ that does not contain $A$, is $X \to ABC$ true.

A more interesting example is the relation scheme R(CITY, ST, ZIP), where ST stands for street address and ZIP for zip code. We expect tuple $(c, s, z)$ in a relation for R only if city $c$ has a building with street address $s$, and $z$ is the zip code for that address in that city. It is assumed that the nontrivial functional dependencies are:

> CITY ST $\to$ ZIP
>
> ZIP $\to$ CITY

That is, the address (city and street) determines the zip code, and the zip code determines the city, although not the street address. One can easily check that {CITY, ST} and {ST, ZIP} are both keys. $\square$

### Axioms for Functional Dependencies

To determine keys, and to understand logical implications among functional dependencies in general, we need to compute $F^+$ from $F$, or at least, to tell, given $F$ and functional dependency $X \to Y$, whether $X \to Y$ is in $F^+$. To do so requires that we have inference rules telling how one or more dependencies imply other dependencies. In fact, we can do more; we can provide a *complete* set of inference rules, meaning that from a given set of dependencies $F$, the rules allow us to deduce all the true dependencies, i.e., those in $F^+$. Moreover, the rules are *sound*, meaning that using them, we cannot deduce from $F$ any false dependency, i.e., a dependency that is not in $F^+$.

The set of rules is often called *Armstrong's axioms*, from Armstrong [1974], although the particular rules we shall present differ from Armstrong's. In what follows we assume we are given a relation scheme with set of attributes $U$, the *universal set* of attributes, and a set of functional dependencies $F$ involving only attributes in $U$. The inference rules are:

A1: *Reflexivity.* If $Y \subseteq X \subseteq U$, then $X \to Y$ is logically implied by $F$. This rule gives the *trivial dependencies*, those that have a right side contained in the left side. The trivial dependencies hold in every relation, which is to say, the use of this rule depends only on $U$, not on $F$.

A2: *Augmentation.* If $X \to Y$ holds, and $Z$ is any subset of $U$, then $XZ \to YZ$. Recall that $X, Y$, and $Z$ are sets of attributes, and $XZ$ is conventional shorthand for $X \cup Z$. It is also important to remember that the given dependency $X \to Y$ might be in $F$, or it might have been derived from dependencies in $F$ using the axioms we are in the process of describing.

A3: *Transitivity.* If $X \to Y$ and $Y \to Z$ hold, then $X \to Z$ holds.

**Example 7.4:** Consider the relation scheme $ABCD$ with functional dependencies $A \to C$ and $B \to D$. We claim $AB$ is a key for $ABCD$ (in fact, it is the only key). We can show $AB$ is a superkey by the following steps:

1. $A \to C$ (given)
2. $AB \to ABC$ [augmentation of (1) by $AB$]
3. $B \to D$ (given)
4. $ABC \to ABCD$ [augmentation of (3) by $ABC$]
5. $AB \to ABCD$ [transitivity applied to (2) and (4)]

To show $AB$ is a key, we must also show that neither $A$ nor $B$ by themselves functionally determine all the attributes. We could show that $A$ is not a superkey by exhibiting a relation that satisfies the given dependencies (1) and (3) above, yet does not satisfy $A \to ABCD$, and we could proceed similarly for $B$. However, we shall shortly develop an algorithm that makes this test mechanical, so we omit this step here. □

### Soundness of Armstrong's Axioms

It is relatively easy to prove that Armstrong's axioms are sound; that is, they lead only to true conclusions. It is rather more difficult to prove completeness, that they can be used to make every valid inference about dependencies. We shall tackle the soundness issue first.

**Lemma 7.1:** Armstrong's axioms are sound. That is, if $X \to Y$ is deduced from $F$ using the axioms, then $X \to Y$ is true in any relation in which the dependencies of $F$ are true.

**Proof:** A1, the reflexivity axiom, is clearly sound. We cannot have a relation $r$ with two tuples that agree on $X$ yet disagree on some subset of $X$. To prove A2, augmentation, suppose we have a relation $r$ that satisfies $X \to Y$, yet there are two tuples $\mu$ and $\nu$ that agree on the attributes of $XZ$ but disagree on $YZ$. Since they cannot disagree on any attribute of $Z$, $\mu$ and $\nu$ must disagree on some attribute in $Y$. But then $\mu$ and $\nu$ agree on $X$ but disagree on $Y$, violating our assumption that $X \to Y$ holds for $r$. The soundness of A3, the transitivity axiom, is a simple extension of the argument given previously that $A \to B$ and $B \to C$ imply $A \to C$. We leave this part of the proof as an exercise. □

### Additional Inference Rules

There are several other inference rules that follow from Armstrong's axioms. We state three of them in the next lemma. Since we have proved the soundness of A1, A2, and A3, we are entitled to use them in the proof that follows.

**Lemma 7.2:**

a) *The union rule.* $\{X \to Y, X \to Z\} \models X \to YZ$.
b) *The pseudotransitivity rule.* $\{X \to Y, WY \to Z\} \models WX \to Z$.

c)   *The decomposition rule.* If $X \rightarrow Y$ holds, and $Z \subseteq Y$, then $X \rightarrow Z$ holds.

**Proof:**

a)   We are given $X \rightarrow Y$, so we may augment by $X$ to infer $X \rightarrow XY$. We are also given $X \rightarrow Z$, so we may augment by $Y$ to get $XY \rightarrow YZ$. By transitivity, $X \rightarrow XY$ and $XY \rightarrow YZ$ imply $X \rightarrow YZ$.

b)   Given $X \rightarrow Y$, we may augment by $W$ to get $WX \rightarrow WY$. Since we are given $WY \rightarrow Z$, transitivity tells us $WX \rightarrow Z$.

c)   $Y \rightarrow Z$ follows from reflexivity, so by the transitivity rule, $X \rightarrow Z$. $\square$

An important consequence of the union and decomposition rules is that if $A_1, \ldots, A_n$ are attributes, then $X \rightarrow A_1, \ldots, A_n$ holds if and only if $X \rightarrow A_i$ holds for each $i$. Thus, singleton right sides on functional dependencies are sufficient. We shall discuss this matter in more detail when we take up the subject of "minimal covers" for sets of functional dependencies.

## Closures of Attribute Sets

Before tackling the completeness issue, it is important to define the closure of a set of attributes with respect to a set of functional dependencies. Let $F$ be a set of functional dependencies on set of attributes $U$, and let $X$ be a subset of $U$. Then $X^+$, the *closure* of $X$ (*with respect to $F$*) is the set of attributes $A$ such that $X \rightarrow A$ can be deduced from $F$ by Armstrong's axioms.[2] The central fact about the closure of a set of attributes is that it enables us to tell at a glance whether a dependency $X \rightarrow Y$ follows from $F$ by Armstrong's axioms. The next lemma tells how.

**Lemma 7.3:** $X \rightarrow Y$ follows from a given set of dependencies $F$ using Armstrong's axioms if and only if $Y \subseteq X^+$; here, the closure of $X$ is taken with respect to $F$.

**Proof:** Let $Y = A_1 \cdots A_n$ for set of attributes $A_1, \ldots, A_n$, and suppose $Y \subseteq X^+$. By definition of $X^+$, $X \rightarrow A_i$ is implied by Armstrong's axioms for all $i$. By the union rule, Lemma 7.2(a), $X \rightarrow Y$ follows.

Conversely, suppose $X \rightarrow Y$ follows from the axioms. For each $i$, $X \rightarrow A_i$ holds by the decomposition rule, Lemma 7.2(c), so $Y \subseteq X^+$. $\square$

## Completeness of Armstrong's Axioms

We are now ready to prove that Armstrong's axioms are complete. We do so by showing that if $F$ is the given set of dependencies, and $X \rightarrow Y$ cannot be proved by Armstrong's axioms, then there must be a relation in which the dependencies of $F$ all hold but $X \rightarrow Y$ does not; that is, $F$ does not logically imply $X \rightarrow Y$.

---

[2] Do not confuse closures of sets of dependencies with closures of sets of attributes, even though the same notation is used for each.

**Theorem 7.1:** Armstrong's axioms are sound and complete.

**Proof:** Soundness is Lemma 7.1, so we have to prove completeness. Let $F$ be a set of dependencies over attribute set $U$, and suppose $X \to Y$ cannot be inferred from the axioms. Consider the relation $r$ with the two tuples shown in Figure 7.1. First we show that all dependencies in $F$ are satisfied by $r$. Intuitively, a dependency $V \to W$ violated by $r$ allows us to "push out" $X^+$ beyond the value that it rightfully has when given set of dependencies $F$.

Suppose $V \to W$ is in $F$ but is not satisfied by $r$. Then $V \subseteq X^+$, or else the two tuples of $r$ disagree on some attribute of $V$, and therefore, could not violate $V \to W$. Also, $W$ cannot be a subset of $X^+$, or $V \to W$ would be satisfied by the relation $r$. Let $A$ be an attribute of $W$ not in $X^+$. Since $V \subseteq X^+$, $X \to V$ follows from Armstrong's axioms by Lemma 7.3. Dependency $V \to W$ is in $F$, so by transitivity we have $X \to W$. By reflexivity, $W \to A$, so by transitivity again, $X \to A$ follows from the axioms. But then, by definition of the closure, $A$ is in $X^+$, which we assumed not to be the case. We conclude by contradiction that each $V \to W$ in $F$ is satisfied by $r$.

| Attributes of $X^+$ | | | | Other attributes | | | |
|---|---|---|---|---|---|---|---|
| 1 | 1 | $\cdots$ | 1 | 1 | 1 | $\cdots$ | 1 |
| 1 | 1 | $\cdots$ | 1 | 0 | 0 | $\cdots$ | 0 |

**Figure 7.1** A relation $r$ showing $F$ does not logically imply $X \to Y$.

Now we must show that $X \to Y$ is not satisfied by $r$. Suppose it is satisfied. As $X \subseteq X^+$ is obvious, it follows that $Y \subseteq X^+$, else the two tuples of $r$ agree on $X$ but disagree on $Y$. But then Lemma 7.3 tells us that $X \to Y$ can be inferred from the axioms, which we assumed not to be the case. Therefore, $X \to Y$ is not satisfied by $r$, even though each dependency in $F$ is. We conclude that whenever $X \to Y$ does not follow from $F$ by Armstrong's axioms, $F$ does not logically imply $X \to Y$. That is, the axioms are complete. $\square$

Theorem 7.1 has some interesting consequences. We defined $X^+$ to be the set of attributes $A$ such that $X \to A$ followed from the given dependencies $F$ using the axioms. We now see that an equivalent definition of $X^+$ is the set of $A$ such that $F \models X \to A$. Another consequence is that although we defined $F^+$ to be the set of dependencies that were logically implied by $F$, we can also take $F^+$ to mean the set of dependencies that follow from $F$ by Armstrong's axioms.

## Computing Closures

It turns out that computing $F^+$ for a set of dependencies $F$ is a time-consuming task in general, simply because the set of dependencies in $F^+$ can be large even if $F$ itself is small. Consider the set

$$F = \{A \rightarrow B_1,\ A \rightarrow B_2, \ldots, A \rightarrow B_n\}$$

Then $F^+$ includes all of the dependencies $A \rightarrow Y$, where $Y$ is a subset of $\{B_1, B_2, \ldots, B_n\}$. As there are $2^n$ such sets $Y$, we could not expect to list $F^+$ conveniently, even for reasonably sized $n$.

At the other extreme, computing $X^+$, for a set of attributes $X$, is not hard; it takes time proportional to the length of all the dependencies in $F$, written out. By Lemma 7.3 and the fact that Armstrong's axioms are sound and complete, we can tell whether $X \rightarrow Y$ is in $F^+$ by computing $X^+$ with respect to $F$. A simple way to compute $X^+$ is the following.

**Algorithm 7.1:** Computation of the Closure of a Set of Attributes with Respect to a Set of Functional Dependencies.

INPUT: A finite set of attributes $U$, a set of functional dependencies $F$ on $U$, and a set $X \subseteq U$.

OUTPUT: $X^+$, the closure of $X$ with respect to $F$.

METHOD: We compute a sequence of sets of attributes $X^{(0)}$, $X^{(1)}$, $\ldots$ by the rules:

1.  $X^{(0)}$ is $X$.
2.  $X^{(i+1)}$ is $X^{(i)}$ union the set of attributes $A$ such that there is some dependency $Y \rightarrow Z$, in $F$, $A$ is in $Z$, and $Y \subseteq X^{(i)}$.

Since $X = X^{(0)} \subseteq \cdots \subseteq X^{(i)} \subseteq \cdots \subseteq U$, and $U$ is finite, we must eventually reach $i$ such that $X^{(i)} = X^{(i+1)}$. Since each $X^{(j+1)}$ is computed only in terms of $X^{(j)}$, it follows that $X^{(i)} = X^{(i+1)} = X^{(i+2)} = \cdots$. There is no need to compute beyond $X^{(i)}$ once we discover $X^{(i)} = X^{(i+1)}$. We can (and shall) prove that $X^+$ is $X^{(i)}$ for this value of $i$. $\Box$

**Example 7.5:** Let $F$ consist of the following eight dependencies:

$$\begin{array}{ll} AB \rightarrow C & D \rightarrow EG \\ C \rightarrow A & BE \rightarrow C \\ BC \rightarrow D & CG \rightarrow BD \\ ACD \rightarrow B & CE \rightarrow AG \end{array}$$

and let $X = BD$. To apply Algorithm 7.1, we let $X^{(0)} = BD$. To compute $X^{(1)}$ we look for dependencies that have a left side $B, D$, or $BD$. There is only one, $D \rightarrow EG$, so we adjoin $E$ and $G$ to $X^{(0)}$ and make $X^{(1)} = BDEG$. For $X^{(2)}$, we look for left sides contained in $X^{(1)}$ and find $D \rightarrow EG$ and $BE \rightarrow C$. Thus, $X^{(2)} = BCDEG$. Then, for $X^{(3)}$ we look for left sides contained in $BCDEG$

and find, in addition to the two previously found, $C \rightarrow A$, $BC \rightarrow D$, $CG \rightarrow BD$, and $CE \rightarrow AG$. Thus $X^{(3)} = ABCDEG$, the set of all attributes. It therefore comes as no surprise that $X^{(3)} = X^{(4)} = \cdots$ . Thus, $(BD)^+ = ABCDEG$. $\square$

Now we must address ourselves to the problem of proving that Algorithm 7.1 is correct. It is easy to prove that every attribute placed in some $X^{(j)}$ belongs in $X^+$, but harder to show that every attribute in $X^+$ is placed in some $X^{(j)}$.

**Theorem 7.2:** Algorithm 7.1 correctly computes $X^+$.

**Proof:** First we show by induction on $j$ that if $A$ is placed in $X^{(j)}$ during Algorithm 7.1, then $A$ is in $X^+$; i.e., if $A$ is in the set $X^{(i)}$ returned by Algorithm 7.1, then $A$ is in $X^+$.

*Basis*: $j = 0$. Then $A$ is in $X$, so by reflexivity, $X \rightarrow A$.

*Induction*: Let $j > 0$ and assume that $X^{(j-1)}$ consists only of attributes in $X^+$. Suppose $A$ is placed in $X^{(j)}$ because $A$ is in $Z$, $Y \rightarrow Z$ is in $F$, and $Y \subseteq X^{(j-1)}$. Since $Y \subseteq X^{(j-1)}$, we know $Y \subseteq X^+$ by the inductive hypothesis. Thus, $X \rightarrow Y$ by Lemma 7.3. By transitivity, $X \rightarrow Y$ and $Y \rightarrow Z$ imply $X \rightarrow Z$. By reflexivity, $Z \rightarrow A$, so $X \rightarrow A$ by another application of the transitivity rule. Thus, $A$ is in $X^+$.

Now we prove the converse: if $A$ is in $X^+$, then $A$ is in the set returned by Algorithm 7.1. Suppose $A$ is in $X^+$, but $A$ is not in that set $X^{(i)}$ returned by Algorithm 7.1. Notice that $X^{(i)} = X^{(i+1)}$, because that is the condition under which Algorithm 7.1 produces an answer.

Consider a relation $r$ similar to that of Figure 7.1; $r$ has two tuples that agree on the attributes of $X^{(i)}$ and disagree on all other attributes. We claim $r$ satisfies $F$. If not, let $U \rightarrow V$ be a dependency in $F$ that is violated by $r$. Then $U \subseteq X^{(i)}$ and $V$ cannot be a subset of $X^{(i)}$, if the violation occurs (the same argument was used in the proof of Theorem 7.1). Thus, $X^{(i+1)}$ cannot be the same as $X^{(i)}$ as supposed.

Thus, relation $r$ must also satisfy $X \rightarrow A$. The reason is that $A$ is assumed to be in $X^+$, and therefore, $X \rightarrow A$ follows from $F$ by Armstrong's axioms. Since these axioms are sound, any relation satisfying $F$ satisfies $X \rightarrow A$. But the only way $X \rightarrow A$ could hold in $r$ is if $A$ is in $X^{(i)}$, for if not, then the two tuples of $r$, which surely agree on $X$, would disagree on $A$ and violate $X \rightarrow A$. We conclude that $A$ is in the set $X^{(i)}$ returned by Algorithm 7.1. $\square$

**Equivalences Among Sets of Dependencies.**

Let $F$ and $G$ be sets of dependencies. We say $F$ and $G$ are *equivalent* if

$$F^+ = G^+$$

It is easy to test whether $F$ and $G$ are equivalent. For each dependency $Y \rightarrow Z$

in $F$, test whether $Y \rightarrow Z$ is in $G^+$ using Algorithm 7.1 to compute $Y^+$ with respect to $G$ and then checking whether $Z \subseteq Y^+$. If some dependency $Y \rightarrow Z$ in $F$ is not in $G^+$, then surely $F^+ \neq G^+$. If every dependency in $F$ is in $G^+$, then every dependency $V \rightarrow W$ in $F^+$ is in $G^+$, because a proof that $V \rightarrow W$ is in $G^+$ can be formed by taking a proof that each $Y \rightarrow Z$ in $F$ is in $G^+$, and following it by a proof from $F$ that $V \rightarrow W$ is in $F^+$.

To test whether each dependency in $G$ is also in $F^+$, we proceed in an analogous manner. Then $F$ and $G$ are equivalent if and only if every dependency in $F$ is in $G^+$, and every dependency in $G$ is in $F^+$.

## Minimal Covers

We can find, for a given set of dependencies, an equivalent set with a number of useful properties. A simple and important property is that the right sides of dependencies be split into single attributes.

**Lemma 7.4:** Every set of functional dependencies $F$ is equivalent to a set of dependencies $G$ in which no right side has more than one attribute.

**Proof:** Let $G$ be the set of dependencies $X \rightarrow A$ such that for some $X \rightarrow Y$ in $F$, $A$ is in $Y$. Then $X \rightarrow A$ follows from $X \rightarrow Y$ by the decomposition rule. Thus $G \subseteq F^+$. But $F \subseteq G^+$, since if $Y = A_1 \cdots A_n$, then $X \rightarrow Y$ follows from $X \rightarrow A_1, \ldots, X \rightarrow A_n$ using the union rule. Thus, $F$ and $G$ are equivalent. $\square$

It turns out to be useful, when we develop a design theory for database schemes, to consider a stronger restriction on covers than that the right sides have but one attribute. We say a set of dependencies $F$ is *minimal* if:

1. Every right side of a dependency in $F$ is a single attribute.
2. For no $X \rightarrow A$ in $F$ is the set $F - \{X \rightarrow A\}$ equivalent to $F$.
3. For no $X \rightarrow A$ in $F$ and proper subset $Z$ of $X$ is $F - \{X \rightarrow A\} \cup \{Z \rightarrow A\}$ equivalent to $F$.

Intuitively, (2) guarantees that no dependency in $F$ is redundant. Incidentally, it is easy to test whether $X \rightarrow A$ is redundant by computing $X^+$ with respect to $F - \{X \rightarrow A\}$. We leave this observation as an exercise.

Condition (3) guarantees that no attribute on any left side is redundant. We also leave as an exercise the fact that the following test checks for redundant attributes on the left. Attribute $B$ in $X$ is redundant for the dependency $X \rightarrow A$ if and only if $A$ is in $(X - \{B\})^+$ when the closure is taken with respect to $F$.

As each right side has only one attribute by (1), surely no attribute on the right is redundant. If $G$ is a set of dependencies that is minimal in the above sense, and $G$ is equivalent to $F$, then we say $G$ is a *minimal cover* for $F$.

**Theorem 7.3:** Every set of dependencies $F$ has a minimal cover.

**Proof:** By Lemma 7.4, assume no right side in $F$ has more than one attribute. We repeatedly search for violations of conditions (2) [redundant dependencies] and (3) [redundant attributes in left sides], and modify the set of dependencies accordingly. As each modification either deletes a dependency or deletes an attribute in a dependency, the process cannot continue forever, and we eventually reach a set of dependencies with no violations of (1), (2), or (3).

For condition (2), we consider each dependency $X \to Y$ in the current set of dependencies $F$, and if $F - \{X \to Y\}$ is equivalent to $F$, then delete $X \to Y$ from $F$. Note that considering dependencies in different orders may result in the elimination of different sets of dependencies. For example, given the set $F$:

$$A \to B \qquad A \to C$$
$$B \to A \qquad C \to A$$
$$B \to C$$

we can eliminate both $B \to A$ and $A \to C$, or we can eliminate $B \to C$, but we cannot eliminate all three.

For condition (3), we consider each dependency $A_1 \cdots A_k \to B$ in the current set $F$, and each attribute $A_i$ in its left side, in some order. If

$$F - \{A_1 \cdots A_k \to B\} \cup \{A_1 \cdots A_{i-1}A_{i+1} \cdots A_k \to B\}$$

is equivalent to $F$, then delete $A_i$ from the left side of $A_1 \cdots A_k \to B$. Again, the order in which attributes are eliminated may affect the result. For example, given

$$AB \to C \qquad A \to B \qquad B \to A$$

we can eliminate either $A$ or $B$ from $AB \to C$, but we cannot eliminate them both.

We leave as an exercise the proof that it is sufficient first to eliminate all violations of (3), then all violations of (2), but not vice versa. $\square$

**Example 7.6:** Let us consider the dependency set $F$ of Example 7.5. If we use the algorithm of Lemma 7.4 to split right sides we are left with:

$$AB \to C \qquad D \to E \qquad CG \to B$$
$$C \to A \qquad D \to G \qquad CG \to D$$
$$BC \to D \qquad BE \to C \qquad CE \to A$$
$$ACD \to B \qquad\qquad CE \to G$$

Clearly $CE \to A$ is redundant, since it is implied by $C \to A$. $CG \to B$ is redundant, since $CG \to D$, $C \to A$, and $ACD \to B$ imply $CG \to B$. Then no more dependencies are redundant. However, $ACD \to B$ can be replaced by $CD \to B$, since $C \to A$ is given, and therefore $CD \to B$ can be deduced from $ACD \to B$ and $C \to A$. Now, no further reduction by (2) or (3) is possible. Thus, one minimal cover for $F$ is that shown in Figure 7.2(a).

Another minimal cover, constructed from $F$ by eliminating $CE \to A$,

$CG \rightarrow D$, and $ACD \rightarrow B$, is shown in Figure 7.2(b). Note that the two minimal covers have different numbers of dependencies. $\square$

<table>
<tr><td>$AB \rightarrow C$</td><td>$AB \rightarrow C$</td></tr>
<tr><td>$C \rightarrow A$</td><td>$C \rightarrow A$</td></tr>
<tr><td>$BC \rightarrow D$</td><td>$BC \rightarrow D$</td></tr>
<tr><td>$CD \rightarrow B$</td><td>$D \rightarrow E$</td></tr>
<tr><td>$D \rightarrow E$</td><td>$D \rightarrow G$</td></tr>
<tr><td>$D \rightarrow G$</td><td>$BE \rightarrow C$</td></tr>
<tr><td>$BE \rightarrow C$</td><td>$CG \rightarrow B$</td></tr>
<tr><td>$CG \rightarrow D$</td><td>$CE \rightarrow G$</td></tr>
<tr><td>$CE \rightarrow G$</td><td></td></tr>
<tr><td>(a)</td><td>(b)</td></tr>
</table>

**Figure 7.2** Two minimal covers.

## 7.4 LOSSLESS-JOIN DECOMPOSITION

The *decomposition* of a relation scheme $R = \{A_1, A_2, \ldots, A_n\}$ is its replacement by a collection $\rho = \{R_1, R_2, \ldots, R_k\}$ of subsets of $R$ such that

$$R = R_1 \cup R_2 \cup \cdots \cup R_k$$

There is no requirement that the $R_i$'s be disjoint. One of the motivations for performing a decomposition is that it may eliminate some of the problems mentioned in Section 7.1.

**Example 7.7:** Let us reconsider the SUP_INFO relation scheme introduced in Section 7.1, but as a shorthand, let the attributes be $S$ (SNAME), $A$ (SADDR), $I$ (ITEM), and $P$ (PRICE). The functional dependencies we have assumed are $S \rightarrow A$ and $SI \rightarrow P$. We mentioned in Section 7.1 that replacement of the relation scheme $SAIP$ by the two schemes $SA$ and $SIP$ makes certain problems go away. For example, in $SAIP$ we cannot store the address of a supplier unless the supplier provides at least one item. In $SA$, there does not have to be an item supplied to record an address for the supplier. $\square$

One might question whether all is as rosey as it looks, when we replace $SAIP$ by $SA$ and $SIP$ in Example 7.7. For example, suppose we have a relation $r$ as the current value of $SAIP$. If the database uses $SA$ and $SIP$ instead of $SAIP$, we would naturally expect the current relation for these two relation schemes to be the projection of $r$ onto $SA$ and $SIP$, that is $r_{SA} = \pi_{SA}(r)$ and $r_{SIP} = \pi_{SIP}(r)$.

How do we know that $r_{SA}$ and $r_{SIP}$ contain the same information as $r$? One way to tell is to check that $r$ can be computed knowing only $r_{SA}$ and $r_{SIP}$.

We claim that the only way to recover $r$ is by taking the natural join of $r_{SA}$ and $r_{SIP}$. The reason is that, as we shall prove in the next lemma, if we let $s = r_{SA} \bowtie r_{SIP}$, then $\pi_{SA}(s) = r_{SA}$, and $\pi_{SIP}(s) = r_{SIP}$. If $s \neq r$, then given $r_{SA}$ and $r_{SIP}$ there is no way to tell whether $r$ or $s$ was the original relation for scheme $SAIP$. That is, if the natural join doesn't recover the original relation, then there is no way whatsoever to recover it uniquely.

### Lossless Joins

If $R$ is a relation scheme decomposed into schemes $R_1, R_2, \ldots, R_k$, and $D$ is a set of dependencies, we say the decomposition has a *lossless join* (with respect to $D$), or is a *lossless-join decomposition* (with respect to $D$) if for every relation $r$ for $R$ satisfying $D$:

$$r = \pi_{R_1}(r) \bowtie \pi_{R_2}(r) \bowtie \cdots \bowtie \pi_{R_k}(r)$$

that is, every relation $r$ is the natural join of its projections onto the $R_i$'s. As we saw, the lossless-join property is necessary if the decomposed relation is to be recoverable from its decomposition.

Some basic facts about project-join mappings follow in Lemma 7.5. First we introduce some notation. If $\rho = (R_1, R_2, \ldots, R_k)$ is a decomposition, then $m_\rho$ is the mapping defined by $m_\rho(r) = \bowtie_{i=1}^{k} \pi_{R_i}(r)$. That is, $m_\rho(r)$ is the join of the projections of $r$ onto the relation schemes in $\rho$. Thus, the lossless join condition with respect to a set of dependencies $D$ can be expressed as: for all $r$ satisfying $D$, we have $r = m_\rho(r)$.

**Lemma 7.5:** Let $R$ be a relation scheme, $\rho = (R_1, \ldots, R_k)$ be any decomposition of $R$, and $r$ be any relation for $R$. Define $r_i = \pi_{R_i}(r)$. Then

a) $r \subseteq m_\rho(r)$.
b) If $s = m_\rho(r)$, then $\pi_{R_i}(s) = r_i$.
c) $m_\rho\big(m_\rho(r)\big) = m_\rho(r)$.

**Proof:**

a) Let $\mu$ be in $r$, and for each $i$, let $\mu_i = \mu[R_i]$.[3] Then $\mu_i$ is in $r_i$ for all $i$. By definition of the natural join, $\mu$ is in $m_\rho(r)$, since $\mu$ agrees with $\mu_i$ on the attributes of $R_i$ for all $i$.

b) As $r \subseteq s$ by (a), it follows that $\pi_{R_i}(r) \subseteq \pi_{R_i}(s)$. That is, $r_i \subseteq \pi_{R_i}(s)$. To show $\pi_{R_i}(s) \subseteq r_i$, suppose for some particular $i$ that $\mu_i$ is in $\pi_{R_i}(s)$. Then there is some tuple $\mu$ in $s$ such that $\mu[R_i] = \mu_i$. As $\mu$ is in $s$, there is some $\nu_j$ in $r_j$ for each $j$ such that $\mu[R_j] = \nu_j$. Thus, in particular, $\mu[R_i]$ is in $r_i$. But $\mu[R_i] = \mu_i$, so $\mu_i$ is in $r_i$, and therefore $\pi_{R_i}(s) \subseteq r_i$. We conclude that $r_i = \pi_{R_i}(s)$.

---

[3] Recall that $\nu[X]$ refers to the tuple $\nu$ projected onto the set of attributes $X$.

c)   If $s = m_\rho(r)$, then by (b), $\pi_{R_i}(s) = r_i$. Thus $m_\rho(s) = \bowtie_{i=1}^k r_i = m_\rho(r)$.  □

Let us observe that if for each $i$, $r_i$ is some relation for $R_i$, and

$$s = \bowtie_{i=1}^k r_i$$

then $\pi_{R_i}(s)$ is not necessarily equal to $r_i$. The reason is that $r_i$ may contain "dangling" tuples that do not match with anything when we take the join. For example, if $R_1 = AB$, $R_2 = BC$, $r_1 = \{a_1 b_1\}$, and $r_2 = \{b_1 c_1, b_2 c_2\}$, then $s = \{a_1 b_1 c_1\}$ and $\pi_{BC}(s) = \{b_1 c_1\} \neq r_2$. However, in general, $\pi_{R_i}(s) \subseteq r_i$, and if the $r_i$'s are each the projection of some one relation $r$, then $\pi_{R_i}(s) = r_i$.

The ability to store "dangling" tuples is an advantage of decomposition. As we mentioned previously, this advantage must be balanced against the need to compute more joins when we answer queries, if relation schemes are decomposed, than if they are not. When all things are considered, it is generally believed that decomposition is desirable when necessary to cure the problems, such as redundancy, described in Section 7.1, but not otherwise.

## Testing Lossless Joins

It turns out to be fairly easy to tell whether a decomposition has a lossless join with respect to a set of functional dependencies.

**Algorithm 7.2:** Testing for a Lossless Join.

INPUT: A relation scheme $R = A_1 \cdots A_n$, a set of functional dependencies $F$, and a decomposition $\rho = (R_1, \ldots, R_k)$.

OUTPUT: A decision whether $\rho$ is a decomposition with a lossless join.

METHOD: We construct a table with $n$ columns and $k$ rows; column $j$ corresponds to attribute $A_j$, and row $i$ corresponds to relation scheme $R_i$. In row $i$ and column $j$ put the symbol $a_j$ if $A_j$ is in $R_i$. If not, put the symbol $b_{ij}$ there.

Repeatedly "consider" each of the dependencies $X \rightarrow Y$ in $F$, until no more changes can be made to the table. Each time we "consider" $X \rightarrow Y$, we look for rows that agree in all of the columns for the attributes of $X$. If we find two such rows, equate the symbols of those rows for the attributes of $Y$. When we equate two symbols, if one of them is $a_j$, make the other be $a_j$. If they are $b_{ij}$ and $b_{lj}$, make them both $b_{ij}$ or both $b_{lj}$, as you wish. It is important to understand that when two symbols are equated, all occurrences of those symbols in the table become the same; it is not sufficient to equate only the occurrences involved in the violation of the dependency $X \rightarrow Y$.

If after modifying the rows of the table as above, we discover that some row has become $a_1 \cdots a_n$, then the join is lossless. If not, the join is lossy (not lossless).  □

**Example 7.8:** Let us consider the decomposition of $SAIP$ into $SA$ and $SIP$ as in Example 7.7. The dependencies are $S \rightarrow A$ and $SI \rightarrow P$, and the initial table is

| $S$ | $A$ | $I$ | $P$ |
|---|---|---|---|
| $a_1$ | $a_2$ | $b_{13}$ | $b_{14}$ |
| $a_1$ | $b_{22}$ | $a_3$ | $a_4$ |

Since $S \rightarrow A$, and the two rows agree on $S$, we may equate their symbols for $A$, making $b_{22}$ become $a_2$. The resulting table is

| $S$ | $A$ | $I$ | $P$ |
|---|---|---|---|
| $a_1$ | $a_2$ | $b_{13}$ | $b_{14}$ |
| $a_1$ | $a_2$ | $a_3$ | $a_4$ |

Since some row, the second, has all $a$'s, the join is lossless.

For a more complicated example, let $R = ABCDE$, $R_1 = AD$, $R_2 = AB$, $R_3 = BE$, $R_4 = CDE$, and $R_5 = AE$. Let the functional dependencies be:

$$A \rightarrow C \qquad DE \rightarrow C$$
$$B \rightarrow C \qquad CE \rightarrow A$$
$$C \rightarrow D$$

The initial table is shown in Figure 7.3(a). We can apply $A \rightarrow C$ to equate $b_{13}$, $b_{23}$, and $b_{53}$. Then we use $B \rightarrow C$ to equate these symbols with $b_{33}$; the result is shown in Figure 7.3(b), where $b_{13}$ has been chosen as the representative symbol. Now use $C \rightarrow D$ to equate $a_4$, $b_{24}$, $b_{34}$, and $b_{54}$; the resulting symbol must be $a_4$. Then $DE \rightarrow C$ enables us to equate $b_{13}$ with $a_3$, and $CE \rightarrow A$ lets us equate $b_{31}$, $b_{41}$, and $a_1$. The result is shown in Figure 7.3(c). Since the middle row is all $a$'s, the decomposition has a lossless join. $\square$

It is interesting to note that one might assume Algorithm 7.2 could be simplified by only equating symbols if one was an $a_i$. The above example shows this is not the case; if we do not begin by equating $b_{13}$, $b_{23}$, $b_{33}$, and $b_{53}$, we can never get a row of all $a$'s.

**Theorem 7.4:** Algorithm 7.2 correctly determines if a decomposition has a lossless join.

**Proof:** Suppose the final table produced by Algorithm 7.2 does not have a row of all $a$'s. We may view this table as a relation $r$ for scheme $R$; the rows are tuples, and the $a_j$'s and $b_{ij}$'s are distinct symbols, each chosen from the domain of $A_j$. Relation $r$ satisfies the dependencies $F$, since Algorithm 7.2 modifies the table whenever a violation of the dependencies is found. We claim that $r \neq m_\rho(r)$. Clearly $r$ does not contain the tuple $a_1 a_2 \cdots a_n$. But for each $R_i$, there is a tuple $\mu_i$ in $r$, namely the tuple that is row $i$, such that $\mu_i[R_i]$ consists of all $a$'s. Thus, the join of the $\pi_{R_i}(r)$'s contains the tuple with all $a$'s, since that tuple agrees with $\mu_i$ for all $i$. We conclude that if the final table from

| A | B | C | D | E |
|---|---|---|---|---|
| $a_1$ | $b_{12}$ | $b_{13}$ | $a_4$ | $b_{15}$ |
| $a_1$ | $a_2$ | $b_{23}$ | $b_{24}$ | $b_{25}$ |
| $b_{31}$ | $a_2$ | $b_{33}$ | $b_{34}$ | $a_5$ |
| $b_{41}$ | $b_{42}$ | $a_3$ | $a_4$ | $a_5$ |
| $a_1$ | $b_{52}$ | $b_{53}$ | $b_{54}$ | $a_5$ |

(a)

| A | B | C | D | E |
|---|---|---|---|---|
| $a_1$ | $b_{12}$ | $b_{13}$ | $a_4$ | $b_{15}$ |
| $a_1$ | $a_2$ | $b_{13}$ | $b_{24}$ | $b_{25}$ |
| $b_{31}$ | $a_2$ | $b_{13}$ | $b_{34}$ | $a_5$ |
| $b_{41}$ | $b_{42}$ | $a_3$ | $a_4$ | $a_5$ |
| $a_1$ | $b_{52}$ | $b_{13}$ | $b_{54}$ | $a_5$ |

(b)

| A | B | C | D | E |
|---|---|---|---|---|
| $a_1$ | $b_{12}$ | $a_3$ | $a_4$ | $b_{15}$ |
| $a_1$ | $a_2$ | $a_3$ | $a_4$ | $b_{25}$ |
| $a_1$ | $a_2$ | $a_3$ | $a_4$ | $a_5$ |
| $a_1$ | $b_{42}$ | $a_3$ | $a_4$ | $a_5$ |
| $a_1$ | $b_{52}$ | $a_3$ | $a_4$ | $a_5$ |

(c)

**Figure 7.3** Applying Algorithm 7.2.

Algorithm 7.2 does not have a row with all $a$'s, then the decomposition $\rho$ does not have a lossless join; we have found a relation $r$ for $R$ such that $m_\rho(r) \neq r$.

Conversely, suppose the final table has a row with all $a$'s. We can in general view any table $T$ as shorthand for the domain relational calculus expression

$$\{a_1 a_2 \cdots a_n \mid (\exists b_{11}) \cdots (\exists b_{kn})(R(w_1) \wedge \cdots \wedge R(w_k))\} \tag{7.1}$$

where $w_i$ is the $i$th row of $T$. When $T$ is the initial table, formula (7.1) defines the function $m_\rho$. In proof, note $m_\rho(r)$ contains tuple $a_1 \cdots a_n$ if and only if for each $i$, $r$ contains a tuple with $a_j$ in the $j$th component if $A_j$ is an attribute of $R_i$ and some arbitrary value, represented by $b_{ij}$, in each of the other attributes.

Since we assume that any relation $r$ for scheme $R$ satisfies the dependencies $F$, we can infer that each of the transformations to the table performed by

Algorithm 7.2 changes the table (by identifying symbols) in a way that does not affect the set of tuples produced by (7.1), as long as that expression changes to mirror the changes to the table. The detailed proof of this claim is complex, but the intuition should be clear: we are only identifying symbols if in (7.1) applied to a relation $R$ which satisfies $F$, those symbols could only be assigned the same value anyway.

Since the final table contains a row with all $a$'s, the domain calculus expression for the final table is of the form.

$$\{a_1 \cdots a_n \mid (\exists b_{11}) \cdots (\exists b_{kn})(R(a_1 \cdots a_n) \wedge \cdots)\} \tag{7.2}$$

Clearly the value of (7.2) applied to relation $r$ for $R$, is a subset of $r$. However, if $r$ satisfies $F$, then the value of (7.2) is $m_\rho(r)$, and by Lemma 7.5(a), $r \subseteq m_\rho(r)$. Thus, whenever $r$ satisfies $F$, (7.2) computes exactly $r$, so $r = m_\rho(r)$. That is to say, the decomposition $\rho$ has a lossless join with respect to $F$. $\square$

Algorithm 7.2 can be applied to decompositions into any number of relation schemes. However, for decompositions into two schemes we can give a simpler test, the subject of the next theorem.

**Theorem 7.5:** If $\rho = (R_1, R_2)$ is a decomposition of $R$, and $F$ is a set of functional dependencies, then $\rho$ has a lossless join with respect to $F$ if and only if $(R_1 \cap R_2) \to (R_1 - R_2)$ or $(R_1 \cap R_2) \to (R_2 - R_1)$. Note that these dependencies need not be in the given set $F$; it is sufficient that they be in $F^+$.

|  | $R_1 \cap R_2$ | $R_1 - R_2$ | $R_2 - R_1$ |
|---|---|---|---|
| row for $R_1$ | $aa \cdots a$ | $aa \cdots a$ | $bb \cdots b$ |
| row for $R_2$ | $aa \cdots a$ | $bb \cdots b$ | $aa \cdots a$ |

**Figure 7.4** A general two row table.

**Proof:** The initial table used in an application of Algorithm 7.2 is shown in Figure 7.4, although we have omitted the subscripts on $a$ and $b$, which are easily determined and immaterial anyway. It is easy to show by induction on the number of symbols identified by Algorithm 7.2 that if the $b$ in the column for attribute $A$ is changed to an $a$, then $A$ is in $(R_1 \cap R_2)^+$. It is also easy to show by induction on the number of steps needed to prove $(R_1 \cap R_2) \to Y$ by Armstrong's axioms, that any $b$'s in the columns for attributes in $Y$ are changed to $a$'s. Thus, the row for $R_1$ becomes all $a$'s if and only if $R_2 - R_1 \subseteq (R_1 \cap R_2)^+$, that is $(R_1 \cap R_2) \to (R_2 - R_1)$, and similarly, the row for $R_2$ becomes all $a$'s if and only if $(R_1 \cap R_2) \to (R_1 - R_2)$. $\square$

**Example 7.9:** Suppose $R = ABC$ and $F = \{A \rightarrow B\}$. Then the decomposition of $R$ into $AB$ and $AC$ has a lossless join, since $AB \cap AC = A$, $AB - AC = B$,[4] and $A \rightarrow B$ holds. However, if we decompose $R$ into $R_1 = AB$ and $R_2 = BC$, we discover that $R_1 \cap R_2 = B$, and $B$ functionally determines neither $R_1 - R_2$, which is $A$, nor $R_2 - R_1$, which is $C$. Thus, the decomposition $AB$ and $BC$ does not have a lossless join with respect to $F = \{A \rightarrow B\}$, as can be seen by considering the relation $r = \{a_1 b_1 c_1, a_2 b_1 c_2\}$ for $R$. Then $\pi_{AB}(r) = \{a_1 b_1, a_2 b_1\}$, $\pi_{BC}(r) = \{b_1 c_1, b_1 c_2\}$, and

$$\pi_{AB}(r) \bowtie \pi_{BC}(r) = \{a_1 b_1 c_1, a_1 b_1 c_2, a_2 b_1 c_1, a_2 b_1 c_2\}$$

which is a proper superset of $r$. $\square$

## 7.5 DECOMPOSITIONS THAT PRESERVE DEPENDENCIES

We have seen that it is desirable for a decomposition to have the lossless-join property, because it guarantees that any relation can be recovered from its projections. Another important property of a decomposition of relation scheme $R$ into $\rho = (R_1, \ldots, R_k)$ is that the set of dependencies $F$ for $R$ be implied by the projection of $F$ onto the $R_i$'s. Formally, the *projection* of $F$ onto a set of attributes $Z$, denoted $\pi_Z(F)$, is the set of dependencies $X \rightarrow Y$ in $F^+$ such that $XY \subseteq Z$. (Note that $X \rightarrow Y$ need not be in $F$; it need only be in $F^+$.) We say decomposition $\rho$ *preserves* a set of dependencies $F$ if the union of all the dependencies in $\pi_{R_i}(F)$, for $i = 1, 2, \ldots, k$ logically implies all the dependencies in $F$.[5]

The reason it is desirable that $\rho$ preserves $F$ is that the dependencies in $F$ can be viewed as integrity constraints for the relation $R$. If the projected dependencies do not imply $F$, then should we represent $R$ by $\rho = (R_1, \ldots, R_k)$, we could find that the current value of the $R_i$'s represented a relation $R$ that did not satisfy $F$, even if $\rho$ had a lossless-join with respect to $F$. Alternatively, every update to one of the $R_i$'s would require a join to check that the constraints were not violated.

**Example 7.10:** Let us reconsider the problem of Example 7.3, where we had attributes CITY, ST, and ZIP, which we here abbreviate $C$, $S$, and $Z$. We observed the dependencies $CS \rightarrow Z$ and $Z \rightarrow C$. The decomposition of the relation scheme $CSZ$ into $SZ$ and $CZ$ has a lossless join, since

$$(SZ \cap CZ) \rightarrow (CZ - SZ)$$

That is, $Z \rightarrow C$. However, the projection of $F = \{CS \rightarrow Z, Z \rightarrow C\}$ onto $SZ$ gives only the trivial dependencies (those that follow from reflexivity), while

---

[4] To make sense of equations like these do not forget that $A_1 A_2 \cdots A_n$ stands for the set of attributes $\{A_1, A_2, \ldots, A_n\}$.

[5] Note that the converse is always true; that is, $F$ always implies all its projections, and therefore implies their union.

the projection onto $CZ$ gives $Z \rightarrow C$ and the trivial dependencies. It can be checked that $Z \rightarrow C$ and trivial dependencies do not imply $CS \rightarrow Z$, so the decomposition does not preserve dependencies.

For example, the join of the two relations in Figure 7.5(a) and (b) is the relation of Figure 7.5(c). Figure 7.5(a) satisfies the trivial dependencies, as any relation must. Figure 7.5(b) satisfies the trivial dependencies and the dependency $Z \rightarrow C$. However, their join in Figure 7.5(c) violates $CS \rightarrow Z$. $\square$

| S | Z |
|---|---|
| 545 Tech Sq. | 02138 |
| 545 Tech Sq. | 02139 |

(a)

| C | Z |
|---|---|
| Cambridge, Mass. | 02138 |
| Cambridge, Mass. | 02139 |

(b)

| C | S | Z |
|---|---|---|
| Cambridge, Mass. | 545 Tech Sq. | 02138 |
| Cambridge, Mass. | 545 Tech Sq. | 02139 |

(c)

**Figure 7.5** A join violating a functional dependency.

We should note that a decomposition may have a lossless join with respect to set of dependencies $F$, yet not preserve $F$. Example 7.10 gave one such instance. Also, the decomposition could preserve $F$ yet not have a lossless join. For example, let $F = \{A \rightarrow B,\ C \rightarrow D\}$, $R = ABCD$, and $\rho = (AB, CD)$.

### Testing Preservation of Dependencies

In principle, it is easy to test whether a decomposition $\rho = (R_1, \ldots, R_k)$ preserves a set of dependencies $F$. Just compute $F^+$ and project it onto all of the $R_i$'s. Take the union of the resulting sets of dependencies, and test whether this set is equivalent to $F$.

However, in practice, just computing $F^+$ is a formidable task, since the number of dependencies it contains is often exponential in the size of $F$. Therefore, it is fortunate that there is a way to test preservation without actually computing $F^+$; this method takes time that is polynomial in the size of $F$.

**Algorithm 7.3:** Testing Preservation of Dependencies.

INPUT: A decomposition $\rho = (R_1, \ldots, R_k)$ and a set of functional dependencies $F$.

OUTPUT: A decision whether $\rho$ preserves $F$.

METHOD: Define $G$ to be $\cup_{i=1}^{k} \pi_{R_i}(F)$. Note that we do not compute $G$; we merely wish to see whether it is equivalent to $F$. To test whether $G$ is equivalent to $F$, we must consider each $X \to Y$ in $F$ and determine whether $X^+$, computed with respect to $G$, contains $Y$. The trick we use to compute $X^+$ without having $G$ available is to consider repeatedly what the effect is of closing $X$ with respect to the projections of $F$ onto the various $R_i$'s.

That is, define an $R$-*operation* on set of attributes $Z$ with respect to a set of dependencies $F$ to be the replacement of $Z$ by $Z \cup ((Z \cap R)^+ \cap R)$, the closure being taken with respect to $F$. This operation adjoins to $Z$ those attributes $A$ such that $(Z \cap R) \to A$ is in $\pi_R(F)$. Then we compute $X^+$ with respect to $G$ by starting with $X$, and repeatedly running through the list of $R_i$'s, performing the $R_i$-operation for each $i$ in turn. If at some pass, none of the $R_i$-operations make any change in the current set of attributes, then we are done; the resulting set is $X^+$. More formally, the algorithm is:

```
Z := X
while changes to Z occur do
    for i := 1 to k do
        Z := Z ∪ ((Z ∩ Ri)+ ∩ Ri) /* closure wrt F */
```

If $Y$ is a subset of the $Z$ that results from executing the above steps, then $X \to Y$ is in $G^+$. If each $X \to Y$ in $F$ is thus found to be in $G^+$, answer "yes," otherwise answer "no." $\square$

**Example 7.11:** Consider set of attributes $ABCD$ with decomposition

$$\{AB, BC, CD\}$$

and set of dependencies $F = \{A \to B, B \to C, C \to D, D \to A\}$. That is, in $F^+$, each attribute functionally determines all the others. We might first imagine that when we project $F$ onto $AB$, $BC$, and $CD$, we fail to get the dependency $D \to A$, but that intuition is wrong. When we project $F$, we really project $F^+$ onto the relation schemes, so projecting onto $AB$ we get not only $A \to B$, but also $B \to A$. Similarly, we get $C \to B$ in $\pi_{BC}(F)$ and $D \to C$ in $\pi_{CD}(F)$, and these three dependencies logically imply $D \to A$. Thus, we should expect that Algorithm 7.3 will tell us that $D \to A$ follows logically from

$$G = \pi_{AB}(F) \cup \pi_{BC}(F) \cup \pi_{CD}(F)$$

We start with $Z = \{D\}$. Applying the $AB$-operation does not help, since

$$\{D\} \cup ((\{D\} \cap \{A, B\})^+ \cap \{A, B\})$$

is just $\{D\}$. Similarly, the $BC$-operation does not change $Z$. However, when we apply the $CD$-operation we get

$$Z = \{D\} \cup ((\{D\} \cap \{C, D\})^+ \cap \{C, D\})$$
$$= \{D\} \cup (\{D\}^+ \cap \{C, D\})$$
$$= \{D\} \cup (\{A, B, C, D\} \cap \{C, D\})$$
$$= \{C, D\}$$

Similarly, on the next pass, the $BC$-operation applied to the current $Z = \{C, D\}$ produces $Z = \{B, C, D\}$, and on the third pass, the $AB$-operation sets $Z$ to $\{A, B, C, D\}$, whereupon no more changes to $Z$ are possible.

Thus, with respect to $G$, $\{D\}^+ = \{A, B, C, D\}$, which contains $A$, so we conclude that $G \models D \rightarrow A$. Since it is easy to check that the other members of $F$ are in $G^+$ (in fact they are in $G$), we conclude that this decomposition preserves the set of dependencies $F$. $\square$

**Theorem 7.6:** Algorithm 7.3 correctly determines if $X \rightarrow Y$ is in $G^+$.

**Proof:** Each time we add an attribute to $Z$, we are using a dependency in $G$, so when the algorithm says "yes," it must be correct. Conversely, suppose $X \rightarrow Y$ is in $G^+$. Then there is a sequence of steps whereby, using Algorithm 7.1 to take the closure of $X$ with respect to $G$, we eventually include all the attributes of $Y$. Each of these steps involves the application of a dependency in $G$, and that dependency must be in $\pi_{R_i}(F)$ for some $i$, since $G$ is the union of these projections. Let one such dependency be $U \rightarrow V$. An easy induction on the number of dependencies applied in Algorithm 7.1 shows that eventually $U$ becomes a subset of $Z$, and then on the next pass the $R_i$-operation will surely cause all attributes of $V$ to be added to $Z$ if they are not already there. $\square$

## 7.6 NORMAL FORMS FOR RELATION SCHEMES

A number of different properties, or "normal forms" for relation schemes with dependencies have been defined. The most significant of these are called "third normal form" and "Boyce-Codd normal form." Their purpose is to avoid the problems of redundancy and anomalies discussed in Section 7.1.

### Boyce-Codd Normal Form

The stronger of these normal forms is called Boyce-Codd. A relation scheme $R$ with dependencies $F$ is said to be in *Boyce-Codd normal form* (BCNF) if whenever $X \rightarrow A$ holds in $R$, and $A$ is not in $X$, then $X$ is a superkey for $R$; that is, $X$ is a key or contains a key. Put another way, the only nontrivial dependencies are those in which a key functionally determines one or more other attributes. In principal, we must look for violating dependencies $X \rightarrow A$ not only among the given dependencies, but among dependencies derived from them. However, we leave as an exercise the fact that if there are no violations among the given set $F$, and $F$ consists only of dependencies with single attributes on the right, then there are no violations among any of the dependencies in $F^+$.

**Example 7.12:** Consider the relation scheme $CSZ$ of Example 7.10, with dependencies $CS \rightarrow Z$ and $Z \rightarrow C$. The keys for this relation scheme are $CS$ and $SZ$, as one can easily check by computing the closures of these sets of attributes and of the other nontrivial sets ($CZ$, $C$, $S$, and $Z$). The scheme $CSZ$ with these dependencies is not in BCNF, because $Z \rightarrow C$ holds in $CSZ$, yet $Z$ is not a key of $CSZ$, nor does it contain a key. $\square$

## Third Normal Form

In some circumstances BCNF is too strong a condition, in the sense that it is not possible to bring a relation scheme into that form by decomposition, without losing the ability to preserve dependencies. Third normal form provides most of the benefits of BCNF, as far as elimination of anomalies is concerned, yet it is a condition we can achieve for an arbitrary database scheme without giving up either dependency preservation or the lossless-join property.

Before defining third normal form, we need a preliminary definition. Call an attribute $A$ in relation scheme $R$ a *prime* attribute if $A$ is a member of any key for $R$ (recall there may be many keys). If $A$ is not a member of any key, then $A$ is *nonprime*.

**Example 7.13:** In the relation scheme $CSZ$ of Example 7.12, all attributes are prime, since given the dependencies $CS \rightarrow Z$ and $Z \rightarrow C$, both $CS$ and $SZ$ are keys.

In the relation scheme $ABCD$ with dependencies $AB \rightarrow C$, $B \rightarrow D$, and $BC \rightarrow A$, we can check that $AB$ and $BC$ are the only keys. Thus, $A$, $B$, and $C$ are prime, and $D$ is nonprime. $\square$

A relation scheme $R$ is in *third normal form*[6] (*3NF*) if whenever $X \rightarrow A$ holds in $R$ and $A$ is not in $X$, then either $X$ is a superkey for $R$, or $A$ is prime. Notice that the definitions of Boyce-Codd and third normal forms are identical except for the clause "or $A$ is prime" that makes third normal form a weaker condition than Boyce-Codd normal form. As with BCNF, we in principle must consider not only the given set of dependencies $F$, but all dependencies in $F^+$ to check for a 3NF violation. However, we can show that if $F$ consists only of dependencies that have been decomposed so they have single attributes on the right, then it is sufficient to check the dependencies of $F$ only.

**Example 7.14:** The relation scheme $SAIP$ from Example 7.7, with dependencies $SI \rightarrow P$ and $S \rightarrow A$ violates 3NF. $A$ is a nonprime attribute, since the only key is $SI$. Then $S \rightarrow A$ violates the 3NF condition, since $S$ is not a superkey.

However, the relation scheme $CSZ$ from Example 7.12 is in 3NF. Since all

---

[6] Yes Virginia, there is a first normal form and there is a second normal form. First normal form merely states that the domain of each attribute is an elementary type, rather than a set or a record structure, as fields in the object model (Section 2.7) can be. Second normal form is only of historical interest and is mentioned in the exercises.

of its attributes are prime, no dependency could violate the conditions of third normal form. $\square$

### Motivation Behind Normal Forms

The purpose behind BCNF is to eliminate the redundancy that functional dependencies are capable of causing. Suppose we have a relation scheme $R$ in BCNF, yet there is some redundancy that lets us predict the value of an attribute by comparing two tuples and applying a functional dependency. That is, we have two tuples that agree in set of attributes $X$ and disagree in set of attributes $Y$, while in the remaining attribute $A$, the value in one of the tuples, lets us predict the value in the other. That is, the two tuples look like

| $X$ | $Y$ | $A$ |
|-----|-----|-----|
| $x$ | $y_1$ | $a$ |
| $x$ | $y_2$ | ? |

Here, $x$, $y_1$, and $y_2$ represent lists of values for the sets of attributes $X$ and $Y$.

If we can use a functional dependency to infer the value indicated by a question mark, then that value must be $a$, and the dependency used must be $Z \to A$, for some $Z \subseteq X$. However, $Z$ cannot be a superkey, because if it were, then the two tuples above, which agree in $Z$, would be the same tuple. Thus, $R$ is not in BCNF, as supposed. We conclude that in a BCNF relation, no value can be predicted from any other, using functional dependencies only. In Section 7.9 we shall see that there are other ways redundancy can arise, but these are "invisible" as long as we consider functional dependencies to be the only way the set of legal relations for a scheme can be defined.

Naturally, 3NF, being weaker than BCNF, cannot eliminate all redundancy. The canonical example is the $CSZ$ scheme of Example 7.12, which is in 3NF, yet allows pairs of tuples like

| $C$ | $S$ | $Z$ |
|-----|-----|-----|
| $c$ | $s_1$ | $z$ |
| ? | $s_2$ | $z$ |

where we can deduce from the dependency $Z \to C$ that the unknown value is $c$. Note that these tuples cannot violate the other dependency, $CS \to Z$.

## 7.7 LOSSLESS-JOIN DECOMPOSITION INTO BCNF

We have now been introduced to the properties we desire for relation schemes: BCNF or, failing that, 3NF. In Sections 7.4 and 7.5 we saw the two most important properties of database schemes as a whole, the lossless-join and dependency-preservation properties. Now we must attempt to put these ideas together, that is, construct database schemes with the properties we desire for

database schemes, and with each individual relation scheme having the properties we desire for relation schemes.

It turns out that any relation scheme has a lossless join decomposition
into Boyce-Codd Normal Form, and it has a decomposition into 3NF that
has a lossless join and is also dependency-preserving. However, there may be
no decomposition of a relation scheme into Boyce-Codd normal form that is
dependency-preserving. The $CSZ$ relation scheme is the canonical example. It
is not in BCNF because the dependency $Z \rightarrow C$ holds, yet if we decompose
$CSZ$ in any way such that $CSZ$ is not one of the schemes in the decomposition,
then the dependency $CS \rightarrow Z$ is not implied by the projected dependencies.

Before giving the decomposition algorithm, we need the following property
of lossless-join decompositions.

**Lemma 7.6:** Suppose $R$ is a relation scheme with functional dependencies $F$.
Let $\rho = (R_1, \ldots, R_n)$ be a decomposition of $R$ with a lossless join with respect
to $F$, and let $\sigma = (S_1, S_2)$ be a lossless-join decomposition of $R_1$ with respect
to $\pi_{R_1}(F)$. Then the decomposition of $R$ into $(S_1, S_2, R_2, \ldots, R_n)$ also has a
lossless join with respect to $F$.

**Proof:** Suppose we take a relation $r$ for $R$, and project it onto $R_1, \ldots, R_n$ to
get relations $r_1, \ldots, r_n$, respectively. Then we project $r_1$ onto $S_1$ and $S_2$ to get
$s_1$ and $s_2$. The lossless-join property tells us we can join $s_1$ and $s_2$ to recover
exactly $r_1$, and we can then join $r_1, \ldots, r_n$ to recover $r$. Since the natural join
is an associative operation, by Theorem 2.1(a), the order in which we perform
the join doesn't matter, so we recover $r$ no matter in what order we take the
join of $s_1, s_2, r_2, \ldots, r_n$. $\square$

We can apply Lemma 7.6 to get a simple but time-consuming algorithm
to decompose a relation scheme $R$ into BCNF. If we find a violation of BCNF
in $R$, say $X \rightarrow A$, we decompose $R$ into schemes $R - A$ and $XA$. These are
both smaller than $R$, since $XA$ could not be all attributes of $R$ (then $X$ would
surely be a superkey, and $X \rightarrow A$ would not violate BCNF). The join of $R - A$
and $XA$ is lossless, by Theorem 7.5, because the intersection of the schemes
is $X$, and $X \rightarrow XA$. We compute the projections of the dependencies for $R$
onto $R - A$ and $XA$, then apply this decomposition step recursively to these
schemes. Lemma 7.6 assures that the set of schemes we obtain by decomposing
until all the schemes are in BCNF will be a lossless-join decomposition.

The problem is that the projection of dependencies can take exponential
time in the size of the scheme $R$ and the original set of dependencies. However,
it turns out that there is a way to find some lossless-join decomposition into
BCNF relation schemes in time that is polynomial in the size of the given set of
dependencies and scheme. The technique will sometimes decompose a relation
that is already in BCNF, however. The next lemma gives some useful properties
of BCNF schemes.

**Lemma 7.7:**

a)   Every two-attribute scheme is in BCNF.

b)   If $R$ is not in BCNF, then we can find attributes $A$ and $B$ in $R$, such that $(R - AB) \rightarrow A$. It may or may not be the case that $(R - AB) \rightarrow B$ as well.

**Proof:** For part (a), let $AB$ be the scheme. There are only two nontrivial dependencies that can hold: $A \rightarrow B$ and $B \rightarrow A$. If neither hold, then surely there is no BCNF violation. If only $A \rightarrow B$ holds, then $A$ is a key, so we do not have a violation. If only $B \rightarrow A$ holds, then $B$ is a key, and if both hold, both $A$ and $B$ are keys, so there can never be a BCNF violation.

For (b), suppose there is a BCNF violation $X \rightarrow A$ in $R$. Then $R$ must have some other attribute $B$, not in $XA$, or else $X$ is a superkey, and $X \rightarrow A$ is not a violation. Thus, $(R - AB) \rightarrow A$ as desired. $\square$

Lemma 7.7 lets us look for BCNF violations in a scheme $R$ with $n$ attributes by considering only the $n(n-1)/2$ pairs of attributes $\{A, B\}$ and computing the closure of $R - AB$ with respect to the given dependencies $F$, by using Algorithm 7.1. As stated, that algorithm takes $O(n^2)$ time, but a carefully designed data structure can make it run in time $O(n)$; in any event, the time is polynomial in the size of $R$. If for no $A$ and $B$ does $(R - AB)^+$ contain either $A$ or $B$, then by Lemma 7.7(b) we know $R$ is in BCNF.

It is important to realize that the converse of Lemma 7.7(b) is not true. Possibly, $R$ is in BCNF, and yet there is such a pair $\{A, B\}$. For example, if $R = ABC$, and $F = \{C \rightarrow A, \ C \rightarrow B\}$, then $R$ is in BCNF, yet $R - AB = C$, and $C$ does functionally determine $A$ (and $B$ as well).

Before proceeding to the algorithm for BCNF decomposition, we need one more observation, about projections of dependencies. Specifically:

**Lemma 7.8:** If we have a set of dependencies $F$ on $R$, and we project them onto $R_1 \subseteq R$ to get $F_1$, and then project $F_1$ onto $R_2 \subseteq R_1$ to get $F_2$, then

$$F_2 = \pi_{R_2}(F)$$

That is, we could have assumed that $F$ was the set of dependencies for $R_1$, even though $F$ presumably mentions attributes not found in $R_1$.

**Proof:** If $XY \subseteq R_2$, then $X \rightarrow Y$ is in $F^+$ if and only if it is in $F_1{}^+$. $\square$

Lemma 7.8 has an important consequence. It says that if we decompose relation schemes as in Lemma 7.6, then we never actually have to compute the projected dependencies as we decompose. It is sufficient to work with the given dependencies, taking closures of attribute sets by Algorithm 7.1 when we need to, rather than computing whole projections of dependencies, which are exponential in the number of attributes in the scheme. It is this observation, together with Lemma 7.7(b), that allows us to take time that is polynomial in the size of the given scheme and the given dependencies, and yet discover some lossless-join, BCNF decomposition of the given scheme.

**Algorithm 7.4:** Lossless Join Decomposition into Boyce-Codd Normal Form.

INPUT: Relation scheme $R$ and functional dependencies $F$.

OUTPUT: A decomposition of $R$ with a lossless join, such that every relation scheme in the decomposition is in Boyce-Codd normal form with respect to the projection of $F$ onto that scheme.

METHOD: The heart of the algorithm is to take relation scheme $R$, and decompose it into two schemes. One will have set of attributes $XA$; it will be in BCNF, and the dependency $X \to A$ will hold. The second will be $R - A$, so the join of $R - A$ with $XA$ is lossless. We then apply the decomposition procedure recursively, with $R - A$ in place of $R$, until we come to a scheme that meets the condition of Lemma 7.7(b); we know that scheme is in BCNF. Then, Lemma 7.6 assures us that this scheme plus the BCNF schemes generated at each step of the recursion have a lossless join.

```
Z := R; /* at all times, Z is the one scheme
    of the decomposition that may not be in BCNF */
repeat
        decompose Z into Z − A and XA, where XA is in BCNF
            and X → A; /* use the subroutine of Figure 7.6(b) */
        add XA to the decomposition;
        Z := Z − A;
until Z cannot be decomposed by Lemma 7.7(b);
add Z to the decomposition
```

(a) Main program.

```
if Z contains no A and B such that A is in (Z − AB)⁺ then
        /* remember all closures are taken with respect to F */
        return that Z is in BCNF and cannot be decomposed
else begin
        find one such A and B;
        Y := Z − B;
        while Y contains A and B such that (Y − AB)⁺ → A do
            Y := Y − B;
        return the decomposition Z − A and Y;
        /* Y here is XA in the main program */
end
```

(b) Decomposition subroutine.

**Figure 7.6** Details of Algorithm 7.4.

The details of the algorithm are given in Figure 7.6. Figure 7.6(a) is the main routine, which repeatedly decomposes the one scheme $Z$ that we do not know to be in BCNF; initially, $Z$ is $R$. Figure 7.6(b) is the decomposition procedure that either determines $Z$ cannot be decomposed, or decomposes $Z$ into $Z - A$ and $XA$, where $X \rightarrow A$. The set of attributes $XA$ is selected by starting with $Y = Z$, and repeatedly throwing out the attribute $B$, the one of the pair $AB$ such that we found $X \rightarrow A$, where $X = Y - AB$. Recall that it does not matter whether $X \rightarrow B$ is true or not. □

**Example 7.15:** Let us consider the relation scheme $CTHRSG$, where $C =$ course, $T =$ teacher, $H =$ hour, $R =$ room, $S =$ student, and $G =$ grade. The functional dependencies $F$ we assume are

$$C \rightarrow T \quad \text{Each course has one teacher.}$$
$$HR \rightarrow C \quad \text{Only one course can meet in a room at one time.}$$
$$HT \rightarrow R \quad \text{A teacher can be in only one room at one time.}$$
$$CS \rightarrow G \quad \text{Each student has one grade in each course.}$$
$$HS \rightarrow R \quad \text{A student can be in only one room at one time.}$$

Since Algorithm 7.4 does not specify the order in which pairs $AB$ are to be considered, we shall adopt the uniform strategy of preserving the order $CTHRSG$ for the attributes and trying the first attribute against the others, in turn, then the second against the third through last, and so on.

We begin with the entire scheme, $CTHRSG$, and the first pair to consider is $CT$. We find that $(HRSG)^+$ contains $C$; it also contains $T$, but that is irrelevant. Thus, we begin the while-loop of Figure 7.6(b) with $A = C$, $B = T$, and $Y = CHRSG$.

Now, we try the $CH$ pair as $\{A, B\}$, but $(RSG)^+$ contains neither $C$ nor $H$. We have better luck with the next pair, $CR$, because $(HSG)^+$ contains $R$. Thus, we have $A = R$, $B = C$, and we set $Y$ to $HRSG$, by throwing out $B$, as usual. With $Y = HRSG$, we have no luck until we try pair $RG$, when we find $(HS)^+$ contains $R$. Thus, we have $A = R$ and $B = G$, whereupon $Y$ is set to $HRS$.

At this point, no further attributes can be thrown out of $Y$, because the test of Lemma 7.7(b) fails for each pair. We may therefore decompose $CTHRSG$ into

1. $HRS$, which plays the role of $XA$, with $X = HS$ and $A = R$, and
2. $Z = CTHRSG - R$, which is $CTHSG$.

We now work on $Z = CTHSG$ in the main program. The list of pairs $AB$ that work and the remaining sets of attributes after throwing out $B$, is:

1. In $CTHSG$: $A = T$, $B = H$, leaves $Y = CTSG$.
2. In $CTSG$: $A = T$, $B = S$, leaves $Y = CTG$.
3. In $CTG$: $A = T$, $B = G$, leaves $Y = CT$.

Surely, $CT$ is in BCNF, by Lemma 7.7(a). We thus add $CT$ to our decomposition. Attribute $T$ plays the role of $A$, so in the main program we eliminate $T$ and progress to the scheme $Z = CHSG$, which is still not in Boyce-Codd normal form.

In $CHSG$, the first successful pair is $A = G$ and $B = H$, which leaves $Y = CSG$. No more pairs allow this scheme to be decomposed by Lemma 7.7(b), so we add $CSG$ to the decomposition, and we apply the main program to the scheme with $A$ removed, that is, $Z = CHS$.

This scheme, we find, cannot be decomposed by Lemma 7.7(b), so it too is in BCNF, and we are done. Notice that we get lossless joins at each stage, if we combine the schemes in the reverse of the order in which they were found. That is, $CHS \bowtie CSG$ is lossless because of the dependency $CS \rightarrow G$; $CHSG \bowtie CT$ is lossless because of the dependency $C \rightarrow T$, and $CTHSG \bowtie HRS$ is lossless because of $HS \rightarrow R$. In each case, the required functional dependency is the one of the form $X \rightarrow A$ that gets developed by the subroutine of Figure 7.6(b). By Lemma 7.6, these lossless joins imply that the complete decomposition, $(HRS, CT, CSG, CHS)$ is lossless. $\square$

### Problems with Arbitrary BCNF Decompositions

In the decomposition of Example 7.15, the four relation schemes store the following kinds of information:

1. The location (room) of each student at each hour.
2. The teacher of each course.
3. Grades for students in courses, i.e., the students' transcripts.
4. The schedule of courses and hours for each student.

This is not exactly what we might have designed had we attempted by hand to find a lossless-join decomposition into BCNF. In particular, we cannot tell where a course meets without joining the $CHS$ and $HRS$ relations, and even then we could not find out if there were no students taking the course. We probably would have chosen to replace $HRS$ by $CHR$, which gives the allocation of rooms by courses, rather than by students, and corresponds to the published schedule of courses found at many schools. Unfortunately, the question of "merit" of different decompositions is not one we can address theoretically. If one does not have a particular scheme in mind, for which we can simply verify that it has a lossless join and that each of its components is in BCNF, then one can try picking $AB$ pairs at random in Algorithm 7.4, in the hope that after a few tries, one will get a decomposition that looks "natural."

Another problem with the chosen decomposition (one which is not fixed by replacing $HRS$ by $CHR$) is that some of the dependencies in $F$, specifically $TH \rightarrow R$ and $HR \rightarrow C$, are not preserved by the decomposition. That is, the projection of $F$ onto $HRS$, $CT$, $CSG$, and $CHS$ is the closure of the following dependencies, as the reader may check.

$$CS \rightarrow G \qquad HS \rightarrow R$$
$$C \rightarrow T \qquad HS \rightarrow C$$

Note that the last of these, $HS \rightarrow C$ is in the projection of $F$ onto $CHS$, but is not a given dependency; the other three are members of $F$ itself. These four dependencies do not imply $TH \rightarrow R$ or $HR \rightarrow C$. For example, the relation for $CTHRSG$ shown below

| $C$ | $T$ | $H$ | $R$ | $S$ | $G$ |
|-----|-----|-----|-----|-----|-----|
| $c_1$ | $t$ | $h$ | $r_1$ | $s_1$ | $g_1$ |
| $c_2$ | $t$ | $h$ | $r_2$ | $s_2$ | $g_2$ |
| $c_2$ | $t$ | $h$ | $r_1$ | $s_3$ | $g_3$ |

satisfies neither $TH \rightarrow R$ nor $HR \rightarrow C$, yet its projections onto $HRS$, $CT$, $CSG$, and $CHS$ satisfy all the projected dependencies.

## Efficiency of BCNF Decomposition

We claim that Algorithm 7.4 takes time that is polynomial in $n$, which is the length of the relation scheme $R$ and the dependencies $F$, written down. We already observed that computing closures with respect to $F$ takes time that is polynomial in $n$; in fact $O(n)$ time suffices if the proper data structures are used. The subroutine of Figure 7.6(b) runs on a subset $Z$ of the attributes, which surely cannot be more than $n$ attributes. Each time through the loop, the set $Y$ decreases in size, so at most $n$ iterations are possible. There are at most $n^2$ pairs of attributes $A$ and $B$, so the test for $(Y - AB)^+ \rightarrow A$ is done at most $n^3$ times. Since this test takes polynomial time, and its time dominates the time of the other parts of the loop body, we conclude that the algorithm of Figure 7.6(b) takes polynomial time.

The principal cost of the main program of Figure 7.6(a) is the call to the subroutine, and this call is made only once per iteration of the loop. Since $Z$ decreases in size going around the loop, at most $n$ iterations are possible, and the entire algorithm is thus polynomial.

## 7.8 DEPENDENCY-PRESERVING 3NF DECOMPOSITIONS

We saw from Examples 7.12 and 7.14 that it is not always possible to decompose a relation scheme into BCNF and still preserve the dependencies. However, we can always find a dependency-preserving decomposition into third normal form, as the next algorithm and theorem show.

**Algorithm 7.5:** Dependency-Preserving Decomposition into Third Normal Form.

INPUT: Relation scheme $R$ and set of functional dependencies $F$, which we assume without loss of generality to be a minimal cover.

OUTPUT: A dependency-preserving decomposition of $R$ such that each relation scheme is in 3NF with respect to the projection of $F$ onto that scheme.

METHOD: If there are any attributes of $R$ not involved in any dependency of $F$, either on the left or right, then any such attribute can, in principle, form a relation scheme by itself, and we shall eliminate it from $R$.[7] If one of the dependencies in $F$ involves all the attributes of $R$, then output $R$ itself. Otherwise, the decomposition $\rho$ to be output consists of scheme $XA$ for each dependency $X \to A$ in $F$. $\square$

**Example 7.16:** Reconsider the relation scheme $CTHRSG$ of Example 7.15, whose dependencies have minimal cover $F$:

$$
\begin{array}{ll}
C \to T & CS \to G \\
HR \to C & HS \to R \\
HT \to R &
\end{array}
$$

Algorithm 7.5 yields the set of relation schemes $CT$, $CHR$, $THR$, $CSG$, and $HRS$. $\square$

**Theorem 7.7:** Algorithm 7.5 yields a dependency-preserving decomposition into third normal form.

**Proof:** Since the projected dependencies include a cover for $F$, the decomposition clearly preserves dependencies. We must show that the relation scheme $YB$, for each functional dependency $Y \to B$ in the minimal cover, is in 3NF. Suppose $X \to A$ violates 3NF for $YB$; that is, $A$ is not in $X$, $X$ is not a superkey for $YB$, and $A$ is nonprime. Of course, we also know that $XA \subseteq YB$, and $X \to A$ follows logically from $F$. We shall consider two cases, depending on whether or not $A = B$.

*Case 1:* $A = B$. Then since $A$ is not in $X$, we know $X \subseteq Y$, and since $X$ is not a superkey for $YB$, $X$ must be a proper subset of $Y$. But then $X \to B$, which is also $X \to A$, could replace $Y \to B$ in the supposed minimal cover, contradicting the assumption that $Y \to B$ was part of the given minimal cover.

*Case 2:* $A \neq B$. Since $Y$ is a superkey for $YB$, there must be some $Z \subseteq Y$ that is a key for $YB$. But $A$ is in $Y$, since we are assuming $A \neq B$, and $A$ cannot be in $Z$, because $A$ is nonprime. Thus $Z$ is a proper subset of $Y$, yet $Z \to B$ can replace $Y \to B$ in the supposedly minimal cover, again providing a contradiction. $\square$

There is a modification to Algorithm 7.5 that avoids unnecessary decomposition. If $X \to A_1, \ldots, X \to A_n$ are dependencies in a minimal cover, then we

---

[7] Sometimes it is desirable to have two or more attributes, say $A$ and $B$, appear together in a relation scheme, even though there is no functional dependency involving them. There may simply be a many-many relationship between $A$ and $B$. An idea of Bernstein [1976] is to introduce a dummy attribute $\theta$ and functional dependency $AB \to \theta$, to force this association. After completing the design, attribute $\theta$ is eliminated.

may use the one relation scheme $X A_1 \cdots A_n$ in place of the $n$ relation schemes $X A_1, \ldots, X A_n$. It is left as an exercise that the scheme $X A_1 \cdots A_n$ is in 3NF.

### Decompositions into Third Normal Form with a Lossless Join and Preservation of Dependencies

As seen, we can decompose any relation scheme $R$ into a set of schemes

$$\rho = (R_1, \ldots, R_k)$$

such that $\rho$ has a lossless join and each $R_i$ is in BCNF (and therefore in 3NF). We can also decompose $R$ into $\sigma = (S_1, \ldots, S_m)$ such that $\sigma$ preserves the set of dependencies $F$, and each $S_j$ is in 3NF. Can we find a decomposition into 3NF that has both the lossless join and dependency-preservation properties? We can, if we simply adjoin to $\sigma$ a relation scheme $X$ that is a key for $R$, as the next theorem shows.

**Theorem 7.8:** Let $\sigma$ be the 3NF decomposition of $R$ constructed by Algorithm 7.5, and let $X$ be a key for $R$. Then $\tau = \sigma \cup \{X\}$ is a decomposition of $R$ with all relation schemes in 3NF; the decomposition preserves dependencies and has the lossless join property.

**Proof:** It is easy to show that any 3NF violation in $X$ implies that a proper subset of $X$ functionally determines $X$, and therefore $R$, so $X$ would not be a key in that case. Thus $X$, as well as the members of $\sigma$, are in 3NF. Clearly $\tau$ preserves dependencies, since $\sigma$ does.

To show that $\tau$ has a lossless join, apply the tabular test of Algorithm 7.2. We can show that the row for $X$ becomes all $a$'s, as follows. Consider the order $A_1, A_2, \ldots, A_k$ in which the attributes of $R - X$ are added to $X^+$ in Algorithm 7.1. Surely all attributes are added eventually, since $X$ is a key. We show by induction on $i$ that the column corresponding to $A_i$ in the row for $X$ is set to $a_i$ in the test of Algorithm 7.2.

The basis, $i = 0$, is trivial. Assume the result for $i - 1$. Then $A_i$ is added to $X^+$ because of some given functional dependency $Y \rightarrow A_i$, where

$$Y \subseteq X \cup \{A_1, \ldots, A_{i-1}\}$$

Then $Y A_i$ is in $\sigma$, and the rows for $Y A_i$ and $X$ agree on $Y$ (they are all $a$'s) after the columns of the $X$-row for $A_1, \ldots, A_{i-1}$ are made $a$'s. Thus, these rows are made to agree on $A_i$ during the execution of Algorithm 7.2. Since the $Y A_i$-row has $a_i$ there, so must the $X$-row. $\square$

Obviously, in some cases $\tau$ is not the smallest set of relation schemes with the properties of Theorem 7.8. We can throw out relation schemes in $\tau$ one at a time as long as the desired properties are preserved. Many different database schemes may result, depending on the order in which we throw out schemes, since eliminating one may preclude the elimination of others.

**Example 7.17:** We could take the union of the database scheme produced for $CTHRSG$ in Example 7.16 with the key $SH$, to get a decomposition that has a lossless join and preserves dependencies. It happens that $SH$ is a subset of $HRS$, which is one of the relation schemes already selected. Thus, $SH$ may be eliminated, and the database scheme of Example 7.16, that is

$$(CT, CHR, THR, CSG, HRS)$$

suffices. Although some proper subsets of this set of five relation schemes are lossless join decompositions, we can check that the projected dependencies for any four of them do not imply the complete set of dependencies $F$. $\square$

## A Cautionary Word About Decompositions

Given tools like Algorithms 7.4 and 7.5, one is often tempted to "decompose the heck" out of a relation scheme. It is important to remember that not every lossless-join decomposition step is beneficial, and some can be harmful. The most common mistake is to decompose a scheme that is already in BCNF, just because it happens to have a lossless-join decomposition that preserves dependencies.

For example, we might have a relation giving information about employees, say $I$, the unique ID-number for employees, $N$, the employee's name, $D$ the department in which he works, and $S$, the salary. Since $I$ is the only key in this situation, we have $I \to A$ for each other attribute $A$. It is therefore possible to decompose this scheme into $IN$, $ID$, and $IS$. This decomposition is easily seen to have a lossless join, because $I$, the only attribute in the intersection of any pair, functionally determines all the attributes; it also clearly preserves the dependencies $I \to NDS$.

However, the scheme $INDS$ is itself in BCNF, and offers significant advantages for the answering of queries relating attributes other than $I$. For example, if we wanted to know the name and salary of all of the employees in the toy department, we would have to join $IN \bowtie ID \bowtie IS$ in the decomposed database scheme, yet we could answer the query without taking any joins if we left the relation scheme intact (and with an index on department, we could answer this query quite efficiently). Further, the decomposed scheme requires that the employee ID number be repeated in many places, although it is not, technically, redundant.

The moral is that when applying the theory of decomposition, one should remember that decomposition is a last resort, used to solve the problems of redundancy and anomalies, not as an end in itself. When applying Algorithm 7.4, we should avoid doing a decomposition, even if Lemma 7.7(b) tells us it can be done, should the scheme already be in BCNF. When using Algorithm 7.5, consider combining the relation schemes that result, should there be no 3NF violations created by doing so.

## 7.9 MULTIVALUED DEPENDENCIES

In previous sections we have assumed that the only possible kind of data dependency is functional. In fact there are many plausible kinds of dependencies, and at least one other, the multivalued dependency, appears frequently in the "real world." Suppose we are given a relation scheme $R$, and $X$ and $Y$ are subsets of $R$. Intuitively, we say that $X \twoheadrightarrow Y$, read "$X$ *multidetermines* $Y$," or "there is a multivalued dependency of $Y$ on $X$," if given values for the attributes of $X$ there is a set of zero or more associated values for the attributes of $Y$, and this set of $Y$-values is not connected in any way to values of the attributes in $R - X - Y$.

Formally, we say $X \twoheadrightarrow Y$ holds in $R$ if whenever $r$ is a relation for $R$, and $\mu$ and $\nu$ are two tuples in $r$, with $\mu[X] = \nu[X]$ (that is, $\mu$ and $\nu$ agree on the attributes of $X$), then $r$ also contains tuples $\phi$ and $\psi$, where

1.  $\phi[X] = \psi[X] = \mu[X] = \nu[X]$.
2.  $\phi[Y] = \mu[Y]$ and $\phi[R - X - Y] = \nu[R - X - Y]$.
3.  $\psi[Y] = \nu[Y]$ and $\psi[R - X - Y] = \mu[R - X - Y]$.[8]

That is, we can exchange the $Y$-values of $\mu$ and $\nu$ to obtain two new tuples $\phi$ and $\psi$ that must also be in $r$. Note we did not assume that $X$ and $Y$ are disjoint in the above definition.

**Example 7.18:** Let us reconsider the relation scheme $CTHRSG$ introduced in the previous section. In Figure 7.7 we see a possible relation for this relation scheme. In this simple case there is only one course with two students, but we see several salient facts that we would expect to hold in any relation for this relation scheme. A course can meet for several hours, in different rooms each time. Each student has a tuple for each class taken and each session of that class. His grade for the class is repeated for each tuple.

| $C$ | $T$ | $H$ | $R$ | $S$ | $G$ |
|-----|-----|-----|-----|-----|-----|
| CS101 | Deadwood | M9 | 222 | Weenie | B+ |
| CS101 | Deadwood | W9 | 333 | Weenie | B+ |
| CS101 | Deadwood | F9 | 222 | Weenie | B+ |
| CS101 | Deadwood | M9 | 222 | Grind | C |
| CS101 | Deadwood | W9 | 333 | Grind | C |
| CS101 | Deadwood | F9 | 222 | Grind | C |

**Figure 7.7** A sample relation for scheme $CTHRSG$.

---

[8] Note we could have eliminated clause (3). The existence of tuple $\psi$ follows from the existence of $\phi$ when we apply the definition with $\mu$ and $\nu$ interchanged.

Thus, we expect that in general the multivalued dependency $C \twoheadrightarrow HR$ holds; that is, there is a set of hour-room pairs associated with each course and disassociated from the other attributes. For example, in the formal definition of a multivalued dependency we may take $X \twoheadrightarrow Y$ to be $C \twoheadrightarrow HR$ and choose

$$\mu = \text{CS101} \quad \text{Deadwood} \quad \text{M9} \quad 222 \quad \text{Weenie} \quad \text{B+}$$
$$\nu = \text{CS101} \quad \text{Deadwood} \quad \text{W9} \quad 333 \quad \text{Grind} \quad \text{C}$$

i.e., $\mu$ is the first tuple, and $\nu$ the fifth, in Figure 7.7. Then we would expect to be able to exchange $\mu[HR] = (\text{M9, 222})$ with $\nu[HR] = (\text{W9, 333})$ to get the two tuples

$$\phi = \text{CS101} \quad \text{Deadwood} \quad \text{M9} \quad 222 \quad \text{Grind} \quad \text{C}$$
$$\psi = \text{CS101} \quad \text{Deadwood} \quad \text{W9} \quad 333 \quad \text{Weenie} \quad \text{B+}$$

A glance at Figure 7.7 affirms that $\phi$ and $\psi$ are indeed in $r$; they are the fourth and second tuples, respectively.

It should be emphasized that $C \twoheadrightarrow HR$ holds not because it held in the one relation of Figure 7.7. It holds because any course $c$, if it meets at hour $h_1$ in room $r_1$, with teacher $t_1$ and student $s_1$ who is getting grade $g_1$, and it also meets at hour $h_2$ in room $r_2$ with teacher $t_2$ and student $s_2$ who is getting grade $g_2$, will also meet at hour $h_1$ in room $r_1$ with teacher $t_2$ and student $s_2$ who is getting grade $g_2$.

Note also that $C \twoheadrightarrow H$ does not hold, nor does $C \twoheadrightarrow R$. In proof, consider relation $r$ of Figure 7.7 with tuples $\mu$ and $\nu$ as above. If $C \twoheadrightarrow H$ held, we would expect to find tuple

$$\text{CS101} \quad \text{Deadwood} \quad \text{M9} \quad 333 \quad \text{Grind} \quad \text{C}$$

in $r$, which we do not. A similar observation about $C \twoheadrightarrow R$ can be made. There are a number of other multivalued dependencies that hold, however, such as $C \twoheadrightarrow SG$ and $HR \twoheadrightarrow SG$. There are also trivial multivalued dependencies like $HR \twoheadrightarrow R$. We shall in fact prove that every functional dependency $X \rightarrow Y$ that holds implies that the multivalued dependency $X \twoheadrightarrow Y$ holds as well. $\square$

## Axioms for Functional and Multivalued Dependencies

We shall now present a sound and complete set of axioms for making inferences about a set of functional and multivalued dependencies over a set of attributes $U$. The first three are Armstrong's axioms for functional dependencies only; we repeat them here.

A1: *Reflexivity for functional dependencies.* If $Y \subseteq X \subseteq U$, then $X \rightarrow Y$.

A2: *Augmentation for functional dependencies.* If $X \rightarrow Y$ holds, and $Z \subseteq U$, then $XZ \rightarrow YZ$.

A3: *Transitivity for functional dependencies.* $\{X \rightarrow Y,\ Y \rightarrow Z\} \models X \rightarrow Z$.

The next three axioms apply to multivalued dependencies.

A4: *Complementation for multivalued dependencies.*

$$\{X \twoheadrightarrow Y\} \models X \twoheadrightarrow (U - X - Y)$$

A5: *Augmentation for multivalued dependencies.* If $X \twoheadrightarrow Y$ holds, and $V \subseteq W$, then $WX \twoheadrightarrow VY$.

A6: *Transitivity for multivalued dependencies.*

$$\{X \twoheadrightarrow Y, Y \twoheadrightarrow Z\} \models X \twoheadrightarrow (Z - Y)$$

It is worthwhile comparing A4–A6 with A1–A3. Axiom A4, the complementation rule, has no counterpart for functional dependencies. Axiom A1, reflexivity, appears to have no counterpart for multivalued dependencies, but the fact that $X \twoheadrightarrow Y$ whenever $Y \subseteq X$, follows from A1 and the rule (Axiom A7, to be given) that if $X \rightarrow Y$ then $X \twoheadrightarrow Y$. A6 is more restrictive than its counterpart transitivity axiom, A3. The more general statement, that $X \twoheadrightarrow Y$ and $Y \twoheadrightarrow Z$ imply $X \twoheadrightarrow Z$, is false. For instance, we saw in Example 7.18 that $C \twoheadrightarrow HR$ holds, and surely $HR \twoheadrightarrow H$ is true, yet $C \twoheadrightarrow H$ is false. To compensate partially for the fact that A6 is weaker than A3, we use a stronger version of A5 than the analogous augmentation axiom for functional dependencies, A2. We could have replaced A2 by: $X \rightarrow Y$ and $V \subseteq W$ imply $WX \rightarrow VY$, but for functional dependencies, this rule is easily proved from A1, A2, and A3.

Our last two axioms relate functional and multivalued dependencies.

A7: $\{X \rightarrow Y\} \models X \twoheadrightarrow Y$.

A8: If $X \twoheadrightarrow Y$ holds, $Z \subseteq Y$, and for some $W$ disjoint from $Y$, we have $W \rightarrow Z$, then $X \rightarrow Z$ also holds.

## Soundness and Completeness of the Axioms

We shall not give a proof that axioms A1–A8 are sound and complete. Rather, we shall prove that some of the axioms are sound, that is, they follow from the definitions of functional and multivalued dependencies, leaving the soundness of the rest of the axioms, as well as a proof that any valid inference can be made using the axioms (completeness of the axioms), for an exercise.

Let us begin by proving A6, the transitivity axiom for multivalued dependencies. Suppose some relation $r$ over set of attributes $U$ satisfies $X \twoheadrightarrow Y$ and $Y \twoheadrightarrow Z$, but violates $X \twoheadrightarrow (Z - Y)$. Then there are tuples $\mu$ and $\nu$ in $r$, where $\mu[X] = \nu[X]$, but the tuple $\phi$, where $\phi[X] = \mu[X]$, $\phi[Z - Y] = \mu[Z - Y]$, and

$$\phi[U - X - (Z - Y)] = \nu[U - X - (Z - Y)]$$

is not in $r$.[9] Since $X \twoheadrightarrow Y$ holds, it follows that the tuple $\psi$, where $\psi[X] =$

---

[9] Recall that we pointed out the definition of multivalued dependencies could require

$\mu[X]$, $\psi[Y] = \nu[Y]$, and

$$\psi[U - X - Y] = \mu[U - X - Y]$$

is in $r$. Now $\psi$ and $\nu$ agree on $Y$, so since $Y \twoheadrightarrow Z$, it follows that $r$ has a tuple $\omega$, where $\omega[Y] = \nu[Y]$, $\omega[Z] = \psi[Z]$, and

$$\omega[U - Y - Z] = \nu[U - Y - Z]$$

We claim that $\omega[X] = \mu[X]$, since on attributes in $Z \cap X$, $\omega$ agrees with $\psi$, which agrees with $\mu$. On attributes of $X - Z$, $\omega$ agrees with $\nu$, and $\nu$ agrees with $\mu$ on $X$. We also claim that $\omega[Z - Y] = \mu[Z - Y]$, since $\omega$ agrees with $\psi$ on $Z - Y$, and $\psi$ agrees with $\mu$ on $Z - Y$. Finally, we claim that $\omega[V] = \nu[V]$, where $V = U - X - (Z - Y)$. In proof, surely $\omega$ agrees with $\nu$ on $V - Z$, and by manipulating sets we can show $V \cap Z = (Y \cap Z) - X$. But $\omega$ agrees with $\psi$ on $Z$, and $\psi$ agrees with $\nu$ on $Y$, so $\omega$ agrees with $\nu$ on $V \cap Z$ as well as on $V - Z$. Therefore $\omega$ agrees with $\nu$ on $V$. If we look at the definition of $\phi$, we now see that $\omega = \phi$. But we claimed that $\omega$ is in $r$, so $\phi$ is in $r$, contrary to our assumption. Thus $X \twoheadrightarrow Z - Y$ holds after all, and we have proved A6.

Now let us prove A8. Suppose in contradiction that we have a relation $r$ in which $X \twoheadrightarrow Y$ and $W \to Z$ hold, where $Z \subseteq Y$, and $W \cap Y$ is empty, but $X \to Z$ does not hold. Then there are tuples $\nu$ and $\mu$ in $r$ such that $\nu[X] = \mu[X]$, but $\nu[Z] \neq \mu[Z]$. By $X \twoheadrightarrow Y$ applied to $\nu$ and $\mu$, there is a tuple $\phi$ in $r$, such that $\phi[X] = \mu[X] = \nu[X]$, $\phi[Y] = \mu[Y]$, and $\phi[U - X - Y] = \nu[U - X - Y]$. Since $W \cap Y$ is empty, $\phi$ and $\nu$ agree on $W$. As $Z \subseteq Y$, $\phi$ and $\mu$ agree on $Z$. Since $\nu$ and $\mu$ disagree on $Z$, it follows that $\phi$ and $\nu$ disagree on $Z$. But this contradicts $W \to Z$, since $\phi$ and $\nu$ agree on $W$ but disagree on $Z$. We conclude that $X \to Z$ did not fail to hold, and we have verified rule A8.

The remainder of the proof of the following theorem is left as an exercise.

**Theorem 7.9:** (Beeri, Fagin, and Howard [1977]). Axioms A1–A8 are sound and complete for functional and multivalued dependencies. That is, if $D$ is a set of functional and multivalued dependencies over a set of attributes $U$, and $D^+$ is the set of functional and multivalued dependencies that follow logically from $D$ (i.e., every relation over $U$ that satisfies $D$ also satisfies the dependencies in $D^+$), then $D^+$ is exactly the set of dependencies that follow from $D$ by A1–A8. □

## Additional Inference Rules for Multivalued Dependencies

There are a number of other rules that are useful for making inferences about functional and multivalued dependencies. Of course, the union, decomposition,

---

only the existence of $\phi$, not the additional existence of $\psi$ as in the third clause of the definition. Thus, the violation of a multivalued dependency can be stated as the absence of $\phi$ (not $\phi$ or $\psi$) from the relation $r$.

and pseudotransitivity rules mentioned in Lemma 7.1 still apply to functional dependencies. Some other rules are:

1.  *Union rule for multivalued dependencies.*

    $$\{X \twoheadrightarrow Y,\ X \twoheadrightarrow Z\} \models X \twoheadrightarrow YZ$$

2.  *Pseudotransitivity rule for multivalued dependencies.*

    $$[X \twoheadrightarrow Y,\ WY \twoheadrightarrow Z] \models WX \twoheadrightarrow (Z - WY)$$

3.  *Mixed pseudotransitivity rule.* $\{X \twoheadrightarrow Y,\ XY \to Z\} \models X \to (Z - Y)$.

4.  *Decomposition rule for multivalued dependencies.* If $X \twoheadrightarrow Y$ and $X \twoheadrightarrow Z$ hold, then $X \twoheadrightarrow (Y \cap Z)$, $X \twoheadrightarrow (Y - Z)$, and $X \twoheadrightarrow (Z - Y)$ hold.

We leave the proof that these rules are valid as an exercise; techniques similar to those used for A6 and A8 above will suffice, or we can prove them from axioms A1–A8.

We should note that the decomposition rule for multivalued dependencies is weaker than the corresponding rule for functional dependencies. The latter rule allows us to deduce immediately from $X \to Y$ that $X \to A$ for each attribute $A$ in $Y$. The rule for multivalued dependencies only allows us to conclude $X \twoheadrightarrow A$ from $X \twoheadrightarrow Y$ if we can find some $Z$ such that $X \twoheadrightarrow Z$, and either $Z \cap Y = A$ or $Y - Z = A$.

## The Dependency Basis

However, the decomposition rule for multivalued dependencies, along with the union rule, allows us to make the following statement about the sets $Y$ such that $X \twoheadrightarrow Y$ for a given $X$.

**Theorem 7.10:** If $U$ is the set of all attributes, then we can partition $U - X$ into sets of attributes $Y_1, \ldots, Y_k$, such that if $Z \subseteq U - X$, then $X \twoheadrightarrow Z$ if and only if $Z$ is the union of some of the $Y_i$'s.

**Proof:** Start the partition of $U - X$ with all of $U - X$ in one block. Suppose at some point we have partition $W_1, \ldots, W_n$, and $X \twoheadrightarrow W_i$ for $i = 1, 2, \ldots, n$. If $X \twoheadrightarrow Z$, and $Z$ is not the union of some $W_i$'s, replace each $W_i$ such that $W_i \cap Z$ and $W_i - Z$ are both nonempty by $W_i \cap Z$ and $W_i - Z$. By the decomposition rule, $X \twoheadrightarrow (W_i \cap Z)$ and $X \twoheadrightarrow (W_i - Z)$. As we cannot partition a finite set of attributes indefinitely, we shall eventually find that every $Z$ such that $X \twoheadrightarrow Z$ is the union of some blocks of the partition. By the union rule, $X$ multidetermines the union of any set of blocks. $\square$

We call the above sets $Y_1, \ldots, Y_k$ constructed for $X$ from a set of functional and multivalued dependencies $D$ the *dependency basis* for $X$ (with respect to $D$).

**Example 7.19:** In Example 7.18 we observed that $C \twoheadrightarrow HR$. Thus, by the complementation rule, $C \twoheadrightarrow TSG$. We also know that $C \to T$. Thus, by axiom A7, $C \twoheadrightarrow T$. By the decomposition rule, $C \twoheadrightarrow SG$. One can check that no single attribute except $T$ or $C$ itself is multidetermined by $C$. Thus, the dependency basis for $C$ is $\{T, HR, SG\}$. Intuitively, associated with each course are independent sets of teachers (there is only one), hour-room pairs that tell when and where the course meets, and student-grade pairs, the roll for the course. □

## Closures of Functional and Multivalued Dependencies

Given a set of functional and multivalued dependencies $D$, we would like to find the set $D^+$ of all functional and multivalued dependencies logically implied by $D$. We can compute $D^+$ by starting with $D$ and applying axioms A1–A8 until no more new dependencies can be derived. However, this process can take time that is exponential in the size of $D$. Often we only want to know whether a particular dependency $X \to Y$ or $X \twoheadrightarrow Y$ follows from $D$. For example, Theorem 7.11, below, requires such inferences to find lossless-join decompositions of relation schemes in the presence of multivalued dependencies.

To test whether a multivalued dependency $X \twoheadrightarrow Y$ holds, it suffices to determine the dependency basis of $X$ and see whether $Y - X$ is the union of some sets thereof. For example, referring to Example 7.19, we know that $C \twoheadrightarrow CTSG$, since $TSG$ is the union of $T$ and $SG$. Also, $C \twoheadrightarrow HRSG$, but $C \twoheadrightarrow TH$ is false, since $TH$ intersects block $HR$ of the dependency basis, yet $TH$ does not include all of $HR$. In computing the dependency basis of $X$ with respect to $D$, a theorem of Beeri [1980] tells us it suffices to compute the basis with respect to the set of multivalued dependencies $M$, where $M$ consists of

1.  All multivalued dependencies in $D$, and
2.  For each functional dependency $X \to Y$ in $D$, the set of multivalued dependencies $X \twoheadrightarrow A_1, \ldots, X \twoheadrightarrow A_n$, where $Y = A_1 \cdots A_n$, and each $A_i$ is a single attribute.

Another theorem of Beeri [1980] gives us a way to extract the nontrivial functional dependencies from the dependency basis computed according to the set of multivalued dependencies $M$. It can be shown that if $X$ does not include $A$, then $X \to A$ holds if and only if

1.  $A$ is a singleton set of the dependency basis for $X$ according to the set of dependencies $M$, and
2.  There is some set of attributes $Y$, excluding $A$, such that $Y \to Z$ is one of the given dependencies of $D$, and $A$ is in $Z$.

Furthermore, Beeri [1980] gives the following polynomial time algorithm for computing the dependency basis of $X$ with respect to $M$. Note that while Theorem 7.10 convinces us that the dependency basis exists, it does not tell us how to find the multivalued dependencies needed to apply the decomposition rule.

**Algorithm 7.6:** Computing the Dependency Basis.

INPUT: A set of multivalued dependencies $M$ over set of attributes $U$, and a set $X \subseteq U$.

OUTPUT: The dependency basis for $X$ with respect to $M$.

METHOD: We start with a collection of sets $S$, which eventually becomes the dependency basis we desire. Initially, $S$ consists of only one set, $U - X$; that is, $S = \{U - X\}$. Until no more changes can be made to $S$, look for dependencies $V \twoheadrightarrow W$ in $M$ and a set $Y$ in $S$ such that $Y$ intersects $W$ but not $V$. Replace $Y$ by $Y \cap W$ and $Y - W$ in $S$. The final collection of sets $S$ is the dependency basis for $X$. $\square$

Since Algorithm 7.6 only causes sets in $S$ to be split, and it terminates when no more splitting can be done, it is straightforward the algorithm takes time that is polynomial in the size of $M$ and $U$. In fact, careful implementation allows the algorithm to run in time proportional to the number of dependencies in $M$ times the cube of the number of attributes in $U$. A proof of this fact and a proof of correctness for Algorithm 7.6 can be found in Beeri [1980].

## Lossless Joins

Algorithm 7.2 helps us determine when a decomposition of a relation scheme $R$ into $(R_1, \ldots, R_k)$ has a lossless join, on the assumption that the only dependencies to be satisfied by the relations for $R$ are functional. That algorithm can be generalized to handle multivalued dependencies, as we shall see in the next section. In the case of a decomposition of $R$ into two schemes, there is a simple test for a lossless join.

**Theorem 7.11:** Let $R$ be a relation scheme and $\rho = (R_1, R_2)$ a decomposition of $R$. Let $D$ be a set of functional and multivalued dependencies on the attributes of $R$. Then $\rho$ has a lossless join with respect to $D$ if and only if

$$(R_1 \cap R_2) \twoheadrightarrow (R_1 - R_2)$$

[or equivalently, by the complementation rule, $(R_1 \cap R_2) \twoheadrightarrow (R_2 - R_1)$].

**Proof:** Decomposition $\rho$ has a lossless join if and only if for any relation $r$ satisfying $D$, and any two tuples $\mu$ and $\nu$ in $r$, the tuple $\phi$ such that $\phi[R_1] = \mu[R_1]$ and $\phi[R_2] = \nu[R_2]$ is in $r$ if it exists. That is, $\phi$ is what we get by joining the projection of $\mu$ onto $R_1$ with the projection of $\nu$ onto $R_2$. But $\phi$ exists if and only if $\mu[R_1 \cap R_2] = \nu[R_1 \cap R_2]$. Thus, the condition that $\phi$ is always in $r$ is exactly the condition that

$$(R_1 \cap R_2) \twoheadrightarrow (R_1 - R_2)$$

or equivalently, $(R_1 \cap R_2) \twoheadrightarrow (R_2 - R_1)$. $\square$

Note that by axiom A7, Theorem 7.5 implies Theorem 7.11 when the only dependencies are functional, but Theorem 7.5 says nothing at all if there are multivalued dependencies that must be satisfied.

## 7.10 FOURTH NORMAL FORM

There is a generalization of Boyce-Codd normal form, called fourth normal form, that applies to relation schemes with multivalued dependencies. Let $R$ be a relation scheme and $D$ the set of dependencies applicable to $R$. We say $R$ is in *fourth normal form* (4NF) if whenever there is, in $D^+$, a multivalued dependency $X \twoheadrightarrow Y$, where $Y$ is not a subset of $X$, and $XY$ does not include all the attributes of $R$, it is the case that $X$ is a superkey of $R$. Note that the definitions of "key" and "superkey" have not changed because multivalued dependencies are present; "superkey" still means a set of attributes that functionally determines $R$.

Observe that if $R$ is in 4NF, then it is in BCNF; i.e., 4NF is a stronger condition than BCNF. In proof, suppose $R$ is not in Boyce-Codd normal form, because there is some functional dependency $X \rightarrow A$, where $X$ is not a superkey, and $A$ is not in $X$. If $XA = R$, then surely $X$ includes a key. Therefore $XA$ does not include all attributes. By A8, $X \rightarrow A$ implies $X \twoheadrightarrow A$. Since $XA \neq R$ and $A$ is not in $X$, $X \twoheadrightarrow A$ is a 4NF violation.

We can find a decomposition of $R$ into $\rho = (R_1, \ldots, R_k)$, such that $\rho$ has a lossless join with respect to $D$, and each $R_i$ is in 4NF, as follows. We start with $\rho$ consisting only of $R$, and we repeatedly decompose relation schemes when we find a violation of 4NF, as in the discussion of the simple but time-consuming decomposition algorithm for BCNF decomposition preceding Algorithm 7.4. If there is a relation scheme $S$ in $\rho$ that is not in 4NF with respect to $D$ projected onto $S$,[10] then there must be in $S$ a dependency $X \twoheadrightarrow Y$, where $X$ is not a superkey of $S$, $Y$ is not empty or a subset of $X$, and $XY \neq S$. We may assume $X$ and $Y$ are disjoint, since $X \twoheadrightarrow (Y - X)$ follows from $X \twoheadrightarrow Y$ using A1, A7, and the decomposition rule. Then replace $S$ by $S_1 = XY$ and $S_2 = S - Y$, which must be two relation schemes with fewer attributes than $S$. By Theorem 7.11, since $(S_1 \cap S_2) \twoheadrightarrow (S_1 - S_2)$, the join of $S_1$ and $S_2$ is lossless with respect to $\pi_S(D)$, which we take in this section to be the set of functional and multivalued dependencies that follow from $D$ and involve only attributes in the set $S$.

We leave it as an exercise the generalization of Lemma 7.6 to sets of functional and multivalued dependencies; that is, the repeated decomposition as above produces a set of relation schemes that has a lossless join with respect

---

[10] We shall discuss later how to find the projection of a set of functional and multivalued dependencies.

to $D$. The only important detail remaining is to determine how one computes $\pi_S(D)$, given $R$, $D$, and $S \subseteq R$. It is a theorem of Aho, Beeri, and Ullman [1979] that $\pi_S(D)$ can be computed as follows.

1. Compute $D^+$.
2. For each $X \to Y$ in $D^+$, if $X \subseteq S$, then $X \to (Y \cap S)$ holds in $S$.[11]
3. For each $X \twoheadrightarrow Y$ in $D^+$, if $X \subseteq S$, then $X \twoheadrightarrow (Y \cap S)$ holds in $S$.
4. No other functional or multivalued dependencies for $S$ may be deduced from the fact that $D$ holds for $R$.

**Example 7.20:** Let us reinvestigate the $CTHRSG$ relation scheme first introduced in Example 7.15. We have several times noted the minimal cover

$$C \to T \qquad CS \to G$$
$$HR \to C \qquad HS \to R$$
$$HT \to R$$

for the pertinent functional dependencies. It turns out that one multivalued dependency, $C \twoheadrightarrow HR$, together with the above functional dependencies, allows us to derive all the multivalued dependencies that we would intuitively feel are valid. We saw, for example, that $C \twoheadrightarrow HR$ and $C \to T$ imply $C \twoheadrightarrow SG$. We also know that $HR \to CT$, so $HR \twoheadrightarrow CT$. By the complementation rule, $HR \twoheadrightarrow SG$. That is to say, given an hour and room, there is an associated set of student-grade pairs, namely the students enrolled in the course meeting in that room and that hour, paired with the grades they got in that course. The reader is invited to explore further the set of multivalued dependencies following from the given five functional dependencies and one multivalued dependency.

To place relation scheme $CTHRSG$ in 4NF, we might start with

$$C \twoheadrightarrow HR$$

which violates the 4NF conditions since $C$ is not a superkey ($SH$ is the only key for $CTHRSG$). We decompose $CTHRSG$ into $CHR$ and $CTSG$. The relation scheme $CHR$ has key $HR$. The multivalued dependency $C \twoheadrightarrow HR$ does not violate fourth normal form for $CHR$, since the left and right sides together include all the attributes of $CHR$. No other functional or multivalued dependency projected onto $CHR$ violates 4NF, so we need not decompose $CHR$ any further.

Such is not the case for $CTSG$. The only key is $CS$, yet we see the multivalued dependency $C \twoheadrightarrow T$, which follows from $C \to T$. We therefore split $CTSG$ into $CT$ and $CSG$. These are both in 4NF with respect to their projected dependencies, so we have obtained the decomposition $\rho = (CHR, CT, CSG)$, which has a lossless join and all relation schemes in fourth normal form.

---

[11] Note that since $X \to Y \cap S$ is also in $D^+$, this rule is equivalent to the rule for projecting functional dependencies given earlier.

It is interesting to note that when we ignore the multivalued dependency $C \twoheadrightarrow HR$, the decomposition $\rho$ does not necessarily have a lossless join, but if we are allowed to use $C \twoheadrightarrow HR$, it is easy to prove by Theorem 7.11 that the join of these relations is lossless. As an exercise, the reader should find a relation $r$ for $CTHRSG$ such that $m_\rho(r) \neq r$, yet $r$ satisfies all of the given functional dependencies (but not $C \twoheadrightarrow HR$, of course). $\square$

## Embedded Multivalued Dependencies

One further complication that enters when we try to decompose a relation scheme $R$ into 4NF is that there may be certain multivalued dependencies that we expect to hold when we project any plausible relation $r$ for $R$ onto a subset $X \subseteq R$, yet we do not expect these dependencies to hold in $r$ itself. Such a dependency is said to be *embedded* in $R$, and we must be alert, when writing down all the constraints that we believe hold in relations $r$ for $R$, not to ignore an embedded multivalued dependency. Incidentally, embedded functional dependencies never occur; it is easy to show that if $Y \rightarrow Z$ holds when relation $r$ over $R$ is projected onto $X$, then $Y \rightarrow Z$ holds in $r$ as well. The same is not true for multivalued dependencies, as the following example shows.

**Example 7.21:** Suppose we have the attributes $C$ (course), $S$ (student), $P$ (prerequisite), and $Y$ (year in which the student took the prerequisite). The only nontrivial functional or multivalued dependency is $SP \rightarrow Y$, so we may decompose $CSPY$ into $CSP$ and $SPY$; the resulting schemes are apparently in 4NF.

The multivalued dependency $C \twoheadrightarrow S$ does not hold. For example, we might have in relation $r$ for $CSPY$ the tuples

| | | | |
|---|---|---|---|
| CS402 | Jones | CS311 | 1988 |
| CS402 | Smith | CS401 | 1989 |

yet not find the tuple

| | | | |
|---|---|---|---|
| CS402 | Jones | CS401 | 1989 |

Presumably Jones took CS401, since it is a prerequisite for CS402, but perhaps he did not take it in 1989. Similarly, $C \twoheadrightarrow P$ does not hold in $CSPY$.

However, if we project any legal relation $r$ for $CSPY$ onto $CSP$, we would expect $C \twoheadrightarrow S$ and, by the complementation rule, $C \twoheadrightarrow P$ to hold, provided every student enrolled in a course is required to have taken each prerequisite for the course at some time. Thus, $C \twoheadrightarrow S$ and $C \twoheadrightarrow P$ are embedded multivalued dependencies for $CSP$. As a consequence, $CSP$ is really not in 4NF, and it should be decomposed into $CS$ and $CP$. This replacement avoids repeating the student name once for each prerequisite of a course in which he is enrolled.

It is interesting to observe that the decomposition $\rho = (CS, CP, SPY)$ has a lossless join if we acknowledge that $C \twoheadrightarrow S$ is an embedded dependency for $CSP$. For then, given any relation $r$ for $CSPY$ that satisfies $SP \rightarrow Y$ and the dependency $C \twoheadrightarrow S$ in $CSP$, we can prove that $m_\rho(r) = r$. Yet we could not prove this assuming only the functional dependency $SP \rightarrow Y$; the reader is invited to find a relation $r$ satisfying $SP \rightarrow Y$ (but not the embedded dependency) such that $m_\rho(r) \neq r$. □

We shall consider embedded multivalued dependencies further in the next section. Here let us introduce the standard notation for such dependencies. A relation $r$ over relation scheme $R$ satisfies the embedded multivalued dependency $X \twoheadrightarrow Y \mid Z$ if the multivalued dependency $X \twoheadrightarrow Y$ is satisfied by the relation $\pi_{X \cup Y \cup Z}(r)$, which is the projection of $r$ onto the set of attributes mentioned in the embedded dependency. Note that there is no requirement that $X$, $Y$, and $Z$ be disjoint, and by the union, decomposition, and complementation rules, $X \twoheadrightarrow Y$ holds in $\pi_{X \cup Y \cup Z}(r)$ if and only if $X \twoheadrightarrow Z$ does, so $X \twoheadrightarrow Y \mid Z$ means the same as $X \twoheadrightarrow Z \mid Y$. As an example, the embedded multivalued dependency from Example 7.21 is written $C \twoheadrightarrow S \mid P$ or $C \twoheadrightarrow P \mid S$.

## 7.11 GENERALIZED DEPENDENCIES

In this section we introduce a notation for dependencies that generalizes both functional and multivalued dependencies. Modeling the "real world" does not demand such generality; probably, functional and multivalued dependencies are sufficient in practice.[12] However, there are some key ideas, such as the "chase" algorithm for inferring dependencies, that are better described in the general context to which the ideas apply than in the special case of functional or multi-valued dependencies. The ideas associated with generalized dependencies also get used in query optimization, and they help relate dependencies to logical rules (Horn clauses), thereby allowing some of this theory to apply to optimization of logic programs as well.

We view both functional and multivalued dependencies as saying of relations that "if you see a certain pattern, then you must also see this." In the case of functional dependencies, "this" refers to the equality of certain of the symbols seen, while for multivalued dependencies, "this" is another tuple that must also be in the relation. For example, let $U = ABCD$ be our set of attributes. Then the functional dependency $A \rightarrow B$ says that whenever we see, in

---

[12] Often, one observes *inclusion dependencies*, as well. These are constraints that say a value appearing in one attribute of one relation must also appear in a particular attribute of some other relation. For example, we would demand of the YVCB database that a customer name appearing in the CUST field of an ORDERS tuple also appear in the CNAME field of the CUSTOMERS relation; i.e., each order must have a real customer behind it. The desire to enforce inclusion dependencies explains the mechanics of insertion and deletion in the DBTG proposal (Section 5.3), and the constraints System R places on a pair of relations that are stored "via set" (Section 6.11). As inclusion dependencies do not influence the normalization process, their theory is mentioned only in the exercises.

some relation $r$, two tuples $ab_1c_1d_1$ and $ab_2c_2d_2$, then $b_1 = b_2$ in those tuples. The multivalued dependency $A \twoheadrightarrow B$ says of the same two tuples that we must also see the tuple $ab_1c_2d_2$ in $r$, which is a weaker assertion than saying $b_1 = b_2$. A convenient tabular form of such dependencies is shown in Figure 7.8.

$$
\begin{array}{cccc}
a & b_1 & c_1 & d_1 \\
a & b_2 & c_2 & d_2 \\
\hline
\end{array}
$$

$$b_1 = b_2$$

(a) The functional dependency $A \to B$.

$$
\begin{array}{cccc}
a & b_1 & c_1 & d_1 \\
a & b_2 & c_2 & d_2 \\
\hline
a & b_1 & c_2 & d_2 \\
\end{array}
$$

(b) The multivalued dependency $A \twoheadrightarrow B$.

**Figure 7.8** Dependencies in tabular notation.

The two dependencies of Figure 7.8 are different in the kind of conclusion they allow us to draw. The functional dependency [Figure 7.8(a)] is called an *equality-generating dependency*, because its conclusion is that two symbols must in fact represent the same symbol. The multivalued dependency [Figure 7.8(b)] is called a *tuple-generating dependency*, because it allows us to infer that a particular tuple is in the relation to which the dependency applies. In the following pages, we wish to allow more than two tuples as hypotheses of dependencies, and we wish to allow various combinations of symbols appearing in their components. The conclusions, though, will continue to be either equalities or new tuples.

Define a *generalized dependency* over a relation scheme $A_1 \cdots A_n$ to be an expression of the form

$$(t_1, \ldots, t_k)/t$$

where the $t_i$'s are $n$-tuples of symbols, and $t$ is either another $n$-tuple (in which case we have a tuple-generating dependency) or an expression $x = y$, where $x$ and $y$ are symbols appearing among the $t_i$'s (then we have an equality-generating dependency). We call the $t_i$'s the *hypotheses* and $t$ the *conclusion*. Intuitively, the dependency means that for every relation in which we find the hypotheses, the conclusion holds. To see the hypothesis tuples, we may have to rename some or all of the symbols used in the hypotheses to make them match the symbols used in the relation. Any renaming of symbols that is done applies to the conclusion as well as the hypotheses, and of course it applies to all occurrences of a symbol. We shall give a more formal definition after some examples and discussion.

Frequently we shall display these dependencies as in Figure 7.8, with the hypotheses listed in rows above a line and the conclusion below. It is sometimes useful as well to show the attributes to which the columns correspond, above a line at the top. In all cases, we assume that the order of the attributes in the relation scheme is fixed and understood.

## Typed and Typeless Dependencies

Frequently, we find, as in Figure 7.8, that each symbol appearing in a generalized dependency is associated with a unique column. Functional and multivalued dependencies have this property, for example. Such dependencies are called *typed*, because we can associate a "type," i.e., an attribute, with each symbol. Dependencies in which some symbol appears in more than one column are called *typeless*.

**Example 7.22:** The second part of Example 7.8 showed that given a certain collection of functional dependencies, the decomposition

$$(AD, AB, BE, CDE, AE)$$

is a lossless-join decomposition. What was really shown there was that any relation that satisfies the functional dependencies $A \rightarrow C$, $B \rightarrow C$, $C \rightarrow D$, $DE \rightarrow C$, and $CE \rightarrow A$ must also satisfy the "join dependency" $\bowtie (AD, AB, BE, CDE, AE)$. In general, a *join dependency* is a typed tuple-generating dependency that says, about a relation $r$ for scheme $R$, that if we project $r$ onto some set of schemes $R_1, \ldots, R_k$, then take the natural join of the projections, the tuples we get are all in $r$. We use the notation $\bowtie (R_1, \ldots, R_k)$ for this dependency.

We can write our example join dependency as in Figure 7.9. In that figure we use blanks to denote symbols that appear only once. The reader may have noticed the similarity between the tabular representation of generalized dependencies and the Query-by-Example notation of Sections 4.4 and 4.5; the convention that a blank stands for a symbol that appears nowhere else is borrowed from there.

In general, the join dependency $\bowtie (R_1, \ldots, R_k)$, expressed in the tabular notation, has one hypothesis row for each $R_i$, and this row has the same symbol as the conclusion row in the columns for the attributes in $R_i$; elsewhere in that row are symbols, each of which appears nowhere else. The justification is that the join dependency says about a relation $r$ that whenever we have a tuple, such as the conclusion row, that agrees with some tuple $\mu_i$ of $r$ in the attributes of $R_i$ for $i = 1, 2, \ldots, k$, then that tuple is itself in $r$. $\square$

| $A$ | $B$ | $C$ | $D$ | $E$ |
|-----|-----|-----|-----|-----|
| $a$ |     |     | $d$ |     |
| $a$ | $b$ |     |     |     |
|     | $b$ |     |     | $e$ |
|     |     | $c$ | $d$ | $e$ |
| $a$ |     |     |     | $e$ |
| $a$ | $b$ | $c$ | $d$ | $e$ |

**Figure 7.9** A join dependency in tabular notation.

## Full and Embedded Dependencies

We shall not require that a symbol appearing in the conclusion of a tuple-generating dependency also appear in the hypotheses. A symbol of the conclusion appearing nowhere else is called *unique*. A generalized dependency is called *embedded* if it has one or more unique symbols and *full* if it has no unique symbols. This use of the term "embedded" generalizes our use of the term in connection with multivalued dependencies. That is, if a multivalued dependency is embedded within a set of attributes $S$, it must have unique symbols in all the components not $S$.

**Example 7.23:** We could write the embedded multivalued dependency

$$C \twoheadrightarrow S \mid P$$

of Example 7.21 as

| $C$ | $S$ | $P$ | $Y$ |
|-----|-----|-----|-----|
| $c$ | $s_1$ | $p_1$ | $y_1$ |
| $c$ | $s_2$ | $p_2$ | $y_2$ |
| $c$ | $s_1$ | $p_2$ | $y_3$ |

Notice that $y_3$ is a unique symbol. $\square$

As a general rule, we can write any embedded multivalued dependency $X \twoheadrightarrow Y \mid Z$ over a set of attributes $U$ by writing two hypothesis rows that agree in the columns for the attributes in $X$ and disagree in all other attributes. The conclusion agrees with both hypotheses on $X$, agrees with the first hypothesis on $Y$, agrees with the second on the attributes in $Z$, and has a unique symbol everywhere else.

The justification is that the embedded multivalued dependency

$$X \twoheadrightarrow Y \mid Z$$

says that if we have two tuples $\mu$ and $\nu$ in relation $r$ that project onto

$$X \cup Y \cup Z$$

to give tuples $\mu'$ and $\nu'$, and $\mu'[X] = \nu'[X]$, then there is some tuple $\omega$ in $r$ that projects to $\omega'$ and satisfies $\omega'[X] = \mu'[X] = \nu'[X]$, $\omega'[Y] = \mu'[Y]$, and $\omega'[Z] = \nu'[Z]$. Notice that nothing at all is said about the value of $\omega$ for attributes in $U - X - Y - Z$. Clearly, we can express all the above in our generalized dependency notation, where $\mu$ and $\nu$ are the first and second hypotheses, and $\omega$ is the conclusion. Since we can only conclude that the tuple $\omega$ has some values in the attributes $U - X - Y - Z$, but we cannot relate those values to the values in $\mu$ or $\nu$, we must use unique symbols in our conclusion.

One reason for introducing the generalized dependency notation is that it leads to a conceptually simple way to infer dependencies. The test works for full dependencies of all sorts, although it may take exponential time, and therefore, is not preferable to Algorithm 7.1 for inferring functional dependencies from other functional dependencies, or to the method outlined before Algorithm 7.6 (computation of the dependency basis) when only functional and multivalued dependencies are concerned. When there are embedded dependencies, the method may succeed in making the inference, but it may also give an inconclusive result. There is in fact, no known algorithm for testing whether an embedded dependency follows logically from others, even when the dependencies are restricted to an apparently simple class, such as embedded multivalued dependencies.

## Generalized Dependencies and Horn Clauses

Notice the similarity between full, tuple-generating dependencies and datalog rules. Since dependencies apply to single relations, the head and all the subgoals of the body have the same predicate symbol, but any datalog rule with no negation and only one predicate symbol can be thought of as a (typeless) tuple-generating dependency. For example, the dependency of Figure 7.8(b) can be written as a rule:

```
r(A,B1,C2,D2) :- r(A,B1,C1,D1) & r(A,B2,C2,D2).
```

We could even view a full equality-generating dependency as a rule with a built-in predicate at the head, and we could make inferences with such rules as with any logical rules. For example, Figure 7.8(a) would appear as

```
B1 = B2 :- r(A,B1,C1,D1) & r(A,B2,C2,D2).
```

However, we should be more careful interpreting embedded dependencies as rules. If we blindly translated the embedded multivalued dependency of Example 7.23 into a rule

```
r(C,S1,P2,Y3) :- r(C,S1,P1,Y1) & r(C,S2,P2,Y2).
```

we would get a rule with a variable, $Y3$, that appears in the head but not in the body. The correct interpretation of such a rule is that, given values of $C$, $S1$, and $P2$ that, together with values for the other variables of the body, satisfy the subgoals of the body, the conclusion of the head is true *for all* values of $Y3$. However, the meaning of the embedded dependency is that *there exists* some value of $Y3$ that makes the head true for these values of $C$, $S1$, and $P2$.

## Symbol Mappings

Before giving the inference test for generalized dependencies, we need to introduce an important concept, the *symbol mapping*, which is a function $h$ from one set of symbols $S$ to another set $T$; that is, for each symbol $a$ in $S$, $h(a)$ is a symbol in $T$. We allow $h(a)$ and $h(b)$ to be the same member of $T$, even if $a \neq b$.

If $\mu = a_1 a_2 \cdots a_n$ is a tuple whose symbols are in $S$, we may apply the symbol mapping $h$ to $\mu$ and obtain the tuple $h(\mu) = h(a_1)h(a_2) \cdots h(a_n)$. If $\{\mu_1, \ldots, \mu_k\}$ is a set of tuples whose symbols are in $S$, and $\{\nu_1, \ldots, \nu_m\}$ are tuples whose symbols are in $T$, we say there is a symbol mapping from the first set of tuples to the second if there is some $h$ such that for all $i = 1, 2, \ldots, k$, $h(\mu_i)$ is $\nu_j$ for some $j$. It is possible that two or more $\mu_i$'s are mapped to the same $\nu_j$, and some $\nu_j$'s may be the target of no $\mu_i$.

**Example 7.24:** Let $A = \{abc, ade, fbe\}$ and $B = \{xyz, wyz\}$. There are several symbol mappings from $A$ to $B$. One has $h(a) = h(f) = x$, $h(b) = h(d) = y$, and $h(c) = h(e) = z$. Thus, $h$ maps all three tuples in $A$ to $xyz$. Another symbol mapping has $g(a) = x$, $g(b) = g(d) = y$, $g(c) = g(e) = z$, and $g(f) = w$. Symbol mapping $g$ sends $abc$ and $ade$ to $xyz$, but sends $fbe$ to $wyz$.
□

Our most important use for symbol mappings is as maps between sets of rows as in Example 7.24. The reader should observe a duality that holds in that situation. We defined symbol mappings as functions on symbols, and when applied to sets of rows, we added the requirement that the mapping applied to each row of the first set is a row of the second set. Dually, we could have defined mappings from rows to rows, and added the requirement that no symbol be mapped by two different rows to different symbols. Thus, in Example 7.24, we could not map $abc$ to $xyz$ and also map $ade$ to $wyz$, because $a$ would be mapped to both $x$ and $w$.

## Formal Definition of Generalized Dependency

With the notion of a symbol mapping, we can formally define the meaning of generalized dependencies. We say a relation $r$ *satisfies* the tuple-generating dependency $(t_1, \ldots, t_n)/t$ if whenever $h$ is a symbol mapping from all the hypotheses $\{t_1, \ldots, t_n\}$ to $r$, we can extend $h$ to any unique symbols in $t$ in such a way that $h(t)$ is in $r$. We also say that $r$ *satisfies* the equality-generating dependency $(t_1, \ldots, t_n)/a = b$ if whenever $h$ is a symbol mapping from the hypotheses to $r$, it must be that $h(a) = h(b)$.

**Example 7.25:** Let $d$ be the generalized dependency in Figure 7.10(a), and let $r$ be the relation of Figure 7.10(b). Notice that $d$ is not the same as the multivalued dependency $A \twoheadrightarrow B$, since the symbol $a_2$, which is a unique symbol in Figure 7.10(a), would have to be $a_1$ instead. In fact, Figure 7.10(a) is an example of a two-hypothesis tuple-generating dependency that is neither a full nor embedded multivalued dependency; such dependencies were called *subset dependencies* by Sagiv and Walecka [1982].

$$
\begin{array}{ccc}
a_1 & b_1 & c_1 \\
a_1 & b_2 & c_2 \\
\hline
a_2 & b_1 & c_2
\end{array}
$$

(a) The dependency $d$.

| $A$ | $B$ | $C$ |
|-----|-----|-----|
| 0 | 1 | 2 |
| 0 | 3 | 4 |
| 0 | 3 | 2 |
| 5 | 1 | 4 |

(b) The relation $r$.

**Figure 7.10** A generalized dependency and a relation satisfying it.

To see that $r$ satisfies $d$, let us consider a symbol mapping $h$ and the tuples of $r$ to which each of the hypotheses of $d$ could be mapped. Since the two hypotheses agree in the $A$-column, and $h(a_1)$ can have only one value, we know that either both hypotheses are mapped to the last tuple of $r$ [if $h(a_1) = 5$], or both are mapped among the first three tuples [if $h(a_1) = 0$]. In the first case, $h$ maps $b_1$ and $b_2$ to 1 and $c_1$ and $c_2$ to 4. Then we can extend $h$ to the unique symbol $a_2$ by defining $h(a_2) = 5$. In that case, $h(a_2 b_1 c_2) = 514$, which is a member of $r$, so we obtain no violation of $d$ with mappings that have $h(a_1) = 5$.

Now consider what happens if $h(a_1) = 0$, so the only possible mappings send the two hypotheses into the first three tuples of $r$. Any such mapping $h$ has $h(b_1)$ equal to either 1 or 3, and it has $h(c_2)$ equal to either 2 or 4. In any of the four combinations, there is a tuple in $r$ that has that combination of values in its $B$ and $C$ components. Thus, we can extend $h$ to the unique symbol $a_2$ by setting $h(a_2) = 5$ if $h(b_1) = 1$ and $h(c_2) = 4$, and setting $h(a_2) = 0$ otherwise.

We have now considered all symbol mappings that map each of the hypotheses of $d$ into a tuple of $r$, and have found that in each case, we can extend the mapping to the unique symbol $a_2$ in such a way that the conclusion of $d$ is present in $r$. Therefore, $r$ satisfies $d$. $\Box$

## Applying Dependencies to Relations

Suppose we have an equality-generating dependency

$$d = (s_1, \ldots, s_k)/a = b$$

and a relation $r = \{\mu_1, \ldots, \mu_m\}$. We can *apply* $d$ to $r$ if we find a symbol mapping $h$ from $\{s_1, \ldots, s_k\}$ to $\{\mu_1, \ldots, \mu_m\}$. The effect of applying $d$ to $r$ using symbol mapping $h$ is to equate the symbols $h(a)$ and $h(b)$ wherever they appear among the $\mu_i$'s; either may replace the other.

If we have a tuple-generating dependency instead, say $e = (s_1, \ldots, s_k)/s$, we *apply* $e$ to $r$ using $h$ by adjoining to $r$ the tuple $h(s)$. However, if $e$ is an embedded dependency, then $s$ will have one or more unique symbols, so $h$ will not be defined for all symbols of $s$. In that case, if $c$ is a unique symbol in $s$, create a new symbol, one that appears nowhere else in $r$, and extend $h$ by defining $h(c)$ to be that symbol. Of course, we create distinct symbols for each of the unique symbols of $s$.

It may be possible, however, the unique symbols can all be replaced by existing symbols of $r$ so that $h(s)$ becomes a member of $r$. In that case, the requirement that $h(s)$ be in $r$ is already satisfied, and we have the option (which we should take, because it simplifies matters) of not changing $r$ at all.

**Example 7.26:** Let us consider the equality-generating dependency

$$(abc, ade, fbe)/a = f$$

applied to the relation $r = \{xyz, wyz\}$. If we use the symbol mapping $g$ of Example 7.24, we find that $g(a) = x$ and $g(f) = w$. We apply the dependency using this symbol mapping, by equating $x$ and $w$; say we replace them both by $x$. Then the effect on $r$ of applying the dependency in this way is to change $r$ into $\{xyz\}$.

Suppose instead we had the tuple-generating dependency

$$(abc, ade, fbe)/abq$$

Then using the same symbol mapping, we would adjoin to $r$ a tuple whose first two components were $g(a) = x$ and $g(b) = y$ and whose third component was a new symbol, not appearing in $r$, say $u$; that is, $r$ becomes $\{xyz, wyz, xyu\}$. However, we could replace $u$ by the existing symbol $z$, and the result would be $xyz$, a tuple already in $r$. Thus, we have the preferred option of leaving $r$ unchanged. $\Box$

## The Chase Algorithm for Inference of Dependencies

Now we can exhibit a process that helps us resolve the question whether $D \models d$, where $D$ is a set of generalized dependencies, and $d$ is another generalized dependency. The procedure is an algorithm when $D$ has full dependencies only. However, if $D$ has some embedded dependencies, it tells the truth if it answers at all, but it may run on forever inconclusively. We call the process the *chase*, because we "chase down" all the consequences of the dependencies $D$.

The intuitive idea behind the chase process is that we start with the hypotheses of the dependency $d$ we wish to test, and we treat them as if they formed a relation. We then apply the given dependencies $D$ to this relation. If we obtain a tuple that is the conclusion of $d$, then we have a proof that $d$ follows from $D$. The reason this test works is that, generalizing Algorithm 7.4, should we fail to draw the desired conclusion, the relation that results when we finish the process is a counterexample; it satisfies $D$ but not $d$.[13]

First suppose that $d$ is a tuple-generating dependency $(t_1, \ldots, t_m)/t$. We begin with the relation $r = \{t_1, \ldots, t_m\}$. We then apply all of the dependencies in $D$, in any order, repeatedly, until either

1.  We cannot apply the dependencies in any way that changes $r$, or
2.  We discover in $r$ a tuple that agrees with $t$ on all components except, perhaps, those places where $t$ has a unique symbol.

However, when applying an equality-generating dependency, if one of the symbols being equated appears in $t$, change the other symbol to that one.

In case (2) above, we conclude that $D \models d$ is true. If (1) holds, but not (2), then we say that $D \models d$ is false. In fact, the resulting $r$ will be a counterexample. To see why, first notice that $r$ satisfies all dependencies in $D$ (or else one of them could be applied).

Second, we must show that $r$ does not satisfy $d$. In proof, note that as we apply equality-generating dependencies to $r$, the symbols in the original rows $t_1, \ldots, t_m$ may change, but there is always a symbol mapping $h$ that sends each symbol of the hypothesis rows to what that symbol has become after these equalities have been performed. Then $h(t_i)$ is in the final relation $r$ for each $i$. When we equate symbols, we do not change symbols in $t$, so $h(a) = a$ for any symbol $a$ that appears in $t$, except for the unique symbols of $t$, for which $h$ is not defined. Thus, if $d$ holds in $r$, that relation must have some tuple that agrees with $t$ on all but the unique symbols. However, (2) was assumed false, so there can be no such tuple in $r$ at the end of the chase process. Thus, $r$ does not satisfy $d$, and therefore serves as a counterexample to $D \models d$.

Now, let us consider the converse, why the implication holds whenever case (2) applies. Recall the proof of Theorem 7.4, which is really a special case of

---

[13] However, there is the problem that if some dependencies are embedded, the process may not stop. In principle, it generates an infinite relation, and that infinite relation forms a counterexample. Unfortunately, with embedded dependencies we cannot tell, as we work, whether the process will go on forever or not, so the "test" is sometimes inconclusive.

our present claim. That is, Algorithm 7.2, the lossless join test, can now be seen as a use of the chase process to test whether $F \models j$, where $j$ is the join dependency made from the decomposition to which Algorithm 7.2 is applied, that is $\bowtie (R_1, \ldots, R_k)$. As in Theorem 7.4, we can see the relation $r$ used in the chase as saying that certain tuples are in a hypothetical relation that satisfies $D$.

Initially, these tuples are the hypotheses $\{t_1, \ldots, t_m\}$ of the dependency being tested. Each time we apply a dependency, we are making an inference about other tuples that must be in this hypothetical relation (if we use a tuple-generating dependency), or about two symbols that must be equal (if we use an equality-generating dependency). Thus, each application is a valid inference from $D$, and if we infer the presence of $t$, that too is valid, i.e., we have shown that any relation containing $t_1, \ldots, t_m$ also contains $t$ (or a tuple that agrees with $t$ on nonunique symbols).

However, the dependency $d$ says more than that a relation that contains the exact tuples $\{t_1, \ldots, t_m\}$ also contains $t$. It says that if any relation whatsoever contains the tuples formed by some symbol mapping $h$ of the $t_i$'s, then $h$ can be extended to the unique symbols of $t$, and $h(t)$ will also be in the relation. We can show this more general statement by following the sequence of applications of dependencies in $D$ during the chase. That is, start with $\{h(t_1), \ldots, h(t_m)\}$ and apply the same sequence of dependencies from $D$ by composing the symbol mapping used to apply each dependency, with the symbol mapping $h$, to get another symbol mapping. The result will be the image, under $h$, of the sequence of changes made to the original relation $r = \{t_1, \ldots, t_m\}$.

We must also explain how to test, using the chase process, whether an equality-generating dependency $(t_1, \ldots, t_m)/a = b$ follows from a set of dependencies $D$. Follow the same process, but end and say yes if we ever equate the symbols $a$ and $b$; say no as for tuple-generating dependencies, if we can make no more changes to $r$, yet we have not equated $a$ and $b$. The validity of the inferences follows in essentially the same way as for tuple-generating dependencies.

We can sum up our claim in the following theorem.

**Theorem 7.12:** The chase process applied to a set of full generalized dependencies $D$ and a (possibly embedded) generalized dependency $d$ determines correctly whether $D \models d$.

**Proof:** Above, we argued informally why the procedure, if it makes an answer at all, answers correctly. We shall not go into further detail; Maier, Mendelzon, and Sagiv [1979] contains a complete proof of the result.

We must, however, show that if $D$ has only full dependencies, then the process is an algorithm; that is, it always halts. The observation is a simple one. When we apply a full dependency, we introduce no new symbols. Thus, the relation $r$ only has tuples composed of the original symbols of the hypotheses of $d$. But there are only a finite number of such symbols, and therefore $r$ is always a subset of some finite set. We have only to rule out the possibility that $r$ exhibits an oscillatory behavior; that is, it assumes after successive applications of dependencies, a sequence of values

$$r_1, r_2, \ldots, r_n = r_1, r_2 \cdots$$

Tuple-generating dependencies always make the size of $r$ increase, while equality-generating dependencies either leave the size the same or decrease it. Thus, the cycle must contain at least one equality-generating dependency. But here, an equality of symbols permanently reduces the number of different symbols, since only the application of an embedded dependency could increase the number of different symbols in $r$, and $D$ was assumed to contain full dependencies only. Thus no cycle could involve an equality-generating dependency and full tuple-generating dependencies only, proving that no cycle exists. We conclude that either we reach a condition where no change to $r$ is possible, or we discover that the conclusion of $d$ is in $r$. $\Box$

$$
\begin{array}{cccc}
a_1 & b_1 & c_1 & d_1 \\
a_1 & b_2 & c_2 & d_2 \\
\hline
a_1 & b_1 & c_2 & d_3
\end{array}
$$

(a) $A \twoheadrightarrow B \mid C$

$$
\begin{array}{cccc}
a_2 & b_3 & c_3 & d_4 \\
a_3 & b_3 & c_4 & d_5 \\
\hline
\end{array}
$$

$$d_4 = d_5$$

(b) $B \to D$

$$
\begin{array}{cccc}
a_4 & b_4 & c_5 & d_6 \\
a_4 & b_5 & c_6 & d_7 \\
\hline
a_4 & b_6 & c_5 & d_7
\end{array}
$$

(c) $A \twoheadrightarrow C \mid D$

**Figure 7.11** Example dependencies.

**Example 7.27:** Example 7.8 was really an application of the chase algorithm to make the inferences $\{S \to A,\ SI \to P\} \models \bowtie (SA, SIP)$ and

$$\{A \rightarrow C, \ B \rightarrow C, \ C \rightarrow D, \ DE \rightarrow C, \ CE \rightarrow A\} \models$$
$$\bowtie (AD, AB, BE, CDE, AE)$$

As another example, we can show that over the set of attributes $ABCD$

$$\{A \twoheadrightarrow B \mid C, \ B \rightarrow D\} \models A \twoheadrightarrow C \mid D$$

We can write the three dependencies involved in tabular notation, as in Figure 7.11.

We begin with the hypotheses of Figure 7.11(c), as shown in Figure 7.12(a). We can apply the dependency of Figure 7.11(a) by using the symbol mapping $h(a_1) = a_4$, $h(b_1) = b_5$, $h(c_1) = c_6$, $h(d_1) = d_7$, $h(b_2) = b_4$, $h(c_2) = c_5$, and $h(d_2) = d_6$. This mapping sends the two hypothesis rows of Figure 7.11(a) to the two rows of Figure 7.12(a), in the opposite order. If we extend $h$ to map $d_3$ to a new symbol, say $d_8$, then we can infer that the tuple $a_4 b_5 c_5 d_8$ is in $r$, as shown in Figure 7.12(b). Then, we can apply the dependency of Figure 7.11(b), using a symbol mapping that the reader can deduce, to map the two hypotheses of Figure 7.11(b) to the second and third rows of Figure 7.12(b) and prove that $d_7 = d_8$. The substitution of $d_7$ for $d_8$ is reflected in Figure 7.12(c). The third tuple in Figure 7.12(c) agrees with the conclusion of Figure 7.11(c), except in the $B$-column, where the latter has a unique symbol, $b_6$. We conclude that the inference is valid. $\square$

| | | | |
|---|---|---|---|
| $a_4$ | $b_4$ | $c_5$ | $d_6$ |
| $a_4$ | $b_5$ | $c_6$ | $d_7$ |

(a) Initial relation.

| | | | |
|---|---|---|---|
| $a_4$ | $b_4$ | $c_5$ | $d_6$ |
| $a_4$ | $b_5$ | $c_6$ | $d_7$ |
| $a_4$ | $b_5$ | $c_5$ | $d_8$ |

(b) After applying Figure 7.11(a).

| | | | |
|---|---|---|---|
| $a_4$ | $b_4$ | $c_5$ | $d_6$ |
| $a_4$ | $b_5$ | $c_6$ | $d_7$ |
| $a_4$ | $b_5$ | $c_5$ | $d_7$ |

(c) After applying Figure 7.11(b).

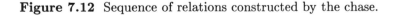

**Figure 7.12** Sequence of relations constructed by the chase.

## EXERCISES

7.1: Suppose we have a database for an investment firm, consisting of the following attributes: $B$ (broker), $O$ (office of a broker), $I$ (investor), $S$ (stock), $Q$ (quantity of stock owned by an investor), and $D$ (dividend paid by a stock), with the following functional dependencies: $S \rightarrow D$, $I \rightarrow B$, $IS \rightarrow Q$, and $D \rightarrow O$.

a) Find a key for the relation scheme $R = BOSQID$.

b) How many keys does relation scheme $R$ have? Prove your answer.

c) Find a lossless join decomposition of $R$ into Boyce-Codd normal form.

d) Find a decomposition of $R$ into third normal form, having a lossless join and preserving dependencies.

7.2: Suppose we choose to represent the relation scheme $R$ of Exercise 7.1 by the two schemes $ISQD$ and $IBO$. What redundancies and anomalies do you forsee?

7.3: Suppose we instead represent $R$ by $SD$, $IB$, $ISQ$, and $BO$. Does this decomposition have a lossless join?

7.4: Suppose we represent $R$ of Exercise 7.1 by $ISQ$, $IB$, $SD$, and $ISO$. Find minimal covers for the dependencies (from Exercise 7.1) projected onto each of these relation schemes. Find a minimal cover for the union of the projected dependencies. Does this decomposition preserve dependencies?

7.5: In the database of Exercise 7.1, replace the functional dependency $S \rightarrow D$ by the multivalued dependency $S \twoheadrightarrow D$. That is, $D$ now represents the dividend "history" of the stock.

a) Find the dependency basis of $I$.

b) Find the dependency basis of $BS$

c) Find a fourth normal form decomposition of $R$.

7.6: Consider a database of ship voyages with the following attributes: $S$ (ship name), $T$ (type of ship), $V$ (voyage identifier), $C$ (cargo carried by one ship on one voyage), $P$ (port), and $D$ (day). We assume that a voyage consists of a sequence of events where one ship picks up a single cargo, and delivers it to a sequence of ports. A ship can visit only one port in a single day. Thus, the following functional dependencies may be assumed: $S \rightarrow T$, $V \rightarrow SC$, and $SD \rightarrow PV$.

a) Find a lossless-join decomposition into BCNF.

b) Find a lossless-join, dependency-preserving decomposition into 3NF.

* c) Explain why there is no lossless-join, dependency-preserving BNCF decomposition for this database.

7.7: Let $U$ be a set of attributes and $D$ a set of dependencies (of any type) on the attributes of $U$. Define $\text{SAT}(D)$ to be the set of relations $r$ over $U$ such that $r$ satisfies each dependency in $D$. Show the following.

a)   $\text{SAT}(D_1 \cup D_2) = \text{SAT}(D_1) \cap \text{SAT}(D_2)$.

b)   If $D_1$ logically implies all the dependencies in $D_2$, then

$$\text{SAT}(D_1) \supseteq \text{SAT}(D_2)$$

7.8: Complete the proof of Lemma 7.1; i.e., show that the transitivity axiom for functional dependencies is sound.

7.9: Complete the proof of Theorem 7.2 by showing that if $X_1 \subseteq X_2$ then $X_1^{(j)} \subseteq X_2^{(j)}$ for all $j$.

7.10: Let $F$ be a set of functional dependencies.

a)   Show that $X \to A$ in $F$ is redundant if and only if $X^+$ contains $A$, when the closure is computed with respect to $F - \{X \to A\}$.

b)   Show that attribute $B$ in the left side $X$ of a functional dependency $X \to A$ is redundant if and only if $A$ is in $(X - \{B\})^+$, when the closure is taken with respect to $F$.

* 7.11: Show that singleton left sides are insufficient for functional dependencies. That is, show there is some functional dependency that is not equivalent to any set of functional dependencies $\{A_1 \to B_1, \ldots, A_k \to B_k\}$, where the $A$'s and $B$'s are single attributes.

** 7.12: Develop the theory of functional dependencies with single attributes on the left and right sides (call them SAFD's). That is:

a)   Give a set of axioms for SAFD's; show that your axioms are sound and complete.

b)   Give an algorithm for deciding whether a set of SAFD's implies another SAFD.

c)   Give an algorithm to test whether two sets of SAFD's are equivalent.

d)   SAFD's look like a familiar mathematical model. Which?

** 7.13: In Theorem 7.3 we used two transformations on sets of functional dependencies to obtain a minimal cover:

*i*)    Eliminate a redundant dependency.

*ii*)   Eliminate a redundant attribute from a left side.

Show the following:

a)   If we first apply (*ii*) until no more applications are possible and then apply (*i*) until no more applications are possible, we always obtain a minimal cover.

b) If we apply first (*i*) until no longer possible, then apply (*ii*) until no longer possible, we do not necessarily reach a minimal cover.

7.14: A relation scheme $R$ is said to be in *second normal form* if whenever $X \to A$ is a dependency that holds in $R$, and $A$ is not in $X$, then either $A$ is prime or $X$ is not a proper subset of any key (the possibility that $X$ is neither a subset nor a superset of any key is not ruled out by second normal form). Show that the relation scheme $SAIP$ from Example 7.14 violates second normal form.

7.15: Show that if a relation scheme is in third normal form, then it is in second normal form.

7.16: Consider the relation scheme with attributes $S$ (store), $D$ (department), $I$ (item), and $M$ (manager), with functional dependencies $SI \to D$ and $SD \to M$.

a) Find all keys for $SDIM$.

b) Show that $SDIM$ is in second normal form but not third normal form.

* 7.17: Give an $O(n)$ algorithm for computing $X^+$, where $X$ is a set of at most $n$ attributes, with respect to a set of functional dependencies that require no more than $n$ characters, when written down.

* 7.18: Complete the proof of Theorem 7.5 by providing a formal proof that in the row for $R_1$, an $a$ is entered if and only if $R_1 \cap R_2 \to A$.

7.19: Complete the proof of Lemma 7.5 by showing that if $r \subseteq s$ then

$$\pi_{R_i}(r) \subseteq \pi_{R_i}(s)$$

7.20: In Example 7.10 we contended that $Z \to C$ does not imply $CS \to Z$. Prove this contention.

7.21: At the end of Section 7.5 it was claimed that $\rho = (AB, CD)$ was a dependency-preserving, but not lossless-join decomposition of $ABCD$, given the dependencies $A \to B$ and $C \to D$. Verify this claim.

7.22: Let $F = \{AB \to C,\ A \to D,\ BD \to C\}$.

a) Find a minimal cover for $F$.

b) Give a 3NF, dependency-preserving decomposition of $ABCD$ into only two schemes (with respect to the set of functional dependencies $F$).

c) What are the projected dependencies for each of your schemes?

d) Does your answer to (a) have a lossless join? If not, how could you modify the database scheme to have a lossless join and still preserve dependencies?

7.23: Let $F = \{AB \rightarrow C,\ A \rightarrow B\}$.

    a)    Find a minimal cover for $F$.

    b)    When (a) was given on an exam at a large western university, more than half the class answered $G = \{A \rightarrow B,\ B \rightarrow C\}$. Show that answer is wrong by giving a relation that satisfies $F$ but violates $G$.

7.24: Suppose we are given relation scheme $ABCD$ with functional dependencies $\{A \rightarrow B,\ B \rightarrow C,\ A \rightarrow D,\ D \rightarrow C\}$. Let $\rho$ be the decomposition $(AB, AC, BD)$.

    a)    Find the projected dependencies for each of the relation schemes of $\rho$.

    b)    Does $\rho$ have a lossless join with respect to the given dependencies?

    c)    Does $\rho$ preserve the given dependencies?

7.25: Show that $(AB, ACD, BCD)$ is not a lossless-join decomposition of $ABCD$ with respect to the functional dependencies $\{A \rightarrow C,\ D \rightarrow C,\ BD \rightarrow A\}$.

7.26: Consider the relation scheme $ABCD$ with dependencies

$$F = \{A \rightarrow B,\ B \rightarrow C,\ D \rightarrow B\}$$

We wish to find a lossless-join decomposition into BCNF.

    a)    Suppose we choose, as our first step, to decompose $ABCD$ into $ACD$ and $BD$. What are the projected dependencies in these two schemes?

    b)    Are these schemes in BNCF? If not, what further decomposition is necessary?

7.27: For different sets of assumed dependencies, the decomposition

$$\rho = (AB, BC, CD)$$

may or may not have a lossless join. For each of the following sets of dependencies, either prove the join is lossless or give a counterexample relation to show it is not.

    a)    $\{A \rightarrow B,\ B \rightarrow C\}$.

    b)    $\{B \rightarrow C,\ C \rightarrow D\}$.

    c)    $\{B \twoheadrightarrow C\}$.

$*$ 7.28: At most how many passes does Algorithm 7.3 (the test for dependency-preservation) need if $F$ is a set of $n$ functional dependencies over $m$ attributes (an order-of-magnitude estimate is sufficient).

$*$ 7.29: Let $F$ be a set of functional dependencies with singleton right sides.

    a)    Show that if a relation scheme $R$ has a BCNF violation $X \rightarrow A$, where $X \rightarrow A$ is in $F^+$, then there is some $Y \rightarrow B$ in $F$ itself such that $Y \rightarrow B$ is a BCNF violation for $R$.

    b)    Show the same for third normal form.

7.30: Show the following observation, which is needed in Theorem 7.8. If $R$ is a relation scheme, and $X \subseteq R$ is a key for $R$ with respect to set of functional dependencies $F$, then $X$ cannot have a 3NF violation with respect to the set of dependencies $\pi_X(F)$.

7.31: Prove that there is no such thing as an "embedded functional dependency." That is, if $S \subseteq R$, and $X \to Y$ holds in $\pi_S(R)$, then $X \to Y$ holds in $R$.

* 7.32. Complete the proof of Theorem 7.9 by showing that axioms A1–A8 are sound and complete. *Hint*: The completeness proof follows Theorem 7.1. To find a counterexample relation for $X \twoheadrightarrow Y$, we generally need more than a two-tuple relation as was used for functional dependencies; the relation could have $2^b$ tuples, if $b$ is the number of blocks in the dependency basis for $X$.

* 7.33: Verify the union, pseudotransitivity, and decomposition rules for multivalued dependencies.

* 7.34: Verify the contention in Example 7.21, that there is a relation $r$ satisfying $SP \to Y$, such that $\pi_{CS}(r) \bowtie \pi_{CP}(r) \bowtie \pi_{SPY}(r) \neq r$. Check that your relation does not satisfy $C \twoheadrightarrow S \mid P$.

7.35: Given the dependencies $\{A \twoheadrightarrow B, \; C \to B\}$, what other nontrivial multivalued and functional dependencies hold over the set of attributes $ABC$?

* 7.36: Prove that in $ABCD$ we can infer $A \twoheadrightarrow D$ from $\{A \twoheadrightarrow B, \; A \to C\}$ in each of the following ways.

   a)   Directly from the definitions of functional and multivalued dependencies.

   b)   From axioms A1–A8.

   c)   By converting to generalized dependencies and "chasing."

* 7.37: Near the beginning of Section 7.10 we claimed that we could project a set of multivalued and functional dependencies $D$ onto a set of attributes $S$ by the following rules (somewhat restated).

   i)    $X \to Y$ is in $\pi_S(D)$ if and only if $XY \subseteq S$ and $X \to Y$ is in $D^+$.

   ii)   $X \twoheadrightarrow Y$ is in $\pi_S(D)$ if and only if $X \subseteq S$, and there is some multivalued dependency $X \twoheadrightarrow Z$ in $D^+$, such that $Y = Z \cap S$.

   Prove this contention.

7.38: Show that the decomposition $(CHR, CT, CSG)$ obtained in Example 7.20 is not lossless with respect the the given functional dependencies only; i.e., the multivalued dependency $C \twoheadrightarrow HR$ is essential to prove the lossless join.

7.39: Use the chase algorithm to tell whether the following inferences are valid over the set of attributes $ABCD$.

    a)  $\{A \twoheadrightarrow B, A \rightarrow C\} \models A \twoheadrightarrow D$

    b)  $\{A \twoheadrightarrow B \mid C, B \twoheadrightarrow C \mid D\} \models A \twoheadrightarrow C \mid D$

    c)  $\{A \twoheadrightarrow B \mid C, A \rightarrow D\} \models A \twoheadrightarrow C \mid D$

  ** d)  $\{A \twoheadrightarrow B \mid C, A \twoheadrightarrow C \mid D\} \models A \twoheadrightarrow B \mid D$

* 7.40: Show that no collection of tuple-generating dependencies can imply an equality-generating dependency.

7.41: State an algorithm to determine, given a collection of functional, (full) multivalued, and (full) join dependencies, whether a given decomposition has a lossless join.

7.42: Show that the multivalued dependency $X \twoheadrightarrow Y$ over the set of attributes $U$ is equivalent to the join dependency $\bowtie (XY, XZ)$, where $Z = U - X - Y$. *Hint*: Write both as generalized dependencies.

7.43: What symbol mapping explains the application of Figure 7.11(b) to Figure 7.12(b) to deduce Figure 7.12(c)?

* 7.44: Show that Theorem 7.11, stated for functional and multivalued dependencies, really holds for arbitrary generalized dependencies. That is, $(R_1, R_2)$ has a lossless join with respect to a set of generalized dependencies $D$ if and only if $(R_1 \cap R_2) \twoheadrightarrow (R_1 - R_2)$.

* 7.45: Show that if decomposition $\rho = (R_1, \ldots, R_k)$ has a lossless join with respect to a set of generalized dependencies $D$, then the decomposition $(R_1, \ldots, R_k, S)$ also has a lossless join with respect to $D$, where $S$ is an arbitrary relation scheme over the same set of attributes as $\rho$.

* 7.46 Show that it is $\mathcal{NP}$-hard ($\mathcal{NP}$-complete or harder—see Garey and Johnson [1979]) to determine:

    a)   Given a relation scheme $R$ and a set of functional dependencies $F$ on the attributes of $R$, whether $R$ has a key of size $k$ or less with respect to $F$?

    b)   Given $R$ and $F$ as in (a), and given a subset $S \subseteq R$, is $S$ in BNCF with respect to $F$?

    c)   Whether a given set of multivalued dependencies implies a given join dependency.

* 7.47: A *unary inclusion dependency* $A \subseteq B$, where $A$ and $B$ are attributes (perhaps from different relations) says that in any legal values of the relation(s), every value that appears in the column for $A$ also appears in the column for $B$. Show that the following axioms

    *i*)   $A \subseteq A$ for all $A$.

    *ii*)  If $A \subseteq B$ and $B \subseteq C$ then $A \subseteq C$.

Are sound and complete for unary inclusion dependencies.

* 7.48: Suppose for some even $n$ we have attributes $A_1, \ldots, A_n$. Also suppose that $A_i \subseteq A_{i+1}$ for odd $i$, that is, $i = 1, 3, \ldots, n-1$. Finally, suppose that for $i = 3, 5, \ldots, n-1$ we have $A_i \rightarrow A_{i-1}$, and we have $A_1 \rightarrow A_n$.

   a)  Show that if relations are assumed to be finite, then all the above dependencies can be reversed; that is,

$$A_2 \subseteq A_1, \ A_2 \rightarrow A_3, \ A_4 \subseteq A_3, \ A_4 \rightarrow A_5, \ldots, A_n \subseteq A_{n-1}, \ A_n \rightarrow A_1$$

   b)  Show that there are infinite relations for which (a) does not hold; that is, they satisfy all the given dependencies but not of their reverses.

* 7.49  Show that if $D$ is a set of functional dependencies only, then a relation $R$ is in BCNF with respect to $D$ if and only if $R$ is in 4NF with respect to $D$.

* 7.50  Show that if $X \rightarrow A_1, \ldots, X \rightarrow A_n$ are functional dependencies in a minimal cover, then the scheme $X A_1 \cdots A_n$ is in 3NF.

## BIBLIOGRAPHIC NOTES

Maier [1983] is a text devoted to relational database theory, and provides a more detailed treatment of many of the subjects covered in this chapter. Fagin and Vardi [1986] and Vardi [1988] are surveys giving additional details in the area of dependency theory. Beeri, Bernstein, and Goodman [1978] is an early survey of the theory that provided the motivation for the area.

### Functional Dependencies

Functional dependencies were introduced by Codd [1970]. Axioms for functional dependencies were first given by Armstrong [1974]; the particular set of axioms used here (called "Armstrong's axioms") is actually from Beeri, Fagin, and Howard [1977]. Algorithm 7.1, the computation of the closure of a set of attributes, is from Bernstein [1976].

### Lossless-Join Decomposition

Algorithm 7.2, the lossless join test for schemes with functional dependencies, is from Aho, Beeri, and Ullman [1979]. The special case of the join of two relations, Theorem 7.5, was shown in the "if" direction by Heath [1971] and Delobel and Casey [1972] and in the opposite direction by Rissanen [1977].

Liu and Demers [1980] provide a more efficient lossless join test for schemes with functional dependencies. Testing lossless joins is equivalent to inferring a join dependency, so the remarks below about inference of generalized dependencies are relevant to lossless-join testing.

### Dependency-Preserving Decomposition

Algorithm 7.3, the test for preservation of dependencies, is by Beeri and Honeyman [1981].

The paper by Ginsburg and Zaiddan [1982] points out that when projected, functional dependencies imply certain other dependencies, which happen to be equality-generating, generalized dependencies, but are not themselves functional. As a result, when we discuss projected dependencies, we must be very careful to establish the class of dependencies about which we speak.

Graham and Yannakakis [1984] discuss "independence," a condition on a decomposition that allows satisfaction of dependencies to be checked in the individual relations of a decomposition.

Gottlob [1987] gives an algorithm to compute a cover for $\pi_R(F)$ directly from $F$; that is, it is not necessary to compute $F^+$ first. However, the algorithm is not guaranteed to run in polynomial time.

### Normal Forms and Decomposition

Third normal form is defined in Codd [1970] and Boyce-Codd normal form in Codd [1972a]. The definitions of first and second normal forms are also found in these papers.

The dependency-preserving decomposition into third normal form, Algorithm 7.5, is from Bernstein [1976], although he uses a "synthetic" approach, designing a scheme without starting with a universal relation. Theorem 7.3, the minimal cover theorem used in Algorithm 7.5, is also from Bernstein [1976]; more restrictive forms of cover are found in Maier [1980, 1983].

The lossless-join decomposition into BCNF given in Algorithm 7.4 is from Tsou and Fischer [1982]. Theorem 7.8, giving a 3NF decomposition with a lossless join and dependency preservation, is from Biskup, Dayal, and Bernstein [1979]. A related result appears in Osborn [1977].

The equivalence problem for decompositions of a given relation was solved by Beeri, Mendelzon, Sagiv, and Ullman [1981]. Ling, Tompa, and Kameda [1981] generalize the notion of third normal form to account for redundancies across several different relation schemes.

Schkolnick and Sorenson [1981] consider the positive and negative consequences of normalizing relation schemes.

### Additional Properties of Decompositions

The problem of adequacy of a decomposition has been considered from several points of view. Arora and Carlson [1978] regard the lossless-join and dependency-preservation conditions as a notion of adequacy, while Rissanen [1977] defines a decomposition to have *independent components* if there is a one-to-one correspondence between relations for the universal scheme that satisfy the dependencies, and projections of relations that satisfy the projected dependencies. Maier, Mendelzon, Sadri, and Ullman [1980] show that these notions are equivalent for functional dependencies, but not for multivalued dependencies.

Honeyman [1983] offers an appropriate definition for what it means for a decomposition (database scheme) to satisfy a functional dependency. Graham, Mendelzon, and Vardi [1986] discuss the extension of this question to generalized dependencies.

## Recognizing Normalized Relations

Osborn [1979] gives a polynomial-time algorithm to tell whether a given relation scheme $R$ is in BCNF, with respect to a given set of dependencies $F$ over $R$.[14] In contrast, Jou and Fischer [1983] show that telling whether $R$ is in third normal form with respect to $F$ is $\mathcal{NP}$-complete.

## Multivalued Dependencies

Multivalued dependencies were discovered independently by Fagin [1977], Delobel [1978], and Zaniolo [1976] (see also Zaniolo and Melkanoff [1981]), although the earliest manifestation of the concept is in Delobel's thesis in 1973.

The axioms for multivalued dependencies are from Beeri, Fagin, and Howard [1977]. The independence of subsets of these axioms was considered by Mendelzon [1979], while Biskup [1980] shows that if one does not assume a fixed set of attributes, then this set minus the complementation axiom forms a sound and complete set. Lien [1979] develops axioms for multivalued dependencies on the assumption that null values are permitted.

Sagiv et al. [1981] show the equivalence of multivalued dependency theory to a fragment of propositional calculus, thus providing a convenient notation in which to reason about such dependencies.

The dependency basis and Algorithm 7.6 are from Beeri [1980]. Hagihara et al. [1979] give a more efficient test whether a given multivalued dependency is implied by others, and Galil [1982] gives an even faster way to compute the dependency basis.

Embedded multivalued dependencies were considered by Fagin [1977], Delobel [1978] and Tanaka, Kambayashi, and Yajima [1979].

## More Normal Forms

Fourth normal form was introduced in Fagin [1977]. In Fagin [1981] we find an "ultimate" normal form theorem; it is possible to decompose relation schemes so

---

14 The reader should not be confused between this result and Exercise 7.46(b). The latter indicates that telling whether a relation scheme $R$ is in BCNF given a set of functional dependencies, *defined on a superset of $R$*, is $\mathcal{NP}$-complete.

that the only dependencies remaining are functional dependencies of a nonkey attribute on a key and constraints that reflect the limited sizes of domains for attributes.

### Join Dependencies

Join dependencies were first formalized by Rissanen [1979]. The condition on relations corresponding to a join dependency on their schemes was considered by Nicolas [1978] and Mendelzon and Maier [1979].

A sound and complete axiomatization for a class slightly more general than join dependencies is found in Sciore [1982].

### Generalized Dependencies

The notion of generalized dependencies was discovered independently several times; it appears in Beeri and Vardi [1981], Paredaens and Janssens [1981], and Sadri and Ullman [1981].

A somewhat more general class, called implicational dependencies in Fagin [1982] and algebraic dependencies in Yannakakis and Papadimitriou [1980], has also been investigated.

### Implications of Generalized Dependencies

The "chase" as an algorithm for inferring dependencies has its roots in the lossless join test of Aho, Beeri, and Ullman [1979]. The term "chase," and its first application to the inference of dependencies, is found in Maier, Mendelzon, and Sagiv [1979]. Its application to generalized dependencies is from Beeri and Vardi [1984b].

The undecidability of implication for generalized tuple-generating dependencies was shown independently by Vardi [1984] and Gurevich and Lewis [1982]. Key results leading to the undecidability proof were contained in earlier papers by Beeri and Vardi [1981] and Chandra, Lewis, and Makowsky [1981].

### Axiomatization of Generalized Dependencies

Several sound and complete axiom systems for generalized dependencies are found in Beeri and Vardi [1984a] and Sadri and Ullman [1981]. Yannakakis and Papadimitriou [1980] gives an axiom system for algebraic dependencies.

### Inclusion Dependencies

Inclusion dependencies were studied by Casanova, Fagin, and Papadimitriou [1982] and Mitchell [1983]. Kanellakis, Cosmadakis, and Vardi [1983] discuss the important special case of unary inclusion dependencies (see Exercise 4.47), where the domain of a single attribute is declared to be a subset of another single attribute.

## Notes on Exercises

Exercise 7.13 (on the order of reductions to produce a minimal cover) is from Maier [1980]. Exercise 7.17 (efficient computation of the closure of a set of attributes) is from Bernstein [1976], although the problem is actually equivalent to the problem of telling whether a context-free grammar generates the empty string.

Exercise 7.32, the soundness and completeness of axioms A1–A8 for functional and multivalued dependencies, is proved in Beeri, Fagin, and Howard [1977]. The algorithm for projecting functional and multivalued dependencies, Exercise 7.37, was proved correct in Aho, Beeri, and Ullman [1979].

Exercise 7.46(a), the $\mathcal{NP}$-completeness of telling whether a relation scheme has a key of given size, is by Lucchesi and Osborn [1978]; part (b), telling whether a relation scheme is in BNCF, is from Beeri and Bernstein [1979], and part (c), inferring a join dependency from multivalued dependencies, is from Fischer and Tsou [1983].

Exercise 7.48 is from Kanellakis, Cosmadakis, and Vardi [1983]; it is the key portion of a polynomial-time algorithm for making inferences of dependencies when given a set of functional dependencies and unary inclusion dependencies.

# CHAPTER 8

Protecting
the
Database
Against
Misuse

There are several dangers from which a DBMS must protect its data:

1. Accidents, such as mistyping of input or programming errors.
2. Malicious use of the database.
3. Hardware or software failures that corrupt data.

Chapters 9 and 10 deal with item (3), as well as with a class of potential programming errors that are caused by concurrent access to the data by several processes. In this chapter we cover the DBMS components that handle the first two problems.

1. *Integrity preservation*. This component of a DBMS deals with nonmalicious data errors and their prevention. For example, it is reasonable to expect a DBMS to provide facilities for declaring that the value of a field AGE should be less than 150. The DBMS can also help detect some programming bugs, such as a procedure that inserts a record with the same key value as a record that already exists in the database.
2. *Security* (or *access control*). Here we are concerned primarily with restricting certain users so they are allowed to access and/or modify only a subset of the database. It might appear that any attempt on the part of a user to access a restricted portion of the database would be malicious, but in fact a programming error could as well cause the attempted access to restricted data.

In this chapter, we give some general principles and some simple examples of how integrity constraints and access control are handled in existing database systems. Sections 8.1 and 8.3 cover integrity and security, respectively, from a general perspective. Section 8.2 discusses integrity in Query-by-Example. In the last three sections we cover three examples of security mechanisms: Query-by-Example, SQL, and OPAL.

## 8.1 INTEGRITY

There are two essentially different kinds of constraints we would like a DBMS to enforce. As discussed at the beginning of Chapter 7, one type is structural, concerning only equalities among values in the database. By far the most prevalent instances of such constraints are what we there called functional dependencies. Many, but not all, functional dependencies can be expressed if the DBMS allows the user to declare that a set of fields or attributes forms a key for a record type or relation.

The need to express functional dependencies is not restricted to relational systems, nor do all relational systems have such a facility, explicitly. For example, the hierarchical system IMS allows the user to declare one field of a logical record type to be "unique," meaning that it serves as a key for that type. A unique field in the root record type serves as a key for database records, as well as for records of the root type. Also, the unique field for any record type, together with the unique fields for all of its ancestor record types, will serve as a key for that record type.

The second kind of integrity constraint concerns the actual values stored in the database. Typically, these constraints restrict the value of a field to some range or express some arithmetic relationship among various fields. For example, a credit union might expect that the sum of the BALANCE field, taken over all members of the credit union, equals the net assets of the union. As another example, if the record for a course contained fields E%, H%, and L%, indicating the percentage of the grade devoted to exams, homework, and labs, we would expect that in each such record the sum of the values in these fields is 100. This is the kind of integrity constraint we shall discuss here.

There are two important issues regarding integrity checking. First we discuss the way constraints can be expressed, and we show how taking "derivatives" of integrity constraints can often lead to an efficient way to perform the checks. Second, we discuss how the system can determine when integrity checks need to be made, and we illustrate with the DBTG approach one way the user can control such checks.

### Query Languages as Integrity Constraint Languages

Many common kinds of integrity constraints can be expressed in the data manipulation language. As we shall see in Section 8.2, it is possible to use the DML, or something very close to the DML, to serve as the integrity-constraint language. In this section, we shall consider the matter abstractly, using relational algebra as our constraint language.

**Example 8.1:** Referring to the YVCB database again, we could write as the containment of two queries the constraint that orders can only be entered if placed by people who are customers, i.e., those listed in the CUSTOMERS relation. These queries can be expressed in any notation; we shall use relational algebra as an example, and write

$$\pi_{\text{CUST}}(\text{ORDERS}) \subseteq \pi_{\text{CNAME}}(\text{CUSTOMERS}) \tag{8.1}$$

$\square$

The integrity constraint (8.1) is really an example of a unary inclusion dependency, mentioned in Exercise 7.46. There are other integrity constraints that cannot be expressed as the containment of one set within another, but can be expressed as the special kind of Horn clause that we have ignored since Section 3.1: the disjunction of negative literals. A Horn clause $\neg p_1 \lor \cdots \lor \neg p_n$ is equivalent to $\neg(p_1 \land \cdots \land p_n)$. We can write this expression as

:- $p_1$ & $\cdots$ & $p_n$

The missing head of the rule should be thought of as "false," so the rule says "$p_1$ and $\cdots$ and $p_n$ implies false," i.e., these atoms cannot all be true simultaneously.

**Example 8.2:** Suppose we want to restrict customers of the YVCB to have nonnegative balances. We could write the constraint

```
:- customers(C,A,B) & B < 0.                              (8.2)
```

This rule says that if we have a customer $C$ with address $A$ and balance $B$, and we also have $B < 0$, then we have a contradiction; i.e., we have inferred "false." Equivalently, it says that we cannot have a value of $B$ which is simultaneously less than 0 and found in the BALANCE component of some CUSTOMERS tuple. $\square$

### Checking Integrity Constraints

Some intelligence must be used when we plan how to check integrity constraints. For example, on inserting a new order, we should realize that only the newly inserted order could violate (8.1), so all we have to do is check its CUST attribute for membership in $\pi_{\text{CNAME}}(\text{CUSTOMERS})$. Similarly, we can check (8.2) on insertion of a new customer by considering only the balance of that new customer, rather than all the customers' balances, as we would do if we took (8.2) literally.

There is a simple technique for getting a good upper bound on what we must do to verify that an integrity constraint is not violated when one or more of the underlying relations change. The idea is related to "semi-naive" evaluation discussed in Algorithm 3.4. In both situations we take the "derivative" of an algebraic expression to find the change in the expression resulting from the changes in relations.

The four monotone operators of relational algebra can be related to "ordinary" arithmetic operations as follows. We can treat Cartesian product as multiplication, union as addition, and both selection and projection as forms of multiplication by a constant. The set difference operator, which is not monotone, gives us some problems because insertion into the database can result in the deletion of tuples from the answer, and vice versa. We can still get bounds on the change to the value of an expression involving set difference, and these bounds will often be useful. We leave the extension of the "derivative" idea to nonmonotone expressions as an exercise.

## Computing Derivatives

The rules for taking the "derivative" of monotone expressions are given below. It should be understood that $\Delta E$, the "change in the value of expression $E$," is really an upper bound on that change, because of the effects of projection, which we shall discuss in the proof of Theorem 8.1, and of union. Suppose we have a database with relations $R_1, \ldots, R_n$, and we insert into each relation $R_i$ the set of tuples $\Delta R_i$ (which may be empty for some $i$'s). Let $E$ be an expression of relational algebra involving the operations $\times$, $\cup$, $\sigma$, and $\pi$. Then $\Delta E$, a set of tuples that includes all of those tuples that were not in the value of $E$ before the $\Delta R_i$'s were inserted into the $R_i$'s, but are in the value of $E$ afterward, is defined by:

1. If $E$ is a constant relation, then $\Delta E = \emptyset$.
2. If $E$ is a relation variable, say $R_i$, then $\Delta E = \Delta R_i$.
3. If $E = \sigma_F(E_1)$ then $\Delta E = \sigma_F(\Delta E_1)$.
4. If $E = \pi_L(E_1)$ then $\Delta E = \pi_L(\Delta E_1)$.
5. If $E = E_1 \cup E_2$ then $\Delta E = \Delta E_1 \cup \Delta E_2$.
6. If $E = E_1 \times E_2$ then $\Delta E = (E_1 \times \Delta E_2) \cup (\Delta E_1 \times E_2) \cup (\Delta E_1 \times \Delta E_2)$.

The same rules apply if the $\Delta R_i$'s are deletions from each of the $R_i$'s. Then, $\Delta E$ is an upper bound on the set of tuples deleted from $E$. However, if we want to develop rules that handle combinations of insertions and deletions at the same time, then we have much of the complexity that we face when we consider set difference with insertions only.

Fortunately, if we are only concerned with checking integrity constraints expressible in monotone relational algebra, then deletions cannot contribute to violations of the constraints. If $E$ is an integrity constraint, a function of database relations $R_1, \ldots, R_n$, we have only to compute $\Delta E$, by the above rules, and check that this relation is empty. As we mentioned, $\Delta E$ is only an upper bound on the set of tuples that newly appear in the value of expression

$E$. However, as we shall show in Theorem 8.1, any tuples in $\Delta E$ that are not newly inserted are tuples that were in the relation denoted by $E$ even before insertion, and thus these are violations of the integrity constraint anyway.

**Example 8.3:** The rule body (8.2) is easily seen equivalent to the relational algebra expression

$$E = \sigma_{B<0}\big(\text{CUSTOMERS}(C, A, B)\big)$$

Then by rule (3),

$$\Delta E = \sigma_{B<0}\big(\Delta \text{CUSTOMERS}(C, A, B)\big)$$

That is, if we insert a new customer or customers (the members of the set of tuples $\Delta$CUSTOMERS), the change in the expression $E$, which represents the violations of the integrity constraint (8.2), is computed by applying the selection for $B < 0$ to the inserted tuple or tuples.

As another, abstract example, consider

$$E = R(A, B) \bowtie S(B, C) = \pi_{1,2,4}\big(\sigma_{\$2=\$3}(R \times S)\big)$$

Then

$$\Delta E = \pi_{1,2,4}\Big(\sigma_{\$2=\$3}\big((R \times \Delta S) \cup (\Delta R \times S) \cup (\Delta R \times \Delta S)\big)\Big) =$$
$$(R \bowtie \Delta S) \cup (\Delta R \bowtie S) \cup (\Delta R \bowtie \Delta S)$$

Note that the above steps did not depend on the particular attributes of $R$ and $S$, and therefore illustrate the fact that natural join also behaves like multiplication as far as the taking of "derivatives" is concerned. □

**Theorem 8.1:** If the $\Delta R_i$'s above are sets of insertions, then $\Delta E$ contains all of the new tuples in the relation produced by expression $E$; if the $\Delta R_i$'s are sets of deletions, then $\Delta E$ contains all of the tuples that are no longer in $E$. In each case, there can be some tuples in $\Delta E$ that are not inserted into (resp. deleted from) $E$, but these tuples are in $E$ both before and after the insertions (resp. deletions).

**Proof:** The proof is an induction on the number of operators in the expression $E$. We shall do only the case of insertions and rule (4), the projection rule. The basis and the remaining cases of the induction are left as an exercise.

Suppose that $E = \pi_L(F)$ [$F$ is $E_1$ in rule (4)], and the values of $E$ and $F$ before the insertion are $E_{old}$ and $F_{old}$; after insertion their values are $E_{new}$ and $F_{new}$. Then by the inductive hypothesis, $F_{new} - F_{old} \subseteq \Delta F$, and the tuples in $\Delta F$ that are not in $F_{new} - F_{old}$ are in both $F_{new}$ and $F_{old}$. Put in an algebraically equivalent way, $\Delta F \subseteq F_{new}$. Now the set of tuples in $E_{new}$ that are not in $E_{old}$ is $\pi_L(F_{new}) - \pi_L(F_{old})$. Call this set $S$; we must show that $S \subseteq \Delta E = \pi_L(\Delta F)$ and that tuples in $\Delta E - S$ are in $E_{old}$ (and therefore in both $E_{new}$ and $E_{old}$, since we assume only insertions are made).

Suppose $\mu$ is in $S$. Then $\mu$ is in $\pi_L(F_{new})$ and not in $\pi_L(F_{old})$. Then there exists a tuple $\nu$ that agrees with $\mu$ in the components on the list $L$, such that $\nu$ is in $F_{new}$; if not, $\mu$ could not be in $\pi_L(F_{new})$. Further, $\nu$ is not in $F_{old}$, or else $\mu$ would be in $\pi_L(F_{old})$. Thus, $\nu$ is in $F_{new} - F_{old}$, which is, by the inductive hypothesis, a subset of $\Delta F$. We conclude $\nu$ is in $\Delta F$. Hence, $\mu$ is in $\pi_L(\Delta F) = \Delta E$, as was to be proved.

For the second part of the induction, we must show that $\Delta E - S$ contains only tuples in $E_{old}$. By the inductive hypothesis, $\Delta F \subseteq F_{new}$. Thus,

$$\Delta E = \pi_L(\Delta F) \subseteq \pi_L(F_{new})$$

and therefore

$$\Delta E - S \subseteq \pi_L(F_{new}) - S \subseteq \pi_L(F_{old})$$

The latter follows since $S = \pi_L(F_{new}) - \pi_L(F_{old})$. But $\pi_L(F_{old}) = E_{old}$, so $\Delta E - S \subseteq E_{old}$, as desired. $\square$

Note that the projection operator can actually introduce tuples into $\Delta E$ that are in both $E_{new}$ and $E_{old}$. That is, we could have, for example,

$$F_{new} = \{01, 02\}$$

and $F_{old} = \{02\}$, with $\Delta F = \{01\}$. If $E = \pi_1(F)$, then

$$\Delta E = \pi_1(\Delta F) = \{0\}$$

while $E_{new} = E_{old} = \{0\}$, so $E_{new} - E_{old} = \emptyset$; that is, there is really no change to the value of expression $E$. A similar situation can occur when we apply rule (5), for union.

### Checking Existence Constraints by Derivatives

An existence constraint like (8.1), which relates two monotone expressions by set inclusion, can also be checked efficiently by taking the derivatives of the two expressions involved. First, we note that if our constraint is $E \subseteq F$, and the relations involved in expression $E$ are disjoint from those involved in $F$, then insertions into the relations of $F$ cannot violate the constraint, and deletions from $E$ cannot violate the constraint. If we insert into a relation involved in $E$, then we compute $\Delta E$. This relation will include all the new tuples of $E$, as well, perhaps, as some old ones. It is certainly sufficient to check that each of these tuples is in $F$. Similarly, if we delete from a relation of $F$, we compute $\Delta F$ and check that none of these tuples are in $E$.

**Example 8.4:** Consider (8.1). Here, $E = \pi_{\text{CUST}}(\text{ORDERS})$, and

$$F = \pi_{\text{CNAME}}(\text{CUSTOMERS})$$

If we insert set of tuples $\Delta\text{ORDERS}$ into ORDERS, we must consider set of names $\Delta E = \pi_{\text{CUST}}(\Delta\text{ORDERS})$, and check that each is in $F$. That is, we must check that the customer name in each inserted order is already a customer in the CUSTOMERS relation. Note that some of the customers placing new orders may already have orders on record, so they are not really "new" customers; they are in $\Delta E$, but not in $E_{new} - E_{old}$, using the notation found in the proof of Theorem 8.1. $\square$

The cases where $E$ or $F$ are not monotone and where these expressions share relations as operands are harder. We leave it as an exercise to develop useful bounds on the set of tuples that must be checked.

## Controlling the Time of Integrity Checks

Instead of trying to check automatically only those integrity checks that could be violated when an insertion or deletion is made, many DBMS's simply allow the user to execute a checking program that is triggered by certain events that the user declares to be triggering events, such as insertion into, or deletion from, a given relation. The general idea is that the integrity constraints are allowed to function as high-level "interrupts," like ON conditions in PL/I.

For example, the DBTG proposal allows ON clauses of the form

ON <command list> CALL <procedure>

in the declaration of DBTG sets and record types. For a DBTG set, the <command list> may include any of INSERT, REMOVE, and FIND. The <procedure> is an arbitrary routine written in the DBTG data manipulation language, which is an extension of COBOL, and thus has full computing capability as well as the ability to access any part of the database. For example, if we declare for DBTG set $S$:

ON INSERT CALL P1

the procedure $P1$ could check that certain fields of the current of run-unit, which is the member record being inserted, are not already present in the selected set occurrence. Thus, these fields, plus a key for the owner record type, functionally determine the rest of the fields of the member type.

The <command list> for an ON clause in a record type declaration can include any of the above three commands that are permitted in DBTG set declarations and also the remaining four: STORE, DELETE, MODIFY, and GET. Such an ON clause is triggered whenever a command in the list is executed and the current of run-unit is of the relevant record type.

## 8.2 INTEGRITY CONSTRAINTS IN QUERY-BY-EXAMPLE

To demonstrate how the ideas of the previous section can be put into practice, we shall discuss integrity in the Query-by-Example system in detail. First, if we review Section 4.5, we note that when a relation is declared in QBE, we are allowed to specify whether each field is key or nonkey. The system then enforces the functional dependency of each nonkey field on the set of key fields taken together. This integrity check is triggered on each insertion or modification of a tuple in the relation, and operations that would cause a violation of the dependency are not done; rather, a warning is printed.

The QBE system maintains a constraint table for each relation. To create a constraint on relation $R$, we call for a table skeleton for $R$. We enter one or more rows representing the constraints into the skeleton. Below the relation name we enter

      I. CONSTR(<condition list>). I.

The first I. refers to the constraint itself and the second I. to the entries defining the constraint, which are in the portion of the row that follows to the right. The <condition list> can consist of any or all of I. (insert), D. (delete), U. (update), and identifiers that represent user defined conditions, to be described subsequently. The terms in the <condition list> indicate when the integrity constraint is to be tested; for example, CONSTR(I.,U.). tells us to test the constraint whenever an insertion or modification occurs in the relevant relation. CONSTR. is short for CONSTR(I.,D.,U.). In principle, the constraint applies to all of the tuples in the relation. However, for many simple constraints, the system can deduce that only the tuple inserted or modified needs to be checked, as we discussed in Section 8.1.

In the rows of the skeleton, we place entries for some or all of the attributes. An entry may be a constant, which says the tuple being inserted, deleted, or modified must have that constant value for that attribute, or the constraint does not apply. An entry may be of the form $\theta c$, where $c$ is a constant and $\theta$ an arithmetic comparison, which says that the corresponding component of a tuple must stand in relation $\theta$ to $c$, whenever the constraint applies to the tuple. An entry can be blank or have a variable name beginning with underscore, which means the tuple can be arbitrary in that attribute. Moreover, there can be additional rows entered in the skeleton for $R$ or in another skeleton; these rows place additional constraints on the values that may appear in the tuple being inserted, deleted, or modified, according to the semantics of the QBE language.

**Example 8.5:** Let us once more consider the YVCB database. To place the constraint on balances that no one owe more than 100 dollars, we could call for a CUSTOMERS skeleton and enter

| CUSTOMERS | NAME | ADDR | BALANCE |
|---|---|---|---|
| I. CONSTR(I.,U.). I. | | | >= -100 |

To guarantee that no order include an item for which no supplier exists, we can call for INCLUDES and SUPPLIES skeletons and enter the information shown in Figure 8.1. This constraint says that the inserted tuple, which defines

a value for _hotdog equal to the value of the ITEM attribute in the inserted
tuple, must be such that some tuple in the SUPPLIES relation has that value
for its ITEM attribute. □

| INCLUDES | O# | ITEM | QUANTITY |
|---|---|---|---|
| I. CONSTR(I.). I. | | _hotdog | |

| SUPPLIES | NAME | ITEM | PRICE |
|---|---|---|---|
| | | _hotdog | |

**Figure 8.1**  Constraint that orders may only include supplied items.

### Defined Triggers for Integrity Checks

In QBE, we may define a condition that, when satisfied by an inserted or
modified tuple, causes an associated integrity check or checks to be made on
that tuple. As mentioned above, in the phrase

> CONSTR(<condition list>).

the <condition list> can include arbitrary character strings as well as I., D.,
and U.. These character strings, called *defined triggers*, are the names of conditions expressed as rows in the QBE language.

**Example 8.6:** Suppose we wish to constrain Zack Zebra so that he cannot owe
as much as 50 dollars. We could write

| CUSTOMERS | NAME | ADDR | BALANCE |
|---|---|---|---|
| ZZlim | Zack Zebra | | |
| I. CONSTR(ZZlim). I. | | | > -50 |

The first row indicates that there is a defined trigger called ZZlim that is "triggered" whenever we modify or insert a tuple for Zebra. The second row says
that if the CUSTOMERS tuple for Zebra is inserted or modified, check that his
new balance is not lower than −49.99. The tuples for other members are not
affected by this constraint. □

### Old-New Constraints

Sometimes one wishes to constrain updates in such a way that there is a relationship between the old and new values for certain attributes. We include

in the constraint specification a line representing the old tuple as well as the constraint tuple itself. Often the QBE language allows the relationship between the old and new tuples to be expressed in the tuples themselves, but if not, a condition box can be used.

**Example 8.7:** To create a constraint that a supplier cannot raise the price of Brie we enter:

| SUPPLIES | NAME | ITEM | PRICE |
|---|---|---|---|
| I. CONSTR(U.). I. | _bmw | Brie | <= _p |
| I. | _bmw | Brie | _p |

The row with the keyword CONSTR. represents the new value, and the other row represents the old value. The presence of I. in the latter row distinguishes the old-new type of constraints from a general constraint requiring more than one row to express, as in the second part of Example 8.5. The presence of variable _bmw in both rows is necessary, or else we would only check that the new price for the supplier involved in the change is less than the price charged for Brie by at least one other supplier. □

### Timing of Constraint Enforcement

The QBE system allows one to enter an entire screenful of commands at once, and this collection of commands may include several insertions, deletions, or updates. It is important to note that integrity constraints are not checked as each command in the collection is executed, but only after all of the commands in the collection are executed. This feature allows us certain freedoms in the order in which we specify commands, as long as the commands are entered together.

Thus, in Example 8.5 we constrained our YVCB database in such a way that we could not place an order for an item not supplied. If we enter as one "screenload" an order for Goat Cheese and fact that Acme now sells Goat Cheese, we would not violate the constraint. However, if the system entered the orders and checked the integrity constraints before entering the new supply information, we would have had an integrity violation.

### The Constraint Table

All integrity constraints declared are available to the user. We can print the constraints pertaining to a relation $R$ if we enter

        P. CONSTR. P.

under the relation name in a skeleton for $R$. Alternatively, we could print only the constraints of specified type; for example

    P. CONSTR(I.).  P.

prints only the insertion constraints.

We can delete a constraint on $R$ by entering under $R$ in a skeleton for this relation

    D. CONSTR(<condition list>).

followed, in the columns for the attributes, by a description of the constraint. Note that a trailing D. is not needed the way a second I. or P. is needed when we insert or print a constraint.

## 8.3 SECURITY

Many of the problems associated with security are not unique to database systems, but must be faced by the designer of an operating system, for example. Therefore, let us touch on some of the techniques common to security for database systems and more general systems, and then turn to some of the specialized problems and techniques germane to existing database systems.

1.  *User identification.* Generally, different users are accorded different rights to different databases or different portions of the database, such as particular relations or attributes. These rights may include the reading of portions of the database, and the insertion, deletion, or modification of data. The most common scheme to identify users is a password known only to the system and the individual. Presumably, the passwords are protected by the system at least as well as the data, although to be realistic, guarantees or proofs of security are nonexistent.

2.  *Physical Protection.* A completely reliable protection scheme must take into account the possibility of physical attacks on the database, ranging from forced disclosure of a password to theft of the physical storage devices. We can protect against theft fairly well by encrypting the data. A high security system needs better identification than a password, such as personal recognition of the user by a guard.

3.  *Maintenance and Transmittal of Rights.* The system needs to maintain a list of rights enjoyed by each user on each protected portion of the database. One of these rights may be the right to confer rights on others. For example, the DBTG proposal calls for DBTG sets, record types, and "areas" (essentially regions of the physical memory) to be protectable; the mechanism could be a password for each protected object. The proposal does not call for a table of user rights to protected objects, and transmission of rights can be handled outside the system, by informing users of passwords, for example. Both System R and the Query-by-Example System (to be discussed further in Section 8.4) maintain a table of rights and permit the granting of rights to others.

Now, let us consider two mechanisms of protection that are specially designed for use in database systems.

## Views as Protection Mechanisms

The view, in addition to making the writing of application programs easier by allowing some redefinition of the conceptual database and promoting logical data independence, serves as a convenient protection mechanism. There are two distinct kinds of view facilities. The first, which we discussed in connection with ISBL and Query-by-Example (Sections 4.2 and 4.5), allows no modification to the view. We call such a view facility *read-only*. There are many situations in which the owner of a database (or of any protectable object for that matter) wishes to give the public the privilege of reading his data but wishes to reserve the privilege of modifying the database to himself or to a limited set of associates. The read-only view is ideal for this purpose.

For example, in ISBL or QBE, we may define a view equal to a given database relation and allow public (read-only) access to this view. There is also the option of creating a view containing only part of the information of a relation, or parts of several relations, thus shielding certain attributes or tuples from public view.

The other type of view permits both reading and writing of the objects that are part of the view, and modifications to the view are reflected in the conceptual scheme. IMS, SQL, and the DBTG proposal permit read/write views to a limited extent. Clearly this facility is more versatile than the read-only view, as far as the design of application programs is concerned.

A serious problem with read/write views is that updates to a view often have side effects on parts of the database that are not in the view. For example, in a hierarchical system, we might have a particular record type in the view, but not its descendants. If we delete an occurrence of that record type, we must delete its descendants as well, for they no longer fit anywhere in the database. This action could be a surprise to the user, or it could be illegal, as we would ordinarily not give a user authorization to delete an object that we would not even allow him to see in his view.

A similar situation occurs in the network model, where we wish to delete an owner record but do not know about its owned records because they are outside the view. Likewise, those relational systems that borrow network and hierarchical ideas for structuring the storage of their relations face the same problems. It is also unclear, in relational systems, what the deletion of some components of a tuple means if there are other attributes of the relation that are outside the view and that therefore should not be deletable by a user seeing only the view. For these reasons, all DBMS's limit the user's ability to update views to a few unambiguous cases.

## The Use of Query Languages to Define Rights

Another important idea concerning security as it pertains to database systems is that the data manipulation language can be used to define the privileges each user has for accessing the database. For example, we may write a selection and projection to be included automatically with every query posed by designated users about a designated relation. This selection and projection have the effect of making certain values invisible.

**Example 8.8:** If a user querying the YVCB database is required to project the CUSTOMERS relation onto NAME and ADDR, whether or not he specifies that projection, then that user cannot see balances. If employees of Acme are required to select for NAME="Acme" in every query about the SUPPLIES relation, then they cannot find the prices charged by other suppliers.

For example, if the latter constraint is declared in Quel, then a query like

```
range of s is SUPPLIES
retrieve (s.price)
    where s.item = "Brie"
```

is automatically translated by the INGRES system into

```
range of s is SUPPLIES
retrieve (s.price)
    where s.item = "Brie"
        and s.name = "Acme"
```

☐

Quel and QBE follow this general approach; we shall discuss Query-by-Example's security mechanism in detail in the next section. The DBTG proposal allows the "privacy lock" for a protectable object to be an arbitrary procedure, so we are able to implement arbitrary checks, expressed in the DBTG data manipulation language, for granting or denying a request to access a protected object. For example, we could check that NAME = "Acme" in every tuple retrieved.

## 8.4 SECURITY IN QUERY-BY-EXAMPLE

The QBE system recognizes the four rights: insert (I.), delete (D.), update (U.), and read (P., for "print"). To confer one or more rights to a relation $R$ upon a person or group of people, the owner of relation $R$ enters a tuple in an $R$ skeleton. Under the relation name $R$ appears the entry

   I. AUTR(<list>). <name> I.

where <list> is a list of one or more of the four rights, I., D., U., and P.; <name> is either the name of the person being given the rights or a variable, representing an arbitrary person. We may omit (<list>) if we intend to grant all four rights, and we may omit <name> if we wish to grant a set of rights to all users.

To complete the row with the AUTR. keyword, we enter variables or constants in some or all of the columns for the attributes. A variable indicates that the right applies to the column. A constant indicates the right applies only to tuples with that constant value in that column. A blank indicates that the column cannot be accessed. Note that this rule differs from the general QBE policy that blanks are synonymous with variables mentioned only once. The full power of the QBE language can be brought to bear to refine the set of tuples in the relation $R$ to which the right is granted. For example, we can use condition boxes to constrain the values of variables, and we can add additional rows that also restrict values of variables.

**Example 8.9:** Let us again use the YVCB database as an example. To give user Zebra the right to read the ORDERS relation we say

| ORDERS | O# | DATE | CUST |
|---|---|---|---|
| I. AUTR(P.). Zebra I. | _n | _d | _c |

To grant Zebra all four access rights to the ORDERS relation we can write

| ORDERS | O# | DATE | CUST |
|---|---|---|---|
| I. AUTR. Zebra I. | _n | _d | _c |

To give anyone the right to read names and balances (but not addresses) from the CUSTOMERS relation, provided the balance is nonnegative, we say

| CUSTOMERS | NAME | ADDR | BALANCE |
|---|---|---|---|
| I. AUTR(P.). _Snake I. | _n | | >= 0 |

Note that the variable _Snake matches any user's name.

As a final example, to allow anyone access to find, from the INCLUDES relation, the order numbers for items supplied by Acme, we may write the command shown in Figure 8.2. □

## Constraints on the Name of the Grantee

We have so far shown two kinds of grants: to anyone or to one specific person. We can use the QBE language to express subsets of the set of users, and we can even allow the set of accessible tuples to be different for different users. The technique is to use a variable for <name> in the AUTR. entry, and to use the same name in the tuple or tuples describing the right granted to each individual user. The system provides a facility to relate the name of the user

| INCLUDES | O# | ITEM | QUANTITY |
|---|---|---|---|
| I. AUTR(P.). _Snake I. | _n | _hotdog | |

| SUPPLIES | NAME | ITEM | PRICE |
|---|---|---|---|
| | Acme | _hotdog | |

**Figure 8.2** Anyone may read order numbers for items supplied by Acme.

to the representation of his name as it appears in the database.

**Example 8.10:** We can give everyone authorization to read only his own balance by:

| CUSTOMERS | NAME | ADDR | BALANCE |
|---|---|---|---|
| I. AUTR(P.). _Snake I. | _Snake | | _b |

☐

## The Authorization Table

As for integrity constraints, all AUTR. statements are placed in a table. From this table we can print the rights granted to an individual concerning a relation, or all grants concerning a relation, in much the same manner as we print integrity constraints. Similarly, the owner of a relation can delete rights from the table concerning that relation.

## 8.5 SECURITY IN SQL/RT

The version of SQL for the IBM PC/RT, which was described in Sections 4.6–4.8, uses a very simple security mechanism. This simplicity is appropriate for a system running on a computer that is in essence a large personal computer, to be shared by a few people at most. The SQL database system runs under the AIX operating system, which is essentially UNIX. Thus, SQL is able to make use of the protection facilities that UNIX provides for files.

UNIX divides the world, as far as access to a file is concerned, into three parts: the owner of the file, the "group" to which the owner belongs, and the rest of the world. Of these, only the notion of a group requires explanation. There is the underlying assumption that users are divided into groups, and the privileges the owner assigns to "group" are available only to those users who are in the same group as the owner. The *privileges* that the owner may grant or withold from himself, his group, or the world are read, write, and execute; the latter is not relevant when access to a database is concerned.

To grant an access privilege to a relation $R$, the owner says one of the six combinations of:

GRANT READ/WRITE/ALL ON $R$ TO GROUP/WORLD

The possible privileges are READ and WRITE; ALL stands for both of these privileges. The privilege of writing includes inserting, deleting, and modifying tuples, as well as other operations such as index creation for the relation, or dropping the relation itself. The read privilege includes only the right to use the relation in queries. The owner is assumed to have all privileges, so there is no need to grant them explicitly.

To cancel a privilege, say

REVOKE READ/WRITE/ALL ON $R$ FROM GROUP/WORLD

Privileges may be granted and revoked for views as well as for relations, and we need to use views if we are to allow anything more refined than all-or-nothing access to relations. The ability to exercise the write privilege on a view is limited, because there are many views we can express in SQL for which no natural translation from the change in the view to the appropriate change in the database exists. SQL/RT permits modification of views only when the view is obtained from a single relation by selection and projection. When projection is involved in the view, we can modify the underlying relation in response to an insertion into the view by padding the inserted tuple with nulls in those attributes not found in the view.

**Example 8.11:** Louise Ledger, manager of the accounting department at the YVCB, is the owner of the CUSTOMERS relation. Other employees in the accounting department are members of the same group as Ledger, and other employees of the YVCB are not. It is desired that:

1. Only Ledger can change balances of customers.
2. Only accounting employees can read balances of customers, insert or delete new customers, or change addresses of customers.
3. All employees can read names and addresses of customers.

Initially, only Ledger has access privileges to CUSTOMERS, so condition (1) is satisfied, but (2) and (3) are not. To permit the second and third types of access, we need a view that has only the NAME and ADDR attributes of CUSTOMERS. All employees will have read access to this view, and accounting department employees will have write access. The view is defined by:

```
CREATE VIEW PUBLIC_CUST(NAME, ADDR) AS
    SELECT NAME, ADDR
    FROM CUSTOMERS;
```

When we insert into PUBLIC_CUST, the new tuple is given a null BALANCE. Deletion from this view is performed by deleting all tuples in CUSTOMERS with the same name and address; there should be only one. Modifications are similarly reflected by modification to all matching tuples of CUSTOMERS.

To grant the proper accesses to the accounting group and to all the users of the database, Ledger should issue the following SQL commands:

```
GRANT READ ON CUSTOMERS TO GROUP;
GRANT READ ON PUBLIC_CUST TO WORLD;
GRANT WRITE ON PUBLIC_CUST TO GROUP;
```

☐

## 8.6 SECURITY IN OPAL/GEMSTONE

The Opal language discussed in Sections 5.6 and 5.7 is part of the Gemstone object-oriented database system. Security issues for Gemstone are addressed through built-in objects and methods of Opal.

The basic unit to which access can be granted or denied is called a *segment*. All objects created are assigned to a segment. In the simplest situation, each user has one segment, containing all of his objects, and there are several owned by the system itself. However, it is possible for users to have more than one segment. For example, to control access on a relation-by-relation or view-by-view basis, as we did in the previous section, we would have to divide objects into segments according to the "relation" to which they belong.

There are three authorizations understood by Gemstone, and they are represented by the Opal symbols #read, #write, and #none.[1] Their meanings should be obvious. The privilege to write includes the privilege to read, and the #none privilege denies all access to the protected segment.

### User Profiles

There is an object called *System* that can be sent messages of various types, some involving security. One of the messages *System* understands is

```
System myUserProfile
```

which returns an object called the *user profile*, the profile belonging to the user who sends *System* the message.

We may send to the user profile object certain messages to read or change some of the facts about the status of the user. One of these facts concerns the *default segment*, which is the "current" segment, the one into which objects

---

[1] Recall from Section 5.6 that "symbols," indicated by the leading #, are essentially internal representations for character strings.

newly created by this user would be placed. If we send the user profile the message

```
defaultSegment
```

we are returned the default segment as an object. We can then send this object messages that read or modify authorizations to that segment. For each segment, we may specify an authorization for the owner, for up to four groups, and for the "world." The forms of the messages are illustrated in the next example.

**Example 8.12:** A user can give himself write authorization, the most general authorization that Gemstone uses, for his own segment by sending the following messages.[2]

```
(1)  ((System myUserProfile)
(2)      defaultSegment)
(3)          ownerAuthorization:  #write.
```

That is, line (1) produces the user profile object as a result. The message sent this object on line (2) produces the default segment object as a result. On line (3), this segment is sent a message that gives the owner of that segment authorization to write into the segment.

Generally, it is not possible to send the

```
ownerAuthorization
```

message, or similar messages, to any segment but one's own.

To authorize the accounting group (represented by the symbol `#accounting`) to read his default segment, a user may say:

```
((System myUserProfile)
    defaultSegment)
        group:  #accounting
        authorization:  #read.
```

Finally, to deny either read or write access to this user's default segment by users not in the accounting group, he can say:

```
((System myUserProfile)
    defaultSegment)
        worldAuthorization:  #none.
```

☐

## Privileges

There are certain activities that require a higher degree of protection than is afforded, through the authorization mechanism, to the reading and writing of

---

[2] In all the following messages, the parentheses are redundant, because messages are applied left-to-right.

objects. These activities include shutting down the system, reading or changing (other people's) passwords, creating new segments, and changing authorization for segments belonging to others.

To provide the necessary security, certain messages can only be sent by users whose profiles explicitly contain the corresponding *privilege*. For example, the privilege

    `SegmentProtection`

allows a user whose profile contains this privilege to change the authorization on other users' segments. Thus, if *Profile* is a variable whose current value is the user profile of user $A$, then user $B$ might send the message

    `Profile worldAuthorization:  #write.`

If the `SegmentProtection` privilege appears in $B$'s user profile, then this action will be taken, and all objects in $A$'s defualt segment will become publicly readable and writable. If $B$ does not have this privilege, the message will not be accepted. Of course, $A$ may send the same message to his own profile without any special privilege.

Curiously, the "privilege" of adding privileges is not itself protected by the privilege mechanism. In principle, any user could send to *Profile* the message

    `Profile addPrivilege:  'SegmentProtection'.`

and gain the `SegmentProtection` privilege for the user whose profile was the current value of *Profile*. The normal way to prevent this situation is to store the user profiles themselves in a segment owned by the "data curator," who is thus the only one who can send such messages legally, as long as write-authorization for this segment is withheld from any other users.

## EXERCISES

8.1: Compute $\Delta E$ for the following expressions $E$.

    a)   $R \times \pi_{A,B}(S)$.

    b)   $(R \cup S) \times \left(\sigma_{A=0}(R) \cup \pi_A(S)\right)$.

\* 8.2: Explain how to extend $\Delta$ to set difference in such a way that the estimates are conservative ($\Delta E$ contains all of the additional tuples of $E$ when insertions are made into the argument relations of $E$) and as close to the minimum set as you can manage.

8.3: Show the law for the derivative of a natural join $E = E_1 \bowtie E_2$:

$$\Delta E = (E_1 \bowtie \Delta E_2) \cup (\Delta E_1 \bowtie E_2) \cup (\Delta E_1 \bowtie \Delta E_2)$$

8.4: Complete the proof of Theorem 8.1 by considering the operators selection, union, and product, and by considering the situation in which the changes to the argument relations are deletions rather than insertions.

* 8.5: Explain how to check whether $E \subseteq F$ holds after insertions to argument relations of expressions $E$ and $F$, when

a)   $E$ and $F$ share arguments.

b)   $E$ and $F$ involve the set difference operator.

8.6: Suppose we have a database consisting of the following relations.

> EMPS(EMP_NO, NAME, ADDR, SALARY, DEPT_NO)
> DEPTS(DEPT_NO, DNAME, MANAGER)

Express the following integrity constraints in the Query-by-Example constraint language.

a)   No employee earns more than $100,000.

b)   No employee in Department number 72 earns more than $50,000.

c)   No employee in the Toy Department earns more than $50,000.

* d)   No two departments have the same number. *Hint*: Use the CNT. (count) operator.

** 8.7: Show that every functional and multivalued dependency can be expressed in the Query-by-Example integrity-constraint language.

8.8: Express in the Query-by-Example authorization language of Section 8.4 the following authorizations for the database of Exercise 8.6.

a)   Anyone can read the EMPS relation, except for the salary attribute.

b)   Any employee can read his own salary.

c)   The manager of a department can read the salary of any employee in his department.

d)   Employee Warbucks can insert and delete EMPS tuples and can modify salaries.

8.9: Repeat Exercise 8.8 (a) and (d) in the SQL/RT authorization mechanism described in Section 8.5. What makes (b) and (c) difficult in SQL/RT?

8.10: Suppose that we create an OPAL database with employee and department objects corresponding to the two relations in Exercise 8.6. Suppose *EmpSegment* is the name of a segment in which all of the employee objects are found, and *DeptSegment* is a segment holding the department objects.

a)   How would we arrange that Warbucks and only Warbucks has write-access to the employee objects?

b)   How would we arrange that all the managers (and only Warbucks and the managers) have read-access to the employee objects?

* c)   How can we arrange that everyone has read-access to the employee objects except for the salary instance variable? *Hint*: Create a "view."

## BIBLIOGRAPHIC NOTES

Fernandez, Summers, and Wood [1980] is a survey of database security and
integrity.

### Integrity

The general idea of integrity constraints through query modification is from
Stonebraker [1975].

The Query-by-Example integrity subsystem discussed in Section 8.2 is
based on Zloof [1978]. This mechanism did not appear in the commercial QBE
discussed in IBM [1978a].

### Authorization

The discussion of security in Query-by-Example in Section 8.4 is taken from
Zloof [1978].

The authorization mechanism of SQL/RT (Section 8.5) is discussed in IBM
[1985b], and authorization in OPAL (Section 8.6) by Servio Logic [1986].

Authorization in INGRES is discussed in Stonebraker and Rubinstein
[1975]. The general idea of security by query modification is from Stonebraker
and Wong [1974].

The paper by Fagin [1978] studies and proves correct an algorithm for
granting authorizations to a database with the possibility that the right to
grant further authorizations can itself be granted. This idea was earlier studied
by Griffiths and Wade [1976].

# CHAPTER 9

Transaction
Management

Until now, our concept of a database has been one in which programs accessing the database are run one at a time (*serially*). Often this is indeed the case. However, there are also numerous applications in which more than one program, or different executions of the same program, run simultaneously (*concurrently*). An example is an airline reservation system, where at one time, several agents may be selling tickets, and therefore, changing lists of passengers and counts of available seats. The canonical problem is that if we are not careful when we allow two or more processes to access the database, we could sell the same seat twice. In the reservations system, two processes that read and change the value of the same object must not be allowed to run concurrently, because they might interact in undesirable ways.

A second example is a statistical database, such as census data, where many people may be querying the database at once. Here, as long as no one is changing the data, we do not really care in what order the processes read data; we can let the operating system schedule simultaneous read requests as it wishes. In this sort of situation, where only reading is being done, we want to allow maximum concurrent operation, so time can be saved. For contrast, in the case of a reservation system, where both reading and writing are in progress, we need restrictions on when two programs may execute concurrently, and we should be willing to trade speed for safety.

In this chapter we shall consider models of concurrent processes as they pertain to database operation. The models are distinguished primarily by the detail in which they portray access to elements of the database. For each model we shall describe a reasonable way to allow those concurrent operations that preserve the integrity of the database while preventing concurrent operations that might, as far as a model of limited detail can tell, destroy its integrity. As a rule, the more detailed the model, the more concurrency we can allow safely.

Section 9.1 introduces most of the necessary concepts, including "locking," the primary technique for controlling concurrency. In Section 9.2 we discuss the simplest model of transactions. That model leads to a discussion of the "two-phase locking protocol" in Section 9.3; that protocol is the most important technique for managing concurrency. Sections 9.4 and 9.6 discuss more realistic models, where reading and writing are treated as distinct operations. Section 9.5 talks about "lock modes" in general; reading and writing are the most common "modes." Access to tree-structured data is covered in Section 9.7.

In Section 9.8 we begin to discuss how the theory must be modified to account for the possibility that software or hardware failures may occur, and in the following section we consider what options exist for containing the effect of an error. Section 9.10 discusses logging and other mechanisms for avoiding the loss of data after a system error. Finally, Section 9.11 discusses all of these issues in the context of "timestamps," which after locking, is the most common approach to concurrency control.

## 9.1 BASIC CONCEPTS

A *transaction* is a single execution of a program. This program may be a simple query expressed in one of the query languages of Chapters 4–5 or an elaborate host language program with embedded calls to a query language. Several independent executions of the same program may be in progress simultaneously; each is a different transaction.

Our model of how a transaction interacts with the database is close to what we discussed in Chapter 4, in connection with the DBTG and IMS systems. A transaction reads and writes data to and from the database, into a private *workspace*, where all computation is performed. In particular, computations performed by the transaction have no effect on the database until new values are written into the database.

### Atomicity

To a large extent, transaction management can be seen as an attempt to make complex operations appear *atomic*. That is, they either occur in their entirety or do not occur at all, and if they occur, nothing else apparently went on during the time of their occurrence. The normal approach to ensuring atomicity of transactions is "serialization," to be discussed shortly, which forces transactions to run concurrently in a way that makes it appear that they ran one-at-a-time (*serially*). There are two principal reasons why a transaction might not be atomic.

1.   In a time-shared system, activities associated with two or more transactions might be done simultaneously or be interleaved. For example, several disk units might be reading or writing data to and from the database at the same time. The time slice for one transaction $T$ might end in the middle of a computation, and activities of some other transaction performed before

$T$ completes.

2. A transaction might not complete at all. For example, it could have to *abort* (terminate) because it tried to perform an illegal calculation (e.g., division by 0), or because it requested some data to which it did not have the needed access privilege. The database system itself could force the transaction to abort for several reasons, which we shall discuss. For example, it could be involved in a deadlock, contending for resources.

In case (1), it is the job of the database system to ensure that, even though things happen in the middle of a transaction, the effect of the transaction on the database is not influenced by those interstitial activities. In case (2), the system must ensure that the aborted transaction has no effect at all on the database or on other transactions.

In reality, transactions are sequences of more elementary steps, such as reading or writing of single items from the database, and performing simple arithmetic steps in the workspace. We shall see that when concurrency control is provided, other primitive steps are also needed, steps which set and release locks, commit (complete) transactions, and perhaps others. We shall always assume that these more primitive steps are themselves atomic. Even though, for example, the end of a time slice could occur in the middle of an arithmetic step, we may, in practice, view that step as atomic, because it occurs in a local workspace, and nothing can affect that workspace until the transaction performing the arithmetic step resumes.

## Items

To manage concurrency, the database must be partitioned into *items*, which are the units of data to which access is controlled. The nature and size of items are for the system designer to choose. In the relational model of data, for example, we could choose large items, like relations, or small items like individual tuples or even components of tuples. We could also choose an intermediate size item, such as a block of the underlying file system, on which some small number of tuples are stored. The size of items used by a system is often called its *granularity*. A "fine-grained" system uses small items and a "coarse-grained" one uses large items.

The most common way in which access to items is controlled is by "locks," which we discuss shortly. Briefly, a *lock manager* is the part of a DBMS that records, for each item $I$, whether one or more transactions are reading or writing any part of $I$. If so, the manager will forbid another transaction from gaining access to $I$, provided the type of access (read or write) could cause a conflict, such as the duplicate selling of an airline seat.[1]

---

[1] Reading and writing are the most common types of access, but we shall see in Section 9.5 that other kinds of access can be controlled by other "lock modes." as well.

Choosing large granularity cuts down on the system overhead needed to maintain locks, since we need less space to store the locks, and we save time because fewer actions regarding locks need to be taken. However, small granularity allows many transactions to operate in parallel, since transactions are then less likely to want locks on the same items.

At the risk of oversimplifying the conclusions of a number of analyses mentioned in the bibliographic notes, let us suggest that the proper choice for the size of an item is such that the average transaction accesses a few items. Thus, if the typical transaction (in a relational system) reads or modifies one tuple, which it finds via an index, it would be appropriate to treat tuples as items. If the typical transaction takes a join of two or more relations, and thereby requires access to all the tuples of these relations, then we would be better off treating whole relations as items.

In what follows, we shall assume that when part of an item is modified, the whole item is modified and receives a value that is unique and unequal to the value that could be obtained by any other modification. We make this assumption not only to simplify the modeling of transactions. In practice, it requires too much work on the part of the system to deduce facts such as: the result of one modification of an item gives that item the same value as it had after some previous modification. Furthermore, if the system is to remember whether part of an item remains unchanged after the item is modified, it may as well divide the item into several smaller items.

## Locks

As we mentioned, a *lock* is an access privilege to a single item, which the lock manager can grant or withhold from a transaction. While our initial model of transactions will have only a single kind of lock, we shall subsequently meet more complex models where there are several kinds of locks. For example, it is normal to use "read-locks," that only allow a transaction to read an item, but not to write a new value, and "write-locks," where both reading and writing (or just writing) is permitted.

As it is typical for only a small subset of the items to have locks on them at any one time, the lock manager can store the current locks in a *lock table*, which consists of records

   (<item>, <lock type>, <transaction>)

The meaning of record $(I, L, T)$ is that transaction $T$ has a lock of type $L$ on item $I$. As we shall see in Section 9.4, it is possible for several transactions to hold locks of certain types on the same item simultaneously. However, the item can almost serve as a key for lock records. Thus, we could, for example, use a hash table with the item field as "key" to store these records. Since the operations the lock manager does on the lock table is to find locks on a given item, insert lock records, and delete lock records, this or a similar data structure will allow efficient management of locks.

## How Locks Control Concurrency

To see the need for using locks (or a similar mechanism) when transactions execute in parallel, consider the following example.

**Example 9.1:** Let us consider two transactions $T_1$ and $T_2$. Each accesses an item $A$, which we assume has an integer value, and adds one to $A$. The two transactions are executions of the program $P$ defined by:

$$P: \quad \texttt{READ A; A:=A+1; WRITE A;}$$

The value of $A$ exists in the database. $P$ reads $A$ into its workspace, adds one to the value in the workspace, and writes the result into the database. In Figure 9.1 we see the two transactions executing in an interleaved fashion,[2] and we record the value of $A$ as it appears in the database at each step.

| $A$ in database | 5 | 5 | 5 | 5 | 6 | 6 |
|---|---|---|---|---|---|---|
| $T_1$: | READ A | | A:=A+1 | | | WRITE A |
| $T_2$: | | READ A | | A:=A+1 | WRITE A | |
| $A$ in $T_1$'s workspace | 5 | 5 | 6 | 6 | 6 | 6 |
| $A$ in $T_2$'s workspace | | 5 | 5 | 6 | 6 | |

**Figure 9.1** Transactions exhibiting a need to lock item $A$.

We notice that although two transactions have each added 1 to $A$, the value of $A$ has only increased by 1. This problem is serious if $A$ represents seats sold on an airplane flight, for example. □

The most common solution to the problem represented by Example 9.1 is to provide a lock on $A$. Before reading $A$, a transaction $T$ must lock $A$, which prevents another transaction from accessing $A$ until $T$ is finished with $A$. Furthermore, the need for $T$ to set a lock on $A$ prevents $T$ from accessing $A$ if some other transaction is already using $A$. $T$ must wait until the other transaction unlocks $A$, which it should do only after finishing with $A$.

---

[2] We do not assume that two similar steps necessarily take the same time, so it is possible that $T_2$ finishes before $T_1$, even though both transactions execute the same steps. However, the point of the example is not lost if $T_1$ writes before $T_2$.

Let us now consider programs that interact with the database not only by reading and writing items but by locking and unlocking them. We assume that a lock must be placed on an item before reading or writing it, and that the operation of locking acts as a synchronization primitive. That is, if a transaction tries to lock an already locked item, the transaction may not proceed until the lock is released by an unlock command, which is executed by the transaction holding the lock. We assume that each transaction will unlock any item it locks, eventually.[3] A schedule of the elementary steps of two or more transactions, such that the above rules regarding locks are obeyed, is termed *legal*.

**Example 9.2:** The program $P$ of Example 9.1 could be written with locks as

$P$:   LOCK A; READ A; A:=A+1; WRITE A; UNLOCK A;

Suppose again that $T_1$ and $T_2$ are two executions of $P$. If $T_1$ begins first, it requests a lock on $A$. Assuming no other transaction has locked $A$, the lock manager grants this lock. Now $T_1$, and only $T_1$ can access $A$. If $T_2$ begins before $T_1$ finishes, then when $T_2$ tries to execute LOCK A, the system causes $T_2$ to wait. Only when $T_1$ executes UNLOCK A will the system allow $T_2$ to proceed. As a result, the anomaly indicated in Example 9.1 cannot occur; either $T_1$ or $T_2$ executes completely before the other starts, and their combined effect is to add 2 to $A$. $\square$

## Livelock

The system that grants and enforces locks on items cannot behave capriciously, or certain undesirable phenomena occur. As an instance, we assumed in Example 9.2 that when $T_1$ released its lock on $A$, the lock was granted to $T_2$. What if while $T_2$ was waiting, a transaction $T_3$ also requested a lock on $A$, and $T_3$ was granted the lock before $T_2$? Then while $T_3$ had the lock on $A$, $T_4$ requested a lock on $A$, which was granted after $T_3$ unlocked $A$, and so on. Evidently, it is possible that $T_2$ could wait forever, while some other transaction always had a lock on $A$, even though there are an unlimited number of times at which $T_2$ might have been given a chance to lock $A$.

Such a condition is called *livelock*. It is a problem that occurs potentially in any environment where processes execute concurrently. A variety of solutions have been proposed by designers of operating systems, and we shall not discuss the subject here, as it does not pertain solely to database systems. A simple way to avoid livelock is for the system granting locks to record all requests that are not granted immediately, and when an item $A$ is unlocked, grant a lock on $A$ to the transaction that requested it first, among all those waiting to lock $A$.

---

[3] Strictly speaking, since some transactions will abort before completing, the system itself must take responsibility for releasing locks held by aborted transactions.

This first-come-first-served strategy eliminates livelocks,[4] and we shall assume from here on that livelock is not a problem.

## Deadlock

There is a more serious problem of concurrent processing that can occur if we are not careful. This problem, called "deadlock," can best be illustrated by an example.

**Example 9.3:** Suppose we have two transactions $T_1$ and $T_2$ whose significant actions, as far as concurrent processing is concerned are:

$$T_1: \quad \text{LOCK A; LOCK B; UNLOCK A; UNLOCK B;}$$
$$T_2: \quad \text{LOCK B; LOCK A; UNLOCK B; UNLOCK A;}$$

Presumably $T_1$ and $T_2$ do something with $A$ and $B$, but what they do is not important here. Suppose $T_1$ and $T_2$ begin execution at about the same time. $T_1$ requests and is granted a lock on $A$, and $T_2$ requests and is granted a lock on $B$. Then $T_1$ requests a lock on $B$, and is forced to wait because $T_2$ has a lock on that item. Similarly, $T_2$ requests a lock on $A$ and must wait for $T_1$ to unlock $A$. Thus neither transaction can proceed; each is waiting for the other to unlock a needed item, so both $T_1$ and $T_2$ wait forever. $\square$

A situation in which each member of a set $S$ of two or more transactions is waiting to lock an item currently locked by some other transaction in the set $S$ is called a *deadlock*. Since each transaction in $S$ is waiting, it cannot unlock the item some other transaction in $S$ needs to proceed, so all wait forever. Like livelock, the prevention of deadlock is a subject much studied in the literature of operating systems and concurrent processing in general. Among the solutions to deadlock are:

1. Require each transaction to request all its locks at once, and let the lock manager grant them all, if possible, or grant none and make the process wait, if one or more are held by another transaction. Notice how this rule would have prevented the deadlock in Example 9.3. The system would grant locks on both $A$ and $B$ to $T_1$ if that transaction requested first; $T_1$ would complete, and then $T_2$ could have both locks.

2. Assign an arbitrary linear ordering to the items, and require all transactions to request locks in this order.

Clearly, the first approach prevents deadlock. The second approach does also, although the reason why may not be obvious. In Example 9.3, suppose $A$ precedes $B$ in the ordering (there could be other items between $A$ and $B$ in the ordering). Then $T_2$ would request a lock on $A$ before $B$ and would find $A$ already locked by $T_1$. $T_2$ would not yet get to lock $B$, so a lock on $B$ would be

---

[4] Although it may cause "deadlock," to be discussed next.

available to $T_1$ when requested. $T_1$ would complete, whereupon the locks on $A$ and $B$ would be released. $T_2$ could then proceed.

To see that no deadlocks can occur in general, suppose we have a set $S$ of deadlocked transactions, and each transaction $R_i$ in $S$ is waiting for some other transaction in $S$ to unlock an item $A_i$. We may assume that each $R_j$ in $S$ holds at least one of the $A_i$'s, else we could remove $R_j$ from $S$ and still have a deadlocked set. Let $A_k$ be the first item among the $A_i$'s in the assumed linear order. Then $R_k$, waiting for $A_k$, cannot hold any of the $A_i$'s, which is a contradiction.

Another approach to handling deadlocks is to do nothing to prevent them. Rather, periodically examine the lock requests and see if there is a deadlock. Draw a *waits-for graph*, whose nodes are transactions and whose arcs $T_1 \rightarrow T_2$ signify that transaction $T_1$ is waiting to lock an item on which $T_2$ holds the lock. Then every cycle indicates a deadlock, and if there are no cycles, neither are there any deadlocks. If a deadlock is discovered, at least one of the deadlocked transactions must be restarted, and its effects on the database must be canceled. This process of abort-and-restart can be complicated if we are not careful about the way transactions write into the database before they complete. The subject is taken up in Section 9.8, and until then we shall assume that neither livelocks nor deadlocks will occur when executing transactions.

## Serializability of Schedules

Now we come to a concurrency issue of concern primarily to database system designers, rather than designers of general concurrent systems. By way of introduction, let us review Example 9.1, where two transactions executing a program $P$ each added 1 to $A$, yet $A$ only increased by 1. Intuitively, we feel this situation is wrong, yet is it not possible that these transactions did exactly what the writer of $P$ wanted? We argue not, because if we run first $T_1$ and then $T_2$, we get a different result; 2 is added to $A$. Since it is always possible that transactions will execute one at a time (serially), it is reasonable to assume that the normal, or intended, result of a transaction is the result we obtain when we execute it with no other transactions executing concurrently. Thus, we shall assume from here on that the concurrent execution of several transactions is correct if and only if its effect is the same as that obtained by running the same transactions serially in some order.

Let us define a *schedule* for a set of transactions to be an order in which the elementary steps of the transactions (lock, read, and so on) are done. The steps of any given transaction must, naturally, appear in the schedule in the same order that they occur in the program of which the transaction is an execution. A schedule is *serial* if all the steps of each transaction occur consecutively. A schedule is *serializable* if its effect is equivalent to that of some serial schedule; we shall make the notion of "equivalent" more precise in the next section.

**Example 9.4:** Let us consider the following two transactions, which might be part of a bookkeeping operation that transfers funds from one account to another.

$T_1$:   READ A; A:=A-10; WRITE A; READ B; B:=B+10; WRITE B;
$T_2$:   READ B; B:=B-20; WRITE B; READ C; C:=C+20; WRITE C;

Clearly, any serial schedule has the property that the sum $A+B+C$ is preserved. In Figure 9.2(a) we see a serial schedule, and in Figure 9.2(b) is a serializable, but not serial, schedule. Figure 9.2(c) shows a nonserializable schedule. Note that Figure 9.2(c) causes 10 to be added, rather than subtracted from $B$ as a net effect, since $T_1$ reads $B$ before $T_2$ writes the new value of $B$. It is possible to prevent the schedule of Figure 9.2(c) from occurring by having all transactions lock $B$ before reading it. □

| $T_1$ | $T_2$ | $T_1$ | $T_2$ | $T_1$ | $T_2$ |
|-------|-------|-------|-------|-------|-------|
| READ A |       | READ A |       | READ A |       |
| A:=A-10 |     |        | READ B | A:=A-10 |      |
| WRITE A |     | A:=A-10 |      |        | READ B |
| READ B |      |        | B:=B-20 | WRITE A |      |
| B:=B+10 |     | WRITE A |      |        | B:=B-20 |
| WRITE B |     |        | WRITE B | READ B |      |
|        | READ B | READ B |      |        | WRITE B |
|        | B:=B-20 |       | READ C | B:=B+10 |     |
|        | WRITE B | B:=B+10 |      |        | READ C |
|        | READ C |        | C:=C+20 | WRITE B |     |
|        | C:=C+20 | WRITE B |      |        | C:=C+20 |
|        | WRITE C |        | WRITE C |        | WRITE C |
| (a) |  | (b) |  | (c) |  |

**Figure 9.2** Some schedules.

Recall that we have defined a schedule to be serializable if its effect is equivalent to that of a serial schedule. In general, it is not possible to test whether two schedules have the same effect for all initial values of the items, if arbitrary operations on the items are allowed, and there are an infinity of possible initial values. In practice, we make some simplifying assumptions about what operations do to items. In particular, it is convenient to assume that values cannot be the same unless they are produced by exactly the same sequence of operations. Thus, we do not regard $(A+10)-20$ and $(A+20)-30$ as producing the same values.

Ignoring algebraic properties of arithmetic causes us to make only "nonfa-

tal" errors, in the sense that we may call a schedule nonserializable, when in
fact it produces the same result as a serial schedule, but we shall never say a
schedule is serializable when in fact it is not (a "fatal" error). Nonfatal errors
may rule out some concurrent operations, and thereby cause the system to run
more slowly than it theoretically could. However, these errors never cause an
incorrect result to be computed, as a fatal error might. Succeeding sections will
use progressively more detailed models that enable us to infer that wider classes
of schedules are serializable, and therefore, to achieve more concurrency while
guaranteeing correctness. We can thus approach, though never reach, the condition where every schedule of every collection of transactions is allowed if its
effect happens to be equivalent to some serial schedule and forbidden otherwise.

## Schedulers

We have seen that arbitrary transactions can, when executed concurrently, give
rise to livelock, deadlock, and nonserializable behavior. To eliminate these
problems we have two tools, schedulers and protocols. The *scheduler* is a portion
of the database system that arbitrates between conflicting requests. We saw,
for example, how a first-come, first-serve scheduler can eliminate livelock. A
scheduler can also handle deadlocks and nonserializability by

1.  Forcing a given transaction to wait, for example, until a lock it wants is
    available, or

2.  Telling the transaction to abort and restart.

It might appear that (2) is never desirable, since we lose the cycles that were
spent running the transaction so far. However, forcing many transactions to
wait for long periods may cause too many locks to become unavailable, as waiting transactions might already have some locks. That in turn makes deadlock
more likely, and may cause many transactions to delay so long that the effect
becomes noticeable, say to the user standing at an automatic teller machine.
Also, in situations where we already have a deadlock, we often have no choice
but to abort at least one of the transactions involved in the deadlock.

## Protocols

Another tool for handling deadlock and nonserializability is to use one or more
protocols, which all transactions must follow. A *protocol*, in its most general
sense, is simply a restriction on the sequences of atomic steps that a transaction
may perform. For example, the deadlock-avoiding strategy of requesting locks
on items in some fixed order is a protocol. We shall see in Section 9.3 the
importance of the "two-phase locking" protocol, which requires that all needed
locks be obtained by a transaction before it releases any of its locks.

The importance of using a nontrivial protocol (i.e., a protocol more restrictive than "any sequence is OK") will be seen throughout this chapter. We shall

see how schedulers that can assume all transactions obey a particular protocol can be made much simpler than those that cannot make such an assumption. For example, there are variants of the two-phase locking protocol that allow a scheduler to guarantee no deadlocks in a simple manner. The overall relationship of the lock manager, scheduler, and protocol is suggested in Figure 9.3

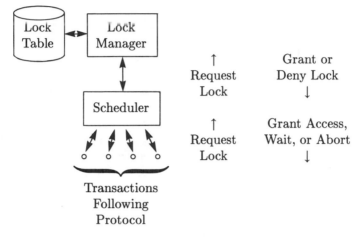

**Figure 9.3** Protocol, scheduler, and lock manager.

## 9.2 A SIMPLE TRANSACTION MODEL

Let us begin by introducing the simplest model of transactions in which we can talk about locking and serializability. In this model, a transaction is viewed as a sequence of lock and unlock statements. Each item locked must subsequently be unlocked. Between a step LOCK A and the next UNLOCK A, a transaction is said to *hold a lock on A*. We assume a transaction does not try to lock an item if it currently holds a lock on that item, nor does it try to unlock an item on which it does not currently hold a lock.

Further, we assume that whenever a transaction locks an item A it reads and writes A. That is, each LOCK step implies reading of the value locked, and each UNLOCK implies writing. We shall see that serializability under this simple lock model implies serializability under more complex lock models. The converse is not true, however; more detailed models allow us to do certain steps concurrently that the simple model implies must be done sequentially.

### Transaction Semantics

In principle, the "meaning" of a transaction is whatever the code that the transaction executes does to the database. In order to understand the design of protocols and schedulers, we need to relate this informal semantics to a reliable computational test that tells whether a given sequence of steps of interleaved transactions is serializable. In a sense, we face the same problem now that we faced in Chapter 3, when we had to relate the informal semantics of datalog programs to a concrete computation in relational algebra.

For the case at hand, we shall define an abstract semantics of transactions. We shall indicate after an example, why this semantics is appropriate, in the sense that when it differs from reality, it does so in a "nonfatal" manner, by prohibiting certain schedules that are in fact serializable, rather than by permitting schedules that are not serializable. Then, we relate the semantics of transactions to a computation, involving graphs, that lets us decide whether a schedule is serializable according to our semantics. In the next section, we discuss a protocol, called "two-phase locking." Transactions obeying this protocol can be scheduled in a serializable manner by a simple scheduler that only checks legality; i.e., it does not allow two transactions to hold locks on the same item at the same time, but permits transactions to proceed otherwise.

Formally, we associate with each pair LOCK A and its following UNLOCK A, a distinct function $f$. This function takes as arguments the values of all items that are locked by the transaction prior to the unlocking of $A$. Note that one transaction may have more than one such function for a given $A$, since, although it is not generally a good idea, we may lock and unlock the same item more than once. Let $A_0$ be the initial value of $A$ before any transactions are executed.

*Values* that $A$ may assume during the execution of the transaction are formulas built by applying these functions to the initial values of the items. Two different formulas are assumed to be different values; this assumption is a formal equivalent to our informal statement in the previous section that we would assume no algebraic laws when determining the effect of transactions on items. Two schedules are *equivalent* if the formulas for the final value of each item are the same in both schedules.

| | | |
|---|---|---|
| LOCK A | LOCK B | LOCK A |
| LOCK B | LOCK C | LOCK C |
| UNLOCK A  $f_1(A,B)$ | UNLOCK B  $f_3(B,C)$ | UNLOCK C  $f_6(A,C)$ |
| UNLOCK B  $f_2(A,B)$ | LOCK A | UNLOCK A  $f_7(A,C)$ |
| | UNLOCK C  $f_4(A,B,C)$ | |
| | UNLOCK A  $f_5(A,B,C)$ | |
| $T_1$ | $T_2$ | $T_3$ |

**Figure 9.4** Three transactions.

**Example 9.5:** In Figure 9.4 we see three transactions and the functions associated with each LOCK—UNLOCK pair; the function appears on the same line as the UNLOCK. For example, $f_1$, associated with $A$ in $T_1$, takes $A$ and $B$ as arguments, because these are the items that $T_1$ reads. Function $f_3$ takes only $B$ and $C$ as arguments, because $T_2$ unlocks $B$, and therefore writes its value, before it locks and reads $A$.

Figure 9.5 shows a possible schedule of these transactions and the resulting effect on items $A$, $B$, and $C$. We can observe that this schedule is not serializable. In proof, suppose it were. If $T_1$ precedes $T_2$ in the serial schedule, then the final value of $B$ would be

$$f_3\big(f_2(A_0, B_0), C_0\big)$$

rather than

$$f_2\big(A_0, f_3(B_0, C_0)\big)$$

If $T_2$ precedes $T_1$, then the final value of $A$ would apply $f_1$ to a subexpression involving $f_5$. Since the actual final value of $A$ in Figure 9.5 does not apply $f_1$ to an expression involving $f_5$, we see that $T_2$ cannot precede $T_1$ in an equivalent serial schedule. Since $T_2$ can neither precede nor follow $T_1$ in an equivalent serial schedule, such a serial schedule does not exist. $\square$

### Fatal and Nonfatal Errors

Note how our assumption that functions produce unique values is essential in the argument used in Example 9.5. For example, if it were possible that

$$f_3\big(f_2(A_0, B_0), C_0\big) = f_2\big(A_0, f_3(B_0, C_0)\big) \tag{9.1}$$

then we could not rule out the possibility that $T_1$ precedes $T_2$. Let us reiterate that our assumption of unique values is not just for mathematical convenience. The work required to enable the database system to examine transactions and detect possibilities such as (9.1), thereby permitting a wider class of schedules to be regarded as serializable, is not worth the effort in general.

An assumption such as the unavailability of algebraic laws is a discrepancy in the nonfatal direction, since it can rule out opportunities for concurrency but cannot lead to a fatal error, where transactions are allowed to execute in parallel even though their effect is not equivalent to any serial schedule. Similarly, our assumption that locks imply both reading and writing of an item is a nonfatal departure from reality. The reader should observe that schedules which are equivalent under our assumption about locks will still be equivalent if, say, a transaction locks an item but does not write a new value. We shall consider in the next sections how relaxing our assumption regarding what happens when locks are taken allows more schedules to be considered serializable, but still only calls schedules serializable if in fact they are.

| | Step | $A$ | $B$ | $C$ |
|---|---|---|---|---|
| (1) | $T_1$: LOCK A | $A_0$ | $B_0$ | $C_0$ |
| (2) | $T_2$: LOCK B | $A_0$ | $B_0$ | $C_0$ |
| (3) | $T_2$: LOCK C | $A_0$ | $B_0$ | $C_0$ |
| (4) | $T_2$: UNLOCK B | $A_0$ | $f_3(B_0, C_0)$ | $C_0$ |
| (5) | $T_1$: LOCK B | $A_0$ | $f_3(B_0, C_0)$ | $C_0$ |
| (6) | $T_1$: UNLOCK A | $f_1(A_0, f_3(B_0, C_0))$ | $f_3(B_0, C_0)$ | $C_0$ |
| (7) | $T_2$: LOCK A | $f_1(A_0, f_3(B_0, C_0))$ | $f_3(B_0, C_0)$ | $C_0$ |
| (8) | $T_2$: UNLOCK C | $f_1(A_0, f_3(B_0, C_0))$ | $f_3(B_0, C_0)$ | $(i)$ |
| (9) | $T_2$: UNLOCK A | $(ii)$ | $f_3(B_0, C_0)$ | $(i)$ |
| (10) | $T_3$: LOCK A | $(ii)$ | $f_3(B_0, C_0)$ | $(i)$ |
| (11) | $T_3$: LOCK C | $(ii)$ | $f_3(B_0, C_0)$ | $(i)$ |
| (12) | $T_1$: UNLOCK B | $(ii)$ | $f_2(A_0, f_3(B_0, C_0))$ | $(i)$ |
| (13) | $T_3$: UNLOCK C | $(ii)$ | $f_2(A_0, f_3(B_0, C_0))$ | $(iii)$ |
| (14) | $T_3$: UNLOCK A | $(iv)$ | $f_2(A_0, f_3(B_0, C_0))$ | $(iii)$ |

Key:

$$(i): \ f_4\Big(f_1\big(A_0, f_3(B_0, C_0)\big), B_0, C_0\Big) \qquad (iii): \ f_6\big((ii), \ (i)\big)$$

$$(ii): \ f_5\Big(f_1\big(A_0, f_3(B_0, C_0)\big), B_0, C_0\Big) \qquad (iv): \ f_7\big((ii), \ (i)\big)$$

**Figure 9.5** A schedule.

An example of a fatal assumption would be to suppose that all transactions wrote values of items that did not depend on the values they read. While some transactions do behave this way, others do not, and scheduling all transactions on this assumption might permit activities to occur in parallel that led to nonserializable behavior.

## A Serializability Test

In order to determine that a given scheduler is correct, we must prove that every schedule it allows is serializable. Thus, we need a simple test for serializability of a schedule.

If we consider Example 9.5 and the argument that the schedule of Figure 9.5 is not serializable, we see the key to a serializability test. We examine a schedule with regard to the order in which the various transactions lock a given item. This order must be consistent with the hypothetical equivalent serial schedule of the transactions. If the sequences induced by two different items force two transactions to appear in different order, then we have a paradox, since both orders cannot be consistent with one serial schedule. We can express this test as a problem of finding cycles in a directed graph. The method is described formally in the next algorithm.

**Algorithm 9.1:** Testing Serializability of a Schedule.

INPUT: A schedule $S$ for a set of transactions $T_1, \ldots, T_k$.

OUTPUT: A determination whether $S$ is serializable. If so, a serial schedule equivalent to $S$ is produced.

METHOD: Create a directed graph $G$ (called a *serialization* graph), whose nodes correspond to the transactions. To determine the arcs of the graph $G$, let $S$ be

$$a_1; \ a_2; \ \cdots \ ; a_n$$

where each $a_i$ is an action of the form

$T_j$: LOCK $A_m$ or $T_j$: UNLOCK $A_m$

$T_j$ indicates the transaction to which the step belongs. If $a_i$ is

$T_j$: UNLOCK $A_m$

look for the next action $a_p$ following $a_i$ that is of the form $T_s$: LOCK $A_m$. If there is one, and $s \neq j$, then draw an arc from $T_j$ to $T_s$. The intuitive meaning of this arc is that in any serial schedule equivalent to $S$, $T_j$ must precede $T_s$.

If $G$ has a cycle, then $S$ is not serializable. If $G$ has no cycles, then find a linear order for the transactions such that $T_i$ precedes $T_j$ whenever there is an arc $T_i \to T_j$. This ordering can always be done by the process known as *topological sorting,* defined as follows. There must be some node $T_i$ with no entering arcs, else we can prove that $G$ has a cycle. List $T_i$ and remove $T_i$ from $G$. Then repeat the process on the remaining graph until no nodes remain. The order in which the nodes are listed is a serial order for the transactions. □

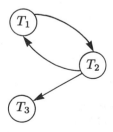

**Figure 9.6** Graph of precedences among transactions.

**Example 9.6:** Consider the schedule of Figure 9.5. The graph $G$, shown in Figure 9.6 has nodes for $T_1$, $T_2$, and $T_3$. To find the arcs, we look at each UNLOCK step in Figure 9.5. For example step (4),

> $T_2$: UNLOCK B

is followed by $T_1$: LOCK B. In this case, the lock occurs at the next step. We therefore draw an arc $T_2 \rightarrow T_1$. As another example, the action at step (8),

> $T_2$: UNLOCK C

is followed at step (11) by $T_3$: LOCK C, and no intervening step locks $C$. Therefore we draw an arc from $T_2$ to $T_3$. Steps (6) and (7) cause us to place an arc $T_1 \rightarrow T_2$. As there is a cycle, the schedule of Figure 9.5 is not serializable. $\square$

```
                                    LOCK A
                                    UNLOCK A
                                                     LOCK A
           time                                      UNLOCK A
            ↓        LOCK B
                     UNLOCK B
                                    LOCK B
                                    UNLOCK B

                 T₁                 T₂               T₃
```

**Figure 9.7** A serializable schedule.

**Example 9.7:** In Figure 9.7 we see a schedule for three transactions, and Figure 9.8 shows its serialization graph. As there are no cycles, the schedule of Figure 9.7 is serializable, and Algorithm 9.1 tells us that the serial order is $T_1$, $T_2$, $T_3$. It is interesting to note that in the serial order, $T_1$ precedes $T_3$, even though in Figure 9.7, $T_1$ did not commence until $T_3$ had finished. $\square$

**Theorem 9.1:** Algorithm 9.1 correctly determines if a schedule is serializable.

**Proof:** Suppose $G$ has a cycle

$$T_{j_1} \rightarrow T_{j_2} \rightarrow \cdots \rightarrow T_{j_t} \rightarrow T_{j_1}$$

Let there be a serial schedule $R$ equivalent to $S$, and suppose that in $R$, $T_{j_p}$ appears first among the transactions in the cycle. Let the arc $T_{j_{p-1}} \rightarrow T_{j_p}$ (take $j_{p-1}$ to be $j_t$ if $p = 1$) be in $G$ because of item $A$. Then in $R$, since $T_{j_p}$ appears before $T_{j_{p-1}}$, the final formula for $A$ applies a function $f$ associated with some LOCK A—UNLOCK A pair in $T_{j_p}$ before applying some function $g$ associated with a LOCK A—UNLOCK A pair in $T_{j_{p-1}}$. In $S$, however, the effect of $T_{j_{p-1}}$ on $A$

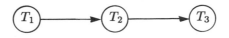

**Figure 9.8** Serialization graph for Figure 9.7.

precedes the effect of $T_{j_p}$ on $A$, since there is an arc $T_{j_{p-1}} \to T_{j_p}$, representing the fact that $T_{j_p}$ uses the value of $A$ produced by $T_{j_{p-1}}$. Therefore, in schedule $S$, $g$ is applied to an expression involving $f$, in the formula for $A$. Thus the final value of $A$ differs in $R$ and $S$, since the two formulas for $A$ are not the same. We conclude that $R$ and $S$ are not equivalent. As $R$ is an arbitrary serial schedule, it follows that $S$ is equivalent to no serial schedule.

Conversely, suppose the serialization graph $G$ has no cycles. Define the *depth* of a transaction in an acyclic serialization graph to be the length of the longest path to the node corresponding to that transaction. For example, in Figure 9.8, $T_1$ has depth 0 and $T_3$ has depth 2. Note that a transaction of depth $d$ can only read values written by transactions of length less than $d$.

We can show by induction on $d$ that a transaction $T$ of depth $d$ reads the same value for each item it locks, both in the given schedule $S$ (from which the serialization graph was constructed) and in the serial schedule $R$ constructed by Algorithm 9.1. The reason is that if transaction $T$ reads a value of item $A$, then in both schedules, the same transaction $T'$ was the last to write $A$ (or in both schedules $T$ is the first to read $A$).

Suppose in contradiction that in $S$, transaction $T$ reads the value of $A$ written by $T'$, but in $R$, it is the value written by $T''$ that $T$ reads. Let

$$T_{i_1}, T_{i_2}, \ldots, T_{i_r}$$

be the sequence of transactions, in order, that lock $A$ in schedule $S$. Then in $G$ there are arcs

$$T_{i_1} \to T_{i_2} \to \cdots \to T_{i_r}$$

In this sequence, $T'$ immediately precedes $T$. Then in the topological sort of $G$, it is not possible that $T''$, which also locks $A$ and therefore appears in the sequence, appears between $T'$ and $T$.

Now, we have established that $T$ reads the value of $A$ written by $T'$ in both schedules $R$ and $S$. We also know that the depth of $T'$ must be less than the depth of $T$, because there is an arc $T' \to T$. By the inductive hypothesis, the value written into $A$ by $T'$ is the same in both schedules. Since this argument applies to any item locked by $T$, we see that $T$ reads the same value for each item it locks. Thus, in both $R$ and $S$, the values written by transaction $T$ for each of the items it locked are the same, proving the induction. $\square$

**Example 9.8:** Let us consider an example of the reasoning behind the second part of the proof of Theorem 9.1. Suppose a transaction $T$ locks items $A$ and $B$, and in a particular schedule $S$, item $A$ is locked, in turn, by $T_1$, $T_2$, and then $T$, while item $B$ is locked by $T_3$, $T_1$, $T_4$, and $T$ in that order (other transactions may lock $A$ or $B$ after $T$ does). Figure 9.9 suggests how the values of $A$ and $B$ are changed, in both $S$ and its equivalent serial schedule $R$.

$$A_0 \rightarrow \rightarrow \rightarrow T_1 \rightarrow T_2 \rightarrow \rightarrow T$$
$$B_0 \rightarrow T_3 \rightarrow T_1 \rightarrow \rightarrow T_4 \rightarrow T$$

**Figure 9.9** Transactions changing values of $A$ and $B$.

Because of the arcs in $G$, we can be sure that in $R$, $T_2$ precedes $T$, and no transaction locking $A$ can come between $T_2$ and $T$. Likewise, reasoning about $B$, we see that $T_4$ precedes $T$ and no transaction locking $B$ comes between them in $R$. The value written by $T$ for $A$ depends only on the values read for $A$ and $B$, and we know that these values were those written by $T_2$ and $T_4$, respectively, in both $R$ and $S$. $\square$

## 9.3 THE TWO-PHASE LOCKING PROTOCOL

The reason we need to understand the conditions under which a schedule is serializable is so that we can select a combination of a scheduler and a protocol that together guarantee any schedule they allow is serializable. In this section we shall introduce what is by far the simplest and most popular approach; Sections 9.7 and 9.11 discuss other techniques that have been used.

This protocol, called the *two-phase protocol*, requires that in any transaction, all locks precede all unlocks. Transactions obeying this protocol are said to be *two-phase*; the first phase is the locking phase, and the second is the unlocking phase. For example, in both Figure 9.4 and Figure 9.7, $T_1$ and $T_3$ are two-phase, while $T_2$ is not.

The two-phase protocol has the property that any collection of transactions obeying the protocol cannot have a legal, nonserializable schedule. That is, the associated scheduler simply grants any lock request if the lock is available, and makes the transaction wait or abort if the lock is unavailable. Moreover, the two-phase protocol is, in a sense to be discussed subsequently, the best general protocol. We first show that the two-phase protocol guarantees serializability.

**Theorem 9.2:** If $S$ is any schedule of two-phase transactions, then $S$ is serializable.

**Proof:** Suppose not. Then by Theorem 9.1, the serialization graph $G$ for $S$ has a cycle,

$$T_{i_1} \to T_{i_2} \to \cdots \to T_{i_p} \to T_{i_1}$$

Then some lock by $T_{i_2}$ follows an unlock by $T_{i_1}$; some lock by $T_{i_3}$ follows an unlock by $T_{i_2}$, and so on. Finally, some lock by $T_{i_1}$ follows an unlock by $T_{i_p}$. Therefore, a lock by $T_{i_1}$ follows an unlock by $T_{i_1}$, contradicting the assumption that $T_{i_1}$ is two-phase. □

Another way to see why two-phase transactions must be serializable is to imagine that a two-phase transaction occurs instantaneously at the moment it obtains the last of its locks (called the *lock point*). Then if we order transactions according to the time at which they reach this stage in their lives, the order must be a serial schedule equivalent to the given schedule. For if in the given schedule, transaction $T_1$ locks some item $A$ before $T_2$ locks $A$, then $T_1$ must unlock $A$ before $T_2$ locks $A$. If $T_1$ is two-phase, then surely $T_1$ obtains the last of its locks before $T_2$ obtains the last of its locks, so $T_1$ precedes $T_2$ in the serial order according to lock points. Thus, the order of transactions we constructed will conform to all the arcs of the serialization graph, and thus, by Theorem 9.1, be an equivalent serial schedule.

## Optimality of Two-Phase Locking

We mentioned that the two-phase protocol in is a sense the most liberal possible protocol. Precisely, what we can show is that if $T_1$ is any transaction that is not two-phase, then there is some other transaction $T_2$ with which $T_1$ could be run in a legal, nonserializable schedule. Suppose $T_1$ is not two-phase. Then there is some step UNLOCK A of $T_1$ that precedes a step LOCK B. Let $T_2$ be:

$T_2$:   LOCK A; LOCK B; UNLOCK A; UNLOCK B

Then the schedule of Figure 9.10 is easily seen to be legal but nonserializable, since the treatment of $A$ requires that $T_1$ precede $T_2$, while the treatment of $B$ requires the opposite.

Note that there are particular collections of transactions, not all two-phase, that yield only serial schedules. We shall consider an important example of such a collection in Section 9.7. However, since it is normal not to know the set of all transactions that could ever be executed concurrently with a given transaction, we are usually forced to require all transactions to be two-phase. Similarly, we could use a more complex scheduler that did not always grant a lock when it was available, and such a scheduler could deal with non-two-phase transactions. This prospect, too, is not attractive in most situations.

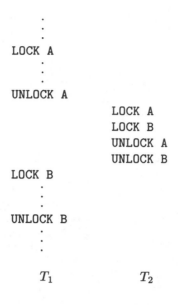

Figure 9.10  A nonserializable schedule.

## 9.4 A MODEL WITH READ- AND WRITE-LOCKS

In Section 9.2 we assumed that every time a transaction locked an item it changed that item. In practice, many times a transaction needs only to obtain the value of the item and is guaranteed not to change that value. If we distinguish between a read-only access and a read-write access, we can develop a more detailed model of transactions that will allow some concurrency forbidden in the model of Section 9.2.[5] Let us distinguish two kinds of locks.

1.  *Read-locks* (or *shared locks*). A transaction $T$ wishing only to read an item $A$ executes RLOCK A, which prevents any other transaction from writing a new value of $A$ while $T$ has locked $A$. However, any number of transactions can hold a read-lock on $A$ at the same time.

2.  *Write-locks* (or *exclusive locks*). These are locks in the sense of Section 9.2. A transaction wishing to change the value of item $A$ first obtains a write-lock by executing WLOCK A. When some transaction holds a write-lock on an item, no other transaction can obtain either a read- or write-lock on the item.

Both read- and write-locks are removed by an UNLOCK statement. As in

---

[5] Note that we still do not have write-only locks. The ability of transactions to write an item without reading it first will be seen in Section 9.6 to complicate greatly the question of serializability.

Section 9.2, we assume no transaction tries to unlock an item on which it does not hold a read- or write-lock, and no transaction tries to read-lock an item on which it already holds any lock. Further, a transaction does not attempt to write-lock an item if it already holds a write-lock on that item, but under some circumstances, it may request a write-lock for an item on which it holds a read-lock. The latter makes sense because a write-lock is more restrictive on the behavior of other transactions than is a read-lock.

## Transaction Semantics

As in Section 9.2, we assume that each time a write-lock is applied to an item $A$, a unique function associated with that lock produces a new value for $A$; that function depends on all the items locked prior to the unlocking of $A$. However, we also assume here that a read-lock on $A$ does not change the value of $A$.

Also as in Section 9.2, we suppose that each item $A$ has an initial value $A_0$, and the effect of a schedule on the database can be expressed by the formulas that are the values of each of the items that were written at least once by the transactions. However, since there might be a transaction that reads items without writing any, or that reads some items only after writing for the last time, we also treat as part of the value of a schedule the values that each item has when it is read-locked by a given transaction. Thus, we may say two schedules are *equivalent* if

1.   They produce the same value for each item, and
2.   Each read-lock applied by a given transaction occurs in both schedules at times when the item locked has the same value.

## From Semantics to Serialization Graphs

Let us now consider the conditions under which we can infer, from the semantics of transactions and schedules, when one transaction must precede another in an equivalent serial schedule. Suppose we have a schedule $S$ in which a write-lock is applied to $A$ by transaction $T_1$, and let $f$ be the function associated with that write-lock. After $T_1$ unlocks $A$, let $T_2$ be one of the (perhaps many) transactions that subsequently read-lock $A$ before any other transaction write-locks $A$. Then surely $T_1$ must precede $T_2$ in any serial schedule equivalent to $S$. Otherwise, $T_2$ reads a value of $A$ that does not involve the function $f$, and no such value is identical to a value that does involve $f$. Similarly, if $T_3$ is the next transaction, after $T_1$, to write-lock $A$, then $T_1$ must precede $T_3$. The argument is essentially that of Theorem 9.1.

Now suppose $T_4$ is a transaction that read-locks $A$ before $T_1$ write-locks $A$. If $T_1$ appears before $T_4$ in a serial schedule, then $T_4$ reads a value of $A$ involving $f$, while in schedule $S$, the value read by $T_4$ does not involve $f$. Thus, $T_4$ must precede $T_1$ in a serial schedule. The only inference we cannot make is that if in $S$ two transactions read-lock the same item $A$ in a particular order, then those transactions should appear in that order in a serial schedule. Rather, the relative order of read-locks makes no difference on the values produced by concurrently executing transactions. These observations suggest that an approach similar to that of Section 9.2 will allow us to tell whether a schedule is serializable.

**Algorithm 9.2:** Serializability test for schedules with read/write-locks.

INPUT: A schedule $S$ for a set of transactions $T_1, \ldots, T_k$.

OUTPUT: A determination whether $S$ is serializable, and if so, an equivalent serial schedule.

METHOD: We construct a serialization graph $G$ as follows. The nodes correspond to the transactions as before. The arcs are determined by the following rules.

1.    Suppose in $S$, transaction $T_i$ read-locks or write-locks item $A$, $T_j$ is the next transaction to write-lock $A$, and $i \neq j$. Then place an arc from $T_i$ to $T_j$.

2.    Suppose in $S$, transaction $T_i$ write-locks $A$. Let $T_m$, $m \neq i$, be any transaction that read-locks $A$ after $T_i$ unlocks its write-lock, but before any other transaction write-locks $A$. Then draw an arc $T_i \rightarrow T_m$.

If $G$ has a cycle, then $S$ is not serializable. If $G$ is acyclic, then any topological sort of $G$ is a serial order for the transactions. $\Box$

**Example 9.9:** In Figure 9.11 we see a schedule of four transactions; Figure 9.12 is the serialization graph for this schedule. The first UNLOCK is step (3), where $T_3$ removes its write-lock from $A$. Following step (3) are read-locks of $A$ by $T_1$ and $T_2$ (steps 4 and 7) and a write-lock of $A$ by $T_4$ at step (12). Thus $T_1$, $T_2$, and $T_4$ must follow $T_3$, and we draw arcs from $T_3$ to each of the other nodes.

Notice that there is nothing wrong with both $T_1$ and $T_2$ holding read-locks on $A$ after step (7). However, $T_4$ could not write-lock $A$ until both $T_1$ and $T_2$ released their read-locks. As another example, $T_4$ releases a read-lock on $B$ at step (5), and the next write-lock on $B$ is by $T_3$, so we draw an arc from $T_4$ to $T_3$. We now have a cycle, so the schedule of Figure 9.11 is not serializable. The complete set of arcs is shown in Figure 9.11. $\Box$

**Theorem 9.3:** Algorithm 9.2 correctly determines if schedule $S$ is serializable.

**Proof:** It is straightforward to argue, whenever we draw an arc from $T_i$ to $T_j$, that in any equivalent serial schedule $T_i$ must precede $T_j$. Thus, if $G$ has a cycle, we may prove as in Theorem 9.1 that no such serial schedule exists. Conversely, suppose $G$ has no cycles. Then an argument like Theorem 9.1 shows that the final value of each item is the same in $S$ as in the serial schedule $R$ that is constructed from the topological sort of $G$. We must also show that

| | $T_1$ | $T_2$ | $T_3$ | $T_4$ |
|---|---|---|---|---|
| (1) | | | WLOCK A | |
| (2) | | | | RLOCK B |
| (3) | | | UNLOCK A | |
| (4) | RLOCK A | | | |
| (5) | | | | UNLOCK B |
| (6) | | | WLOCK B | |
| (7) | | RLOCK A | | |
| (8) | | | UNLOCK B | |
| (9) | WLOCK B | | | |
| (10) | | UNLOCK A | | |
| (11) | UNLOCK A | | | |
| (12) | | | | WLOCK A |
| (13) | UNLOCK B | | | |
| (14) | | RLOCK B | | |
| (15) | | | | UNLOCK A |
| (16) | | UNLOCK B | | |

**Figure 9.11** A schedule.

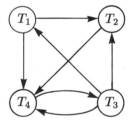

**Figure 9.12** Serialization graph of Figure 9.11.

corresponding read-locks on item $A$ obtain the same value in $R$ and $S$. But this proof is easy, since the arcs of $G$ guarantee the write-locks on $A$ that precede the given read-lock must be the same in $R$ and $S$ and that they must occur in the same order. $\square$

## The Two-Phase Protocol

As with the model in the previous section, a two-phase protocol, in which all read- and write-locks precede all unlocking steps, is sufficient to guarantee serializability. Moreover, we have the same partial converse, that any transaction in which some UNLOCK precedes a read- or write-lock can be run in a nonserializable way with some other transaction. We leave these results as exercises.

## 9.5 LOCK MODES

We saw in the previous section that locks can be issued in different "flavors," called *lock modes*, and different modes have different properties when it comes to deciding whether a lock of one mode can be granted while another transaction already has a lock of the same or another mode on the same item. In Section 9.4, the two modes were "read" and "write," and the rules regarding the granting of locks were:

1. A read-lock can be granted as long as no write-lock is held on the same item by a different transaction.
2. A write-lock can be granted only if there are no read- or write-locks held on the same item by a different transaction.

Note that these rules do not apply to the situation where a transaction is requesting a lock and also holds another lock on the same item.

### Lock Compatibility Matrices

We can summarize the rules for read- and write-locks by a *lock compatibility matrix*. The rows correspond to the mode of lock being requested, and the columns correspond to the mode of lock already held by another transaction. The entries are $Y$ (yes, the requested lock may be granted), and $N$ (no, it may not be granted). The lock compatibility matrix for read and write is shown in Figure 9.13.

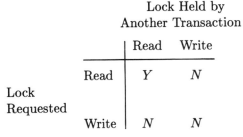

Figure 9.13 Lock compatibility matrix for read and write.

## General Sets of Lock Modes

More complex sets of lock modes can be developed and used. The principle we must follow when deciding what the entry for row $L$ and column $M$ should be is whether the operations corresponding to lock modes $L$ and $M$ commute; i.e., is the final result unaffected by the order in which the two operations are done? For example, when $L$ and $M$ are both "read," their order is unimportant, so the (Read, Read) entry in Figure 9.13 is $Y$. However, the order in which a read and a write are performed generally does affect the value read, and therefore might affect the final result.

**Example 9.10:** Suppose we allow, in addition to read- and write-locks, an *incr-lock*, which allows the holder to add or subtract atomically a constant to or from the current value of an item, without reading that item. Then the order in which two incrementations takes place does not affect the final result. However, reading and writing do not commute with incrementation. Thus, the compatibility matrix for read-, write-, and incr-locks is the one given in Figure 9.14. $\square$

|       | Read | Write | Incr |
|-------|------|-------|------|
| Read  | $Y$  | $N$   | $N$  |
| Write | $N$  | $N$   | $N$  |
| Incr  | $N$  | $N$   | $Y$  |

**Figure 9.14** Compatibility of read, write, and increment.

The serializability test of Algorithm 9.2 generalizes to arbitrary compatibility matrices. We construct a serialization graph by putting an arc $T_1 \to T_2$ whenever in the given schedule a lock of an item $A$ in mode $L$ by $T_1$ precedes a lock by $T_2$ on $A$ in mode $M$, and the entry in row $M$ and column $L$ is "$N$."[6] As before, the test for serializability is the test for absence of cycles in the graph.

---

[6] It should be noted that $T_1$ may not be the last transaction prior to $T_2$ to lock $A$ in a mode incompatible with $M$. Since some $T_3$ between them may lock $A$ in a mode that forbids the granting of $M$, but is not itself forbidden by a lock in mode $L$, we must draw arcs from both $T_1$ and $T_3$ to $T_2$. In the read/write case, we could take advantage of the simplicity of the compatibility matrix for read and write to omit the arc $T_1 \to T_2$ if $T_3$ write-locked $A$; for then we knew arcs $T_1 \to T_3$ and $T_3 \to T_2$ would be present.

```
ILOCK A
UNLOCK A
                    ILOCK  A
                    UNLOCK A
                    ILOCK  B
                    UNLOCK B
       ILOCK B
       UNLOCK B

         T₁                  T₂
```

**Figure 9.15** Schedules with incr-locks.

**Example 9.11:** Consider the schedule of Figure 9.15, where ILOCK means a lock in "increment" mode. According to the compatibility matrix of Figure 9.14, no items are locked in incompatible modes, so no arcs in the serialization graph are needed, as shown in Figure 9.16(a). Either order, $T_1T_2$ or $T_2T_1$ is an equivalent serial order for the schedule of Figure 9.15. That makes sense, because the relative order in which $A$ and $B$ are incremented by the two transactions is unimportant; the result will be the same in any case.

(a) With incr-locks.                    (b) With write-locks.

**Figure 9.16** Serialization graphs for Example 9.11.

On the other hand, if we did not have incr-locks, we would have to use write-locks in Figure 9.15, because read-locks do not permit items to be changed in any way, including incrementation. Then we would get the serialization graph of Figure 9.16(b) from the schedule of Figure 9.15, with WLOCK replacing ILOCK. That graph is cyclic, so the schedule of Figure 9.15 is not serializable when write-locks are used. □

## 9.6 A READ-ONLY, WRITE-ONLY MODEL

A subtle assumption with profound consequences that was made in Sections 9.2 and 9.4 is that whenever a transaction writes a new value for an item $A$, then it previously read the value of $A$, and more importantly, the new value of $A$ depends on the old value. A more realistic model would admit the possibility that a transaction reads a set of items (the *read-set*) and writes a set of items (the *write-set*), with the option that an item $A$ could appear in either one of these sets, or both.

**Example 9.12:** Any transaction that queries a database but does not alter it has an empty write-set. In the transaction

```
READ A; READ B; C:=A+B; A:=A-1; WRITE C; WRITE A
```

the read-set is $\{A, B\}$ and the write-set is $\{A, C\}$. $\square$

### Semantics of Transactions and Schedules

Our semantics of transactions differs from the model of Section 9.4 only in one point. We do not assume that write-locking an item implies that the item is read. Thus, associated with each write-lock on an item $A$ is a function that computes a new value for $A$ only in terms of the read-set of the transaction. In particular, this new value does not depend on the old value of $A$ if $A$ is not in the read-set.

When attributing semantics to schedules, we shall abandon the requirement of Section 9.4 that the value of item $A$ read by a transaction is significant, whether or not that value affects the final value of any item in the database. Should we care about the values read by a read-only transaction, then we can modify the transaction to write an imaginary item. Thus, two schedules are equivalent if and only if they produce the same values for each database item written, as functions of the initial values of the items read.

### Two Notions of Serializability

Following the pattern of Sections 9.2 and 9.4, we should define a schedule to be "serializable" if it is equivalent to some serial schedule. Unfortunately, this definition leads to difficulties, such as the fact that a simple graph-theoretic test does not exist in this model as it did in the previous models. Thus, equivalence to a serial schedule is considered only one possible definition of "serializability," and it is usually referred to as *view-serializability*. This notion of serializability will be discussed later in the section.

A more useful definition of serializability is called *conflict-serializability*. This notion is based on local checks regarding how pairs and triples of transactions treat a single item. We shall now develop the mechanics needed to define conflict-serializability and to present a graph-theoretic test for this property, albeit a more complicated test than was needed for previous models.

### Serialization Graphs for Read-Only, Write-Only Transactions

When we allow write-only access, we must revise our notion of when one transaction is forced to precede another in an equivalent serial schedule. One important difference is the following. Suppose (in the model of Section 9.4), that in given schedule $S$, the transaction $T_1$ wrote a value for item $A$, and later $T_2$ wrote a value for $A$. Then we assumed in Section 9.4 that $T_2$ write-locked $A$ after $T_1$ unlocked $A$, and by implication, $T_2$ used the value of $A$ written by $T_1$ in computing a new value. Therefore, when dealing with serializability, it was taken for granted that in a serial schedule $R$ equivalent to $S$, $T_1$ appears before $T_2$, and, incidentally, that no other transaction $T$ write-locking $A$ appears between $T_1$ and $T_2$. One gets the latter condition "for free" in Algorithm 9.2, since that algorithm forced $T$ to appear either before $T_1$ or after $T_2$ in $R$, whichever was the case in $S$.

However, if we assume that $T_2$ has written its value for $A$ without reading $A$, then the new value of $A$ is independent of the old; it depends only on the values of items actually read by $T_2$. Thus, if between the times that $T_1$ and $T_2$ write their values of $A$, no transaction reads $A$, we see that the value written by $T_1$ "gets lost" and has no effect on the database. As a consequence, in a serial schedule, we need not have $T_1$ appearing before $T_2$ (at least as far as the effect on $A$ is concerned). In fact, the only requirement on $T_1$ is that it be done at a time when some other transaction $T_3$ will later write $A$, and between the times that $T_1$ and $T_3$ write $A$, no transaction reads $A$.

We can now formulate a new definition of a serialization graph, based on the semantics that the values written by a transaction are functions only of the values read, and distinct values read produce distinct values written. The conditions under which one transaction is required to precede another are stated informally (and not completely accurately) as follows. If in schedule $S$, transaction $T_2$ reads the value of item $A$ written by $T_1$, then

1.  $T_1$ must precede $T_2$ in any serial schedule equivalent to $S$.
2.  If $T_3$ is a transaction that writes $A$, then in any serial schedule equivalent to $S$, $T_3$ may either precede $T_1$ or follow $T_2$, but may not appear between $T_1$ and $T_2$.

There are also two details needed to make the above definition an accurate one. First, there are "edge effects" involving the reading of an item before any transaction has written it or writing an item that is never rewritten. These rules are best taken care of by postulating the existence of an *initial transaction* $T_0$ that writes every item, reading none, and a *final transaction* $T_f$ that reads every item, writing none.

The second detail concerns transactions $T$ whose output is "invisible" in the sense that no value $T$ writes has any effect on the value read by $T_f$. Note that this effect need not be direct, but could result from some transaction $T'$ reading a value written by $T$, another transaction $T''$ reading a value written by $T'$, and so on, until we find a transaction in the chain that writes a value read by $T_f$. Call a transaction with no effect on $T_f$ *useless*. Our second modification of the above rules is to rule out the possibility that $T_2$, in (1) and (2) above, is a useless transaction.[7]

## Testing for Useless Transactions

It is easy, given a schedule $S$, to tell which transactions are useless. We create a graph whose nodes are the transactions, including the dummy transaction $T_f$ assumed to exist at the end of $S$. If $T_1$ writes a value read by $T_2$, draw an arc from $T_1$ to $T_2$. Then the useless transactions are exactly those with no path to $T_f$. An example of this algorithm follows the discussion of a serializability test.

## Conflict-Serializability

The simple serialization graph test of previous sections does not work here. Recall that there are two types of constraints on a potential serial schedule equivalent to a given schedule $S$.

1.  *Type 1 constraints* say that if $T_2$ reads a value of $A$ written by $T_1$ in $S$, then $T_1$ must precede $T_2$ in any serial schedule. This type of constraint can be expressed graphically by an arc from $T_1$ to $T_2$.

2.  *Type 2 constraints* say that if $T_2$ reads a value of $A$ written by $T_1$ in $S$, then any $T_3$ writing $A$ must appear either before $T_1$ or after $T_2$. These cannot be expressed by a simple arc. Rather, we have a pair of arcs $T_3 \rightarrow T_1$ and $T_2 \rightarrow T_3$, one of which must be chosen.

The above constraints apply to the dummy initial and final transactions, but do not apply to useless transactions.

Then schedule $S$ is said to be *conflict-serializable* if there is some serial schedule that respects all the type 1 and type 2 constraints generated by $S$. As we saw in Theorems 9.1 and 9.3, the notions of view- and conflict-serializability are equivalent in the simpler models of Sections 9.2 and 9.4. We shall, however, see that conflict-serializability implies view-serializability, but not vice versa, in the present model. There is a relatively easy-to-state test for conflict-serializability, which is one reason we prefer this notion, even though it misses detecting some serializable schedules.

## The Polygraph Test for Conflict-Serializability

A collection of nodes, arcs, and pairs of alternative arcs has been termed a *polygraph*. A polygraph is *acyclic* if there is some series of choices of one arc from each pair that results in an acyclic graph in the ordinary sense. The obvious conflict-serializability test is to construct the appropriate polygraph and

---

[7] We cannot simply remove useless transactions from $S$, since the portion of the system that schedules transactions cannot know that it is scheduling a transaction that will later prove to be useless.

determine if it is acyclic. Unfortunately, testing a polygraph for acyclicness is a hard problem; it has been shown $\mathcal{NP}$-complete by Papadimitriou, Bernstein, and Rothnie [1977]. We summarize the construction in the next algorithm.

**Algorithm 9.3:** Conflict-Serializability Test for Transactions with Read-Only and Write-Only Locks.

INPUT: A schedule $S$ for a set of transactions $T_1, T_2, \ldots, T_k$.

OUTPUT: A determination whether $S$ is conflict-serializable, and if so, an equivalent serial schedule.

METHOD:

1.  Augment $S$ by appending to the beginning a sequence of steps in which a dummy transaction $T_0$ writes each item appearing in $S$ and appending to the end steps in which dummy transaction $T_f$ reads each such item.
2.  Begin the creation of a polygraph $P$ with one node for each transaction, including dummy transactions $T_0$ and $T_f$. Temporarily, place an arc from $T_i$ to $T_j$ whenever $T_j$ reads an item $A$ that in the augmented $S$ was last written by $T_i$.
3.  Discover the useless transactions. A transaction $T$ is useless if there is no path from $T$ to $T_f$.
4.  For each useless transaction $T$, remove all arcs entering $T$.
5.  For each remaining arc $T_i \to T_j$, and for each item $A$ such that $T_j$ reads the value of $A$ written by $T_i$, consider each other transaction $T \neq T_0$ that also writes $A$. If $T_i = T_0$ and $T_j = T_f$, add no arcs. If $T_i = T_0$ but $T_j \neq T_f$, add the arc $T_j \to T$. If $T_j = T_f$, but $T_i \neq T_0$, add the arc $T \to T_i$. If $T_i \neq T_0$ and $T_j \neq T_f$, then introduce the arc pair $(T \to T_i, T_j \to T)$.
6.  Determine whether the resulting polygraph $P$ is acyclic. For this step there is no substantially better method than the exhaustive one. If there are $n$ arc pairs, try all $2^n$ choices of one arc from each pair to see if the result is an acyclic graph.[8] If $P$ is acyclic, let $G$ be an acyclic graph formed from $P$ by choosing an arc from each pair. Then any topological sort of $G$, with $T_0$ and $T_f$ removed, represents a serial schedule equivalent to $S$. If $P$ is not acyclic, then no serial schedule equivalent to $S$ exists. $\square$

**Example 9.13:** Consider the schedule of Figure 9.17. The arcs constructed by step (2) of Algorithm 9.3 are shown in Figure 9.18; for clarity, the arcs are labeled with the item or items justifying their presence. In understanding how Figure 9.18 was created it helps first to observe that the schedule of Figure 9.17 is legal, in the sense that two transactions do not hold write-locks, or a read-and

---

[8] Obviously one can think of some heuristics to make the job somewhat simpler than it appears at first glance. For example, if one of a pair of arcs causes a cycle with existing arcs, we must choose the other of the pair. However, there are cases where neither arc in a pair causes an immediate cycle, yet our choice influences what happens when we try to select arcs from other pairs.

| | $T_1$ | $T_2$ | $T_3$ | $T_4$ |
|---|---|---|---|---|
| (1) | | | RLOCK A | |
| (2) | RLOCK A | | | |
| (3) | WLOCK C | | | |
| (4) | UNLOCK C | | | |
| (5) | | | RLOCK C | |
| (6) | WLOCK B | | | |
| (7) | UNLOCK B | | | |
| (8) | | | | RLOCK B |
| (9) | UNLOCK A | | | |
| (10) | | UNLOCK A | | |
| (11) | | | WLOCK A | |
| (12) | | | | RLOCK C |
| (13) | | WLOCK D | | |
| (14) | | | | UNLOCK B |
| (15) | | | UNLOCK C | |
| (16) | | RLOCK B | | |
| (17) | | | UNLOCK A | |
| (18) | | | | WLOCK A |
| (19) | | UNLOCK B | | |
| (20) | | | | WLOCK B |
| (21) | | | | UNLOCK B |
| (22) | | UNLOCK D | | |
| (23) | | | | UNLOCK C |
| (24) | | | | UNLOCK A |

Figure 9.17  A schedule.

write-lock simultaneously. Thus, we may assume all reading and writing occurs at the time the lock is obtained, and we may ignore the UNLOCK steps.

Let us consider each read-lock step in turn. The read-locks on $A$ at steps (1) and (2) read the value "written" by the dummy transaction $T_0$. Thus, we draw arcs from $T_0$ to $T_1$ and $T_2$. At step (5) $T_3$ reads the value of $C$ written by $T_1$ at step (3), so we have arc $T_1 \rightarrow T_3$. At step (8), $T_4$ reads what $T_1$ wrote at step (6), so we have arc $T_1 \rightarrow T_4$, and so on. Finally, at the end, $T_f$ "reads" $A, B, C$, and $D$, whose values were last written by $T_4$, $T_4$, $T_1$, and $T_2$, respectively, explaining the three arcs into $T_f$.

Now we search for useless transactions, those with no path to $T_f$ in Figure 9.18; $T_3$ is the only such transaction. We therefore remove the arc $T_1 \rightarrow T_3$ from Figure 9.18.

In step (5) of Algorithm 9.3 we consider the arcs or arc pairs needed to prevent interference of one write operation with another. An item like $C$ or $D$ that is written by only one nondummy transaction does not figure into step (5). However, $A$ is written by both $T_3$ and $T_4$, as well as dummy transaction $T_0$. The value written by $T_3$ is not read by any transaction, so $T_4$ need not appear in any particular position relative to $T_3$. The value written by $T_4$ is "read" by $T_f$. Therefore, as $T_3$ cannot appear after $T_f$, it must appear before $T_4$. In this case, no arc pair is needed; we simply add to $P$ the arc $T_3 \rightarrow T_4$. The value of $A$ written by $T_0$ is read by $T_1$ and $T_2$. As $T_3$ and $T_4$ cannot appear before $T_0$, we place arcs from $T_1$ and $T_2$ to $T_3$ and $T_4$; again no arc pair is necessary.

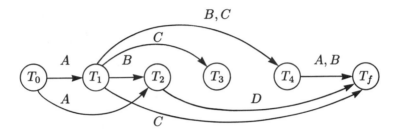

**Figure 9.18** First step in construction of a polygraph.

Item $B$ is written by $T_1$ and $T_4$. The value of $B$ written by $T_4$ is read only by $T_f$, so we need arc $T_1 \rightarrow T_4$. The value of $B$ written by $T_1$ is read by $T_2$ and $T_4$. The writing of $B$ by $T_4$ cannot interfere with the reading of $B$ by $T_4$. Thus no requirement that "$T_4$ precedes $T_1$ or follows $T_4$" is needed. However, $T_4$ must not be interposed between $T_1$ and $T_2$, so we add the arc pair $(T_4 \rightarrow T_1, T_2 \rightarrow T_4)$. The resulting polygraph is shown in Figure 9.19, with the one arc pair shown dashed. Note that arc $T_1 \rightarrow T_3$, removed in step (4), returns in step (5).

If we choose arc $T_4 \rightarrow T_1$ from the pair we get a cycle. However, choosing $T_2 \rightarrow T_4$ leaves an acyclic graph, from which we can take the serial order $T_1$, $T_2, T_3, T_4$. Thus, the schedule of Figure 9.17 is serializable. $\square$

Algorithms 9.1 and 9.2 are correct in the strong sense that they produce an equivalent serial schedule if and only if there is one, according to the semantics of transactions used in Sections 9.2 and 9.4, respectively. Algorithm 9.3 is not that strongly correct. If it finds a serial schedule, then that schedule is surely equivalent to the given schedule, under the semantics of read-only, write-only transactions of this section. However, if it fails to find a serial schedule, it only means that there is no serial schedule that meets the type-1 and type-2 constraints on transaction order. Thus, after proving this weaker form of

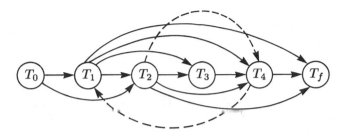

**Figure 9.19** Final polygraph.

correctness for Algorithm 9.3, we shall consider an example of a schedule that has an equivalent serial schedule, according to our transaction semantics, i.e., it is view-serializable, yet it fails the test of Algorithm 9.3. We shall also discuss why there is not much use in regarding view-serializable schedules to be "serializable."

**Theorem 9.4:**

a) If Algorithm 9.3 succeeds on given schedule $S$, then there is a serial schedule equivalent to $S$ under the read-only, write-only semantics.

b) If Algorithm 9.3 fails on $S$, then there is no serial schedule that meets the type-1 and type-2 constraints for $S$.

**Proof:** (a) Suppose first that the resulting polygraph is acyclic. That is, there is some choice between arcs in each pair that results in an acyclic graph $G$. The construction of $P$ in Algorithm 9.3 assures that each nonuseless transaction, including $T_f$, reads the same copy of each item in $S$ as it does in the serial schedule resulting from a topological sort of $G$. Thus, the corresponding values produced for each item are the same in both schedules.

(b) Conversely, suppose there is a serial schedule $R$ that meets the type-1 and type-2 constraints generated by given schedule $S$. Then by the reasoning used in Theorem 9.1, if $T_i \rightarrow T_j$ is any arc introduced in step (2) and not removed in step (4), $T_i$ must precede $T_j$ in $R$. Suppose the arc pair

$$(T_n \rightarrow T_i, T_j \rightarrow T_n)$$

is introduced in step (5). Then $T_n$ cannot appear between $T_i$ and $T_j$ in $R$. Pick arc $T_n \rightarrow T_i$ from the pair if $T_n$ precedes $T_i$ in $R$, and pick $T_j \rightarrow T_n$ otherwise. The linear order implied by $R$ will be consistent with this choice from arc pairs. Similarly, a single arc added in step (5) must be consistent with this linear order, so we have a way of constructing, based on $R$, an acyclic graph from polygraph $P$. $\square$

## The Two-phase Protocol, Again

As with the previous models, a two-phase protocol, requiring each transaction to do all locking before any unlocking, guarantees conflict-serializability of any legal schedule. To see why, let us suppose $S$ is a legal schedule of transactions obeying the two-phase protocol. Suppose $(T_3 \to T_1, T_2 \to T_3)$ is an arc pair in the polygraph $P$. Then there is some item $A$ such that $T_2$ reads the copy of $A$ written by $T_1$. If in $S$, $T_3$ unlocks $A$ before $T_1$ read-locks $A$, then select $T_3 \to T_1$ from the pair. If $T_3$ write-locks $A$ after $T_2$ unlocks it, select $T_2 \to T_3$. No other possibilities exist, since the arc pair was placed in $P$ by Algorithm 9.3.

We now have a graph $G$ constructed from $P$. Suppose $G$ has a cycle $T_1 \to T_2 \to \cdots \to T_n \to T_1$. Surely, neither dummy transaction can be part of a cycle. Examination of Algorithm 9.3 and the above rules for constructing $G$ from $P$ indicates that for every arc $T_i \to T_{i+1}$ (with $T_{n+1} = T_1$) in the cycle, there is an item $A_i$ such that in $S$, $T_i$ unlocks $A_i$ before $T_{i+1}$ locks $A_i$. By the two-phase protocol, $T_{i+1}$ must unlock $A_{i+1}$ after it locks $A_i$. Thus $T_1$ unlocks $A_1$ before $T_{n+1}$ locks $A_n$. But $T_{n+1}$ is $T_1$, and the two-phase protocol forbids $T_1$ from unlocking $A_1$ before it locks $A_n$. We have thus proved the following theorem.

**Theorem 9.5:** In the model of this section, if transactions obey the two-phase protocol, then any legal schedule is serializable. $\square$

## View-Serializability

There is a subtlety in the model of this section that allows certain schedules to have the same effect as a serial schedule on all the items, yet not be conflict-serializable; i.e., they fail the test of Algorithm 9.3. Intuitively, the problem is that some, but not all, of the effects of a transaction may be made invisible by other transactions. The next example, illustrates this phenomenon.

**Example 9.14:** Consider the three transactions of Figure 9.20. Because $T_2$ reads the value of $A$ written by $T_1$, we have a type-1 arc $T_1 \to T_2$. Because $T_1$ reads the value of $C$ written by $T_2$ we likewise have an arc $T_2 \to T_1$, so the transactions of Figure 9.20 are not conflict-serializable. The polygraph for Figure 9.20 is shown in Figure 9.21; note that it is an ordinary graph, with no pairs of alternative arcs.

Yet the schedule of Figure 9.20 is equivalent to a serial schedule, and in fact, the order of $T_1$ and $T_2$ is immaterial; the only real requirement is that $T_3$ follow both. The reason is that $T_3$ writes new values of $B$ and $D$ before any other transaction reads the values written by $T_1$ or $T_2$. If we, say, run $T_1$ then $T_2$ and finally $T_3$ in a serial order, the value $T_1$ produces for $D$ will be wrong (because it uses the initial value of $C$, rather than the value written by $T_2$). However, after $T_3$ runs, the value of $D$ becomes correct again, in the sense that it agrees with what the schedule of Figure 9.20 produces. Thus, the schedule

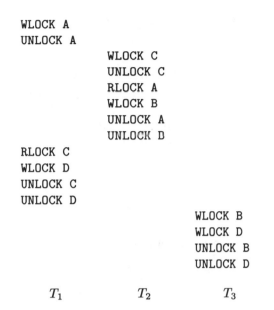

```
WLOCK A
UNLOCK A
              WLOCK C
              UNLOCK C
              RLOCK A
              WLOCK B
              UNLOCK A
              UNLOCK D
RLOCK C
WLOCK D
UNLOCK C
UNLOCK D
                            WLOCK B
                            WLOCK D
                            UNLOCK B
                            UNLOCK D

      T₁            T₂            T₃
```

$$T_1 \qquad\qquad T_2 \qquad\qquad T_3$$

**Figure 9.20** View-serializable transactions.

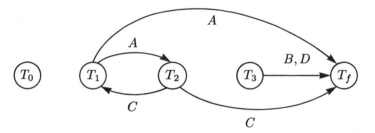

**Figure 9.21** Polygraph for Figure 9.20.

of Figure 9.20 is view-serializable. $\square$

   Unfortunately, it is $\mathcal{NP}$-complete to determine whether a schedule is view-serializable (Yannakakis [1984]). Perhaps more importantly, there is something unsatisfying about the claim that the schedule of Figure 9.20 is "serializable." What would happen if $T_3$ had never occurred, or if the system failed before $T_3$ ran? If the scheduler had permitted the interleaving of $T_1$ and $T_2$ it would have to be sure that $T_3$ would be executed before any transaction could read the values of $B$ or $D$. Since that is far from a realistic assumption, schedulers based on view-serializability are not found in practice.

## 9.7 CONCURRENCY FOR HIERARCHICALLY STRUCTURED ITEMS

There are many instances where the set of items accessed by a transaction can be viewed naturally as a tree or forest. Some examples are:

1.  Items are logical records in a database structured according to the hierarchical model.
2.  Items are nodes of a B-tree (recall Section 6.5).
3.  Items of various sizes are defined, with small items nested within larger ones. For example, a relational database could have items at four levels:
    *i*)   The entire database,
    *ii*)   Each relation,
    *iii*)   Each block in which the file corresponding to a relation is stored, and
    *iv*)   Each tuple.

There are two different policies that could be followed when items are locked. First, a lock on an item could imply a lock on all its descendant items. This policy saves time, as locking many small items can be avoided. For example, in situation (3) above, a transaction that must read an entire relation can lock the relation as a whole, rather than locking each tuple individually. The second policy is to lock an item without implying anything about a lock on its descendants. For example, if we are searching a B-tree, we shall read a node and select one of its children to read next. In this case, it is preferable not to lock all descendants at the time we read a node. We shall consider these policies, in turn.

### A Simple Protocol for Trees of Items

Let us revert to the model of Section 9.2 using only the LOCK and UNLOCK operations.[9] We assume that locking an item (node of a tree) does not automatically lock any descendants. As in Section 9.2, only one transaction can lock an item at a time. We say a transaction obeys the *tree protocol* if

1.  Except for the first item locked (which need not be the root), no item can be locked unless a lock is currently held on its parent.
2.  No item is ever locked twice by one transaction.

Observe that a transaction obeying the tree protocol need not be two-phase. For example, it might lock an item $A$, then lock its child $B$, unlock $A$ and lock a child of $B$. This situation is quite realistic, for example, in the case that the transaction is performing an insertion into a B-tree. If $B$ is a node of the B-tree that has room for another pointer, then we know that no restructuring of the tree after insertion can involve the parent of $B$. Thus, after

---

[9]   The bibliographic notes contain pointers to generalizations of this protocol, where both read- and write-locks are permitted.

examining $B$ we can unlock the parent $A$, thereby allowing concurrent updates to the B-tree involving descendants of $A$ that are not descendants of $B$.

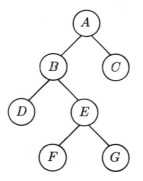

**Figure 9.22** A hierarchy of items.

**Example 9.15:** Figure 9.22 shows a tree of items, and Figure 9.23 is the schedule of three transactions $T_1$, $T_2$, and $T_3$, obeying the tree protocol. Note that $T_1$ is not two-phase, since it locks $C$ after unlocking $B$. $\square$

**The Tree Protocol and Serializability**

While we shall not give a proof here (see Silberschatz and Kedem [1980]), all legal schedules of transactions that obey the tree protocol are serializable. The algorithm to construct a serial ordering of the transactions begins by creating a node for each transaction. Suppose $T_i$ and $T_j$ are two transactions that lock the same item (at different times, of course). Let FIRST($T$) be the item first locked by transaction $T$. If FIRST($T_i$) and FIRST($T_j$) are independent (neither is a descendant of the other), then the tree protocol guarantees that $T_i$ and $T_j$ do not lock a node in common, and we need not draw an arc between them. Suppose therefore, without loss of generality, that FIRST($T_i$) is an ancestor of FIRST($T_j$). If $T_i$ locks FIRST($T_j$) before $T_j$ does, then draw arc $T_i \rightarrow T_j$. Otherwise draw an arc $T_j \rightarrow T_i$.

It can be shown that the resulting graph has no cycles, and any topological sort of this graph is a serial order for the transactions. The intuition behind the proof is that, at all times, each transaction has a frontier of lowest nodes in the tree on which it holds locks. The tree protocol guarantees that these frontiers do not pass over one another. Thus, if the frontier of $T_i$ begins above the frontier of $T_j$, it must remain so, and every item locked by both $T_i$ and $T_j$ will be locked by $T_j$ first.

|       |            |          |          |
|-------|------------|----------|----------|
| (1)   | LOCK A     |          |          |
| (2)   | LOCK B     |          |          |
| (3)   | LOCK D     |          |          |
| (4)   | UNLOCK B   |          |          |
| (5)   |            | LOCK B   |          |
| (6)   | LOCK C     |          |          |
| (7)   |            |          | LOCK E   |
| (8)   | UNLOCK D   |          |          |
| (9)   |            |          | LOCK F   |
| (10)  | UNLOCK A   |          |          |
| (11)  |            |          | LOCK G   |
| (12)  | UNLOCK C   |          |          |
| (13)  |            |          | UNLOCK E |
| (14)  |            | LOCK E   |          |
| (15)  |            |          | UNLOCK F |
| (16)  |            | UNLOCK B |          |
| (17)  |            |          | UNLOCK G |
| (18)  |            | UNLOCK E |          |
|       | $T_1$      | $T_2$    | $T_3$    |

**Figure 9.23** A schedule of transactions obeying the tree protocol.

**Example 9.16:** Let us reconsider the schedule of Figure 9.23. In this schedule we have FIRST($T_1$) = $A$, FIRST($T_2$) = $B$, and FIRST($T_3$) = $E$. $T_1$ and $T_2$ both lock $B$, and $T_1$ does so first, so we have arc $T_1 \rightarrow T_2$. Also, $T_2$ and $T_3$ each lock $E$, but $T_3$ precedes $T_2$ in doing so. Thus we have arc $T_3 \rightarrow T_2$. The precedence graph for this schedule is shown in Figure 9.24, and there are two possible serial schedules, $T_1, T_3, T_2$ and $T_3, T_1, T_2$. $\square$

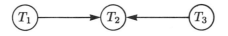

**Figure 9.24** Serialization graph for Figure 9.23.

### A Protocol Allowing Locks on Subtrees

We now consider the second kind of hierarchy, a nested structure. It is convenient, when the hierarchy of items includes some that are subsets of other items, as in our introductory example (3):

database–relations–blocks–tuples

to assume that a lock on an item implies a lock on all its descendants. For example, if a transaction must lock most or all the tuples of a relation, it may as well lock the relation itself. At a cost of possibly excluding some concurrent operations on the relation, the system does far less work locking and unlocking items if we lock the relation as a whole.

However, indiscriminate locking can result in illegal schedules, where two transactions effectively hold a lock on the same item at the same time. For example, suppose transaction $T_1$ locks $E$ of Figure 9.22 (and therefore, by our new assumptions, also locks $F$ and $G$). Then let $T_2$ lock $B$, thereby acquiring a conflicting lock on $E$, $F$ and $G$. To avoid this conflict, a protocol has been devised in which a transaction cannot place a lock on an item unless it first places a "warning" at all its ancestors. A warning on item $A$ prevents any other transaction from locking $A$, but it does not prevent it from also placing a warning at $A$ or from locking some descendant of $A$ that does not have a warning.

This approach is patterned after that used for concurrency control in System R. What we present here is a simplification of the ideas found in that system, which uses both read- and write-locks, as well as warnings for both types of locks. We shall here consider transactions to consist of operations:

1. LOCK, which locks an item and all its descendants. No two transactions may hold a lock on an item at the same time.
2. WARN, which places a "warning" on an item. No transaction may lock an item on which some other transaction has placed a warning.
3. UNLOCK, which removes a lock and/or a warning from an item.

The semantics of transactions follows that of Section 9.2. When an item is locked, its value, and the values of all its descendants, are assumed to change in a way that depends uniquely on the values of all the items (and their descendants) locked by the transaction. However, placing a warning on an item does not, by itself, allow the value of that item or any of its descendants to change.

A transaction obeys the *warning protocol* on a hierarchy of items if

1. It begins by placing a lock or warning at the root.
2. It dos not place a lock or warning on an item unless it holds a warning on its parent.[10]
3. It does not remove a lock or warning unless it holds no locks or warnings on its children.

---

[10] Note that there is no need to place a lock on an item if a lock on its parent is already held.

4.   It obeys the two-phase protocol, in the sense that all unlocks follow all
     warnings and locks.

We assume that this protocol acts in conjunction with the simple scheduler that
allows any lock to be placed on an item $A$ only if no other transaction has a
lock or warning on $A$, and allows a warning to be placed on $A$ as long as no
transaction has a lock on $A$.

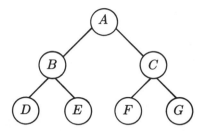

**Figure 9.25**  A hierarchy.

**Example 9.17:** Figure 9.25 shows a hierarchy, and Figure 9.26 is a schedule
of three transactions obeying the warning protocol. Notice, for example that at
step (4) $T_1$ places a warning on $B$. Therefore, $T_3$ was not able to lock $B$ until
$T_1$ unlocked its warning on $B$ at step (10). However, at steps (1)–(3), all three
transactions place warnings on $A$, which is legal.

The lock of $C$ by $T_2$ at step (5) implicitly locks $C$, $F$, and $G$. We assume
that any or all of these items are changed by $T_2$ before the lock is removed at
step (7). $\Box$

**Theorem 9.6:** Legal schedules of transactions obeying the warning protocol
are serializable.

**Proof:** Parts (1)–(3) of the warning protocol guarantee that no transaction
can place a lock on an item unless it holds warnings on all of its ancestors. It
follows that at no time can two transactions hold locks on two ancestors of the
same item. We can now show that a schedule obeying the warning protocol is
equivalent to a schedule under the model of Section 9.2, in which all items are
locked explicitly (not implicitly, by locking an ancestor). Given a schedule $S$
satisfying the warning protocol, construct a schedule $R$ in the model of Section
9.2 as follows.

1.   Remove all warning steps, and their matching unlock steps.
2.   Replace all locks by locks on the item and all its descendants. Do the same
     for the corresponding unlocks.

Let $R$ be the resulting schedule. Its transactions are two-phase because those of
$S$ are two-phase, by part (4) of the warning protocol. We have only to show that

| | | | |
|---|---|---|---|
| (1)  | WARN A   |          |          |
| (2)  |          | WARN A   |          |
| (3)  |          |          | WARN A   |
| (4)  | WARN B   |          |          |
| (5)  |          | LOCK C   |          |
| (6)  | LOCK D   |          |          |
| (7)  |          | UNLOCK C |          |
| (8)  | UNLOCK D |          |          |
| (9)  |          | UNLOCK A |          |
| (10) | UNLOCK B |          |          |
| (11) |          |          | LOCK B   |
| (12) |          |          | WARN C   |
| (13) |          |          | LOCK F   |
| (14) | UNLOCK A |          |          |
| (15) |          |          | UNLOCK B |
| (16) |          |          | UNLOCK F |
| (17) |          |          | UNLOCK C |
| (18) |          |          | UNLOCK A |
|      | $T_1$    | $T_2$    | $T_3$    |

**Figure 9.26** A schedule of transactions satisfying the warning protocol.

$R$ is legal, since we know that every legal schedule of two-phase transactions is serializable by Theorem 9.2.

Suppose in contradiction that in $R$, two transactions $T_1$ and $T_2$ hold locks on item $A$ at the same time. Then in $S$, $T_1$ must have held a lock on some ancestor $B$ of $A$, at the same time $T_2$ held a lock on an ancestor $C$ of $A$ (any of $A$, $B$, and $C$ could be the same). Suppose without loss of generality that $B$ is an ancestor of $C$. If, in $S$, $T_1$ locks $B$ before $T_2$ places a warning on $B$, then $T_2$ can never place a warning on $B$ until $T_1$ unlocks $B$. By condition (2) of the warning protocol, $T_2$ cannot lock $C$ until $T_1$ unlocks $B$, contrary to our assumption that the locks on $B$ and $C$ were held simultaneously.

The remaining possibility is that $T_2$ locks $C$ before $T_1$ locks $B$. But then, by condition (3) of the warning protocol, $T_2$ holds a lock or warning on $B$ until it releases its lock on $C$. Thus, in $S$, $T_1$ was prohibited from locking $B$ while $T_2$ locks $C$, another contradiction. $\square$

## Compatibility Matrix For Warnings and Locks

The matrix of Figure 9.27 expresses the definition of LOCK and WARN. This compatibility matrix is no different from the matrix of Figure 9.13, which expressed

|        | Warn | Lock |
|--------|:----:|:----:|
| Warn   |  $Y$ |  $N$ |
| Lock   |  $N$ |  $N$ |

**Figure 9.27** Compatibility of warn and lock.

the compatibility of read- and write-locks. However, we should not suppose that a warning is really the same as a read-lock. The difference between read/write locks on one hand, and warn/lock on the other is that in the latter case, one accesses items through a hierarchy, placing warnings and locks all along a path to the desired item. In the read/write lock case, each item is locked directly, independently of locks held on any other item.

In fact, one can use both read and write versions of locks and warnings for each type of lock. For example, a single transaction could place both a read-lock and a warning-to-write lock on the same item in a hierarchy. The exercises explore the way locks of these modes interact.

## 9.8 HANDLING TRANSACTION FAILURES

Until now, we have assumed that each transaction runs happily to completion. In practice, there are several reasons why a transaction might perform some actions and then abort (terminate without completing).

1. The transaction fails for some reason. The user interrupts it, an arithmetic failure such as division by zero occurs, or it tries to access an item of the database for which it does not have access privileges, for example.
2. The scheduler detects a deadlock, and decides to abort the transaction so it can release its locks and allow other transactions to proceed.
3. As we shall discuss in Sections 9.9 and 9.11, there are certain scheduling algorithms that sometimes need to abort a transaction to enforce serializability.
4. A software or hardware error causes the entire database system to fail.

The simplest to deal with are failures of a single transaction, such as (1)–(3) above. It is harder to handle failures of the software system, since usually all the transactions active at the time of the crash will have to be redone. Unless we are careful how transactions are managed, we shall have lost some essential information about what was going on at the time of the crash, and it will be impossible to resume operations correctly, from that time. Still more serious is a media failure, where the data in the permanent database is lost. The only way to recover from a media failure is to have a backup copy of the database up-to-date at all times.

The methods for recovery from system-wide software and hardware failures will be discussed in Section 9.10. Here, we consider only the problems caused by single-transaction failures or by the scheduler's decision to abort a transaction.

### Commitment of Transactions

When dealing with transactions that may abort, it helps to think of *active* transactions, which have not yet reached the point at which we are sure they will complete, and *completed* transactions, which we are sure cannot abort for any of the reasons suggested by (1)–(3) above, such as an attempted illegal step or involvement in a deadlock. The point in the transaction's execution where it has completed all of its calculation and done everything, such as ask for locks, that could possibly cause the transaction to abort, we call the *commit point*. In what follows, we shall assume that COMMIT is an action taken by transactions, just like locking, writing, and computation in the workspace are steps. In Section 9.10 we shall see that particular actions must be taken when reaching the commit point, but for the moment, let us simply regard the COMMIT action as marking the commit point of the transaction.

### Transactions That Read "Dirty" Data

In several of the examples we have seen so far, transactions read items that had been written by other transactions, and the reading occurred prior to the commit point of the writing transaction. For example, in Figure 9.17, $T_3$ reads $C$ at step (5), and the value it reads was written by $T_1$ at step (4), yet $T_1$ could not possibly have committed until step (7), when it wrote the value of $B$.[11] Data written into the database by a transaction before that transaction commits is called *dirty* data.

We are severely punished for reading dirty data in any situation where the writing transaction could abort. The following example illustrates what can happen.

**Example 9.18:** Consider the two transactions of Figure 9.28. Fundamentally these transactions follow the model of Section 9.2, although to make clear certain details of timing, we have explicitly shown commitment, reads, writes, and the arithmetic done in the workspace of each transaction. We assume that the WRITE action stores a value in the database, while arithmetic steps, such as (3), are done in the workspace and have no effect on the database.

Suppose that after step (14) transaction $T_1$ fails, perhaps because division by 0 occurred at step (14), or because a deadlock involving other transactions caused the scheduler to decide to abort $T_1$. We have to take the following actions.

---

[11] Recall we have assumed that writing of an item occurs at the time that item is unlocked.

```
(1)       LOCK A
(2)       READ A
(3)       A:=A-1
(4)       WRITE A
(5)       LOCK B
(6)       UNLOCK A
(7)                      LOCK A
(8)                      READ A
(9)                      A:=A*2
(10)      READ B
(11)                     WRITE A
(12)                     COMMIT
(13)                     UNLOCK A
(14)      B:=B/A
```

$$T_1 \qquad\qquad T_2$$

**Figure 9.28** A schedule.

1. $T_1$ still holds a lock on item $B$. That lock must be removed by the system.
2. The value of $A$ written by $T_1$ at step (4) must be restored to the value $A$ had prior to step (1). There appears not to be a record of the old value of $A$; when we discuss recovery from crashes in Section 9.10 we shall see it is essential in this situation that we have written the old value of $A$ into a "journal" or "log."
3. The value of $A$ read by $T_2$ at step (8) is now wrong. $T_2$ has performed an incorrect calculation and written its result in $A$. Thus, not only do we have to restore the value of $A$ from before step (1), we have to undo all effects of $T_2$ and rerun that transaction.[12]
4. Suppose that some other transaction $T_3$ read the value of $A$ between steps (13) and (14). Then $T_3$ is also using invalid data and will have to be redone, even if, like $T_2$, it has already reached its commit point. Further, any transaction that read a value written by $T_3$ will have to be redone, and so on. □

The phenomenon illustrated in point (4) of Example 9.18 is called *cascading rollback*. It is the consequence of our decision to allow $T_2$ read dirty data. That is, once we allow even one transaction to read dirty data, then completion of any transaction $T$ is no guarantee that sometime in the far future it will be discovered that $T$ read a value which should not have been there, and therefore

---

[12] In this simple example, nothing but $A$ was changed by $T_2$.

$T$ must be redone.

### Strict Two-Phase Locking

Since this situation is generally not tolerable, it is normal to use the following version of the two-phase locking protocol, which is called *strict two-phase locking*.

1. A transaction cannot write into the database until it has reached its commit point.
2. A transaction cannot release any locks until it has finished writing into the database; therefore locks are not released until after the commit point.

**Example 9.19:** $T_2$ of Figure 9.28 is not quite a strict two-phase transaction. For it to be strict, the COMMIT at line (12) would have to be moved prior to the WRITE at line (11). □

Clearly condition (2) is necessary to avoid cascading rollback, for without it, another transaction could read a value written by a transaction that later aborted. Condition (1) is also important. True, until the lock is released, no other transaction can read the dirty data, but if we find the writing transaction has to abort, we may have no way to restore the old value of the item written. Section 9.10 will discuss ways, such as logging, to solve that problem.

If all transactions obey the strict two-phase locking protocol, we know that a value, once found in the database, was written by a committed transaction, and a committed transaction cannot abort. Thus, no cascading rollback is possible, and once a transaction commits, writes its data into the database, and releases its locks, that transaction is a permanent part of history; it will never need to be rolled back or redone.

## 9.9 AGGRESSIVE AND CONSERVATIVE PROTOCOLS

In the previous section we saw why writing and unlocking at the very end of a transaction is a wise strategy. We might ask whether it makes sense to begin transactions in a special way, such as by taking all of the locks the transaction needs. The answer is that there are different options, even among strict two-phase protocols, that can be "right" in certain situations. We do not face a problem as severe as cascading rollback, but our choice affects the performance that we can obtain from the system. There are two performance issues that need to be faced.

1. We want the best possible throughput, i.e., the largest possible rate of transaction completion for a machine of given processing speed and for a given mix of transactions.

2.   We want any particular transaction to finish without too much delay.

Sometimes, (1) and (2) are incompatible, and there are situations where no user is waiting around for a transaction to finish, so (2) is not important. There could even be situations where (1) is not vital, because we have much more than adequate computing power for the transactions being processed.

The choice of protocol and scheduler affects (1), the throughput, in several ways.

a)   Cycles spent deciding whether to grant or deny locks, maintaining lock tables, enqueueing and dequeueing waiting transactions, detecting and resolving deadlocks, and so on, are cycles that do not contribute to the execution of transactions. We wish to minimize the time spent on these operations, which is the *overhead* of scheduling transactions concurrently.

b)   The cycles spent on transactions that later abort are wasted and do not contribute to throughput. Moreover, additional cycles may have to be spent finding and releasing locks of aborted transactions.

c)   If the protocol used is not strict two-phase, then additional cycles must be spent restoring the database after a transaction aborts and checking for and fixing cascading rollback problems.

If we assume strict two-phase locking, (c) is not an issue. Then the competition is really between (a) and (b); shall we try to avoid aborting transactions as much as possible, in particular by using a protocol and scheduler that avoids deadlock,[13] or shall we opt for simplicity of the scheduler, hoping to save more time managing locks than we lose by occasionally having to resolve deadlocks?

We can classify protocols as

1.   *Aggressive*, meaning that they try to proceed as quickly as possible, even if there is the possibility that they will be led to a situation where they must abort, and

2.   *Conservative*, meaning that the protocol tries to avoid performing the beginning part of a transaction if it is not sure the transaction can complete.

Different protocols can exhibit different degrees of aggressiveness. We shall here consider only locking protocols, but in Section 9.11 we shall consider some other protocols of the aggressive and conservative variety, that do not use locks.

## A Conservative Protocol

The most conservative version of two-phase locking is for each transaction $T$ to request all of the locks it will ever need, at the beginning of the transaction. The scheduler grants the locks and allows $T$ to proceed if all the locks are available.

---

[13] Of course, we cannot avoid aborting transactions altogether, because there are always system errors and transaction-specific errors such as illegal database access, that leave us no choice.

If one or more locks are unavailable, $T$ is put on a queue to wait. This scheme clearly avoids deadlock resulting from competition for locks (which is the only resource that, in our model, can cause deadlock).

We must be more careful if livelock is to be avoided. To prevent livelock, the scheduler cannot allow a transaction $T$ to proceed, even if all of its desired locks are available, as long as any transaction in the queue is waiting for one of the locks $T$ needs. Furthermore, once a transaction enters the queue, it cannot proceed, even when all of its locks are available, if there is another transaction ahead of it in the queue that wants any of the same locks.[14]

**Example 9.20:** Suppose there is a sequence of transactions

$$U_0, V_1, U_1, V_2, U_2, \ldots$$

with the property that each $U_i$ locks item $A$, while each $V_i$ locks $B$ and $C$. Suppose also that a transaction $T_1$ is initiated immediately after $U_0$, and $T_1$ needs locks on $A$ and $B$. Then $T_1$ must wait for its lock on $A$ and is placed on the queue. However, before $U_0$ terminates, $V_1$ initiates and is granted locks on $B$ and $C$. Thus, when $U_0$ terminates, it releases the lock on $A$, but now, $B$ is unavailable, and $T_1$ cannot proceed. Before $V_1$ terminates, $U_1$ initiates, which again prevents $T_1$ from proceeding when $V_1$ releases its lock on $B$. In this manner, $T_1$ can wait in the queue forever.

However, following the livelock-prevention policy described above, the scheduler should not grant a lock on $B$ to $V_1$, because $T_1$ is waiting on the queue, and $T_1$ wants a lock on $B$. Thus, the correct action by the scheduler when $V_1$ requests its locks is to place $V_1$ on the queue behind $T_1$. Then, when $U_0$ finishes, the locks on both $A$ and $B$ become available and are granted to $T_1$. When $T_1$ finishes, its lock on $B$ is released and given to $V_1$, along with the lock on $C$, which we assume has remained available.

A similar example can be developed where, if we do not follow the livelock-prevention policy outlined above, $T_1$ waits at the front of the queue forever, never in a situation where all of its locks are available at once, while transactions behind it on the queue are repeatedly given all of their locks. This construction is left as an exercise. □

**Theorem 9.7:** Suppose that we use a protocol in which all locks are obtained at the beginning of the transaction, and we use a scheduler that allows a transaction $T$ (which may be on the queue or not) to receive its requested locks if and only if:

1. All of the locks are available, and

---

[14] We can, though, grant locks to a transaction not at the head of the queue if all the locks are available, and no transaction ahead of it on the queue wants any of those locks. Thus, strictly speaking, our "queue" is not a true queue.

2.   No transaction ahead of $T$ on the queue wants any of the locks requested
     by $T$.

Then livelocks and deadlocks resulting from contention for locks cannot occur.

**Proof:** That deadlocks do not occur is an immediate consequence of (1); no
transaction that holds a lock can ever be in a situation where it is waiting for
another lock.

To see that no livelocks can occur, suppose transaction $T$ is placed on the
queue. At this time, there are only a finite number of transactions ahead of $T$
on the queue, say $U_1, \ldots, U_k$. The locks desired by the first of these, $U_1$, will
all be released within a finite amount of time, and none of them can be granted
to any other transaction. Thus, $U_1$ initiates after a finite amount of time and
is removed from the queue. We can argue similarly about $U_2, \ldots, U_k$. Thus, $T$
eventually reaches the head of the queue, and it too will be granted its locks
after a finite amount of time. Thus, no livelock occurs. $\Box$

While the conservative protocol seems attractive, there are two drawbacks.

1.   Transactions may be delayed unnecessarily, because they need a certain
     lock late in their execution that they are required to take at the beginning.
     If that lock is unavailable, the transaction cannot begin, even though it
     could do a number of steps without the lock.
2.   Transactions must lock any item they might need, even though they may
     have to do some computation to tell whether or not they really need the
     lock.

**Example 9.21:** In Figure 9.29 we see an SQL query to find the customers who
ordered Brie. Let us assume that items are physical blocks, each containing a
few tuples from one of the relations ORDERS or INCLUDES, or from part of
an index structure. Let us also assume that there is a secondary index on ITEM
for INCLUDES and a primary index on O# for ORDERS, perhaps among other
indices.

```
SELECT CUST
FROM ORDERS, INCLUDES
WHERE ORDERS.O# = INCLUDES.O#
    AND ITEM = 'Brie';
```

**Figure 9.29** Find who ordered Brie.

The most efficient way to answer the query is to enter the ITEM index,
read-locking blocks as we need them, to find the tuples of INCLUDES that
have "Brie" in the ITEM component. Then, with the set of order numbers that
include Brie, we enter the O# index on ORDERS, to find the tuples for these

orders, again locking index blocks and blocks of the ORDERS relation as we go.

If we had to lock initially every block we might need during the execution of the query of Figure 9.29, we would have to ask for a lock on every block of the two relations and the two indices. Or, if we were using a hierarchy of locks, we would take locks on the entire relations and indices. However, if we can let the query run while we decide on the locks we want, we could begin with a lock on the root of the ITEM index, examine it to find the next step on the path to the Brie tuples, and so on. Typically, we would wind up locking only a small fraction of the blocks.

The advantage to limiting the number of blocks that get locked is that we can allow updating, insertion, and deletion to go on in parallel with our query, as long as those operations don't require the rewriting of any of the blocks our query accesses. Additionally, by taking locks as we need them, our query is allowed to proceed even if, say, an ORDERS tuple we needed was being written during the time we accessed the INCLUDES relation. □

## Aggressive Protocols

The most aggressive version of two-phase locking requests a lock on an item immediately before reading or writing the item. If an item is to be written after reading, the read-lock is taken first and upgraded to a write-lock when needed. Of course locks can only be released after all of the locks are taken, or we are outside the realm of two-phase locking, and nonserializable behavior becomes possible. Also, locks still must be released at the end if we wish to follow the strict protocol.

As was mentioned, this aggressive behavior can lead to deadlocks, where two or more transactions are each waiting to acquire a lock that another has, and none can proceed. The possibility that locks will be upgraded from read to write introduces another possibility for deadlock. For example, $T_1$ and $T_2$ each hold a read-lock on item $A$ and cannot proceed without upgrading their locks to a write-lock, as each wants to write a new value of $A$. There is a deadlock, and either $T_1$ or $T_2$ must abort and run again.

Incidentally, one might suppose that we could avoid deadlocks by the trick of ordering the items and having each transaction lock items in order. The problem is that when running transactions like Figure 9.29 aggressively, we cannot choose the order in which many of the blocks are locked. We have to traverse the index in the way it was designed to be traversed, for example. If the index is, say a B-tree, we could order the blocks top-to-bottom, so locking would occur in the right order, but how to we decide on the order for the index on ITEMS, relative to the index on O# for ORDERS? If we place the latter first, Figure 9.29 cannot get its locks in the right order. If we place the former first, then we have problems with a query that runs in the opposite direction from Figure 9.29, e.g., "find all the items ordered by Zack Zebra."

## Choosing an Aggressive or Conservative Protocol

Suppose that the nature of items and transactions is such that the chances of two transactions trying to lock the same item is very small. Then the probability of deadlock is very likely to be small, and an aggressive protocol is best. Aborting transactions will not reduce throughput by much, and by being aggressive we are avoiding the excess locking and unnecessary transaction delay that was illustrated in Example 9.21.

On the other hand, suppose that the typical transaction locks a large enough fraction of the items that unavailable locks are the norm rather than a rare occurrence. In this case, there is a high probability that a transaction will be involved in a deadlock, and if we are too aggressive, the probability that any given transaction will complete is small. Thus, the cost in wasted cycles may be too great, and a conservative protocol can easily turn out to be more efficient.

## 9.10 RECOVERY FROM CRASHES

In Section 9.8 we considered what must be done to handle single transactions that fail. Now, we must consider the more difficult cases of software and hardware failure. Such failures come in two degrees of seriousness, depending on what is lost. Memory can be divided into *volatile storage*, whose contents will not survive most failures such as loss of power, and *stable storage*, which can survive all but the most serious physical problems such as a head crash on a disk or a fire. Memory and cache are examples of volatile storage, while disks and tapes are stable. In what follows, we shall often use "secondary storage" as a synonym for "stable storage," and "main memory" may be regarded as meaning "volatile storage."

We shall refer to loss of volatile storage only as a *system failure*, while loss of stable storage is termed a *media failure*. A database system that does not lose data when a failure of one of these types occurs is said to be *resilient* in the face of that kind of failure.

## The Log

The most common tool for protecting against loss of data in the face of system failures is the *log* or *journal*, which is a history of all the changes made to the database, and the status of each transaction. That is, the following events are recorded by appending records to the end of the log.

1.  When a transaction $T$ initiates, we append record $(T, \textbf{begin})$.

2. When transaction $T$ asks to write a new value $v$ for item $A$, we first append record $(T, A, v)$. If there is the possibility that we shall have to undo transactions, as we discussed in Example 9.18, then this record must also include the old value of $A$. Also, if item $A$ is a large object, such as a relation or memory block, we would be better off letting $v$ be an encoding of the changes in $A$ (e.g., "insert tuple $\mu$") than the entire new value of $A$.

3. If transaction $T$ commits, we append $(T, \textbf{commit})$.

4. If transaction $T$ aborts, we append $(T, \textbf{abort})$.

**Example 9.22:** The following is really an example of how a log could be used to handle transaction abort, but it will illustrate several points about logs and system failures. Suppose we execute the fourteen steps of Figure 9.28, after which $T_1$ aborts. Since a system that allows the schedule of Figure 9.28 evidently is not using strict two-phase locking, we must allow for the fact that rollback of transactions is possible, and therefore, when we write new value $v$ for an item $A$ that had old value $w$, we write the record $(T, A, w, v)$. To allow actual values to be computed, we shall assume that item $A$ starts with the value 10.

Figure 9.30 shows the records written into the log and indicates the step at which the log entry is written. As we shall see, it is essential that the log entry be written before the action it describes actually takes place in the database. □

| Step | Entry |
|---|---|
| Before (1) | $(T_1, \textbf{begin})$ |
| (4) | $(T_1, A, 10, 9)$ |
| Before (7) | $(T_2, \textbf{begin})$ |
| (11) | $(T_2, A, 9, 18)$ |
| (12) | $(T_2, \textbf{commit})$ |
| After (14) | $(T_1, \textbf{abort})$ |

**Figure 9.30** Log entries for Figure 9.28.

Example 9.22 also suggests how the system could use the log to recover from the failure which we suppose happened after step (14) of Figure 9.28. It will also suggest some of the problems faced when we do not use the strict protocol. First, we examine the log and discover that $T_1$ has aborted, and therefore we must roll back the database to its state before $T_1$ began. It is not hard to find the record $(T_1, \textbf{begin})$ by scanning backwards from the end of the log. We can also find the record $(T_1, A, 10, 9)$ and discover that 10 is the value that must be restored to $A$.

What is not so obvious is that $T_2$ must be redone. Although evidently $T_2$ wrote $A$, the log does not record that $T_2$ read $A$ after $T_1$ wrote $A$. Thus, if we are going to deal with cascading rollback, we need to record read actions as well as write actions in the log. Worse, we now have to redo $T_2$ with the proper value of $A$, which is 10, in place of the value 9 that it used before. However, while we have the record $(T_2, \mathbf{begin})$ on the log, and $T_2$ is presumably a unique identifier for that transaction, we don't know exactly what code $T_2$ represents. Thus, if we are going to redo $T_2$ we need to keep an indication of what procedure underlies the transaction $T_2$. Moreover, we need to keep that code around indefinitely, since there is no limit to how much time could elapse between the running of a transaction and the discovery that it was involved in a cascading rollback.

## Some Efficiency Considerations

Recall from Section 6.1 that the cost of reading and writing data found on secondary storage is primarily the cost of moving blocks between main and secondary storage. Since only secondary storage is stable, whenever we want the ability to recover from system failures we must keep data on secondary storage, even if the database is small enough that it could fit completely in main memory. Typically, blocks of the database are moved in and out of main memory, and the system remembers in a *page table* the blocks that are currently in main memory. The portion of the system that moves blocks (pages) in and out of main memory is often termed the *page manager*, and the strategy it uses to decide on the page that must be sent back to secondary storage when space for a new page is needed we call the *paging strategy*.

A block $B$ of the database, once read into main memory, may be used for many reads and writes before it is written out into secondary storage again. That will occur either because

1.  We are lucky, and some general-purpose paging strategy left $B$ in main memory for a long time, or
2.  A special-purpose paging strategy used by the database system has recognized that $B$ is likely to be used several times and elected to keep it in main memory.

When we keep a log, we have, in effect, two copies of the database. On updating an item, we have a choice of writing the item itself into secondary storage or writing the corresponding log entry into secondary storage, or both. Before we take one of these steps, the change will be lost if the system crashes. For efficiency's sake, we would like to write only one into secondary storage, but which one?

A monent's thought tells us we are frequently better off writing the log into stable storage. The reason is that the log is created as a stream of data, and we can store many log records, say 10–100, on a single block. If we have $n$ write-records per log block, then we need to do only $1/n$th as much block writing as if we wrote the block of the affected item each time a write occurred. Of course, the paging strategy will probably cause some fraction of the database blocks to be written out anyway, during the time it takes to fill up one log block. Yet we are still likely to save time if we write log blocks into stable storage as they are created (or after each transaction, which we shall see is required) and write database blocks into stable storage only when required by the paging manager.

## A Resilient Protocol

We are now ready to discuss a protocol that is resilient in the face of system failures. There are several other methods in use, but this one is probably the simplest to understand and implement; others are mentioned in the bibliographic notes. This protocol is called the *redo* protocol, because to recover from system failure we have only to redo certain transactions, never undo them as was the case in Example 9.22.

The redo protocol is a refinement of strict two-phase locking. On reaching the commit point of a transaction $T$, the following things must happen in the order indicated.

1. For each item $A$ for which a new value, $v$, is written by the transaction $T$, append $(T, A, v)$ to the log.
2. Append the record $(T, \textbf{commit})$ to the log.
3. Write to stable storage the block or blocks at the end of the log that have not yet been written there. At this point, $T$ is said to be *committed*.
4. For each item $A$, write its new value $v$ into the place where $A$ belongs in the database itself. This writing may be accomplished by bringing the block for $A$ to main memory and doing the update there. It is optional to write the block of $A$ back into stable storage immediately.

**Example 9.23:** In Figure 9.31 we see a transaction $T$ following the redo protocol, and next to $T$ we see the log entries made in response to $T$. The commit point is reached between steps (3) and (4); we assume all calculations in the workspace are performed between steps (3) and (4). The log is written into stable storage between steps (6) and (7). □

## The "Redo" Recovery Algorithm

When a system failure occurs, we execute a *recovery algorithm* that examines the log and restores the database to a *consistent* state, i.e., one that results from the application of some sequence of transactions. It is also necessary that any locks held at the time of the crash be released by the system, since either the transaction that held them will be reexecuted and will ask for them again, or the transaction has already committed but not released its locks. In the latter case, the transaction will not be resumed, and so will not have an opportunity

| (1) |  | $(T, \textbf{begin})$ |
|------|--------|------|
| (2) | LOCK A | |
| (3) | LOCK B | |
| (4) | | $(T, A, v)$ |
| (5) | | $(T, B, w)$ |
| (6) | | $(T, \textbf{commit})$ |
| (7) | WRITE A | |
| (8) | WRITE B | |
| (9) | UNLOCK A | |
| (10) | UNLOCK B | |

**Figure 9.31** Transaction following the redo protocol.

to release the locks itself.

If transactions follow the redo protocol, we can repair the database by executing the following simple *redo algorithm*. Examine the log from the most recent entry back into history, and determine which transactions $T$ have a log record $(T, \textbf{commit})$. For each such transaction $T$ we examine each write-record $(T, A, v)$ and write the value $v$ for the item $A$ into the database that exists in stable storage. Note that $v$ may already be the value of $A$ at that time, since the original execution of $T$ may have progressed far enough that the change reached stable storage.

Transactions that did not yet write their **commit** record in the log, or that wrote an **abort** record, are ignored by the redo algorithm; it is as if they never ran. Observe that such transactions cannot have had any effect on the database, either in main or secondary storage, because of the order in which steps are taken in the redo protocol. It is not desirable that such transactions are lost, but there is nothing more we can do given only the log with which to create a stable state. As we have $(T, \textbf{begin})$ records in the log, we can at least print a warning that transaction $T$ did not complete, if we find $(T, \textbf{begin})$ but not $(T, \textbf{commit})$.[15]

Once we determine which transactions committed, we can scan the log in the forward direction. Each time we come to a record $(T, A, v)$, where $T$ is a committed transaction, we write $v$ into item $A$. Notice that we have no way of telling from the log whether the copy of $A$ belonging to the database had already been updated to correspond to this log record. It is possible that

1.   The crash occurred so soon after the $(T, \textbf{commit})$ record was placed in the log that there was no time to update the copy of $A$ in main memory, or

---

[15] If we include the procedure and arguments that constituted the transaction $T$, along with the **begin** record, we can rerun $T$ after reestablishing a consistent state.

2. The copy of $A$ in main memory was updated, but the crash occurred before the block holding $A$ was written into stable memory.

We cannot tell whether one of these cases holds, or if the writing of $A$ is in fact unnecessary. However, it doesn't matter, because either way, the value of $A$ winds up as $v$ in the database copy on secondary storage.[16] The reason is that we have recorded actions on the log in a way that makes their effect on the database *idempotent*; that is, the effect of applying the update any positive number of times is the same as applying it once. Consider in contrast what would happen had we recorded actions like "add 1 to $A$" on the log. This operation is not idempotent, so we would have to know for certain whether the update had been applied to stable storage before we allowed it to be redone. Because that is not something we can know, we are constrained to express updates in an idempotent way, such as by giving the new value as we have done.

Idempotence is also important if there is another crash during the time we are executing the redo algorithm. When the system is again operational, we simply begin the redo algorithm again, knowing that no updates performed or not performed during the previous attempt at recovery can affect our present execution of the redo algorithm.

**Example 9.24:** Consider the steps of Figure 9.31, supposing that a system failure occurs at some point. If the failure is prior to step (6), $T$ will not have committed as far as the log is concerned, so when we execute the redo algorithm, we ignore the update steps (4) and (5). If the crash occurs immediately after step (6), then $T$ has committed as far as the log is concerned, and when we recover we perform steps (4) and (5), thereby updating the values of $A$ and $B$ in stable storage. Since steps (7) and (8) were never done, we are certainly updating $A$ and $B$ with their values from transaction $T$ for the first time.

If the crash occurs after step (7), then $A$ will have been written before, but may or may not have its value written in stable storage [the writing of step (7) could have been in the main-memory copy of $A$'s block only]. Either way, the correct thing will be done when the redo algorithm performs the write indicated by step (4). Similarly, if the crash occurs later than step (7), we store the correct values in $A$ and $B$, regardless of whether they were correct already.

Finally, note that during recovery, all locks held by transactions must be released. If not, a crash occurring between steps (6) and (9), followed by recovery, would leave locks on $A$ and $B$, even though transaction $T$ had completed. □

---

[16] That is, unless a later update to $A$ appears in the log.

## Checkpointing

One might suppose from our example that recovery only involved scanning the log for entries made by the most recent transaction or a few recent transactions. In truth, there may be no limit to how far back in the log we must look. We need to find a point far enough back that we can be sure any item written before then has had its main-memory copy written into stable storage.

Unfortunately, depending on the paging strategy used, it may be hard or easy to find such a point, or to be sure one exists. In the extreme case, the entire database fits into main memory, and there is thus no reason why the page manager ever needs to write a page onto secondary memory. Thus, a database system needs occasionally to perform a *checkpoint* operation, which guarantees that any prior writes have been copied to stable storage. The easiest way to perform checkpointing is to do the following.

1.  Temporarily forbid the initiation of transactions and wait until all active transactions have either committed or aborted.

2.  Find each block whose main-memory copy has been updated but not re-copied into secondary memory. A bit associated with each page in the page table can warn us that the page has been modified.

3.  Copy the blocks found in (2) into secondary storage.

4.  Append to the end of the log a record indicating that a checkpoint has occurred, and copy the end of the log onto stable storage.

If we need to recover from a crash, we run the redo algorithm, but we only consult the log as far back as the most recent checkpoint. In fact, the log prior to the most recent checkpoint record will never be consulted for recovery from a system failure, and as long as that part of the log is not needed for any other purpose, such as to help recover from a media failure or to act as a record of activity in case of a security violation, it can be discarded.

**Example 9.25:** If we decide to do a checkpoint during the time that transaction $T$ of Figure 9.31 runs, we must wait until after step (10).[17] By the end of step (10), the values of $A$ and $B$ have at least been written into main memory. To perform the checkpoint, the values of $A$ and $B$ (and any other items that weer updated in main memory only) are written into secondary memory. A checkpoint record is appended to the log somewhere after step (10). If we need to recover from a later crash, the existence of the checkpoint record will prevent the redo algorithm from consulting the log as far back as transaction $T$. That is the right thing to do, because the effects of $T$ and previous transactions have already appeared in stable storage, and so were not lost during the crash. $\Box$

Evidently, checkpointing incurs some cost; not only might we have to do a

---

[17] If a crash occurs before then, the checkpoint will not have occurred and will not be written into the log.

lot of writing from main to secondary storage, but we need to delay transactions that want to initiate during the checkpoint process. Fortunately, checkpointing does not have to occur too frequently, since as long as crashes are rare, we prefer to spend a lot of time recovering (examining a long log) than to spend a lot of time during normal operation protecting against a time-consuming recovery process.

### Protecting Against Media Failures

Everything we have said so far was intended to help deal with system failures, but not with media failures, where the stable database itself is destroyed. Media failures can result from a "head crash" of a disk, a fire, or a small child with a large magnet running amok in the computer room; a nuclear holocaust will also do the trick. Clearly, there is nothing that will prevent loss of data in all these situations, but we can do better than what happens in most computer systems, where a head crash usually results in a message

```
We had a head crash; all your work of
the past week has been destroyed.
```

In many general-purpose computer systems, the main protection against a media failure is periodic backups, or *archiving*. For example, once a night. a backup copy is made of every file that has been changed since the last backup. If a file is changed during the backup, it may or may not have its change recorded on the backup, and nobody cares too much except the owner of the file. That casualness is sufficient for some database systems, but there are also some critical database applications where we must make the probability that anything gets lost in a media failure as low as possible; electronic banking systems and airline reservation systems are two examples.

Our principal tool for assuring resiliency against media failures is the (almost) continuous creation of an archive copy of the entire database. If we keep the archive copy on a set of disks distinct from those used for the "real" database, and we keep the two sets of disks sufficiently far apart that they are unlikely both to be destroyed at the same time, then we have good protection against losing data irretrievably. We can modify our techniques of logging and checkpointing to accommodate the creation of an archive copy of the database by observing the following points.

1. The log itself must be duplicated. When we write a block of the log to secondary memory, we must also copy that log block into the archive. If a media failure occurs between the times that the two copies are made, then that portion of the log will or will not survive, depending on which copy's medium failed. The transaction whose commitment caused the attempt to write the log into stable storage thus may or may not appear to have committed, but that is the worst loss that can occur. On recovery, we can

issue a message that the transaction was lost, since we shall find a **begin** record in one of the logs.

2. When checkpointing, we must make sure that any blocks that were modified since the last checkpoint are also copied into the archive. These blocks include those that were in main memory at the time the current checkpoint operation started, and which therefore will be copied into the stable storage of the database itself during the checkpoint operation. Also included are blocks that were previously written into the stable storage of the database, during the normal operation of the page manager. These blocks can be found by examining the log, since the last checkpoint, for items whose values have been written at least once.

## 9.11 TIMESTAMP-BASED CONCURRENCY CONTROL

Until this section, we have assumed that the only way to assure serializable behavior of transactions was to maintain and enforce locks on items. There are other ways one could enforce serializability as well. As an extreme example, the scheduler could construct the conflict graph based on all reads and writes it has issued to active transactions, and only allow an additional access to take place if it does not cause a cycle in that graph. While such a scheme is possible, it is hardly practical. However, another approach has been used in practice, and it is appropriate in situations where aggressive locking makes sense, that is, when it is unlikely that two transactions executing at about the same time will need to access the same item.

The general idea is to give each transaction a "timestamp," which indicates when the transaction began. For example, the scheduler could be called when each transaction begins and a timestamp issued then, or a timestamp could be issued to a transaction the first time the scheduler is asked for access to any item.

With two-phase locking, the order in which transactions reach their lock points (obtain the last of their locks) is the serial order that is guaranteed to be equivalent to the actual schedule. With the timestamp approach, the equivalent serial order is simply the order of the transactions' timestamps. These two approaches are incommensurate; a schedule could be equivalent to the lock-point-based serial schedule and not to the timestamp-based serial schedule, or vice-versa, as the next example shows.

**Example 9.26:** Consider the transactions of Figure 9.32. Since $T_2$ initiated before $T_1$, the timestamp-based serial order is $T_2, T_1$. On the other hand, if locking is used to serialize these transactions, then evidently, $T_1$ got a lock on $C$ before $T_2$ did. Thus, $T_1$ reached its lock point before step (3), while $T_2$ could not reach its lock point until after step (3). It follows that if locking is used, the equivalent serial order is $T_1, T_2$. Since the final value of $C$ is the one written by $T_2$, we conclude that in this case, the order based on lock points agrees with the actual schedule. Put another way, if we use two-phase locking, the schedule seen in Figure 9.32 is a possible schedule, but if we use timestamps to control concurrency, we could not allow such a sequence of events.

```
(1)                        READ B
(2)        READ A
(3)        WRITE C
(4)                        WRITE C

              T₁            T₂
```

**Figure 9.32** Schedule serializable by locks, not timestamps.

On the other hand, consider the schedule of Figure 9.33. We can tell that $T_2$ did not reach its lock point until after step (7), because $T_1$ had a lock on $B$ until that time, and therefore, $T_2$ could not have locked $B$ until that time. However, $T_3$ finished by step (6), and therefore reached its lock point before $T_2$ did. Thus, in a serial schedule based on lock points, $T_3$ precedes $T_2$. However, evidently, in a serial order based on the time of initiation, $T_2$ precedes $T_3$. Which of these orders can be correct? Only the order $T_2, T_3$ could appear in an equivalent serial schedule, because in Figure 9.33, $T_3$ writes a value of $A$ after $T_2$ reads $A$, and if the serial order had $T_3$ before $T_2$, then $T_2$ would erroneously read the value written by $T_3$. Thus, Figure 9.33 is an example of a schedule we could see if timestamps were used to control concurrency, but not if locking were used. □

```
(1)    READ A
(2)              READ A
(3)                         READ D
(4)                         WRITE D
(5)                         WRITE A
(6)              READ C
(7)    WRITE B
(8)              WRITE B

          T₁         T₂         T₃
```

**Figure 9.33** Schedule serializable by timestamps, not locks.

The point of Example 9.26 is that neither locking nor timestamps can be said to dominate the other. Each permits some schedules that the other forbids. Since we generally want a concurrency control method that permits as many serializable schedules as possible, we cannot rule out either timestamps or locking on the basis of the set of schedules they permit.

## Establishing Timestamps

If all transactions must go through the scheduler to get their timestamps, then timestamps may be created by having the scheduler keep a count of the number of transactions it has ever scheduled, and assigning the next number to each transaction in turn. Then, we can be sure that no two transactions get the same timestamp, and that the relative order of timestamps corresponds to the order in which the transactions initiated. An alternative approach is to use the value of the machine's internal clock at the time a process initiates, as that process' timestamp.

   If there are several processes that can assign timestamps, e.g., because:

1.   The database system is running on a machine with more than one processor, and several incarnations of the scheduler are possible, or
2.   The database is distributed over several machines, as discussed in Chapter 10,

then we must choose a unique suffix of some fixed length for each processor, and we must append this suffix to each timestamp generated by that processor. For example, if there were no more than 256 processors, we could append an 8-bit sequence to each timestamp, to identify the processor. We must also arrange that the counts or clocks used by each processor remain roughly in synchronism; how to do so is explained in Section 10.6.

## Enforcing Serializability by Timestamps

Now, we must consider how timestamps are used to force those transactions that do not abort to behave as if they were run serially. The particular scheme we describe is analogous to a locking scheme using read- and write-locks; we could have a timestamp-based system that did not distinguish between reading and writing (analogous to the simple locking scheme of Section 9.2). We could even have a timestamp-based scheme that distinguished more kinds of access, such as incrementation, as we discussed in Example 9.10.

   In the read/write scheme, we associate with each item in the database two times, the *read-time*, which is the highest timestamp possessed by any transaction to have read the item, and the *write-time*, which is the highest timestamp possessed by any transaction to have written the item. By so doing, we can maintain the fiction that each transaction executes instantaneously, at the time indicated by its timestamp.

We use the timestamps associated with the transactions, and the read- and write-times of the items, to check that nothing physically impossible happens. What, we may ask, is not possible?

1. It is not possible that a transaction can read the value of an item if that value was not written until after the transaction executed. That is, a transaction with a timestamp $t_1$ cannot read an item with a write-time of $t_2$, if $t_2 > t_1$. If such an attempt is made, the transaction with timestamp $t_1$ must abort and be restarted with a new timestamp.

2. It is not possible that a transaction can write an item if that item has its old value read at a later time. That is, a transaction with timestamp $t_1$ cannot write an item with a read-time $t_2$, if $t_2 > t_1$. The transaction with timestamp $t_1$ must abort and be restarted with a new timestamp.

Notice that the other two possible conflicts do not present any problems. Not surprisingly, two transactions can read the same item at different times, without any conflict. That is, a transaction with timestamp of $t_1$ can read an item with a read-time of $t_2$, even if $t_2 > t_1$. Less obviously, a transaction with timestamp $t_1$ need not abort if it tries to write an item $A$ with write-time $t_2$, with $t_2 > t_1$. We simply do not write anything into $A$. The justification is that in the serial order based on timestamps, the transaction with timestamp $t_1$ wrote $A$, then the transaction with timestamp $t_2$ wrote $A$. However, between $t_1$ and $t_2$, apparently no transaction read $A$, or else the read-time of $A$ would exceed $t_1$ when the transaction with timestamp $t_1$ came to write, and that transaction would abort by rule (2).

To summarize, the rule for preserving serial order using timestamps is the following. Suppose we have a transaction with timestamp $t$ that attempts to perform an operation $X$ on an item with read-time $t_r$ and write-time $t_w$.

a) Perform the operation if $X = $ READ and $t \geq t_w$ or if $X = $ WRITE, $t \geq t_r$, and $t \geq t_w$. In the former case, set the read-time to $t$ if $t > t_r$, and in the latter case, set the write-time to $t$ if $t > t_w$.

b) Do nothing if $X = $ WRITE and $t_r \leq t < t_w$.

c) Abort the transaction if $X = $ READ and $t < t_w$ or $X = $ WRITE and $t < t_r$.

**Example 9.27:** Let us review the transactions of Figure 9.1, which are shown in Figure 9.34, with the read-time (RT) and write-time (WT) of item $A$ indicated as it changes. Suppose that $T_1$ is given timestamp 150 and $T_2$ has timestamp 160. Also, assume the initial read- and write-times of $A$ are both 0. Then $A$ would be given read-time 150 when $T_1$ reads it and 160 at the next step, when it is read by $T_2$. At the fifth step, when $T_2$ writes $A$, $T_2$'s timestamp, which is 160, is not less than the read-time of $A$, which is also 160, nor is it less than the write-time, which is 0. Thus the write is permitted, and the write-time of $A$ is set to 160. When $T_1$ attempts to write at the last step, its timestamp, which is 150, is less than the read-time of $A$ (160), so $T_1$ is aborted, preventing the

|        | $T_1$       | $T_2$       | $A$       |
|--------|-------------|-------------|-----------|
|        | 150         | 160         | RT=0      |
|        |             |             | WT=0      |
| (1)    | READ A      |             | RT=150    |
| (2)    |             | READ A      | RT=160    |
| (3)    | A:=A+1      |             |           |
| (4)    |             | A:=A+1      |           |
| (5)    |             | WRITE A     | WT=160    |
| (6)    | WRITE A     |             |           |
|        | $T_1$ aborts |            |           |

**Figure 9.34** Transactions of Figure 9.1 using timestamps.

anomaly illustrated in Figure 9.1.

A similar sequence of events occurs if the timestamp of $T_1$ is larger than that of $T_2$. Then, $T_2$ aborts at step (5). $\square$

**Example 9.28:** Figure 9.35 illustrates three transactions, with timestamps 200, 150, and 175, operating on three items, $A$, $B$, and $C$, all of which are assumed to have read and write-times of 0 initially. The last three columns indicate changes to the read-times and write-times of the items.

|        | $T_1$       | $T_2$       | $T_3$       | $A$       | $B$       | $C$       |
|--------|-------------|-------------|-------------|-----------|-----------|-----------|
|        | 200         | 150         | 175         | RT=0      | RT=0      | RT=0      |
|        |             |             |             | WT=0      | WT=0      | WT=0      |
| (1)    | READ B      |             |             |           | RT=200    |           |
| (2)    |             | READ A      |             | RT=150    |           |           |
| (3)    |             |             | READ C      |           |           | RT=175    |
| (4)    | WRITE B     |             |             |           | WT=200    |           |
| (5)    | WRITE A     |             |             | WT=200    |           |           |
| (6)    |             | WRITE C     |             |           |           |           |
|        |             | $T_2$ aborts |            |           |           |           |
| (7)    |             |             | WRITE A     |           |           |           |

**Figure 9.35** Transactions controlled by timestamps.

At step (6), an attempt to write $C$ is made. However, the transaction doing the writing, $T_2$, has a timestamp of 150, and the read-time of $C$ is then 175. Thus, $T_2$ cannot perform the write and must be aborted. Then, at step (7), $T_3$ tries to write $A$. As $T_3$ has a timestamp, 175, that is bigger than the read-time of $A$, which is 150, $T_3$ need not abort. However, the write-time of $A$ is 200, so the value of $A$ written by $T_3$ is not entered into the database, but rather is discarded. $\square$

## Maintaining Timestamp Data

When we use locks, we save a lot of time and space by keeping in the lock table only facts about currently locked items. That is, there is a "default" status of "no locks," which applies to any item not mentioned in the lock table. In contrast, it appears that every item will eventually be given both a read-time and a write-time, other than the initial time (which was 0 in Examples 9.27 and 9.28, e.g.). We might then suppose that the table of timestamps must include entries for all items, or that the timestamps themselves must be stored with the items.

If the number of items is small, and the items themselves are large, then storing timestamps with items is feasible. However, if items are small, as often they are, we need to take advantage of a default value that will cover most of the items, and avoid storing the items with default timestamps explicitly. The "trick" is to realize that any item's read- or write-time that is less than the timestamp of all the active transactions may as well be $-\infty$, because the serialization rule for timestamps only cares about the relative values of the transaction's timestamp and the read- and write-times of the items it accesses. Thus, we can maintain the earliest active timestamp, updating it as transactions abort and commit, thereby becoming inactive. When the earliest active time-stamp increases, we can delete the timestamp entries that are earlier than the new earliest active timestamp. The deleted timestamps become $-\infty$, which by the argument above does not change the decisions made by a timestamp-based scheduler.

## Logs and Cascading Rollback

The scheme described above only works if we assume no transaction aborts. The problem is that a transaction may write a new value for an item, and later abort, leaving the value it wrote to be read by some other transaction. The transaction that read this "dirty" data must abort, and transactions that read what this transaction wrote must abort, and so on. The situation is one of cascading rollback, as discussed in Section 9.8.

We can handle this problem if we maintain a log, as described in the Section 9.10; the log is essential anyway, if our system is to be resilient. As in Example 9.22, when cascading rollback is a prospect, we need to append a record with the old value as well as the new, whenever a new value is written. If the likelihood that two transactions initiating at about the same time access the same item is low, then cascading rollback will be rare, and performance will not suffer seriously because of it. Since the timestamp concurrency control algorithm that we described here is an aggressive strategy, we probably only want to use it when access conflicts are rare anyway.

When we allow writing into the database before the commit point of a transaction is reached, we also face problems if we must recover from a system failure; it matters not whether concurrency control is maintained by timestamps, locking or another mechanism. We still need to place records $(T, \textbf{begin})$, and $(T, \textbf{commit})$ or $(T, \textbf{abort})$ on the log for each transaction $T$. However, it is no longer adequate to simply redo the transactions $T$ for which $(T, \textbf{commit})$ appears. If that record does not appear, then we also must undo any writes of $T$, using the old value that was placed in the log record for this purpose. Further, undoing $T$ may result in cascading rollback, just as if $T$ had aborted.

## Strict Timestamp-Based Concurrency Control

To avoid cascading rollback, and to allow the redo algorithm of Section 9.10 to suffice for recovery from system failures, we can adopt may of the ideas used for locking-based algorithms. First, we can perform all updates in the workspace, and write into the database only after the transaction reaches its commit point. This approach is analogous to strict two-phase locking, as discussed in Section 9.8, and we shall refer to this protocol as "strict" as well. As in Section 9.10, we perform our writes in two stages. First a record is written into the log, which is copied to stable storage; second the value is written into the database itself. Also as before, a **commit** record is written on the log between the two stages.

When we use timestamps, there is a subtlely that strictness introduces. We abort transaction $T$ if we try to write an item $A$ and find the read-time of $A$ exceeds $T$'s timestamp. Thus, the checking of timestamps must be done prior to the commit point, because by definition, a transaction may not abort after reaching its commit point.

Suppose, for example, $T$ has timestamp 100, and $T$ decides to write $A$. It must check that the read-time of $A$ is less than 100, and it must also change the write-time of $A$ to 100; if it does not change the write-time now, another transaction, say with a timestamp of 110, might read $A$ between now and the time $T$ reaches its commit point. In that case, $T$ would have to check again on the read-time of $A$ (which is now 110) and abort after $T$ thought it reached its commit point.

However, now we are faced with the situation where $T$ has changed the write-time of $A$, but has not actually provided the database with the value supposedly written at that time; $T$ cannot actually write the value, because $T$ still might abort, and we wish to avoid cascading rollback. The only thing we can do is to give transaction $T$ what amounts to a lock on $A$ that will hold between the time $T$ changes the write-time of $A$ and the time $T$ provides the corresponding value. If $T$ aborts during that time, the lock must be released and the write-time of $A$ restored.[18]

There are two different approaches to making the checks that are needed when a transaction $T$ read or writes an item $A$:

1.  Check the write-time of $A$ at the time $T$ reads $A$, and check the read-time of $A$ at the time $T$ writes the value of $A$ in its workspace, or

2.  Check the read-time of $A$ (if $T$ wrote $A$) and the write-time of $A$ (if $T$ read $A$) at the time $T$ commits.

In either case, when writing $A$, we must maintain a lock on $A$ from the time of the check to the time the value is written. However, in approach (1), these locks are held for a long time, while in (2) the lock is held for a brief time, just long enough for the other items written by $A$ to have similar checks made on their read-times. On the other hand, strategy (2), often called *optimistic* concurrency control, checks timestamps later than (1), and therefore will abort more transactions than (1).

To summarize, the steps to be taken to commit a transaction running under the optimistic strategy, item (2) above, are the following.

*i)*   When the transaction $T$ finishes its computation, we check the read-times of all items $T$ wants to write into the database; "locks" are taken on all these items. If any have a read-time later than the timestamp of $T$, we must abort $T$. Also check the write-times of items read by $T$, and if any are too late, abort $T$. Otherwise, $T$ has reached its commit point.

*ii)*  Write $T$'s values into the log.

*iii)* Append a **commit** record for $T$ to the log and copy the tail of the log into stable storage.

*iv)*  Write $T$'s values into the database.

*v)*   Release the "locks" taken in step (*i*).

If we use strategy (1), then the only difference is that step (*i*) is not done. Rather, the "locks" will have been taken, and the checks made, during the running of the transaction.

## A Multiversion Approach

To this point we have assumed that when we write a new value of an item, the old value is discarded. However, there are some applications where it is desirable to keep the history of an item available in the database. For example, a hospital may wish to store not only a patient's temperature today, but his temperature throughout his stay. The hospital may in fact wish to retain records

---

[18] If we do not restore the write-time, then a transaction with timestamp 90, say, might assume it did not have to write its value of $A$ because its value would be overwritten before being read in the equivalent serial schedule.

of a patient's condition indefinitely, because that information is relevant in the event of future treatment.

Even if we do not wish to keep old values indefinitely, keeping them for a while can help reduce the need for transaction abort at a small cost in extra space. Each time an item is written (with the exception noted below), we create a new version and give it a write-time equal to the timestamp of the transaction doing the writing. When a transaction with timestamp $t$ wishes to read an item $A$, it finds the version of $A$ with the highest write-time not exceeding $t$ and reads that version.

The only way we can have a problem is if a transaction $T$ with timestamp $t$ wishes to write $A$, and we find that there is a version $A_i$ of $A$ with a write-time less than $t$ and a read time greater than $t$. For the transaction that read $A_i$ had a timestamp bigger than $t$, and therefore should have read the value written by $T$, which has timestamp $t$, rather than the earlier version that it did read. The only way to fix things now is to abort $T$.

**Example 9.29:** The use of multiple versions does not help with the problem of the transactions of Figure 9.1, which we discussed in connection with time-stamps in Example 9.27 (Figure 9.34). Let $A_0$ be the version of $A$ which exists before the transactions $T_1$ and $T_2$ run. At steps (1) and (2), the read-time of $A_0$ is raised first to 150, then 160. At step (5), $T_2$ writes a new version of $A$, call it $A_1$, which gets write-time 160. At step (6), $T_1$ tries to create a new version of $A$, but finds that there is another version, $A_0$, with a read-time (160) bigger than $T_1$'s timestamp (150) and a write-time (0) less than $T_1$'s timestamp. Thus, $T_1$ must still abort. $\square$

| | $T_1$ | $T_2$ | $A_0$ | $A_1$ | $B_0$ | $B_1$ |
|---|---|---|---|---|---|---|
| | 100 | 200 | RT=0 | | RT=0 | |
| | | | WT=0 | | WT=0 | |
| (1) | READ A | | RT=100 | | | |
| (2) | | READ A | RT=200 | | | |
| (3) | | WRITE B | | | | WT=200 |
| (4) | READ B | | | | RT=100 | |
| (5) | WRITE A | | | WT=100 | | |

**Figure 9.36** A multiversion schedule.

**Example 9.30:** Consider the schedule of Figure 9.36. Two transactions, $T_1$ with timestamp 100 and $T_2$ with timestamp 200 access items $A$ and $B$. The initial versions of these items we call $A_0$ and $B_0$, and we assume these have read- and write-times of 0. $T_2$ creates a new version of $B$ with write-time 200, and $T_1$ creates a new version of $A$ with write-time 100; we call these $B_1$ and $A_1$, respectively. The advantage of multiple versions is seen at step (4), where $T_1$ reads $B$. Since $T_1$ has timestamp 100, it needs to see the value of $B$ that existed at that time. Even though $T_2$ wrote $B$ at step (3), the value $B_0$, which existed from time 0 to time 199, is still available to $T_1$, and this value is the one returned to $T_1$ by the scheduler. $\square$

Multiversion scheduling is the most conservative variety of timestamp-based concurrency control that we have covered. It clearly causes fewer aborts than the other approaches studied in this section, although it causes some aborts that conservative two-phase locking would not cause (the latter causes none at all). The disadvantages of multiversion scheduling are that:

1. We use extra space,
2. The retrieval mechanism is more complicated than for single-version methods, and
3. The DBMS must discover when an old version is no longer accessible to any active transaction, so the old version can be deleted.

We leave the discovery of an algorithm to achieve (3) as an exercise.

## Summary

There are four variants of timestamp-based concurrency control that we have considered in this section.

1. Unconstrained, with cascading rollback possible.
2. Check read- and write-times when an item is read from the database or written in the workspace.
3. Check read- and write-times just before the commit point (optimistic concurrency control).
4. Multiversion method. Here we could handle the read- and write-time checks as in any of (1)–(3); we shall assume (2).

The relative advantages of each are summarized in Figure 9.37.

## Restart of Transactions

The timestamp-based methods we have covered do not prevent livelock, a situation where a transaction is aborted repeatedly. While we expect transactions to be aborted rarely, or the whole approach should be abandoned in favor of the locking methods described earlier, we should be aware that the potential for cyclic behavior involving only two transactions exists.

**Example 9.31:** Suppose we have transaction $T_1$ that writes $B$ and then reads $A$, while $T_2$ writes $A$ and then reads $B$.[19] If $T_1$ executes, say with timestamp

---

[19] These transactions may read and write other items, so writing before reading need not

|                   | Locks | Abort       | Rollback           | Weak Point              |
| ----------------- | ----- | ----------- | ------------------ | ----------------------- |
| Unconstrained     | None  | Possible    | Cascading Aborts   | Rollback                |
| Check when read or write occurs | Long Time | Possible | Redo Algorithm | Locking |
| Optimistic        | Short Time | More Likely | Redo Algorithm | Aborts              |
| Multiversion      | None  | Less Likely | Redo Algorithm     | Flushing Useless Values |

**Figure 9.37** Advantages of different timestamp methods.

100, and $T_2$ executes with timestamp 110, we might find that $T_2$ wrote $A$ before $T_1$ read it. In that case, $T_1$ would abort, because it cannot read a value with a write-time greater than its own timestamp. If we immediately restart $T_1$, say with timestamp 120, it might write $B$ before $T_2$ reads it, causing $T_2$ to abort and restart, say with timestamp 130. Then the second try at $T_2$ might write $A$ before the second try of $T_1$ reads $A$, causing that to abort, and so on. The pattern is illustrated in Figure 9.38. □

|     | $T_1$ 100 | $T_2$ 110 | $T_1$ 120 | $T_2$ 130 | $A$ RT=0 WT=0 | $B$ RT=0 WT=0 |
| --- | ------- | ------- | ------- | ------- | ------------- | ------------- |
| (1) | WRITE B |         |         |         |               | WT=100        |
| (2) |         | WRITE A |         |         | WT=110        |               |
| (3) | READ A  |         |         |         |               |               |
| (4) |         |         | WRITE B |         |               | WT=120        |
| (5) |         | READ B  |         |         |               |               |
| (6) |         |         |         | WRITE A | WT=130        |               |
| (7) |         |         | READ A  |         |               |               |

**Figure 9.38** Indefinite repetition of two conflicting transactions.

The solution to the problem indicated by Example 9.31 is not easy to find. Probably the simplest approach is to use a random number generator to select a random amount of time that an aborted transaction must wait before restarting.

---

mean that the transactions are unrealistic.

In principle, new transactions could arise forever to cause a given transaction to abort each time it is run. However, if few transactions conflict, then the probability of having to restart a given transaction $k$ times shrinks as $c^k$, where $c$ is some constant much less than one. Further, the random delay each time a transaction aborts guarantees that the probability that a cyclic behavior like Figure 9.38 will go on for $k$ cycles shrinks in the same fashion.

## EXERCISES

9.1: In Figure 9.39 we see a schedule of four transactions. Assume that write-locks imply reading, as in Section 9.4. Draw the serialization graph and determine whether the schedule is serializable.

| | $T_1$ | $T_2$ | $T_3$ | $T_4$ |
|---|---|---|---|---|
| (1) | | RLOCK $A$ | | |
| (2) | | | RLOCK $A$ | |
| (3) | | WLOCK $B$ | | |
| (4) | | UNLOCK $A$ | | |
| (5) | | | WLOCK $A$ | |
| (6) | | UNLOCK $B$ | | |
| (7) | RLOCK $B$ | | | |
| (8) | | | UNLOCK $A$ | |
| (9) | | | | RLOCK $B$ |
| (10) | RLOCK $A$ | | | |
| (11) | | | | UNLOCK $B$ |
| (12) | WLOCK $C$ | | | |
| (13) | UNLOCK $A$ | | | |
| (14) | | | | WLOCK $A$ |
| (15) | | | | UNLOCK $A$ |
| (16) | UNLOCK $B$ | | | |
| (17) | UNLOCK $C$ | | | |

**Figure 9.39** A schedule.

9.2: Repeat Exercise 9.1 under the assumptions of Section 9.6, where a write-lock does not imply that the value is read.

* 9.3: In Figure 9.40 are two transactions. In how many ways can they be scheduled legally? How many of these schedules are serializable?

```
LOCK   A          LOCK   B
LOCK   B          UNLOCK B
UNLOCK A          LOCK   A
UNLOCK B          UNLOCK A

      $T_1$                 $T_2$
```

**Figure 9.40** Two schedules.

9.4: Give an example of why the assumption of Section 9.2, that a unique function can be associated with each time that a transaction locks an item, is too strong. That is, give a schedule of transactions that Algorithm 9.1 says is not serializable, but that actually has the same effect as some serial schedule.

9.5: Prove that if a transaction on a tree of items does not obey the tree protocol, then there is some transaction (that, in fact, does obey the tree protocol) such that the two transactions have a legal schedule that is not serializable.

9.6: Suppose we are using timestamp-based concurrency control. Reinterpret the operations of Figure 9.39 as if RLOCK were a READ operation, WLOCK were WRITE, and the UNLOCK steps did not exist. Which, if any of the four transactions in Figure 9.22 abort on the assumption that the timestamps of $T_1$ through $T_4$ are respectively

a)   300, 310, 320, and 330.

b)   250, 200, 210, and 275.

In each case, what are the final read and write times of $A$, $B$, and $C$?

* 9.7: Suppose we have three transactions that obey the tree protocol on the hierarchy of Figure 9.25 in Section 9.7. The first transaction locks $A, B, C$, and $E$; the second locks $C$ and $F$; the third locks $B$ and $E$. In how many ways can these transactions be scheduled legally?

** 9.8: A generalization of the warning protocol of Section 9.7 allows both read-and write-locks and warnings regarding these locks, with the obvious semantics. There are thus in principle sixteen lock modes an item may be given by a transaction, corresponding to the sixteen subsets of two kinds of lock and two kinds of warning. However, some combinations are useless. For example, it is not necessary to place a read-warning and a write-warning on the same item, since a write-warning forbids any action that a read-warning does. In how many different lock modes might a transaction wish to place an item? Give the compatibility matrix for these lock modes. For example, two transactions can each place a read-warning on an item, but one cannot place a read-lock when the other has a write-warning.

9.9: Two lock modes are *equivalent* in a given compatibility matrix if they have identical rows and columns. Show that there are only five inequivalent lock modes in your table from Exercise 9.8.

* 9.10: Suppose a set of items forms a directed, acyclic graph ($DAG$). Show that the following protocol assures serializability.

   *i*)   The first lock can be on any node.

   *ii*)  Subsequently, a node $n$ can be locked only if the transaction holds a lock on at least one predecessor of $n$, and the transaction has locked each predecessor of $n$ at some time in the past.

* 9.11: Show that the following protocol is also safe for DAG's.

   *i*)   The first lock can be on any node.

   *ii*)  Subsequently, a transaction can lock a node only if it holds locks on a majority of its predecessors.

* 9.12: Show that two-phase locking is necessary and sufficient for serializability in the model of Section 9.4 (read-locks and write-locks that imply reading).

9.13: In Example 9.10 we claimed that incrementation does not commute with either reading or writing. Give examples to show that is the case.

* 9.14: Instead of storing locks in a lock table, we could store locks with the items themselves. What problems would this approach cause? *Hint*: Consider the number of block accesses needed, on the assumption that a lock table fits in main memory, but the entire database does not. Also, what data structure would be necessary to store locks with items, assuming a lock mode like READ, which can be held by several transactions at once, were used?

* 9.15: Timestamps could also be stored with items instead of in a table. To what extent do the disadvantages of doing so with locks (as mentioned in Exercise 9.14) apply to timestamps?

* 9.16: Let us consider a database with a relation $R$ representing accounts at a bank. Suppose that items are tuples of $R$; i.e., each tuple is locked separately. There are many transactions that write new values of the BALANCE attribute of $R$, so many that it is unlikely for there to be a time when none of the tuples of $R$ are write-locked. Occasionally, we wish to run a long transaction that sums all the balances of $R$. Some potential problems are:

   *i*)   Lack of serializability; i.e., the sum of the balances does not reflect the situation that existed at any time in the history of the bank.

   *ii*)  Livelock; i.e., the sum-of-balances transaction has to wait indefinitely.

*iii*) Long delays; i.e., the short transactions must wait for the sum-of-balances to complete.

*iv*) Cascading rollback in case of system failure.

*v*) Inability to recover from system (not media) failures.

Indicate which of these problems may occur if we use each of the following concurrency-control strategies.

a) Strict two-phase locking, with locks taken at the time a transaction needs them.

b) Strict two-phase locking, with all locks taken at the beginning of the transaction.

c) Nonstrict two-phase locking, with locks taken at the time they are needed and released as soon after the lock point as they are no longer needed.

d) Non-two-phase locking, with locks taken immediately before reading or writing and released immediately after reading or writing.

e) Timestamp-based, optimistic concurrency control, with timestamps checked at the end of the transaction.

f) As in (e), but with timestamps checked when the items are read or written.

g) A multiversion, timestamp-based scheme, with appropriate versions read, and timestamps checked at the time of writing.

* 9.17: How do the fraction of cycles lost to aborted transactions compare in the situation of Exercise 9.16, for the seven concurrency-control methods listed?

* 9.18: Suppose that in the situation of Exercise 9.16 we instead used a hierarchy of items and the "warning protocol." That is, it is possible to place a read- or write-warning on the entire relation $R$. How would this approach fare with respect to problems $(i)$–$(v)$ mentioned in Exercise 9.16?

* 9.19: Extend the idea of warnings on a hierarchy of items to timestamp-based concurrency control.

* 9.20: In Example 9.20 we mentioned that it was possible for transaction $T_1$ to wait at the beginning of the queue forever, if locks could be given to following transactions on the queue, should all locks that such a transaction needs be available. Give an example of such a situation.

9.21: In Figure 9.41 is a list of transactions and the items they lock. We suppose that these five transactions become available to initiate in the order shown. $T_1$, the first to initiate, finishes after $T_3$ becomes available but before $T_4$ does. No other transaction finishes until after all five become available. Suppose we use the conservative, deadlock- and livelock-avoiding protocol of Theorem 9.7. Indicate the order in which the transactions actually

| Transaction | Locks Items |
|:-----------:|:-----------:|
| $T_1$ | $\{A, B\}$ |
| $T_2$ | $\{A, C\}$ |
| $T_3$ | $\{B, C\}$ |
| $T_4$ | $\{B\}$ |
| $T_5$ | $\{C\}$ |

**Figure 9.41** Transactions for Exercise 9.20.

initiate and the queue at each step.

* 9.22: Suppose we have a database that occupies 10,000 blocks, and 1,000 blocks will fit in main memory. Also assume each transaction reads and writes in 10 blocks, with all blocks equally likely to be accessed. The paging strategy is to write a random block back into secondary memory whenever space for a new block is needed.

   a) What is the average number of blocks per transaction read or written to or from main memory, if we copy into secondary storage all blocks accessed by a transaction at the time that transaction commits?

   b) Repeat (a) on the assumption that we only write blocks into secondary storage if they are thrown out of main memory by the paging strategy.

   c) Suppose we want to minimize the total number of block accesses, including both normal operation and the work that must be done reading the log and redoing transactions. Each log block may be assumed to hold the records for five transactions. What is the optimal number of transactions to wait between checkpoints, assuming a system failure occurs after every $10^5$ transactions?

9.23: Verify that $T_2$ aborts in Figure 9.34 if $T_1$ has a larger timestamp than $T_2$.

9.24: Does the multiversion approach of Section 9.11 solve the problem of the transactions in Figure 9.1 if $T_2$ has a smaller timestamp than $T_1$?

* 9.25: Suggest an appropriate data structure for maintaining read- and write-times, and deleting those that are earlier than the timestamp of the earliest active transaction.

9.26: Does the schedule of Figure 9.36 succeed (no transaction aborts) if single versions of items are used? Show what happens when the transactions are run.

* 9.27: Give an algorithm to tell when an old version in a multiversion system is no longer necessary.

## BIBLIOGRAPHIC NOTES

Much of the theory and practice of transaction management was first organized in the survey by Gray [1978]. Papadimitriou [1986] is an excellent summary of the theory of concurrency control in database systems, and Bernstein, Hadzilacos, and Goodman [1987] is likewise an important study of the theory and pragmatics of the subject. The organization of concurrency-control policies into families such as "strict," "aggressive," and "conservative," which we have followed here, comes from the latter text.

### Serializability

Eswaran, Gray, Lorie, and Traiger [1976] is the origin of the notion of serializability as the appropriate notion of correctness for concurrent database systems. Similar ideas appeared in Stearns, Lewis, and Rosenkrantz [1976], which includes the notion of a serialization graph.

   The model of Section 9.6 and the polygraph-based serializability test are from Papadimitriou, Bernstein, and Rothnie [1977] and Papadimitriou [1979].

### Locking

The two-phase locking protocol is from Eswaran, Gray, Lorie, and Traiger [1976].

   Some recent studies of the performance of different locking policies are found in Tay, Goodman, and Suri [1985], Tay, Suri, and Goodman [1985], and Franaszek and Robinson [1985].

### Lock Modes

The theory of lock modes is discussed in Korth [1983]. Stonebraker [1986] discusses the use of lock modes as a technique for implementing more expressive query languages, such as logic-based languages.

### Lock Granularity

The choice of lock granularity is discussed by Gray, Lorie, and Putzolo [1975] and Reis and Stonbraker [1977, 1979].

### Non-Two-Phase Locking

Two-phase locking is necessary and sufficient to assure serializability when an abstract model of transactions, such as appeared in Sections 9.2, 9.4, and 9.6, is used. If we model transactions in more detail, e.g., by using normal semantics for arithmetic operations, then we can use less restrictive protocols and still have serializability. This theory has been developed by Kung and Papadimitriou [1979], Yannakakis, Papadimitriou, and Kung [1979], Yannakakis

[1982a], Papadimitriou [1983], and Yannakakis [1984].

There have also been studies of particular algorithms that apply to specific situations. The tree protocol discussed in Section 9.7, is from Silberschatz and Kedem [1980]. A generalized version with read- and write-locks appears in Kedem and Silberschatz [1980]. The DAG protocol of Exercise 9.10 is from Yannakakis, Papadimitriou, and Kung [1979], and that of Exercise 9.11 from Kedem and Silberschatz [1979]. Further extensions are found in Buckley and Silberschatz [1985].

## Serializability for Hierarchies

The "warning protocol" is a simplification of ideas (sketched in Exercises 9.8 and 9.9) described in Gray, Putzolo, and Traiger [1976]. Carey [1983] discusses the theory of granularity hierarchies.

## Timestamp-Based Concurrency Control

The SDD-1 distributed database system (Bernstein, Goodman, Rothnie, and Papadimitriou [1978]) implemented timestamps as a concurrency control mechanism. Some of the theory for these methods is developed in Bernstein and Goodman [1980b] and Kung and Robinson [1981].

## Multiversion Systems

Reed [1978] was an early work proposing multilevel concurrency control. The formal study of multiversion scheduling began with Papadimitriou and Kanellakis [1984]. Later work was done by Bernstein and Goodman [1983] and Hadzilacos and Papadimitriou [1985].

## Predicate Locks

An interesting proposal in Eswaran, Gray, Lorie, and Triager [1976] is that locks should be taken on predicates. For example, consider what happens in the situation of Exercise 9.16 if, while balances are being summed, another transaction inserts a new tuple with a new balance. That tuple wasn't locked by the summing transaction because it didn't exist. Yet in principle, it should have been locked; i.e., it should not have been created until after the sum was complete. The trouble comes from our inability to lock the set of all balances, existing or not. Hunt and Rosenkrantz [1979] discuss the complexity of maintaining such *predicate locks*.

## Concurrency Control for Special Structures

Concurrent access to B-trees has received considerable attention. Bayer and Schkolnick [1977], Ellis [1980], Lehman and Yao [1981], Sagiv [1985], and Biliris [1987] cover the subject.

Other data structrures and their concurrent access are discussed by Manber and Ladner [1984] and Ellis [1987].

## Recovery

Two surveys of recovery techniques are Bernstein, Goodman, and Hadzilacos [1983], and Haerder and Reuter [1983]. In each, the distinction between "undoing," having to roll back completed transactions, and "redoing," having to redo partially-completed transactions as we discussed in Section 9.10, is made, and many algorithms are classified accordingly.

Many studies of the performance of different recovery strategies have been made, including Chandy, Browne, Dissly, and Uhrig [1975], Gelenbe and Derochette [1978], Reuter [1984], Agrawal and DeWitt [1985], and Garcia-Molina and Kent [1985].

The design of logs is discussed by Aghili and Severance [1982].

Hadzilacos [1982] considers how to minimize the cost of rolling back transactions.

For the theory and complexity of recovery algorithms, see Yannakakis and Papadimitriou [1985] and Hadzilacos and Yannakakis [1986].

An approach not classifiable under the "undo/redo" umbrella is *shadow paging*, a technique used in System R (Gray et al. [1981], Lorie [1977]). With shadow paging, two copies of all the blocks (pages) being modified by a transaction are kept, and the new copy atomically replaces the original at the moment a transaction commits.

## Nested Transactions

An improvement in our understanding of the semantics of transactions can be achieved if we view (presumably) atomic transactions as composed of smaller atomic steps; these "atomic" steps are in fact composed of smaller atomic steps, and so on, perhaps for many levels. The theory of serializability and concurrency control under such a model was developed by Beeri, Bernstein, Goodman, Lai, and Shasha [1982].

More recent investigations of the model include Weikum [1986] and Fekete, Lynch, Meritt, and Weihl [1987].

## Deadlocks

Holt [1972] is a fundamental paper on deadlocks, including the "waits-for" graph.

The theory of deadlocks in database systems is developed by Lipski and Papadimitriou [1981], Soisalon-Soininen and Wood [1982], and Yannakakis [1982].

# CHAPTER 10

Distributed
Database
Management

Our model of transaction management in Chapter 9 was that of a single computer operating on a database located on the secondary storage devices of that computer. In fact, databases frequently are distributed over many computers and their storage devices. In such a database, notions like two-phase locking become far more complex than they are when transactions are processed by a single machine. In this chapter we shall discuss the generalization of the concurrency control mechanisms of the previous chapter to the distributed environment. We also give algorithms for distributed commitment of transactions, distributed deadlock detection, and recovery from crashes in a distributed system.

## 10.1 DISTRIBUTED DATABASES

A distributed database consists of a collection of *nodes* or *sites*, each of which represents one computer and its associated secondary storage devices. Possibly some nodes have little or no secondary storage, and other nodes are only secondary storage, with the minimal computing power needed to store and retrieve data. Some pairs of nodes are connected by *links*, allowing data or messages to be transmitted from one of the pair of nodes to the other, in either direction.

For example, a collection of workstations on a local-area network could hold a distributed database, with part of the data at each workstation. The workstations are the nodes, and there is a "link" between every pair of nodes, because the network permits a message to be sent directly from any node to any other.

Other distributed databases have their nodes separated much more widely than the mile or so that limits the extent of a local-area network. For example, a bank might have a computer at each branch, and that computer would store the information about the accounts at that branch. The connections among nodes could be dedicated telephone lines, for example. While it is possible that there is a link from every node to every other, it is more likely that only a subset of the possible links exist.

Whether we are talking about a local-area network or a more widely distributed network, it should be apparent that communication between nodes is likely to be costly. In the local-area network, the capacity is large, but small messages such as "please grant me a lock on item $A$" bear considerable overhead. In a network composed of phone lines, the rate at which data can be transmitted is low compared with the instruction-execution speed of a computer. In either case, we are motivated to keep communication to a minimum as we execute transactions, manage locks or timestamps, and commit transactions.

### Resiliency of Networks

Naturally, a distributed database is vulnerable to a failure at any of its nodes. The links between nodes may also fail, either because the link itself fails, or because the computer at either end fails. We would like the distributed database system to continue to function when a link or node fails; i.e., the system should be *resilient* in the face of network failure.

One way to promote resiliency is to keep more than one copy of each item, with different copies at different sites. If we do so, then part of the transaction management problem for the distributed database is to guarantee that all of the copies have the same value; more specifically, we must ensure that changes to an item with several copies appears to be an atomic operation. That is especially difficult if one of the copies of item $A$ is at a node that has failed. When a node $N$ with a copy of $A$ fails, we may access other copies of $A$; that ability is what the redundancy provided by the multiple copies buys. When node $N$ eventually recovers, it is necessary that the changes made to $A$ at the other nodes are made at $N$ as well.

A more complex failure mode occurs when a link or links fail and thereby partition the network into two or more pieces that cannot communicate. For example, any tree becomes disconnected if a nonleaf node fails, or if any link fails.

**Example 10.1:** The failure of node $D$ in the tree of Figure 10.1 disconnects the tree into three pieces $\{A, B, C\}$, $\{E\}$, and $\{F, G, H\}$. The failure of the link $(B, D)$ separates the network into two pieces, $\{A, B, C\}$ and $\{D, E, F, G, H\}$. $\square$

Disconnection of the network makes it more difficult to keep the database system operational. For one problem, all the copies of an item may be in one block of the network partition, and the other blocks cannot access that item. For another problem, in different blocks, different changes may be made to the same item, and these changes will have to be integrated when the network

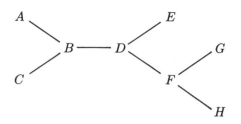

**Figure 10.1** Tree network.

is reconnected. Thus, when designing a network, there is an advantage to providing enough links that the network does not partition often. For example, linking the nodes in a circle protects against disconnection in the face of the failure of any one node or one link.

### Local and Global Items

As we have seen, that which we think of logically as an item may in fact be composed of many *fragments*, distributed among the nodes. For example:

1.  An item may have several identical copies, each of which is a "fragment." For resiliency, the fragments are stored at different sites.
2.  An item may be physically partitioned into several disjoint pieces. For example, a bank may maintain one relation

    ACCOUNTS(NUMBER, BALANCE)

    that is partitioned so the tuples for the accounts of each branch are physically located at that branch.
3.  Some combination of (1) and (2) may occur. For example, backup copies of the accounts at all the branches in a district are kept at the district office, and a copy of the entire ACCOUNTS relation is kept at the bank's main office.

It is, therefore, necessary to distinguish between an item in the *global* or *logical* sense, which is the item as seen from the point of view of the database as a whole, and *local* or *physical* items, which are the individual copies of an item that exist in the database.[1] For example, we wish to think about the action of locking a logical item as an atomic action. In reality, the action of taking a lock on logical item $A$ involves taking locks on the physical copies of $A$, and these lower-level actions may be separated in time, with many other intervening actions. We must, therefore, think carefully about how the action

---

[1] The distinction between "logical" and "physical" here should not be confused with the use of the same terms in Section 1.2.

of taking a logical lock is translated into taking physical locks, in such a way that the logical lock appears to be granted as an atomic action.

### Global Transactions, Local Subtransactions, and Serializability

Similarly, global transactions may be composed of many local subtransactions, each executing at a different site, and it is the job of the database system to assure that the global transactions behave in a serializable manner. The notion of "serializability" in a distributed database is a natural generalization of the definition given in Chapter 9. A schedule of transactions on a distributed database is *serializable* if its effect on the logical items is the same as that of the transactions executing serially, that is, one-at-a-time, with each in its turn performing all of its subtransactions at all the sites before the next transaction begins.

**Example 10.2:** Suppose transaction $T$ transfers \$10 from account $A$ to account $B$. Suppose also that $T$ is initiated at node $N_1$, copies of $A$ exist at nodes $N_2$ and $N_3$, and copies of $B$ exist at $N_4$ and $N_5$. Then $T$ must initiate two subtransactions that deduct 10 from the physical copies of item $A$ at $N_2$ and $N_3$, and also must initiate two subtransactions that add 10 to the physical copies of $B$ at $N_4$ and $N_5$. Thus, the global transaction $T$ consists of local transactions at each of the five nodes $N_1, \ldots, N_5$, and the effects of these transactions must be coordinated and made serializable. For example, the change to one copy of an item must not be made in the permanent database if the same change to the other copy is not guaranteed to be made eventually. That requirement holds even if, say, $N_3$ fails after $A$ is updated at $N_2$. In that case, we must be sure that $A$ will be updated at $N_3$ when that node recovers. $\Box$

## 10.2 DISTRIBUTED LOCKING

Our first task, as we extend concurrency control concepts from the single-site case to the distributed case, is to consider how locks on logical, or global, items can be built from locks on physical, or local, items. The only thing we can do with physical items is take a lock on a single physical copy $A_i$ of a logical item $A$, by requesting the lock from the lock manager that is local to the site of $A_i$.

Whatever we do with physical copies must support the properties we expect from locks on the logical items. For example, if we use read- and write-locks, then we need to know that at no time can two transactions hold write-locks, or a read- and a write-lock, on the same logical item. However, any number of transactions should be able to get read-locks on the same logical item at the same time.

If there is but one copy of an item, then the logical item is identical with its one physical copy. Thus, we can maintain locks on the logical item if and only if we maintain locks on the copy correctly. Transactions wishing to lock an item $A$ with one copy send lock-request messages to the site at which the copy resides. The lock manager at that site can grant or deny the lock, sending a back a message with its decision in either case.

However, if there are several copies of an item, then the translation from physical locks to logical locks can be accomplished in several ways, each with its advantages. We shall consider some of these approaches and compare the numbers of messages required by each.

### Write-Locks-All—Read-Locks-One

A simple way to maintain logical locks is to maintain ordinary locks on copies of items, and require transactions to follow a protocol consisting of the following rules defining locks on logical items.

1. To obtain a read-lock on logical item $A$, a transaction may obtain a read-lock on any copy of $A$.
2. To obtain a write-lock on logical item $A$, a transaction must obtain write-locks on all the copies of $A$.

This strategy will be referred to as *write-locks-all*.

At each site, the rules for granting and denying locks on copies are exactly the same as in Chapter 9; we can grant a read-lock on the copy as long as no other transaction has a write-lock on the copy, and we can only grant a write-lock on the copy if no other transaction has either a read- or write-lock on the copy.

The effect of these rules is that no two transactions can hold a read- and write-lock on the same logical item $A$ at the same time. For to hold a write-lock on logical item $A$, one transaction would have to hold write-locks on all the physical copies of $A$. However, to hold a read-lock on $A$, the other transaction would have to hold a read-lock on at least one copy, say $A_1$. But the rules for locks on the physical copy $A_1$ forbid a transaction from holding a read-lock at the same time another transaction holds a write-lock. Similarly, it is not possible for two transactions to hold write-locks on $A$ at the same time, because then there would have to be conflicting write-locks on all the physical copies of $A$.

### Analysis of Write-Locks-All

Let us see how much message traffic is generated by this locking method. Suppose that $n$ sites have copies of item $A$. If the site at which the transaction is running does not know how many copies of $A$ exist, or where they are, then we may take $n$ to be the total number of sites.[2] To execute WLOCK A, the trans-

---

[2] It is worth noting that considerable space and effort may be required if each site is to maintain an accurate picture of the entire distributed database, at least to the extent

action must send messages requesting a lock to all $n$ sites. Then, the $n$ sites will reply, telling the requesting site whether or not it can have the lock. If it can have the lock, then the $n$ sites are sent copies of the new value of the item. Eventually, a message UNLOCK A will have to be sent, but we may be able to attach this message to messages involved in the commitment of the transaction, as discussed in Sections 10.4 and 10.5.

The messages containing values of items may be considerably longer than the lock messages, since, say, a whole relation may be transmitted. Thus, we might consider sending only the changes to large items, rather than the complete new value. In what follows, we shall distinguish between

1.   *Control messages*, which concern locks, transaction commit or abort, and other matters of concurrency control, and
2.   *Data messages*, which carry values of items.

Under some assumptions, control and data messages cost about the same, while under other conditions, data messages could be larger and/or more expensive. It is unlikely that control messages will be more costly than data messages. Sometimes, we shall have the opportunity to attach control messages to data messages, in which case we shall count only the data message.

When a transaction write-locks a logical item $A$, we saw by the analysis above that it needed to send $2n$ control messages and $n$ data messages. If one of $A$'s copies is at the site running the transaction, we can save two control messages and one data message, although we must still request and reserve a lock at the local site. If one or more sites deny the lock request, then the lock on $A$ is not granted.

To obtain a read-lock, we have only to lock one copy, so if we know a site at which a copy of $A$ exists, we can send RLOCK A to that site and wait for a reply granting the lock or denying the lock request. If the lock is granted, the value of $A$ will be sent with the message. Thus, in the simplest case, where we know a site at which $A$ can be found and the lock request is granted, only two messages are exchanged, one control (the request), and one data (the reply, including the value read). If the request is denied, it probably does not pay to try to get the read-lock from another site immediately, since most likely, some transaction has write-locked $A$, and therefore has locks on all the copies.

## The Majority Locking Strategy

Now let us look at another, seemingly rather different protocol for defining locks on logical items.

---

of knowing what items exist throughout the database, and where the copies are. For this reason, among others, there is an advantage to using large items in a distributed environment.

1.  To obtain a read-lock on logical item $A$, a transaction must obtain read-locks on a majority of the copies of $A$.
2.  To obtain a write-lock on logical item $A$, a transaction must obtain write-locks on a majority of the copies of $A$.

We call this strategy the *majority* approach.

To see why majority locking works, note that two transactions each holding locks on $A$ (whether they are read- or write-locks doesn't matter) would each hold locks on a majority of the copies. It follows that there must be at least one copy locked by both transactions. But if either lock is a write-lock, then there is a lock conflict for that copy, which is not permitted by the lock manager at its site. Thus, we conclude that two transactions cannot hold write-locks on logical item $A$ simultaneously, nor can one hold a read-lock while the other holds a write-lock. They can, of course, hold read-locks on an item simultaneously.

### Analysis of Majority Locking

To obtain a write-lock, a transaction must send requests to at least a majority of the $n$ sites having copies of the item $A$. In practice, the transaction is better off sending requests to more than the minimum number, $(n + 1)/2$,[3] since, for example, one site may not answer, or another transaction may be competing for the lock on $A$ and already have locks on some copies. While a transaction receiving a denial or no response at all from one or more sites could then send the request to additional sites, the delay inherent in such a strategy makes it undesirable unless the chances of a failed node or a competing transaction are very small. We shall, however, take as an estimate of the number of request messages the value $(n + 1)/2$ and use the same value for the number of response messages. Thus, assuming the lock is granted, $n + 1$ control messages are used. Eventually $n$ data messages with a new value of $A$ will be sent, as well.

For a read, we must again send requests to at least $(n + 1)/2$ nodes and receive this number of replies, at least one of which will be a data message including the value that is read along with the lock on this copy of $A$. If the transaction runs at the site of one of the copies, we can omit this message. Thus, we estimate the number of messages for a read operation at $n$ control messages and one data messages (including a control portion).

### Comparison of Methods

Before proceeding to some other methods for distributed locking, let us compare the write-locks-all and majority methods. Each uses $n$ data messages for a write and one data message for a read. Write-locks-all uses $2n$ control messages for a write and one for a read, while majority uses $n+1$ for write and $n$ for read. Thus,

---

[3] In what follows, we assume $n$ is odd, and use $(n + 1)/2$ for the more precise $\lceil (n + 1)/2 \rceil$.

if an equal number of read and write-locks are requested by typical transactions, there is no advantage to either method. On the other hand, if most locks are for reading, the write-locks-all method is clearly preferable, and if write-locks dominate, we might prefer the majority method.

The two methods differ in a subtle way that affects the likelihood of a deadlock. Using the write-locks-all approach, two transactions, each trying to write logical item $A$, that begin at about the same time are likely each to manage to obtain a lock on at least one copy of $A$. The result is a deadlock, which must be resolved by the system, in one of a number of costly ways. In comparison, under the majority approach, one of two competing transactions will always succeed in getting the lock on the item, and the other can be made to wait or abort.

## A Generalization of the Two Previous Methods

The two strategies we have mentioned are actually just the extreme points in a spectrum of strategies that could be used. The "$k$-of-$n$" strategy, for any $n/2 < k \leq n$, is defined as follows:

1. To obtain a write-lock on logical item $A$, a transaction must obtain write-locks on any $k$ copies of $A$.
2. To obtain a read-lock on logical item $A$, a transaction must obtain read-locks on any $n - k + 1$ copies of $A$.

To see that the method defines locks properly, observe that if one transaction held a read-lock on logical item $A$, it would hold read-locks on $n - k + 1$ copies of $A$, while if another transaction simultaneously held a write-lock on $A$, it would hold write-locks on $k$ copies of $A$. Since there are only $n$ copies of $A$, some copy is read-locked and write-locked by different transactions at the same time, an impossibility. Similarly, if two transactions simultaneously hold write-locks on logical item $A$, then each holds locks on $k$ copies of $A$. Since $k > n/2$, some copy is write-locked by both transactions at the same time, another impossibility.

What we referred to as "write-locks-all" is strategy $n$-of-$n$, while the majority strategy is $(n + 1)/2$-of-$n$. As $k$ increases, the strategy performs better in situations where reading is done more frequently. On the other hand, the probability that two transactions competing for a write-lock on the same item will deadlock, by each obtaining enough locks to block the other, goes up as $k$ increases. It is left as an exercise that we cannot do better. That is, if the sum of the number of copies needed for a read-lock and a write-lock, or for two write-locks is $n$ or less, then physical locks do not imply logical locks.

## Primary Copy Protocols

A rather different point of view regarding lock management is to let the responsibility for locking a particular logical item $A$ lie with one particular site, no matter how many copies of the item there are. At the extreme, one node of the network is given the task of managing locks for all items; this approach is the "central node method," which we describe shortly. However, in its most general form, the assignment of lock responsibility for item $A$ can be given to any node, and different nodes can be used for different items.

A sensible strategy, for example, is to identify a *primary site* for each item. For example, if the database belongs to a bank, and the nodes are bank branches, it is natural to consider the primary site for an item that represents an account to be the branch at which the account is held. In that case, since most transactions involving the account would be initiated at its primary site, frequently locks would be obtained with no messages being sent.

If a transaction, not at the primary site for $A$, wishes to lock $A$, it sends one message to the primary site for $A$ and that site replies, either granting or withholding the lock. Thus, locking the logical item $A$ is the same as locking the copy of $A$ at the primary site. In fact, there need not even be a copy of $A$ at the primary site, just a lock manager that handles locks on $A$.

## Primary Copy Tokens

There is a more general strategy than the simple establishment of a primary site for each item. We postulate the existence of *read-tokens* and *write-tokens*, which are privileges that nodes of the network may obtain, on behalf of transactions, for the purpose of accessing items. For an item $A$, there can be in existence only one write-token for $A$. If there is no write-token, then there can be any number of read tokens for $A$. If a site has the write-token for $A$, then it can grant a read or write-lock on $A$ to a transaction running at that site. A site with only a read-token for $A$ can grant a read-lock on $A$ to a transaction at that site, but cannot grant a write-lock. This approach is called the *primary copy token* method.

If a transaction at some site $N$ wishes to write-lock $A$, it must arrange that the write-token for $A$ be transmitted to its site. If the write-token for $A$ is already at the site, it does nothing. Otherwise, the following sequence of messages is exchanged:

1.  $N$ sends a message to all sites requesting the write-token.

2.  Each site $M$ receiving the request replies, either:

    a)  $M$ either has no (read or write) token for $A$, or it has, but is willing to relinquish it so $N$ can have a write-token.

    b)  $M$ has a read- or write-token for $A$ and will not relinquish it (because some other transaction is either using the token, or $M$ has reserved that token for another site).

In case (a), $M$ must remember that $N$ has asked it for the token, but does not know whether it can have it yet [another site could answer (b)]. $M$ "reserves" the token for $N$; doing so prevents another site $P$ from also being told by $M$ that it has no objection to $P$'s obtaining the token.[4]

3.   If all sites reply (a) to $N$, then $N$ knows it can have the write-token. It sends a message to each site that replied (a), telling it that $N$ has accepted the write-token, and they should destroy whatever tokens they have for $A$. If some site replies (b), then $N$ cannot have the write-token, and it must send messages to the nodes that replied (a) telling them they can cease reserving the write-token for $A$, and may allow another site to get that token.

To read $A$, essentially the same process takes place, except that if the local site has any of the read-tokens for $A$, no messages need to be sent. In (2) above, the responding site $M$ does not object [send message (b)] if it has a read-token for $A$, only if it has a write-token. In (3), if $N$ is allowed to obtain a read-token for $A$, then only write-tokens, not read-tokens, are destroyed at other sites.

## More Comparisons Among Methods

Evidently, the primary copy token method uses considerably more messages than the other methods so far; both reading and writing can use $3m$ control messages, where $m$ is number of nodes in the network, while other methods use a number of messages that is proportional to the number of copies of an item, at worst. On the other hand, the primary copy token approach averages much less than $3m$ control messages per lock operation when one site runs most of the transactions that reference a particular item. Then the write-token for that item will tend to reside at that site, making control messages unneeded for most transactions. Thus, a direct comparison with the $k$-of-$n$ methods is not possible; which is preferable depends on the site distribution of the transactions that lock a particular item.

Similarly, we cannot compare the primary site method directly with the write-locks-all method; while the former uses smaller numbers of messages on the average, the latter has the advantage when most locks are read-locks on copies that are not at the primary site for that item. It appears that the primary site approach is more efficient than the $k$-of-$n$ methods for $k > 1$. However, there are other considerations that might enter into the picture. For example, the primary site method is vulnerable to a failure at the primary site

---

[4] The reason we must be careful is that there might be no tokens for $A$ at all. For example, none might have been created, or the last one could have been lost, because the node holding it failed. If we did not use "reservations," two sites could ask for the write-token for $A$ at the same time, and each be told by all of the sites (including each other) that they did not have any token on $A$. Then, each would create a write-token for $A$ and there would be two tokens when at most one should exist.

for an item, as the sites must then detect the failure and send messages to agree on a new primary site. In comparison, $k$-of-$n$ type strategies can continue locking that item with no interruption.

We can also compare primary copy token methods with the primary site approach. In the later method, a write requires two control messages to request and receive a lock from the primary site, then $n$ data messages, as usual, to write the new value. Reading requires a control message asking for a lock and a data message in response, granting the request and sending the value. If all transactions referencing $A$ run at the primary site for $A$, then the two approaches are exactly the same; no messages are sent, except for the obligatory writes to update other copies of $A$, if any. When other sites do reference $A$, the primary site method appears to save a considerable number of messages.

However, the token method is somewhat more adaptable to temporary changes in behavior. For example, in a hypothetical bank database, suppose a customer goes on vacation and starts using a branch different from his usual one. Under the primary site method, each transaction at the new branch would require an exchange of locking messages. In comparison, under the token approach, after the first transaction ran at the new branch, the write-token for the account would reside at that branch as long as the customer was on vacation.

### The Central Node Method

The last approach to locking that we shall consider is that in which one particular node of the network is given the responsibility for all locking. This method is almost like the primary site method; the only difference is that the primary site for an item, being the one *central* node, may not be a site that has a copy of the item. Thus, a read-lock must be garnered by the following steps:

1. Request a read-lock from the central node.
2. If not granted, the central node sends a message to the requesting site to that effect. If granted, the central node sends a message to a site with a copy of the item.
3. The site with the copy sends a message with the value to the requesting site.

Hence, the central node method often requires an extra control message to tell some other site to ship the value desired. Similarly, when writing, the site running the transaction must often send an extra message to the central node telling it to release the lock. In the primary site method, this message would be included with the messages committing the transaction.

Therefore, it seems that the central node approach behaves almost like the primary site method, but slower. Moreover, while it does not show in our model, which only counts messages without regard for destination, there is the added disadvantage that most of the message traffic is headed to or from one node, thus creating a potential bottleneck. Additionally, this method is especially vulnerable to a crash of the central node.

However, the algorithm has its redeeming features, also in areas not covered by our model. For example, under certain assumptions about loads on the system, there is an advantage to be had by bundling messages to and from the central site. The case for the central node approach is made by Garcia-Molina [1979].

### Summary

The relative merits and demerits of the various approaches are summarized in Figure 10.2. We use $n$ for the number of copies of an item and $m$ for the total number of nodes. We assume in each case that the lock is granted and we ignore the possible savings that result if we can read or write at the same site as the transaction, thus saving a data message. The tabulation of Figure 10.2 counts only control messages, since each write requires $n$ data messages, and each read requires one data message, no matter what the locking method.

| Method | Control Msgs. to Write | Control Msgs. to Read | Comments |
|---|---|---|---|
| Write-Locks-All | $2n$ | 1 | Good if read dominates |
| Majority | $\geq n + 1$ | $\geq n$ | Avoids some deadlock |
| Primary Site | 2 | 1 | Efficient; some vulnerability to crash |
| Primary Copy Token | $0\text{--}4m$ | $0\text{--}4m$ | Adapts to changes in use pattern |
| Central Node | 3 | 2 | Vulnerable to crash; efficiencies may result from centralized traffic pattern |

**Figure 10.2** Advantages and disadvantages of distributed locking methods.

## 10.3 DISTRIBUTED TWO-PHASE LOCKING

From the last section, we see that it is feasible to define locks on logical items in various ways. Now, we must consider how to use locking to ensure the serializability of transactions that consist of several subtransactions, each running at a different site. Recall that a schedule of transactions in a distributed environment is a sequence of events, each occurring at one site. While several sites may perform actions simultaneously, we shall break ties arbitrarily, and assume that, according to some global clock, there is a linear order to events. A schedule is *serial* if it consists of all the actions for one transaction, followed by all the actions for another, and so on. A schedule is *serializable* if it is equivalent, in its effect on the database, to a serial schedule.

Recalling the strong relationship between serializability and two-phase locking from Section 9.3, let us consider how two-phase locking can be generalized to the distributed environment. Our first guess might be that at each node, the subtransactions should follow the two-phase protocol. However, that is not enough, as the following example shows.

**Example 10.3:** Suppose that logical transaction $T_1$ has two subtransactions:

1. $T_{1.1}$, which runs at site $S_1$ d writes a new value for copy $A_1$ of logical item $A$, and

2. $T_{1.2}$, which runs at site $S_2$ and writes the same new value for copy $A_2$ of $A$.

Also, transaction $T_2$ has two subtransactions, $T_{2.1}$ running at $S_1$ and writing a new value of $A_1$, and $T_{2.2}$, running at $S_2$ and writing the same value into $A_2$. We shall assume that write-locks-all is the protocol followed by these transactions for defining locks on logical items, but as we shall see, other methods cause similar problems.

| $T_{1.1}$ | $T_{2.1}$ | $T_{1.2}$ | $T_{2.2}$ |
|-----------|-----------|-----------|-----------|
| WLOCK $A_1$ | | | WLOCK $A_2$ |
| UNLOCK $A_1$ | | | UNLOCK $A_2$ |
| | WLOCK $A_1$ | WLOCK $A_2$ | |
| | UNLOCK $A_1$ | UNLOCK $A_2$ | |
| At $S_1$ | | At $S_2$ | |

**Figure 10.3** Transactions with two-phase locking at each node.

For the example at hand, we see in Figure 10.3 a possible schedule of actions at the two sites. Pairs of events on each line could occur simultaneously, or we could assume they occur in either order; it doesn't matter. Evidently, the situation at site $S_1$ tells us that $T_{1.1}$ must precede $T_{2.1}$ in the serial order. At

$S_2$ we find that $T_{2.2}$ must precede $T_{1.2}$. Unfortunately, a serial order must be formed not just from the subtransactions, but from (logical) transactions. Thus, if we choose to have $T_1$ precede $T_2$, then $T_{1.2}$ precedes $T_{2.2}$, violating the local ordering at $S_2$. Similarly, if the serial order is $T_2, T_1$, then the local ordering at $S_1$ is violated. In fact, in the order of events indicated in Figure 10.3, the two copies of $A$ receive different final values, which should immediately convince us that no equivalent serial order exists.

The problem indicated above is not restricted to write-locks-all. For example, suppose we use the primary site method of locking. We can modify Figure 10.3 by letting $A_1$ be the sole copy of $A$ and letting $A_2$ be the sole copy of another logical item $B$. Therefore, $S_1$ and $S_2$ are the primary sites for $A$ and $B$, respectively. The schedule of Figure 10.3 is still not serializable, since the final value of $B$ is that written by $T_1$ and the final value of $A$ is what $T_2$ writes. In fact, notice that all the locking methods of Section 10.2 become the same when there is only one copy of each item; thus this problem of nonserializability comes up no matter what method we use. □

### Strict Two-Phase Locking

The problem illustrated by Example 10.3 is that in order for distributed transactions to behave as if they are two-phase locked, we must consider not only the local schedules, but the global schedule of actions, and that schedule must be two-phase locked. The consequence is that a subtransaction of $T$ cannot release any lock if it is possible that another subtransaction of $T$ at another site will later request a lock. For example, $T_{1.1}$ of Figure 10.3 violated this principle by unlocking $A_1$ before $T_{1.2}$ got its lock on $A_2$.

Thus, each subtransaction of a given transaction must inform the other subtransactions that it has requested all of its locks. Only after all subtransactions have reached their individual lock points has the transaction as a whole reached its lock point, after which the subtransactions may release their locks. The problem of all subtransactions agreeing that they have reached the lock point is one example of a *distributed agreement problem*. We shall study another, the distributed agreement to commit, in the next section. It will then become clear that distributed agreement, especially in the face of possible network failures, is very complex and expensive. Thus, the sending of control messages to establish that the subtransactions have reached their lock points is not normally sensible.

Rather, there are many reasons to insist that transactions in a distributed environment be strict, that is, they unlock only after reaching their commit point. For example, Section 9.8 discussed the problem of reading dirty data and consequent cascading rollback, e.g., which strict two-phase locking solves. If our transactions obey the strict protocol, then we can use the commit point as the lock point. The subtransactions agree to commit, by a process described in the next section, and only after committing are locks released.

In a situation like Figure 10.3, $T_{1.1}$ and $T_{2.2}$ would not release their locks at the second line, if the strict protocol were followed. In this case, there would be a deadlock between $T_1$ and $T_2$, since each has a subtransaction that is waiting for a lock held by a subtransaction of the other. We shall discuss distributed deadlock detection in Section 10.8. In this case, one of $T_1$ and $T_2$ has to abort, along with all of its subtransactions.

## 10.4 DISTRIBUTED COMMITMENT

For the reason just discussed (supporting distributed two-phase locking), as well as for the reasons discussed in Sections 9.8 and 9.10 (resiliency), it is necessary for a distributed transaction to perform a commit action just before termination. The existence of subtransactions at various sites complicates the process considerably.

Suppose we have a transaction $T$ which initiated at one site and spawned subtransactions at several other sites. We shall call the part of $T$ that executes at its home site a subtransaction of the logical transaction $T$; thus logical $T$ consists solely of subtransactions, each executing at a different site. We distinguish the subtransaction at the home site by calling it the *coordinator*, while the other subtransactions are the *participants*. This distinction is important when we describe the distributed commitment process.

In the absence of failures, distributed commitment is conceptually simple. Each subtransaction $T_i$ of logical transaction $T$ decides whether to commit or abort. Recall, $T_i$ could abort for any of the reasons discussed in Chapter 9, such as involvement in a deadlock or an illegal database access. When $T_i$ decides what it wants to do, it sends a `vote-commit` or `vote-abort` message to the coordinator. If the `vote-abort` message is sent, $T_i$ knows the logical transaction $T$ must abort, and therefore $T_i$ may terminate. However, if $T_i$ sends the `vote-commit` message, it does not know whether $T$ will eventually commit, or whether some other subtransaction will decide to abort, thus causing $T$ to abort.

Thus, after voting to commit, $T_i$ must wait for a message from the coordinator. If the coordinator receives a `vote-abort` message from any subtransaction, it sends `abort` messages to all of the subtransactions, and they all abort, thus aborting the logical transaction $T$. If the coordinator receives `vote-commit` messages from all subtransactions (including itself), then it knows that $T$ may commit. The coordinator sends `commit` messages to all of the subtransactions. Now, the subtransactions all know that $T$ can commit, and they take what steps are necessary at their local site to perform the commitment, e.g., writing in the log and releasing locks.

It is useful to visualize the subtransactions changing state in response to their changes in knowledge about the logical transaction. In Figure 10.4, the

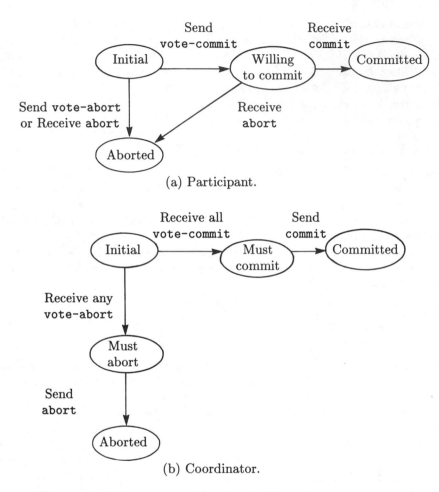

(a) Participant.

(b) Coordinator.

**Figure 10.4** State transactions for distributed commitment.

transitions among states are indicated. The following comments are useful in understanding the diagram.

1.  Do not forget to distinguish between *voting* messages, which are sent by participant transactions to the coordinator, and *decision* messages sent by the coordinator to the participants.

2.  The coordinator is a participant, and in principle sends messages to itself, although we do not "pay" for these messages with network traffic. For example, the coordinator might decide to abort because it divides by zero, which we regard, in Figure 10.4(b), as if the coordinator had "received" a `vote-abort` message from itself.

3.  The Committed and Aborted states really are not entered until the sub-transactions perform whatever steps are required, such as releasing locks and writing in the log.

4.  When a participant is in the Initial state, it will eventually decide to send `vote-abort` or `vote-commit`, entering the Aborted or Willing-to-commit states, respectively. This decision is based on the circumstances of the participant; for example, it "decides" to abort if the system tells it that it is involved in a deadlock and must abort.

5.  It is also possible that a participant will enter the Aborted state because the coordinator tells it to. That may happen if some other participant has decided to abort and informed the coordinator, which relays the message to all participants.

6.  The use of a coordinator is not essential. All participants could broadcast their votes to all others. However, the number of messages would then be proportional to the square of the number of participants, rather than linearly proportional to this number. Commitment algorithms of this type are discussed in the exercises.

### Blocking of Transactions

When there are network failures, the simple distributed commitment protocol of Figure 10.4 can lead to *blocking*, a situation where a subtransaction at a site that has not failed can neither commit nor abort until failures at other sites are repaired. Since a site may be down indefinitely, and since the blocked subtransaction may be holding locks on items, which it cannot release, we are in a difficult situation indeed. There are many circumstances that can cause blocking; perhaps the simplest is the following.

**Example 10.4:** Suppose a subtransaction $T_i$ holds a lock on one copy of item $A$, and $T_i$ reaches its commit point. That is, $T_i$ sends `vote-commit` to its coordinator and enters the state Willing-to-commit in Figure 10.4(a). After a long time, $T_i$ receives neither a `commit` nor an `abort` message from the coordinator. We claim that $T_i$ must remain in this state and hold its lock on the local copy of $A$; i.e., $T_i$ is blocked. Any other action can lead to an error.

1.  If $T_i$ decides to commit without instructions from the coordinator, it may be that some other subtransaction with a local copy of $A$ decided to abort, but the coordinator has failed and cannot tell $T_i$ to abort. If $T_i$ commits, another transaction may read the local copy of $A$, which should not have been changed; i.e., the local copy of $A$ is dirty data.

2.  If $T_i$ decides to abort without instructions from the coordinator, it could be that the coordinator received `vote-commit` messages from all participants, but afterward, the network failed, cutting $T_i$ off from the coordinator. However, some other participants were not cut off from the coordinator;

they received the `commit` message and wrote new values for their copies of $A$. Thus, the copies of $A$ no longer hold the same value.

Other options could be considered, such as releasing the lock on $A$ without committing or aborting. However, all options can lead to an inconsistent value for the copies of $A$, because $T_i$ is in a state where it does not know whether the logical transaction of which $T_i$ is a part will eventually commit or abort, and there are scenarios where either could happen. $\square$

## Two-Phase Commit

The most common approach to distributed commitment is a variant of the simple algorithm of Figure 10.4. The protocol is called *two-phase commit*, because of the two phases, voting followed by decision, that we see in Figure 10.4. Two-phase commit does not avoid all blocking, but it does reduce the likelihood of blocking. We shall later mention an improvement, called "three-phase commit," which does avoid blocking when nodes fail (although not necessarily when the network disconnects).

Two-phase commit offers two improvements over the simplest protocol. First, subtransactions measure the time since a response message was first expected, and if the message is delayed so long that it is probable a network failure has occurred, the subtransaction "times out," entering a state from which it will attempt to recover. The most serious problem, as we saw in Example 10.4, is when a participant is in the Willing-to-commit state, and a *timeout* occurs, i.e., the elapsed time since it sent the `vote-commit` message exceeds a preset time limit. To help avoid blocking, such a transaction sends a message `help-me` to all other participants.

On receiving a `help-me` message:

1. A participant in the Committed state replies `commit`. It can do so safely, because it must have received the `commit` message from the coordinator, and thus knows that all participants have voted to commit.
2. A participant that is in the Aborted state can send the `abort` message, because it knows that the transaction must abort.
3. A participant that has not voted yet (i.e., one in the Initial state) can help resolve the problem by deciding arbitrarily to abort, so it too makes an `abort` reply and sends `vote-abort` to the coordinator.[5]
4. A participant in the Waiting-to-commit state cannot help resolve the problem, so it makes no reply.

A blocked transaction that receives an `abort` or `commit` message follows that instruction, going to the appropriate state. That this choice is always correct

---

[5] We leave as an exercise the observation that should a participant in the Initial state decide to commit in this situation there is the possibility of inconsistent data.

is expressed by the following theorem.

**Theorem 10.1:** A participant $T_i$ that sends a `help-me` message

a) Cannot receive both `commit` and `abort` as replies from different participants.

b) Cannot receive `commit` from a participant if the coordinator can eventually send `abort`.

c) Cannot receive `abort` from a participant if the coordinator can eventually send `commit`.

**Proof:** $T_i$ can receive `commit` only if some other participant has received `commit`, which means the coordinator has already sent `commit`. Thus, (b) follows.

$T_i$ can receive `abort` in cases (2) and (3) above. In case (2), the sending participant either

a) Has received `abort` from the coordinator, or

b) Has decided to abort.

In case (a), the coordinator has already sent `abort`; in case (b), it will receive, or has received, `vote-abort`, or it will fail, and so can never send `commit`. In case (3), the sending participant has not voted previously, so the coordinator has sent neither `commit` nor `abort`. However, that participant now sends `vote-abort`, so the coordinator can never send `commit`. Thus, (c) follows.

For (a), we noted above that $T_i$ receives `commit` from a participant only if the coordinator has sent `commit`. Thus, cases (2) and (3) are impossible, so $T_i$ cannot also receive `abort` from a participant. □

The second modification to Figure 10.4 that two-phase commit uses is to initiate the voting by a `begin-vote` message sent by the coordinator to all participants. Under some circumstances, this message could be dispensed with, as each subtransaction could assume it was to vote as soon as possible. However, as we just saw, if recovery from the Willing-to-commit state is necessary, then each subtransaction needs to know the other participants, from whom it requests help. We cannot necessarily know the full set of participants when each subtransaction is created, because the transaction may execute conditional statements, and use different subtransactions in different branches (see Example 9.21, for the effect of conditionals in transactions). Thus, a possible function of the `begin-vote` message is to transmit the full list of participants, in case help is necessary.

Figure 10.5 shows the state transitions of the two-phase commit protocol, both for the participants and for the coordinator. The points made in connection with Figure 10.4 still apply. In addition, we note that when a participant times out in the Willing-to-commit state, it goes to the Recover state, from which it issues the `help-me` message. It then goes to the Blocked state, and waits for a `commit` or `abort` message from another participant. If it never re-

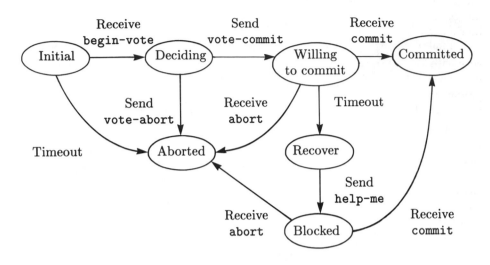

(a) Participant.

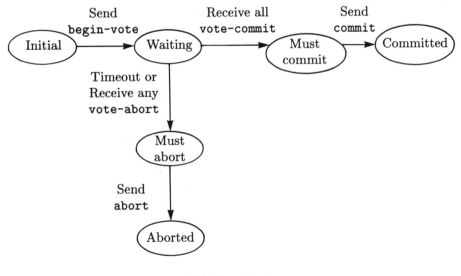

(b) Coordinator.

**Figure 10.5** Two-phase Commit.

ceives one, because all other participants are either cut off from the sender, failed, or also in the Willing-to-commit state, then this participant remains blocked.

There are two other conditions under which a timeout occurs and some action to avoid blocking occurs. In Figure 10.5(b), the coordinator times out if, after it sends begin-vote, one or more participants do not vote, after a predetermined and long time limit. If so, the coordinator decides to abort and sends abort messages to all the participants that can hear it [6] Of course, participants that are cut off from the coordinator at this time will not get the message; they remain blocked, if they heard the earlier begin-vote, voted to commit, and are unable to recover successfully when they time out.

The last place a timeout can occur is in Figure 10.5(a), where a participant has finished its task and a long time elapses, during which it is never asked to vote. Possibly the coordinator has failed or been cut off from this participant. The participant decides to abort, so it can release its locks. Not shown in Figure 10.5(a) is the fact that if subsequently, this participant does get a begin-vote message from its coordinator, it simply votes to abort. Some additional points about the transitions of Figure 10.5 follow.

1.  A transaction may have entered the Aborted or Committed state and still be asked to send messages in response to a help-me. There is nothing wrong with the supposition that a nonactive transaction will respond to messages. In reality, the system consults its log and responds for the transaction. In fact, normally all messages and state changes are managed by the system, rather than being built into transactions.

2.  In the blocked state, it makes sense to repeat the help-me message after a while, in the hope that a node that was failed or disconnected will now be available to help. In many systems, a node that recovers from a failure will make its presence known anyway, since it must find out about what happened to the transactions it was involved in and the items they changed. Thus, a blocked subtransaction can resend help-me whenever a node with a participant subtransaction reestablishes communication.

### Recovery

In addition to logging all of the information discussed in Section 9.10, a distributed system that is resilient against network failures must enter into the log at each site the messages it sends and receives. When a node recovers, or becomes reconnected to parts of the network that it could not reach for a while, it is the responsibility of that node to find out what has happened to the

---

[6] Notice that deciding to abort in ambiguous situations is always safe as long as no participant can then decide to commit; that possibility is what makes the Willing-to-commit state the source of most of the complexity.

transactions it was running when the failure or disconnection occurred. The log at a node tells it what subtransactions began but did not commit at that node. If the begin-vote message was received, that is recorded in the log, and with it the participants in the vote are listed. Thus, the recovering node knows whom to ask about the outcome.

For example, participant $T_i$ might have received the begin-vote message, voted to commit, and then failed. The coordinator may have sent commit, which $T_i$ never heard. However, some other participant, perhaps the coordinator, certainly knows that the decision was to commit, so it can tell the node of $T_i$ that it too should commit. As another example, if the begin-vote is recorded in the log, but no vote is recorded, then surely the coordinator timed out while waiting for a response, so we know that the decision to abort was made, and $T_i$ can abort.

## 10.5 A NONBLOCKING COMMIT PROTOCOL

The two-phase commit protocol that we discussed in the previous section does not avoid blocking, although it reduces the probability of blocking below what the simplest voting scheme (Figure 10.4) produces. No scheme can avoid blocking (or worse, causing different participants to make different commit/abort decisions) in situations where the network may disconnect. However, we can reduce the number of situations where blocking occurs by adding an additional phase to the commitment process.

Intuitively, the two-phase commit protocol allows a participant to commit as soon as it knows that all participants have voted to commit. In a "three-phase commit," a participant does not commit until it not only knows that all participants have voted to commit, but it knows that all participants know that too (or they have failed, and will know it when they recover).

**Example 10.5:** Let us see why merely knowing that everyone is willing to commit, without knowing that they all know that fact, can be inadequate. In two-phase commit, a participant $T_i$ might send vote-commit and then be cut off from the coordinator. The coordinator might collect the votes and send commit to another participant $T_j$. Then, the coordinator and $T_j$ both fail or are cut off. Now, $T_i$, and any participants it can talk to, are in the Willing-to-commit state, but do not know whether all participants are willing to commit; therefore, they block. However, $T_j$ knew that all were willing, and so committed. The fact that $T_j$ committed, before it knew that $T_i$ knew everyone was willing to commit, forces $T_i$ to block. $\Box$

In a *three-phase commit*, there is a third round of messages. The second message from the coordinator (which we now call prepare-commit rather than commit), tells all participants that all are willing to commit, as before. However, a participant does not commit upon receiving this message. Rather, it acknowledges its receipt with a message `ready-commit`.[7] In the third phase, the coordinator collects all of these messages, and when all are received, it sends `commit` messages to all, which lets them know that everyone knows that everyone is willing to commit; at that point, the participants commit.

While the distinction between "knowing" and "knowing that everyone knows" appears subtle, it is in fact fundamental in understanding what distributed commit algorithms (and many other distributed operations) do. Hadzilacos [1987] characterizes the entire family of two-phase commit protocols as those where a participant commits as soon as it knows everyone is willing to commit. While we discussed only one such protocol, a "centralized" version with a coordinator, there are other versions where, for example, all participants communicate with each other, or information is passed around a ring of participants. Similarly, all known variants that are called "three-phase" allow a participant to commit as soon as it knows that all know that all are willing to commit.

## A Model of Failures

We are going to present a variant of three-phase commit that can be shown to avoid blocking as long as failures take a reasonable, but limited form. In particular, we assume that:

1.  Only node failures occur, and the network never disconnects into two or more groups of live nodes that cannot communicate with the other groups. For example, an Ethernet generally has the property that it can support communication between any two live nodes, no matter how many have failed, assuming the net itself has not failed.
2.  When a node fails, it does not communicate at all. It cannot send false messages (e.g., send `abort` when it should send `commit`), and it does not send some messages while omitting others.
3.  When a node fails, it is out of action for the duration of the commitment process for any one transaction. That is, a node that fails will know it failed when it recovers, and will not resume participation in commitment processes without first announcing itself to the other nodes and finding out what has happened, as discussed at the end of the previous section.
4.  A node that has not failed will respond to a request for a message within a time that is shorter than the timeout period used to detect failed nodes.
5.  The network does not lose messages, and delivers messages from node $A$ to node $B$ in the order they were received.[8]

---

[7] In the simple model of failures that we shall discuss here, this acknowledgement is not needed. However, the acknowledgement can help detect certain errors, such as a lost message, and so is generally included in three-phase commit protocols.

[8] It is possible, however, that if $A$ sends a message to $B$, then a message to $C$, the latter

We shall now describe a protocol that guarantees no transaction will block, as long as failures conform to the assumptions above.

### Three-Phase Commit

We shall give a simple version of a three-phase commit protocol that, under the failure model just described, assures that as long as one or more processors remain alive during the commitment process, no processor is blocked. Our version eliminates the `ready-commit` acknowledgements in the second phase, because, as we shall see, it is unnecessary. However, an implementation of the algorithm would probably include that acknowledgement, since it protects against certain other failure modes like lost or garbled messages.

Figure 10.6 formalizes the discussion above of a commitment protocol with a third phase to determine that all participants know of the willingness of all to commit. In Figure 10.6(a) are the transitions of the participants. We omit what happens when the Recover state is entered; that will be described separately. Figure 10.6(b) shows the transitions of the coordinator.

In Phase 1, the coordinator sends `begin-vote` to all participants, and each votes, exactly as in two-phase commit. Phases 2 and 3 occur only if the coordinator receives `vote-commit` from all participants. In Phase 2, the coordinator sends `prepare-commit` to all participants, and in Phase 3, the coordinator sends `commit`, and the participants receiving it commit.

There are several places where a failure could occur, resulting in one or more of these messages not being received. As with two-phase commit, a sub-transaction waiting for a message times out after a period sufficiently long that the sending subtransaction has surely failed. First, the participants may not receive the expected `begin-vote` from the coordinator. As shown in Figure 10.6(a), such a participant merely aborts. If other participants did receive the `begin-vote` message, they will discover the coordinator has failed while they are waiting for a `prepare-commit` message.

The second place where a timeout can occur is while the coordinator is waiting for votes. If any do not arrive within the timeout period, then, as in two-phase commit, the coordinator decides to abort the transaction.

Third, a participant that is willing to commit may time out waiting for a `prepare-commit` or `abort` message. If so, it goes to a recovery state, which we shall describe later.

Finally, the last place a timeout can occur is when a participant that is in the Ready-to-commit state does not get the `commit` message from the coordinator. In this situation too, we go to the recovery state, where the live participants will resolve the problem.

---

may receive its message first.

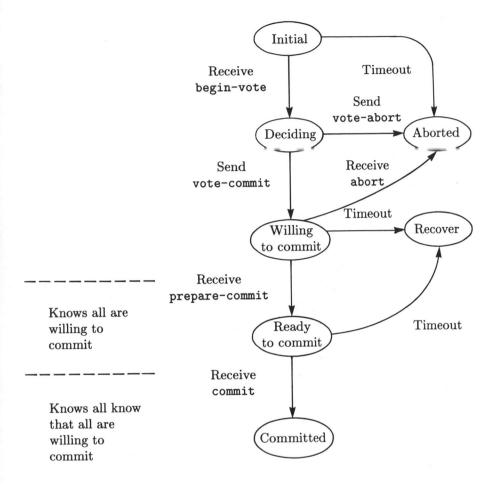

**Figure 10.6(a)** Participant in three-phase commit.

Our first (but erroneous) thought is that the two messages, `prepare-commit` and `commit`, which the coordinator sends in sequence to the participants, cannot both be necessary. That is, the receipt of `prepare-commit` assures the participant that `commit` will eventually be sent, unless the coordinator fails; in the latter case, surely the coordinator would have sent `commit` if it could. However, if we eliminate one of the messages, then we are back to two-phase commit, and Example 10.5 should convince the reader that participants can block, even under our restrictive failure model. Furthermore, if we interleave the two messages, say by sending both to one participant, then both to a second participant, and so on, we again behave like two-phase commit, and blocking is possible. In fact, the reader can show as an exercise that

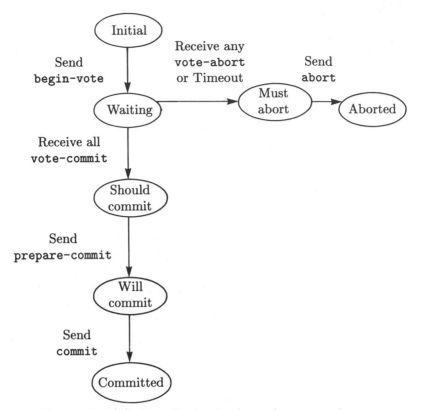

**Figure 10.6(b)**  Coordinator in three-phase commit.

should the coordinator send any `commit` message prior to sending the last of the `prepare-commit` messages, then blocking is possible.

What is essential about three-phase commit is that the coordinator sends all of the `prepare-commit` messages out before it sends any `commit` message. The intuitive reason is that the `prepare-commit` message informs each participant that all are willing to commit. If any participant $T_i$ receives `commit`, it knows that the coordinator has sent all its `prepare-commit` messages, and thus every participant that is still live has received `prepare-commit` or is about to do so, since the message could be delayed but not lost by the network. That is, the receipt of a `commit` message by $T_i$ tells $T_i$ that all know all are willing to commit.

Technically, $T_i$ only knows that every participant $T$ either knows that all are willing to commit, or $T$ will know it shortly, or $T$ will fail before it receives the `prepare-commit`. However, since the protocol of Figure 10.6 only involves messages between the coordinator and participants, and because assumption (5) assures us messages are not lost, it can be assumed that messages are received instantaneously. That is, when $T_i$ commits, every participant has either received prepare-commit or has already failed. The reason is that if some $T_j$ actually fails after the time $T_i$ receives commit, but before $T_j$ receives prepare-commit, then there would be no observable change in the activity of the network if we assumed that $T_j$ had failed before $T_i$ received commit. What we have shown is that it is impossible for two participants to be simultaneously in the Willing-to-commit and Committed states, respectively. This fact and other useful observations about the protocol of Figure 10.6 are summarized in the following lemma.

**Lemma 10.1:** Prior to transactions entering the recovery state, and under the (justifiable) assumption that messages are delivered instantaneously, the following states are incompatible.

a)   One (live or failed) participant cannot have entered the Committed state while any live participant is still in the Willing-to-commit state.

b)   One (live or failed) participant cannot have entered the Aborted state while another (live or failed) participant has entered the Committed state, or any live participant has entered the Ready-to-commit state.[9]

**Proof:** For (a), we note that in order for a participant to enter the Committed state before any recovery takes place, it must receive a commit message. By the argument given above, we know that every live participant has (on the assumption of instantaneous messages) received prepare-commit, and therefore has left the Willing-to-commit state.

We leave (b) as an exercise. The reader has only to examine Figure 10.6 and argue that a prepare-commit message cannot be sent if one or more participants have aborted. □

### Recovery in Three-Phase Commit

The consequence of Lemma 10.1 is that we cannot have a failed participant that has aborted if any live transaction has reached as far as the Ready-to-commit state, and we cannot have a failed participant that has committed if any live transaction is still in the Willing-to-commit state. Thus, when one or more participants detect the need for recovery, because of a timeout, we have only to arrange that each live participant discloses to the others its state, or more precisely, its state just before it entered the Recovery state. If all are in Willing-to-commit or Aborted, then we know no failed participant has committed, and it is safe for all to abort. If any has reached the Ready-to-commit state or the

---

[9] In fact, it is not even possible for a failed participant to have entered Ready-to-commit, but we state the conditions this way because we want them to be weak enough that they are preserved during the recovery process.

Committed state, then no failed transaction can have aborted, so it is safe for all to commit.

In the latter case, the distributed commitment process must be taken by steps. That is, any participants still in the Willing-to-commit state must first be brought to the Ready-to-commit state, and then all those in that state must be made to commit. The reason we must continue in stages is that at any time, more participants may fail, and we must avoid creating a situation where one participant is in Willing-to-commit while another has already committed.

## Electing a New Coordinator

As with two- or three-phase commit in general, the recovery process can be conducted in several different ways. As we have considered only the centralized, or coordinator-based approach, because it tends to save messages, let us continue with that approach now. Then as soon as one participant realizes recovery is needed, it sends a message to all the other participants. Several participants may reach this conclusion at about the same time, so many redundant messages will be sent in the worst case, but not in the typical case.

Then, the live participants must attempt to elect a new coordinator, because the only time we enter the Recovery state is if a participant has timed out waiting for the coordinator to send a message. Each participant knows the original set of participants, although some now are failed. We may assume that the participants are numbered $T_1, \ldots, T_k$, and the lowest-indexed live participant will be the new coordinator. Since $T_1$ may have failed, we cannot just assume $T_1$ is the new coordinator. Rather, each participant must make known to the others that it is live. If done properly, at most one live participant will conclude that it is the new coordinator (because it never heard from any lower-numbered participant).

One relatively efficient way to make the decision is for each $T_i$ to send a message with its index, $i$, to $T_{i+1}, T_{i+2}, \ldots, T_k$ in that order. However, if $T_i$ receives a message from a lower-numbered participant, then $T_i$ knows it is not the coordinator, and so stops sending messages. Most participants will stop sending messages very quickly, but if some messages are delayed inordinately,[10] then on the order of $k^2$ messages could be sent.

After this step, each live participant will have a notion of who the new coordinator is. If no failures occurred during the election, then all will have the same notion. However, if the lowest-numbered participant failed during the election, then there may be disagreement regarding who is the coordinator.

---

[10] Note we are no longer assuming messages are sent instantaneously; that assumption was justified only by the pattern of messages (to and from the coordinator) that is present in the basic three-phase commit algorithm.

**Example 10.6:** Suppose there are participants $T_1, \ldots, T_4$. Also suppose that during the election, the following sequence of events occurs.

1. $T_1$ sends a message to $T_2$ before $T_2$ can send its own message to $T_3$. Thus, $T_2$ never sends any messages.
2. $T_1$ fails.
3. $T_3$ sends a message to $T_4$. $T_4$ is thereby inhibited from sending any messages.

The net effect of these events is that $T_2$ thinks $T_1$ is the coordinator, while $T_3$ and $T_4$ both think $T_3$ is the coordinator. After a suitable timeout period, so it can be determined that no more messages are being sent, $T_3$ starts its roll as coordinator by requesting the state of all participants.[11] □

It is easy to show that no more than one live participant can think it is the new coordinator. For suppose $T_i$ and $T_j$ both are live and think they are the coordinator, where $i < j$. Since $T_i$ thinks it is the coordinator, it never received a message from any participant lower than $i$. Thus, it continued to send out messages to the participants numbered above $i$, and in particular to $T_j$. Thus, $T_j$ would not think it is the coordinator.

It is possible that no live participant thinks it is the coordinator, in which case the live participants will time out waiting for the recovery to begin. They will then elect a new coordinator.

### The Recovery Algorithm

With these tools, we can describe an appropriate recovery algorithm to use with three-phase commit. This recovery strategy has the property that it never causes a participant to block, as long as at least one participant remains live. Unfortunately, it is not possible to avoid blocking in a situation where all participants fail, and then one recovers and finds it is in the Willing-to-commit state. As discussed in Example 10.4, in connection with two-phase commit, such a participant cannot rule out the possibility that some other participant is aborted, nor can it rule out the possibility that another committed. Thus, it must block and wait for more participants to recover. The steps taken for recovery are summarized as follows:

1. The live participants elect a new coordinator.
2. The new coordinator sends messages to all participants requesting their state immediately prior to recovery, which must be Aborted, Willing-to-commit, Ready-to-commit, or Committed. Failed participants, of course, will not reply, so the coordinator waits for the timeout period and then

---

[11] The timeout period need not be long. It can be based on the expected time for each $T_i$ to receive a message from $T_1$. If some $T_i$ thinks it is the coordinator and isn't, it will get a message to that effect from some participant.

assumes it has all the "votes" it is ever going to receive.

3.  If any Ready-to-commit or Committed states were found, the coordinator decides to commit the transaction. By Lemma 10.1, no participant could have aborted in this case. If only Aborted and Willing-to-commit responses were received, then the coordinator decides to abort the transaction.

4.  If the decision was to abort the transaction, then the coordinator sends abort to each participant. If the decision was to commit then the coordinator sends

    a)  prepare-commit to every participant in the Willing-to-commit state, and then

    b)  commit to every participant that was not already in the Committed state.

As long as the coordinator does not fail, the above steps will complete; the fact that other participants may fail meanwhile does not affect the algorithm. If the coordinator fails at any intermediate point, one of the participants will discover this fact through the timeout mechanism, and the entire process will begin again at step (1). If the recovery algorithm stops at some intermediate point, the effect may be that some state changes have occurred, e.g., from Willing-to-commit to Abort or to Ready-to-commit. The important property of the algorithm is that the pairs of states that Lemma 10.1 said were impossible remain impossible.

**Lemma 10.2:** Conditions (a) and (b) of Lemma 10.1 hold at all times during the above recovery algorithm.

**Proof:** There are a number of details that we leave for the reader to check. For one example, in step (4), some $T_i$ could go from the Willing-to-commit state to the Aborted state. No violation of Lemma 10.1(b) could occur, because the coordinator only decides to abort if there are no live participants in states other than Aborted and Willing-to-commit. Then Lemma 10.1(a) says that there can be no live or failed participant in the Committed state, which implies that part (b) continues to hold.[12] $\square$

**Theorem 10.2:** The three-phase commit algorithm described above does not block, as long as at least one participant does not fail. Also, it makes a consistent decision, in the sense that two participants cannot abort and commit, respectively.

**Proof:** Since the recovery algorithm always makes a decision, each time it is invoked it either completes or a failure causes it to time out and be run again. Eventually, the algorithm will either succeed, or the last participant will fail.

---

[12] As an exercise, the reader should find a scenario in which several rounds of recovery are necessary, during which a participant gets into the Ready-to-commit state then fails, and the final decision is to abort.

Thus, the transaction does not block.

For the correctness of the algorithm, Lemma 10.2 tells us that the conditions of Lemma 10.1 are preserved by recovery, and of course, Lemma 10.1 tells us they hold before recovery. If the outcome is that the transaction commits, then Lemma 10.1(b) says that no failed transaction can be in the Aborted state. If the transaction aborts, Lemma 10.1(b) implies that no failed participant can be in the Committed state. Failed participants that recover and find themselves in states other than Committed or Aborted will inquire of the nodes live at that time to (if possible) determine what the decision was.[13] □

## 10.6 TIMESTAMP-BASED, DISTRIBUTED CONCURRENCY

The timestamp approach to concurrency control, covered in Section 9.11, can be carried over to distributed databases. In essence, transactions run at any site, and they read and write any copy when they will, leaving their timestamp at the site of the copy as the read- or write-time of the copy, respectively. Of course, if they write a new value for one copy of an item, they must write the same value into all copies of that item, and a distributed commitment algorithm along the lines of Sections 10.4 and 10.5, must be used before any of the values are written into the database.

As in Section 9.11, we need some way of checking that the transaction is not doing something impossible, such as reading a value before it would have been written if the transactions were run in the serial order according to timestamps. In Section 9.11, we used timestamps and read- and write-times for items, in order to maintain a behavior that mimicked a serial order. Recall that the hypothetical serial order is one in which a transaction is assumed to run instantaneously at the time given by its timestamp.

This approach is still valid in the distributed environment. However, the "timestamp" notion must be generalized to apply to distributed databases. For nondistributed systems, timestamps were assumed given out by the computer system at large. If there is but one computer, this assumption surely can be satisfied. But what if computers at many sites are assigning timestamps? How do we know they can do so consistently?

### Distributed Timestamps

While it may not be obvious, the most elementary approach to distributed timestamping actually works. That is, we may let the computers at each node of the network keep their own clocks, even though the clocks cannot possibly run in synchronism. To avoid the same timestamp being given to two transactions, we

---

[13] In unfortunate circumstances, these participants will find none of the participants that made the final decision live at the moment, and then the recovering participant must block.

require that the last $k$ bits of the "time" be a sequence that uniquely identifies the node. For example, if there were no more than 256 nodes, we could let $k = 8$ and give each node a distinct eight-bit sequence that it appended to its local clock, as the low-order bits, to form the timestamp.

Even setting aside the theory of relativity, it is not realistic to suppose that all of the clocks at all of the nodes are in exact synchronism. While minor differences in the clocks at two nodes are of no great consequence, a major difference can be fatal. For example, suppose that at node $N$, the clock is five hours behind the other clocks in the system. Then, on the assumption that most items are read and written within a five hour period, a transaction initiating at $N$ will receive a timestamp that is less than the read- and write-times of most items it seeks to access. It is therefore almost sure to abort, and transactions, in effect, cannot run at $N$.

There is, fortunately, a simple mechanism to prevent gross misalignment of clocks. Let each message sent bear its own timestamp, the time at which the message left the sending node according to the clock of the sender. If a node ever receives a message "from the future," that is, a message with a timestamp greater than its current clock, it simply increments its clock to be greater than the timestamp of the received message. If, say, a node was so inactive that it did not discover that its clock had become five hours slow, then the first time it ran a transaction it would receive a message telling it to abort the transaction it was running. That message would include the "correct time." The node would then update its clock and rerun the transaction with a realistic timestamp. We shall thus assume from here on that the creation of timestamps that have global validity is within the capability of a distributed DBMS.

### A Timestamp-Based Algorithm

Next, let us consider the steps necessary to read and write items in such a way that the effect on the database is as if each transaction ran instantaneously, at the time given by its timestamp, just as was the case in Section 9.11. As in Section 10.1, we shall consider the elementary step to be an action on a copy of an item, not on the copy itself. However, when dealing with timestamps, the elementary steps are not locking and unlocking, but examining and setting read- and write-times on copies.

Many of the locking methods discussed in Section 10.2 have timestamp-based analogs. We shall discuss only one, the analog of write-locks-all. When reading an item $A$, we go to any copy of $A$ and check that its write-time does not exceed the timestamp of the transaction doing the reading. If the write-time is greater than the timestamp, we must abort the transaction.[14] Looking

---

[14] In terms of the distributed commitment algorithms discussed in Sections 10.4–5, the subtransaction attempting to write must vote to abort.

for another copy of $A$ to read is a possible alternative strategy, but it is likely to be futile.

When writing $A$, we must write all copies of $A$, and we must check that for each, the read-time is less than the timestamp of the transaction. If the read-time of any copy exceeds the timestamp, the transaction must abort. If the read-time is less than the timestamp, but the write-time exceeds the timestamp, then we do not abort, but neither do we write the item, for the reason discussed in Section 9.11.

It is easy to check that by following these rules, a transaction can never read a value that was created "in the future," nor can a transaction write a value if a value written previously will be read in the future. Thus, the method is guaranteed to produce an effect equivalent to that of the serial order in which transactions occur in the order of their timestamps.

### Locking Vs. Timestamps

The timestamp approach saves some messages, even compared to the best of the methods mentioned in Figure 10.2. A read takes only one control message and one data message to request and receive the data, while a write takes $n$ data messages to do the writing if $n$ is the number of sites with copies.

The other side of the coin, as for the nondistributed case, is that timestamp methods will cause many transactions to abort and restart if there are frequent situations where two transactions are trying to access the same item at the same time. Thus, neither approach can be said to dominate the other.

## 10.7  RECOVERY OF NODES

As we mentioned in Sections 10.4 and 10.5, when a node fails and then recovers, it cannot simply resume operation. To begin, it must examine its log and determine what transactions were being committed when it failed. Often, it will not be able to tell from its log whether a transaction ultimately committed or aborted; thus it must send a message to at least one of the other participants to determine what happened.

However, getting up-to-date on these transactions is not sufficient. While a node $N$ was down, transactions involving items with copies at $N$ may have run, even though there is no record of such transactions at $N$. In the discussion of Sections 10.4 and 10.5, we assumed that all sites with copies of an item $A$ were live at the beginning, and the only problem was that some of these sites might fail during the running of the transaction.

In reality, it is quite possible that a site $N$ fails and does not recover for a long time. The fact that $N$ is failed will be discovered by each other site $M$ as soon as a transaction initiating at $M$ tries to access a copy of some data item $A$ with a copy at $N$. If $N$ has the only copy of $A$, the transaction must abort, and there is nothing else we can do. However, if there are other copies of $A$, then we can proceed as if the copy at $N$ did not exist. When $N$ recovers, it not only has the responsibility to find out about the transactions being committed or aborted when it failed, but now it must find out which of its items are out of date, in the sense that transactions have run at the other sites and modified copies of items that, like $A$, are found at $N$ and also at other nodes.

### Obtaining Up-to-Date Values

When the failed site resumes activity, it must obtain the most recent values for all its items. We shall suggest two general strategies for doing so.

1.  If site $M$ discovers that site $N$ has failed, $M$ records this fact in its log. When $N$ recovers, it sends a message to each site. If $M$ receives such a message, $M$ examines its log back to the point where it discovered $N$ had failed, and sends the most recent value it has for all items it holds in common with $N$.[15] The values of these items must be locked while the recovery of $N$ is in progress, and we must be careful to obtain the most recent value among all of the sites with copies. We can tell the most recent values, because all transactions that have committed a value for item $A$ must have done so in the same order at all the sites of $A$, provided we have a correct locking method. If we are using timestamp-based concurrency control, the write-times of the values determine their order.

2.  All copies of all items may be assigned a write-time, whether or not time-stamp concurrency control is in use. When a site $N$ recovers, it sends for the write-times of all its items, as recorded in the other sites. These items are temporarily locked at the other sites, and the current values of items with a more recent write-time than the write-time at $N$ are sent to $N$.

This description merely scratches the surface of the subject of crash management. For example, we must consider what happens when a site needed to restore values to a second site has itself failed, or if a site fails while another is recovering. The interested reader is encouraged to consult the bibliographic notes for analyses of the subject.

## 10.8 DISTRIBUTED DEADLOCKS

Recall from Section 9.1 that we have simple and elegant methods to prevent deadlock in single-processor systems. For example, we can require each transaction to request locks on items in lexicographic order of the items' names. Then it will not be possible that we have transaction $T_1$ waiting for item $A_1$ held by

---

[15] Note that under the methods of locking and commitment described in this chapter, $M$ must discover $N$ has failed if there is a transaction that involves any item held by both $N$ and $M$, so $N$ will hear of all its out-of-date items.

$T_2$, which is waiting for $A_2$ held by $T_3$, and so on, while $T_k$ is waiting for $A_k$ held by $T_1$. That follows because the fact that $T_2$ holds a lock on $A_1$ while it is waiting for $A_2$ tells us $A_1 < A_2$ in lexicographic order. Similarly, we may conclude $A_2 < A_3 \cdots A_k < A_1$, which implies a cycle in the lexicographic order, an impossibility.

With care, we can generalize this technique to work for distributed databases. If the locking method used is a centralized one, where individual items, rather than copies, are locked, then no modification is needed. If we use a locking method like the $k$-of-$n$ schemes, which lock individual copies, we can still avoid deadlocks if we require all transactions to lock copies in a particular order:

1. If $A < B$ in lexicographic order, then a transaction $T$ must lock all the copies of $A$ that it needs before locking any copies of $B$.

2. The copies of each item $A$ are ordered, and a transaction locks all copies of $A$ that it needs in that order.

Even if it is possible under some circumstances to avoid deadlock by judicious ordering of copies, there is a reason to look elsewhere for a method of dealing with deadlocks. We discussed in Example 9.21 why it is sometimes difficult to predict in advance the set of items that a given transaction needs to lock. If so, then locking needed items in lexicographic order is either not possible or requires the unnecessary locking of items.

In the remainder of this section we shall take a brief look at some general methods for deadlock detection and deadlock avoidance that do not place constraints on the order in which a transaction can access items. First, we consider the use of timeouts to detect and resolve deadlocks. Next, the construction of a waits-for graph is considered as a detection mechanism. Finally, we consider a timestamp-based approach to avoiding deadlocks altogether.

## Deadlock Resolution by Timeout

A simple approach to detecting deadlocks is to have a transaction time out and abort if it has waited sufficiently long for a lock that it is likely to be involved in a deadlock. The timeout period must be sufficiently short that deadlocked transactions do not hold locks too long, yet it must be sufficiently long that we do not often abort transactions that are not really deadlocked.

This method has a number of advantages. Unlike the waits-for-graph approach to be described next, it requires no extra message traffic. Unlike the timestamp-based methods to be described, it does not (usually) abort transactions that are not involved in a deadlock. It is prone, however, to aborting all or many of the transactions in a deadlock, rather than one transaction, which is generally sufficient to break the deadlock.

**Waits-for-Graphs**

We mentioned in Section 9.1 that a necessary and sufficient test for a deadlock in a single-processor system is to construct a *waits-for graph*, whose nodes are the transactions. The graph has an arc from $T_1$ to $T_2$ if $T_1$ is waiting for a lock on an item held by $T_2$. Then there is a deadlock if and only if there is a cycle in this graph. In principle, the same technique works in a distributed environment. The trouble is that at each site we can maintain easily only a *local* waits-for graph, while cycles may appear only in the *global* waits-for graph, composed of the union of the local waits-for graphs.

**Example 10.7:** Suppose we have transactions $T_1$ and $T_2$ that wish to lock items $A$ and $B$, located at nodes $N_A$ and $N_B$, respectively. $A$ and $B$ may be copies of the same item or may be different items. Also suppose that at $N_A$, (a subtransaction of) $T_2$ has obtained a write-lock on $A$, and (a subtransaction of) $T_1$ is waiting for that lock. Symmetrically, at $N_B$ $T_1$ has a lock on $B$, which $T_2$ is waiting for.

(a) Local waits-for graph at $N_A$.

(b) Local waits-for graph at $N_B$.

(c) Global waits-for graph.

**Figure 10.7**  Global deadlock detection.

The local waits-for graphs at $N_A$ and $N_B$ are shown in Figure 10.7(a) and (b); clearly each is acyclic. However, the union of these graphs is the cycle shown in Figure 10.7(c). As far as we can tell at either of the sites $N_A$ or $N_B$, there might not be a deadlock. For example, from $N_A$ alone, we cannot be sure that anything prevents $T_2$ from eventually committing and releasing its lock on $A$, then allowing $T_1$ to get the lock. $\square$

Example 10.7 illustrates why in order to detect cycles it is necessary to send messages that allow a global waits-for graph to be constructed. There are several ways this task could be accomplished:

1.  Use a central node to receive updates to the local waits-for graphs from all of the sites periodically. This technique has the advantages and disadvantages of centralized methods of locking: it is vulnerable to failure of the central node and to concentration of message traffic at that site,[16] but the total amount of traffic generated is relatively low.

2.  Pass the current local waits-for graphs among all of the sites, preferring to append the local graph to another message headed for another site if possible, but sending the local graph to each other site periodically anyway. The amount of traffic this method generates can be much larger than for the central-node method. However, if the cost of messages is relatively invariant to their length, and frequently waits-for information can be "piggybacked" on other messages, then the real cost of passing information is small.

### Timeliness of Waits-for Graphs

In either method described above, the union of the local waits-for graphs that any particular site knows about currently does not have to reflect the situation that existed globally at any particular time. That doesn't prevent the detection of deadlocks, since if a cycle in the global waits-for graph exists, it won't go away until the deadlock is resolved by aborting at least one of the transactions involved in the cycle. Thus, the arcs of a cycle in the global graph will eventually all reach the central node (in method 1) or reach some node (in method 2), and the deadlock will be detected.

However, errors in the opposite direction can occur. There can be *phantom* deadlocks which appear as cycles in the union of the local waits-for graphs that have accumulated at some site, yet at no time did the global waits-for graph have this cycle.

**Example 10.8:** The transaction $T_2$ in Example 10.7 might decide to abort for one of several reasons, shortly after the local graph of Figure 10.7(a) was sent to the central site. Then the graph of Figure 10.7(b) might be sent to the central site. Before an update to Figure 10.7(a) can reach the central site, that node constructs the graph of Figure 10.7(c). Thus, it appears that there is a deadlock, and the central node will select a victim to abort. If it selects $T_2$, there is no harm, since $T_2$ aborted anyway. However, it could just as well select $T_1$, which would waste resources. $\Box$

### Timestamp-Based Deadlock Prevention

We mentioned schemes that avoid deadlocks by controlling the order in which

---

[16] Note that in comparison, centralized, or coordinator-based distributed commit protocols use different nodes for different transactions, and so do not suffer these disadvantages.

items are locked by any given transaction, e.g., locking in lexicographic order or taking all locks at once. There also are schemes that do not place constraints on the order in which items are locked or accessed, but still can assure no deadlocks occur. These schemes use timestamps on transactions, and each guarantees that no cycles can occur in the global waits-for graph. It is important to note that the timestamps are used for deadlock avoidance only; access control of items is still by locking.

In one scheme, should (a subtransaction of) $T_1$ be waiting for (a subtransaction of) $T_2$, then it must be that the timestamp of $T_1$ is less than the timestamp of $T_2$; in the second scheme, the opposite is true. In either scheme, a cycle in the waits-for graph would consist of transactions with monotonically increasing or monotonically decreasing timestamps, as we went around the cycle. Neither is possible, since when we go around the cycle we come back to the same timestamp that we started with.

We now define the two deadlock avoidance schemes. Suppose we have transactions $T_1$ and $T_2$ with timestamps $t_1$ and $t_2$, respectively, and a subtransaction of $T_1$ attempts to access an item $A$ locked by a subtransaction of $T_2$.

1.   In the *wait-die* scheme, $T_1$ waits for a lock on $A$ if $t_1 < t_2$, i.e., if $T_1$ is the older transaction. If $t_1 > t_2$, then $T_1$ is aborted.

2.   In the *wound-wait* scheme, $T_1$ waits for a lock on $A$ if $t_1 > t_2$. If $t_1 < t_2$, then $T_2$ is forced to abort and release its lock on $A$ to $T_1$.[17]

In either scheme, the aborted transaction must initiate again with the same timestamp, not with a new timestamp. Reusing the original timestamp guarantees that the oldest transaction, in either scheme, cannot die or be wounded. Thus, each transaction will eventually be allowed to complete, as the following theorem shows.

**Theorem 10.3:** There can be neither deadlocks nor livelocks in the wait-die or the wound-wait schemes.

**Proof:** Consider the wait-die scheme. Suppose there is a cycle in the global waits-for graph, i.e., a sequence of transactions $T_1, \ldots, T_k$ such that each $T_i$ is waiting for release of a lock by $T_{i+1}$, for $1 \le i < k$, and $T_k$ is waiting for $T_1$. Let $t_i$ be the timestamp of $T_i$. Then $t_1 < t_2 < \cdots < t_k < t_1$, which implies $t_1 < t_1$, an impossibility. Similarly, in the wound-wait scheme, such a cycle would imply $t_1 > t_2 > \cdots > t_k > t_1$, which is also impossible.

To see why no livelocks occur, let us again consider the wait-die scheme. If

---

[17]   Incidentally, the term "wound-wait" rather than "kill-wait" is used because of the image that the "wounded" subtransaction must, before it dies, run around informing all the other subtransactions of its transaction that they too must abort. That is not really necessary if a distributed commit algorithm is used, but the subject is gruesome, and the less said the better.

| Method | Messages | Phantom aborts | Other |
|---|---|---|---|
| Timeout | None | Medium number | Can abort more than one transaction to resolve one deadlock |
| Waits-for Graph Centralized | Medium traffic | Few | Vulnerable to node failure, bottlenecks |
| Waits-for Graph Distributed | High traffic | Few | |
| Timestamp | None | Many | |

**Figure 10.8** Comparison of deadlock-handling methods.

$T$ is the transaction with the lowest timestamp, that is, $T$ is the oldest transaction that has not completed, then $T$ never dies. It may wait for younger transactions to release their locks, but since there are no deadlocks, those locks will eventually be released, and $T$ will eventually complete. When $T$ first initiates, there are some finite number of live, older transactions. By the argument above, each will eventually complete, making $T$ the oldest. At that point, $T$ is sure to complete the next time it is restarted. Of course, in ordinary operation, transactions will not necessarily complete in the order of their age, and in fact most will proceed without having to abort.

The no-livelock argument for the wound-wait scheme is similar. Here, the oldest transaction does not even have to wait for others to release locks; it takes the locks it needs and wounds the transactions holding them. □

**Comparison of Methods**

Figure 10.8 summarizes the advantages and disadvantages of the methods we have covered in this section. The column labeled "Messages" refers to the message traffic needed to detect deadlocks. The column "Phantom aborts" refers to the possibility that transactions not involved in a deadlock will be required to abort.

## EXERCISES

10.1: Suppose we have three nodes, 1, 2, and 3, in our network. Item $A$ has copies at all three nodes, while item $B$ has copies only at 1 and 3. Two transactions, $T_1$ and $T_2$ run, starting at the same time, at nodes 1 and 2, respectively. Each transaction consists of the following steps:

RLOCK $B$; WLOCK $A$; UNLOCK $A$; UNLOCK $B$;

Suppose that at each time unit, each transaction can send one message to one site, and each site can read one message. When there is a choice of sites to send or receive a message to or from, the system always chooses the lowest numbered site. Additional messages are placed in a queue to be sent or received at the next time units. Simulate the action of the network under the following concurrency rules.

a)    Write-locks-all.
b)    Majority locking.
c)    Primary site, assumed to be node 1 for $A$ and 3 for $B$.
d)    Primary copy token, with initially sites 2 and 3 holding read tokens for $A$, and 1 holding the write token for $B$.
e)    Timestamp-based concurrency control, assuming the timestamp of $T_1$ exceeds that of $T_2$, and both are greater than the initial read- and write-times for all the copies.

* 10.2: Show that in order for no two link failures to disconnect a network of $n$ nodes, that network must have at least $3n/2$ edges. Also show that there are networks with $\lceil 3n/2 \rceil$ edges that cannot be disconnected by the failure of two links.

* 10.3: How many edges must an $n$-node network have to be resilient against the failure of any $k$ links?

* 10.4: Suppose that we have an incrementation lock mode, as in Example 9.10, in addition to the usual read and write. Generalize the $k$-of-$n$ methods to deal with all three kinds of locks.

* 10.5: Some distributed environments allow a *broadcast* operation, in which the same message is sent by one site to any desired subset of the other sites. Redo the table of Figure 10.2 on the assumption that broadcasts are permitted and cost one message each.

10.6: Suppose that a logical read-lock requires that $j$ physical copies be read-locked, and a logical write-lock requires write-locks on $k$ copies. Show that if either $j + k \leq n$ or $k \leq n/2$, then logical locks do not work as they should (thus, the $k$-of-$n$ strategies are the best possible).

* 10.7: Determine the average number of messages used by the primary-copy token method of defining locks, on the assumption that, when it is desired to lock some item $A$,

    *i*) 50% of the time a write token for $A$ is available at the local site (and therefore there is no read-token).

    *ii*) 40% of the time a read-token for $A$ is available at the local site.

    *iii*) 10% of tho timo noithor a road- nor write-token for $A$ is available at the local site.

    *iv*) Whenever a desired token is not available locally, all sites are willing to give up whatever tokens they have to the requesting site, after the necessary exchange of messages.

10.8: What happens when the transactions of Figure 10.3 are run under the lock methods other than write-locks-all?[18]

* 10.9: We can perform a distributed two-phase commit without a coordinator if we have each of the $n$ participants send their votes to all other participants.

    a) Draw the state-transition diagram for each participant, including actions to be taken if recovery is necessary.

    b) How many messages are necessary?

    c) If broadcast operations are permitted, how many operations are necessary?

    d) Is blocking of transactions possible? If so, give an example.

10.10: Repeat Exercise 10.9 for three-phase commit without a coordinator.

10.11: Another approach to distributed two-phase commit is to arrange the participants in a ring, and expect them to pass and accumulate votes around the ring, starting and returning to the coordinator. Then the coordinator passes the outcome of the vote around the ring. In the case that one or more nodes fail, participants can skip positions around the ring to find the next live participant. Repeat the questions of Exercise 10.9 for this model.

10.12: Repeat Exercise 10.11 for three-phase commit.

10.13: In Example 10.4 we asserted that if participant $T_i$ gave up its locks without either committing or aborting, then an inconsistency among copies of a logical item could occur. Give a scenario to show that is the case.

10.14: We also claimed that, during recovery in two-phase commit, should a participant that has not yet voted decide to commit, then an inconsistency was possible. Offer a scenario to justify this claim.

---

[18] Note: Example 10.3 talks about similar pairs of transactions and their behavior under the other lock methods. We are interested in the exact transactions of Figure 10.3.

10.15: Suppose there are four participants, $T_1$ (the coordinator), $T_2$, $T_3$, and $T_4$, in a two-phase commit. Describe what happens if the following failures occur. In each case, indicate what happens during recovery (if the recovery phase is entered), and tell whether any transaction blocks.

a) $T_1$ fails after sending `vote-commit` to $T_2$ and $T_3$, but not $T_4$.

b) $T_2$ fails after sending `vote-abort`; the other participants vote to commit.

c) $T_2$ fails before voting; the other participants vote to commit.

d) All vote to commit, but $T_1$ fails before sending out any `commit` messages.

e) All vote to commit, and $T_1$ fails after sending `commit` to $T_2$ (only).

f) All vote to commit, and $T_1$ sends `commit` to all, but $T_2$ fails before receiving the `commit` message.

10.16: Repeat Exercise 10.15 for three-phase commit. However, in (d)–(f), the `commit` message should be replaced by `prepare-commit`.

10.17: Show that in three-phase commit, if the coordinator sends `commit` to even one participant before sending `prepare-commit` to all, then erroneous behavior (or blocking) is possible under the failure model of Section 10.5.

10.18: Is erroneous behavior or blocking possible in three-phase commit if the failure model of Section 10.5 is modified to allow messages to get lost even if there is no (permanent) node or link failure? Assume that there is no acknowledgement of `prepare-commit` messages, but a participant waiting for `commit` may time out and go to the Recover state. What if `prepare-commit` messages have to be acknowledged?

10.19: Complete the proof of Lemma 10.1(b).

10.20: Consider the leader election algorithm described in Section 10.5 applied to a set of $k$ participants.

* a) Show that the algorithm can use as many as $\Omega(k^2)$ messages.

b) Suppose that all messages take the same time. Show that only $O(k)$ messages are used, assuming no failures.

** c) What if all messages take the same time, but there are failures during the leader election? Give the maximum number of messages that can be sent, as a function of $k$.

10.21: Complete the proof of Lemma 10.2.

10.22: Give a scenario for the recovery algorithm of three-phase commit in which several rounds of recovery are necessary, and the ultimate decision is to abort, even though some participant gets into the Ready-to-commit state.

10.23: Describe a timestamp-based analog of majority locking.

10.24: Suppose that there are three items $A_1$, $A_2$, and $A_3$ at sites $S_1$, $S_2$, and $S_3$, respectively. Also, there are three transactions, $T_1$, $T_2$, and $T_3$, with $T_i$ initiated at site $S_i$, for $i = 1, 2, 3$. The following six events happen, sequentially:

> $T_1$ locks $A_1$; $T_2$ locks $A_2$; $T_3$ locks $A_3$;
> $T_1$ asks for a lock on $A_2$; $T_2$ asks for a lock on $A_3$;
> $T_3$ asks for a lock on $A_1$.

a)  Suppose we pass local waits-for graphs around, piggybacking them on messages such as lock requests. Show the picture of the global waits-for graph obtained by each of the three sites after the above sequence of actions. Is a deadlock detected?

b)  What additional messages (containing local waits-for graphs), if any, need to be sent so that one site detects deadlock.

c)  Suppose we use the wait-die strategy to prevent deadlocks. Show what happens if the timestamps $t_i$ for $T_i$ are in the order $t_1 < t_2 < t_3$.

d)  Repeat (c) on the assumption that $t_1 > t_2 > t_3$.

e)  Repeat (c) for the wound-wait scheme.

f)  Repeat (e) on the assumption that $t_1 > t_2 > t_3$.

## BIBLIOGRAPHIC NOTES

As was mentioned in Chapter 9, many of the key ideas in concurrency and distributed systems were enunciated by Gray [1978], and an extensive, modern treatment of the subject can be found in Bernstein, Hadzilacos, and Goodman [1987].

Additional surveys of distributed database systems are Rothnie and Goodman [1977], Bernstein and Goodman [1981], and the text by Ceri and Pelagatti [1984].

### Distributed Concurrency Control

The $k$-of-$n$ family of locking strategies is from Thomas [1975, 1979]. The primary site method is evaluated by Stonebraker [1980], the central node technique in Garcia-Molina [1979], and primary-copy token methods in Minoura [1980].

Timestamp-based, distributed concurrency control is discussed in Bernstein and Goodman [1980b]. The method of maintaining global timestamps in a distributed system is by Lamport [1978].

Additional methods are covered in Bayer, Elhardt, Heller, and Reiser [1980], while Traiger, Gray, Galtieri, and Lindsay [1982] develop the concepts underlying distributed concurrency control.

Some of the complexity theory of distributed concurrency control is found in Kanellakis and Papadimitriou [1981, 1984].

Performance analysis for distributed concurrency control can be found in Badal [1980], Agrawal, Carey, and Linvy [1985], and Wolfson [1987].

## Distributed Commitment Algorithms

Two-phase commit is from Lampson and Sturgis [1976] and Gray [1978]. Three-phase commit is from Skeen [1981].

The complexity of commit protocols is examined in Dwork and Skeen [1983] and Ramarao [1985]. Segall and Wolfson [1987] discuss minimal-message algorithms for commit, assuming no failures.

The knowledge-theoretic definition of two- and three-phase commitment is taken from Hadzilacos [1987].

Leader election in distributed database systems is covered by Garcia-Molina [1982]. Peleg [1987] gives references and optimal algorithms for leader election in many cases, although the model does not take into account failure during the election.

## Recovery

The works by Menasce, Popek, and Muntz [1980], Minoura [1980] Skeen and Stonebraker [1981], and Bernstein and Goodman [1984] contain analyses of the methods for restoring crashed, distributed systems.

Many other algorithms have been proposed for maintaining replicated data, allowing partition of the network, and then restoring or updating copies correctly when the network becomes whole. See Eager and Sevcik [1983], Davidson [1984], Skeen and Wright [1984], Skeen, Cristian, and El Abbadi [1985], and El Abbadi and Toueg [1986].

## Distributed Deadlocks

Menasce and Muntz [1979] and Obermarck [1982] give distributed deadlock detection algorithms. Timestamp-based deadlock detection (wait-die and wound-wait) are from Stearns, Lewis, and Rosenkrantz [1976] and Rosenkrantz, Stearns, and Lewis [1978].

The complexity of distributed deadlock detection is treated by Wolfson and Yannakakis [1985].

## Systems

One of the earliest distributed database system experiments was the SDD-1 system. Its distributed aspects are described in Bernstein, Goodman, Rothnie, and Papadimitriou [1978], Rothnie et al. [1980], Bernstein and Shipman [1980], Bernstein, Shipman, and Rothnie [1980], Hammer and Shipman [1980], and Bernstein, Goodman, Wong, Reeve, and Rothnie [1981]. See also the comment on the system by McLean [1981].

Distributed INGRES is discussed in Epstein, Stonebraker, and Wong [1978] and Stonebraker [1979].

The Alpine distributed file system of Xerox PARC, which deals with many database-system issues, can be found in Brown, Kolling, and Taft [1984].

System R*, IBM's experimental distributed version of System R, is described by Mohan, Lindsay, and Obermarck [1986].

# BIBLIOGRAPHY

Abiteboul, S. and S. Grumbach [1987]. "COL: a language for complex objects based on recursive rules," unpublished memorandum, INRIA, Le Chesnay, France.

Abiteboul, S. and R. Hull [1987]. "IFO: a formal semantic data model," *Proc. Third ACM Symp. on Principles of Database Systems*, pp. 119–132.

Aghili, H. and D. G. Severance [1982]. "A practical guide to the design of differential files for recovery of on-line databases," *ACM Trans. on Database Systems* **7**:4, pp. 540–565.

Agrawal, R., M. J. Carey, and M. Linvy [1985]. "Models for studying concurrency control performance: alternatives and implications," *ACM SIGMOD Intl. Conf. on Management of Data*, pp. 108–121.

Agrawal, R. and D. J. DeWitt [1985]. "Integrated concurrency control and recovery mechanisms: design and performance evaluation," *ACM Trans. on Database Systems* **10**:4, pp. 529–564.

Aho, A. V., C. Beeri, and J. D. Ullman [1979]. "The theory of joins in relational databases," *ACM Trans. on Database Systems* **4**:3, pp. 297–314. Corrigendum: *ACM Trans. on Database Systems* **8**:2, pp. 287.

Aho, A. V., J. E. Hopcroft, and J. D. Ullman [1974]. *The Design and Analysis of Computer Algorithms*, Addison-Wesley, Reading Mass.

Aho, A. V., J. E. Hopcroft, and J. D. Ullman [1983]. *Data Structures and Algorithms* Addison-Wesley, Reading Mass.

Aho, A. V., B. W. Kernighan, and P. J. Weinberger [1979]. "Awk—a pattern scanning and processing language," *Software Practice and Experience* **9**, pp. 267–279.

Aho, A. V., B. W. Kernighan, and P. J. Weinberger [1988]. *The AWK programming Language*, Addison-Wesley, Reading Mass.

Aho, A. V. and J. D. Ullman [1979]. "Optimal partial match retrieval when fields are independently specified," *ACM Trans. on Database Systems* **4**:2, pp. 168–179.

ANSI [1975]. "Study group on data base management systems: interim report," *FDT* **7**:2, ACM, New York.

Apt, K. R. [1987]. "Introduction to logic programming," TR–87–35, Dept. of CS, Univ. of Texas, Austin. To appear in *Handbook of Theoretical Computer Science* (J. Van Leeuwen, ed.), North Holland, Amsterdam.

Apt, K. R., H. Blair, and A. Walker [1985]. "Towards a theory of declarative knowledge," unpublished memorandum, IBM, Yorktown Hts., N. Y.

Apt, K. R. and J.-M. Pugin [1987]. "Maintenance of stratified databases viewed as a belief revision system," *Proc. Sixth ACM Symp. on Principles of Database Systems*, pp. 136–145.

Apt, K. R. and M. H. Van Emden [1982]. "Contributions to the theory of logic programming," *J. ACM* **29**:3, pp. 841–862.

Armstrong, W. W. [1974]. "Dependency structures of data base relationships," *Proc. 1974 IFIP Congress*, pp. 580–583, North Holland, Amsterdam.

Arora, A. K. and C. R. Carlson [1978]. "The information preserving properties of certain relational database transformations," *Proc. Intl. Conf. on Very Large Data Bases*, pp. 352–359.

Astrahan, M. M. and D. D. Chamberlin [1975]. "Implementation of a structured English query language," *Comm. ACM* **18**:10, pp. 580–587.

Astrahan, M. M., et al. [1976]. "System R: a relational approach to data management," *ACM Trans. on Database Systems* **1**:2, pp. 97–137.

Astrahan, M. M., et al. [1979]. "System R: a relational database management system," *Computer* **12**:5, pp. 43–48.

Bachman, C. W. [1969]. "Data structure diagrams," *Data Base* **1**:2, pp. 4–10.

Badal, D. S. [1980]. "The analysis of the effects of concurrency control on distributed database system performance," *Proc. Intl. Conf. on Very Large Data Bases*, pp. 376–383.

Balbin, I. and K. Ramamohanarao [1986]. "A differential approach to query optimization in recursive deductive databases," TR–86/7, Dept. of CS, Univ. of Melbourne.

Bancilhon, F. [1986]. "A logic-programming/object-oriented cocktail," *SIGMOD Record*, **15**:3, pp. 11–21.

Bancilhon, F. and S. Khoshafian [1986]. "A calculus for complex objects," *Proc. Fifth ACM Symp. on Principles of Database Systems*, pp. 53–59.

Bancilhon, F. and R. Ramakrishnan [1986]. "An amateur's introduction to recursive query-processing strategies," *ACM SIGMOD Intl. Conf. on Management of Data*, pp. 16–52.

Baroody, J. A. Jr. and D. J. DeWitt [1981]. "An object-oriented approach to database system implementation," *ACM Trans. on Database Systems* **6**:4, pp. 576–601.

Bayer, R. [1985]. "Query evaluation and recursion in deductive database systems," unpublished memorandum, Technical Univ. of Munich.

Bayer, R., K. Elhardt, H. Heller, and A Reiser [1980]. "Distributed concurrency control in database systems," *Proc. Intl. Conf. on Very Large Data Bases*, pp. 275–284.

Bayer, R. and E. M. McCreight [1972]. "Organization and maintenance of large ordered indices," *Acta Informatica* **1**:3, pp. 173–189.

Bayer, R. and M. Schkolnick [1977]. "Concurrency of operating on B-trees," *Acta Informatica* **9**:1, pp. 1–21.

Beck, L. L. [1978]. "On minimal sets of operations for relational data sublanguages," TR–CS–7802, Southern Methodist Univ., Dallas, Tex.

Beech, D. [1987]. "Groundwork for an object database model," unpublished memorandum, Hewlett-Packard, Palo Alto, CA.

Beeri, C. [1980]. "On the membership problem for functional and multivalued dependencies," *ACM Trans. on Database Systems* **5**:3, pp. 241–259.

Beeri, C. and P. A. Bernstein [1979]. "Computational problems related to the design of normal form relation schemes," *ACM Trans. on Database Systems* **4**:1, pp. 30–59.

Beeri, C., P. A. Bernstein, and N. Goodman [1978]. "A sophisticate's introduction to database normalization theory," *Proc. Intl. Conf. on Very Large Data Bases*, pp. 113–124.

Beeri, C., P. A. Bernstein, N. Goodman, M. Y. Lai, and D. E. Shasha [1983]. "A concurrency control theory for nested transactions," *Proc. Second ACM Symp. on Principles of Database Systems*, pp. 45–62.

Beeri, C., R. Fagin, and J. H. Howard [1977]. "A complete axiomatization for functional and multivalued dependencies," *ACM SIGMOD Intl. Conf. on Management of Data*, pp. 47–61.

Beeri, C. and P. Honeyman [1981]. "Preserving functional dependencies," *SIAM J. Computing* **10**:3, pp. 647–656.

Beeri, C., A. O. Mendelzon, Y. Sagiv, and J. D. Ullman [1981]. "Equivalence of relational database schemes," *SIAM J. Computing* **10**:2, pp. 352–370.

Beeri, C., S. Naqvi, R. Ramakrishnan, O. Shmueli, and S. Tsur [1987]. "Sets and negation in a logic database language (LDL1)," *Proc. Sixth ACM Symp. on Principles of Database Systems*, pp. 21–37.

Beeri, C. and M. Y. Vardi [1981]. "The implication problem for data dependencies," *Automata, Languages and Programming* (S. Even and O. Kariv, eds.), pp. 73–85, Springer-Verlag, New York.

Beeri, C. and M. Y. Vardi [1984a]. "Formal systems for tuple- and equality-generating dependencies," *SIAM J. Computing* **13**:1, pp. 76–98.

Beeri, C. and M. Y. Vardi [1984b]. "A proof procedure for data dependencies," *J. ACM* **31**:4, pp. 718–741.

Bentley, J. L. [1975]. "Multidimensional binary search trees used for associative searching," *Comm. ACM* **18**:9, pp. 507–517.

Bentley, J. L. and J. H. Friedman [1979]. "Data structures for range searching," *Computing Surveys* **11**:4, pp. 397–410.

Bentley, J. L. and D. Stanat [1975]. "Analysis of range searches in quad trees," *Information Processing Letters* **3**:6, pp. 170–173.

Bernstein, P. A. [1976]. "Synthesizing third normal form relations from functional dependencies," *ACM Trans. on Database Systems* **1**:4, pp. 277–298.

Bernstein, P. A. and N. Goodman [1980a]. "What does Boyce-Codd normal form do?" *Proc. Intl. Conf. on Very Large Data Bases*, pp. 245–259.

Bernstein, P. A. and N. Goodman [1980b]. "Timestamp-based algorithms for concurrency control in distributed database systems," *Proc. Intl. Conf. on Very Large Data Bases*, pp. 285–300.

Bernstein, P. A. and N. Goodman [1981]. "Concurrency control in distributed database systems," *Computing Surveys* **13**:2, pp. 185–221.

Bernstein, P. A. and N. Goodman [1983]. "Multiversion concurrency control—theory and algorithms," *ACM Trans. on Database Systems* **8**:4, pp. 463–483.

Bernstein, P. A. and N. Goodman [1984]. "An algorithm for concurrency control and recovery in replicated, distributed databases," *ACM Trans. on Database Systems* **9**:4, pp. 596–615.

Bernstein, P. A., N. Goodman, and V. Hadzilacos [1983]. "Recovery algorithms for database systems," *Proc. 1983 IFIP Congress*, pp. 799–807, North Holland, Amsterdam.

Bernstein, P. A., N. Goodman, J. B. Rothnie Jr., and C. H. Papadimitriou [1978]. "Analysis of serializability of SDD-1: a system of distributed databases (the fully redundant case)," *IEEE Trans. on Software Engineering* **SE4**:3, pp. 154–168.

Bernstein, P. A, N. Goodman, E. Wong, C. L. Reeve, and J. B. Rothnie, Jr. [1981]. "Query processing in a system for distributed databases (SDD-1)," *ACM Trans. on Database Systems* **6**:4, pp. 602–625.

Bernstein, P. A., V. Hadzilacos, and N. Goodman [1987]. *Concurrency Control and Recovery in Database Systems* Addison-Wesley, Reading Mass.

Bernstein, P. A. and D. W. Shipman [1980]. "The correctness of concurrency control mechanisms in a system for distributed databases (SDD-1)," *ACM Trans. on Database Systems* **5**:1, pp. 52–68.

Bernstein, P. A., D. W. Shipman, and J. B. Rothnie, Jr. [1980]. "Concurrency control in a system for distributed databases (SDD-1)," *ACM Trans. on Database Systems* **5**:1, pp. 18–51.

Bidiot, N. and R. Hull [1986]. "Positivism vs. minimalism in deductive databases," *Proc. Fifth ACM Symp. on Principles of Database Systems*, pp. 123–132.

Biliris, A. [1987]. "Operation specific locking in B-trees," *Proc. Sixth ACM Symp. on Principles of Database Systems*, pp. 159–169.

Biskup, J. [1980]. "Inferences of multivalued dependencies in fixed and undetermined universes." *Theoretical Computer Science* **10**:1, pp. 93–106.

Biskup, J., U. Dayal, and P. A. Bernstein [1979]. "Synthesizing independent database schemas," *ACM SIGMOD Intl. Conf. on Management of Data*, pp. 143–152.

Blasgen, M. W., et al. [1981]. "System R: an architectural overview," *IBM Systems J.* **20**:1, pp. 41–62.

Bocca, J. [1986]. "EDUCE: a marriage of convenience: Prolog and a Relational Database," *Symp. on Logic Programming*, pp. 36–45, IEEE, New York.

Bolour, A. [1979]. "Optimality properties of multiple key hashing functions," *J. ACM* **26**:2, pp. 196–210.

Bosak, R., R. F. Clippinger, C. Dobbs, R. Goldfinger, R. B. Jasper, W. Keating, G. Kendrick, and J. E. Sammet [1962]. "An information algebra," *Comm. ACM* **5**:4, pp. 190–204.

Boyce, R. F., D. D. Chamberlin, W. F. King, and M. M. Hammer [1975].

"Specifying queries as relational expressions: the SQUARE data sublanguage," *Comm. ACM* **18**:11, pp. 621–628.

Brodie, M. L. [1984]. "On the development of data models," in Brodie, Mylopoulos, and Schmidt [1984], pp. 19–48.

Brodie, M. L. and J. Mylopoulos [1986]. *On Knowledge Base Management Systems*, Springer-Verlag, New York.

Brodie, M. L., J. Mylopoulos, and J. W. Schmidt [1984]. *On Conceptual Modeling*, Springer-Verlag, New York.

Brown, M. R., K. Kolling, and E. A. Taft [1984]. "The Alpine file system," CSL–84–4, Xerox, Palo Alto.

Buckley, G. N. and A. Silberschatz [1985]. "Beyond two-phase locking," *J. ACM* **32**:2, pp. 314–326.

Burkhard, W. A. [1976]. "Hashing and trie algorithms for partial match retrieval," *ACM Trans. on Database Systems* **1**:2, pp. 175–187.

Burkhard, W. A., M. L. Fredman, and D. J. Kleitman [1981]. "Inherent complexity trade-offs for range query problems," *Theoretical Computer Science* **16**:3, pp. 279–290.

Cardenas, A. F. [1979]. *Data Base Management Systems*, Allyn and Bacon, Boston, Mass.

Carey, M. J. [1983]. "Granularity hierarchies in concurrency control," *Proc. Second ACM Symp. on Principles of Database Systems*, pp. 156–165.

Casanova, M. A., R. Fagin, and C. H. Papadimitriou [1984]. "Inclusion dependencies and their interaction with functional dependencies," *J. Computer and System Sciences* **28**:1, pp. 29–59.

Ceri, S. and G. Pelagatti [1984]. *Distributed Databases: Principles and Systems*, McGraw-Hill, New York.

Chamberlin, D. D., et al. [1976]. "SEQUEL 2: a unified approach to data definition, manipulation, and control," *IBM J. Research and Development* **20**:6, pp. 560–575.

Chamberlin, D. D., et al. [1981]. "A history and evaluation of System R," *Comm. ACM* **24**:10, pp. 632–646.

Chandra, A. K. and D. Harel [1980]. "Computable queries for relational database systems," *J. Computer and System Sciences* **21**:2, pp. 156–178.

Chandra, A. K. and D. Harel [1982]. "Structure and complexity of relational queries," *J. Computer and System Sciences* **25**:1, pp. 99–128.

Chandra, A. K. and D. Harel [1985]. "Horn clause queries and generalizations," *J. Logic Programming* **4**:1, pp. 1–15.

Chandra, A. K., H. R. Lewis, and J. A. Makoswky [1981]. "Embedded implicational dependencies and their inference problem," *Proc. Thirteenth Annual ACM Symp. on the Theory of Computing*, pp. 342–354.

Chandy, K. M., J. C. Browne, C. W. Dissly, and W. R. Uhrig [1975]. "Analytic models for rollback and recovery strategies in database systems," *IEEE Trans. on Software Engineering* **SE-1**:1, pp. 100–110.

Chen, P. P. [1976]. "The entity-relationship model: toward a unified view of data," *ACM Trans. on Database Systems* **1**:1, pp. 9–36.

Childs, D. L. [1968]. "Feasibility of a set-theoretical data structure—a general structure based on a reconstituted definition of relation," *Proc. 1968 IFIP Congress*, pp. 162–172, North Holland, Amsterdam.

Cincom [1978]. *OS TOTAL Reference Manual*, Cincom Systems, Cincinnati, Ohio.

Clark, K. L. [1978]. "Negation as failure," in Gallaire and Minker [1978], pp. 293–322.

Clocksin, W. F. and C. S. Mellish [1981]. *Programming in Prolog*, Springer-Verlag, New York.

CODASYL [1971]. *CODASYL Data Base Task Group April 71 Report*, ACM, New York.

CODASYL [1978]. *COBOL J. Development*, Materiel Data Management Center, Quebec, Que. Earlier editions appeared in 1973 and 1968.

Codd, E. F. [1970]. "A relational model for large shared data banks," *Comm. ACM* **13**:6, pp. 377–387.

Codd, E. F. [1972a]. "Further normalization of the data base relational model," in *Data Base Systems* (R. Rustin, ed.) Prentice-Hall, Englewood Cliffs, New Jersey.pp. 33–64.

Codd, E. F. [1972b]. "Relational completeness of data base sublanguages," *ibid.* pp. 65–98.

Codd, E. F. [1975]. "Understanding relations," *FDT* **7**:3–4, pp. 23-28, ACM, New York.

Codd, E. F. [1979]. "Extending the data base relational model to capture more meaning," *ACM Trans. on Database Systems* **4**:4, pp. 397–434.

Comer, D. [1978]. "The difficulty of optimum index selection," *ACM Trans. on Database Systems* **3**:4, pp. 440–445.

Comer, D. [1979]. "The ubiquitous B-tree," *Computing Surveys* **11**:2, pp. 121–138.

Cooper, E. C. [1980]. "On the expressive power of query languages for relational databases," TR–14–80, Aiken Computation Lab., Harvard Univ.

Culik, K. II, Th. Ottmann, and D. Wood [1981]. "Dense multiway trees," *ACM Trans. on Database Systems* **6**:3, pp. 486–512.

Cullinane [1978]. *IDMS DML Programmer's Reference Guide,* Cullinane Corp., Wellesley, Mass.

Date, C. J. [1986]. *An Introduction to Database Systems,* two volumes, Addison-Wesley, Reading Mass.

Davidson, S. B. [1984]. "Optimism and consistency in partitioned distributed database systems," *ACM Trans. on Database Systems* **9**:3, pp. 456–482.

Dayal, U. and P. A. Bernstein [1982]. "On the correct translation of update operations on relational views," *ACM Trans. on Database Systems* **7**:3, pp. 381–416.

Dayal, U. and J. M. Smith [1986]. "PROBE: a knowledge-oriented database management system," in Brodie and Mylopoulos [1986], pp. 227–258.

Delobel, C. [1978]. "Normalization and hierarchical dependencies in the relational data model," *ACM Trans. on Database Systems* **3**:3, pp. 201–222. See also, "Contributions theoretiques a la conception d'un systeme d'informations," doctoral dissertation, Univ. of Grenoble, Oct., 1973.

Delobel, C. and R. C. Casey [1972]. "Decomposition of a database and the theory of boolean switching functions," *IBM J. Res. Devel.* **17**:5, pp. 370–386.

DiPaola, R. A. [1969]. "The recursive unsolvability of the decision problem for a class of definite formulas," *J. ACM* **16**:2, pp. 324–327.

Dwork, C. and D. Skeen [1983]. "The inherent cost of nonblocking commitment," *Proc. Second ACM Symp. on Principles of Distributed Computing,* pp. 1–11.

Eager, D. and K. Sevcik [1983]. "Achieving robustness in distributed database systems," *ACM Trans. on Database Systems* **8**:3, pp. 354–381.

El Abbadi, A., and S. Toueg [1986]. "Availability in partitioned, replicated databases," *Proc. Fifth ACM Symp. on Principles of Database Systems*, pp. 240–251.

Ellis, C. S. [1980]. "Concurrent search and insertion in 2-3 trees," *Acta Informatica* **14**:1, pp. 63–86.

Ellis, C. S. [1987]. "Concurrency in linear hashing," *ACM Trans. on Database Systems* **12**:2, pp. 195–217.

El Masri, R. and G. Wiederhold [1979]. "Data model integration using the structural model," *ACM SIGMOD Intl. Conf. on Management of Data*, pp. 191–202.

Epstein, R., M. Stonebraker, and E. Wong [1979]. "Distributed query processing in a relational database system," *ACM SIGMOD Intl. Conf. on Management of Data*, pp. 169–180.

Eswaran, K. P., J. N. Gray, R. A. Lorie, and I. L. Traiger [1976]. "The notions of consistency and predicate locks in a database system," *Comm. ACM* **19**:11, pp. 624–633.

Fagin, R. [1977]. "Multivalued dependencies and a new normal form for relational databases," *ACM Trans. on Database Systems* **2**:3, pp. 262–278.

Fagin, R. [1978]. "On an authorization mechanism," *ACM Trans. on Database Systems* **3**:3, pp. 310–319.

Fagin, R. [1981]. "A normal form for relational databases that is based on domains and keys," *ACM Trans. on Database Systems* **6**:3, pp. 387–415.

Fagin, R. [1982]. "Horn clauses and database dependencies," *J. ACM* **29**:4, pp. 952–983.

Fagin, R., J. Nievergelt, N. Pippenger, and H. R. Strong [1979]. "Extendible hashing—a fast access method for dynamic files," *ACM Trans. on Database Systems* **4**:3, pp. 315–344.

Fagin, R. and M. Y. Vardi [1986]. "The theory of data dependencies—a survey," in *Mathematics of Information Processing* (M. Anshel and W. Gewirtz, eds.), *Symposia in Applied Mathematics* **34**, pp. 19–72.

Fekete, A., N. Lynch, M. Merritt, and W. Weihl [1987]. "Nested transactions and read/write locking," *Proc. Sixth ACM Symp. on Principles of Database Systems*, pp. 97–111.

Fernandez, E. B., R. C. Summers, and C. Wood [1980]. *Database Security and Integrity*, Addison-Wesley, Reading Mass.

Fillat, A. I. and L. A. Kraning [1970]. "Generalized organization of large databases: a set theoretic approach to relations," MIT MAC TR–70, June, 1970.

Finkel, R. A. and J. L. Bentley [1974]. "Quad trees, a data structure for retrieval on composite keys," *Acta Informatica* 4:1, pp. 1–9.

Fischer, P. C. and D.-M. Tsou [1983]. "Whether a set of multivalued dependencies implies a join dependency is $\mathcal{NP}$-hard," *SIAM J. Computing* 12:2, pp. 259 266.

Fischer, P. C. and D. Van Gucht [1984]. "Weak multivalued dependencies," *Proc. Third ACM Symp. on Principles of Database Systems*, pp. 266–274.

Fishman, D. H., et al. [1986]. "Iris: an object-oriented DBMS," STL–86–15, Hewlett-Packard, Palo Alto.

Fong, A. C. and J. D. Ullman [1976]. "Induction variables in very high-level languages," *Proc. Third ACM Symp. on Principles of Programming Languages*, pp. 104–112.

Franaszek, P. and J. T. Robinson [1985]. "Limitations on concurrency in transaction processing," *ACM Trans. on Database Systems* 10:1, pp. 1–28.

Fredman, M. F. [1981]. "A lower bound on the complexity of orthogonal range queries," *J. ACM* 28:4, pp. 696–705.

Frost, R. [1986]. *Introduction to Knowledge Base Systems*, MacMillan, New York.

Furtado, A. L. [1978]. "Formal aspects of the relational model," *Information systems* 3:2, pp. 131–140.

Galil, Z. [1982]. "An almost linear time algorithm for computing a dependency basis in a relational database," *J. ACM* 29:1, pp. 96–102.

Gallaire, H. and J. Minker [1978]. *Logic and Databases*, Plenum Press, New York.

Gallaire, H., J. Minker, and J.-M. Nicolas [1981]. *Advances in Database Theory*, Vol. I, Plenum Press, New York.

Gallaire, H., J. Minker, and J.-M. Nicolas [1983]. *Advances in Database Theory*, Vol. II, Plenum Press, New York.

Gallaire, H., J. Minker, and J.-M. Nicolas [1984]. "Logic and databases: a deductive approach," *Computing Surveys* 16:1, pp. 154–185.

Garcia-Molina, H. [1979]. "Performance comparison of update algorithms for distributed databases," Part I: Tech. Note 143, Part II: Tech. Note 146, Digital

Systems Lab., Stanford Univ.

Garcia-Molina, H. [1982]. "Elections in a distributed computing system," *IEEE Trans. on Computers* **C-31**:1, pp. 48–59.

Garcia-Molina, H. and J. Kent [1985]. "An experimental evaluation of crash recovery algorithms," *Proc. Fourth ACM Symp. on Principles of Database Systems*, pp. 113–121.

Garey, M. R. and D. S. Johnson [1979]. *Computers and Intractability: A Guide to the Theory of NP-Completeness*, Freeman, San Francisco.

Gelenbe, E. and D. Derochette [1978]. "Performance of rollback recovery systems under intermittent failures," *Comm. ACM* **21**:6, pp. 493–499.

Gelfond, M. and V. Lifschitz [1988]. "The stable model semantics for logic programming," unpublished memorandum, Dept. of CS, Stanford Univ.

Gelfond, M., H. Przymusinska, and T. C. Przymusinski [1986]. "The extended closed world assumption and its relationship to parallel circumscription," *Proc. Fifth ACM Symp. on Principles of Database Systems*, pp. 133–139.

Genesereth, M. R. and N. J. Nilsson [1988]. *Logical Foundatations of Artificial Intelligence*, Morgan-Kaufmann, Los Altos.

Ginsberg, M. [1988]. *Nonmonotonic Reasoning*, Morgan-Kaufmann, Los Altos.

Ginsburg, S. and S. M. Zaiddan [1982]. "Properties of functional dependency families," *J. ACM* **29**:3, pp. 678–698.

Goldberg, A. and D. Robson [1980]. *Smalltalk-80: The Language and Its Implementation*, Addison-Wesley, Reading Mass.

Gonzalez-Rubio, R., J. Rohmer, and A. Bradier [1987]. "An overview of DDC: a delta driven computer," DSG/CRG/87007, Bull, Louveciennes, France.

Gotlieb, C. C. and F. W. Tompa [1973]. "Choosing a storage schema," *Acta Informatica* **3**:3, pp. 297–319.

Gottlob, G. [1987]. "Computing covers for embedded functional dependencies," *Proc. Sixth ACM Symp. on Principles of Database Systems*, pp. 58–69.

Graham, M. H., A. O. Mendelzon, and M. Y. Vardi [1986]. "Notions of dependency satisfaction," *J. ACM* **33**:1, pp. 105–129.

Gray, J. N. [1978]. "Notes on database operating systems," in *Operating Systems: an Advanced Course* (R. Bayer, R. M. Graham, and G. Seegmuller, eds.), Springer-Verlag, New York.

Gray, J. N., et al. [1981]. "The recovery manager of the system R database manager," *Computing Surveys* **13**:2, pp. 223–242.

Gray, J. N., R. A. Lorie, and G. R. Putzolo [1975]. "Granularity of locks in a shared database," *Proc. Intl. Conf. on Very Large Data Bases*, pp. 428–451.

Gray, J. N., G. R. Putzolo, and I. L. Traiger [1976]. "Granularity of locks and degrees of consistency in a shared data base," in *Modeling in Data Base Management Systems* (G. M. Nijssen, ed.), North Holland, Amsterdam.

Greenblatt, D. and J. Waxman [1978]. "A study of three database query languages," in Shneiderman [1978], pp. 77–98.

Griffiths, P. P. and B. W. Wade [1976]. "An authorization mechanism for a relational database system," *ACM Trans. on Database Systems* **1**:3, pp. 242–255.

Gudes, E. and S. Tsur [1980]. "Experiments with B-tree reorganization," *ACM SIGMOD Intl. Conf. on Management of Data*, pp. 200–206.

Gurevich, Y. and H. R. Lewis [1982]. "The inference problem for template dependencies," *Proc. First ACM Symp. on Principles of Database Systems*, pp. 221–229.

Hadzilacos, T. and C. H. Papadimitriou [1985]. "Some algorithmic aspects of multiversion concurrency control," *Proc. Fourth ACM Symp. on Principles of Database Systems*, pp. 96–104.

Hadzilacos, T. and M. Yannakakis [1986]. "Deleting completed transactions," *Proc. Fifth ACM Symp. on Principles of Database Systems*, pp. 43–46.

Hadzilacos, V. [1982]. "An algorithm for minimizing roll back cost," *Proc. First ACM Symp. on Principles of Database Systems*, pp. 93–97.

Hadzilacos, V. [1987]. "A knowledge-theoretic analysis of atomic commitment protocols," *Proc. Sixth ACM Symp. on Principles of Database Systems*, pp. 129–134.

Haerder, T. and A. Reuter [1983]. "Principles of transaction oriented database recovery—a taxonomy," *Computing Surveys* **15**:4, pp. 287–317.

Hagihara, K., M. Ito, K. Taniguchi, and T. Kasami [1979]. "Decision problems for multivalued dependencies in relational databases," *SIAM J. Computing* **8**:2, pp. 247–264.

Hammer, M. and D. McLeod [1981]. "Database description with SDM: a semantic database model," *ACM Trans. on Database Systems* **6**:3, pp. 351–386.

Hammer, M. and D. Shipman [1980]. "Reliability mechanisms for SDD-1: a system for distributed databases," *ACM Trans. on Database Systems* **5**:4, pp. 431–466.

Harel, D. [1986]. "Logic and databases: a critique," *SIGACT News* **18**:1, pp. 68–74.

Heath, I. J. [1971]. "Unacceptable file operations in a relational data base," *ACM SIGFIDET Workshop on Data Description, Access, and Control*, pp. 19–33.

Heiler, S. and A. Rosenthal [1985]. "G-WHIZ: a visual interface for the functional model with recursion," *Proc. Intl. Conf. on Very Large Data Bases*, pp. 209–218.

Held, G. and M. Stonebraker [1978]. "B-trees reexamined," *Comm. ACM* **21**:2, pp. 139–143.

Holt, R. C. [1972]. "Some deadlock properties in computer systems," *Computing Surveys* **4**:3, pp. 179–196.

Honeyman, P. [1982]. "Testing satisfaction of functional dependencies," *J. ACM* **29**:3, pp. 668–677.

Hull, R. and R. King [1987]. "Semantic database modeling: survey, applications, and research issues," CRI–87–20, Computer Research Inst., USC.

Hull, R. and C. K. Yap [1984]. "The format model, a theory of database organization," *J. ACM* **31**:3, pp. 518–537.

Hunt, H. B. III and D. J. Rosenkrantz [1979]. "The complexity of testing predicate locks," *ACM SIGMOD Intl. Conf. on Management of Data*, pp. 127–133.

IBM [1978a]. *Query-by Example Terminal Users Guide*, SH20–2078–0, IBM, White Plains, N. Y.

IBM [1978b]. IMS/VS publications, especially GH20–1260 (*General Information*), SH20–9025 (*System/Application Design Guide*), SH20–9026 (*Application Programming Reference Manual*), and SH20–9027 (*Systems Programming Reference Manual*), IBM, White Plains, N. Y.

IBM [1984]. "SQL/data system application programming for VM/system product," SH24–5068–0, IBM, White Plains, N. Y.

IBM [1985a]. "SQL/RT database programmer's guide," IBM, White Plains, NY.

IBM [1985b]. "Easy SQL/RT user's guide," IBM, White Plains, NY.

Imielinski, T. [1986]. "Query processing in deductive database systems with incomplete information," *ACM SIGMOD Intl. Conf. on Management of Data*, pp. 268–280.

Imielinski, T. and W. Lipski [1984]. "Incomplete information in relational databases," *J. ACM* **31**:4, pp. 761–791.

Immerman, N. [1982]. "Relational queries computable in polynomial time," *Proc. Fourteenth Annual ACM Symp. on the Theory of Computing*, pp. 147–152.

Jaeschke, G. and H.-J. Scheck [1982]. "Remarks on the algebra of non first normal form relations," *Proc. First ACM Symp. on Principles of Database Systems*, pp. 124–138.

Jarke, M., J. Clifford, and Y. Vassiliou [1984]. "An optimizing Prolog front end to a relational query system," *ACM SIGMOD Intl. Conf. on Management of Data*, pp. 296–306.

Jou, J. H. and P. C. Fischer [1983]. "The complexity of recognizing 3NF relation schemes," *Information Processing Letters* **14**:4, pp. 187–190.

Kambayashi, Y. [1981]. *Database a Bibliography*, Computer Science Press, Rockville, Md.

Kanellakis, P. C., S. S. Cosmadakis, and M. Y. Vardi [1983]. "Unary inclusion dependencies have polynomial time inference problems," *Proc. Fifteenth Annual ACM Symp. on the Theory of Computing*, pp. 264–277.

Kanellakis, P. C. and C. H. Papadimitriou [1981]. "The complexity of distributed concurrency control," *Proc. Twenty-Second Annual IEEE Symp. on Foundations of Computer Science*, pp. 185–197.

Kanellakis, P. C. and C. H. Papadimitriou [1984]. "Is distributed locking harder?," *J. Computer and System Sciences* **28**:1, pp. 103–120.

Kedem, Z. and A. Silberschatz [1979]. "Controlling concurrency using locking protocols." *Proc. Twentieth Annual IEEE Symp. on Foundations of Computer Science*, pp. 274–285.

Kedem, Z. and A. Silberschatz [1980]. "Non-two phase locking protocols with shared and exclusive locks," *Proc. Intl. Conf. on Very Large Data Bases*, pp. 309–320.

Keller, A. [1985]. "Algorithms for translating view updates into database updates for views involving selections, projections, and joins," *Proc. Fourth ACM Symp. on Principles of Database Systems*, pp. 154–163.

Kellogg, C., A. O'Hare, and L. Travis [1986]. "Optimizing the rule-data interface in a KMS," *Proc. Intl. Conf. on Very Large Data Bases*, pp. 42–51.

Kent, W. [1979]. "Limitations of record-based information models," *ACM Trans. on Database Systems* 4:1, pp. 107–131.

Kerschberg, L., A. Klug, and D. C. Tsichritzis [1977]. "A taxonomy of data models," in *Systems for Large Data Bases* (Lockemann and Neuhold, eds.), North Holland, Amsterdam, pp. 43–64.

Khoshafian, S. N. and G. P. Copeland [1986]. "Object identity," *OOPSLA '86 Proceedings*, ACM, New York, pp. 406–416.

Kim, W. [1979]. "Relational database systems," *Computing Surveys* 11:3, pp. 185–210.

Klug, A. [1981]. "Equivalence of relational algebra and relational calculus query languages having aggregate functions," *J. ACM* 29:3, pp. 699–717.

Knuth, D. E. [1968]. *The Art of Computer Programming*, Vol. 1, *Fundamental Algorithms*, Addison-Wesley, Reading Mass.

Knuth, D. E. [1973]. *The Art of Computer Programming*, Vol. 3, *Sorting and Searching*, Addison-Wesley, Reading Mass.

Korth, H. F. [1983]. "Locking primitives in a database system," *J. ACM* 30:1, pp. 55–79.

Korth, H. F. and A. Silberschatz [1986]. *Database System Concepts*, McGraw-Hill, New York.

Kowalski, R. A. [1974]. "Predicate logic as a programming language," *Proc. 1974 IFIP Congress*, pp. 569–574, North Holland, Amsterdam.

Kuhns, J. L. [1967]. "Answering questions by computer; a logical study," RM-5428-PR, Rand Corp., Santa Monica, Calif.

Kung, H.-T. and C. H. Papadimitriou [1979]. "An optimality theory of concurrency control for databases," *ACM SIGMOD Intl. Conf. on Management of Data*, pp. 116–126.

Kung, H.-T. and J. T. Robinson [1981]. "On optimistic concurrency control," *ACM Trans. on Database Systems* 6:2, pp. 213–226.

Kunifuji, S. and H. Yokuta [1982]. "PROLOG and relational databases for fifth-generation computer systems," TR002, ICOT, Tokyo.

Kuper, G. M. [1987]. "Logic programming with sets," *Proc. Sixth ACM Symp. on Principles of Database Systems*, pp. 11–20.

Kuper, G. M. and M. Y. Vardi [1984]. "A new approach to database logic," *Proc. Third ACM Symp. on Principles of Database Systems*, pp. 86–96.

Kuper, G. M. and M. Y. Vardi [1985]. "On the expressive power of the logical data model," *ACM SIGMOD Intl. Conf. on Management of Data*, pp. 180–189.

Lacroix, M. and A. Pirotte [1976]. "Generalized joins," *SIGMOD Record* 8:3, pp. 14–15.

Lamport, L. [1978]. "Time, clocks, and the ordering of events in a distributed system," *Comm. ACM* 21:7, pp. 558–565.

Lampson, B. and H. Sturgis [1976]. "Crash recovery in a distributed data storage system," unpublished memorandum, Xerox PARC, Palo Alto, CA.

Larson, P. [1978]. "Dynamic hashing," *BIT* 18:2, pp. 184–201.

Larson, P. [1982]. "Performance analysis of linear hashing with partial expansions," *ACM Trans. on Database Systems* 7:4, pp. 565–587.

Lehman, P. L. and S. B. Yao [1981]. "Efficient locking for concurrent operations on B-trees," *ACM Trans. on Database Systems* 6:4, pp. 650–670.

Lein, Y. E. [1979]. "Multivalued dependencies with null values in relational databases," *Proc. Intl. Conf. on Very Large Data Bases*, pp. 61–66.

Levien, R. E. [1969]. "Relational data file: experience with a system for propositional data storage and inference execution," RM–5947–PR, Rand Corp., Santa Monica, Calif.

Levien, R. E. and M. E. Maron [1967]. "A computer system for inference execution and data retrieval," *Comm. ACM* 10:9, pp. 715–721.

Le, V. T. [1985]. "General failure of logic programs," *J. Logic Programming* 2:2, pp. 157–165.

Lien, Y. E. [1979]. "Multivalued dependencies with null values in relational databases," *Proc. Intl. Conf. on Very Large Data Bases*, pp. 61–66.

Lifschitz, V. [1985]. "Closed world databases and circumscription," *Artificial Intelligence* 28:1, pp. 229–235.

Lifschitz, V. [1988]. "On the declarative semantics of logic programs," in Minker [1988].

Ling, T. W., F. W. Tompa, and T. Kameda [1981]. "An improved third normal form for relational databases," *ACM Trans. on Database Systems* 6:2, pp. 329–346.

Lipski, W. Jr. [1981]. "On databases with incomplete information," *J. ACM* **28**:1, pp. 41–70.

Lipski, W. and C. H. Papadimitriou [1981]. "A fast algorithm for testing for safety and deadlocks in locked transaction systems," *J. Algorithms* **2**:2, pp. 211–226.

Litwin, W. [1980]. "Linear hashing: a new tool for file and table addressing," *Proc. Intl. Conf. on Very Large Data Bases*, pp. 212–223.

Litwin, W. [1984]. "MALPHA, A Multidatabase manipulation language," *Proc. IEEEDEC*, April, 1984.

Liu, L. and A. Demers [1980]. "An algorithm for testing lossless joins in relational databases," *Information Processing Letters* **11**:1, pp. 73–76.

Lloyd, J. W. [1984]. *Foundations of Logic Programming*, Springer-Verlag, New York.

Lorie, R. A. [1977]. "Physical integrity in a large segmented database," *ACM Trans. on Database Systems* **2**:1, pp. 91–104.

Lucchesi, C. L. and S. L. Osborn [1978]. "Candidate keys for relations." *J. Computer and System Sciences* **17**:2, pp. 270–279.

Lueker, G. S. [1978]. "A data structure for orthogonal range queries," *Proc. Nineteenth Annual IEEE Symp. on Foundations of Computer Science*, pp. 28–33.

Lum, V. and H. Ling [1970]. "Multi-attribute retrieval with combined indices," *Comm. ACM* **13**:11, pp. 660–665.

Maier, D. [1980]. "Minimum covers in the relational database model," *J. ACM* **27**:4, pp. 664–674.

Maier, D. [1983]. *The Theory of Relational Databases*, Computer Science Press, Rockville, Md.

Maier, D. [1986]. "A logic for objects," TR CS/E–86–012, Oregon Graduate Center, Beaverton, Ore.

Maier, D., A. O. Mendelzon, F. Sadri, and J. D. Ullman [1980]. "Adequacy of decompositions in relational databases," *J. Computer and System Sciences* **21**:3, pp. 368–379.

Maier, D., A. O. Mendelzon, and Y. Sagiv [1979]. "Testing implications of data dependencies," *ACM Trans. on Database Systems* **4**:4, pp. 455–469.

Maier, D., Y. Sagiv, and M. Yannakakis [1981]. "On the complexity of testing implications of functional and join dependencies," *J. ACM* **28**:4, pp. 680–695.

Maier, D., J. Stein, A. Otis, and A. Purdy [1986]. "Development of an object-oriented DBMS," *OOPSLA '86 Proceedings*, ACM, New York, pp. 472–482.

Maier, D. and D. S. Warren [1988]. *Computing with Logic: Logic Programming with Prolog*, Benjamin Cummings, Menlo Park, CA.

Manber, U. and R. E. Ladner [1984]. "Concurrency control in a dynamic search structure," *ACM Trans. on Database Systems* **9**:3, pp. 439–455.

Manna, Z. and R. Waldinger [1985]. *The Logical Basis for Computer Programming*, Addison-Wesley, Reading Mass.

Maurer, W. D. and T. G. Lewis [1975]. "Hash table methods," *Computing Surveys* **7**:1, pp. 5–20.

McCarthy, J. [1980]. "Circumscription—a form of nonmonotonic reasoning," *Artificial Intelligence* **13**:1, pp. 27–39.

McLean, G. [1981]. "Comments on SDD-1 concurrency control mechanisms," *ACM Trans. on Database Systems* **6**:2, pp. 347–350.

Menasce, D. A. and R. R. Muntz [1979]. "Locking and deadlock detection in distributed data bases," *IEEE Trans. on Software Engineering* **SE-5**:3, pp. 195–202.

Menasce, D. A., G. J. Popek, and R. R. Muntz [1980]. "A locking protocol for resource coordination in distributed databases," *ACM Trans. on Database Systems* **5**:2, pp. 103–138.

Mendelzon, A. O. [1979]. "On axiomatizing multivalued dependencies in relational databases," *J. ACM* **26**:1, pp. 37–44.

Mendelzon, A. O. and D. Maier [1979]. "Generalized mutual dependencies and the decomposition of database relations," *Proc. Intl. Conf. on Very Large Data Bases*, pp. 75–82.

Minker, J. [1982]. "On indefinite databases and the closed world assumption," *Proc. Sixth Conf. on Automated Deduction* (D. Loveland, ed.), Springer-Verlag, New York.

Minker, J. [1987]. "Perspectives in deductive databases," CS–TR–1799, Dept. of CS, Univ. of Maryland.

Minker, J. [1988]. *Foundations of Deductive Databases and Logic Programming*, Morgan-Kaufmann, Los Altos.

Minoura, T. [1980]. "Resilient extended true-copy token algorithm for distributed database systems," Ph. D. Thesis, Dept. of EE, Stanford Univ., Stanford, Calif.

Minsky, N. H. and D. Rozenshtein [1987]. "Law-based approach to object-oriented programming," *Proc. 1987 OOPSLA Conf.*

Mitchell, J. C. [1983]. "Inference rules for functional and inclusion dependencies," *Proc. Second ACM Symp. on Principles of Database Systems*, pp. 58–69.

Moffat, D. S. and P. M. D. Gray [1986]. "Interfacing Prolog to a persistent data store," *Proc. Third Intl. Conf. on Logic Programming*, pp. 577–584.

Mohan, C., B. G. Lindsay, and R. Obermarck [1986]. "Transaction management in the R* Distributed database management system," *ACM Trans. on Database Systems* 11:4, pp. 378–396.

Morris, K., J. F. Naughton, Y. Saraiya, J. D. Ullman, and A. Van Gelder [1987]. "YAWN! (yet another window on NAIL!)," to appear in *Database Engineering*.

Morris, K., J. D. Ullman, and A. Van Gelder [1986]. "Design overview of the NAIL! system," *Proc. Third Intl. Conf. on Logic Programming*, pp. 554–568.

Morris, R. [1968]. "Scatter storage techniques," *Comm. ACM* 11:1, pp. 38–43.

MRI [1978]. *System 2000 Reference manual*, MRI Systems Corp., Austin, Tex.

Naish, L. [1986]. "Negation and control in Prolog," Lecture Notes in Computer Science **238**, Springer-Verlag, New York.

Naqvi, S. [1986]. "Negation in knowledge base management systems," in Brodie and Mylopoulos [1986], pp. 125–146.

Nicolas, J. M. [1978]. "Mutual dependencies and some results on undecomposable relations," *Proc. Intl. Conf. on Very Large Data Bases*, pp. 360–367.

Obermarck, R. [1982]. "Distributed deadlock detection algorithm," *ACM Trans. on Database Systems* 7:2, pp. 187–208.

Olle, T. W. [1978]. *The Codasyl Approach to Data Base Management*, John Wiley and Sons, New York.

Orenstein, J. A. and T. H. Merrett [1984]. "A class of data structures for associative searching," *Proc. Fourth ACM Symp. on Principles of Database Systems*, pp. 181–190.

Osborn, S. L. [1977]. "Normal forms for relational databases," Ph. D. Thesis, Univ. of Waterloo.

Osborn, S. L. [1979]. "Testing for existence of a covering Boyce-Codd normal form," *Information Processing Letters* 8:1, pp. 11–14.

Ozsoyoglu, G. and H. Wang [1987]. "On set comparison operators, safety, and QBE," unpublished memorandum, Dept. of CSE, Case Western Reserve Univ., Cleveland, Ohio.

Ozsoyoglu, M. Z. and L.-Y. Yuan [1985]. "A normal form for nested relations," *Proc. Fourth ACM Symp. on Principles of Database Systems*, pp. 251–260.

Paige, R. and J. T. Schwartz [1977]. "Reduction in strength of high level operations," *Proc. Fourth ACM Symp. on Principles of Programming Languages*, pp. 58–71.

Papadimitriou, C. H. [1979]. "The serializability of concurrent database updates," *J. ACM* **26**:4, pp. 631–653.

Papadimitriou, C. H. [1983]. "Concurrency control by locking," *J. ACM* **12**:2, pp. 215–226.

Papadimitriou, C. H. [1986]. *The Theory of Database Concurrency Control*, Computer Science Press, Rockville, Md.

Papadimitriou, C. H., P. A. Bernstein, and J. B. Rothnie Jr. [1977]. "Computational problems related to database concurrency control," *Proc. Conf. on Theoretical Computer Science*, Univ. of Waterloo, Waterloo, Ont.

Papadimitriou, C. H. and P. C. Kanellakis [1984]. "On concurrency control by multiple versions," *ACM Trans. on Database Systems* **9**:1, pp. 89–99.

Paredaens, J. and D. Jannsens [1981]. "Decompositions of relations: a comprehensive approach," in Gallaire, Minker, and Nicolas [1980].

Peleg, D. [1987]. "Time-optimal leader election in general networks," unpublished memorandum, Dept. of CS, Stanford Univ.

Perl, Y., A. Itai, and H. Avni [1978]. "Interpolation search—a log log $n$ search," *Comm. ACM* **21**:7, pp. 550–553.

Pirotte, A. [1978]. "High level data base query languages," in Gallaire and Minker [1978], pp. 409–436.

Przymusinski, T. C. [1986]. "An algorithm to compute circumscription," unpublished memorandum, Dept. of Math. Sci., Univ. of Texas, El Paso.

Przymusinski, T. C. [1988]. "On the declarative semantics of stratified deductive databases and logic programs," in Minker [1988].

Ramakrishnan, R., F. Bancilhon, and A. Silberschatz [1987]. "Safety of recursive Horn clauses with infinite relations," *Proc. Sixth ACM Symp. on Principles of Database Systems*, pp. 328–339.

Ramarao, K. V. S. [1985]. "On the complexity of commit protocols," *Proc. Fourth ACM Symp. on Principles of Database Systems*, pp. 235–244.

Reed, D. P. [1978]. "Naming and synchronization in a decentralized computer system," Ph. D. thesis, Dept. of EECS, MIT, Cambridge, Mass.

Reis, D. R. and M. Stonebraker [1977]. "Effects of locking granularity in a database management system," *ACM Trans. on Database Systems* **2**:3, pp. 233–246.

Reis, D. R. and M. Stonebraker [1979]. "Locking granularity revisited," *ACM Trans. on Database Systems* **4**:2, pp. 210–227.

Reiter, R. [1978]. "On closed world databases," in Gallaire and Minker [1978], pp. 55–76.

Reiter, R. [1980]. "Equality and domain closure in first-order databases," *J. ACM* **27**:2, pp. 235–249.

Reiter, R. [1984]. "Towards a logical reconstruction of relational database theory," in Brodie, Mylopoulos, and Schmidt [1984], pp. 191–233.

Reiter, R. [1986]. "A sound and sometimes complete query evaluation algorithm for relational databases with null values," *J. ACM* **33**:2, pp. 349–370.

Reuter, A. [1984]. "Performance analysis of recovery techniques," *ACM Trans. on Database Systems* **9**:4, pp. 526–559.

Rissanen, J. [1977]. "Independent components of relations," *ACM Trans. on Database Systems* **2**:4, pp. 317–325.

Rissanen, J. [1979]. "Theory of joins for relational databases—a tutorial survey," *Proc. Seventh Symp. on Mathematical Foundations of C. S.*, Lecture notes in CS, **64**, Springer–Verlag, pp. 537–551.

Rivest, R. L. [1976]. "Partial match retrieval algorithms," *SIAM J. Computing* **5**:1, pp. 19–50.

Robinson, J. T. [1981]. "The K-D-B tree; a search structure for large, multidimensional dynamic indices," *ACM SIGMOD Intl. Conf. on Management of Data*, pp. 10–18.

Robinson, J. T. [1986]. "Order preserving linear hashing using dynamic key statistics," *Proc. Fifth ACM Symp. on Principles of Database Systems*, pp. 91–99.

Rosenberg, A. L. and L. Snyder [1981]. "Time- and space-optimality in B-trees," *ACM Trans. on Database Systems* **6**:1, pp. 174–193.

Rosenkrantz, D. J., R. E. Stearns, and P. M. Lewis II [1978]. "System level concurrency control for distributed data base systems," *ACM Trans. on Database Systems* **3**:2, pp. 178–198.

Ross, K. A. and R. W. Topor [1987]. "Inferring negative information in deductive database systems," TR 87/1, Dept. of CS, Univ. of Melbourne.

Ross, K. A. and A. Van Gelder [1988]. "Unfounded sets and well-founded semantics for general logic programs," to appear in *Proc. Seventh ACM Symp. on Principles of Database Systems.*

Roth, M., H. F. Korth, and A Silberschatz [1984]. "Theory of non-first-normal-form relational databases," TR–84–36, Dept. of CS, Univ. of Texas, Austin.

Rothnie, J. B. Jr., et al. [1980]. "Introduction to a system for distributed databases (SDD-1)," *ACM Trans. on Database Systems* **5**:1, pp. 1–17.

Rothnie, J. B. Jr. and N. Goodman [1977]. "A survey of research and development in distributed database management," *Proc. Intl. Conf. on Very Large Data Bases*, pp. 48–62.

Rothnie, J. B. Jr. and T. Lozano [1974]. "Attribute based file organization in a paged memory environment," *Comm. ACM* **17**:2, pp. 63–69.

Rustin, R. (ed.) [1974]. *Proc. ACM/SIGMOD Conf. on Data Models: Data-Structure-Set vs. Relational,* ACM, New York.

Sadri, F. and J. D. Ullman [1981]. "Template dependencies: a large class of dependencies in relational databases and their complete axiomatization," *J. ACM* **29**:2, pp. 363–372.

Sagiv, Y. [1985]. "Concurrent operations on B-trees with overtaking," *Proc. Fourth ACM Symp. on Principles of Database Systems*, pp. 28–37.

Sagiv, Y. [1987]. "Optimizing datalog programs," *Proc. Sixth ACM Symp. on Principles of Database Systems*, pp. 349–362.

Sagiv, Y., C. Delobel, D. S. Parker, and R. Fagin [1981]. "An equivalence between relational database dependencies and a fragment of propositional logic," *J. ACM* **28**:3, pp. 435–453.

Sagiv, Y. and S. Walecka [1982]. "Subset dependencies and a completeness result for a subclass of embedded multivalued dependencies," *J. ACM* **29**:1, pp. 103–117.

Samet, H. [1984]. "The quad tree and related hierarchical data structures," *Computing Surveys* **16**:2, pp. 187–260.

Scheuermann, P. and M. Ouksel [1982]. "Multidimensional B-trees for associative searching in database systems," *Information Systems* **7**:2, pp. 123–137.

Schkolnick, M. and P. Sorenson [1981]. "The effects of denormalization on database performance," RJ3082, IBM, San Jose, Calif.

Schmid, H. A. and J. R. Swenson [1976]. "On the semantics of the relational model," *ACM SIGMOD Intl. Conf. on Management of Data*, pp. 9–36.

Sciore, E. [1979]. "Improving semantic specification in the database relational model," *ACM SIGMOD Intl. Conf. on Management of Data*, pp. 170–178.

Sciore, E. [1982]. "A complete axiomatization of full join dependencies," *J. ACM* **29**:2, pp. 373–393.

Sciore, E. and D. S. Warren [1986]. "Towards an integrated database-Prolog system," *Proc. First Intl. Conf. on Expert Database Systems*, pp. 801–815, Benjamin-Cummings, Menlo Park CA.

Segall, A. and O. Wolfson [1987]. "Transaction commitment at minimal communication cost," *Proc. Sixth ACM Symp. on Principles of Database Systems*, pp. 112–118.

Servio Logic [1986]. "Programming in OPAL," Servio Logic Development Corp., Beaverton, Oregon.

Shepherdson, J. C. [1984]. "Negation as failure: a comparison of Clark's completed data base and Reiter's closed world assumption," *J. Logic Programming* **1**:1, pp. 51–79.

Shipman, D. W. [1981]. "The functional data model and the data language DAPLEX," *ACM Trans. on Database Systems* **6**:1, pp. 140–173.

Shmueli, O. [1987]. "Decidability and expressiveness aspects of logic queries," *Proc. Sixth ACM Symp. on Principles of Database Systems*, pp. 237–249.

Shneiderman, B. (ed.) [1978]. *Database: Improving Usability and responsiveness*, Academic Press, New York.

Sibley, E. (ed.) [1976]. *Computer Surveys* **8**:1, March, 1976.

Silberschatz, A. and Z. Kedem [1980]. "Consistency in hierarchical database systems," *J. ACM* **27**:1, pp. 72–80.

Skeen, D. [1981]. "Nonblocking commit protocols," *ACM SIGMOD Intl. Conf. on Management of Data*, pp. 133–142.

Skeen, D., F. Cristian, and A. El Abbadi [1985]. "An efficient fault-tolerant algorithm for replicated data management," *Proc. Fourth ACM Symp. on Prin-*

*ciples of Database Systems*, pp. 215–229.

Skeen, D. and M. Stonebraker [1981]. "A formal model of crash recovery in a distributed system," *Proc. Fifth Berkeley Workshop on Distributed Data Management and Computer Networks*, pp. 129–142.

Skeen, D. and D. D. Wright [1984]. "Increasing availability in partitioned database systems," *Proc. Fourth ACM Symp. on Principles of Database Systems*, pp. 290–299.

Smith, J. M. and D. C. P. Smith [1977]. "Database abstractions: aggregation and generalization," *ACM Trans. on Database Systems* **2**:2, pp. 105–133.

Snyder, L. [1978]. "On B-trees reexamined," *Comm. ACM* **21**:7, pp. 594.

Software AG [1978]. *ADABAS Introduction*, Software AG of North America, Reston, Va.

Soisalon-Soininen, E. and D. Wood [1982]. "An optimal algorithm for testing safety and detecting deadlocks," *Proc. First ACM Symp. on Principles of Database Systems*, pp. 108–116.

Stearns, R. E., P. M. Lewis II, and D. J. Rosenkrantz [1976]. "Concurrency control for database systems," *Proc. Seventeenth Annual IEEE Symp. on Foundations of Computer Science*, pp. 19–32.

Stonebraker, M. [1975]. "Implementation of integrity constraints and views by query modification," *ACM SIGMOD Intl. Conf. on Management of Data*, pp. 65–78.

Stonebraker, M. [1979]. "Concurrency control and consistency of multiple copies in distributed INGRES," *IEEE Trans. on Software Engineering* **SE-5**:3, pp. 188–194.

Stonebraker, M. [1980]. "Retrospection on a database system," *ACM Trans. on Database Systems* **5**:2, pp. 225–240.

Stonebraker, M. [1986]. "Triggers and inference in database systems," in Brodie and Mylopoulos [1986], pp. 297–314.

Stonebraker, M. and L. A. Rowe [1977]. "Observations on data manipulation languages and their embedding in general purpose programming languages," TR UCB/ERL M77–53, Univ. of California, Berkeley, July, 1977.

Stonebraker, M. and L. A. Rowe [1986a]. "The design of Postgres," *ACM SIGMOD Intl. Conf. on Management of Data*, pp. 340–355.

Stonebraker, M. and L. A. Rowe [1986b]. "The Postgres papers," UCB/ERL M86/85, Dept. of EECS, Univ. of Calif., Berkeley

Stonebraker, M. and P. Rubinstein [1976]. "The INGRES protection system," *Proc. ACM National Conf.*, pp. 80–84.

Stonebraker, M. and E. Wong [1974]. "Access control in a relational database management system by query modification," *Proc. ACM National Conf.*, pp. 180–187.

Stonebraker, M., E. Wong, P. Kreps, and G. Held [1976]. "The design and implementation of INGRES," *ACM Trans. on Database Systems* 1:3, pp. 189–222.

Tanaka, K., Y. Kambayashi, and S. Yajima [1979]. "Properties of embedded multivalued dependencies in relational databases," *J. IECE of Japan* 62:8, pp. 536–543.

Tanimoto, S. L. [1987]. *The Elements of Artificial Intelligence*, Computer Science Press, Rockville, Md.

Tarski, A. [1955]. "A lattice theoretical fixpoint theorem and its applications," *Pacific J. Math.* 5:2, pp. 285–309.

Tay, Y. C., N. Goodman, and R. Suri [1985]. "Locking performance in centralized databases," *ACM Trans. on Database Systems* 10:4, pp. 415–462.

Tay, Y. C., R. Suri, and N. Goodman [1985]. "A mean value performance model for locking in databases: the no-waiting case," *J. ACM* 32:3, pp. 618–651.

Thomas, R. H. [1975]. "A solution to the update problem for multiple copy databases which use distributed control," Rept. 3340, Bolt Beranek, and Newman, Cambridge, Mass.

Thomas, R. H. [1979]. "A majority consensus approach to concurrency control," *ACM Trans. on Database Systems* 4:2, pp. 180–219.

Todd, S. J. P. [1976]. "The Peterlee relational test vehicle—a system overview," *IBM Systems J.* 15:4, pp. 285–308.

Traiger, I. L., J. N. Gray, C. A. Galtieri, and B. G. Lindsay [1982]. "Transactions and consistency in distributed database systems," *ACM Trans. on Database Systems* 7:3, pp. 323–342.

Tsichritzis, D. C. and A. Klug (eds.) [1978]. *The ANSI/X3/SPARC Framework*, AFIPS Press, Montvale, N. J.

Tsichritzis, D. C. and F. H. Lochovsky [1982]. *Data Models*, Prentice-Hall, Englewood Cliffs, New Jersey.

Tsou, D.-M. and P. C. Fischer [1982]. "Decomposition of a relation scheme into Boyce-Codd normal form," *SIGACT News* 14:3, pp. 23–29. Also appears in *Proc. 1980 ACM Conf.*

Tsur, S. and C. Zaniolo [1986]. "LDL: a logic-based data-language," *Proc. Intl. Conf. on Very Large Data Bases*, pp. 33–41.

Ullman, J. D. [1982]. *Principles of Database Systems*, Computer Science Press, Rockville, Md.

Ullman, J. D. [1987]. "Database theory—past and future," *Proc. Sixth ACM Symp. on Principles of Database Systems*, pp. 1–10.

Van Emden, M. H. and R. A. Kowalski [1976]. "The semantics of predicate logic as a programming language," *J. ACM* **23**:4, pp. 733–742.

Van Gelder, A. [1986]. "Negation as failure using tight derivations for general logic programs," *Proc. Symp. on Logic Programming*, IEEE, pp. 127–139.

Van Gelder, A. and R. W. Topor [1987]. "Safety and correct translation of relational calculus formulas," *Proc. Sixth ACM Symp. on Principles of Database Systems*, pp. 313–327.

Van Gucht, D. and P. C. Fischer [1986]. "Some classes of multilevel relational structures," *Proc. Fifth ACM Symp. on Principles of Database Systems*, pp. 60–69.

Vardi, M. Y. [1982]. "Complexity of relational queries," *Proc. Fourteenth Annual ACM Symp. on the Theory of Computing*, pp. 137–145.

Vardi, M. Y. [1983]. "Inferring multivalued dependencies from functional and join dependencies," *Acta Informatica* **19**:2, pp. 305–324.

Vardi, M. Y. [1984]. "The implication and finite implication problems for typed template dependencies," *J. Computer and System Sciences* **28**:1, pp. 3–28.

Vardi, M. Y. [1985]. "Querying logical databases," *Proc. Fourth ACM Symp. on Principles of Database Systems*, pp. 57–65.

Vardi, M. Y. [1986]. "On the integrity of databases with incomplete information," *Proc. Fifth ACM Symp. on Principles of Database Systems*, pp. 252–266.

Vardi, M. Y. [1988]. "Fundamentals of dependency theory," in *Trends in Theoretical Computer Science* (E. Borger, ed.), pp. 171–224, Computer Science Press, Rockville, Md.

Vassiliou, Y. [1979]. "Null values in database management—a denotational semantics approach," *ACM SIGMOD Intl. Conf. on Management of Data*, pp. 162–169.

Vassiliou, Y. [1980]. "Functional dependencies and incomplete information,"

*Proc. Intl. Conf. on Very Large Data Bases*, pp. 260–269.

Walker, A. [1986]. "Syllog: an approach to Prolog for nonprogrammers," in *Logic Programming and its Applications* (M. van Canaghem and D. H. D. Warren, eds.), Ablex.

Warren, D. H. D. [1981]. "Efficient processing of interactive relational database queries expressed in Prolog," *Proc. Intl. Conf. on Very Large Data Bases*, pp. 272–282.

Weikum, G. [1986]. "A theoretical foundation of multi-level concurrency control," *Proc. Fifth ACM Symp. on Principles of Database Systems*, pp. 31–42.

Wiederhold, G. [1983]. *Database Design*, McGraw-Hill, New York.

Wiederhold, G. [1986]. "Views, objects, and databases," *Computer*, Dec., 1986.

Wiederhold, G. [1987]. *File Organization for Database Design*, McGraw-Hill, New York.

Wiederhold, G. and R. El Masri [1980]. "The structural model for database design," *Proc. Intl. Conf. on the Entity-Relationship Approach to System Analysis and Design* (P. P. Chen, ed.), North Holland, Amsterdam.

Willard, D. E. [1978a]. "New data structures for orthogonal range queries," TR–22–78, Aiken Computation Lab., Harvard Univ.

Willard, D. E. [1978b]. "Predicate-oriented database search algorithms," TR–20–78, Aiken Computation Lab., Harvard Univ.

Willard, D. E. and G. S. Lueker [1985]. "Adding range restriction capability to dynamic data structures," *J. ACM* **32**:3, pp. 597–617.

Wolfson, O. [1987]. "The overhead of locking (and commit) protocols in distributed databases," *ACM Trans. on Database Systems* **12**:3, pp. 453–471.

Wolfson, O. and M. Yannakakis [1985]. "Deadlock-freedom (and safety) of transactions in a distributed database," *Proc. Fourth ACM Symp. on Principles of Database Systems*, pp. 105–112.

Yannakakis, M. [1982a]. "A theory of safe locking policies in database systems," *J. ACM* **29**:3, pp. 718–740.

Yannakakis, M. [1982b]. "Freedom from deadlock of safe locking policies," *SIAM J. Computing* **11**:2, pp. 391–408.

Yannakakis, M. [1984]. "Serializability by locking," *J. ACM* **31**:2, pp. 227–245.

Yannakakis, M. and C. H. Papadimitriou [1980]. "Algebraic dependencies," *J. Computer and System Sciences* **25**:1, pp. 2–41.

Yannakakis, M. and C. H. Papadimitriou [1985]. "The complexity of reliable concurrency control," *Proc. Fourth ACM Symp. on Principles of Database Systems*, pp. 230–234.

Yannakakis, M., C. H. Papadimitriou, and H.-T. Kung [1979]. "Locking policies: safety and freedom from deadlock," *Proc. Twentieth Annual IEEE Symp. on Foundations of Computer Science*, pp. 283–287.

Yao, A. C., and F. F. Yao [1976]. "The complexity of searching a random ordered table," *Proc. Seventeenth Annual IEEE Symp. on Foundations of Computer Science*, pp. 173–177.

Zaniolo, C. [1976]. "Analysis and design of relational schemata for database systems," doctoral dissertation, UCLA, July, 1976.

Zaniolo, C. [1984]. "Database relations with null values," *J. Computer and System Sciences* **28**:1, pp. 142–166.

Zaniolo, C. [1985]. "The representation and deductive retrieval of complex objects," *Proc. Intl. Conf. on Very Large Data Bases*, pp. 458–469.

Zaniolo, C. [1986]. "Safety and compilation of nonrecursive Horn clauses," *Proc. First Intl. Conf. on Expert Database Systems*, pp. 167–178, Benjamin-Cummings, Menlo Park, CA.

Zaniolo, C. and M. A. Melkanoff [1981]. "On the design of relational database schemata," *ACM Trans. on Database Systems* **6**:1, pp. 1–47.

Zloof, M. M. [1975]. "Query-by-Example: operations on the transitive closure," IBM RC 5526, Yorktown Hts., N. Y.

Zloof, M. M. [1977]. "Query-by-Example: a data base language," *IBM Systems J.* **16**:4, pp. 324–343.

Zloof, M. M. [1978]. "Security and integrity within the Query-by-Example data base management language," IBM RC 6982, Yorktown Hts., N. Y.

Zook, W., K. Youssefi, N. Whyte, P. Rubinstein, P. Kreps, G. Held, J. Ford, R. Berman, and E. Allman [1977]. *INGRES Reference Manual*, Dept. of EECS, Univ. of California, Berkeley.

# INDEX

616